REPORTING FROM WASHINGTON

Reporting from Washington

THE HISTORY OF THE
WASHINGTON PRESS CORPS

———

Donald A. Ritchie

OXFORD
UNIVERSITY PRESS

2005

OXFORD
UNIVERSITY PRESS

Oxford University Press, Inc., publishes works that further
Oxford University's objective of excellence
in research, scholarship, and education.

Oxford   New York
Auckland   Cape Town   Dar es Salaam   Hong Kong   Karachi
Kuala Lumpur   Madrid   Melbourne   Mexico City   Nairobi
New Delhi   Shanghai   Taipei   Toronto

With offices in
Argentina   Austria   Brazil   Chile   Czech Republic   France   Greece
Guatemala   Hungary   Italy   Japan   Poland   Portugal   Singapore
South Korea   Switzerland   Thailand   Turkey   Ukraine   Vietnam

Published by Oxford University Press, Inc.
198 Madison Avenue, New York, New York 10016
www.oup.com

Oxford is a registered trademark of Oxford University Press

Library of Congress Cataloging-in-Publication Data
Ritchie, Donald A., 1945–
Reporting from Washington : the history of the Washington
press corps / Donald A. Ritchie
p. cm.
Includes bibliographical references and index.
ISBN-13: 978-0-19-517861-6
ISBN-10: 0-19-517861-0
1. Journalism—Objectivity—United States—History—20th century.
2. Press and politics—United States—History—20th century.
3. Journalism—Political aspects—United States—History—20th century.
4. Reporters and reporting—United States—History—20th century.
I. Title.
PN4888.O25R58   2005
071'.53-dc22   2004018892

1 3 5 7 9 8 6 4 2

Printed in the United States of America
on acid-free paper

For Anne, Jennifer, Andrea, and Cami

Men and women who trust you as a reporter provide you with the bulk of your news. Most of the time it comes from the well where you have been lowering your bucket for a long time, getting fresh, sweet facts from springs that never seem to run dry.

—Jack Bell, Associated Press

Contents

Preface

Washington, D.C., is a reporter's town. It seems thick with correspondents for newspapers and magazines, radio and television, wire services and web sites; columnists and commentators; independents and stringers. More Washingtonians hold press passes than hold office. Prime space within the White House and the Capitol is reserved for reporters, and outside on the lawns and balconies of government buildings television cameras have become regular fixtures. Tourists are more likely to recognize the TV correspondents than the politicians they are interviewing. The National Press Club holds highly coveted forums for newsmakers. The Gridiron Club, the White House Correspondents Association, and the Radio and Television Correspondents Association host annual dinners where journalists and politicians socialize. News bureaus honeycomb the downtown, while the local Washington newspapers can blanket the city with reporters. As the Washington press corps grew from a few hundred reporters to many thousands over the course of the twentieth century, these abundant signs of power and preeminence elevated the press corps into an unofficial fourth branch of the government, with an irreplaceable role in the federal system of checks and balances.[1]

With its expansion in size and influence, however, the Washington press corps encountered mounting skepticism from the American public. From the Great Depression through the Cold War, newspapers and radio and television networks pumped up their reporting on the federal government. But these same organizations ended the twentieth century by trimming their Washington budgets and their news coverage of government and politics. By then, opinion polls showed reporters ranking lower than politicians in public standing, with three-quarters of American adults perceiving some form of media bias. The prevalent dissatisfaction with Washington press coverage prompted a range of conflicting theories. Some critics accused the press corps of having forged cozy alliances with the power elite, while others complained of an excessively negative, adversarial coverage of those in power. Critics with pronounced ideological leanings detected that reporters were slanting the news in the opposite direction. The left assailed the mainstream media as a "transmission belt for official opinion." The right made the press corps's "liberal bias" an article of faith. Some blamed reporters for straying away from objective reporting and

into news analysis. A movement alternatively known as public or civic journalism pinned the blame on objectivity itself for turning reporters into stenographers, and lamented that the media had "abdicated its duty to help the
public think beyond instinctive reactions."[2]

Washington correspondents as a whole profess to report the news objectively. Their jobs require an ability to stand apart and avoid taking sides. Objective reporting stands as the requisite for acquiring trust and credibility,
although pure objectivity is an ideal rather than an attainable goal. Everyone,
even a reporter, views events through his or her individual perceptions and
values. Was it likely, asked *National Review* publisher William Rusher, that journalists, upon entering their profession, had undergone some miraculous transformation and emerged "shriven and pure, purged of all bias"? To compensate
for this human tendency, news departments employ editors to filter out opinion and maintain balanced coverage. Despite such safeguards, the very selection of what to cover, whom to interview, what to ask, and what prominence
to give the story reflects personal predispositions. Bias in the news will remain
a matter of consequence, as what is reported, and what is distorted or overlooked, will shape public attitudes, make political careers, and influence political agendas.[3]

The mantra of media bias has too often conflated news analysis with slanted
reporting. Correspondents and commentators walk a line between an objectivity that accepts everything at face value and interpretation that reflects their
opinions rather than the facts. Historically, Washington reporting has operated on a scale ranging from advocacy to objectivity. When the first newspaper correspondents arrived at the capital early in the nineteenth century, they
reported for partisan papers whose politics they explicitly reflected in their
dispatches. Straightforward news reporting emerged out of the wire services.
During the Civil War, the Washington correspondent for the Associated Press
apologized for reporting "merely dry matters of fact and detail." Because his
reports went out to papers of all political leanings, he explained, he had to
strip out the slightest hint of opinion. Later in the century, commercial advertising and corporate ownership weaned newspapers off of party patronage,
and editors aimed to purge partisanship entirely from their news columns.
They built a firewall between the news and editorial pages, told reporters to
stick to the facts, and relied on columnists to supply opinion. "Reporters were
to report the news as it happened, like machines, without prejudice, color, and
without style; all alike," Lincoln Steffens learned when he worked for the *New
York Post* in the 1890s. "Humor or any sign of personality in our reports was
caught, rebuked, and, in time, suppressed."

Yet, not all of the press espoused strict objectivity. The newspaper mogul
William Randolph Hearst demanded that his papers do more than simply print
the news as it happened. His "new journalism" would not wait for things to
turn up, he said, "It turns them up." Hearst's papers advocated his political

causes, and followed his personal political drift from left to right. Other segments of the press gravitated toward issue advocacy and practiced journalism as a form of moral engagement. For decades, for instance, the black press filled a gaping void in national news coverage by reporting on and promoting the struggle for equal rights. Advocacy, like objectivity, has a long and honorable tradition in the media, although taking sides runs the risk of alienating audiences and advertisers, and of having one's reporting dismissed as slanted.[4]

Washington journalism's code of objectivity was aptly expressed in a notice that the eminent columnist, correspondent, and bureau chief James Reston posted at the *New York Times* bureau in June 1963:

> We are obviously going into a savage debate on civil rights, probably for the rest of the year. I urge everybody who writes on this subject in the news to be vigilant about seeing that both sides get a fair shake. We don't want to come to the end of this debate and have anybody say that we used the news columns to play up the *Times*'s editorial policy, or that we used inflammatory language in our reporting of the events. The story is obviously going to be inflammatory enough.[5]

Journalism schools and professional literature drummed the same message into reporters, as have many angry letters to the editor. The quest for objectivity required reporters to suppress their own views and let the facts speak for themselves. Submerging self was more than a matter of style, it was "a habit of mind, even a trait of character," lectured Louis Lyons, who as director of the prestigious Nieman Fellowships offered selected journalists a year's sabbatical at Harvard and influenced the cream of Washington reporters. Objective reporters needed to be neutral observers, not participants. They recorded the opinions of others, not their own. They told the public what happened, not what to think about it. Not every story might be balanced, but reputations for fairness were built in the aggregate. As one editor at the *Washington Post* explained, "We know what our values and standards are, and that's why errors or lapses or imperfections that come into the paper don't undermine our overall fairness and accuracy."[6]

Yet moments arose when journalists found it impossible to remain neutral. In the 1920s, the *New York Times* reporter Charles Hambidge was covering a heated civic meeting when a reporter for the *New York Herald*, Leland Stowe, jumped up from the press table to join in the debate. "I never saw anything like it," the astonished Hambidge commented. "If this sort of thing is allowed, it bodes no good for journalism." Of the two reporters, however, it was Stowe who went on to win a Pulitzer Prize. Forty years later, the eminent television news broadcaster Howard K. Smith walked away from a lucrative contract with CBS rather than allow the network to dilute his coverage of civil rights demonstrations in the South. He joined those reporters who refused to worship impartiality "as the true be-all and end-all of journalism," as *Time* magazine correspondent John L. Steele described it. On controversial issues from

McCarthyism to the Vietnam War, many members of the press corps concluded that strict objectivity favored conventional wisdom and blurred the
truth. "Bias has no place in good journalism, but neither does blind patriotism," asserted J. Robert Port, who headed an investigative team for the Associated Press, "and I'm not ashamed to acknowledge that I make moral judgments
as an investigative reporter." Thomas Winship, who served as a Washington
correspondent and bureau chief on his way to becoming editor of the *Boston
Globe*, took an early stand against American intervention in Vietnam. He justified it as one of those "fundamental issues which come along in a lifetime
which have such overriding moral importance that you just can't be neutral."[7]

Washington correspondents tilted to the left on enough of these moral issues to convince conservative politicians from Robert Taft to Richard Nixon
and Newt Gingrich that the press corps stood collectively against them. Conservative alienation reached its apex during Nixon's administration, which
deliberately aimed "to turn objectivity into an issue and a subject of public
debate." Nixon's first vice president, Spiro Agnew, drew national applause by
targeting the media as a bastion of liberal eastern elitists. Even some liberal
journalists agreed that the press corps lacked a sufficient diversity of views.
News organizations sought greater balance on their op-ed pages and airwaves,
until the conservative niche grew so prominent that the left began asking whatever happened to the liberal media. Beyond ideology, economic and cultural
biases infused national reporting. Washington correspondents evolved into a
highly educated upper class, observed Russell Baker, who had worked his way
up through the ranks of Washington journalism. "They belong to a culture for
which the American system works exceedingly well. Which is to say, they are,
in the pure sense of the word, extremely conservative." If Washington reporters showed any persistent partiality, it was toward those who held power–and
who, therefore, held the information they sought. As vexed and abused by reporters as so many politicians felt, the Washington press corps has always paid
the greatest attention to those in authority.[8]

The real price of everything, according to Adam Smith, is the toil and trouble
of acquiring it. For journalists in Washington, the price of success can be measured in the accumulation of knowledgeable sources, the higher placed the
better. Maintaining such sources requires mutual trust. Despite their natural
antagonisms, government officials and reporters cannot do without each other.
One side craves publicity to promote careers and policies. The other side de-
pends on making contact with the right people to gain reliable information.
Candor and credibility depend heavily on the confidence that officials have in
the reporters and their news outlets. "Every veteran correspondent worth his
salt has one or more such private sources," wrote one seasoned reporter; "the
fortunate ones have several, covering a wide range of governmental activity."[9]

To build confidence among their sources, Washington reporters over time
have crafted formal and informal rules, and none of these is more important

than that which establishes how to attribute the information gathered. Reporters and officials alike understand the distinctions between what is on and off the record, not for attribution, or on deep background. The press corps has a proud history of refusing to divulge confidential sources. Twice during the nineteenth century, Washington correspondents were imprisoned in the Capitol in unsuccessful attempts to force them to reveal the source of leaked government secrets. Countless other leak investigations ended just as ineffectively. The journalists' rules and practices established the desired harmony between themselves and the politicians they covered, but this harmony bred contentment and complacency. By the 1920s, the press corps's conspicuous compatibility with the political establishment caused the media critic H. L. Mencken to blast Washington correspondents as "a class of many of almost incredible credulity." Mencken considered the average Washington correspondent "honest enough, as honesty goes in the United States. . . . What ails him mainly is that he is a man without sufficient force of character to resist the blandishments that surround him from the moment he sets foot in Washington."[10]

What most shook the press corps from complacency was the periodic intrusion of new technology. From the telegraph to radio, television, and digital electronics, technological innovations not only speeded delivery of the news but stimulated competition within the media. Each invention introduced a new group of reporters who felt less bound by their predecessors' rules and traditions. Over time, the outsiders invariably forced the veteran insiders to adjust to new practices. But initially reporters for each new media met stiff resistance from the press corps's establishment. Since 1880, the U.S. government has ceded the authority to determine who qualifies for a press pass to cover the Capitol, the White House, and the federal agencies to members of the press corps themselves. Reporters elect committees of correspondents who grant formal accreditation, thereby defining, and restricting, their own trade. The newspapermen who ran the original press gallery in the U.S. Congress set rules that denied press passes to magazine writers and radio broadcasters. The excluded correspondents petitioned Congress and received their own separate galleries, from which they in turn excluded newcomers who failed to meet their rules. As a result, the U.S. Congress, alone among national legislatures, divides its press galleries according to media technologies. Both the print and broadcast galleries became perplexed over how to classify Internet reporters, fearing that setting too loose a definition would allow anyone with a web site to apply for a press pass. In addition to denying access to new technologies, for decades the fraternal rules of the press galleries also excluded women and minorities, and limited access for foreign correspondents and American reporters who worked for government agencies. Hard-fought battles eventually opened the press galleries to greater diversity, by race, gender, and technology, and repeatedly redefined Washington reporting.

While reporters seek sources, sources seek reporters. Leaks became a prime instrument of government. In the 1940s, Bruce Catton—who toiled as a Washington correspondent before devoting himself to writing history—defined leaks as information that officials were "either unwilling or unready" to reveal formally but would divulge to reporters they trusted not to reveal their sources. Reporters, likewise, needed to have some confidence in their sources' proximity to the actual events and their honesty in conveying them. These collaborations resulted in stories attributed to "a usually reliable source," "administration officials," "sources close to the investigation," and "high-level sources." Willard Edwards, who covered Washington for the *Chicago Tribune* from the 1930s to the 1970s, admitted that when all else failed he would cite himself as "a veteran Washington observer." Sometimes the "informed sources" were simply other reporters—despite recurring warnings from bureau chiefs: "Don't use reporters as sources. They often know less than you do." Reporters joked that their colleagues who cited "sources that cannot be disclosed" usually had not "the dimmest notion where they are." Government sources used leaks to float trial balloons they could later disavow, to sabotage programs they opposed, and to undermine their rivals. But leaks also allowed the public to get a glimpse of policies still in the making, and of the insiders' reservations about those policies. As Bruce Catton reasoned, "our particular form of government wouldn't work without it."[11]

The twentieth century was replete with attempts by those running the government to manipulate reporters by controlling and distorting the flow of information. But manipulation was not always necessary to make reporters receptive to the government's agenda. The press corps generally shared a similar worldview with those in power, and embraced the prevailing national consensus. From the New Deal through the New Frontier, reporters favored an active federal government and a strong presidency, until the Vietnam War and Watergate scandal shook their confidence and eroded the consensus. "There are no issues anymore, just questions of character. There's no confidentiality, just leaks and scoops," said House Speaker Tip O'Neill of the erosion of relations between reporters and politicians. Negative press contributed to government's slippage in public approval, which in turn reduced the national appetite for government news. As the percentage of eligible voters dwindled at the ballot box, readers and viewers drifted away from hard news. Editors and producers sought more human-interest stories from beyond the Beltway, and Washington news bureaus shrank accordingly. During the 1990s, the advent of twenty-four-hour news cycles on cable television channels and web sites convinced some "news personalities" to adopt highly-opinionated, confrontational styles, on the assumption that they had to be entertaining in order keep the audience's attention. Alternative media mixed opinion and attitude into their news reporting and taunted the traditional press to "abandon the false god of objectivity" and "let people speak far more freely."[12]

This history of reporting from Washington begins in 1932, when the combination of radio and Franklin D. Roosevelt broke the newspapers' hold on public opinion and transformed the Washington press corps and its nineteenth-century practices. It opens with a violent clash between the U.S. Army and an army of the unemployed on the streets of the capital, events that literally rocked the press corps out of a decade of lethargy and left them ripe for the political revolution that would soon follow. It ends with appalling acts of international terrorism in New York City and Washington that once more riveted public attention on the news from the federal government. Between those milestones, the press corps's fortunes ebbed and flowed along with those of the government it covered. Before 1932, newspapers had trouble recruiting talented staff for their Washington bureaus. Foreign correspondents regarded the American capital as a hardship post. Until then, New York City rather than Washington stood as the nation's news center. The national capital provided poor soil even for its local papers, due to a scarcity of commercial advertising and a transient population. All of that changed with the growth of the federal government during the New Deal and Second World War. More than anyone else, Franklin Roosevelt made Washington a hub of national and international news, a trend that was further locked in place during the long Cold War. During these decades the size and status of the Washington press corps swelled until the "media elite" stood equal to the political establishment.

In his immensely popular novel *Advise and Consent*, the former Washington correspondent Allen Drury employed the press corps as a Greek chorus, identified not by their names but by their news outlets. This device advanced the plot brilliantly but diminished the corps's individualism. His novel fanned my earliest interests in Washington politics and media as a teenage reader. Later as a teacher, I showed the Hollywood film version of *Advise and Consent* to my classes, pointing out the real reporters who appeared in it as extras. Unlike *Advise and Consent*, this study names the members of the press corps and brings them to the foreground, assigning the politicians to the role of extras. The narrative is organized not by presidential administrations or other political benchmarks, but corresponds to the various types of Washington reporting in much the same way that the press galleries separate reporters by media. Its aim is a collective biography of an intelligent, ambitious, shrewd, curious, skeptical, sometimes cynical, occasionally gullible, but always competitive corps of correspondents. Politicians may dream of circumventing them, yet the Washington reporters continue to provide most of the information that the public receives about its government.[13]

Once when I served as a judge to present the Everett Dirksen award for the best congressional reporting, the historians and political scientists on the panel were favorably inclined toward the analytical writers from the weekly journals of news and opinion. Another panelist, the White House correspondent Helen Thomas, took us to task for undervaluing those reporters who worked on their feet, under short deadlines without the luxury of lengthy contemplation. The reporters she described fill the corridors of the Capitol any day that Congress is in session, standing alone or in clusters outside closed meetings, alongside elevator banks, and at the subway entrances, ready to ambush members for an attributable quote or an off-the-record assessment. Under pressure to get the story quickly and to get it right, these reporters scramble to move beyond official handouts, develop their own sources, and scoop the rest of the pack. Thomas's insights into the work culture of Washington reporters swung the jury that year. (She had arrived late, having just covered an Easter egg roll on the White House lawn, where reporters had been kept away from the president in a roped-off area. "They'd put ropes around our necks if they could get it away with it," she commented.)

News is a perishable commodity. Yesterday's newspapers are discarded; broadcasts fade into the ether; breaking news on the Internet is eventually deleted. While libraries and archives diligently preserve the print, broadcast, and electronic versions of the news, those who study journalism often collect much of their evidence as it occurs. In this respect, I have had the unusual advantage of participatory observation, something closer to the realm of the anthropologist than the historian. As a historian who has worked for the U.S. Senate since 1976, I have interacted with Washington reporters on almost every workday—and on a few weekends—answering their questions about the precedents, personalities, and peculiarities of the Senate. The Senate historians are professional and nonpartisan, taking no sides on political issues. Feeling the need to stand behind the information we provide, I have never requested that any of my remarks be "off the record," although sometimes on more sensitive subjects I have been greatly relieved when reporters chose not to quote me directly.

One year I kept a record of the number of calls that I took from journalists. From January 2 until October 17, 2001 (when I had to stop because the Hart Senate Office Building was evacuated due to an anthrax incident), I logged 331 calls from newspaper reporters, magazine writers, columnists, broadcasters, and fact-checkers; from ABC, CBS, NBC, PBS, CNN, Fox, MSNBC, C-SPAN, Fugi TV, NPR, and Radio Free Europe; from the Associated Press, *Atlanta Constitution, Baltimore Sun, Bergen Record, Boston Globe, Chicago Tribune, Christian Science Monitor, Ft. Worth Star-Telegram, Great Falls Tribune, The Hill, Houston Chronicle, Las Vegas Sun, Los Angeles Times, Milwaukee Journal, New Orleans Picayune, Newark Star-Ledger, New York Daily News, New York Post, New York Times, Newsday, Orlando Sentinel, Philadelphia Inquirer, Providence Journal, Roll Call, San Jose Mercury News, St. Petersburg Times, Tulsa World, USA Today,* and the *Washington Post;* from Copley, Gannett, Hearst, Knight-Ridder, McClatchey, Newhouse, and States News Service; from *Congressional Quarterly, Editor & Publisher, Kiplinger, National Journal, Nation, New Republic, New Yorker, Newsweek, People, San Francisco Magazine, Slate,* and *Time;*

from the offices of Evans and Novak, Helen Thomas, the McLaughlin Group, and George Will; and from the *Asahi Shimbun, Frankfurter Rundshau,* and *Nikkei* news bureaus.

On a memorable afternoon, the syndicated columnist Joseph Alsop stopped by the Senate Historical Office, ostensibly to interview me about Washington history for his memoirs, although he did most of the talking. Over the years, I have hunted for clues in Senate records for investigative reporters, provided data for columnists, explained American history to foreign correspondents, and taken reporters on backstairs tours of the Capitol, from the top of the dome to the bathtubs in the basement. I have appeared on radio and television news broadcasts, and gotten glimpses of their operations from the inside. I have watched reporters at work in the press galleries, and conversed with them at Capitol receptions, where I met James Reston, Fred Friendly, Mary McGrory, and many others who appear throughout this book. The National Press Club has occasionally invited me to participate in their functions, and I have served as an advisor to the Washington Press Foundation's Women in Journalism oral history project. I have attended some of the black-tie dinners of the Radio and Television Correspondents Association as the guest of C-SPAN, and the Gridiron Club's white-tie dinner as the guest of Mary Kay Quinlan, a Washington correspondent turned professor. But I have never worked as a journalist, and make no pretension of being part of their community. Like the journalists I studied, I have attempted to write about them as an entirely neutral observer.

My earlier book on this subject, *Press Gallery: Congress and the Washington Correspondents*, examined the first 130 years of Washington reporting. That book reviewed the careers of individual newspaper reporters who represented distinctive stages in the evolution of their craft. In continuing that story over the past seventy years, I retained the primary focus on reporters but otherwise altered the format to accommodate the vast changes in the government and in journalism. Where Congress had previously occupied center stage and dominated the news from Washington, it was displaced by the peremptory presidency. Where the Washington press corps had formerly been compact and homogeneous, it had grown enormously in size and complexity. This account follows the development of newspaper news bureaus, radio commentators, television broadcasters, wire services, columnists, investigative reporters, foreign correspondents, minority journalists, and the local Washington media. Rather than designate a single journalist to represent each stage, I selected clusters of individuals and institutions, sometimes polar opposites, to shed light on some aspect of Washington reporting through their disparate approaches to getting the news. The topical chapters are arranged in roughly chronological order from the 1930s through the 1990s, introducing each media at its point of preeminence.

Since beginning this project in 1980, I have accumulated several file cabinets of clippings, sifted through manuscripts and oral histories, conducted formal interviews, and held numerous informal conversations with reporters. I also acquired a few shelves of memoirs by Washington journalists, the largest share through Washington's annual Vassar book sale, now lamentably ended after a half century of trading in used books. Historians have tended to over-look these reflective accounts by professional eyewitnesses, even as they cited the same authors' contemporary news articles. Provoked to exasperation, the prominent book reviewer Jonathan Yardley once declared that no American journalist had ever written an autobiography worth reading, although he later acknowledged an occasional exception. Regardless of their literary quality, I found that reporters' memoirs contained vast supplies of useful insights and telling anecdotes. It was a further asset that the Vassar alumnae had tapped the libraries of notable Washingtonians, so that many of the hard-to-find, out-of-print, and sometimes privately printed volumes that I acquired were also autographed by the reporters to their sources. My copy of *The Fourth Branch of Government,* for instance, is inscribed by author Douglass Cater "To Gover-nor [Adlai] Stevenson, Who is not unfamiliar with the dilemmas of this book!"[14]

After the publication of *Press Gallery,* I appeared on Brian Lamb's *Booknotes* program on C-SPAN. Shortly afterward, a verbatim transcript arrived in the mail, alerting me to C-SPAN's practice of posting almost all of its hour-long *Booknotes* interviews on its web site. As an abundance of the hundreds of au-thors interviewed on the long-running program were Washington journalists, the transcripts of their interviews added personal commentary that invariably went beyond the contents of their books. In drawing upon many of those in-terviews, I benefited from Brian Lamb's ability to get people to speak perhaps more candidly about their subjects and themselves than they anticipated.

Washington is awash in documentary resources on the media. The Library of Congress counts the personal papers of leading Washington journalists among its collections, along with back issues of the publications for which they wrote, and tapes of the programs on which they appeared. The Senate Library, directed by Greg Harness, has a comprehensive collection of congres-sional documents and related books, along with newspapers from across the country and magazines of all political hues, and a truly outstanding staff of reference librarians. The Washington Press Foundation's Women in Journalism oral history interviews—conducted by Mary Marshall Clark, Kathleen Currie, Margot Knight, Donita Moorhus, and Anne Ritchie—proved an invaluable resource. The University of Maryland's Broadcasting Archives, directed by Tom Connors, offered a rich collection related to radio and television, and I owe spe-cial thanks to Michael Henry for his help in obtaining illustrations from that collection. Larry Janezich, the superintendent of the Senate radio & TV gallery, and Bob Petersen, the former superintendent of the Senate press gallery, granted me access to the minutes of the Standing Committees of Correspondents.

The Freedom Forum, the Newseum, and the National Press Club invited me to participate in programs featuring Washington journalists. At one event,

Sarah McClendon delivered commentary on my paper and questioned it in a vigorous style well familiar to the presidents she had confronted at press conferences. A panel of veteran journalists at a seminar on "Eisenhower and the Media" in Gettysburg, Pennsylvania, deepened my appreciation of the key role of the wire services. I delivered a talk on John F. Kennedy's press relations to the Capitol Historical Society, which was broadcast on C-SPAN, gave the Armstrong Lecture at Bradley University on newspaper columnists during the Vietnam War, and discussed the symbiotic relations between politicians and the press in addresses to the Australian Centre for American Studies at the University of Sydney, the Woodrow Wilson Center, and the American Political Science Association's Congressional Fellows. A version of several presentations that I made on the racial integration of the press galleries, before the Organization of American Historians, the American Journalism Historians Association, and the Smithsonian's National Museum of American History, was published in the winter 1996 issue of *Media Studies Journal*.

Other assistance for this study came from Patrick Cox at the Institute for News Media History at the University of Texas, and from the Franklin D. Roosevelt, Harry S. Truman, Dwight D. Eisenhower, John F. Kennedy and Lyndon B. Johnson presidential libraries. The Wisconsin Historical Society provided oral histories relating to Joseph R. McCarthy and the press. Former NBC correspondent Sander Vanocur gave me copies of his insightful video documentaries, *The Postwar Congress and the Media* and *The Television Presidency*, produced by the Freedom Forum.

The unpredictable schedules of working reporters made it difficult to conduct formal interviews with them, but because so many reporters interviewed me as part of their jobs, I often gathered information from them during the same encounters. Among those with whom I have had informative discussions that helped compose this book were Joseph Alsop, Griffing Bancroft, Bob Barr, Jackie Calmes, Clay Claiborne, Bob Clark, Chris Collins, Sidney Davis, Helen Dewar, Robert Donovan, Al Eisele, Fred Frommer, William Gordon, Fred Graham, David Grann, Richard Harwood, Janet Hook, Phil Jones, Fritz Joubert, Herb Kaplow, Lew Ketchum, Kathy Kiely, Larry Knudson, Keith Kyle, Brian Lamb, Don Larrabee, David Lawsky, Finlay Lewis, Bill MacDougall, Roy McGhee, Neil MacNeil, Chris Matthews, Mike Michelson, Bruce Morton, Roger Mudd, John Mulligan, Don Oberdorfer, Mike Posner, Elaine Povitch, Mark Preston, Mary Kay Quinlan, Susan Rasky, Chalmers Roberts, Nan Robertson, Paul Rodriguez, William Sheehan, Isabel Shelton, Martin Schram, Al Spivak, Sheryl Gay Stolberg, Jim Talbert, George Tames, Evan Thomas, Helen Thomas, Alden Todd, Martin Tolchin, Frank Van Der Linden, Sander Vanocur, and George Will.

I am also grateful to Gini Blodgett, Barbara Vandergrift, and Christina Hostetter at the National Press Club, and to former White House and Senate curator James Roe Ketchum, for their advice and assistance. Alden Todd gave me access to some of the papers of his father, Laurence Todd. Ann Wood, a former Washington correspondent who was active in the Counter-Gridiron movement, shared with me her personal collection of clippings and correspondence. James Sayler, formerly of the *Washington Star*, the *New York Times* Washington bureau, and the Congressional Research Service, generously shared observations from his research on Arthur Krock. David Dunaway of the University of New Mexico sharpened my thinking about radio history. Matthew Wasniewski of the House Office of History and Preservation shared insights from his study of Walter Lippmann. Mark Feldstein, a journalist-turned-historian, reviewed the chapters on television and investigative reporting from his own experiences in those fields. Harry Liebersohn translated from German portions of Manfried Zapp's writings. Rodney Joseph, Betty Koed, James Sayler, and Nancy Toff each thoroughly and thoughtfully scrutinized the entire manuscript. My colleagues in the Senate Historical Office, Richard Baker, Betty Koed, Beth Hahn, Karen Paul, Heather Moore, Diane Boyle, Mary Baumann, and Rachael Abarca have provided professional support and good company. My most heartfelt thanks go to my personal muses—my wife, two stepdaughters, and granddaughter—to whom this book is dedicated.

REPORTING FROM WASHINGTON

Prologue

Washington, D.C., 1932

An army of the unemployed marched on Washington in 1932, disrupting the capital and the sedate existence of its press corps. A good many Washington reporters had grown accustomed to gathering news through press releases and briefings, routines they called "no more exciting than knitting." Now they were sent out to cover a "bonus expeditionary force" of desperate veterans of the World War, who had come to urge the passing of a bill that would grant early payment of a promised veteran's bonus, not due for another dozen years. When the government attempted to dislodge the marchers from their camps near Pennsylvania Avenue, the protest turned violent. United Press reporter Bill Kerby normally patrolled the quiet corridors of the Interior Department, but he was standing on Pennsylvania Avenue, just a few blocks from the Capitol, when the first fighting erupted between the veterans and the police. Bricks flew, shots rang out, and in the commotion some of the bonus marchers seized Kerby as a hostage.

"I'm a reporter," he protested.

"Newspapers are capitalist tools," replied his captors.

"But I work for the *Daily News*," Kerby lied, citing the only Washington newspaper in sympathy with the marchers. Once freed, he ran to a telephone booth to report that the Bonus Riots had begun.[1]

Rioting on Pennsylvania Avenue turned virtually every Washington reporter into a "combination of police reporter and war correspondent," wrote the *New York Times* correspondent Delbert Clark. Members of the press corps had long regarded themselves as the cream of the journalism profession, although they reported from a dreary political center devoid of the cultural amenities that made other world capitals glitter. Washington, D.C., had flourished during the First World War, only to shrink again in peace. The prestige of the Washington press corps similarly slipped during the 1920s. Luther Huston of the *New York Times* recalled that "editors and reporters elsewhere had a tendency to speak of their Washington colleagues in falsetto tones—spats and canes and tea at 4 p.m."[2]

The federal government had moved from New York City more than a century earlier, but Manhattan remained America's news capital. Its profusion of newspapers created the nation's highest concentration of reporters. The New York correspondents dismissed Washington's daily papers as "sycophantic, provincial and banal." The major wire services maintained their headquarters in New York, as did the first radio networks, whose programs tapped the entertainment and financial resources along the Hudson rather than the political outpost on the Potomac. In 1932 the *New York Times* had trouble convincing any of its top reporters to head its Washington bureau. Big city reporters such as the *Chicago Tribune's* Walter Trohan were dismayed at having to leave the metropolitan bustle for "little more than a sleepy town." Trohan swore that a man could read the newspaper in the middle of one of Washington's broad avenues with little danger of being run down.[3]

During the Jazz Age of the 1920s, Americans more avidly followed the exploits of baseball players, prizefighters, gangsters, and silent film stars than politicians and diplomats. Newspapers accordingly cut back on political news to provide more space for sports, crime, and movies. Washington reporters of the era "delighted in prolonged snoozes." Their bureaus went for days without getting a story on the front pages. New tabloid newspapers, designed for easier reading on streetcars and subways, further compressed news in favor of bigger pictures and bolder headlines. Even the stately *New York Times* ran six columns of front-page stories on Jack Dempsey's heavyweight boxing victory in 1921, and just a single column that same day on the signing of the peace treaty with Germany. Washington correspondents responded to this competition by magnifying the leaders they covered. Generally sympathetic to the conservative Republican administrations of the decade, the press corps tried to promote the pallid Warren G. Harding and Calvin Coolidge as updated versions of Theodore Roosevelt and Woodrow Wilson. "A few months of association with the gaudy magnificoes of the town, and they pick up its meretricious values, and are unable to distinguish men of sense and dignity from mountebanks," Baltimore's resident critic H. L. Mencken wrote of the Washington press corps. "A few clumsy overtures from the White House, and they are rattled and undone. They come in as newspaper men, trained to get the news and eager to get it; they end as tin-horn statesmen, full of dark secrets and unable to write the truth if they tried."[4]

After eight years of Harding and Coolidge, the press corps greeted the election of Herbert Hoover with universal relief. They hailed Hoover as a "superman" who would elevate the presidency and boost their reporting. As commerce secretary, he had been "the best single news source" in town. Yet after Washington reporters celebrated his elevation to the presidency, they watched in dismay as he dismantled most of the public relations apparatus that had gotten him there. Once inaugurated president, Hoover preferred to deal with a select group of friendly reporters, and divorced himself from the rest of the Washington correspondents. The resentful press corps suspected that his past cordiality had been simply a calculated maneuver for advancement. Ike Hoover, the chief usher at the White House since the days of Benjamin Harrison, wondered why his new boss gave so little consideration to the reporters who collectively shaped the national image of all presidents. Within a year the alienated press corps was writing, "Why has Hoover failed?"[5]

The stock market crash of 1929, followed by a wave of bank failures, bankruptcies, and widespread unemployment, soon had movie audiences hissing at Hoover's face in the newsreels, even in the capital. The press corps reported the economic catastrophe and also suffered from it. By 1932 the *Washington Post* was bankrupt and the new National Press Building faced foreclosure. Newspapers slashed expenses and cut paychecks in half. The less fortunate lost their jobs as Washington news bureaus closed down. More papers depended on wire service reports instead of hiring their own correspondents. Displaced reporters quit the trade or subsisted as stringers and freelance writers. Other unemployed Americans took more direct action, and in December 1931 a thousand jobless victims of the Great Depression staged a hunger march on Washington. With visions of violent insurrection, anxious editors at the *Washington Post* urged President Hoover "to crush violence with a sledge hammer of law, not in belated or wavering fashion, but instantly, on the spot, whenever any hand is raised against the public peace."[6]

In the spring of 1932 a larger army of twenty thousand war veterans marched into Washington, bringing along their families, other unemployed folks, and a few radical agitators. The core of bonus marchers camped in shanties on the empty land across the Anacostia River from Washington, while fringe groups squatted in some partially demolished buildings along Pennsylvania Avenue that were being cleared for construction of the Federal Triangle. The veterans put up makeshift shacks that reporters noted were "chalked over with sassy slogans." They paraded to Capitol Hill, where the bonus bill passed the House of Representatives only to be blocked in the Senate. With veterans picketing outside and filling the Senate galleries, Vice President Charles Curtis nervously called in the Marines, who set up machine guns on the Capitol steps. Editors at the Washington bureau of the United Press (UP) deleted any reference to the machine guns from news dispatches, not wanting the story to sound "too alarmist." But the local Washington newspapers quaked as if "a horde of drunkards and maniacs were hovering on the hillside like Genghis Khan's army," wrote Associated Press correspondent Marguerite Young.[7]

The bonus marchers took the news that the Senate had defeated their bill in stunned silence. "Tell them to sing 'America,'" the Hearst columnist Elsie Robinson whispered to one of their leaders, and when the marchers burst into song they won praise for their patriotic restraint. Congress hastily adjourned and left town, and President Hoover hoped that the marchers would follow their lead. Viewing the protest as misguided but lawful, Hoover discounted the inflammatory press reports about Communist domination of the Bonus March (propaganda that the Communist Party itself spread to boost its public image). The Quaker president encouraged a peaceful dispersal of the protesters by offering them free rides home. Most accepted, but a few of the more militant marchers lingered behind.

Meanwhile, a building contractor with salvage rights to the half-demolished buildings on Pennsylvania Avenue threatened to sue the government for time and money lost, and the Washington police moved to evict the veterans occupying the area. Tipped off in advance, the UP's Washington bureau stationed its reporters and office boys along Pennsylvania Avenue, with orders to telephone as soon as anyone saw fighting break out. When the police arrived, the squatters pelted them with rubble from the ruined buildings, and the police opened fire. The battle broke out just a stone's throw from the Associated Press office, and AP reporter Bess Furman said the stones were flying fast.[8]

President Hoover reluctantly authorized the U.S. Army to surround the riot area and assist in clearing the buildings, but General Douglas MacArthur, the army's chief of staff, exceeded his orders and adopted a more sweeping plan to rid the capital of insurrection. As reporters and other civilians gawked on the sidewalks, infantrymen and mounted cavalry from Fort Myer paraded down Pennsylvania Avenue. Tanks rolled after them. Soldiers lobbed tear gas, and the cavalry charged, swinging the flat end of their sabers. The infantry followed with fixed bayonets. "Tear gas bombs were popping across the street," wrote UP reporter Joseph Baird. "Steel helmeted doughboys were hurling them left and right." Himself a former Marine, Baird had never faced tear gas without a gas mask. Weeping and choking, he rushed into a drug store "to flash word to the office that the gas attack had begun." The advancing soldiers ordered reporters to move back, and those who responded too slowly were driven away with bayonets. When a cavalryman galloped toward one group of reporters, they beat a hasty retreat to a nearby cigar store. Sir Willmott Lewis, the Washington correspondent for the *Times* of London, stood his ground. "I say, I'm press," he shouted, waving his press card and umbrella. The blunt side of a saber across his well-tailored trousers finally sent the British correspondent dashing for cover. Franklyn Waltman of the *Baltimore Sun* was too slow to scale a wall and had the seat of his pants lacerated by another soldier's saber. The AP's Herbert Plummer and the International News Service's Harry Ward both required medical treatment after the fracas.[9]

Hoover never disavowed MacArthur's insubordination, and the army insisted that its actions had been provoked. Investigative reporter Paul Y. Anderson of the *St. Louis Post-Dispatch* disputed the army's claims, describing how men, women, and children had "fled shrieking across the broken ground, falling into excavations as they strove to avoid the rearing hoofs and saber points." He had seen "dozens of women grab their children and stagger out of the area with streaming, blinded eyes while the bombs fizzed and popped all around them." The infantry had "harried thousands of veterans and spectators through the streets . . . raining gas bombs on them as they fled," leaving children "choking and screaming" on the sidewalk. "This gas was intended for spectators," Anderson asserted. The secretary of war denied that army troops had deliberately burned the squatters' shanties, but Anderson reported that the soldiers had brought drums of kerosene with them and that he had seen an infantry-man going into a store to purchase a carton of matches. "The gas-masked infantry had begun burning the shacks nearest the river," Laurence Todd reported for the Federated Press, a labor news service. "Clouds of white tear gas rose slowly against the red glare of the flames."[10]

The sharp differences between what the government said and what the reporters saw outraged the press corps. Yet, the editors of most of the papers for which they reported backed the use of military force to rout the marchers. Editors at the *Washington Post* had watched the troops advance from the safety of their office windows and declared that the veterans had only themselves to blame. The Washington bureau chief for the *New York Times*, Arthur Krock, had removed himself to Manhattan, where he dismissed the incident as a scuffle and blamed it all on "demagogic politicians" in Congress for deluding the veterans. William Randolph Hearst's *Washington Times* ran the headline: "Use of Force Was Necessary." Even the pro-labor *Washington Daily News* at first supported the military's actions, until its staff held a protest meeting and forced a reversal of editorial judgment in the next edition. The White House promptly canceled its subscription. Despite the many editorial endorsements, the news reports, photographs, and newsreels of army tanks and soldiers driving American veterans from the national capital undermined what little remained of President Hoover's popularity.[11]

Radio had no reporters of its own in Washington to cover the confrontation. Ted Church, the Washington director of special events for the Columbia Broadcasting System, pleaded with various newspaper reporters to describe the riots on the airwaves of his fledgling network. When no journalist was willing to take the assignment, Church reported the story himself. The National Broadcasting Corporation had better luck in persuading the managing editor of the *Washington Evening Star* to deliver its breaking news.[12]

For Washington reporters, getting caught up in the Bonus Riots raised doubts about the neutral, objective reporting of the news. It was hard for correspondents who had inhaled gas and felt the prod of a bayonet not to sympathize with the marchers. Sir Willmott Lewis informed readers of the *Times* of London that he detected no sign of public gratitude toward the troops "among the crowds with which your Correspondent mingled during the eviction. They were mostly well dressed and respectable people who were driven with the veterans, blocks away from the 'bonus camps' by cavalry sabers, fixed bayonets, and tear gas." The Bonus March galvanized the press corps, confronting them with the realities of the depression beyond press conferences, congressional debates, and presidential pronouncements. "So all the misery and suffering had come finally to this—soldiers marching with their guns against American citizens," recorded the UP congressional correspondent Thomas Stokes. Having been hit by a cavalryman's saber, Stokes "had nothing but bitter feelings toward Herbert Hoover that night." Shortly afterward, many of the same correspondents headed for Chicago to cover the Democratic National Convention, although many papers such as the insolvent *Washington Post* had so slashed their budgets that they could not afford to send their own reporters to cover the nomination of New York's governor, Franklin D. Roosevelt.[13]

Within a year after the Bonus March, Roosevelt's New Deal had transformed Washington, D.C., making it at last "the capital of the U.S.," as *Fortune* magazine proclaimed. Previously, Washington reporters had identified the U.S. Senate as "the choicest assignment," and derided the White House as "devoid of allurements to all except chess players and gentlemen in need of sleep." Then, Franklin Roosevelt seized the press's attention away from the Capitol and fixed it on the White House. The president's press staff shaped Roosevelt's public image more thoroughly than that of any of his predecessors, literally staging his every move to camouflage his paralysis from polio. News reporters and photographers willingly cooperated in this deception, which succeeded in focusing public attention on Roosevelt's policies rather than on his health. The New Deal changed the whole calendar of Washington reporting. For more than a century the press corps had timed its arrivals and departures according to the sessions of Congress, often spending less than half the year at the capital. Roosevelt made reporters readjust to the year-round pace of the chief executive. News from Washington gripped the nation as never before in peacetime. "I had never worked harder than in the Hundred Days, as one bill after another barreled from the White House up to Capitol Hill," reminisced the *New York Times* correspondent Turner Catledge. "We reporters were running around in circles trying to keep up with the new bills, much less figure out what they meant."[14]

Politicized by the Bonus Riots and the depression, sentiments within most of the Washington press corps shifted appreciably to the left. Reporters came to expect the federal government to take the lead in rebuilding the national economy. At the same time, public demand for news of the New Deal reactivated many Washington bureaus. During Roosevelt's presidency, the number of reporters accredited to the press galleries doubled. Larger bureaus expanded and single-reporter shops multiplied. Women reporters began breaking barriers that limited entry to the "man's world" of political reporting. Radio broadcasters added to the mix—although radio news remained in arrested development until the Second World War. Washington reporters also emerged from anonymity. For years, most of their stories had been identified only as "special from our Washington correspondent," until depression-ridden newspapers awarded them bylines in lieu of salary increases. Bylines built national reputations, and a favored few gained even greater glory by writing signed columns of opinion. Reinvigorated editorial pages also helped Washington's dismal local newspapers earn some respect during the 1930s. From out of a cloud of tear gas had emerged modern Washington journalism.[15]

1

The News Bureaus and the New Deal

By the time that Franklin D. Roosevelt entered the White House in 1933, three hundred news bureaus operated in Washington. The most influential of these represented the half dozen papers that the president read in bed every morning, principally the *New York Times, New York Herald Tribune, Chicago Tribune, Baltimore Sun, Washington Post,* and *Washington Times-Herald.* Roosevelt tended to skim over their critical editorial pages, the bulk of the nation's press having editorially opposed his election. He paid closer attention to the news stories, feeling confident that he could sway public opinion more through the reporters than through their editors and publishers. The buoyant president was "a smooth propagandist," *Detroit News* correspondent Blair Moody observed. "Every reporter in Washington knows that, and Mr. Roosevelt knows they all know it. He is trying to 'sell' the New Deal to the public, and makes no bones about it." Roosevelt instituted twice-weekly press conferences where he all but seduced the reporters who packed into the Oval Office. Roosevelt's approach to the economic crisis he had inherited bolstered his support within the Washington press corps, with most reporters favoring his bold initiatives for reform and recovery. Despite this partiality, Roosevelt had an uneasy and sometimes stormy relationship with Washington's most influential news bureaus. No matter how artfully he flattered and rewarded their correspondents, he could not control the news they reported.[1]

When the sociologist Leo Rosten conducted a poll of the Washington correspondents in 1936, they ranked the *New York Times* "the most fair and reliable" paper and the *Chicago Tribune* "the least fair and reliable." The *Times* operated the largest newspaper bureau in Washington, trailing only the Associated Press and United Press bureaus in staff size. The *Times* fielded more correspondents at the capital than the struggling *Washington Post* employed on its entire national reporting staff. Publisher Adolph S. Ochs intended the *Times* to be the nation's "paper of record," and the epitome of objective journalism. Ochs had once contemplated eliminating the editorial page entirely to prevent any suspicion of bias in his paper—or in any way offending his advertisers. His insistence on straightforward news reporting led *Times* editors to trim down Washington dispatches to the point where they did little more than reproduce official reports, speeches, and court rulings. To the reporters' despair, the "desk men" at the *Times* meticulously stripped out any opinion, emotion, or style from their writing.[2]

At the bottom of the poll, the *Chicago Tribune*'s detractors pointed out that its "least fair and reliable" reputation had not been built overnight. Immodestly billing itself the "World's Greatest Newspaper," the *Chicago Tribune* perpetuated an old-fashioned style of personal journalism in the image of its formidable publisher, Colonel Robert R. McCormick. Its news columns advocated McCormick's views, and his hates became the *Tribune*'s. The low rating of its Washington bureau reflected the staff's excessive deference to their publisher rather than the quality of their reporting. Colonel McCormick sent good reporters to Washington but subverted their efforts at objectivity. He ran the Washington bureau personally through long-distance telephone calls and wires that would "crackle with Morse sparks." McCormick ordered his bureau chief, Arthur Sears Henning, to rewrite lead stories and take a more critical line against politicians and policies that he deplored. The ever-obliging Henning simply tossed away his original copy and produced a new text closer to the latest editorial line. Colonel McCormick regarded his Washington reporters as foot soldiers who would obey orders unquestionably, and he made them aware that a worker in a "news factory" was as replaceable as a worker in a cannery. Knowing how carefully the publisher would scrutinize their work, they tried hard to anticipate his reactions, causing other Washington reporters to wonder whether the *Tribune*'s correspondents actually believed the news stories they slanted.[3]

Arthur Sears Henning never ventured far from his bureau without leaving phone numbers where his publisher could reach him at any moment. A dapper man with a knack for unloading his administrative duties onto others, Henning was Washington's highest-paid bureau chief, thanks to drawing dual salaries from McCormick's newspaper and his radio station WGN. "Henning lived above the rest of us," recalled *Tribune* reporter Willard Edwards, who described his chief as "the kind of a guy that used a cane when he didn't need one." For all his affectations, Henning had worked his way up from a sports stringer to police reporter before being tapped for the *Chicago Tribune*'s Washington bureau. When offered the job, Henning had hesitated as Washington's news "did not bulk large compared with the news of Chicago" and seemed to promise few of the "big stories that every reporter aspired to cover." He took it only after his editor pointed out that Congress met just a few months each year, which made a Washington assignment "a snap."[4]

Henning stepped off the train in Washington in 1909 just in time to encounter his bureau chief's coffin being shipped back to Chicago. The *Tribune* installed John Callan O'Laughlin as the new chief, with Henning filling out the two-man bureau. O'Laughlin went on to serve as the unofficial press agent for Theodore Roosevelt's "Bull Moose" campaign for president (in those days, the *Chicago Tribune* touted Roosevelt's progressive reforms). The *Tribune* promoted Henning to bureau chief, and he held that title for more than thirty years. "Henning was a scholar, a gentleman and a gourmet," commented another of his reporters, Walter Trohan, "but hardly a bureau chief." Trohan had admired Henning's weekly review of Washington events that ran on the paper's front page each Sunday, but he was appalled to discover that all Henning had been doing was pasting introductions onto clippings from the *New York Herald Tribune* and *New York Times*. That Henning's plagiarism escaped exposure indicated how little notice East Coast journalists paid to the *Chicago Tribune*.[5]

The *Tribune* got by with a small Washington bureau by tapping occasional stringers, mostly women who could not find regular employment. By 1933 the explosion of New Deal activity made it plain that the paper needed a larger full-time staff. Colonel McCormick had already drifted from reform to reaction, but he extended a grace period to his old Groton schoolmate, Franklin Roosevelt. Henning dutifully portrayed Roosevelt as "a man with lines of pain, or will power, and of courage written into his face," and praised his leadership during the legislative rush of the New Deal's first hundred days. The honeymoon ended when Roosevelt's National Recovery Administration set codes to regulate employment in the newspaper business. McCormick demanded that the codes include freedom-of-the-press provisions, which Roosevelt considered superfluous. The *Tribune*'s White House correspondent, John Boettiger, brought up the issue at a press conference, and Roosevelt deflected it flippantly, "Well, look, John, you tell Bert McCormick that he is seeing things under the bed." The correspondents all laughed, but McCormick saw no humor in the challenge. The *Tribune* swiftly shifted into the anti-Roosevelt camp.[6]

Roosevelt thought highly enough of the *Tribune*'s Washington bureau to hire several of its reporters for government public relations jobs, and another of them, John Boettiger, quit when he married the president's daughter. Searching for replacements for these pro–New Deal defectors, the *Tribune* dispatched a trio of tough-minded reporters from the Chicago staff. Willard Edwards, Chesly Manly, and Walter Trohan would give the Roosevelt administration no end of trouble.[7]

Willard Edwards came to Washington in 1933 as a temporary replacement, and stretched his stay to forty years. A Prohibition-era police reporter, Edwards had gone on his first assignment to a barbershop where two men sat in barber chairs, lather on their faces and bullet holes in their foreheads. He earned a reputation as the paper's best all-around reporter, but the demands of the job left him with a serious drinking problem—a reporter "had to have one in Chicago in the '20s," he shrugged. In Washington, bureau chief Henning told Edwards to "go up and cover the Senate," without further instruction, not even directions on how to find the Senate chamber. Edwards had no strong political leanings at first and he rarely bothered to read his paper's editorials. He wrote a favorable profile of Senator Burton K. Wheeler from Montana, unaware that his publisher abhorred the senator. "Has Edwards hired out to

Wheeler?" the Colonel telegraphed the bureau. Thereafter, Willard Edwards read the *Tribune* editorials religiously. "I was conscious what our line was, and I didn't violate that line," he explained. When he realized that Colonel McCormick regarded the New Deal "with a loathing that can't be described," Edwards's reporting adopted a matching attitude.[8]

Neither of the two other Chicago police reporters that joined the *Tribune*'s Washington bureau in 1934 needed to adjust his politics. The young Texan Chesly Manly was deeply conservative in politics and religion, and viewed the New Deal as riddled with "Godless Communists." On Capitol Hill, Manly developed his best sources among the president's most implacable foes, who fed him scoops that established his reputation for being "dogged in the pursuit of facts." The other newcomer, Walter Trohan, had been born in Pennsylvania but grew up in Chicago, so he could describe himself as "a Midwesterner in speech and thought." The conservative Trohan replaced the liberal Boettiger at the White House. A gregarious man with a sparkling Irish wit, Trohan made many friends among New Deal officials while needling them with provocative questions. The White House would leak stories to him, calculating that the material would have greater effect—and seem less likely to have come from the president—if it appeared in a paper as hostile as the *Tribune*.[9]

On a visit to Chicago to dedicate a bridge near the *Tribune* tower, Roosevelt was greeted with a giant banner: "Undominated *Chicago Tribune*, The World's Greatest Newspaper." Back at the White House, he called out jovially at his next press conference, "Come up here, Walter Trohan, I want to see an undominated reporter." Everyone laughed because they regarded the *Tribune* reporters as very much dominated by their publisher, whose constant interventions undermined much of their credibility. While the *Tribune*'s Washington correspondents admitted tailoring stories to fit their publisher, they insisted that it was their job to scrutinize and criticize government actions, and that the public had a right to hear more than the government's official line. The sin of slanting with which they were accused, Trohan liked to point out, would later become acceptable among liberal journalists "under the dignified term of interpretation."[10]

In Washington, the *Chicago Tribune* topped the *New York Times* only in location. Its bureau occupied a suite of offices three flights above the *Times* bureau in the Albee Building near the White House. As the capital's oldest and largest newspaper bureau in the 1930s, the *New York Times* had ten men and one woman. Read universally by high-level government officials and the rest of the Washington press corps, the *New York Times* exerted a powerful influence on both government policy and news reporting from Washington. When Arthur Krock took over the *Times* bureau in 1932, Walter Lippmann congratulated him for assuming "the most influential and important single job in American journalism."[11]

Krock did not want the job. A self-described "country boy from Kentucky," he had developed a taste for the bright lights of New York. He relished the free tickets that the *Times* procured for opening nights on Broadway, and enjoyed leisurely weekends of polo matches at the Long Island estates of his wealthy friends, a lifestyle out of the pages of *The Great Gatsby*. The son of a Jewish father and Protestant mother, Krock resisted any religious identity and became a lifelong agnostic. A family financial crisis had forced him to drop out of Princeton University and started him reporting in Louisville. In 1909 the *Louisville Times* sent him to Washington, and soon afterward the paper and its bureau merged into the prestigious *Louisville Courier-Journal.* Six years later Krock returned to Louisville as editor of the *Courier-Journal.* He held the post until forced out by the paper's new owner, Robert Worth Bingham.[12]

Moving to New York, first as a publicity agent for the Motion Picture Producers and Distributors, Krock joined the editorial staff of the *New York World*, headed by Walter Lippmann. On almost every issue, Krock found himself a "mind apart" from Lippmann. Their relations strained further when Lippmann accused him of leaking early news reports to friends of his stockbroker. Krock switched to the *New York Times,* from which he denigrated the *World* as "a crusader, and crusading invariably creeps into the columns labeled news." Arthur Krock felt more at home with his new paper's unadorned, objective news. Publisher Adolph Ochs—a fellow Southerner from Chattanooga, Tennessee—had banned comics, crossword puzzles, and other trendy features from his paper, with his standard comment, "I won't have a dern thing to do with it." At the *Times,* Krock wrote editorials and got a byline in the Sunday news supplement.[13]

Convinced that he had "shaken off the dust of Washington permanently," Krock was dismayed when the *Times* sent him back to head its largest news operation outside of New York. The bureau's longtime chief Richard Oulahan (President Hoover's closest friend in the press corps) had died suddenly in December 1931. Several top men at the *Times* had declined to replace him. Ochs's son-in-law and chief of staff, Arthur Hays Sulzberger, implored Krock to take over the Washington bureau on a temporary basis. After he got the bureau running effectively, he could return to New York. Krock's wife and son would stay in their Manhattan apartment while he commuted for weekends. "I felt more or less like an executioner in asking him to go," Sulzberger confided to Ochs, "since it involves breaking up his family for the time being."[14]

In a thick cloud of cigar smoke, Krock strode into the Washington bureau in February 1932. Close examination showed him that while the bureau's reporters each held a regular beat, the lines between them so overlapped that several of them might interview the same official independently and file different versions of the same story. Krock wanted greater specialization, so that reporters would know as much about their subject areas as "the men who are making the news." He also dismantled an entrenched seniority system that paid the bureau's hardest-working staff the least. Within five months, he felt that he had completed his reorganization and made plans to leave. To head the bureau, Krock singled out Turner Catledge, a thirty-year-old Mississippian whom he admired as an ambitious reporter and an amusing storyteller (both men shared a fondness for the "darky" stories of their Southern roots). Krock planned to go back to New York as the *Times*'s political editor, and visit Washington occasionally to coach Catledge. Instead, the worsening depression made the *Times* management eager to have a more experienced man in the post, and they asked Krock to stay there a little longer.[15]

Both in New York and Washington, the *New York Times* viewed the *New York Herald Tribune* as its chief rival. The two differed markedly in style. The *Times* was an editor's paper, devoid of color and proud of being called the "Good Gray Lady" of American journalism. The *Herald Tribune* boasted of being a writer's paper that encouraged sprightly copy. It ran a smaller Washington bureau than the *Times*, but installed a shrewd competitor, Bert Andrews, as bureau chief. Many late night phone calls from New York urged Krock to seek verification of something that appeared in the *Herald Tribune*. The *Times* compensated for its less aggressive style with an abundance of staff. Other reporters quipped that press conferences had to start by introducing all the *New York Times* reporters to each other. Most Washington bureaus consisted of a couple of reporters who filed "specials" to their papers on a range of government issues. *Times* reporters could specialize, develop well-placed sources, and write with greater authority. "We are not here to duplicate the A.P.," the *Times* reporter Felix Belair explained. The bureau aimed to "mine the town for news the A.P. doesn't have or won't have until we get it in the paper."[16]

During the hectic years of the New Deal, Washington datelines dominated the front page of the *New York Times*. No matter how much news the bureau filed, editors in New York wanted more. When big news broke, the bureau staff would count the bylines on the next day's front page with satisfaction and would post compliments from New York on the bulletin board. At other times, the Washington staff groaned over how their dispatches had been "butchered" by deskmen who stripped out adjectives, added information from the wire service dispatches, garbled leads, and then peppered them with queries about their accuracy and completeness. As bureau chief, Arthur Krock reflexively sided with his staff. He assumed that a reporter on the spot understood the situation better than an editor in New York, and he doubted that the bullpen of night editors grasped the subtleties of Washington's political culture. Krock insisted that the New Yorkers route all questions through his bureau's news desk and not call reporters directly. Editors in New York bristled at such "petty griping," and reminded him of the biblical admonition that "the branch cannot bear fruit of itself, except it abide in the vine."[17]

In Washington, Krock became highly influential because he was "THE correspondent of THE *New York Times*," assessed the *Washington Post* reporter

Chalmers Roberts. "Even though he had a big bureau, he was THE correspondent." Holding the official title of "Washington Correspondent," Krock for years had the bureau's only regular byline. He filed daily news stories and a signed editorial page column that allowed him a freedom of expression denied to the rest of his staff. His column came about after Walter Lippmann had launched one for the rival *Herald Tribune*. Arthur Hays Sulzberger proposed that Krock contribute a column for the daily and Sunday *Times*, stretching the paper's traditional definition of the news to "include coverage of what men were thinking as well as what they were doing." The elderly Adolph Ochs remained skeptical, but Lester Markel, editor of the Sunday edition, argued that the paper owed its readers more than facts. "Background—or interpretation—is *not* opinion," Markel reasoned. A newspaper ought to give the essential facts with enough interpretation "to make those facts understandable." After Ochs relented, Krock's column, first called "From Washington" and later "In the Nation," began in 1933 and ran until 1966.[18]

Mindful of his publisher's caution, Krock offered a more restrained column than did most of his syndicated competitors. "In the Nation" usually recapitulated issues, and it reflected Krock's extensive reading in history, economics, and political theory. Occasional flashes of humor, irony, and insider gossip relieved its stately, old-fashioned prose. Krock regarded himself as a liberal in the Woodrow Wilson mold, but in actuality he stood still as events transformed the political landscape around him. His increasing skepticism of New Deal liberalism rankled other reporters at the *Times*, who yearned for more left-leaning opinion in the paper. Politicians, by contrast, disapproved of the *Times*'s Washington correspondent expressing any opinion at all. Krock persisted against all criticism, managing to write the lead story of the day, churn out his column, and run the bureau. He would shut himself up in his office to write, stalking out periodically to stop at a reporter's desk. He rarely held staff meetings or socialized with his reporters, who never dared call him anything other than "Mr. Krock."[19]

The *Times* bureau chief maintained an aloof distance from much of the Washington press corps, lunching at the exclusive Metropolitan Club rather than the National Press Club, and avoiding press conferences. "Krock used to be a good reporter," the other correspondents scoffed, "but now he's a journalist." He returned their disdain by dismissing the pack as "often stupid, devoted to the 'huddle' instead of original research in the quest for news, intent on appearing on radio programs and Gridiron dinners." Krock preferred to hobnob with the top politicians, diplomats, and financiers, who kept him well informed. In later years, however, he realized bitterly that many of those whom he had considered personal friends had actually been trying to use him.[20]

The 1932 presidential election pitted two of Krock's old friends against each other. He had known the incumbent Herbert Hoover and the challenger Franklin Roosevelt since he covered them both during the Wilson administration. In 1920, when Roosevelt ran as the Democratic candidate for vice president, Krock had handled publicity for the Democratic National Committee. He had spent a night at Hyde Park, advising the candidate, and he never forgot "how young and hand-some he was and how young and charming his wife was." When he joined the *New York Times*'s editorial staff, Krock exchanged light-hearted notes with Gov-ernor Roosevelt. After Roosevelt routed Hoover in the presidential race, at the depth of the depression, an interminable five months stood between the No-vember election and the inauguration in March. The economy crumbled, banks failed, mortgages were foreclosed, and workers lost their jobs, yet the outgoing and incoming presidents barely spoke to each other. Desperate to convince his successor to continue his policies, Hoover turned to their mutual friend Arthur Krock as a go-between. It took years for Krock to recognize the mistake he made by agreeing. His intervention pegged himself as "a Hoover man" and severely strained his relations with the new president. "I don't know how the *hell* I got into this," Krock later wondered. "Why was I so officious in those days?"[21]

In his initial reporting on the New Deal, Krock praised Roosevelt with exu-berance. "If swift decision and action, vast political power and willingness to use it are the chief prerequisites in the pilot, Franklin D. Roosevelt in a week has displayed them all," he informed his readers. "Gone is the fortress that was the White House; the formal, uneasy place that was the Executive Office; the wild-cat cage that was Congress." FDR was "the boss, the dynamo, the works." Similar sentiments were widespread within the press corps. The pro-Hoover columnist Mark Sullivan reasoned that it would be "almost unpatriotic" to make things difficult for Roosevelt as he tried to lift the nation out of the depression. New Dealers filled with "shocking ideas" poured into Washington, often straight from college campuses, eager to reform and regulate the economy. Krock had no trouble establishing sources among the ebullient newcomers, who loved to talk about what they were doing. What surprised him, however, was his inability to interview the president.[22]

A month after the inauguration, Krock contacted the White House for an appointment with Roosevelt. He advised Roosevelt's appointment secretary Marvin McIntyre (formerly a reporter for Krock in Louisville) that he had seen President Hoover whenever he wanted, and that as the Washington corre-spondent for "the largest paper in Mr. Roosevelt's home city and state," he felt entitled to continued access. McIntyre took the matter to the press secretary Stephen Early, commenting, "This is bound to come up sooner or later, and I think we should have a confab and definitely determine what the policy is to be about fair haired boys." Roosevelt's staff feared that granting private interviews would result either in "an endless process" or only a "privileged few" getting to see the president. They remained mindful of the resentment over Hoover's exclusive dealings with a select circle of friendly correspondents—whom the excluded reporters had referred to as the "trained seals." Indignant when his applications were repeatedly rejected, Krock demanded to know whether it was the president's policy "not to receive any individual newspaper correspondents, regardless of their past relations to him or the position of the newspapers they represent in the American journalistic structure."[23]

Even without formal interviews, Krock got invited to family dinners at the White House and engaged in plenty of "bull sessions" with volatile New Dealers who provided him with some impressive scoops. Two front-page stories in April 1933 confirmed his worth to the *New York Times*. On April 14, he revealed that Roosevelt intended to mobilize government-business relations to end the depression, a tip Krock picked up during lunch with Senator Robert Wagner of New York. At his next press conference, Roosevelt feigned ignorance, saying that all he knew was what he read in the *Times*. Two weeks later, the administration publicly proposed the National Industrial Recovery Act. On April 19, Krock again beat the press corps with advance word that the United States would stop exporting gold, an offhand tip he had gotten from a Treasury Department official. Roosevelt did not deny the *Times* story, leading Krock to conclude that it had been a trial balloon, floated to test the public's reaction. Yet as the columnist Raymond Clapper pointed out, Roosevelt hated being second-guessed. As an improviser who rarely knew for certain where he was heading, the president preferred that reporters wait until after he had made up his mind before they signaled his moves. Krock's scoops got on his nerves.[24]

Rather than give exclusive interviews, Roosevelt dealt with reporters as a group at his regular press conferences. "He insulted them, lectured them, and made them laugh," the United Press reporter Merriman Smith recalled in describing these conferences. "He called them liars and used the mighty weight of his high office against the press in pile-driving fashion." Then, with a jaunty wave of his cigarette and a first-name greeting, he won their forgiveness. A reporter who asked a hostile question, sometimes planted by an editor, would get presidential responses with elaborately formal courtesy that often included a greeting to the antagonistic editor. Most reporters liked Roosevelt, but they said it was essentially a "friendship of convenience." They were doing their job, collecting news, and Roosevelt served an endless source of interesting items. "They knew that he knew what they wanted, and that it was to his political interest to give them a great deal of information," explained Laurence Todd, by then the Washington correspondent for the Soviet news agency TASS. "They laughed at his jokes, respected his injunctions upon publication of advance-release statements and speeches, and knew—as they had not under previous administrations—that he would play no favorites."[25]

A noticeably missing figure from the mob that gathered at presidential press conferences was Arthur Krock. The *Times* bureau chief found it demeaning to line up like "so many street-idlers waiting for a parade to go by" before rushing into the Oval Office to jockey for position near the president's desk. He also found it inhibiting to hear the president declare something "off-the-record" that a reporter could have learned, and reported, from another source. By staying away and relying on the *Times* correspondent at the White House to cover the conferences, Krock preserved his freedom to break stories the administration hoped to suppress. So conspicuous was his absence that Roosevelt asked him about it. Krock genially replied that the president made it hard for him to preserve his objectivity, "You charm me so much that when I go back to write comment on the proceedings, I can't keep it in balance." Absence did not preclude Krock's planting questions with his White House correspondent. "I suppose Arthur told you to ask that one," Roosevelt responded to one pointed question. Piqued by Krock's truancy, Roosevelt belittled him as "Li'l Arthur" (a play on the hillbilly comic strip "Li'l Abner") to the amusement of other reporters.[26]

As their relationship frayed, the president and the bureau chief craved the same thing. They both wanted someone else to head the *New York Times* bureau in Washington. Krock yearned to return to New York as editorial page editor and to turn the bureau over to Turner Catledge. That would have suited Roosevelt fine, but the New Deal had made Arthur Krock indispensable to the *Times* in Washington. When nothing had changed by 1934, the president directly appealed to *Times* publisher Adolph Ochs. Krock was spreading misinformation that people took as truth because of the *Times*'s reputation for accuracy, Roosevelt complained. Ochs shrewdly asked Krock to draft his reply. The bureau chief took wry pleasure in declining to remove himself and had his publisher declare, "I am sure if you would discuss the article with Mr. Krock personally he could enlighten you with respect to other details." Krock later mused that a chronicler of government activities who tried not only to report what happened but to explain what it meant "sits in a hot spot." He accused the Roosevelt administration of seeking to turn the press into "official gazettes" that printed official press releases uncritically. But to keep the White House doors open to his bureau, Krock blunted his criticism by defending the president against charges about government assaults on freedom of the press. "No Chief Executive has ever answered so many questions as Mr. Roosevelt," he wrote in the *Times*, "and he does not stand on form."[27]

A Christmas greeting from Press Secretary Steve Early drew from Krock another protest over the cold shoulder the White House was giving him. "I am not conscious of having done any more or less than my duty in what I have written about the Administration," he complained; "certainly there has been no unfriendly motive on my part." He had been friendly toward the president, his press secretary, and other White House aides for years, yet he had been "made conscious in many ways of something amounting almost to hostility on the part of the President, who certainly went out of his way the other day to do textually what he had on several previous occasions done verbally before a couple of hundred newspaper men—and that was to disparage things I had written or had been written under my direction." If Roosevelt had grievances with him, Krock pleaded, he should discuss them with him personally.[28]

Angry over not gaining freer access, Krock could not help but observe how skillfully Roosevelt had won over the other correspondents. It was hard for any reporter to criticize a president after playing cards or going swimming with him, or dining at his table. The Roosevelt administration employed "more ruthlessness, intelligence, and subtlety in trying to suppress legitimate, unfavorable comment" than any other he had known, he later insisted. The president had so generously spread patronage among journalists that the *Baltimore Sun*'s Frank Kent commented there were "almost as many newspaper men in the New Deal as there are in the press gallery." Taking public relations posts in the new federal agencies, the former correspondents helped the working press cope with the New Deal's dizzying pace. To understand and explain complex economic issues on deadline, reporters relied increasingly on government press releases, a practice that led to "some of the best reporting, and also some of the worst," commented the *New York Times*'s night editor Neil MacNeil. "The correspondent who believes all he is told will find it easy, for nowhere is news more available." Press releases improved the quality of technical information available, but Arthur Krock dismissed the diet of handouts as "an incentive to laziness on the part of the press."[29]

In line with its care and feeding of the press, Roosevelt's White House opened a larger pressroom off the main entrance of the West Wing, providing correspondents with desks, typewriters, telephones, and a poker table. Franklin and Eleanor Roosevelt elevated the journalists' status by inviting them to social functions as guests rather than as reporters. The Roosevelts hosted annual receptions for White House correspondents, had groups of them in for Sunday night scrambled-egg suppers, and threw picnics for them at Hyde Park. With both the president and his wife traveling extensively, reporters could get to know them on long journeys. Once when presidential travel disrupted a reporter's wedding plans, Roosevelt arranged for the bride to get press credentials so they could turn the trip into a honeymoon. Harrison Salisbury, who reported then for the United Press and later for the *New York Times*, viewed all this skeptically. "I knew Roosevelt's tricks," he recorded. "They were so obvious: dances for the press in the Blue Room, the little birthday notes, the Christmas parties; good fun, but there had to be a bill."[30]

Economic recovery slowed in 1934, the Supreme Court struck down key New Deal programs, and populist criticism from Senator Huey Long and Father Charles Coughlin shook the Roosevelt administration. The president abandoned his efforts to win business cooperation and adopted a more confrontational strategy. His shift to the left alienated many publishers, who worried about the impact of the New Deal's labor and tax policies on their newspapers. Conservative columnists now decried Roosevelt's "dictatorial" aspirations and accused him of trying to "sovietize" America. Some liberal reporters also grew disenchanted with the president because of his tendency to float stories and disavow them whenever it suited his purposes. The president blamed the mounting press criticism on editors and publishers, arguing that "special bureau chiefs down here write what the owner of the newspaper tells them to write, and they leave out half the truth."[31]

Arthur Krock strayed closer to the administration's congressional opposition, and the more out of step with the New Deal that he became, the happier he would have been to abandon Washington completely. But Adolph Ochs's death in April 1935 handed Krock another setback. Arthur Hays Sulzberger, taking over as publisher, said that he felt uneasy about making immediate changes in the paper and preferred to have his Washington bureau chief stay in place for the time being. Further cementing Krock's position was the Pulitzer Prize he earned in 1935 for the "clearness and terseness of style" and "fair, judicious, well-balanced and well-informed, interpretive writing" of his Washington coverage.[32]

At this juncture, Krock forged an alliance with Joseph P. Kennedy, the financier whom Roosevelt had appointed to head the new Securities and Exchange Commission. Kennedy's influential friends lobbied for Krock's endorsement, and when Krock responded with a column of fulsome praise, Kennedy welcomed him as an ally. The *Washington Post* reporter Ernest K. Lindley observed that Krock and Kennedy shared "expensive tastes, conservative economic views and a love for banter, and they were therefore a perfect fit." They formed a close bond. Kennedy lavished gifts on Krock, and the correspondent spent so much time at Kennedy's home, ghostwriting his speeches and a campaign book, *I'm for Roosevelt*, in which Kennedy endorsed the president's reelection, that some family members assumed that the correspondent must have been working on retainer. It was the affluent lifestyle and gracious hospitality that attracted Krock to Kennedy, along with the opportunity to play behind-the-scenes advisor to a potential president.[33]

Joe Kennedy returned Krock's favors by defending the *Times* bureau chief to the president. He measured Krock's support of the New Deal at "95 percent." "Oh, but that other 5 percent!" Roosevelt sighed. In 1936, Krock halfheartedly endorsed the president as "neither as much of an opportunist as the Republicans insisted nor as great a humanitarian as the Democrats proclaimed." That was enough to improve his relations modestly with the president. Roosevelt appreciated editorial support from the *New York Times* at a time when about two-thirds of the nation's newspapers opposed his reelection. He was also pleased to hear rumors that the *Times* at long last planned to recall Krock to New York. At the Democratic convention that year, Krock alerted Turner Catledge that he did not expect to return to Washington after the campaign, and advised Catledge to move into his vacated office. By the fall, however, Catledge had to move out again when New York sent Krock back to Washington.[34]

A thoroughly exasperated Roosevelt then made a personal overture to Turner Catledge. Expressing his disdain for Krock, the president offered Catledge direct access to see him without consulting his bureau chief. Catledge reported all this back to Krock, who thought it no surprise that the president would try to undermine his authority. What Catledge drew from the incident was Roosevelt's dislike for "anyone or anything that had independent status. He was repeatedly intrigued with the idea of bringing *The Times* to heel." Roosevelt soon detected that his tactic had misfired and reversed course. He invited Krock to spend the night at Hyde Park, to indicate that they were still friends, and during the evening outlined a "great design" for an international peace conference to avoid war. Krock asked permission to write about the plan, and Roosevelt promised not to deny it. But when public reaction proved unfavorable, the president technically kept his pledge by keeping silent and having his agriculture secretary, Henry Wallace, declare Krock's story false.[35]

Flush with success from his landslide reelection in 1936, and counting on the enormous congressional majorities that had ridden on his coattails, Roosevelt announced a stunning plan to add extra justices to the Supreme Court (where the predominantly conservative justices had ruled much of the early New Deal unconstitutional). "There has been little else in the newspapers," Interior Secretary Harold Ickes recorded in his diary, since the president's plan to "pack" the Court was read in Congress. Democrats split over the plan, with opponents allying themselves with Republicans against it. The *New York Times* joined the many papers that editorially denounced any tampering with the Supreme Court. Relishing the chance to surprise the press and confound its predictions, Roosevelt had failed to test the water in advance. He was caught off guard by the intensely negative public reaction. "One of the major functions of the press in a democracy is to act as a cushion for unpleasant news," explained Neil MacNeil. Had Roosevelt leaked the plan, he could have modified it to mute the hostile response.[36]

Scrambling to regroup, Roosevelt broke his rule against giving journalists exclusive interviews and granted one to Arthur Krock. Despite his past criticism, Krock agreed with Roosevelt that several of the justices were "twenty years behind the times—insensible to social change." Krock notified Press Secretary Steve Early that the *Times*'s Sunday magazine wanted him to write about the battle over the Supreme Court. The president could use the opportunity to calm public anxieties, Krock advised, and he offered to let the White House review the article before its publication. On February 13, 1937, after four years of trying, Krock formally interviewed President Roosevelt. He took no notes and instead rushed back to the *Times* bureau to reconstruct the talk from memory. Then he sent the text back to the White House staff, warning them not to edit out those portions that mirrored the president's philosophy. "No one cares what I *think* the President thinks," he explained, "and it would be an impertinence on my part to seem to be writing that." They made only cursory changes. Given the news value of the story, the *Times* ran it on the front page, under a discrete headline: "The President Discusses His Political Philosophy." The interview won Krock his second Pulitzer Prize.[37]

Irate members of the White House press corps could not believe that "Li'l Arthur" had gotten an exclusive interview. At his next press conference, Roosevelt swore that it would not happen again. Indeed, Roosevelt never granted another exclusive for-attribution interview to a Washington correspondent. As for Krock, he fell from the president's good graces as soon as his next critical article appeared. "I am a walking allergy to Presidents," he later joked, "that soon becomes insufferable." Krock grievously offended Roosevelt by reporting that Joseph P. Kennedy would be the next ambassador to Great Britain, at a time when the incumbent ambassador, Robert Worth Bingham (the same man who had years earlier forced Krock out of his editorship in Louisville) lay dying in a hospital. Convinced that Krock was cultivating Kennedy to run for president, Roosevelt warned his new ambassador that Krock's friendship "has done you more harm in the past few years than all of your enemies put together." Krock could never write anything decent "without qualifying it by some nasty dig at the end of the praise," Roosevelt complained, dismissing him as "a social parasite whose surface support can be won by entertainment and flattery, but who in his heart is a cynic who has never felt warm affection for anybody—man or woman." Kennedy lost no time in making sure that the president's letter got back to his friend and ally Krock. In his correspondence with Krock, the ambassador was critical of the Roosevelt administration, inspiring Krock to pass along Kennedy's letters to the White House to ingratiate himself with Roosevelt's staff. The White House leaked them to the *Chicago Tribune,* which speculated that Kennedy was poised to run for president. Kennedy threatened to sue the *Tribune.* Krock blamed the leak on the New Dealers, but he had meanly contributed to the mess.[38]

It seemed odd that the Washington bureau chief of the *New York Times,* that paradigm of eastern liberalism, had emerged as the New Deal's most influential critic in the press. Washington had no shortage of conservative columnists, but their overt biases against Roosevelt diminished their impact. By contrast, Krock had delivered his blows in a low-key manner. During Roosevelt's second term, Krock began hitting harder. He landed his mightiest blow on a presidential favorite, Harry Hopkins, whom Roosevelt had nominated for secretary of commerce. Krock's column quoted Hopkins as saying, "We shall tax and tax, and spend and spend, and elect and elect." The statement had already appeared in other papers but had not resonated until Krock gave it prominence in the *Times.* Harry Hopkins vehemently denied having said it. The Senate Commerce Committee called Krock to testify at the nomination hearings, but he declined to identify his source. He modestly pointed out that the quote had appeared in syndicated columns that reached many millions of people, while his went to "only a humble 570,000 a day."[39]

The editorial page editorship of the *New York Times* fell vacant in 1938, and once again Arthur Krock saw himself passed over for a candidate more congenial to his publisher. Despite Krock's denial of his Jewish heritage, he believed that Arthur Hays Sulzberger was reluctant to do anything that would further the perception that the *Times* was a "Jewish newspaper." Sulzberger said as much to Joseph Kennedy, who had expressed disappointment that his friend had not been promoted, yet it was strange reasoning given that Krock's byline figured more prominently on the front page than it would have on the masthead. More likely, it served as an excuse for Sulzberger to keep the prickly Krock at a distance. Krock resigned himself to permanent exile and grasped control of the Washington bureau more firmly, running it as an independent fiefdom. To his surprise, Krock found that he was satisfied to stay in the capital, where he decided he had more freedom to speak his mind than he would have had writing editorials. The death in 1938 of his estranged wife, Marguerite, who had remained in New York, also freed Krock to marry Martha Blair, a society columnist for the *Washington Times-Herald*.[40]

Both the bureau chief and the *New York Times* opposed Roosevelt's unprecedented bid for a third term in 1940, and Krock allowed his personal animosity to surface in his lead story on the president's reelection: "Over an apparently huge popular minority, which under the electoral college system was not able to register its proportion of the total vote in terms of electors, President Roosevelt was chosen yesterday for a third term, the first American in history to break the tradition which began with the Republic." Faced with four more years of Franklin Roosevelt, Krock tendered his resignation as bureau chief, on the grounds that the president might take revenge against the paper. Sulzberger declined to accept this offer, however. When the *Times* reporter Charles Hurd asked the president how it felt to be so criticized, Roosevelt airily waved it aside. "If the newspapers report what I do and say," he said with seeming assurance, "I am not concerned about the editorials or the columnists." Yet at the same time the president ordered the Secret Service to bar from his press conferences a half dozen of the most critical correspondents, Arthur Krock among them. Press Secretary Steve Early promptly rescinded the order and explained to the correspondents, "Well, I couldn't let the boss make a damned fool of himself, could I?"[41]

The Second World War put the internationalist *New York Times* back in Roosevelt's camp, and further alienated the isolationist *Chicago Tribune* from the White House. The *Tribune* condemned Roosevelt for what it saw as his maneuvering the nation into the war without adequate military preparedness. The *Tribune* was then facing new competition from the department store heir Marshall Field, who was about to launch the *Chicago Sun* as a pro–New Deal paper. Field enticed Turner Catledge away from the *New York Times* as the new paper's managing editor. Field also sought an Associated Press franchise, but Colonel McCormick blocked the AP from extending its invaluable service to his new rival, an action that caused Roosevelt's Justice Department to file an antitrust suit against the AP. The *Sun* was due to rise for the first time on December 4, 1941, and the *Tribune* desperately wanted a blockbuster story to eclipse it. The Washington bureau obliged when reporter Chesly Manly obtained a top-secret document labeled "Victory Program" from the isolationist Senator Burton K. Wheeler. The report estimated the amount of troops and matériel that would be necessary to win a war against Germany and Japan. Manly copied key excerpts, which appeared on the front page of the *Chicago Tribune* on December 4 under the banner headline "FDR's WAR PLANS!"[42]

The *Tribune*'s White House correspondent Walter Trohan opposed publishing this story on the grounds that the military planned for almost any contingency, and he warned that there could be harsh repercussions from the government. The *Tribune*'s managing editor also had second thoughts, but Colonel McCormick said "Publish it." The report raised a storm among isolationists on Capitol Hill, and Senator Wheeler, without mentioning his own role in leaking the document, demanded a congressional investigation. President Roosevelt declined to answer questions on the matter and referred reporters to his secretary of war, who questioned the "loyalty and patriotism" of the newspapers that published the story. Roosevelt's silence led some to speculate that he welcomed the leak as a way of provoking war while simultaneously discrediting the nation's leading isolationist newspaper. Within days, the Japanese attack on Pearl Harbor made the *Tribune*'s leak seem utterly irresponsible. Yet Walter Trohan concluded that he had been wrong to oppose its publication. The public had a right to know what its leaders were planning, especially when it conflicted with what they were saying. Trohan noted wryly that thirty years later the *Tribune*'s harshest critics published the Pentagon Papers.[43]

In June 1942 the *Chicago Tribune* published an even more reckless story on Japanese naval capacity on the eve of the Battle of Midway, giving clues from which the Japanese could have surmised that the United States had broken their codes. A *Tribune* reporter in the Pacific had written the story, but it appeared under a Washington dateline to disguise its source. Stunned by this breach of national security, Navy Secretary Frank Knox (formerly publisher of the rival *Chicago Daily News*) demanded that the government prosecute the *Tribune* under federal espionage laws. A grand jury was impaneled, but the navy realized that the Japanese must not have read the *Chicago Tribune*, as they had not changed their codes after the report. Rather than draw the enemy's attention to the breach of security, the navy withdrew its complaint and the case collapsed. The code-breaking incident consumed countless hours for the *Tribune*'s Washington bureau, which bore the brunt of the "censorship storm," with FBI agents interviewing its reporters and tapping their phones.[44]

Once the United States entered the war, the American press operated under military and voluntary constraints, and President Roosevelt no longer felt it

necessary to keep reporters constantly informed. His biweekly press conferences continued, but now he traveled in secret, usually with only three wire
service reporters. Even the tradition of not flying a flag over the White House
during the president's absences was discontinued. While Roosevelt kept the
press "comfortably distant" for the rest of his presidency, he began inviting
select groups of correspondents and columnists for off-the-record background
briefings. Arthur Krock did not make the list, and it irked him to discover that
the *Times* columnist Anne O'Hare McCormick, who wrote on world affairs
out of the New York offices, had attended such a closed session without telling
him. "Of course, the president has consistently sought to shut off my information sources," Krock groused. "But I don't think *The Times* in any way should
help him do it."[45]

The war disrupted the Washington news bureaus. Some reporters went
abroad as war correspondents, others as combatants, just as the war was putting a premium on news from the capital. To augment his staff, Krock hired
the aggressive political reporter Bill Lawrence away from the United Press, and
lured Turner Catledge back from the *Chicago Sun*. Catledge had come to doubt
that he would ever succeed Krock as bureau chief, and soon afterward he accepted a position back in New York, on his way to becoming the *New York
Times*'s managing editor. While Krock rebuilt the bureau, he was not at all
pleased to acquire the rising star James "Scotty" Reston, a Scottish-born American sportswriter turned diplomatic correspondent. Reston had covered the
London blitz for the *Times* until an illness sent him stateside for recuperation.
When Reston was assigned to Washington, Krock complained that New York
was turning his bureau into "a damned displaced persons' office."[46]

As a green correspondent in the Senate press gallery, Scotty Reston failed to
report that his paper's general manger, Colonel Julius Adler, had been nominated to be an army general. "It's a good thing you don't work for Colonel
McCormick on the *Tribune* in Chicago!" commented Adler, accepting the
reporter's profuse apologies. Nor did Reston win much favor from bureau chief
Krock by publishing his first book, *Prelude to Victory*, in which he assailed
America's prewar isolationism and unpreparedness. The *New York Times Book
Review* gave it front-page prominence, which whetted Reston's appetite for
more analytical writing. His pleas left Arthur Krock unimpressed. Reporters
in his bureau could dabble with analysis in the Sunday "Review of the Week"
section, he decreed, but not in their daily news reporting. Krock showed no
remorse when Reston chose to return to London to work for the U.S. Office of
War Information, and he tried to block the young reporter's return to the bureau the next year. All the major beats were already covered, Krock explained,
so reinserting Reston would disrupt "the machinery of the bureau." Arthur
Sulzberger's insistence made the bureau chief relent, but Krock continued to
withstand Reston's appeals to write interpretive reports. Suspecting that Krock

did not want his own standing as a columnist diluted by having his reporters do anything more than report the news, Reston toyed with an offer to write a column for the rival *Herald Tribune*. To prevent him from leaving the *Times*, Krock finally consented to let Reston write occasional news analysis—by which he meant interpretive writing, not editorials. The editors would retain the right to eliminate anything from news analysis that had "an emotional content or editorial slant."[47]

What softened Krock was James Reston's extraordinary talent for scoops. Krock had assigned him to the backwater beat of collecting news at Washington's embassies. It was Reston's good fortune that the Allies were convening at the Georgetown estate Dumbarton Oaks in 1944 to plan for a postwar United Nations. Among the Nationalist Chinese delegation, Reston encountered a former intern at the *Times*, Chen Yi. As the Chinese disliked some of the proposals being circulated, they had no objection to their premature release. The obliging Chen Yi slipped the position papers to Reston, who raced back to present his windfall to his bureau chief as if it were "the sort of thing I 'picked up' every day or so." Looking like he had just won the Kentucky Derby, Krock agreed that publication of the position papers would not jeopardize national security. The *Times* began publishing one paper a day, agonizing its competitors and infuriating the State Department. For this exclusive, Reston won his first Pulitzer Prize and the everlasting respect of his bureau chief. Sent to San Francisco to report on the creation of the United Nations, Reston disappeared on the day that Britain's foreign secretary Anthony Eden was due to make a major announcement. Other *Times* staffers wondered what had happened to him, but when the door to the conference room swung open Scotty Reston walked in arm-in-arm with Eden. Squeezed in the back of the crowded room, Arthur Krock turned to a colleague and said, "You have to hand it to the little guy." Krock accepted Reston as a regular member of the Washington bureau, although he reminded New York that "two columnists in the Washington Bureau . . . was one too many." For his part, Reston agreed to conform to the "light regimentation" of the bureau, so long as he was spared from any "picayune assignments."[48]

Scotty Reston concentrated on foreign affairs while Arthur Krock focused on politics, specifically on President Roosevelt's "outrageous" bid for a fourth term. The *Times* reversed its editorial defection of four years earlier and endorsed Roosevelt in 1944, but Krock's columns sharply diverged from his paper's editorial line. He offered to step down as bureau chief if Roosevelt won reelection. "I am *persona non grata* at the White House," Krock reminded his publisher, "which the President has emphasized often by attentions to other *Times* executives and writers, and his election to a fourth term will mean that the 'non' in that phrase will assume capital letters." Once again, Sulzberger declined to remove him, although he chided Krock that the *Times* had reached its editorial decision out of concern for international affairs and he wished that the columnist had been "guided a bit more by similar consideration."[49]

Arthur Krock grew accustomed to his fate as bureau chief, and a mellowed Roosevelt grew resigned to Krock's staying there. Privately, the president admitted "a certain affection" for the crusty but dependable fixture at the *Times* bureau. Krock frequently disagreed with the president's policies but retained some admiration for his experimental approach to government. The depression and Second World War had called for dramatic new directions, he agreed, even if his own sentiments remained rooted in past principles. Krock was the last Washington bureau chief for the *Times* to have been born in the nineteenth century, James Reston observed, and he "regarded it as a personal misfortune that he took over the bureau just when the Roosevelt revolution changed the world he loved." Yet Krock appreciated that he owed his own prominence to Roosevelt's putting Washington at the center of the world map. By 1945 the *New York Times* could not get enough newsprint to publish all the news its Washington bureau was sending back daily.[50]

The president and the bureau chief last crossed paths at the White House correspondents' annual dinner on March 22, 1945. Krock had heard reports about Roosevelt's declining health but had seen little of him during the war. The expression on Krock's face as the ailing president was wheeled past him caused Roosevelt to laugh. "Cheer up, Arthur," he exclaimed. "Things have seldom been as bad as you said they were." Three weeks later, Roosevelt died. In the *Times*'s lead story, Krock wrote that despite all the rumors about Roosevelt's health, "the fact stunned the Government and the citizens of the world." He reported that "men's hats were off, and the tears that were shed were not to be seen only on the cheeks of women. Some Presidents have been held in lukewarm esteem here, and some have been disliked by the local population, but Mr. Roosevelt held a high place in the rare affections of the capital."[51]

Having outlasted the New Deal, Arthur Krock headed the *New York Times* Washington bureau until 1953. By then, the capital's most prestigious news bureau had gone stale. The rest of the press corps gossiped that *Times* reporters, with the notable exception of Scotty Reston, did little or no original digging for news stories. On Capitol Hill, the *Times*'s congressional staff gained reputations as the most habitual card players in the press galleries. The relentlessness with which New York editors stripped away the slightest style from their copy had drained the reporters' initiative, and Krock had contributed to the morass by presiding over the bureau rather than managing it. For more than twenty years, Krock held onto a job he had not wanted until finally, to stop James Reston from accepting an offer to head the editorial page of the *Washington Post*, he stepped down as bureau chief in Reston's favor. Rather than return to New York, however, Krock chose to remain in Washington, where he continued to write his "In the Nation" column for another thirteen years.[52]

Krock also outlasted the *Chicago Tribune*'s bureau chief Arthur Sears Henning, who fell from grace for perpetuating his newspaper's most embarrassing error. Like every other political expert in 1948, Henning expected Governor Thomas E. Dewey to win the presidency handily. At 9:00 a.m. on Election Day, before most votes had been cast, let alone counted, Henning confidently wrote the next day's lead announcing Dewey's victory. That evening, when election returns showed Harry Truman running stronger than expected, Henning obstinately ignored them. "Oh, that's just nonsense; that's nonsense," he assured nervous colleagues. "Forget it, the AP is all wrong." Henning headed to WGN's radio studios to report on the Republican sweep, and in his absence the *Tribune*'s editors revised his story and recalled the first edition. They gathered up most copies, but forgot about the newsstand in the *Tribune*'s own lobby. It was there that the rival *Chicago Herald Examiner* gleefully bought a stack of papers for display. On the same day that a victorious President Truman held aloft the *Tribune*'s infamous "DEWEY DEFEATS TRUMAN" headline, Colonel McCormick terminated Henning's thirty-four-year tenure as Washington bureau chief.[53]

The Washington correspondents' designation of the *Chicago Tribune* as the "least fair and reliable" paper underestimated its Washington bureau, which throughout the Roosevelt years had fielded a team of able and aggressive reporters. What kept the *Tribune*'s bureau from standing taller was not its reporters but its idiosyncratic publisher, for whom they twisted the news to suit his opinions. The pliant Arthur Henning treaded his paper's editorial line, while Arthur Krock's intransigence reinforced the firewall between Washington reporting and editorials at the *New York Times*. Krock's own columns regularly differed from his paper's editorials as he grew increasingly disaffected with an administration that the *Times* supported. Nor did the *Times*'s editors and publisher impose their own values on their Washington reporters, most of whom were far more approving of the New Deal than was their bureau chief. The contrast between the *Times* and *Tribune* bureaus in this respect could not have been starker.

Colonel McCormick's death in 1954 liberated the *Chicago Tribune*'s reporters. In later years its Washington bureau grew in size and stature. By the end of the century it had seventeen journalists accredited to the congressional press galleries, compared to sixty-five from the *New York Times*'s bureau. The *Tribune*'s parent company mushroomed into a multimedia conglomerate that absorbed other newspapers, radio and television stations, and web sites. That put the *Chicago Tribune*'s Washington reporters under the same roof with reporters for the *Los Angeles Times, Baltimore Sun, Hartford Courant,* and *Newsday,* all owned by the Tribune Company. Yet its Washington bureau managed to retain an "outsider" tradition in an "insider" town. James Warren, who headed the bureau in the 1990s, lambasted prominent Washington correspondents for such practices as accepting generous honoraria for speaking to special interest groups, and berated the Gridiron Club for the coziness it perpetuated between the press and the politicians. Warren deemed the culture of Washington journalism "a world in which access becomes a god," where "the rule is sucking up to power." He instructed *Tribune* reporters to cover Washington as if they were foreign correspondents who had to explain back home "the strange ways of this town."[54]

The Washington bureau of the *New York Times* underwent its own transformation. Its traditional "low-intensity warfare" with the editors in New York persisted long after Arthur Krock stepped aside. James Reston turned the bureau into an even greater powerhouse by building a staff that included Russell Baker, Max Frankel, David Halberstam, Anthony Lewis, and Tom Wicker—known collectively as "Scotty's Boys"—and such able women reporters as Marjorie Hunter, Nan Robertson, and Eileen Shanahan. Reston eventually made the move that had always eluded Arthur Krock. In 1968 he went to New York to become the *Times*'s executive editor. It was a job he neither relished nor excelled in. He took it chiefly to protect the Washington bureau from New York's further attempts to curtail its autonomy. As soon as he could, Reston relinquished the editorship to return to Washington and write his columns. Other Washington bureau chiefs, from Clifton Daniel to Max Frankel, Howell Raines, Gerald Boyd (the bureau's first African American chief), and Jill Abramson (its first woman bureau chief), were promoted into editorships in New York. Once these bureau chiefs had left Washington, most made a point of trying to rein in the notoriously independent bureau. Despite perennial charges that its top reporters were too intimate with the power elites they covered, the *New York Times*'s Washington bureau continued to set the pace for the rest of the Washington press corps and to make life uncomfortable for those in power.[55]

2

Race, Rules, and Reporting

The Washington press corps remained exclusively white until President Roosevelt's press secretary, Stephen Early, kneed a black policeman in the groin during the 1940 campaign. His rash act set in motion a chain of events that finally toppled racial barriers for African American journalists at the White House and Capitol. Until then, black reporters had been shut out of Franklin Roosevelt's press conferences and denied seats in the congressional press galleries, and the resistance they encountered came not from the politicians but from the reporters who ran the White House Correspondents Association and the Standing Committee of Correspondents in the Senate and House. Integration of the Washington press corps was a slow and painful process, complicated by white reporters' intolerance or indifference, discord within the black press, and rancor between men and women journalists of both races. Change came only after the politicians overruled the press corps.[1]

Other than crime stories, the mainstream, mass-circulation press ignored the African American community. White newspapers rarely hired black reporters. Black journalists found work instead on small, black-owned weekly newspapers, which collectively reached some two million readers. As white reporters rarely read anything their black counterparts wrote, they had little appreciation for the constraints under which the black press operated. The lack of equal access to the news made it particularly difficult for black reporters to cover the nation's capital. Black readers eagerly sought news about New Deal policies that affected them, but black reporters could not get admitted to government press conferences or even get on the distribution lists for agency press releases. "Washington had been traditionally a barren wasteland for news of interest to the black press," observed Enoch Waters, an editor of the black paper the *Chicago Defender.* "A black reporter had as little chance of interviewing a cabinet officer as of getting an interview with God." During the New Deal, black reporters could turn to the Black Cabinet, a small circle of high-ranking black government officials that included Mary McLeod Bethune, William Hastie, Ralph Bunche, and Robert Weaver, who offered the most reliable pipeline of federal news. Other tips came from government secretaries and custodians, who passed along overheard conversations or documents retrieved from mimeograph machines. Occasionally, a sympathetic white official might offer information, but black reporters often could only find out what was going on by reading the *New York Times*.[2]

Washington, D.C., retained elements of formal racial segregation until the 1960s, although the presence of the federal government prevented the enactment of Jim Crow laws. Whites and blacks rode side by side on Washington's streetcars until the cars crossed the Potomac into Virginia and blacks had to move to the rear. Whites and blacks lived in close proximity in many of the District's neighborhoods, but their children attended separate schools. Public parks, pools, and golf courses were segregated by race, and hotels, theaters, and restaurants catered to either white or black clientele. A few federal cafeterias served everyone equally, but not the dining rooms at the U.S. Capitol, the ultimate symbol of American democracy. Because Washington segregated more by custom than by law, northern white transplants generally accepted the city's racial divisions as natural—if they noticed them at all. Even members of the "liberal media" resisted racial integration. Just as the White House pressroom and congressional press galleries remained white, the National Press Club admitted no black members.[3]

The mainstream press laid claim to objective reporting and viewed black newspapers as advocates on a single issue. Black reporters acknowledged the truth in such charges. "All civil rights," a reader once complained to the reporter Simeon Booker. "Hell, I can't even get the weather from your paper." For Booker, civil rights was his beat. Black reporters aimed not to duplicate the news available in the rest of the press but to provide what white reporters had overlooked. They reported from an unabashedly racial perspective. When a tornado killed 132 people in Woodward, Oklahoma, the *Baltimore Afro-American* ran the headline: "Sole Colored Resident of Okla. Town Unhurt in Tornado." In a column for the *Chicago Defender,* the poet Langston Hughes argued that "the readers of the Negro papers are mainly those who still need a voice to say what they still want and have not yet gotten—namely full citizenship, full equality, full civil rights, job rights, and an absence from fear, want, and contempt." Yet while African Americans read black newspapers or heard their stories by word of mouth, the Swedish sociologist Gunnar Myrdal observed that most white Americans were entirely unaware of the black press and its "bitter and relentless criticism of themselves."[4]

With the sole exception of the *Atlanta Daily World*, all black newspapers in 1940 put out weekly, semi-weekly, or semi-monthly editions. After the *Daily World*, the strongest black papers in terms of circulation and revenue were the *Chicago Defender* and *Pittsburgh Courier*. These were more than local papers, as all three sought national markets by publishing different municipal and regional editions wherever they found sizeable black readerships. The *Chicago Defender* put out local and national editions, while the *Pittsburgh Courier* produced editions for the Far South, Midwest, Pacific Coast, New York City, Chicago, Detroit, and Washington, D.C. The Scott News Syndicate included some fifty-five widely scattered weekly papers that reprinted much of their material from the *Atlanta Daily World*. This practice pitted black papers from distant cities against one another, directly competing for the same readers and the same limited advertising revenue.[5]

Financially strapped black newspapers could not afford to send full-time correspondents to Washington. Two newspaper services emerged to fill the void: the Associated Negro Press (ANP), and the National Negro Publishers Association (NNPA). The ANP dated back to 1919, when Claude Barnett started it. A Tuskegee Institute graduate, Barnett aimed to apply the philosophy of Booker T. Washington to journalism by creating a black-run business that would promote racial betterment. Twice a week the ANP compiled and mailed news stories to member papers, charging them modest fees to print whatever items they chose. Barnett encouraged the reciprocal sharing of news among the ANP's member papers, but because the papers often targeted the same markets, their publishers resisted sharing news with competitors. The ANP itself was based in Chicago and compiled some of its news by rewriting copy from the *Chicago Defender,* where Barnett had once worked. The *Defender* refused to subscribe to the ANP. "He's stealing my news and selling to other papers for a profit," complained publisher Robert Abbott, overlooking the fact that the *Defender* rewrote some of its own content from the *Chicago Tribune*.[6]

With a small grant from the Julius Rosenwald Fund in 1939, the ANP opened a full-time bureau in Washington and appointed Alvin White as its correspondent. Observing that the reporter was so light-skinned that he could have "passed for white," Claude Barnett had high hopes for his admission into the White House pressroom, but White still encountered racial barriers. Black reporters had been petitioning President Roosevelt for admission to his press conferences since 1933. Press Secretary Steve Early had repeatedly explained that the White House Correspondents Association, not the Roosevelt administration, decided on press credentials. The association had rules that limited attendance at press conferences to reporters for daily newspapers. They barred reporters for all weekly papers, white or black, in order to keep attendance at the press conferences small enough to fit the tight confines of the Oval Office. Yet Early somehow found ways to bend the rules to admit favored white journalists who would not otherwise have qualified, from the radio broadcaster Walter Winchell to the weekly magazine writer I. F. Stone, so long as their presence suited the administration's purposes.[7]

New Deal liberals regarded the Virginia-born Early (a grandnephew of the Confederate general Jubal Early) as racially prejudiced. Early certainly worried that Eleanor Roosevelt's backing of civil rights would hurt the president politically, and he tried hard to steer her away from black leaders. He begged her not to break the Correspondents Association's rule against admitting reporters for weekly publications to her own press conferences. "I have taken care of the Negro requests for the President's press conferences and if Mrs.

Roosevelt opens hers it just makes the President more vulnerable," he appealed to the first lady's secretary. Whatever his biases, Early reasoned that black reporters would raise questions about civil rights, to which any answer could offend some part of the New Deal coalition. By avoiding specifics, Franklin Roosevelt could create the impression of commitment to equal rights without aggravating southern Democrats in Congress, and without losing a single southern state in any of his four presidential campaigns.[8]

Then on a trip to New York City during the presidential election of 1940, Early inadvertently made himself an issue, at a time when Roosevelt was actively campaigning for support among black voters. The press secretary intervened to help a group of White House officials and Washington correspondents pass through a police line to catch up with the presidential party. Early confronted a police sergeant, got pushed, and pushed back. In the ensuing melee, he kneed a black policeman. Republicans quickly capitalized on the incident by distributing broadsides throughout Harlem, urging black voters to repay "this kick in the groin by a punch in the eye to all New Dealers on election day." Distressed that he might have damaged the president's chances of reelection, Early enlisted White House correspondents to sign a statement affirming that his action had been neither deliberate nor racially motivated. Eleanor Roosevelt assured black leaders that the hot-tempered Early would have reacted the same way to a policeman of any race. Repercussions from the incident finally dissipated when the injured police officer announced that he still intended to vote for Roosevelt.[9]

Grateful at having survived the crisis, Steve Early sought to make amends by admitting a black reporter to the president's press conferences. Black editors had been conducting a letter-writing campaign to waive the rules of admission for Louis Lautier, a Justice Department stenographer who freelanced for several black newspapers. Early concluded that this presumably pliable government employee might solve the problem. In January 1941 the press secretary met privately with Lautier and advised him that he could comply with the rules by applying for admission to the press conferences as a reporter for the *Atlanta Daily World*. Getting wind of the deal in Chicago, Claude Barnett bristled that a civil servant "would hardly be the person to hold such a position," and he notified the White House that the ANP counted the *Daily World* among its member papers.[10]

One way or another, a black reporter's accreditation depended on the cooperation of the sole daily black newspaper, the *Atlanta Daily World*. Yet the *Daily World* would not abandon the competitive advantage it held against its rivals. In May 1941 the paper's owner, A. S. Scott, applied for membership to the White House press corps on behalf of the "World's Only Negro Daily." Early forwarded this request to the White House Correspondents Association and said that if Lautier met the association's qualifications "we will have to admit him." As the *Daily World* failed to specify Lautier as its reporter, however, the Correspondents Association rejected the application on the grounds that "only those stationed regularly in Washington are eligible for membership." A perplexed Early watched his solution unravel. He promised Eleanor Roosevelt that the first black reporter who presented legitimate credentials from a daily newspaper would be admitted automatically. "There is one such daily newspaper printed in the United States—in Atlanta," Early explained. "The editor of this paper has never appointed a Washington correspondent, although he has been advised of his right to do so."[11]

After Pearl Harbor, the ANP redoubled its efforts to publish Washington news from the black perspective. Claude Barnett grew impatient with Alvin White's inability to get a press pass and suspected that he was not pursuing the matter vigorously enough. White replied that he had never managed to meet the chairman of the Standing Committee of Correspondents, who always seemed to be out. "Apparently the fellow had been tipped off to give the Negro the 'run around,'" Barnett determined. "Those lounges maintained by the Senate and House are really like clubs," he commented on the press galleries. "I suspect therein lies part of the reluctance to admit us."[12]

A united front within the black press might have strengthened its case, but the Associated Negro Press was at that point engaged in head-on competition from the newly formed National Negro Publishers Association. Prior to the founding of the NNPA, publishers of the largest black newspapers had concluded that there was little advantage in a news service, such as the ANP, that was available to all papers regardless of size. They aimed to create an association that they would operate to meet their own needs, by fielding their own correspondents to develop exclusive stories. The driving force behind the NNPA, John Sengstacke, had recently succeeded his uncle, Robert Abbott, as publisher of the *Chicago Defender*. Sengstacke's uncle had warned him that the black publishers "weren't speaking to each other and wouldn't join in an organization designed to serve for the betterment of all." True to form, the older publishers boycotted the NNPA's first organizational meeting in Chicago in 1941, but many younger publishers attended, and they agreed to support a news service more directly under their control than Barnett's ANP. By 1942, Sengstacke had opened a Washington office for the *Chicago Defender* and hired as his part-time Washington correspondent Harry S. McAlpin, a lawyer who worked as an aide to Mary McLeod Bethune at the National Youth Administration. The ANP's Alvin White complained that both McAlpin and Lautier were using their government posts to get news before he could, and he grumbled about "these namby pamby guys getting fat on the government payroll and also on individual newspapers."[13]

During World War II, the black press came under fire for its crusade to integrate the armed services. The conservative columnist Westbook Pegler accused them of "exploiting the war emergency as an opportunity to push the aspirations of the colored people," and charged them with "inflammatory bias." The NAACP's chairman Walter White warned that continued editorial criticism of segregation in the military might lead to government harassment. Indeed, there were indications that the government might deny newsprint as a means of silencing critical black papers. Agents of the Federal Bureau of Investigation identified the black press as "a strong provoctor [*sic*] of discontent among Negroes" and raised the specter of prosecution for sedition. The black press evaded indictment, thanks largely to the efforts of John Sengstacke. Meeting in 1942 with Attorney General Francis Biddle, Sengstacke offered to tone down the papers' rhetoric in return for greater access to official news. "Nobody will talk to us," he pointed out. "So, what do you expect us to publish?" If black reporters could not get information from the heads of federal agencies, they had to do the best they could. The attorney general, who had previously given no thought to the restrictions on black reporters, agreed to call other cabinet members and ask for their cooperation. Biddle also suggested to the president that he admit a black correspondent to his press conferences.[14]

John Sengstacke next met with Steve Early to work out the details for a White House press pass. By November 1943 the White House Correspondents Association agreed to accredit an NNPA reporter. But several more months elapsed before the NNPA could afford to set up its own Washington bureau, underwritten by the *Baltimore Afro-American*'s editor, Carl Murphy, and to designate the *Chicago Defender*'s Harry McAlpin as its full-time Washington correspondent. In February 1944 the NNPA convened a conference in Washington. Roosevelt, then running for his fourth term, invited thirteen NNPA editors and publishers to the White House. Three days later Harry McAlpin joined the rest of the White House press corps at an Oval Office press conference. "I'm glad to see you, McAlpin," said the president as he shook his hand, "and very happy to have you here."[15]

Harry McAlpin broke the race barrier only because politicians had stretched the rules for him. The White House accepted him as the "full-time" correspondent for the *Atlanta Daily World* despite a Secret Service report showing that the weekly *Chicago Defender* paid most of his salary. Although the *Daily World*'s general manager, C. A. Scott, was willing to acknowledge McAlpin as one of his correspondents out of solidarity with the rest of the black press, a deep division of opinion existed within the paper's hierarchy. Other members of the Scott family dissented in a telegram to the president: "McAlpine [*sic*] is unknown here, never worked for the *Atlanta Daily World*, never lived here. . . . Obviously there is some error." Not about to eject McAlpin in an election year, Early pocketed their protest.[16]

Questions lingered about McAlpin's status. When Franklin Roosevelt died in April 1945, the White House Correspondents Association excluded the sole black reporter at the White House from the pool of reporters covering the funeral services in the East Room. Expecting a large number of family, friends, and government officials, the new press secretary, Jonathan Daniels, had asked the Correspondents Association to limit the press pool to twelve newspaper and radio correspondents. At first, McAlpin was part of the pool, but on the morning of the funeral his name disappeared from the roster and two white reporters were added. In his column, McAlpin recorded that he had gotten into the press conferences only because President Roosevelt had ordered that he be given press credentials. "But Roosevelt is now gone and the white press, through the White House Correspondents Association, has made its first move to try to again exclude the Negro."[17]

With a reporter at the White House, the black press set its sights on the congressional press galleries, where no African American had sat since Frederick Douglass, the famous pre–Civil War abolitionist, who had reported during Reconstruction. Rules adopted in 1880 to ban lobbyists from the press gallery had required that reporters file stories by telegraph to daily newspapers in order to be accredited. So long as the black press consisted of weekly papers, the rule effectively eliminated all black reporters from the gallery. Harry McAlpin continued to apply, citing his connection to the *Atlanta Daily World*. Yet despite his White House pass, the Capitol's Standing Committee of Correspondents rejected his application on the grounds that most of his work went to the NNPA, which serviced predominantly weekly publications. Whichever way he turned, McAlpin was stymied. The newspaper press gallery refused to admit him because he reported for weekly rather than daily papers. The periodical press gallery would not admit him because he reported for newspapers rather than magazines. Both galleries argued that making an exception for McAlpin would flood their limited space with other applicants from weekly papers. It was a specious argument, as very few weekly papers could afford a resident correspondent in Washington. McAlpin had no doubt that the Standing Committee's actions had been influenced "by my racial identity rather than by the flimsy technicality publicly stated."[18]

For years, the Associated Negro Press had sought accreditation by "playing by the rules," only to see its rival, the NNPA, advance by going over the heads of the white correspondents. "There is no reason to shed briny tears over our failure to win entrance first," Claude Barnett comforted his disappointed Washington correspondent when McAlpin got his press pass to the White House. "We will get in." After Alvin White resigned to take a better paying job in the wartime government, the ANP replaced him with Ernest S. Johnson, a brash and impulsive young reporter whom Barnett hoped could succeed where the cautious White had failed. Although a hustler for news, Johnson quickly found it physically impossible for one man to cover all of Washington. He needed access to the press galleries and press offices to get news releases and interviews.[19]

Johnson's applications to the congressional press galleries claimed that he reported by telegraph to the *Atlanta Daily World* and the new *Dayton Daily Bulletin*. The ANP had agreed to underwrite his telegraph dispatches to the *Daily*

World for at least a week until the paper recognized their value and paid for the service itself. However, the *Daily World* refused to declare Johnson its correspondent. In addition, the Standing Committee of Correspondents questioned the size of the *Dayton Daily Bulletin*'s circulation. "Quote them 10,000 if necessary and let them jump in the river," a frustrated Johnson advised Barnett.[20]

Even without congressional press passes, the ANP's Johnson and NNPA's McAlpin carried on a spirited competition for Washington news. The hardworking Johnson managed to best McAlpin on many stories. Distressed over the ANP's exclusives, the NNPA publishers dropped McAlpin only months after getting him into the White House. They handed the assignment to Louis Lautier, but McAlpin refused to surrender his White House press card, and Lautier could attend press conferences only with temporary passes. By 1946 both Washington bureaus had fallen into disarray. Lautier and McAlpin bickered over the NNPA's press pass and Ernest Johnson resigned from the ANP over a salary dispute.[21]

Black reporters remained outside the press galleries until the Eightieth Congress convened in January 1947. The Senate opened with a debate on whether to seat Mississippi senator Theodore Bilbo, a notorious racist. This issue held intense interest for black readers, so Louis Lautier stood in line to get a seat in the crowded public galleries. It rankled him that white reporters failed to cover news that blacks so eagerly sought. Lautier noted that when Clarence Mitchell Jr. of the NAACP and Senator Wayne Morse testified on the same day about pending labor legislation, the white press reported only Morse's testimony. Now that Republicans had returned to the majority in both the Senate and House for the first time since the depression, southern Democrats no longer chaired the key committees. Lautier took his case to Senator C. Wayland "Curley" Brooks of Illinois, the new Republican chairman of the Rules Committee. The time seemed ripe for change. Editorials in both the *Washington Post* and *New York Herald Tribune* recommended amending the rules to admit Lautier, and Senator Brooks was eager for the *Chicago Defender* to endorse his reelection. Louis Martin, then editor of the *Defender*, came to Washington to appeal to Brooks on Lautier's behalf.[22]

Chicago Sun-Times reporter Griffing Bancroft chaired the Standing Committee of Correspondents that year and he cast the sole vote in favor of accrediting Lautier. Bancroft believed it was time for a black man to be admitted to the press galleries. "I don't think the others felt it was so important," he later reflected. Opposition from the other committee members rested "more or less on a technicality" over whether Lautier was the bona fide correspondent of the *Atlanta Daily World*. The committee was responsible for insulating the press galleries from political interference, Bancroft acknowledged. "We wanted the press galleries to be run by the press," without the Rules Committee overturning its decisions. Bancroft proposed that the Rules Committee study the problem of weekly papers and explore ways of providing additional gallery space (the press gallery at the time had more than seven hundred members but seats inside the chamber for only ninety-three). Perhaps not coincidentally, the smaller periodical press gallery chose that moment to admit its first black member, Percival S. Prattis, as Washington correspondent for *Our World,* a New York–based magazine with a circulation of 250,000.[23]

Less concerned with institutional reform than with resolving the immediate problem, Senator Brooks instructed the Standing Committee that it could "very easily answer this question by admitting one man." The issue of gallery space could be dealt with sometime in the future. The Senate Rules Committee responded by voting unanimously to admit Louis Lautier. As the Rules Committee's jurisdiction extended no further than the Senate galleries, the ban still existed on the House side, but the Standing Committee conceded defeat and accredited Lautier to both the Senate and House galleries. The *New York Times*'s Washington correspondent Arthur Krock blasted the Senate for forcing the Standing Committee of Correspondents to violate its rules "only because the reporter affected by them is a Negro." Other correspondents speculated that the only problem Senator Brooks wanted to solve was winning reelection. Harry McAlpin added that the senator had lost friends among black reporters by his insistence that Lautier's admission alone would solve the "Negro press problem."[24]

Contrary to Senator Brooks's expectations, the Standing Committee already had a second black applicant. Alice Dunnigan had applied for a press pass as the Washington correspondent for the Associated Negro Press. As a wartime clerk in the Department of Labor, Dunnigan had moonlighted as a stringer for the ANP. When Ernest Johnson quit, Dunnigan inherited his post by default. None of the men whom Claude Barnett tried to hire would work for the dismal salary he was paying. At the Capitol, Dunnigan tried to follow other reporters into the press gallery. "I'm a newspaper reporter, and I'm going wherever those newsmen are going," she told the Capitol policeman who stopped her. He explained that she needed a press pass. Knowing nothing about ANP's long fight for accreditation, Dunnigan applied because she saw it as her right as a reporter. When Lautier won admittance, she assumed the door had opened for him because he was a man. Then she discovered that the ANP had never bothered to endorse her application. "For years we have been trying to get a man accredited to the Capitol Galleries and have not succeeded," Claude Barnett chided. "What makes you think that you—a woman—can accomplish this feat?" To Barnett's astonishment, the Standing Committee granted Alice Dunnigan accreditation in July 1947. She immediately applied to the White House and the Department of State, and became the first African American reporter to hold all three coveted press passes.[25]

Fully accredited, the NNPA's Louis Lautier and ANP's Alice Dunnigan encountered vastly different receptions in the press galleries. Lautier, the more experienced and professional of the two, won speedy acceptance into the male fraternity of Washington journalism. Dunnigan, as an outsider who battled against the system, suffered doubly from discrimination. "Race and sex were twin strikes against me from the beginning," she wrote. "I don't know which of these barriers were the hardest to break down. I think sex was more difficult, because I not only had to convince members of the other race of my capacity, but had to fight against discrimination of Negro men, as well as against envy and jealousy of female members of my own race."[26]

Louis Lautier was born in Louisiana, and attended Straight College (later Dilliard University) in New Orleans, Morris Brown College in Atlanta, and Howard Law School in Washington. Married, with one child, he commuted from his home in Arlington, Virginia, to a civil service post as a legal stenographer for the Justice Department, picking up extra income as a freelance reporter for assorted black newspapers. Lautier devoted most of his reporting to exposing the injustices and absurdities of racial segregation in the capital and the federal government. Black publishers occasionally used him to lobby around Washington on such issues as ending racial segregation in the armed forces.[27]

After 1947, Lautier made the House press gallery his regular base of operations, from which he covered Congress, the White House, and the rest of Washington for the NNPA. He knew that he was setting precedents that would open the way for the acceptance of other black reporters and he behaved accordingly. Other reporters described him as a prim and tidy man, quiet, considerate, and highly principled, but neither very opinionated nor a crusader. Lautier ate lunch with the white reporters in part of the Senate restaurant reserved for the press. He listened more than he talked, occasionally injecting a wry remark into the conversation. The press corps also appreciated Lautier's stenographic skills, and after press conferences other reporters checked the accuracy of their quotes against his. "We looked on Mr. Lautier as an authority on the Negro," recalled the *Washington Post* correspondent Edward T. Folliard, "and we would go to him for help just like you would talk to a science reporter on missiles." As Lautier was a lifelong Republican, leaders of his party also turned to him for advice and assistance. Once when Simeon Booker attended a gathering at the home of Vice President Richard Nixon, he received an effusive welcome. The Nixons escorted Booker and his wife through their home and into the kitchen where they introduced them to a black employee as Mr. and Mrs. Louis Lautier. Booker corrected Pat Nixon and noted, "She was apologetic, but I wondered what on earth they wanted Louis Lautier to do after such a VIP welcome."[28]

The *Chicago Defender*'s Enoch Waters wrote that Lautier's Washington reporting proved the value of the NNPA's news service, but that his one-man effort "was doomed by its inability to produce a greater volume and a greater variety of copy which would have made the NNPA service at least equal to and perhaps more attractive than ANP." To everyone's surprise, Alice Dunnigan, despite her lack of professional training, demonstrated a drive that made her a formidable competitor. Never collegial with Lautier, she later claimed that the opposition she met as a woman correspondent in the Capitol press galleries "came mainly from a black man." White reporters might have disapproved of her presence, she noted, but they never bothered her because they never felt threatened by her. They just ignored her.[29]

Alice Dunnigan struggled mightily for whatever status she achieved. The daughter of a Kentucky sharecropper, she had grown up determined to keep out of "the white folk's kitchen." Working her way through the Kentucky Normal and Industrial Institute, she became a teacher, and while teaching in a rural school she married a tobacco farmer. When that unhappy union ended in divorce, she took an unpaid position as a fund-raiser for a black college. Her salary and expenses came from whatever money she raised. As a publicity effort, she sent a poem she had written about the school to a black newspaper. The editor invited her to contribute other items—without pay—and published her occasional articles and opinion pieces. A second marriage, to Charles Dunnigan, produced a son. She returned to her hometown of Russellville, Kentucky, to teach again. Her husband lived with her during the school term while she collected a salary, but disappeared during the summer months for "a gay carefree life, enlivened with booze, babes and ballyhoo." To support her son, Dunnigan worked as a cook and cleaning woman during school vacations. She regarded domestic work as demeaning, but found nothing else open for a black woman in the South.[30]

Eventually, her newspaper writing came to the attention of the editor for the *Kentucky Reporter*, who proposed that she write a column on health, homemaking, and women's issues—"Scribbles from Alice's Scrapbook"—once again without pay. Dunnigan also sent a few articles to the *Louisville Defender*. Then the editor of the *Louisville Leader*, the city's oldest black newspaper, asked why she had not contributed to his paper. When the school term ended, she accepted an offer to move to Louisville and work for the *Leader* at five dollars a week—two dollars more than her domestic work had paid. "At least the work would be dignified, the experience wonderful, and the contacts great," she decided.[31]

Dunnigan enrolled at the nearest black college that offered courses in journalism and returned to teach in Russellville to pay her bills. In 1942, feeling confined by her marriage and the limited opportunities in Kentucky, she responded to a wartime recruitment poster for government clerk-typists and took the civil service typing test, against her husband's wishes. When an offer from the Labor Department arrived, she quit her teaching job, her hometown, and her marriage. The $1,440-a-year government salary more than doubled what she earned as a teacher, but she had not counted on the high cost of living in wartime Washington. Looking for contacts that might lead to a living wage, Dunnigan joined the United Federal Workers of America (an integrated union of federal employees), and the Southern Conference for Human Welfare. Both later made the attorney general's list of Communist-front organizations. She enrolled in night school at Howard University and took courses in economics and statistics, gaining a professional-level appointment at the Office of Price Administration. That job lasted until the end of the war. With the OPA scheduled for abolition, Dunnigan's job ended in December 1946.[32]

Since coming to Washington, Dunnigan had reported part-time for the Associated Negro Press, being paid on a "space-rate" basis of a half-cent a word. After Ernest Johnson quit as the ANP's Washington correspondent, Dunnigan applied to replace him. Claude Barnett expressed doubt that a woman could handle his biggest national assignment, but he gave her an opportunity to prove herself while he looked for a man to take the job. Barnett knew that he was dealing with a novice when he read her copy. "I don't know what sort of writing experience you had," he lectured, "but it certainly was not modern newspaper writing." He admonished her to avoid words like "today" and "yesterday," which were irrelevant for weekly papers, not to use "we," and to submit stories with a "Negro slant." During her probationary period, ANP paid her only for the stories they used. Her monthly checks gradually improved along with her writing skills, but when she finally got a regular salary, it was insufficient to sustain herself and her son. Dunnigan supplemented her income with magazine writing, especially about restaurants that swapped her free meals for favorable reviews.[33]

Dunnigan's less-than-subsistence wages made her job more difficult than her white colleagues might have suspected. To reduce the rent for her basement apartment, in the mornings she stoked the building's coal furnace and hauled out the ashes. She rode trolleys around Washington, as taking a cab meant "good-bye to lunch money." Sensitive to criticism about her unstylish clothes, she spent large portions of her income on a wardrobe suitable for covering White House functions.[34]

The White House press office invited Dunnigan aboard Harry Truman's campaign train to the West Coast in June 1948. Claude Barnett refused to pay her expenses, saying that it was not worth a thousand dollars for his cash-strapped service. Besides, he pointed out, the *Chicago Defender* and *Pittsburgh Courier* were both sending reporters on the president's train, and the ANP could pick up news from them. Dunnigan approached the presidential assistant for minority affairs and suggested that the Democratic Party "quietly" underwrite her expenses, but he declined on the grounds that other correspondents, who had paid in full, would protest if they found out that she had been subsidized. Undeterred, she took out a personal loan.[35]

Aboard the presidential train, the two black men representing the *Defender* and *Courier* kept their distance from Alice Dunnigan. "They were having a wonderful time themselves and appeared to be on a pleasure trip rather than a working one," she recorded, assuming that men did not take their work as seriously as women, because "they don't have to work as hard as women to get recognition." It was a white reporter from the *Washington Post*, the veteran correspondent Edward Folliard, who advised her on how to cover the trip.

Avoid the "canned" press releases, Folliard counseled. Get off the train at every stop. Mingle with the people, and pick up "real live color for your story." As logical as that sounded, race complicated her task. The ANP required that Dunnigan's stories have a "Negro angle," but in many western towns she could see few black faces among those who met the president's train. One of her stories opened with the observation: "Not a single Negro was seen in the crowd of hundreds of people."

President Truman avoided mentioning civil rights, until an unscheduled midnight stop in Montana. There, he answered a question from the crowd by observing that "civil rights is as old as the Constitution of the United States and as new as the Democratic platform of 1944," and intimated that it would be part of the platform in 1948. Dunnigan got her big story, and it was an exclusive as the other two black reporters had not gotten off the train to cover the impromptu event. When they begged her to share her notes to keep them from looking bad, she refused. Her stubborn competitiveness broke an unwritten rule of the Washington press corps that reporters traveling as a pack on presidential trips would not scoop one another. If someone missed a story, the others shared what they had. Failure to cooperate could get a reporter excluded from other pooled information.[36]

During Truman's campaign, the Democratic Speakers Bureau paid Dunnigan to make a promotional tour of Kentucky for the ticket. She counted on Truman's upset victory to reward her with a political appointment. When nothing materialized, she appealed to the Democratic National Committee to create a position for her where she could be "very beneficial to the Negro press and very influential in attracting Negro voters." That plan failed for the lack of an endorsement from Representative William Dawson, who vetted all African American appointments to the DNC. Her boss, Claude Barnett, disapproved of Dunnigan's "dabbling in politics," but could not afford to raise her salary enough to discourage her from taking other part-time jobs. In 1950 she accepted a civil service position as a clerk-typist at the Washington Navy Yard, confining her news reporting to the evenings and weekends, mostly by interviewing over the phone and rewriting press releases. Despite her complaints about the ANP's low pay, Dunnigan could not abandon reporting without losing her unparalleled access to the highest levels of government.[37]

Alice Dunnigan harbored her deepest resentment for her rival Louis Lautier, who earned four times her salary, had staff assistance and an office, and was authorized to send his stories straight to the NNPA's member papers. She routed hers through the ANP in Chicago, which allowed Lautier to get into print well ahead of her. The ANP refused to grant her that privilege, however, as Claude Barnett still lacked confidence in her ability. He frequently rewrote her copy, and had to keep reminding her of the particular needs of a black national news service. In 1954 she was in the House press gallery when Puerto Rican nationalists fired shots into the chamber and wounded five representatives.

Dunnigan rushed to call the ANP in Chicago and breathlessly report the story. When Barnett learned that neither of the two black representatives, William Dawson or Adam Clayton Powell, had been shot, he told her, "You've got no story."[38]

Another formidable competitor to both Dunnigan and Lautier appeared when the *Chicago Defender* sent Ethel Payne to Washington as its correspondent in 1953. Although still a weekly when she arrived, the *Defender* went daily in 1956, which facilitated her press accreditation. The daughter of a Chicago Pullman car porter, she had worked in Tokyo as an army hostess in a Special Service Club, where she kept a diary of her observations on black army life and on relations between African Americans and Japanese. When the Korean War began in 1950, a *Defender* reporter arranged for his paper to print excerpts from Payne's diary. Her critical commentary got her into trouble with army officials, but also got her a reporting job with the *Defender*. Payne returned to Chicago, took some courses in journalism at Northwestern University, and wrote feature articles for the paper. Her stories dealing with the adoption of African American babies won an award from the Illinois Press Association and a job offer from another newspaper. To keep her with the *Defender,* her editors made her their Washington correspondent. "I was a one-person operation," she later reflected on the stark realities of the job. "I had no staff. So the best I could do was build up sources. And fortunately I was able to do that—at the Pentagon, the State Department, the White House. I was unable to cover everything at one time, but when people saw I was serious, they began sending me stories and tips."[39]

Ethel Payne's arrival proved costly for Alice Dunnigan as the *Chicago Defender* canceled the unsigned column of Washington news she had been writing for seventy-five dollars a month—a quarter of her income. To make up the difference, Dunnigan wrote a "Washington Inside Out" column for the *Pittsburgh Courier* and freelanced for the *Baltimore Afro-American*, above and beyond her ANP reporting. She also wrote occasionally for the *Louisville Defender*, the *Amsterdam News*, and a Nigerian newspaper, *Pilot.* The quiet and reserved Dunnigan suffered by comparison to the "big, bad and bold" Payne, but, despite differences in personality and style, both women were liberal Democrats and staunch supporters of the civil rights movement. Both women attended President Dwight D. Eisenhower's press conferences and got into trouble for raising questions about his administration's commitment to equal rights for all.[40]

The chief Washington lobbyist for the NAACP, Clarence Mitchell Jr., himself a former reporter for the *Baltimore Afro-American*, planted questions for the president with the two women. Dunnigan, for instance, asked Eisenhower about his plans to name a new chairman for the Government Contract Compliance Committee, forcing him to admit that he was unaware of the vacancy. A few months later he made the appointment. Eisenhower fended off Dunnigan's questions by referring her to the departments that handled the issues she was raising, leaving it unclear whether he did not know the answers or did not want to commit himself. Ethel Payne also saw herself "as an advocate as much as being a newspaper person," and got on the president's nerves. In July 1954 she asked whether the administration planned to support legislation banning segregation in interstate travel. A clearly annoyed Eisenhower rasped that he would do what was fair but would support no "special group of any kind." Reporters at the press conference were taken aback by his angry tone.[41]

The confrontation made the front page of the *Washington Star,* and some of the black newspapers that carried Payne's reports criticized her. "Oooh! I was pilloried by the black press as being over-assertive," she recalled. Even her own mother thought she had needlessly upset the president. But the director of the NNPA, Sherman Briscoe, reassured her that if she had disconcerted Eisenhower, "at least he is aware there is a problem here, and you have done your job." At the ANP, Claude Barnett, a lifelong Republican, chided Alice Dunnigan for leaning too hard on the president. Neither woman had much of a chance to ask any questions after that. Although they stood out from the mostly white male audience of the press conferences, they turned invisible to the president. Having called on Ethel Payne seven times during his first two years in office, Eisenhower recognized her only twice more during the next six years. He similarly stopped calling on Dunnigan. Their work came under heightened scrutiny. The Standing Committee of Correspondents called Dunnigan on the carpet for moonlighting as a clerk-typist and threatened to revoke her press credentials unless she quit her government job. The White House press office also questioned Ethel Payne about editorial work she had done for a Congress of Industrial Organizations (CIO) publication. Both women suspected Louis Lautier of being the informant against them.[42]

Lautier came to Eisenhower's defense in his syndicated column and assailed "the two gal reporters" for asking the president embarrassing questions. Dunnigan commented that Eisenhower liked to call on Lautier because he raised nonconfrontational questions and did not always ask about civil rights. Ethel Payne saw Lautier as "a water boy for the White House," but she gave him credit for being "the right kind of person" to break the racial barriers in the Washington press corps. He was unassuming and dignified. "If we had to wait for some pushy, aggressive reporter like me to be the first," she commented, "we still wouldn't be in the press gallery."[43]

Lautier broke yet another barrier in 1955 by becoming the first African American member of the National Press Club. A social club with standing committees on entertainment, games, golf, and the bar, the Press Club was also a professional organization whose luncheons for prominent newsmakers made it a handicap for a reporter not to belong. The Press Club barred blacks both as members and as guests. The leftist columnist I. F. Stone publicly resigned in 1943 when the club refused to serve his luncheon guest, William Hastie, the dean of Howard University's law school. (The club made exceptions only for the press officers from African embassies, who could be associate members.) When Lautier tried to join, Lee Nichols of United Press and columnist Drew Pearson, both Quakers, sponsored his application. The membership committee approved but a group of members filed a petition of disapproval. The line within the club seemed drawn between older and younger members rather than between southerners and northerners. Advocates of Lautier's admission were surprised when Frank Holeman, a southerner who reported for the *New York Daily News*, agreed that "the time is right" to admit him. As the club's vice president–elect, Holeman was politically savvy enough to want the fracas to be over before he became president the following year. It fell instead to Lucian Warren of the *Buffalo Courier-Express* to preside over the tense business meeting to vote on the nomination. Unable to resolve the dispute, the leadership put Lautier's application up to a referendum of the entire membership. That vote took place on February 4, 1955, and Lautier was approved by a margin of 377 to 281. Only one member resigned in protest. "My only reason for asking membership is to have access to the noted speakers at the club," Lautier said. After being admitted, he stopped by only sporadically to eat lunch or to read the wire service tickers.[44]

Lautier opened the door, but Dunnigan and Payne could not follow him because the National Press Club remained resolutely men only. Women journalists in Washington had formed their own Women's National Press Club, whose membership was also all white. In 1948, May Craig offered to sponsor Alice Dunnigan for membership. To acquaint her with some of the other members, Craig arranged a private dinner, but Dunnigan felt uneasy in the company of the quick-talking, assertive women journalists and stayed silent through the meal. No offer of membership followed until seven years later when Lautier integrated the National Press Club. Embarrassed by their own discrimination, the Women's National Press Club unanimously invited Dunnigan to join. Alice Dunnigan later cited her membership in the club as one of the best things to happen to her during her newspaper career because it "opened avenues for many exclusive stories and personal interviews with prominent dignitaries." Yet she also resented her "seven years of waiting for professional liberals to decide whether they could, in good faith, accept just one minority into their sacred society."[45]

Louis Lautier and Alice Dunnigan broke racial barriers in the press galleries in 1947, the same year that Jackie Robinson first played for the Brooklyn Dodgers, but the Washington press corps integrated far more slowly than baseball did. The editor of the *Washington Evening Star* blamed the failure of the press to hire more black reporters on the paucity of blacks who wanted news jobs. The more liberal *Washington Post* had the lowest percentage of black readers of the five leading Washington papers. In the 1930s the *Post* had hired a black schoolteacher, Edward H. Lawson, to cover "colored" news. Its general reporting staff remained all white until 1952, when managing editor Ben Gilbert hired Simeon Booker. The *Post*'s first black general reporter came with stellar credentials, having won journalism awards for his reporting in Cleveland and spent a year as a Nieman Fellow at Harvard, but Booker found working for the *Post* a frustrating experience. Others on the staff greeted him coolly and made him feel uncomfortable when using either the paper's cafeteria or its restrooms. He could not flag cabs or get through police lines to report on fires in white neighborhoods. Editors kept Booker from covering civil rights demonstrations against department stores that advertised in the *Post*. They ran his stories far back in the paper. Fatigued and angry, he quit after a year and became the Washington bureau chief for *Ebony* and *Jet* magazines.[46]

Simeon Booker called covering Washington during the Eisenhower administration as a black reporter a "pathetic chore." Eisenhower's sense of order, and of federal authority, prompted him to send troops to Little Rock, Arkansas, to uphold court-ordered school desegregation. But the president worried that paying too much attention to civil rights would ignite a potentially explosive situation. Booker stopped attending Eisenhower's press conferences because the president would not talk about the topics that most concerned his readers. Other than Louis Lautier, black reporters had trouble making contact with Eisenhower's top-level staff. Presidential press secretary James Hagerty treated the black press as too unimportant to cultivate. With black papers stepping up their criticism of Eisenhower, the president's advisor on race relations, E. Frederick Morrow, struggled to mend fences. He urged the president to "recognize Negro newsmen" at his press conferences, and he arranged for Eisenhower to address the National Negro Publishers Association in 1958. Morrow drafted a speech for the occasion, but Eisenhower chose to speak extemporaneously. "In his typically honest manner," Morrow observed, Eisenhower told the group that even though laws assured citizens equal rights, racial prejudice remained "deeply rooted in the hearts of men." Eisenhower asked them to "have patience," but from the expressions on the faces of the four hundred black journalists in the audience, Morrow could tell that they felt they had been patient for too long. From the audience, Simeon Booker judged it "one of Eisenhower's most disastrous adventures with Negroes," and noted that the remarks received little applause.[47]

Dwight Eisenhower remained perplexed over the black reporters' fixation on civil rights. After he had retired to his Gettysburg farm, Eisenhower granted Simeon Booker an interview. Near its end, the former president interjected: "Tell me. You've been here 45 minutes and all you've asked me are questions about civil rights. Is that all you're interested in?" Booker replied, "Well, Mr. President, you spoke out on other issues while you were President, but no one knew how you really felt about the major civil rights issues." Eisenhower scratched his chin thoughtfully.[48]

During Eisenhower's presidency, Washington had changed dramatically as "white flight" from the city combined with black migration from the South to make African Americans the majority population by 1960. For white reporters, black Washington seemed as remote and mysterious as Ulaanbaator. The columnist Stewart Alsop had to ask a black friend, Clarence Hunter of the *Washington Star*, to lead him on an expedition through the city's black neighborhoods, which he could barely locate on his own. The election of John F. Kennedy promised greater federal attention to civil rights. At his first presidential press conference Kennedy pointedly called on both Alice Dunnigan and Ethel Payne. He named an African American, Andrew Hatcher, as associate press secretary. Kennedy also let the White House Press Photographers Association know that he would not attend its annual dinners if they did not admit black photographers.[49]

The Kennedy administration freed Alice Dunnigan to quit the ANP. Constantly at loggerheads with Claude Barnett over her starvation wages, she resigned in 1961 to join the staff of the President's Commission on Equal Employment Opportunity. Her modest government salary tripled what she earned as a journalist. The job came as a reward for her service during the campaign as a press aide for Democratic vice presidential candidate Lyndon Johnson. In July 1961 the commission sent Dunnigan as its representative to the annual NAACP convention in Philadelphia. Tapping her long association with the NAACP's public relations office, she gained access to the pressroom and sat at the press table at the banquet. Once again Dunnigan encountered her old rival, Louis Lautier. He made no secret of his resentment of her presence in the press facilities and sent protest letters to the NAACP's executive director as well as to Vice President Johnson.

The two antagonists met again in September at the National Baptist Convention in Kansas City, Missouri, where another public relations officer had given Dunnigan press status. Lautier stormed that she had no business in the pressroom or "running all around the country at the taxpayer's expense." Dunnigan replied that her presence there would give him "something else to write more letters about." The shouting match marked their last encounter. Lautier retired from the NNPA that September to become special assistant to the chairman of the Republican National Committee, where he wrote a column called "Looking at the Record" which the RNC distributed to the black press. He died of a heart attack the following year at age sixty-five. Alice Dunnigan remained in the federal government until the Nixon administration forced her retirement in 1970. She spent many of her last years settling old scores in her autobiography, *A Black Woman's Experience: From School House to White House*, before her death in 1983 at age seventy-seven.[50]

The black newspaper services for which Alice Dunnigan and Louis Lautier had reported helped demolish racial barriers, but as the mass-circulation press awoke to devote more attention to civil rights and to African Americans in general, it undermined the black press. Successful black magazines such as *Ebony* and *Jet* further undercut the weekly newspapers. To stay alive, the black papers shifted their attention from national to local news. Clients of the Associated Negro Press fell steadily into arrears until their unpaid accounts put the news service out of business in 1964. As a final gesture, Claude Barnett offered the ANP to the National Negro Publishers Association. Adamant to the end, the publishers rejected his proposal. Not long after, following the death of publisher Carl Murphy, who for years had maintained their Washington bureau, the NNPA's Washington service similarly succumbed. Alice Dunnigan "wept bitter tears" at her old boss Barnett's death in 1967. She recognized it as the end of an era in black journalism, but given the transformation of conditions for black reporters during her years as a Washington correspondent, she knew that the struggle had been worth waging.[51]

3

Radio Voices

"What does it matter on radio?" quipped a Washington correspondent, expressing his indifference to getting his facts wrong on an early radio broadcast. To newspaper reporters, radio news seemed as fleeting as the airwaves that carried it, but their own papers' management did not share their cavalier attitude. Publishers recognized radio as potential competition for advertising revenue, and editors resented radio's ability to scoop them on fast breaking news. As the general manager of the *Trenton Times* complained in 1931, "How can an eight-column banner line on some spot news happening hold the same thrill after it has been heard over the radio?" Afraid that newspapers might not survive if "headline-minded" Americans got used to radio's condensed version of events, the newspapers launched a preventive war. For a decade they fought radio's ability to broadcast the news, and denied its Washington correspondents press passes. Not until the Second World War would radio news finally find its voice.[1]

From the start, radio aspired to report the news, although it fumbled its first big story. Broadcasting from an experimental station in the Bronx, the pioneering radio engineer Lee de Forest announced election returns for the 1916 presidential race between President Woodrow Wilson and his Republican challenger, Charles Evans Hughes. Taking his news from a direct wire from the *New York American,* de Forest spent six hours on the air before declaring Hughes the victor and signing off at 11:00 that evening. The next morning's returns from California reelected Wilson. America's entry into the First World War suspended commercial radio development, as the navy commandeered all available broadcasting frequencies for ship-to-shore communications. Civilian radio began anew after the war, and this time Pittsburgh's station KDKA correctly called Warren G. Harding's landslide victory in 1920. Three years later, Moses Koenigsberg, head of Hearst's International News Service, was at his club when a member rushed in shouting that President Harding was dead. Koenigsberg dismissed the story out of hand. He considered it "almost insulting" that some stockbroker would presume to have news of that magnitude ahead of a leading newspaperman like himself. "I know it's true," the broker stood his ground, "I just got it over my radio set."[2]

Intrigued by radio's possibilities, newspaper publishers began buying stations with the intention of using them to sell their papers. Long before the 1920s were over, however, the majority had abandoned their stations as too expensive. News was only a minuscule portion of radio schedules crowded with music, serial dramas, and sports. Broadway's ready supply of talent made Manhattan the natural center for radio. All that Washington could offer was a limitless supply of politicians eager to talk. With Washington playing a minor role on the air, the press corps relegated the handful of radio news broadcasters among them to second-class status. On Capitol Hill, the Standing Committee of Correspondents denied radio reporters access to the press galleries—unless they also reported for a daily newspaper. The National Press Club allowed radio broadcasters to join and pay dues, but not to vote or hold office.[3]

Radio adopted an "easy and breezy" tone, and coached its announcers not to talk over the listeners' heads. Radio news came to depend as much on delivery as on content. As an announcer for station WOC (World of Chiropractic) in Davenport, Iowa, the young Ronald Reagan learned that the secret of announcing was to make reading sound like unrehearsed conversation, and he worked to perfect his own persuasive sell. Through inflection, cadence, and resonance, news announcers could inform, reassure, and entertain. Radio news broadcasters generally tried to deliver the news objectively, although vocal qualities sometimes gave them away by indicating personal disapproval or acclamation—a form of acoustic advocacy. Some Washington broadcasters, such as Edward P. Morgan, regarded objectivity on the radio as a hopelessly unattainable virtue. "It would be more accurate (if not more objective)," Morgan insisted, "to measure our balance by the degrees by which we are able to control our subjectivity in this business of dealing so intimately with human conflict."[4]

The tendency of radio commentators to draw conclusions and express opinions troubled officials in both government and the radio industry. Around the world, most governments either owned or controlled radio broadcasting within their boundaries. In the United States, radio operated as a private enterprise under federal regulation. In 1927, Congress created the Federal Radio Commission to prevent a single corporation or network from dominating the air. Recognizing the new medium's potential for propaganda, politicians aimed to ensure that the airwaves would never fall under the control of a "radio trust." The Federal Radio Commission defined the airwaves as a public utility, assigned radio frequencies, required stations to operate "in the public interest," and established a fairness doctrine that mandated equal time for opposing views. While protecting radio from a monopolizing interest, the regulations made it more vulnerable than newspapers to government intervention.[5]

Brisk sales of radio sets before championship boxing matches and the World Series during the 1920s demonstrated audiences' hunger to listen in on live events. In 1925 the *Chicago Tribune*'s station WGN arranged to broadcast live reports from the Scopes "Monkey Trial" in Dayton, Tennessee, via telephone hookups. WGN's connections broke down during the trial, but its much-ballyhooed experiment demonstrated the same basic technology that later enabled independent radio stations to be linked into national networks. A central studio sent programs by phone lines to multiple stations, which broadcast them from transmitting towers. Reliance on telephone lines made it seem inevitable that the American Telephone & Telegraph Company (AT&T) would dominate network radio. AT&T founded the New York station WEAF with the specific intention of linking it to a network of "radiotelephone" stations in other cities. AT&T charged programmers for the use of radio airtime the same way it did for phone calls. In August 1922, WEAF aired radio's first paid commercial, a ten-minute program promoting a housing project in Jackson Heights, Queens.[6]

Among the first advertisers, the *Brooklyn Eagle* paid WEAF to air weekly commentary by its chief editorial writer Hans von Kaltenborn. Supremely opinionated, Kaltenborn had been chafing at censorship from his paper whenever he criticized society's "sacred cows," and he anticipated gaining greater freedom of expression over the radio. But when Kaltenborn chided a judge who was about to preside over a phone rate case, AT&T executives begged him to exercise some prudence. He caused another flap with anti-union remarks that threatened the phone company's labor relations. Then he rebuked Secretary of State Charles Evans Hughes for having brusquely rejected diplomatic recognition for the Soviet Union. Hughes happened to hear the broadcast on the Washington station WRC, which was carrying selected WEAF programs from New York. "Secretary Hughes did not like what I said," Kaltenborn later commented, "particularly since my opinions were expressed in his own home in the hearing of his guests." Hughes protested and the phone company decided to let Kaltenborn's contract expire. In selling airtime, AT&T had never anticipated that it might be held accountable for the contents of the broadcasts or that the enterprise might jeopardize its standing as a regulated public utility.[7]

During the early 1920s, AT&T had viewed the Radio Corporation of America (RCA, the largest manufacturer of radio sets) as a likely rival and had refused to allow RCA to rent its phone lines to form its own network. As it became nervous over the potential liabilities of its radio venture, however, the phone company opted to lease out its telephone lines to others rather than to operate any stations itself. In 1926, AT&T sold WEAF to RCA, which made the station its flagship for the new National Broadcasting Company. Over the next decade, NBC expanded from 19 affiliated stations to 148, divided into Red, Blue and Orange Networks (the Orange Network operated only on the West Coast). A second network, the Columbia Broadcasting System, got underway the next year with 11 stations and grew to 115 within its first decade. In 1934, the *Chicago Tribune*'s WGN joined in a cost-sharing arrangement with four other stations to form the Mutual Broadcasting Service. By 1939, Mutual linked more than one hundred previously independent affiliates. A fourth national network, the American Broadcasting Company, emerged in 1943, when the federal government ordered RCA to divest itself of its Blue Network.[8]

Newspapers published daily listings of radio programs for their readers, but the resentful publishers decided to restrict radio's use of wire service news reports. Associated Press members took the most rigid stance by restricting radio's use of AP news to late-breaking bulletins and announcements of "transcendent" public interest. The AP's hungrier rivals, the United Press and the International News Service, showed more tolerance of the new media and gave radio news their dispatches gratis in return for on-air attribution. When H. V. Kaltenborn quit the *Brooklyn Eagle* to do a daily radio news show on another New York station, the AP cut off his access to its wire services. The commentator simply went to the United Press bureau, where he stood unobtrusively near a printer to pick up news for his program.[9]

The radio networks eased into regular news reporting. During the 1920s, NBC's popular noontime *National Farm and Home Hour* added a five-minute segment of general news stories on the assumption that not all farm families read a daily newspaper. David Lawrence, publisher of the Washington-based *United States Daily* (the forerunner of *U.S. News and World Report*), provided the news, and lent reporter H. R. Baukhage to read it on the air. Baukhage developed such a national following that he started his own program, *Baukhage Talking* (so named for his signature opening for each program). In 1930, NBC experimented with a regularly scheduled fifteen-minute evening news program, *Literary Digest Topics in Brief,* featuring the flamboyant *Chicago Tribune* reporter Floyd Gibbons. His staccato delivery and fortunate scheduling before the popular comedy show *Amos 'n' Andy* made his news program immensely popular. Away from the microphone, Gibbons's excessive drinking offended the teetotalist president of his sponsor, the *Literary Digest.* When the *Literary Digest* refused to renew his contract, NBC replaced Gibbons with the sober and reliable Lowell Thomas, who remained a durable fixture on radio long after the *Literary Digest* closed down.[10]

NBC may have pioneered with news broadcasts but its challenger CBS billed itself as the "News Network." CBS's founding president, William Paley, worried that broadcasting news ahead of the newspapers might trigger a backlash of bad publicity, but his public relations consultant, Edward Bernays, reminded him that CBS was competing with NBC, not with the newspapers. On Bernays's advice, Paley hired a tough-minded reporter and night city editor for the *New York Times,* Edward Klauber, to run the network. Assuming that radio audiences cared more about reliable information than an announcer's personal views, Klauber set about building a news department that would match the *Times*'s standards of objectivity. Nor did it escape CBS executives that their advertisers, hesitant to offend consumers with controversial viewpoints, felt more comfortable sponsoring straight news programs than analysis. Klauber handled CBS's day-to-day administration and hired Paul White from United Press to run CBS News. To broadcast the news, they hired two veteran print journalists: H. V. Kaltenborn and Frederic William Wile.[11]

From time to time, the New York–based Kaltenborn imperiously descended upon the capital to attend the president's press conferences or some other high-profile event. Fred Wile, by contrast, operated exclusively out of Washington. The Indiana-born Wile graduated from Notre Dame, where his German-Jewish father was a business advisor to the school's founder. Wile went abroad for a Chicago paper to cover the Boer War, and then got hired by the *London Daily Mail* as its Berlin correspondent. At the outbreak of the First World War, the Germans seized him as a suspected British spy, but his American citizenship won his freedom and a cash settlement for wrongful arrest. Repatriated, Wile joined the *Washington Evening Star,* where he wrote a syndicated column that, his detractors said, adhered to the *Star'*s policy of rarely saying much of any importance about anything.[12]

Fred Wile dabbled in radio on the side with a weekly Washington news commentary on NBC, drawing on the sources he cultivated as an affable back-slapper. He became the first radio newscaster to broadcast directly from the U.S. Capitol. He did radio reports for five years at no salary, strictly "for love and glory." As he wrote in his memoirs, he finally decreed that "unless NBC pays up, Wile would shut up!" NBC agreed to pay him twenty-five dollars a week, which CBS doubled when it hired him away. By 1931, Wile was earning $250 per broadcast and riding around in a chauffeured limousine. He studiously avoided partisanship in his commentary, pointing out that as a resident of the voteless District of Columbia he had not cast a presidential ballot since 1896. Still, he slipped in just enough opinion to provide some cover for the more outspoken Kaltenborn, who believed that Wile's commentary "justified *me* in giving my own opinions on foreign problems as he gave them on Washington problems."[13]

During the depression, the advertising revenues of newspapers dropped while radio's share rose. Advertisers sensed that the hard times had stimulated the public's appetite for radio news. "Instead of seeking diversion from his troubles, as you'd expect," one radio programmer marveled, "the average American seems to hanker for bad news. He can't hear enough about the state of the nation and the state of the world." More anxious about losing advertisers than readers, the American Newspaper Publishers Association urged newspapers to renew efforts to cut radio off from wire service reports. Competition among the wires, however, undermined this resistance. When the United Press offered to sell election returns to CBS and NBC at a reduced rate, protests from newspapers forced the UP to raise its fees. CBS withdrew from the arrangement, but, before that development became public, the Associated Press panicked over the challenge from the UP and offered its own election returns to radio at no cost at all. UP similarly reversed its policy, and by election night all of CBS's teleprinters were running again.[14]

Franklin Roosevelt's victory in 1932 was such a foregone conclusion that radio provided few surprises that election night. Even so, newspaper editors were apoplectic over having been scooped by radio's election returns. The following spring, AP member papers voted to shut off wire service news to all radio networks. If an AP newspaper owned a radio station, it had to pay an additional fee to broadcast AP news. The newspapers carefully monitored local radio news broadcasts and hauled stations into court over violations of the ban. But NBC suffered little from the ban because of its creative, and only, news writer, Abel Schechter. A former *New York World* reporter and AP editor, Schechter created what he called a "Scissors and Paste-Pot Press Association" by clipping leads from various newspapers and rewriting them into patchwork scripts. (Rather than collect the news, commentator Lowell Thomas confessed, NBC "swiped it.") Schechter supplemented this method by phoning additional sources. Across the country, NBC affiliates sent him daily reports on local news, and if something caught his eye he would call local officials for more details. Schechter discovered that his sources regarded radio more as a form of entertainment than a source of hard news and talked more willingly to him than they would to newspaper reporters. Phone interviews also translated smoothly into news scripts. "When a man tells me in his own words just what happened, that's perfect radio," Schechter realized.[15]

The ban on wire service news prompted CBS to organize its own news service, underwritten by General Mills. News director Paul White set up news bureaus in Washington, Chicago, and Los Angeles; arranged for affiliate stations to provide local news; purchased news from the Dow-Jones ticker service and a British news agency; and recruited scores of stringers. The CBS news service generated copy for the network's news commentators and for three short daily news broadcasts. Its first year of operation, 1933, proved a heavy news year, between the New Deal and the rise of Nazi Germany, but the news service met the challenge due to White's intense competitive drive against both newspapers and NBC.[16]

In Washington, reporters for the CBS news service applied for congressional press gallery passes but confronted rules that strictly excluded those who did not report for a daily newspaper. Radio correspondents such as Kaltenborn and Wile held press passes because they also appeared in print. Unwilling to revise the rules or share the cramped press galleries with a despised rival, the Standing Committee of Correspondents rejected CBS's bid. The *Washington Evening Star* went further by refusing to publish the daily program listings for CBS's Washington station. Frank B. Noyes, publisher of the *Star* and head of the Associated Press, loftily explained that, "we propose to pursue our policy of not advertising our competitors."[17]

Big money finally brokered a truce in the press-radio war. The Standard Oil Company of New Jersey contracted to sponsor a daily five-minute news program, the *Esso Reporter*, on NBC, for so much money that the UP agreed to ignore the newspapers' protests and sell its news to the program. In December 1933 print and broadcast media met at the bargaining table. "You could tell from the start that these were peace conferences because of the warlike attitude of all the participants," commented CBS's Paul White. The newspapers agreed to provide wire services dispatches to radio, and the networks promised not to broadcast any headline news less than twelve hours old, save for bulletins. Radio agreed that its news programs would not be commercially sponsored and would be broadcast only twice daily, after the morning and afternoon papers had appeared on the newsstands. Disappointed, White called the outcome "about as satisfactory as Versailles." As confining as the rules seemed, they established a regular schedule for news broadcasts that made listeners accustomed to tuning in at set times for the news. Radio also artfully dodged the sponsorship ban by exempting Kaltenborn, Wile, and others, calling them "commentators" rather than news reporters. But the compromise stunted the networks' growth as news vendors. Radio listeners heard only summaries of stories they could have already read in the newspapers. "Perhaps this is the final niche of radio in the structure of the news; perhaps it is merely a temporary truce," mused journalism critic Will Irvin in the mid-1930s. "But if radio ever cancels this agreement and comes into full competition with the newspaper, it may transform the relations between journalism and the public."[18]

During Franklin Roosevelt's inauguration in March 1933, CBS commentator H. V. Kaltenborn drove up and down Pennsylvania Avenue broadcasting over the airwaves from a two-way radio, describing what he saw and speculating freely on the new president's policies. One disgusted print reporter remarked, "I wish I could be as sure of a few things as that guy is about everything." Politicians took broadcasting more seriously than radio's newspaper rivals. President Roosevelt seized on the medium as another way of combating the nation's overwhelmingly Republican-leaning newspaper publishers. During the campaign, his robust radio voice had counteracted questions about his health. Now, faced with a national economic emergency, the radio networks promised Roosevelt the right of way whenever he wanted it. Eight days after his inauguration he accepted the offer and went on the air to tell the nation how he planned to solve the banking crisis. He picked a Sunday night, when radio audiences were at their largest, but waited until 10:00 p.m. to avoid preempting the nation's favorite programs. Roosevelt addressed his 40 million listeners like an old friend. He outlined the economic situation in simple terms and offered reassurances. After his second radio talk, on May 7, CBS's Washington director likened it to a "fireside chat," and the label stuck. Over the next twelve years, the president delivered twenty-eight fireside chats that extolled his administration's accomplishments and assailed his opponents. They made grand theater, but audiences also stayed loyal because he always gave them substantive information.[19]

Congress cooperated by rescheduling the annual State of the Union message from the afternoon to the evening to reach more listeners. Conservative senators complained that New Deal supporters dominated the airwaves, so the networks offered them free time for rebuttal. Roosevelt's critics spoke with many voices, however, and never mounted a unified challenge. Other members of the administration showed less enthusiasm for radio than did the president. When they spoke to a newspaper reporter, they usually saw the resulting article, but if they missed the radio broadcast, they had no idea how their remarks had been used. Washington officials were so indifferent about keeping radio appointments that the networks resorted to sending limousines to fetch them, to ensure that guests appeared at the studios on schedule.[20]

While Congress permitted radio to cover its joint session to hear the president's State of the Union address, both the House and Senate refused to allow radio to cover their own debates—a decision that further retarded Washington news broadcasting. A Senate committee held hearings on whether to wire the Senate chamber for broadcasting, but the Senate Democratic leader Joseph T. Robinson protested that radio would cause the "virtual abolition of the press gallery, since the radio reports might displace the newspaper accounts." Robinson questioned how much interest the public would have for the Senate's protracted debates. House leaders shared similar doubts, and newspapers applauded the legislature's reluctance to air its debates. The White House, by contrast, courted the commentators. Press Secretary Steve Early invited H. V. Kaltenborn to observe a typical day in the White House, and the radio star boasted of his license to "walk in and out of rooms and talk to anyone I pleased."[21]

Radio clearly contributed to Roosevelt's reelection in 1936. His Republican challenger, Kansas governor Alf Landon, never mastered the art of radio speaking. Roosevelt's campaign manager, James A. Farley, credited the broadcast media for the Democratic landslide. No matter what the newspapers wrote, Farley beamed, "the harmful effect was largely washed away as soon as the reassuring voice of the President of the United States started coming through the ether into the family living room." The election results certified the print media's diminishing influence.[22]

Politicians shared the airwaves with a new class of radio news commentators who earned incomes far in excess of the average reporter. CBS had originally paid Kaltenborn a hundred dollars a week for his two broadcasts, and he supplemented his income by freelance writing and lecturing. Once he got a sponsor for his network broadcasts, however, a soaring income eliminated his need to travel the exhausting lecture circuit. With his precisely enunciated speech and Teutonic authority, Kaltenborn achieved star status—he even played himself in the Hollywood film *Mr. Smith Goes to Washington*. Even greater celebrity and salary went to the glib Broadway gossip columnist Walter

Winchell, whose dishing the dirt on radio made sponsors sit up and pay attention to radio news commentary. Winchell launched a regular Sunday night
program on NBC in 1930 to promote his syndicated newspaper column. He
mixed a dollop of serious news into a heap of gossip. Because there were no
Sunday evening newspapers, Winchell, as a "commentator" free from radio
news restrictions, could claim any late-breaking wire dispatch that he read on
the air as an exclusive. The program caught the public's attention, and its ratings captivated advertisers.[23]

Despite the mass audiences that these opinionated news commentators attracted, they made network executives terribly uncomfortable. When CBS's
highly popular commentator Boake Carter drifted further into the isolationist
camp, listeners complained that Carter spoke more cordially about Nazi Germany than about the American State Department. His sponsor canceled his
contract and CBS fired him. Carter resurfaced on the Mutual network but
never regained his influence. CBS also abandoned its practice of selling airtime to speakers after the radio priest Father Charles Coughlin began blaming
the depression on international bankers and delivering anti-Semitic sermons.
Instead of selling public affairs time slots, CBS decided to promote speakers of
its own choosing, and in 1935 it hired the young Edward R. Murrow to recruit
broadcasters. Murrow had no prior experience in journalism, learning the news
business from the head of the network, Ed Klauber. Two years later, Klauber
sent Murrow to London to arrange for European participation in CBS programs. Murrow was there when Europe went to war in 1939 and he took to the
air himself, becoming radio's most authoritative news commentator.[24]

Washington had few radio stars—but those few reaped the medium's financial reward. The New York Times had the largest Washington bureau, but the
Chicago Tribune's Arthur Sears Henning was the capital's highest paid Washington bureau chief. His enviable salary came from the weekly radio addresses he
made over Chicago's WGN and the National Mutual network. After Arthur Krock
won the Pulitzer Prize in 1935, he received an attractive monetary offer from
NBC to address public issues from its Washington studio, but the New York Times
denied its permission. Just as the Times refused to syndicate Krock's "In the Nation" column, it insisted on exclusive rights for what he said as well as what he
wrote. Determined that his reporters not be distracted by the lure of broadcasting, publisher Arthur Hayes Sulzberger reiterated to Krock: "The point is that
the newspaper comes first and must always come first."[25]

The local Washington newspapers also approached radio with caution. Not
until 1939 did the capital's most profitable newspaper, the Evening Star, acquire a radio station, WMAL, an affiliate of the Blue Network, which later
became ABC. The station broadcast the news directly from the Star's headquarters on Pennsylvania Avenue. The Star's publishers counted on radio bulletins to allow them to discontinue costly extra editions of the paper. In 1944
the Star's morning rival, the Washington Post, acquired a small independent

station, WINX, not realizing that its previous owners derived most of their income by broadcasting race results and the daily "numbers" for local gamblers. Publisher Eugene Meyer switched to classical music and sacrificed the station's audience. WINX had no network affiliation and practically no equipment with which to broadcast outside its studios. To cover President Roosevelt's return to Washington after the 1944 election, the station's engineers strung together a hundred yards of cable, which was all it owned. Announcer Bill Gold was attempting to interview the president, who was sitting in his limousine, when the cable came undone. Gold begged him to wait until they could fix it. A newspaper photo that showed the president doubled over on the backseat of the car caused speculation that he was in pain—but Roosevelt was actually leaning forward because Gold could not stretch out his hand-held microphone any closer. The *Post* sold WINX when it acquired majority ownership of the Washington CBS station WTOP. CBS had considered selling the station to the *Evening Star,* but during the negotiations the *Star's* publisher, Sam Kauffmann, asked CBS president Frank Stanton how much of CBS was Jewish-owned. "All of it, Mr. Kauffmann," replied Stanton, who took the deal to the *Post.*[26]

WINX's technical limitations were typical of radio's problem with "on the spot" news coverage. Most news shows originated from studios. The stunning broadcast of the zeppelin *Hindenburg's* explosion in 1937 occurred only by chance—the Chicago radio announcer Herbert Morrison happened to be making an experimental recording of his observations when the airship burst into flames. Radio bulletins followed within minutes of the explosion, but the recording of Morrison's anguished eyewitness account did not air until the next day. The lack of variety in the nightly newscasts turned audiences to the dramatized *March of Time* series, in which actors portrayed players in the news to the accompaniment of background music and sound effects. Then events in Europe, coupled with advances in technology, provided dramas that radio could broadcast live without any need for special effects.[27]

The Second World War gave a professional boost to radio news. Network news departments raced to find news announcers and commentators who knew what they were talking about. "Professional news analysts, converted reporters, military experts, and political philosophers have been put on the air," applauded the radio columnist for the *Washington Post.* Americans anxiously tuned in for radio news from Munich, where British and French diplomats tried to appease Adolf Hitler in 1938. The Munich crisis marked the first time that the majority of American radio stations carried news on the hour and on the half-hour. On CBS, the correspondent H. V. Kaltenborn conducted a "Munich marathon," giving more than a hundred extemporaneous broadcasts, and setting up live links with Edward R. Murrow in London and William L. Shirer in Berlin. As one radio producer marveled, "You could wake Kaltenborn up at four o'clock in the morning and just say 'Czechoslovakia,' one word, and he'd talk for thirty minutes on Czechoslovakia." Yet Kaltenborn's commentary troubled CBS executives, who were concerned that his opinions might offend government regulators, sponsors, and listeners. Aware that antiwar groups were complaining about Jewish control of the American media, William Paley promised to keep news on CBS "militantly nonpartisan." When Kaltenborn violated that code, CBS news chief Ed Klauber begged him to make his remarks less personal. Rather than saying, "I think," or "I believe," Klauber wanted to hear, "there are those who believe" or "some experts say." A stubborn Kaltenborn insisted that his listeners ought to know what was on his mind. Despite the success of his Munich broadcasts, Kaltenborn considered conditions at CBS untenable and jumped to NBC, which offered a contract that guaranteed his freedom of speech.[28]

Munich proved to radio that its real strength lay in broadcasting eyewitness reports of momentous events, and that some opinion in these reports was probably inevitable. Even a straightforward radio commentator such as Edward R. Murrow could make it clear through words or inflection what he thought. What bothered the newspaper columnist Walter Lippmann was that some commentators seemed compelled to make their programs seem momentous by delivering the news "in hot, moist, and fervent voice, conveying a mood of breathless alarm and mounting danger." Lippmann was describing the kind of commentary that the Mutual network thrived upon. Rather than encourage neutral presentation of the news, in the CBS model, Mutual offered a range of voices from left to right. Its most provocative speaker was the Washington commentator Fulton Lewis Jr., who overflowed with righteous indignation against Franklin Roosevelt and the New Deal. Lewis possessed radio's "voice with a snarl." A fellow Mutual commentator, Wythe Williams, observed that Lewis was too caustic to be popular with either Washington officialdom or other Washington reporters, but this same quality made for high ratings. At his peak, five hundred radio stations ran Lewis's program, making him Mutual's "Most Valuable Property."[29]

The son of a prominent Washington attorney, Fulton Lewis Jr. was born in Georgetown and raised in high society. He flitted away his college years at the University of Virginia by leading a dance orchestra, and then dropped out of law school to take a job with Hearst's morning *Washington Herald*. The paper's small staff and paltry salaries offered him quick advancement from cub reporter to city editor. He could spend his fifteen-dollar-a-week paycheck on his country club dues and live off of his family's assets. His marriage to the daughter of the chairman of the Republican National Committee attracted First Lady Lou Henry Hoover and two thousand other Washingtonians to their wedding. Not until his fortunes tumbled with the stock market crash did Lewis take either his finances or his journalism all that seriously. He investigated irregularities in the federal payments that airlines received for carrying airmail and produced an explosive story on government overpayments—too explosive for the *Herald* to publish. Lewis turned his notes over to a congressional investigation that eventually resulted in the government's cancellation of all airmail contracts. His paper finally recognized his talents and gave him a syndicated column on "The Washington Sideshow."[30]

Lewis tried radio without success in the 1920s and signed off for a decade until he was called to substitute for a vacationing commentator at a local station. He enjoyed that experience more than his first foray into radio, but his words spilled out in a mix of slang and clichés, and his voice grew strident with excitement. Yet he managed to impress the station's manager, William Dolph, by showing up on time and sober (unlike so many of the print reporters Dolph had hired), and by sounding passionate. "Announcers who can read the news perfectly are a dime a dozen," Dolph decided. "I've asked perhaps a hundred announcers to tell me the news just after they read it, and not one ever came close. They don't know what they're reading, and they don't care. Fulton reads from a script, sure, but it's a script that he himself has written at the last moment. . . . He gets excited and loses his place, but you know a guy like that just can't be phony."[31]

Taking a gamble and a substantial cut in pay, Lewis gave up his newspaper writing to do radio commentary on the Washington station WOL. By 1937, Mutual was broadcasting his program nationally as *The Top of the News*. When Fred Wile retired, Mutual advertised Fulton Lewis Jr. as the only national news commentary originating from Washington. With the smallest news operation of any of the radio networks, Mutual depended heavily on its Washington outlet for national news. Lewis filled that void, although he started without commercial sponsorship and in a sacrifice slot against NBC's popular *Amos 'n' Andy* show. Somehow his news program flourished and made him the heart of the Mutual network.[32]

Politically conservative, Fulton Lewis developed his sources among the right wing of both parties in Congress, and specialized in unearthing scandals within the liberal Roosevelt administration. Lewis prided himself on being a "legman," someone who specialized in gathering his own news on site, which made a congressional press pass a necessity. But after he switched from newspapers to radio, the print journalists who ran the gallery revoked his credentials. They disdained radio reporters' pretensions of equality. The Washington columnist Joseph Alsop, for instance, owned no radio and his partner on the column, Robert Kintner, listened only to *The March of Time* on Sunday evenings. "The way we saw it," Kintner commented, "if the broadcasters wanted somebody to tell the news from Washington, they could pay a working newspaperman to give a talk every once in a while." Denied a place to write his reports or from which to broadcast inside the Capitol, Lewis had to sit in the public galleries, where gallery rules prohibited note taking. Other radio reporters met the press gallery's requirements by taking extra assignments from smaller newspapers, but Lewis stubbornly lobbied Congress for a separate radio gallery.[33]

His crusade seemed little more than a publicity stunt, so reporters were stunned when the politicians in Congress—eager for more radio coverage—responded favorably. In the summer of 1939 Congress voted to establish the House and Senate radio galleries. Fulton Lewis Jr. won election as the first president of the Radio Correspondents Association. H. R. Baukhage represented NBC in the radio gallery, and CBS hired Albert L. Warner away from his post as Washington bureau chief of the *New York Herald Tribune.* Only two reporters for the Transradio Press Service used the new radio galleries on a daily basis, however; one covering the Senate and the other the House. The radio galleries could not have handled a bigger crowd. The House of Representatives created office space for radio newscasters by walling off a narrow gap between two elevators, and reserved just five seats for them in the visitors' gallery. The Senate provided a small room beside the spacious press gallery and set aside a few seats in a side gallery for radio reporters.[34]

Members of Congress often forgot to send their press releases to the radio gallery. Print reporters loathed making space for their radio counterparts at press tables in congressional hearings. Yet the recognition offered by an official gallery started a trend. Within a week after the radio galleries were established, White House press conferences followed suit by accrediting the radio reporters. Press conferences now became "news conferences," although print reporters noted that whenever White House secretaries summoned them to briefings they still shouted "Press!" Agency officials also began accommodating broadcasters, and the State, War, and Navy Departments created special radio sections in their public relations offices.[35]

When CBS transferred the young Eric Sevareid to Washington in 1940, the regulars in the White House pressroom greeted his arrival with derisive cries of "Make way for the com-men-ta-*tor!*" mocking his pretentious status. NBC's novice radio journalist David Brinkley sensed that he had been chosen to cover the White House solely for being "tall, white, Protestant and neatly dressed." Feeling inadequately prepared for the job, for months Brinkley kept silent at Roosevelt's press conferences. No such doubts troubled Fulton Lewis Jr. The cocky commentator maneuvered himself close to the president's desk and always tried to ask several questions. On the air, Lewis treated the packed press conferences as if they had been a personal meeting, intoning: "The president told me today. . . ."[36]

Just as the Capitol's radio galleries were opening in September 1939, Lewis scored another coup by arranging a national broadcast for the famed aviator Charles A. Lindbergh. Back from a tour of Nazi Germany, and impressed by the German military build-up, Lindbergh warned Americans to stay out of another European war. An undercurrent of anti-Semitism ran through Lindbergh's isolationism, and he feared that Jewish influence over the media would push the nation into war. After meeting with Lewis in 1939, Charles

Lindbergh recorded in his diary: "We are disturbed about the effect of the Jewish influence in our press, radio, and motion pictures. It may become very serious. Lewis told us of one instance where Jewish advertising firms threatened to remove all their advertising from the Mutual system if a certain feature were permitted to go on the air. The threat was powerful enough to have the feature removed."

Mixing paranoia and pragmatism, Lewis worried about the powerful control sponsors exercised. Having seen how reliance on a single advertiser had silenced Boake Carter, once that sponsor had soured on him, Lewis marketed his program to a multitude of local businesses. For a minimal price, each had the prestige of advertising on a national broadcast, even though its message aired only locally. The more sponsors that he signed, the higher Lewis's income rose.[37]

By nightly attacking the Roosevelt administration, Fulton Lewis Jr. made himself the radio commentator "whom New Dealers like least," judged Edwin A. Lahey, a Washington correspondent for the Knight newspapers. Lewis assailed wartime economic restrictions, public housing, and organized labor. He attacked government price controls throughout the war, and then, once these controls were lifted, blamed the sharp rise in prices on the "wide-eyed theorists and statisticians" in the Office of Price Administration. Lewis's opposition to the Roosevelt administration led him to speak at the 1944 Republican National Convention, causing one radio critic to identify him as "a campaigner, not . . . a commentator." Responding to complaints of his political bias, the Mutual Broadcasting Company pointed to the pro–New Deal commentators whom it also aired. None of them, however, matched Lewis's popularity, and by the end of the war his programs were reaching some 10 million people on more than 150 stations.[38]

The most popular radio news commentators had distinctive voices. "You tune into Walter Winchell and without hearing his name, you know it is Winchell," said NBC's Abel Schechter. H. V. Kaltenborn's clipped enunciation mixed his childhood German with Midwestern English and a Harvard accent. Edward R. Murrow's resonance and Fulton Lewis Jr.'s stridency gave personality to their voices that enabled audiences to envision them. "After all it is more than just news knowledge that is important in radio," Schechter explained, "it is the show business, how you throw your voice." A deep voice by itself was insufficient; the speaker needed tonal variety to give it life. Such prerequisites sent prospective broadcasters to speech instructors. A notable exception to the rule was Elmer Davis, who succeeded despite the ordinariness of his flat, Midwestern voice. A refreshing break from announcers who enunciated like Shakespearean actors, Davis adopted a low-keyed, "shirt-sleeve" approach to the news. Critics praised his five-minute nightly newscasts for offering "more grain and less chaff" than his competitors, and cited him as a model news broadcaster.[39]

The antithesis of Fulton Lewis Jr. in every respect, Elmer Davis escaped from a strict Baptist upbringing in Aurora, Indiana, by going to Oxford as a Rhodes Scholar. There he disappointed his parents by abandoning the classics for a career as a writer. "I cannot bear the thought of your wasting all these golden opportunities for reaching professional distinction by using your abilities in the preparation of foolish stories," his father reprimanded him. When Davis returned to the United States, he took a job with the *New York Times*. Moving up the ranks from cub reporter to feature writer, he won high praise for his political reporting before stunning *Times* editors in 1924 by quitting to write fiction.[40]

At the *Times*, Davis had worked closely enough with Ed Klauber to have him as the best man at his wedding. Once Davis went freelance, Klauber arranged for him to speak on CBS, under the assumption that he would be more readily available than a working reporter, but Davis's audition impressed no one. He returned to writing novels and magazine articles. (*Harper's* published more of his submissions than those of any other freelance writer of the era.) When Europe went to war again in 1939, Davis yearned to be in on the story, and he accepted Ed Klauber's invitation to substitute for H. V. Kaltenborn. This time, Davis's delivery scored. He projected a decency and rationality that listeners found reassuring amidst a world crisis.[41]

CBS retained Elmer Davis for a nightly five-minute news program. Their prime-time slot, at 8:55 p.m. eastern time, attracted high ratings and eager sponsors (commercials cut his actual airtime to three-and-a-half minutes). The tight schedule left little room for commentary, and as an alumnus of the *New York Times* Davis appreciated CBS's desire for objectivity, but he still worried that "objectivity had leaned so far over backwards that it had become unobjective." Although he offered mostly straight facts, he sometimes communicated his sentiments and editorialized "by inflection." Whenever CBS president William Paley suspected that Davis's leanings had become too obvious, he would take the broadcaster to lunch to remind him of the network's policy of neutrality. Davis would agree to try harder, but he found it impossible to suppress his admiration for Franklin Roosevelt or his loathing for Nazi Germany.[42]

Davis won a Peabody Award in 1940 for his on-air talks with Edward R. Murrow in London and Thomas Grandin in Paris. CBS's young European correspondents held Davis as a role model. "It hasn't been possible for me to hear all of your talks but I'm proud to be working with you," Murrow wrote to him. "I have hopes that broadcasting is to become an adult means of communications at last. I've spent a lot of time listening to broadcasts from many countries during the past month and yours stand out as the best example of fair, tough minded, interesting talking I've heard." Davis returned the high esteem for Murrow, despite feeling "faintly scandalized that such good reporting can be done by a man who never worked on a newspaper in his life." The Washington correspondent Robert Kintner, who also made the transition from print to radio, identified Davis and Murrow as the two men who "first gave broadcast journalism real stature and importance."[43]

Reporting on the Japanese attack on Pearl Harbor on December 7, 1941, Elmer Davis won further praise for his ability to suppress any sign of tension in his voice. At other times, he could not restrain his irritation over criticism of the president. "Well, you may not like Mr. Roosevelt," he commented on the air, "but if he loses the war we all lose it with him." Not surprisingly, Davis came to mind when the president was searching for someone sympathetic to head the Office of War Information (OWI). In June 1942 Davis informed his radio audience: "This is my last broadcast, as I have been called into government service."[44]

The Washington press corps warmly welcomed "Uncle Elmer," and counted on him to battle the bureaucracy and pry out the wartime news they needed. They were surprised and disappointed, however, when Davis kept his distance. He rarely ventured into the National Press Club to share confidences with old colleagues, and some reporters grumbled that he had gone "high hat." What kept Davis away was his preoccupation with an intractable bureaucracy. Four agencies had been hastily thrown together to form the Office of War Information, and Davis felt like "a man who married a four-time widow and was trying to raise her children all by her previous husbands." The OWI never knit together as an organization and remained rife with factions. Its talented writers, all proud individualists, complained that the OWI prevented them from writing the "honest and objective story of the war," and many of them noisily resigned.[45]

The Office of War Information had two contradictory missions: to provide straight news at home and propaganda abroad. Ideological divisions within the staff further complicated the effort. Through the Voice of America, the OWI broadcast radio news to war-torn Europe, for which it depended on refugees to deliver its foreign language reports. Staff members joked that this often meant choosing between a Communist and a Nazi. Some of the area specialists seemed far more intent on propagandizing against the Soviet Union than against Germany. In deference to the wartime alliance with the U.S.S.R., Davis suppressed anti-Communist rhetoric, and word spread that the agency was harboring Communists on its payroll. Staff dissidents formed an anti-Communist underground to collect internal evidence of alleged subversion, which they leaked to the press. Congressional conservatives denounced Elmer Davis for recruiting "as fine an aggregation of pinkos as was ever crowded under one roof," and the acerbic columnist Westbrook Pegler condemned the OWI as a "hideout for privileged intellectuals, New Deal cowards, and Communists." Others on the agency's staff resented these charges as groundless. "I got hot under the collar at the snide suggestion that the OWI preferred Reds," said Herbert Brucker, a Republican who came to the OWI from the Columbia School of Journalism, where others on the faculty had regarded him as "hopelessly conservative."[46]

For help in running the agency, Davis dipped into radio to recruit CBS's Ed Klauber and NBC's Abel Schechter. Having been forced into early retirement from CBS, Klauber jumped at the chance to become Davis's second-in-command. "The more mess and trouble you are in, OWI is in and the war effort is in," he volunteered, "the more I would like to help." A tough-minded manager, Klauber compensated for his boss's bureaucratic innocence. Davis, for instance, deprived his agency of direct access to the Oval Office by declining an offer to meet daily with President Roosevelt to discuss war news. He said that he did not want to bother the president. Davis was surprised by the deep aversion that military and civilian government agencies showed toward releasing bad news. Nor had he expected the suspicions in Congress about ideological bias at his agency. Turning to his strength, Davis briefly delivered his own news broadcasts about the war for the OWI. But he refused to use his radio time to defend the agency, and he eventually gave up the program because he found it impossible to be the voice of the government. He felt he could not speak for the president if Roosevelt had not approved what he had to say, "which he was much too busy to do." As a government official, he could not publicly disagree with government policies. Nor in fairness to other radio commentators could he use his inside knowledge to scoop them.[47]

Davis's personal reputation survived the war intact, but despite his hopes that the Office of War Information might have a postwar peacekeeping function, the Truman administration speedily abolished it. The Voice of America was transferred to the State Department, and Elmer Davis went back to radio news, although he did not return to New York. Instead, he joined the growing ranks of Washington broadcasters, which by then included Drew Pearson on ABC, Eric Sevareid on CBS, Richard Harkness on NBC, and Fulton Lewis Jr. on Mutual. The rising status of Washington radio reporters was reflected in the 1948 amendments to the National Press Club's rules that gave full active membership to those who wrote or edited news for radio or the newly emerging medium of television—although the rules still eliminated announcers, who were considered entertainers. Radio bureaus in the capital grew comparable in size to the larger newspaper bureaus.[48]

When Davis returned to CBS, he asked to do a full fifteen minutes of commentary, but the network proposed another five-minute program. He chose to accept an offer from the fledgling ABC network, headed by the former Washington correspondent Robert Kintner, to deliver two fifteen-minute evening news programs each week, alternating with Raymond Gram Swing. Soon afterward, Swing retired from radio and Davis took over all the weeknight programs. Even with the extra time, Davis found it difficult to explain the complicated issues of the early Cold War. It seemed to him that instead of competing with newspapers for comprehensiveness, the networks showed more interest in competing with each other. Davis resisted the impulse to hype the news and stripped his commentary of emotion-laden words. The Washington columnist Joseph Alsop, in a bid to do his own radio commentary, had finally bought a radio and started listening to some of the news broadcasters. Alsop admired Elmer Davis's ability to present the news in tabloid style, noting that he commented briefly on several major events rather than addressing any one of them in depth. Among the radio commentators, Alsop observed, "The very grand ones chiefly express their own opinions; the very popular ones chiefly deal in gossip." What distinguished radio from newspapers, he decided, was "the curious power of the voice." Unfortunately for Alsop, his own upper-class blend of Connecticut Yankee and Harvard Yard sounded too aloof for radio, while the flat voice of Elmer Davis retained its popular appeal.[49]

ABC offered Davis the opportunity to appear as its on-air editorial columnist, but he turned it down, feeling that radio needed to express a wider diversity of viewpoints, and that ABC was already "as a whole somewhat to the left of center." Davis located his own politics somewhere "to the left of the organization Democrats and to the right of the fellow-traveling Laborites." His beliefs placed him in the current mainstream of the press corps, and in 1949 fellow correspondents elected him chairman of the Radio Correspondents Association (which governed the radio gallery that Fulton Lewis Jr. had founded).[50]

Davis and Lewis soon found themselves at odds over the Red scare that followed World War II. The Grand Alliance had dissolved into Cold War, and Fulton Lewis Jr. had wholeheartedly joined the anti-Communist crusade to root subversives out of the government. His radio program denounced the State Department as riddled with Communists and their cohorts, and cheered on the congressional investigating committees. On the opposite wavelength, Elmer Davis defended the targets of those investigations and assailed the demagogic tactics of smears, innuendo, and guilt by association. Davis compared the investigations to "never-ending serial melodramas, like soap operas," and he decried the irresponsible accusations being made by Senator Joseph R. McCarthy.[51]

Elmer Davis grew so irate over McCarthy that he allowed his passions to spill into his reporting. "In his latter days, Elmer Davis became almost too violent a partisan to be an ideal reporter," judged James Reston of the *New York Times*. On the air, Fulton Lewis Jr. attacked Davis for purporting to be "a great factual reporter," when he had once belonged to the left-leaning American Labor Party. One listener complained: "I am becoming convinced, reluctantly however, that Fulton Lewis Jr. has been right all along in his seeming belief that there must be something in your past associations with the left wing crowd and a former pro-commie crowd that you were desperately anxious to have remain undisclosed." Davis replied that Lewis knew full well that he had left the Labor Party *"because the Communists were infiltrating it, as did all the decent members when we were unable to keep the Communists out."* But Lewis continued to repeat the allegations on the air.[52]

Davis associated with the left, while Lewis marched with the right. Lewis made headlines with a broadcast that accused the late president Roosevelt's assistant Harry Hopkins of having deliberately provided the Soviet Union with uranium to build an atomic bomb. He drew his account from a former Lend-Lease inspector in Montana, Colonel G. Racey Jordan, who had recorded quantities of wartime materials passing through the state on their way to the U.S.S.R. The House Un-American Activities Committee (HUAC) investigated and verified that the Soviets had shipped a staggering 1.7 million pounds of documents via Montana, including small quantities of uranium. Government witnesses explained that the uranium shipments had been designed to divert Soviet attention from American research on the bomb. Harry Hopkins had indeed provided classified information to Soviet intelligence agents—as part of his back-channel diplomacy on the president's behalf. Colonel Jordan had tried unsuccessfully to set himself up in business with the Soviets after the war, and the FBI dismissed his story as a self-serving fabrication. His testimony before HUAC was nowhere near as explosive as Lewis's broadcast had promised, and the committee quickly lost interest. Elmer Davis and Edward R. Murrow both condemned Fulton Lewis Jr.'s reckless reporting and *Life* magazine accused him of deliberate distortion of the news. "Personally, I think Jordan and Lewis are much alike," commented Eric Sevareid, "—a pair of blowhards with childish illusions of grandeur." Lewis's credibility had suffered seriously.[53]

Fulton Lewis Jr. crossed another line by lending his own ghostwriter, Ed Nellor, to write speeches for Senator McCarthy. In turn, Nellor collected material from McCarthy's office for Lewis's broadcasts. With Nellor as the go-between, Lewis threw himself wholeheartedly into McCarthy's campaign to unseat Maryland senator Millard Tydings in 1952. He repeatedly attacked Tydings on his radio programs, and denied the senator equal time to reply, on the grounds that if every politician received equal time then radio would have to "ban all political news, whenever an election is forthcoming." On this point, Elmer Davis agreed with Lewis, "for perhaps the only time in my life." The two commentators, coming from opposite perspectives, reached a shared sense that total objectivity in news reporting was impossible.[54]

Both broadcasters got involved in the 1952 presidential elections, on opposite sides. Lewis lavished praise on the Republican vice presidential candidate Richard Nixon, a close friend whom he frequently entertained at his 275-acre estate in southern Maryland. At the Republican convention that year, Lewis rented an expensive suite and extended generous hospitality. "How can a man have a hotel bill for twelve hundred dollars a day?" his business manager wondered. "But Fulton does!" After Nixon received the nomination for vice president, he embraced the commentator and said, "Except for you, Fulton, it never would have happened!" Lewis also defended Nixon when allegations arose that a group of Nixon's California business friends had been secretly funding his personal expenses, and urged his radio listeners to appeal to General Eisenhower not to drop Nixon from the ticket. Elmer Davis acted more circumspectly, although not more neutrally. He made financial contributions to the Democratic candidate Adlai Stevenson, and criticized Eisenhower so frequently that he drew complaints from some of his corporate sponsors.[55]

Davis's persistent condemnations of Joe McCarthy attracted return fire. The anti-Communist writer, J. B. Matthews, a McCarthy ally, claimed that Davis "personified the practice of broadcasting myths in the guise of news," and accused him of having harbored Communists at the OWI. Matthews did not call Davis a Communist sympathizer, but said that he held "an irrational anger toward all ex-Communists associated with the mythical monster of McCarthyism." Davis responded by tagging McCarthy's supporters as "poor, ignorant people who are easily gulled." Liberals such as the comedian Groucho Marx applauded Davis's broadcasts as "a breath of fresh air in a fairly polluted world," but the emotional confrontation took its toll on the commentator. Davis suffered a stroke in 1953 and cut back his nightly news shows to once a week. Martin Agronsky, who headed the Radio and Television Correspondents Association, reported that Davis's colleagues in the media missed listening to his news program, but added that one radio man had said, "Lucky Elmer... think of all the horror he is missing while the rest of us have to sit in on these hearings day after day." Davis never regained his health. He died in 1958, widely commended for recognizing that the greatest internal menace to the United States was the assault on freedom of thought.[56]

Fulton Lewis Jr.'s identification with McCarthyism unraveled his career. Riding on the crest of his radio popularity, he returned to newspapers with a syndicated column. Running, at first, with his picture on the front pages of Hearst's flagship paper, the *New York Journal-American*, the column soon slid into the back pages and lost his picture. (The press critic A. J. Liebling compared taking away the photograph of a columnist to "stripping the chevrons from a noncommissioned officer.") On the radio, Lewis spent his energy defending America from "CIO-backed Communist left-wing crackpots," and invited his friend Joe McCarthy on as a frequent guest. After McCarthy's censure in 1954, Lewis's radio audience trailed off until it consisted of a core of such right-wing groups as the John Birch Society. Lewis conceded that he attracted "a very considerable amount of lunatic fringe that adheres like lint to the coattails of the conservative side of the American picture. Why I can't say.

. . . you cannot control those who follow you down the street." His longtime assistant, Ed Nellor, who had written hundreds of Lewis's columns and scripts, finally quit in protest, tagging Lewis "a consummate con man." Lewis failed in an attempt to switch to television. As the columnist Marya Mannes observed, television made people's "destructive qualities" too explicit. Fulton Lewis Jr. remained an angry, alienated voice on radio, speaking to dwindling audiences until his death in 1966.[57]

Technological changes shook radio's conventions. The arrival of portable tape recorders after the Second World War—radio's equivalent of the print reporter's pencil and notebook—changed the sounds of radio news. Radio reporters began to make recordings of government news conferences and felt they were "no longer regarded as second-rate journalists." Griffing Bancroft, a newspaper reporter whom CBS Radio hired to cover Capitol Hill, attributed the change in status to the "Murrow era," when radio networks "decided that it was better to have somebody who knew what the hell he was talking about" rather than a news reader with an actor's voice. "That's why they hired me," said Bancroft. "I'd had fifteen years in the news business before I ever got to a microphone." Yet radio's rising professional status occurred just as television appeared on the horizon.[58]

Then came television, with which the radio networks had been tinkering for decades. NBC made its first experimental TV broadcast from atop the Empire State Building in 1930, causing the New York Times to predict that while it took radio years to reach its potential audience, television would "find an audience waiting for it." The audience had to wait until after the Second World War, when the Federal Communications Commission belatedly issued licenses for commercial television broadcasting. NBC had pressed for action, but CBS wanted the FCC to wait until the technology had improved, anticipating "seven lean years" before television could turn profitable. In 1946 government regulators sided with NBC. CBS's predictions proved unduly pessimistic. By 1950, Americans owned five million TV sets, and the new medium was turning a profit by attracting advertising away from radio.[59]

Elmer Davis and Fulton Lewis Jr. spent their last years losing listeners to television. A 1949 survey found that once families had television sets there was a sharp decline in their radio listening, although surveys showed that radio news commentators continued to hold an "above-average appeal in TV homes." The transition from radio to television proved as traumatic for newscasters as the switch to talking pictures had been for silent film stars. The dean of radio commentators, H. V. Kaltenborn, complained that television's complicated formats and cumbersome technology required too much nervous energy to allow him to do "anything important in this new form of radio." To NBC's rising news star David Brinkley, Kaltenborn said bluntly that he hated television. Other big names in radio news thought that television offered only the novelty of attaching pictures to the headlines, while radio permitted more thoughtful analysis. They insisted that radio gave listeners physical mobility, from the kitchen to the car, and "mobility of mind" as well, as word pictures could tell more than film. The public's enthusiasm for television reminded Kaltenborn of his early radio days "when people wrote excited letters to say they had actually heard me without troubling to comment on what they heard." He concluded sadly that despite its flaws television would inevitably triumph due to "the greater advertising impact of the combination of sight and sound."[60]

Television's triumph upended radio news. The networks split their radio and television productions into separate and competing entities. As advertisers turned to television, radio slashed its rates and promoted itself as the new low-priced medium. The campaign failed. In 1956, CBS Radio suffered its first unprofitable year ever, dropping into a seven-year slump. Reading the balance sheets, William Paley felt as if he were watching the tide going out. Radio filled the airwaves with rock 'n' roll, but revenues reached rock bottom in 1960, when radio ad sales were down 75 percent from their high in 1948. CBS Radio canceled its soap operas and serials and turned to news for low-cost programming. The network's flagship outlet in New York adopted an all-news format, and stations in other cities followed its lead. Billing themselves as newspapers of the air, news radio stations offered a drumbeat of headlines and wire service reports. That format began to fall out of favor in the 1980s, when federal deregulation reduced public service requirements and allowed stations to cut costs by eliminating news departments in favor of syndicated talk shows. After that, fewer radio stations maintained their own Washington correspondents. In 1987 the FCC also dropped the federal "fairness doctrine," which had permitted editorializing on the air so long as there was reasonable opportunity for the expression of conflicting views. President Ronald Reagan vetoed congressional attempts to reinstate the fairness doctrine and preserve some balance. Deregulation facilitated commercial radio's turn from hard news to hot air.[61]

By then, Fulton Lewis Jr.'s "voice with a snarl" had found its reincarnation in Rush Limbaugh, whose nationally syndicated broadcasts brought millions of listeners back to AM radio. Limbaugh was fired as a Kansas City radio commentator for expressing his conservative political opinions too stridently, but in 1988 he landed at another station and turned his vitriol into a virtue, gleefully attacking feminists, environmentalists, and liberal politicians. Once syndicated, his populist rhetoric attracted radio's biggest audience, listeners whom Limbaugh described as being "fed up with the single version of events they were getting from the mainstream media elite."

Echoes of Elmer Davis lingered in the calm tones of Bob Edwards, on the nation's second most popular radio program. Edwards anchored National Public Radio's *Morning Edition* for the first twenty-five years after its inception in 1979. He originally tried to emulate Edward R. Murrow's style, until he

learned to relax and be himself. His detached manner appealed to a generation of radio listeners he called "smart, aware, involved," who were likely to
identify with the groups whom Limbaugh disparaged. Neither abrasive nor
adversarial, Edwards drew opinions out of those he interviewed rather than
expressing his own. The format of his Washington-based program made room
for everything from cowboy poets to geographic expeditions, but he kept its
primary focus on serious, in-depth reporting on government and politics.
"Commercial radio has abandoned news," Edwards declared. "They do a lot of
talk, and they may talk about public affairs, but not news."[62]

4

The Friends of Joe McCarthy

Political sentiments in the Washington press corps swung to the left during the New Deal and remained there, fanning resentment of a liberal bias in the news. The leader of the Republican Party's conservative wing, Senator Robert Taft, blamed the media for his loss of the presidential nomination to General Dwight D. Eisenhower in 1952. Despite Eisenhower's landslide victory that fall, his running mate, Richard Nixon, smarted for years over reports that Washington correspondents had largely voted for the Democratic candidate. As Democrats had controlled the executive branch and Congress for most of the previous twenty years, Washington reporters had naturally developed a network of sources among Democratic office holders. A small band of conservative journalists resisted this trend and cultivated their sources among the opposition. Although they portrayed themselves as a beleaguered minority, they were not an inconsequential force. Some of them represented powerful newspaper chains such as Hearst and Scripps-Howard, whose editorial positions leaned decidedly toward the right. Others attracted national audiences via their radio broadcasts. They were fairly prominent and popular members of the press corps until they made the mistake of siding with a freewheeling senator from Wisconsin. The friends of Joe McCarthy soared with his celebrity and then crashed with his censure.[1]

For a politician, Joseph R. McCarthy spoke to reporters with rare candor. In the fall of 1949, halfway through his first Senate term, he freely admitted nervousness over his chances of reelection in 1952. "I know if I had to run today, I'd have a potful of trouble," he told a reporter for the *Milwaukee Journal*. At a racetrack near Washington, McCarthy buttonholed the Hearst columnist George Dixon and asked how he could get more publicity. Hire a press agent, Dixon suggested, recommending Jim Walter, a *Washington Times-Herald* reporter. Through a misunderstanding, McCarthy contacted George Waters, the *Times-Herald*'s hard-drinking, down-on-his-luck former city editor. Waters spent only a few months on the senator's staff, working out of a basement office in the Senate Office Building, but in that time he helped make Joe McCarthy a household name.[2]

It was no aberration that a reporter played a key role in activating McCarthyism. Conservative journalists openly sided with the senator's crusade, which they saw as a corrective to liberals' indifference to subversion in government. Not only did they report McCarthy's speeches, they often wrote them for him. Sympathetic reporters and columnists drifted in and out of the senator's office, serving as paid and unpaid members of his staff, providing advice, and fueling his suspicions. In return, they picked up inside information about his investigations. One of the senator's antagonists, army counsel John G. Adams, believed that McCarthy benefited from the fact that many reporters "were too lazy to check the facts." But Adams added, "He was helped even more by a few reporters who had reason to know that McCarthy was distorting the truth and chose to ignore it."[3]

When George Waters joined McCarthy's staff in January 1950, the senator was getting ready to deliver a Lincoln's Birthday address before a string of Republican clubs from West Virginia to South Dakota. McCarthy suggested that he could talk about subversion in government. To Waters that sounded like "pretty old stuff," but he promised that as a good newspaperman he could always dig up something. Going to the Senate press gallery, Waters sought out *Chicago Tribune* correspondent Willard Edwards, whose series on Communism in the government had been running in the *Tribune* and its sister paper, the *Washington Times-Herald*. Edwards obliged by turning over his files, and Waters then recruited Ed Nellor, another *Times-Herald* reporter (and ghostwriter for Fulton Lewis Jr.), to help him assemble the material. What they produced was a series of talking points rather than a formal speech.[4]

Later, not even McCarthy could reconstruct precisely what he had said in Wheeling, West Virginia. The *Wheeling Intelligencer* reported that the senator blamed America's foreign policy blunders that had allowed communism to spread in Europe and Asia on Communist infiltration in the State Department. "While I cannot take the time to name all of the men in the State Department who have been named as members of the Communist Party and members of a spy ring," the paper quoted him, "I have here in my hand a list of 205 that were known to the Secretary of State as being members of the Communist Party and who nevertheless are still working and shaping the policy of the State Department." An abridged version of the *Intelligencer*'s story went national on the Associated Press wire. At various stops on the tour, McCarthy altered the number of "card-carrying Communists" and demoted them from spies to security risks. His charges generated headlines, particularly after the State Department denied them. "Are we getting some publicity out of it?" the senator asked when he called his office.[5]

Startled by the deluge of press attention, Joe McCarthy came back "nearly insane with excitement," as his secretary described him. Reporters were clamoring for names, however, and the Senate Foreign Relations Committee appointed a subcommittee to investigate his charges. McCarthy's notes from Wheeling offered little help in constructing a reply. He had statistics rather than names, and his original source, Willard Edwards, could not provide any more detailed information. McCarthy called the newspaper publisher William Randolph Hearst Jr. and begged for help, admitting that he had shot his mouth off. Hearst agreed to lend some of his reporters, who moved into McCarthy's office as a team. They turned up a House Appropriations Committee report on security in the State Department, but the report identified the problem cases by number, without names. It was the reporter Ed Nellor who obtained a key to the list that enabled McCarthy's team to craft a more substantive version of the Wheeling speech for the senator to deliver on the Senate floor. Energized by the experience, McCarthy set out on a sweeping campaign to alert America about Communist infiltration of their government, but not with his hapless press secretary. George Waters went off to Hollywood as a scriptwriter, and spent his last years telling tales about how he had gotten Joe McCarthy started as a Red hunter.[6]

Waters was correct when he called subversion "old stuff" in 1950. A dozen years before anyone had labeled it McCarthyism, the House Un-American Activities Committee (HUAC) began hunting Communists in New Deal relief agencies.[7] Chaired by the Texas Democrat Martin Dies, the committee's grandstanding earned it contempt from the press corps; Commentator Raymond Clapper said that Washington reporters considered the Dies committee "90 per cent hogwash"—although that did not stop them from reporting on its hearings. The liberal reporter Marquis Childs of the St. Louis Post-Dispatch was convinced that Dies staged his hearings to produce outbursts of confrontation "made to order for a certain section of the press." Franklin Roosevelt also put little stock in HUAC's accusations—he laughed heartily when the committee listed his own mother as a contributor to a Communist front.

The Communist Party regarded Roosevelt's New Deal as makeshift and beholden to corporate capitalism, but the party forged a "popular front" with liberals during the 1930s to promote civil rights, organize unskilled labor, and fight fascism. Throughout the depression, non-Communist leftists had signed petitions, attended rallies, and made financial contributions to groups that would later be identified as Communist fronts. The party's ideological and financial dependence on the Soviet Union led it to endorse the Nazi-Soviet Friendship Pact of 1939, which shocked and alienated countless party members and fellow travelers (and put the Communists temporarily on the side of American isolationists). After Germany invaded Russia, the party reversed direction again. Once the United States allied with the Soviet Union during the war, the American Communists disbanded as a political party and openly promoted Roosevelt's reelection in 1944, although Roosevelt formally disavowed their support.[8]

In the wake of finance capitalism's collapse in the early 1930s, the New Deal had offered an alternative to communism by aiming to reform capitalism rather than to overthrow it. That distinction did not prevent New Deal liberals from finding common cause with the Communists on specific issues nationally, and internationally. While members of the Roosevelt administration suspected that a few Communists held government posts, they regarded this as a manageable problem. In 1943 the president's assistant David K. Niles advised Harry Hopkins to meet with representatives of the National Council of American-Soviet Friendship. "Yes I know this outfit very well," Niles explained. "It is a 'front' organization, but as long as the party line is on our side it will do a good job. Edwin Smith, who signs this letter [requesting the meeting] is a former Commissioner of the National Labor Relations Board. No doubt he is a party boy."[9]

The depression at home and fascism abroad helped the Communist Party recruit thousands of Americans attracted by Marxist certitude and comradeship. A highly disciplined political party with utopian goals appealed to those who felt that capitalism had failed and that only radical tactics could overcome injustice and oppression—even if that meant defending an oppressive Soviet regime. During the 1930s, the U.S. Communist Party functioned openly, publishing the *Daily Worker*, holding public meetings, collecting petitions, and running candidates for office; but a small wing operated sub rosa, aiding Soviet intelligence agents engaged in espionage. Whittaker Chambers, who served as a courier to the underground Communist operatives in Washington, observed that a person could be active in the party for years "without completely understanding the nature of communism or the political methods that follow inevitably from its vision."[10]

Regardless of what individual party members knew, revelations of subversive activities would later implicate by association the entire radical left. Charges of having been an espionage agent, party member, or fellow traveler would blend together indistinctly. In 1939, after Chambers broke with the party, he advised government officials that there were Communists operating within the State Department. *Washington Daily News* reporter Will Allen stumbled onto the story and passed it along to the FBI, expecting the agents to reward him with an exclusive on their investigation. The FBI was preoccupied with other wartime investigations, however, and simply referred the reporter back to the State Department. Two years passed before FBI agents questioned Chambers. Meanwhile, the Army Signal Corps was intercepting messages between Moscow and Soviet agents in the United States. Known as Project Venona, it amassed thousands of cables, but cryptologists were unable to break the Soviet code until 1946. When the code was cracked, Venona confirmed the existence of a pervasive espionage network that had penetrated the highly secret Manhattan Project and obtained Roosevelt's negotiating strategies at Yalta.[11]

The defection of another Communist courier, Elizabeth Bentley, caused the Soviet Union to abort most of its American espionage operations, recalling operatives or sending them into hiding. The defection of Igor Gouzenko, a Soviet code clerk in Canada, and conversion to anti-Communism by Louis Budenz, a former editor of the U.S. *Daily Worker*, raised public alarm. By the time their stories broke, the wartime marriage of convenience between the

Soviet Union and the United States had dissolved into a frigid divorce. The first sensational spy revelations of the early Cold War aided the Republican Party's campaign to recapture the majority in Congress in 1946, and goaded President Truman into signing an executive order that created loyalty boards, to screen suspected civil servants, and made Communist sympathies grounds for dismissal from federal service. Rather than calm national fears, Truman's actions only convinced people of a looming danger to their national security.[12]

Under its new Republican management, HUAC seemed primarily intent—in the words of columnist Murray Kempton—on getting noticed. A headline-grabbing investigation of "Hollywood Reds" raised snickers from the Washington press corps. When House Democrats won back the majority in the 1948 elections, they would likely have abolished HUAC, except for some spectacular revelations that had unexpectedly emerged during the previous special summer session. President Truman, in a bold move to jumpstart his seemingly hopeless campaign for reelection, called Congress back into special session in July 1948. The Republican majority's unwillingness to enact all the reforms promised in their platform handed Truman his campaign slogan about the "Do-Nothing Congress." Taking advantage of the special session, however, HUAC called Elizabeth Bentley to testify, and her disclosures of a Washington spy network produced banner headlines.

To reinforce Bentley's charges, HUAC subpoenaed Whittaker Chambers, and he created an even greater stir by publicly naming Alger Hiss, a former assistant secretary of state then heading the Carnegie Endowment for World Peace. Hiss promptly telegraphed the committee to demand a hearing, thereby setting up a dramatic confrontation that guaranteed greater media attention. Hiss so adamantly denied the accusations against him that several committee members apologized, and reporters stepped forward to shake his hand. In view of Hiss's impeccable New Deal credentials, liberal journalists felt predisposed to believe his denials. At the National Press Club bar, Hiss's supporters lambasted Chambers's defenders as wildly irresponsible. The investigation might well have ended except for the insistence of freshman California representative Richard Nixon, who had been irritated by Hiss's "insolent" testimony. Nixon agreed to chair a special subcommittee to continue the probe—although the *Washington Post* reporter Mary Spargo offered the friendly warning that if his hunch proved wrong he would be "a dead duck" politically.[13]

Seeking allies in the press, Nixon invited Felix Morley, a former editor of the *Washington Post* and founder of the anti-Communist newsletter *Human Events*, to accompany him to Chambers's farm in Westminster, Maryland. Morley declined, suspecting the congressman of being concerned more with personal ambition than with national security. Nixon then turned to Bert Andrews, Washington bureau chief for the citadel of eastern liberal Republicanism, the *New York Herald Tribune*. Andrews had won a Pulitzer Prize for his critical reporting on HUAC. He had also covered Alger Hiss at the State

Department, and had recommended Hiss to head the Carnegie Endowment. An aggressive reporter in search of a scoop, Andrews readily agreed to visit Chambers's farm as an impartial witness. Both he and Nixon came away convinced that Chambers was telling the truth. The *Herald Tribune*'s bureau chief offered to collaborate with Nixon, trading seasoned advice in return for inside information. Paternally, Andrews lectured the young congressman against repeating the sloppy proceedings that had so discredited HUAC in the eyes of the press corps. He coached Nixon on how to handle the Hiss-Chambers confrontation, and alerted him to the notorious Pumpkin Papers—the reels of microfilm containing government records obtained from Hiss that Chambers had hidden in a hollowed-out pumpkin. "My liberal friends don't love me no more, nor you," Andrews cabled Nixon when the Pumpkin Papers surfaced. "But facts are facts and these are dynamite."

The evidence now linked Hiss to charges of espionage, and when Chambers repeated the allegations of disloyalty on the radio news show *Meet the Press*, Hiss sued him for libel. The suit eventually resulted in Hiss's conviction and imprisonment for perjury. Nixon's triumphs in the Hiss case became Andrews's headlines. (Andrews later played another pivotal role in Nixon's career by introducing him to General Eisenhower.) At the rival *New York Times* Washington bureau, James Reston called Andrews "a hell-raiser from San Diego, who wouldn't commit murder for a good story but would certainly consider it." The *Times* "didn't admire Bert's tactics," Reston commented, "but we had to deal with his successes."[14]

Ralph de Toledano, who reported for *Newsweek*, called the Hiss trial a litmus test in which many "true-blue 'liberals'" came out "a disconcerting pink." A former fellow traveler himself, de Toledano joined the small band of reporters in the courtroom who had made anti-Communism their beat. The bulk of the press corps treated them as pariahs, and after de Toledano avowed Hiss's guilt in his reporting, a lot of reporters stopped talking to him. For their part, liberal journalists found it exasperating to be scolded from the right by the same people who had previously assailed them from the left. The radio news commentator Elmer Davis thought it no accident that so many disillusioned ex-Communists became "extreme reactionaries." Seeing no middle ground between good and evil, they simply transposed their notions of what was good and what was evil.[15]

The tensions among courthouse journalists peaked during Hiss's first trial, which ended in a hung jury. By the second trial, the faith of Hiss's supporters had dwindled. Only one reporter was still willing to wager de Toledano that Hiss would be acquitted. Conservatives took Hiss's conviction for perjury, on January 21, 1950, as their vindication. That Communist conspiracies had not been figments of their imagination, said de Toledano, gave them a "sense of moral ascendancy." It also made them more receptive to Joe McCarthy's message from Wheeling three weeks later. Hard-line anti-Communists in the press corps viewed the fiery Wisconsin senator as a tough street fighter who would force the public to confront the clear and present danger of internal subversion. In their enthusiasm, they averted their eyes from McCarthy's questionable motives and blatant recklessness, thereby squandering their moral standing. "We became partisans," de Toledano acknowledged, "and by the dialectics of the situation, we took over some of the characteristics of our antagonists."[16]

Joe McCarthy had nothing to do with the Hiss case, but it had everything to do with building his national reputation. Hiss's conviction served as a backdrop, along with the Communist takeover in China and the Soviet Union's testing of thermonuclear weapons, against which McCarthy laid out his conspiracy theories. He offered his audiences a plausible explanation for the perplexing news of the day: Communist infiltrators were deliberately scuttling U.S. foreign policy. "Senator McCarthy seems to have tapped, quite accidentally, a reservoir of long-hidden malice," wrote Max Ascoli, editor of *The Reporter* magazine. Jack Bell, the chief AP correspondent on Capitol Hill, agreed that McCarthy's charges "hit home to a people vastly disturbed by the implications of Alger Hiss's conviction."[17]

Before he emerged as an anti-Communist crusader, Joe McCarthy had garnered a reputation in Washington as a tireless publicity seeker. The *Saturday Evening Post* had pegged him as "The Senate's Remarkable Upstart" for calling a press conference immediately upon arriving in Washington. Reporters wanted to know why a freshman senator would face the press with nothing new to announce. McCarthy then stunned them by suggesting that striking coal miners be drafted and that the union president be court-martialed and shot. After his glib pronouncements, McCarthy looked sheepishly around the room, as United Press reporter Allen Drury observed, "wanting us to like him and wanting to be friends." Most of the correspondents did like McCarthy, despite his loose talk. They assumed that he would acquire some discretion once he had been around a little longer.[18]

Senator McCarthy went to remarkable lengths to accommodate the press. He presented wheels of Wisconsin cheeses and cases of Wisconsin beer to the National Press Club. He cooked dinner for a group of newswomen. He helped reporters find apartments during Washington's postwar housing shortage. He left his Senate office door open and invited reporters to put their feet on his desk while chatting with him. He solicited reporters' opinions and introduced amendments they suggested. He gave out the phone numbers of the bars where he could be reached late at night and promised to return all calls. He joined their poker games—although reporters regarded him as a poor player who liked to "bull the game" too much, betting and raising with nothing in his hand. At a National Press Club outing to the Charles Town, West Virginia, racetrack in June 1949, McCarthy rode in the club's "Freakness" races. His horse ran last, but he won another race astride a mule.[19]

The senator could bluff his way artfully out of the most embarrassing questions. When a *Congressional Quarterly* reporter questioned McCarthy about problems with his income taxes, he produced his tax forms while carrying on "a non-stop monologue, which was laced with irrelevancies." The reporter looked at his income tax returns and tried to listen at the same time, unable to make sense out of either the documents or the patter. McCarthy handled Richard Rovere, Washington correspondent for the *New Yorker,* in the same manner when Rovere pressed him for evidence regarding his charges that American soldiers had mistreated German prisoners of war. The senator turned over a pile of photostats, carbon copies, and newspaper clippings, impressive as a collection but revealing very little individually. He assumed that the sheer bulk of his material would convince people, regardless of its quality. The Gridiron Club aptly spoofed McCarthy's technique in a 1952 skit: "Well it just so happens I have here—[opens brief case and yanks out blue prints and documents, waves them and stuffs them rapidly back in brief case]—there, gentlemen, you have studied the evidence."[20]

The *New York Times* correspondent Bill Lawrence freely criticized McCarthy, yet the two men enjoyed each other's company, eating and drinking together, "both in excess," Lawrence admitted. The senator also maintained a friendship with Jack Anderson, the congressional legman for the liberal columnist Drew Pearson. Craving gossip and sensation for his daily newspaper columns and Sunday broadcasts, Pearson dispatched a squad of reporters to scour Washington for new leads, urging them to "dramatize wrongs" that would capture the public's attention. Jack Anderson (who got his job when Pearson fired one of his reporters for being a "card-carrying Communist") counted McCarthy among his most willing collaborators on Capitol Hill. The senator did not hesitate to reveal Republican Party secrets, going so far as to let Anderson listen on an extension while he chatted with party leaders. Because Anderson had heard everything for himself, McCarthy could deny having leaked it. Before 1950, Pearson's columns were studded with favorable references to McCarthy, a pattern that ended abruptly with the Wheeling speech. Even then, when McCarthy was searching frantically for evidence to support his accusations, Jack Anderson rooted through Pearson's files to provide some raw data that McCarthy could use. Anderson tried to discourage Pearson from attacking their best source in Congress. "He may be a good source, Jack," Pearson replied, "but he's a bad man."[21]

McCarthy might have extricated himself from his accusations of government subversion after Wheeling if Democrats had not insisted on investigating the charges. When a subcommittee chaired by Senator Millard Tydings of Maryland looked into his accusations, McCarthy diverted the press corps's attention by promising to name the top Russian spy in America, the "boss of Alger Hiss." He whispered to reporters that his target was a Johns Hopkins University professor, Owen Lattimore, a distinguished scholar of the Far East and an occasional consultant to the State Department on Asian policy. Jack Anderson passed this information along to Drew Pearson, who decided to force McCarthy's hand by revealing on his Sunday night radio program that the senator intended to name Lattimore as a spy. Abroad at the time, Professor Lattimore returned to defend himself before the Tydings subcommittee, where he vehemently denounced McCarthy's "reign of terror." In Arthur Krock's opinion, Lattimore easily bested McCarthy. The columnist compared the senator's record to a baseball team down nine to nothing in the seventh inning. Then Louis Budenz, the former *Daily Worker* editor turned anti-Communist informant, saved the game by testifying that party officials had regarded Lattimore as a Communist.[22]

That evening, McCarthy appeared before the American Society of Newspaper Editors meeting in Washington. "I knew it would be thus," he intoned melodramatically, "that vilification, smear and falsehoods would follow, peddled by the Reds, their minions, and the egg-sucking phony liberals who litter Washington . . . and clutter American thinking with their simple-minded arguments." McCarthy went on: "Some of them write columns for your newspapers." The audience greeted him at first with perfunctory applause but warmed as he proceeded. The editors had had their fill of pussyfooting politicians, Arthur Krock surmised, and they suspected their own Washington correspondents of glossing over official deficiencies "for reasons of personal friendship." So they were thrilled to hear someone in power speak so bluntly. By the conclusion of his remarks, the applause swelled appreciably.[23]

Freda Utley, an ex-Communist who wrote for the libertarian weekly *The Freeman,* had first alerted McCarthy to Lattimore. But she had only cataloged a "deadly parallel" between Lattimore's statements and Stalin's, and never called Lattimore a Soviet agent. When McCarthy magnified Utley's charges beyond her evidence, she excused his exaggerations as necessary to shock the public into paying attention. Even unsympathetic reporters found McCarthy's charges hard to disprove. Because concealment and lies were basic to any conspiracy, and as neither the Truman administration nor the FBI would release the pertinent files, reporters lacked the evidence to assess the senator's allegations. Most reporters told the story without taking sides, and only a few journalists openly defended the beleaguered professor. The ex-Communist literary critic Granville Hicks cautioned them not to rush to Lattimore's defense simply on the assumption that he "must be innocent because McCarthy says he's guilty." ABC radio commentator Elmer Davis (under whom Lattimore had worked in the Office of War Information's Pacific bureau) rebutted Hicks's reasoning. Accepting that argument, Davis warned, "would mean that the anti-Communist Left must keep its mouth shut, leave the field to McCarthy, and regard everyone whom he accuses as guilty until he proves his innocence."[24]

Liberal reporters taunted that Joe McCarthy could not find a Communist in Red Square on May Day. Conservative journalists also recognized the senator's amateurism and impulsiveness. Like the young writer William F. Buckley Jr., however, they refused to allow "McCarthy's distasteful techniques" to blind them to the desirability of his goals. The issue was not McCarthy's manners, Buckley exhorted. "It is treason in the State Department." On a less lofty plane, conservative newspaper reporters benefited from McCarthy because he kept their bylines on the front pages almost daily. Given their urge to scoop—or avoid being scooped—few reporters could afford to ignore McCarthy's accusations. A surprising exception had been the Hearst press, which held back from reporting on McCarthy's activities for a month after the Wheeling speech. Because the senator had privately confessed his lack of evidence to him, William Randolph Hearst Jr. was waiting to see whether the staff he had lent could build a convincing case. Finally, on March 16, 1950, the *New York Daily Mirror* ran an editorial, "Go to it, Joe McCarthy," signaling other Hearst papers to fall into line. Banging the drum most loudly for the cause were three Hearst columnists, Fulton Lewis Jr., George Sokolsky, and Westbrook Pegler.[25]

The *Chicago Tribune* enlisted for the crusade, despite the skepticism of its chief Washington correspondent, Walter Trohan. He had gotten burned years earlier when he ran a House Un-American Activities Committee "Red list." A wrongly identified man had sued the *Tribune* for libel and had reaped a substantial out-of-court settlement. "When I saw I was caught with my pants down, I offered to make a settlement out of my own pocket," Trohan told other reporters, but Colonel McCormick had insisted on paying it. The case made Trohan leery of reproducing unsubstantiated charges coming out of congressional committees. His colleague Willard Edwards, the *Tribune*'s congressional correspondent, did not share Trohan's caution. Edwards thought Joe McCarthy "just fitted into what we had been saying long before." When he reported the senator's reconstructed Wheeling address in the Senate, Edwards gave no indication of his own role in the original speech, nor did he question the claims that went beyond his original research. He simply asserted that McCarthy had disclosed "data from the State Department's own files." Other journalists regarded Edwards as the senator's tool, and suspected him of planting information to use McCarthy as a quotable source and to protect himself from libel suits. Edwards resented these accusations. He reminded reporters that he had barely known McCarthy when George Waters first solicited his help, and he insisted that McCarthy had tinkered with the material and distorted his conclusions. "I was very indignant about it being attributed to me," Edwards later fumed about the Wheeling speech. "It was full of errors."[26]

McCarthy's staff later approached Edwards with material they had collected on Communists at the National Labor Relations Board (NRLB), and asked him to draft a speech. Edwards read through the material and decided that there was enough there for the senator to raise questions about "Communist influences" in the NLRB. Later in the press gallery, he cringed to hear McCarthy deviate from the text and make the unsupported claim that the National Labor Relations Board was "honeycombed with members of the Communist Party." Yet Edwards remained a loyal supporter and publicist. "I considered McCarthy a good news source," he explained. "I cultivated him for that. For a while I functioned as almost a member of McCarthy's staff. I'd go out and investigate things for him." Edwards accepted McCarthy's charges at face value. After publishing his allegations against Lattimore as fact, Edwards said he never felt perturbed "by the thought that I should check everything he said."[27]

The conservative columnist Holmes Alexander felt torn over McCarthy's accusations against Owen Lattimore. Living in Baltimore, Alexander had gotten to know the Johns Hopkins professor personally, and while he considered Lattimore slanted to the left, he considered the evidence against him entirely circumstantial. Alexander also begged Maryland senator Millard Tydings to stay "a safe distance from the contagion of McCarthyism," but the senator had insisted upon standing for fair play and free speech.[28]

Rather than discredit Joe McCarthy, Tydings's investigation established him as the standard-bearer of the anti-Communist movement. Willard Edwards thought that Tydings's obvious hostility only made McCarthy look better. The hearings inspired McCarthy to set out on an extraordinary campaign to defeat Tydings in the next election. Reporter Ed Nellor, who hung around McCarthy's office writing speeches and snappy remarks for the senator, worked for the Mutual Radio commentator Fulton Lewis Jr., and also for the *Washington Times-Herald*. Nellor helped consolidate those forces behind the Republican candidate for Tydings's seat, John Marshall Butler. Colonel McCormick's *Chicago Tribune* owned the *Washington Times-Herald*, and the Colonel appointed his niece, Ruth "Bazy" Miller, as the Washington paper's publisher. She readily took up McCarthy's crusade and at his request, the *Times-Herald* prepared a four-page tabloid that trashed Tydings's career, complete with a composite photograph of Tydings and Communist Party leader Earl Browder. A half-million copies of the tabloid blanketed Maryland. On the radio, Fulton Lewis Jr. assailed Tydings for "whitewashing" McCarthy's charges. The combined publicity barrage helped the obscure Butler unseat the veteran Tydings. When a Senate subcommittee criticized the intervention of outsiders in the Maryland campaign, McCarthy pointed to the *Times-Herald*'s extensive circulation in Maryland and to Fulton Lewis Jr.'s nightly broadcasts throughout the state. He added characteristically, "Strangely the subcommittee made no mention of the *Washington Post* or Drew Pearson, who always bleed whenever a Communist is scratched, and who were vigorously and violently supporting Millard Tydings and opposing John Marshall Butler."[29]

In Illinois, another of McCarthy's vociferous critics, Majority Leader Scott Lucas, was also defeated in 1950, while voters in California promoted Richard Nixon to the Senate. The press widely portrayed these races as a victory for

McCarthy's brand of anti-Communism. Joe McCarthy glided on the prevailing winds of public opinion. Months after his Wheeling speech, the arrest of Julius and Ethel Rosenberg on espionage charges, and Communist North Korea's invasion of South Korea, convinced a growing number of Americans that McCarthy must have known what he was talking about. When President Truman fired General Douglas MacArthur from his post as commander of United Nations forces in Korea, McCarthy further stirred the waters by accusing Truman's secretary of defense, General George C. Marshall, of having aided and abetted international communism. Standing in the Senate, McCarthy read a lengthy tome on Marshall that had been written by the Washington journalist Forrest Davis. Davis's colleague on the libertarian magazine *The Freeman*, John Chamberlain, believed that Davis admired McCarthy "because the Bad Boy from Wisconsin was a Quixotic fighter." Davis donated to McCarthy his own book-length manuscript, which denounced General Marshall's "retreat from victory" in Asia. McCarthy adopted Davis's work as his own, but went beyond its bounds in a speech before the Senate in which he accused Marshall of being part of a "conspiracy so immense and an infamy so black as to dwarf any previous such venture in the history of man." McCarthy published the speech as a booklet, without acknowledging Davis as the original author. Davis kept silent about the senator's embellishments, but *The Freeman* thereafter concentrated on McCarthy's anti-Communist objectives without defending the senator himself.[30]

Columnist Holmes Alexander had listened from the press gallery while McCarthy denounced General Marshall, and he rated it an unimpressive performance. The senator stumbled through half of his speech and inserted the rest in the *Congressional Record* as if it had been read. "Senator, it's only fair to say that I'm against you," Alexander said when he introduced himself afterward. "What's one more writer jumping on my neck?" McCarthy replied disarmingly. "Tell me your beef." When Alexander accused him of maligning one of the witnesses who appeared before his committee, McCarthy commented on the man's membership in various front organizations. That was just guilt by association, Alexander protested; it proved nothing. "Nope. It doesn't," said McCarthy. "But is this the sort of jerk you want in the State Department?" McCarthy claimed that other senators were sending him names of people to expose. "We don't want to touch this fellow, but you do it, Joe," he quoted them as saying. "Your hands are already bloody." As Alexander began to take McCarthy more seriously, he gradually joined his camp. Previously, Alexander had held Ohio senator and majority leader Robert Taft as his hero, and said that his columns "prospered best" in Taft's political territory, but after Taft's death in 1953 the columnist sought a new idol. He found it in Joe McCarthy's "shaggy dog" personality and his aggressive crusade against subversion and espionage.[31]

Newspapers owned by McCormick, Hearst, and Scripps-Howard rooted for McCarthy, but while they reached millions of readers, their correspondents constituted only a small fraction of the Washington press corps. Polls indicated that eight out of ten Washington reporters disliked McCarthy. Yet whenever the cry "McCarthy's up!" went through the Senate press gallery, conservatives and liberals alike rushed to hear his latest rampage. McCarthy himself felt satisfied enough with his press coverage to declare that "85 percent of the newsmen do an outstanding job of reporting the news that should be reported."[32]

Joe McCarthy's friends in the press corps joined his bandwagon out of a mixture of good intentions, zealotry, and personal ambition. They could see that publicity intoxicated him, and acknowledged his "sins of exaggeration," but they connected his extreme accusations with his extraordinary public support. Television covered his hearings and curious spectators packed his committee rooms. "You should have seen the people go agog when McCarthy would come though the corridors," recalled one Senate staff member. "You could hardly walk along, they were all wanting to get his autograph and touch him or speak to him." As McCarthy achieved folk hero status, his circle of supporters expanded to include "intellectuals, place-seekers, reputable newspapermen, crackpots," Ralph de Toledano observed, "all basking in the sudden respectability of anti-communism." Willard Edwards suspected that even some liberal journalists admired McCarthy because he "dared to take on anybody and anything in sight—the entire establishment," and because he had "outfought, outwitted or outrun" so many of his antagonists. [33]

Indirectly, McCarthy benefited from the postwar budget cutting that had decimated many of the Washington news bureaus. Bureaus that fielded only one or two reporters could hardly conduct extensive investigative reporting, and leaned instead on the wire services. The AP's Washington bureau never had fewer than three reporters handling McCarthy's hearings, with two additional editors in the office editing the copy. Yet all the wire services stuck to a neutral, just-the-facts style of reporting. John L. Steele, who covered McCarthy day and night for two years for the United Press, later claimed that his job was "*not* to put Senator McCarthy and his work in focus, but to take his speeches, his words, and with as much sensationalism and speed as possible—and always with a straight face—spread them as gospel in the name of 'straight' reporting." Hearst's International News Service (INS) struggled to maintain its objectivity, even as Hearst newspapers editorially boosted McCarthy. INS reporter William Theis accused all three wires of being "so goddamn objective that McCarthy got away with everything, bamboozling the editors and the public." Wire reporters rushed to report McCarthy's charges as soon as he made them because they were trapped by their techniques, said another INS alumnus, Charles Seib. "If he said it, we wrote it; the pressures were to deliver."

Editors who wanted more critical analysis of McCarthy complained that the wire services never labeled "smears as smears or nonsense as nonsense," but simply passed along accusations as if they were responsible statements. Editors who supported McCarthy attributed anything critical of him on the wire services to their "left-wing bias."[34]

A reporter who criticized McCarthy could expect him to retaliate. On the TV news program *Meet the Press*, McCarthy turned the inquisition around on the *St. Louis Post-Dispatch*'s columnist and correspondent Marquis Childs by demanding to know whether he had written certain statements about China, the Soviet Union, and Alger Hiss. "He reeled off one alleged quote after another," Childs recalled, "all taken out of context by a researcher on his staff." Caught by surprise, Childs felt that he had been made to look foolish. On another *Meet the Press*, Frank McNaughton of *Time* magazine asked an innocuous question to which McCarthy gruffly replied: "I have no respect for you or for *Time* and I will answer none of your questions." In response to a more hostile question from the *New York Times*'s William S. White, McCarthy cooed: "I am *glad* to answer any question from my dear friend, Bill White." The astonished White found this public embrace disconcerting. As they left the broadcasting studio, McCarthy gave him a wide grin and said: "I fixed you up back there, hey?"

Broadcasters felt McCarthy's sting most directly because he aimed his fire at their sponsors, encouraging his supporters to contact sponsors and demand they abandon broadcasters who opposed him. Adam Hats dropped Drew Pearson's program, and Martin Agronsky's sponsorship fell so low that ABC affiliates pressured the network to cancel his fifteen-minute news program. After a stormy meeting of the network's affiliates, ABC president Robert Kintner summoned Agronsky from Washington to his New York office. "I was asked to bring to your attention the concern throughout the network about the way you've been covering McCarthy," Kintner explained, and then asked, "Are you going to change the way you're covering McCarthy?" Agronsky said, "no." "That's what I figured you'd say," Kintner replied. "Let's go to lunch."[35]

During the 1952 presidential primaries, most of the Washington press corps resented Senator Robert Taft's isolationism and his tolerance of Joe McCarthy's assault on civil liberties. Columnist Joseph Alsop decried the spectacle of Taft "marching forward to the Republican nomination, flanked by the *Chicago Tribune* publisher Colonel Robert McCormick and Senator McCarthy, preceded by William Randolph Hearst's favored columnist Westbrook Pegler and radio commentator Fulton Lewis, Jr., beating their peculiar anti-communist drums." Alsop and other Washington journalists swung behind General Dwight D. Eisenhower's candidacy, trusting that the general could defeat Taft and restrain McCarthy. With Eisenhower campaigning against Communism and corruption, Republicans not only won back the White House but took majorities in both the House and Senate. Joe McCarthy was swept into a second Senate term and returned to Washington to chair the Permanent Subcommittee on Investigations, with a license to investigate anything he wanted.[36]

A haphazard administrator, Chairman McCarthy took the advice of the Hearst columnist George Sokolsky and hired Roy Cohn as his chief counsel. Cohn was a brash young New York attorney who had prosecuted subversives for the Truman Justice Department. Some of McCarthy's friends in the press considered it a disastrous choice. Ralph de Toledano regarded Cohn as rich, spoiled, undisciplined, and unscrupulous, and he was a Democrat to boot. McCarthy also added to his subcommittee's staff the volatile Howard Rushmore, a former Communist who had become a feature writer for the Hearst chain.[37]

Under McCarthy and Cohn, the Permanent Subcommittee on Investigations lurched from one spectacular inquiry to the next, rarely finishing one before plunging into another. This stretched his staff perilously thin, so McCarthy tapped sympathetic newspaper reporters for witnesses to interrogate and questions to ask. Taking testimony behind closed doors where reporters and television cameras were prohibited enabled McCarthy to offer his version of the interrogation to waiting reporters, and thus shape the next day's headlines. Witnesses often had to wait days or weeks before they were able to testify in a public hearing and present their side openly. At these public sessions, the chairman basked in television lights, commenting that the presence of television kept press coverage of the hearings more accurate, "because when millions of people see what is going on, they don't quite like what some of the left-wingers say." The bright lights also tended to blind observers to the inconclusiveness of the hearings. Nathaniel Weyl, a former Communist turned cooperative witness, pointed to the unfairness of these investigations, when even those who could disprove the accusations leveled against them suffered irreparable damage. "The public had neither the time nor the inclination to study the labyrinth of charges and countercharges," Weyl pointed out. "All that it was likely to remember about a man was that he had been accused."[38]

In February 1953, as McCarthy's subcommittee prepared to open hearings on infiltration of the Voice of America, his staff prepped Willard Edwards for a lurid story on the uncovering of a sabotage plot. Edwards's story ran before McCarthy had taken a word of sworn testimony. "Despite the rigid secrecy ordered by the McCarthy staff," the reporter boasted, he had "elicited much information concerning the evidence being gathered." Edwards outlined a "fantastic situation" by which anti-Communist employees at the Voice of America had banded together into a "Loyal American Underground" to collect evidence that would reveal the "Red influence" within their agency. With a mental agility that enabled him to leap broad gaps in the evidence, McCarthy transformed the reports of disgruntled staff about waste and mismanagement into "deliberate sabotage." The Senate inquiry caused consternation at the Voice of America headquarters in New York, where Willard Edwards described subpoenas "fluttering on desks like pigeons in Union Square." The televised hearings rocked the agency—until the subcommittee dropped the investigation and moved on to something else, having established no proof of Communist sabotage at the VOA. In the subcommittee's wake, some top administrators lost their jobs, a distraught employee committed suicide, and morale within the agency plummeted.[39]

Roy Cohn made his friend G. David Schine the unpaid "chief consultant" to the subcommittee, despite his scant credentials for the job. The two self-indulgent young men operated in a heady, unrestrained atmosphere that fostered sadistic treatment of witnesses. An investigation of the books stocked by the U.S. Information Agency's libraries overseas gave McCarthy carte blanche to call any author whose book the government might have purchased to question the authors' personal politics in order to discredit the USIA. Among those interrogated was one of his most outspoken critics, the editor of the *New York Post*, James Wechsler, who as a college student and member of the Young Communist League had written *Revolt on the Campus* in 1935. Wechsler later broke with the Communists and his anti-Communist editorial line at the *Post* regularly drew fire from the *Daily Worker*. Wechsler was astonished when McCarthy asked whether he had actually inspired the *Daily Worker*'s attacks upon himself as a form of cover. "That way madness lies," the conservative James Burnham wrote, castigating McCarthy's logic. "By this kind of reasoning, no one could ever prove his loyalty. If you support Communist objectives, you are obviously a Communist; if you attack them, this is a deception maneuver, and you are still a Communist." Liberals suspected that the hearings were intended to silence the press, and indeed many of the witnesses before McCarthy's subcommittee were asked both "Do you read the *Daily Worker*?" and "Do you read the *New York Post*?"[40]

The editors of the left-wing weekly *National Guardian*, James Aronson and Cecil Belfrage, were called to testify in 1953. They wanted to protest the hearings as a violation of their First Amendment protection of freedom of the press, but their lawyers convinced them that only the Fifth Amendment offered them a safe refuge. Belfrage was not a U.S. citizen, however, so taking the Fifth led to his deportation. Aronson, who had previously reported for the *New York Post* and *New York Times*, saw Senator McCarthy glare ominously at reporters for those papers during the hearing. Aronson met with reporters outside the hearing room to explain why he refused to answer any questions about his politics, and was dismayed that his former colleagues showed so little interest in his self-defense. The brief article that appeared in the *New York Times* emphasized that he no longer wrote for the paper.[41]

McCarthy's wandering attention finally settled on the Army Signal Corps at Fort Monmouth, New Jersey. He set out to make a case that several engineers who had been suspended as security risks had actually been engaged in espionage. At one of the many closed-door sessions he held, reporters watched an ashen-faced witness being escorted from the hearing. Senator McCarthy informed them that the witness had broken down and cried after "some rather vigorous cross-examination by Roy Cohn." The senator solemnly added, "I have just received word that the witness admits that he was lying the first time and now wants to tell the truth," proclaiming it the "most important development" of the investigation. In the *Chicago Tribune*'s lead story the next day, Willard Edwards hyped McCarthy's charges, writing "an army signal corps employee suddenly burst into tears, hysterically confessing perjury." The chairman asked reporters not to identify the witness, but they published his name anyway. Carl Greenblum, a technician at the army facility, had a hammer and sickle painted on his house after his name appeared in the papers. He later explained to the press that the death of his mother two days earlier had left him emotionally distraught. He had sent word that he wanted to tell his story over from the beginning, which McCarthy interpreted to mean that he had lied earlier, "but that certainly was not the case."[42]

The closed hearings made it practically impossible for reporters to verify what the chairman told them, and caused what Army Secretary Robert Stevens considered "very exaggerated headlines that had little relation to the facts that were being developed at Fort Monmouth." Having promised stunning revelations of a spy ring masterminded by Julius Rosenberg, McCarthy's investigation got nowhere until it stumbled upon the army dentist Irving Peress, who had been promoted and honorably discharged despite his refusal to answer questions about membership in the Communist Party. "Who promoted Peress?" became McCarthy's rallying cry. The senator lost his temper with Peress's commanding officer, General Ralph Zwicker, and declared him "not fit to wear that uniform." This intemperate attack on a decorated military officer shocked even McCarthy's friends, and a *Chicago Tribune* editorial suggested that he learn to "distinguish the role of investigator from the role of avenging angel." Radio commentator H. V. Kaltenborn, previously sympathetic to McCarthy, called the senator's outburst a sign that he had grown "completely egotistic, arrogant, narrow-minded, reckless and irresponsible."[43]

White House aides advised reporters that President Eisenhower would rise to the army's defense at his next press conference. Yet Ike chose merely to praise General Zwicker and request that more courtesy be shown toward witnesses at congressional hearings. The columnist Joseph Alsop turned to Willard Edwards and snarled, "The yellow son of a bitch!" Realizing that Eisenhower had offered McCarthy an olive branch, Edwards rushed to the Senate Office Building. He arrived just as McCarthy was handing out copies of a press release sharply rebuking the president. "Cancel that," Edwards begged, but McCarthy persisted. From that day on, Edwards considered it "all downhill" for Senator McCarthy. Forced to take sides between their president and their colleague, congressional Republicans implored McCarthy to tone down his accusations. "When you fellows . . . find a Communist the press gives the story about an inch of space with a headline to match," McCarthy scoffed. "On the other hand, when I give out a statement I announce that I have the proof which shows that I have discovered hundreds of communists in some government agency, then the press puts my statement on page one with banner headlines."[44]

Led by the *New York Times* and *Washington Post*, much of the press intensified its fire on McCarthy. The conservative Washington correspondent Allen Drury complained that newspapers seemed to have only three ways of dealing with news in those days. It was either, "He Didn't Mention McCarthy But We Know He Meant To, So We'll Do It For Him," or "He Said Five Thousand Words on Something Else And Fifteen On McCarthy And It's Up To Us To Put It In Proper Perspective," or "Nobody Even Thought About McCarthy And We Just Can't Conceal Our Surprise." The senator might have had a knack for planting himself in the center of things, Drury conceded, but most of his publicity came from the media's "sick obsession" with him.[45]

As McCarthy's investigation of the army heated up, the army charged that McCarthy and Roy Cohn were using the hearings as "blackmail" to win special treatment for David Schine, who had been drafted into the army as a private. McCarthy countercharged that the army was holding Schine "hostage" to restrain the investigation. The Permanent Subcommittee on Investigations looked into these charges, forcing the senator to step aside temporarily as chairman and appear as a defendant. Television covered the public Army-McCarthy hearings, and ABC president Robert Kintner, an implacable anti-McCarthyite, made sure that his network carried them live, gavel to gavel. TV had given McCarthy the immense national audience he craved, but it ultimately became the technological noose by which he hung himself. The senator had provoked agonized discussions in many Washington news bureaus over how to cover someone they thought was lying, and whether employing news analysis to challenge his assertions would somehow undermine their objectivity. Television cameras instead looked over the heads of the reporters and showed the senator just as he was. His belligerent, bullying, disruptive tactics played poorly on the small screen, and even Roy Cohn described his behavior as "demanding, dictatorial and obstructive."[46]

Within the press corps, McCarthy's supporters came to realize that they had bet on the wrong horse. Ed Nellor, the reporter who said he wrote "maybe 500 speeches" for the senator, left McCarthy's office after he ignored Nellor's pleas not to take on the army. Walter Trohan of the *Chicago Tribune* begged the senator to tone down his rhetoric and concluded ruefully, "McCarthy's love of the sensational made life difficult for his supporters." Trohan's colleague, Willard Edwards, described Joe McCarthy as "irresponsible in the way that an overgrown boy is careless when his size belies his years." He just "never grew up." Edwards sent warnings to the *Tribune*'s editors about McCarthy's excesses, but "they never paid any attention to them."[47]

Whittaker Chambers also came to view McCarthy as a charlatan after the senator tried to use him in a cynical public relations ploy. When McCarthy opposed Eisenhower's nomination of Charles Bohlen to be ambassador to the Soviet Union because of Bohlen's past association with Alger Hiss, he told reporters that he was going to consult with Chambers at his farm. Chambers had no information about Bohlen. The senator stopped by for only a brief visit and then hid from the press for the rest of the weekend to leave the impression that they were locked in secret discussions. This stunt convinced Chambers to warn other conservatives to keep their distance from McCarthy, whose "flair for the sensational, his inaccuracies and distortions, his tendency to sacrifice the greater objective for the momentary effect, will lead him and us into trouble."[48]

McCarthy loyalists in the press corps began to bail out. Among them were Howard Rushmore, McCarthy's erstwhile research director, who began writing skeptically of his investigations for the *New York Journal-American,* and Frederick Woltman of the *New York World-Telegram and Sun,* whom Scripps-Howard had advertised as its "premier 'Red-baiter.'" Woltman praised McCarthy's crusade until he grew suspicious that the senator was embroidering his charges to attract headlines. After trying to stop McCarthy from calling Secretary of State Dean Acheson a "traitor," Woltman was stunned to see a news photograph of McCarthy beaming at an encounter with a grim-faced Acheson in a Senate elevator. That McCarthy could smile at a man he had just accused of treason indicated to Woltman that he was "getting a kick out of it." In his five-part review, "The McCarthy Balance Sheet," Woltman ripped into McCarthy's record and accused him of having turned anti-Communism into a political football. His "disgraceful, scatter-brained, inept, misleading and unfair investigations" had undermined government morale and thrown the whole process of congressional investigation into disrepute. This sweeping indictment signaled Scripps-Howard's abandonment of Joe McCarthy for having tried "to destroy the Eisenhower administration when it's grappling with a world crisis."[49]

McCarthy's stature eroded with the Army-McCarthy hearings. During this slide, the columnist Murray Kempton visited the senator's office late one day and observed him "talking to the reporters, wearily, abstractedly, like a loser on election night, not so much grim as drained of his emotional capital, half wondering if it is all worth it." McCarthy lost his chairmanship when his party lost the majority in the November elections. By December, half of his Republican colleagues in the Senate had joined with the Democrats in voting to censure him. The first time that McCarthy rose to speak after the new Congress convened a month later everyone in the press gallery rushed to hear the censured senator's latest attack. Leaning over for a better view, AP correspondent Jack Bell watched the majority leader Lyndon B. Johnson "winking covertly and knowingly to the other Democrats sitting smugly listening to the swish of the knife." McCarthy's speech generated not much of a story. The next time that reporters heard the familiar cry, "McCarthy's up!" no one moved. "That was the day that really sealed McCarthy's fate," recorded Robert C. Albright in the *Washington Post*.[50]

Ignored by the press corps, McCarthy's news value diminished. To Eisenhower, that confirmed his theory that turning off the spigot of publicity would cause McCarthyism to dry up. Had the press snubbed McCarthy before his censure, however, his supporters would have charged bias, or worse. Willard Edwards regarded the post-censure blackout as a reflection of the press corps's guilt for having "made" McCarthy. When McCarthy encountered television cameras outside the Foreign Relations Committee room, he dashed over waving copies of his latest press release, but no one would take it. One of his supporters started printing and distributing copies of his Senate speeches because the Washington papers barely mentioned them. Ruth Watt, chief clerk of the Permanent Subcommittee on Investigations, noticed that whenever McCarthy sent out a press release, "you never saw it unless it was on the back page." Being in the papers got into his blood, she thought, and being ignored "broke his heart, really." The White House press office adopted a policy of not responding to anything the senator said, and Eisenhower joked that McCarthyism had become McCarthywasm.[51]

Severed from publicity, McCarthy drank himself into an early grave, leaving behind many damaged reputations, among his supporters as well as the targets of his investigations. Reporter May Craig, who covered the Maine delegation for the Gannett papers, had praised McCarthy as an "amazing dynamo" and endorsed his campaign to root subversives from the government. "Those who despise McCarthy and think he just is riding the popular horse of anti-Communism are likely to underestimate the anti-Communist feeling in this country," she wrote in her column. Such sentiments caused the liberal columnist Doris Fleeson to move out of the office she shared with Craig at the National Press Building, and ruptured Craig's long-standing friendship with Maine senator Margaret Chase Smith. Senator Smith went so far as to recommend that Gannett drop Craig as its Washington correspondent.[52]

Among broadcasters, the ratings for the pro-McCarthy radio commentator Fulton Lewis Jr. steadily declined, and ABC-TV terminated the contract of gossip columnist and commentator Walter Winchell. During McCarthy's heyday, Winchell had tapped his friendship with Roy Cohn to broadcast a string of "firsts" about those whom McCarthy planned to subpoena next. Before long, Winchell's opponents in the press began calling him a "McCarthy stooge," and a "McCarthyite," labels that alienated his sponsors. The same month that·he lost his television show, Winchell apologized for calling the *New York Post* and its editor James Wechsler sympathetic to Communism, in return for Wechsler dropping his libel suit. The *Post* celebrated Winchell's apology as "a dramatic setback for McCarthyism." Ralph de Toledano, who had lost faith in McCarthy during the Voice of America hearings but could not bring himself to attack him publicly, blamed his association with the senator for costing him a job with CBS.[53]

"If the Communists had wanted to pick someone to attack them, they couldn't have done better," Willard Edwards commented. McCarthy's freewheeling style "killed anti-Communism for years." The movement suffered a further blow when the *Chicago Tribune* sold off the *Washington Times-Herald* to the *Washington Post* in 1954. "It meant that there was no local morning paper on his side, and the local morning paper is everything in Washington," said Edwards. The sale cost McCarthy editorial support and denied Edwards a regular outlet at the capital. The *Chicago Tribune* was not widely distributed in Washington, and even Edwards stopped reading the paper after he retired to the Washington suburbs.[54]

Communist subversion was no longer a credible political issue. Liberals agreed on the external threat of communism, William F. Buckley Jr. observed, but regarded anyone who raised it as an internal issue "at best deluded, at worst suffering from paranoia." The Hearst columnist George Sokolsky called Senator McCarthy's censure a political maneuver to make his name abhorrent and "to frighten off any senator, journalist, or radio commentator who chose to support him or his cause." Sokolsky's close identification with McCarthy led his friends to observe that "when the Wisconsin Senator lost, the New York columnist lost." The columnist Holmes Alexander came to the conclusion that the major newspapers were deliberately blacklisting his columns and refusing to review his books. Within the press corps he encountered "a supercilious greeting here, a clumsy attempt at snubbing there," and realized that his connections with McCarthy would forever define his journalism. "In the years that followed," Alexander wrote, "I worked on at my columns, my articles and my books but I thought and thought about the McCarthy story."[55]

Advocacy by the band of conservative journalists had undermined their standing as reporters. At the same time, many liberal reporters were expressing unease over objectivity. Within the Washington press corps came complaints that the constraints of objective reporting had perpetuated McCarthy's distortions rather than clarifying them. William S. White, who labored on "the McCarthy beat" for the *New York Times,* concluded that journalists should discard their blinders and insert "an extra dimension" of interpretation into their reporting. The *Washington Post*'s cartoonist Herblock, who enjoyed complete editorial freedom, felt that "conscientious newspapers found themselves reporting his crooked charges with a straight face because their standards of objectivity required them to give space to a United States senator who manufactured news." His publisher, Philip L. Graham, disagreed. Graham expected that the pressures and time constraints of daily deadlines would always make it difficult for reporters to sift through controversial charges and counter-charges. "And even in stories like the McCarthy story," Graham added, "I confess that I am fearful of our using our power unfairly when we try to print the 'whole truth' instead of merely being 'objective.'"[56]

Ultimately, Joe McCarthy's impact proved more anti-ideological than anti-Communist. Having begun as a movement to stigmatize the left, McCarthyism marginalized the right. "In the end vindictiveness reigned," wrote Ralph de Toledano, "directed primarily against the Senator, and those who supported him found themselves marked, misrepresented, and therefore embittered." The friends of Joe McCarthy had believed that ridding Communists from the government trumped individual rights and justified the means to that end. Convincing themselves that traitors had sabotaged U.S. foreign policy, the McCarthyites underestimated the actual accomplishments of the Truman and Eisenhower administrations. The architects of America's Cold War strategies, whom McCarthy relentlessly assailed, eventually prevailed. McCarthy's own ruin flattened political discourse and narrowed the range of acceptable argument, fostering a Cold War political consensus that left little room for his supporters.[57]

5

News Center of the World

While Joe McCarthy hunted for Reds in the government, reporters for the Soviet news agency TASS could watch him from the congressional press galleries. The columnist Joseph Alsop mused that "anybody could go anywhere; you didn't even need a card to get in the White House, and even Larry Todd got into the press conferences, and nobody thought anything about it." He was referring to Laurence Todd, the mild-mannered, scholarly correspondent for TASS. Both the liberal columnist Drew Pearson and the conservative *Chicago Tribune* correspondent Walter Trohan counted Todd as a personal friend, regardless of his employer. By the time the Cold War started, on the heels of World War II, Todd had represented TASS in Washington for two decades and had become the dean of the State Department's press corps. His press pass let him dine in the State Department cafeteria, a hub of office gossip, and attend off-the-record briefings on matters of national security. American officials assumed that TASS reporters were Communists at best and spies at worst, yet when anti-Communists in Congress tried to expel TASS from the press galleries, the State Department and the Standing Committee of Correspondents rallied to its defense. Even TASS belonged to what members of the press corps referred to as the "international fraternity of reporters."[1]

Foreign correspondents tended to blur the lines between objectivity and advocacy. At times they functioned as quasi-diplomats, intelligence gatherers, interpreters, propagandists, lobbyists, and other extensions of their nations' embassies. Like diplomats, their mission was to report home on developing events in another land. For foreign correspondents stationed in Washington that meant explaining an exceptional, trend-setting society with a non-parliamentary government unlike the political systems in most of their own nations. Foreign correspondents usually had to grapple with a second language, strange customs, and deadlines that stretched across many time zones. They struggled to develop sources among officials who were unlikely to read what they wrote or hear what they broadcast. They contended with resentment from American reporters for taking up limited space or for asking questions at crowded press briefings. They were expected to cover the entire federal government and often the rest of the United States as well. Very few foreign news organizations could afford a large staff in Washington. By necessity, their correspondents relied on news reported by the American media, which extended the influence of the Washington press corps globally.[2]

Long before Washington reached the status of a world capital, it attracted curious foreign visitors. From Alexis de Tocqueville to Charles Dickens and Fanny Trollope, nineteenth-century Europeans came to observe and record the novelty of the new American republic. During the Civil War, correspondents for the leading newspapers of London, Paris, and Berlin stationed in the United States reported on the military and political battles. After the war, the *London Daily News* formed a news-sharing syndicate with the *New York Tribune,* and other foreign papers found American partners to minimize the costs of overseas reporting. In 1893, the three major European news associations— Reuters in Great Britain, Havas in France, and Wolff in Germany—reached an agreement with the Associated Press. They would provide world news to the AP in return for the AP's coverage of the United States. The AP could open news bureaus abroad, but it could not sell foreign news directly to non-U.S. customers.[3]

The few European papers that sent special correspondents to the United States were more interested in America's finances than its politics, so they stationed their reporters in New York. Americans regarded Washington as a center of corruption and intrigue, Henry Adams observed, but "foreigners only know it as dull." Alone among the major nations of the world, the United States had no capital, wrote the astute British ambassador, Lord Bryce. By capital he meant not just a seat of government but "the favored residence of the great and powerful," and the center of "the creative power of a country." It was cosmopolitan New York, the great commercial and entertainment center, that offered an abundance of newspapers and magazines from which foreign correspondents could repackage the news for home consumption. One British journalist marveled that New York offered him "the American Government in tabloid form in a modest flat five minutes from my hotel." In 1900 only a single foreign newspaper, the *Kölnische Zeitung* (Cologne Gazette), maintained an exclusive correspondent in Washington. Other overseas papers relied on the moonlighting services of American journalists such as Edward S. Little, who reported for the *San Francisco Bulletin* while also covering Washington for the *London Morning Leader* and the *Montreal Star.* In similar arrangements, the *New York World's* editorial writers Walter Lippmann and Arthur Krock, before he went to the *New York Times,* supplemented their incomes as American correspondents for the *Manchester Guardian.*[4]

On occasion, the New York–based foreign correspondents would organize excursions to Washington, where they expressed astonishment at the openness of the American government. It was often easier for them to see the president of the United States than their own prime ministers at home. No sentries stood in front of government buildings early in the twentieth century, and no one seemed to be keeping their movements under surveillance. Despite this accessibility, they found it hard to fathom a government that separated power between a Congress, in place of a parliament, and a president, instead of a monarch, and maintained such a complex system of checks and balances between them. Maurice Low, an Englishman who reported for the *London Morning Post* and the *Boston Globe* at the turn of the century, advised his British readers not to underestimate America for its idiosyncrasies. "Uncle Sam's ambitions are boundless," Low predicted. "He wants to be the biggest thing in all creation, and he knows he will be eventually."[5]

The Times of London set the model for foreign correspondents. That preeminent paper owed its ascendancy largely to its foreign reporting, which fed Victorian-era Britain's appetite for world news and imperial glory. Before *The Times* hired a colonial reporter, it consulted with the British Colonial Office, which in turn counted on those reporters for intelligence. *The Times* had contented itself with a single American correspondent based in New York, until an assassin's bullet ended William McKinley's presidency and put the dynamic Theodore Roosevelt in the White House in 1901. *The Times* then felt the need for an observer in Washington, but its top choices all regarded the assignment as tantamount to exile. The paper's foreign editor coaxed his leading European corespondents with glowing descriptions of Washington as "the blue ribbon of journalism" and predicted that "*The Times* Correspondent in Washington could become the most important man in America after the President." The best he could come up with, however, was the engineering supplement editor, Robert Percival Porter, who at least knew the territory. Porter had been raised in the United States, where he had acquired an American accent and political connections. He reported as "Our Own Correspondent at Washington" but preferred to live in Manhattan and send his inexperienced assistant, Arthur Willert, to Washington. The young man "worked like a dog" and filed so many stories that *The Times* eventually sacked Porter and appointed Willert as its first full-fledged Washington correspondent.[6]

Arthur Willert's reporting also impressed personnel at the British embassy, who used the reporter as their unofficial press attaché. When Great Britain declared war on Germany in 1914, Willert tried to explain American neutrality to his incredulous readers. He advised his editor that he felt it "incumbent to be more pro-American in print than I am in private." Willert wanted to resign and join the British Army, but *The Times* ordered him to remain at his post. "You grumble at being marooned in Washington," his publisher, Lord Northcliffe, reassured him, "but as a matter of fact you are doing a very great service to the Empire." The British government needed his help in combating the formidable propaganda campaign being conducted by the German ambassador, Count J. H. A. von Bernstorff, who cultivated the Washington press corps by offering inside views of their own State Department's negotiations with Germany over submarine warfare in the Atlantic. "He told as much as he dared," the *Baltimore Sun* correspondent J. Fred Essary wrote of von Bernstorff, "more, in many instances, than was discreet." Willert countered with his own public relations campaign, including serving as press agent for a special British diplomatic mission that his publisher led to Washington. When the war ended, the British government awarded Arthur Willert with a knighthood and appointed him as head of the Foreign Office's news department.[7]

Once the United States entered the First World War, it created a Committee on Public Information headed by the journalist George Creel. The Creel Committee promoted reporting favorable to the Allied war effort. It also set about defining the rules by which the foreign press corps could cover the war news in America. It underwrote the Association of Foreign Press Correspondents in the United States and paid for first-class travel fares and hotel accommodations so that its members could tour American industrial centers to impress upon their readers the nation's military and economic capabilities. At the war's end, the Creel Committee also paid for the foreign correspondents to come to Washington and watch the Senate debate the Treaty of Versailles and the League of Nations. So many took up the offer that members of the National Press Club said they gave the club "the appearance of a diplomatic anteroom." Once the fog of war had lifted, many journalists both foreign and American came to regret having docilely submitted to the Creel Committee's manipulation, and that lingering memory would haunt the federal government's efforts to influence war news during World War II.[8]

In the peacetime of the 1920s U.S. government patronage evaporated, prompting the foreign correspondents to reconstitute themselves as an independent Foreign Press Association "to safeguard the rights and privileges of correspondents and promote ties of friendship between all our racial elements." Reflecting their preferred base of operations, the association met in a New York speakeasy and made sporadic expeditions to Washington, where their embassies fortunately did not observe Prohibition. The few foreign correspondents who worked out of Washington complained of being "a vassal state of New York." They joined with returning American war correspondents to form the Overseas Writers Club, which was based in Washington. Yet another organization emerged in the 1920s when Secretary of State Henry Stimson attempted to exclude foreign reporters from his regular news briefings. The *Baltimore Sun*'s diplomatic correspondent Drew Pearson led a revolt that resulted in the founding of the State Department Correspondents Association. From then on the diplomatic correspondents themselves screened press eligibility, just as correspondents handled accreditation at the White House and Capitol. A charter member of all three organizations was *The Times*'s replacement for Arthur Willert, Willmott Harsant Lewis.[9]

Born in Wales, and educated in Heidelberg and Paris, Willmott Lewis went to the Far East as editor of the *North China Daily News* in Shanghai and the *Manila Times*, British-owned papers published for English-speakers living abroad. While in the Philippines, he befriended an American army officer, John

J. Pershing. General Pershing later headed the American Expeditionary Force to Europe, and invited Lewis to handle his press relations. That exposure brought Lewis to the attention of Lord Northcliffe, who hired him to cover postwar Washington for *The Times*. From 1920 until his retirement in 1947, Lewis held a joint portfolio as *The Times*'s Washington correspondent and as Great Britain's "Ambassador Incognito." The urbane Lewis dated Baltimore's Wallis Warfield, later Simpson—the future Duchess of Windsor—and married Ethel Noyes, whose father headed the *Washington Star* and the Associated Press. From their Georgetown mansion, Quality Hill, they entertained in a grand manner, although Lewis's American press colleagues called him just plain Bill.

Lewis rarely bothered to attend press conferences or spend much time at the State Department's pressroom. He gathered his news mostly from other Washington reporters at the National Press Club's card tables, repaying their tips with a ready supply of epigrams and quips that they used in their own writing. It was Lewis who coined the much-reprinted aphorism when a Supreme Court justice changed his vote in order to derail Franklin Roosevelt's plan to "pack" the Supreme Court with additional justices: "A Switch in Time that Saved Nine." For such apt expressions, his friends called him "Bonmott." Lewis was in the card room as usual in 1931 when word came that King George VI had made him a knight of the British Empire. To celebrate, his closest friends—among them Drew Pearson, radio commentator Frederic William Wile, and TASS correspondent Larry Todd—threw a dinner for Sir Willmott and Lady Lewis at the Mayflower Hotel, where reporters in formal attire wore old convention badges and campaign buttons in lieu of diplomatic decorations. When asked what difference a knighthood made, he replied, "Well, I'll tell you, old boy, Willmott Lewis used to fetch $250 a lecture. Sir Willmott Lewis gets $500."[10]

As Europe again drifted toward war in the late 1930s, Sir Willmott escalated his diplomacy for the empire, presenting its cause as a lecturer and radio personality, and as a much sought-after guest at Washington's dinner parties. He used his rumbling bass voice to good effect on the radio, where he was "a master at tweaking the noses of dictators," noted the *Washington Post* columnist Harlan Miller. He also nudged British diplomats into better relations with the Washington press corps. Because the stiff-necked British ambassador, Sir Ronald Lindsay, held the American press at arm's length, Lewis acted as the chief point of contact between the embassy and the Washington correspondents. Once when a journalist finally managed to question the British ambassador, he got the sour reply, "Haven't you seen Willmott Lewis?" Younger British journalists who began arriving in Washington in larger numbers during the 1930s and 1940s found Lewis's style distasteful, however. Rather than get their news at the Press Club, they intended to do their own interviewing. When the *Sunday Times* of London sent over a young Czechoslovakian Jewish refugee,

Henry Brandon, the aging Willmott Lewis offered him a crash course in American politics, but Brandon preferred to ask American journalists for help. Brandon was surprised at how many of his British colleagues remained in New York. He overheard an argument between the correspondents for London's *News Chronicle* and *Daily Express* over the best place to cover the war. The *News Chronicle* reporter insisted that Washington had become the "front line." The *Daily Express* man retorted that "even though the guns may be fired in Washington, the shells still explode in New York."[11]

Franklin D. Roosevelt had made Washington more hospitable by welcoming foreign correspondents to his press conferences. The president charmed the foreign writers and won glowing reports of his policies. One foreign correspondent admitted that they found it "embarrassing to adopt any other attitude toward him." Willmott Lewis praised Roosevelt's internationalism and launched a wartime newsletter, *Foreign Correspondence,* for American readers. Most likely subsidized by the British government, the newsletter endorsed Roosevelt's use of "the great powers of his office in the teeth of wild opposition to provide such safeguards and measures of defense as he could devise." At the same time, Lewis stopped charging lecture fees and began giving pro bono talks on Anglo-American solidarity to women's clubs, colleges, and chambers of commerce. After the war, he retired both the newsletter and himself. Rather than return to Great Britain, Sir Willmott remained in Georgetown in his last years. He lunched at the National Press Club on the day he died.[12]

Foreign correspondents also took to the airwaves. The British Broadcasting Corporation first employed U.S. radio commentators to broadcast from America, but when that arrangement proved unsatisfactory it sent a British correspondent, Felix Green, to open a bureau in New York in 1935. He performed satisfactorily until Britain went to war. As a religious pacifist, Green declined to peddle wartime propaganda and lost his job. The BBC turned to the suave correspondent for the *Manchester Guardian,* Alistair Cooke. Shuttling between New York and Washington, Cooke observed that his British colleagues in the press corps felt compelled to perform as missionaries. Rather than preach to his hosts in the hope of winning coverts to British policies, Cooke thought it more valuable to educate his British radio listeners on the Americans. After the war, he started delivering a weekly "Letter from America" over the BBC. His listeners were more likely to hear about the Miss America pageant than the latest foreign policy debates—an approach that kept his "Letter from America" on the air for fifty-eight years. "Politicians and diplomats come and go," said one British ambassador, "but Cooke's weekly lessons have, for half a century, translated one nation for the understanding of another."[13]

The fascists made a much clumsier presence in Washington. Italian dictator Benito Mussolini initially impressed the National Press Club's president J. Fred Essary, who proposed making Il Duce an honorary club member. Essary got the approval of the club's board of governors, but when he posted Mussolini's name on the club's bulletin board TASS correspondent Larry Todd spearheaded the petition drive that blocked his membership. A chagrined Essary could not understand why anyone would want to "stir up trouble" against such an anti-Communist bulwark. Later the Nazis, led by Kurt George Wilhelm Luedecke, correspondent for the National Socialist Press Bureau, targeted Washington. Luedecke's mission was to win support for the Nazi regime among American reporters and officials, but he fell victim to an internal party struggle within the Nazi Party and to protect himself wound up confessing his pro-Nazi activities to the House Un-American Activities Committee.

The Nazis also took over the official German news agency that had been represented in Washington since 1927 by Kurt Sell. The roly-poly, round-faced, pink-cheeked Sell could "walk on eggs adroitly" and he managed to avoid political debates as if he had diplomatic immunity. Sell became known to American radio listeners for providing English summaries of speeches delivered by Joseph Goebbels and other German officials. "Herr Sell, the best known of the German correspondents in this country," the *New York Times* reported, " has many friends among his American colleagues." Sell assured fellow reporters in the State Department pressroom that he personally opposed fascism and that he filed his dispatches without political coloring. Yet because Sell's family lived in Germany, he succumbed to Nazi pressure. Having previously lived modestly, he began hosting elaborate social functions at Washington's best hotels, where American reporters and isolationist politicians mingled with German embassy staff. "Vast quantities of Germany food were served, and oceans of fine German beer," wrote one correspondent, while guests sang along with a Bavarian band. Sell also kept the embassy apprised of the president's off-the-record comments at press conferences. The Secret Service kept tabs on him, but most of the press corps felt sorry for him.[14]

In 1939 Manfred Zapp, whom the FBI pegged as a "not-too-astute" propaganda agent, descended on Washington. He represented the German Transocean News Service, a Nazi front that masqueraded as a private news organization. Zapp kept in close contact with the Germany embassy staff, with whom he boasted of his contacts with "many circles and all sorts of people" from whom he could secure confidential information. He had no trouble obtaining press credentials as a foreign correspondent, but reporters at the National Press Club advised President Roosevelt not to speak so freely when Zapp attended his press conferences. Late in 1940 the House Un-American Activities Committee subpoenaed Zapp's records and exposed his subversive activities. By March 1941 the Justice Department indicted him for not registering as a foreign agent and shut down Transocean. The Germans retaliated by arresting the United Press reporter in Germany Richard C. Hottelet on trumped up charges of espionage, and exchanging him for Zapp. Back in Berlin, Zapp published a critical account of American politics, in which he accused Roosevelt of having hypnotized the press corps with his charm. Kurt Sell was also deported back to Germany. He soon reemerged in the neutral port of Lisbon, where he watched American arrivals and departures, read American newspapers, and filed reports to Berlin. Sell later claimed to have secretly collaborated with American diplomats. By war's end, he had lost everything he owned in Germany and desperately enlisted the support of his friends in the Washington press corps to return to the United States. During his fifteen years in Washington, Sell swore, "I never spoke or wrote a word of propaganda." He managed to get a visa in 1946, but it was canceled after Drew Pearson denounced him on a Sunday night radio broadcast. Sell took a job with a newspaper in the American zone in Germany, complaining that he had "no more relatives to go to, no home, no coal, little food." He died there the following year.[15]

Unlike the lingering affection that American reporters showed toward Kurt Sell, they turned a cold shoulder to Masuo Kato, who reported for the Japanese news agency Domei. Educated in the United States, Kato had kindled warm friendships during his previous stint in Washington from 1937 to 1940. Yet on his second tour of duty, in the spring of 1941, the University Club no longer could find a room for him. Nor would the Kenwood Country Club renew his membership. Former colleagues at the National Press Club went out of their way to avoid him. Rumors spread that Kato was actually a Japanese naval officer posing as a newspaperman. On Sunday afternoon, December 7, 1941, the correspondent was riding in a Washington taxi when a radio bulletin reported the Japanese attacks on Pearl Harbor and Manila. "God damn Japan," the taxi driver swore. "We'll lick the hell out of those bastards now." When FBI agents arrested Kato the next day, no one in the press corps came to his defense. He was shipped back to Tokyo as part of a prisoner exchange. In 1945, when Japan formally surrendered aboard the battleship U.S.S. *Missouri* in Tokyo Bay, Masuo Kato covered it as a Japanese newsman. Astonished to see Kato in civilian clothes, Associated Press reporter Ben Grant exclaimed, "Then you really weren't a commander in the Navy, after all!"[16]

Except in times of war, the "international fraternity" transcended politics. Some of the most conservative Washington correspondents rallied in support of the first Washington correspondent for the Soviet newspaper *Izvestiya*, Vladimir Romm, after he went on trial during Stalin's purges. Heading a group of Washington correspondents, Arthur Krock cabled Moscow that they had found Romm "a true friend and advocate of the U.S.S.R." Never had he shown the slightest infidelity to the Communist government, and he "did more than any other Soviet envoy to popularize the Stalin regime in this country." Despite the intervention of his U.S. friends, Romm confessed his disloyalty and disappeared into Stalin's work camps.[17]

Most remarkable of all was the press corps's casual acceptance of Laurence Todd during his quarter century as Washington correspondent for TASS. Larry

Todd did not fit the stereotype of a Bolshevik. A homegrown American radical, he had spent a hardscrabble childhood on a farm in western Michigan. While a student at the University of Michigan, Todd was inspired by the Socialist labor leader Eugene V. Debs to join the Socialist Party. He regularly voted for Debs for president. Years later as a reporter he was thrilled to meet Debs and wrote that the old man still possessed "the burning eyes of our Marxist saint of old." Todd reported labor news for E. W. Scripps's *San Francisco News*, and then moved to Washington for Scripps's United Press in 1911. Hearst's International News Service then hired him as its State Department correspondent, and he reported on every secretary of state from William Jennings Bryan to Dean Acheson.

After taking a brief leave from journalism to serve as secretary to a Socialist member of Congress, Todd signed on with the Federated Press, a cooperative news service launched during the wave of strikes in 1919 to provide articles for labor and radical newspapers across "the grimy industrial map of the country." Although its masthead proclaimed that its news dispatches "must at all times be kept free from propaganda," the news service rejected the notion that newspapers reported without bias. "The Federated Press is very careful about facts," said its managing editor, Carl Haessler, "but they are presented with a decided pro-labor interpretation just as we believe the capitalist press interprets news so that it becomes pro-capitalist." As the Federated Press's Washington correspondent, Todd typed news items onto mimeograph stencils, ran them off onto legal-size sheets, and mailed them twice a week to subscribers. Because the news service numbered the Communist Party's *Daily Worker* among its subscribers, critics called it a Communist front, but Todd's articles were insufficiently ideological to appear often in the pages of the *Worker*. (Association with the *Daily Worker* may have tarred the Federated Press, but because the *Worker* was a daily newspaper it preserved the news service's eligibility for congressional press gallery accreditation during periods when all its other members were labor weeklies.)[18]

The Russian Revolution fascinated Todd and he visited the Soviet Union twice during the 1920s. The dispatches he sent to the Federated Press argued that Communism had given the Russians social insurance, public health programs, better housing and schools, and "freedom to think and read in every field except the field of political capitalism." The Russians tolerated censorship and police control, he assumed, as "necessary discipline and insurance against the return of civil war and czarism." His glowing dispatches came to the attention of Kenneth Durant, the American representative of the Telegraph News Service of the Soviet Union, TASS. The wealthy Durant handled American public relations for the Bolshevik government, working out of Greenwich Village. He hired Todd to report part-time for TASS from Washington, allowing him to keep his connection to the Federated Press. TASS stipulated that none of its reporters could be members of a political party or carry on any political activities. For other Americans who reported for TASS, this edict usually required them to resign from the Communist Party. For Todd, it precluded his joining the party. He understood that writing for TASS meant he was working for the Soviet government, but he felt no pressure to slant his news to meet the party line. Although he gave other reporters the impression of "restraining only with some difficulty his opinion of American bourgeois and reactionaries," he insisted that he made his reports factually reliable and noncontroversial. He provided the facts and let Moscow supply any interpretation.[19]

Todd's standing in the State Department pressroom rose after the U.S. formally recognized the U.S.S.R. in 1933. State Department officials began asking his opinions about Soviet policies, despite his demurral that all he knew about the Soviet Union was what he read in the newspapers. Once the Soviets opened an embassy in Washington, TASS raised Todd's salary and asked him to quit the Federated Press, promising job security in return. Other TASS reporters in the United States spent their time culling newspapers, magazines, government reports, and press releases for items to send to Moscow, but Kenneth Durant wanted Todd to check the facts that appeared in mainstream publications and filter out capitalist biases. As a Washington correspondent, Todd worked alone in a cramped bureau at the National Press Building, down the hall from the *Daily Worker*'s bureau. Occasionally, Durant would join him, as did the *New York Times*'s Moscow correspondent, Walter Duranty, during his Washington visits. Sympathetic to the Soviet regime, Duranty felt more comfortable writing at the TASS office than at the *Times*'s bureau, under the frosty gaze of bureau chief Arthur Krock.[20]

Few Americans heard of Larry Todd until a dinner party in the spring of 1934 catapulted him into the headlines. His friend Alice Barrows invited Todd and a small group of left-leaning, lower-level New Dealers to her suburban Virginia home to meet her former boss, Dr. William Wirt, the superintendent of schools in Gary, Indiana. Dr. Wirt proved himself a monumental bore who monopolized the dinner conversation and continued his monologue while Todd drove him back to Washington. To everyone's astonishment, a few months later Wirt testified before a House committee that he had attended a private party where the TASS reporter and group of New Deal radicals had engaged in "revolutionary talk." Wirt accused Todd of comparing Franklin D. Roosevelt to the Socialist Alexander Kerensky (who had led Russia just before the Bolsheviks seized power). "We have Roosevelt in the middle of the stream," Wirt quoted Todd, "and we will keep him there until we replace him with a Stalin." The Hearst press headlined the "communistic plot," but Walter Trohan of the *Chicago Tribune* snorted at the idea of "the mild and scholarly" Larry Todd as a conspirator. Called to testify before Congress, Todd swore that he had never mentioned Kerensky, and that he had interrupted the talkative Dr. Wirt to defend Franklin Roosevelt as the strongest president since Lincoln. Wirt turned out to have lifted the Kerensky quote from a book by *Washington Post* correspondent Ernest K. Lindley. With that finding, the House committee dismissed his allegations. At the White House, Press Secretary Steve Early chuckled as he introduced the TASS correspondent to President Roosevelt: "This is Larry Todd, Dr. Wirt's friend."[21]

When the publicity turned sour, congressional conservatives charged that Dr. Wirt had been "literally crucified" by the "New Dealish and pro-Communist" Washington press corps. Later revelations that Communist spy cells had indeed operated in Washington revived Wirt's charges, and Alice Barrows and her dinner guests were called repeatedly before investigating committees. (Barrows later took the Fifth Amendment.) Twenty years later, at the height of the McCarthy era, the Red-hunting writer J. B. Matthews resurrected the dinner as the centerpiece of an essay on "Communism and the New Deal." Citing Wirt's claims, Matthews argued that liberals had blocked efforts to root Communists out of the government by their "anti-anti-Communist" tactics. Offering no new evidence, Matthews cited the very presence of a TASS reporter as ipso facto proof of the dinner guests' disloyalty.[22]

The news that Todd supplied to the Soviet Union sometimes reached American audiences circuitously. In the propaganda battles for American public opinion during the months before the United States entered the Second World War, British agents traced the course of one rumor they had spread. The story first appeared on August 15, 1941, in the pro-British *New York Post*. Todd picked it up from the *Post* and cabled it to Moscow, where the Soviet newspapers reprinted it. British correspondents in Moscow then sent the story to London, where the United Press cabled it back to the United States. By August 19 the story had resurfaced in the *New York Herald Tribune, Daily News,* and *Daily Mirror.*

Once the United States entered the Second World War in alliance with the Soviet Union, Todd's standing in Washington was elevated—even as his role in TASS diminished. In wartime, the Washington bureau expanded from Todd's one-man operation to five news writers and two teletype operators. Todd headed the Washington bureau but New York ran all operations. One new recruit in the Washington bureau noticed that when she dictated her reports from Congress and the State Department over the phone, they went straight to New York by teletype rather than to her Washington bureau chief. A defector later estimated that 90 percent of all TASS correspondents belonged to Soviet military intelligence during the war. Their press passes provided them with entry to the highest levels in government.[23]

Larry Todd was no spy, but he understood the intelligence value of open information that was not readily available to the general public. In 1945 a delegation from the American Society of Newspaper Editors (ASNE) visited Russia and on their return presented an eighteen-thousand-word report to President Truman. They took a stack of press releases to the National Press

Building but arrived late on a Saturday evening after most of the news bureaus had closed. They shoved their press releases into mail slots until they came to the TASS bureau, where they found its staff busy at work. The editors described bureau chief Laurence Todd as "a monument of courtesy," who took the press release and asked for the complete eighteen-thousand-word report. "Not for newspaper publication, perhaps," Todd explained, "but our foreign staffs will wish to see the entire report." The press statement garnered only a six-hundred-word AP dispatch. Only TASS and the ASNE's own magazine, *Editor & Publisher,* distributed the report in full.[24]

When the Grand Alliance collapsed into Cold War, Washington correspondents found it difficult to fathom how the earnest Larry Todd could serve such a ruthless government. Todd became an apologist for the Soviet regime, insisting that it remained committed to world peace. His very presence at press conferences agitated government officials. The chairman of the Joint Committee on Atomic Energy, Senator Brien McMahon, refused to answer off the record whenever a TASS reporter was present. Senator Richard Russell closed the Senate hearings on General Douglas MacArthur's firing in part because TASS had placed a standing order for the transcripts of the public hearings. In this hostile atmosphere, Todd stopped asking questions at press conferences, concerned that anything he said might raise speculations over Soviet motives. He spent much of his time at the House Un-American Activities Committee hearings. When Whittaker Chambers testified before HUAC, he felt unnerved by a "rather owlish newsman" who stared at him from the press table. A *Time* magazine reporter explained, "That's the TASS man."[25]

Todd's presence also made other correspondents uncomfortable. In 1947 the Overseas Writers Club, in which he had been active for years, abruptly altered its rules to exclude American citizens who reported for foreign news agencies. In 1951 the president of the American Society of Newspaper Editors proposed that Congress retaliate against the imprisonment of an AP reporter in Czechoslovakia by banning TASS from the press galleries, charging that TASS reporters were Soviet agents who ought to be "sent back to Russia." Quietly, however, the Department of State intervened on behalf of TASS, as excluding the Soviet news agency in Washington would undoubtedly result in the expulsion of American reporters from Communist countries. The Standing Committee of Correspondents unanimously refused to eject TASS, withstanding the public hysteria of the Red scare. TASS reporters had to register under the Foreign Agents Registration Act, but so did correspondents for the French and Chinese news services. Larry Todd expressed irritation that American newspapers had devoted so much space to the fulminating of "a reactionary editor," but he felt relieved that his colleagues in the gallery had resisted the "mob action" against his bureau.[26]

A more insidious threat came from Moscow. At the end of World War II, the defection of several covert operatives prompted the Soviets to disband their espionage units in the United States. Soviet leaders turned to TASS as a convenient cover for intelligence gathering, and decreed that their own nationals should run the news agency in the United States. They retired Kenneth Durant and placed the New York office under a Soviet intelligence officer. In 1948 they replaced the seasoned head of their Washington bureau with a thirty-year-old Soviet aviation engineer. The Soviet hierarchy assumed that an engineer could handle anything, but Todd found his replacement unskilled in journalism and uninformed about Washington. The young engineer resisted his attempts to educate him and instead expounded party rhetoric. The author Howard Fast, then a member of the U.S. Communist Party, described these new TASS reporters as entirely "ignorant of America."[27]

Despite his demotion, Todd had no other options than to stay with TASS. No one else would hire an ex-TASS reporter in the McCarthy era. He had remarried, was raising a school-age daughter, and needed the income. Then, in 1952, TASS unceremoniously retired him on a modest pension. Four years later, when the Senate Internal Security Subcommittee called Todd to testify about his career with TASS, he astonished the senators by swearing under oath that he had never been a member of the Communist Party, had never attended a Communist meeting, and had never made a public speech on behalf of the party. His job had prohibited him from doing any of those things. He also told the senators that he had no recollection of having met Alger Hiss at the State Department, although he was not surprised when they exhibited documents showing that Hiss knew who he was. "For many years I was stationed—I had a desk in the press room at the State Department," he explained, "and I saw a good many of these people around then." Hiss undoubtedly knew him by sight because he was fairly well known, said Todd. "After all, I served forty years in the press gallery."[28]

No model employer, TASS sent Todd a teletype message that abruptly canceled his pension. His son Alden, a freelance journalist, went to the United Nations in New York and confronted the Soviet foreign minister, Andrei Gromyko. "How is your father?" Gromyko inquired solicitously. "He doesn't know it, but he's dying of cancer," Alden reported. Within weeks, the Soviet bureaucracy had restored the pension. Larry Todd died in 1957 and was mourned, according to the *Washington Evening Star*, by "a wide circle of friends in the news-gathering field."[29]

At the end of the Cold War it was verified that TASS reporters had served as extensions of Soviet intelligence. Yuri Shvets, a KGB officer who worked as a TASS correspondent in Washington during the 1980s, later described his work as essentially reading U.S. newspapers for bits of information and transmitting what he found to the KGB headquarters in Moscow. In 1989, TASS director Leonid Kravchenko described his correspondents as "stringers" for the KGB who filed intelligence reports along with their news stories. By 1992, following the collapse of the Soviet Union, TASS was melded into ITAR, the Information Telegraph Agency of Russia. Although state-supported, the new service could not afford to field anywhere near as many foreign correspondents as the old regime.[30]

The Cold War ensured that the largest number of American correspondents who reported Washington news overseas were actually employees of the U.S. government. Soon after the United States entered the Second World War it created the Voice of America, which transmitted its first message on February 24, 1942, in German, promising to tell the truth. VOA swiftly began speaking in many tongues, depending heavily on recent refugees from Europe as broadcasters. Some of its staff saw themselves as purveyors of "free, fair and uncensored news" to their homelands, while others used broadcasts as a form of moral suasion. Some of the Europeans were more anti-Communist than anti-Nazi, and internal staff squabbles developed that would later have devastating consequences. The Voice operated under the Office of War Information, headed by Elmer Davis, who tried to instill within the OWI a commitment to reliable, authoritative, and balanced news broadcasting, even in the service of wartime propaganda. But this did not mean the Voice had the freedom to broadcast whatever its reporters thought. VOA was often on a collision course with the State Department, such as the time a Voice commentator called Italy's Victor Emanuel III a "moronic little king." The young *New York Times* reporter Jack Gould heard the broadcast on his shortwave radio and wrote a front-page story on how the Voice had contradicted the American government's policy of encouraging the king to take Italy out of the war. (Gould later became the *Times*'s first television critic.) Arthur Krock picked the story up in his column and warned that overseas listeners would naturally assume that what they heard on the Voice of America reflected the government's official positions. Elmer Davis pressed the Voice to broadcast more hard news and less opinion, but the sour taste lingered and as soon as the war ended the Voice of America was transferred to the Department of State.[31]

Postwar budget cuts decimated the VOA until the Cold War made its services seem crucial again. While the Voice broadcast into the Soviet Union and Eastern Europe, its most successful program was Willis Conover's long-running *Music USA*, a jazz show that attracted millions of loyal listeners. Conover never intended to "sell America," but the music he played had a liberating effect that trumped propaganda. On the news side, the European émigrés who broadcast in their languages pursued a rigorously anti-Soviet line and formed a network they called the Loyal American Underground to collect evidence to prove that Communist sympathizers were sabotaging the Voice. They made their allegations to Senator Joe McCarthy, who launched a much-publicized investigation that wrecked havoc within the agency, forcing staff resignations and dismissals. Administrators argued that their broadcasts would be more effective as a reliable source of news rather than as an overt purveyor of propaganda, in the Soviet model, but the McCarthy probes encouraged Voice broadcasts to adopt a more stridently anti-Communist tone. Not until 1960 did the Voice emerge from the shadow of McCarthyism by adopting a charter that pledged that its news would be accurate and comprehensive, even if that meant reporting American social and economic ills.[32]

President John F. Kennedy intended to revitalize American overseas broadcasting by appointing the CBS news broadcaster Edward R. Murrow to head the U.S. Information Agency, the Voice of America's parent agency. Murrow lent his personal prestige to the overseas news organization, improving its relations with Congress, and restoring its staff's self-confidence. During his Senate confirmation hearings, Murrow pledged to make the USIA "an objective reporting agency" that would provide "editorial balance" in its depictions of the United States. Republican senator Homer Capehart, a former vacuum cleaner salesman from Indiana, disliked what he heard and advised Murrow that his mission should be to market the United States to the world, just like selling a Buick or a Cadillac, and never to admit any defects in the product. But Murrow rejected the notion of telling America's story "only in superlatives." Overseas news broadcasts had to face American problems honestly or lose credibility, he insisted. No one pointed out that the same politicians who usually protested media bias were urging Murrow to slant the news.[33]

In another peculiarity of the Cold War, the same press galleries that preserved accreditation for TASS denied it to the Voice of America, because it was a government agency. The Radio and Television Correspondents Association even considered expelling four prominent American broadcasters who had accepted fees to speak on VOA broadcasts. One of the chastised broadcasters, CBS's Eric Sevareid, was flabbergasted that American correspondents had more of a problem accepting the legitimacy of an American news agency than of a Soviet one. "The TASS agents, in my opinion, work to injure the American government," Sevareid pointed out, "the four of us were trying to help the American government." Another of those under threat of expulsion, Richard L. Strout, the Washington correspondent for the *Christian Science Monitor* and a columnist for the *New Republic*, protested that the propriety of the broadcasts was a concern between himself and his employer, not a matter for a committee of colleagues. Strout's resignation from the press galleries caused the Standing Committee to rescind the rule as "both unenforceable and unfair," as the U.S. government did not directly control the content of VOA programs. Still the efforts to open the galleries to Voice correspondents met continued resistance from purists such as Arthur Krock, who warned that accrediting employees of any government agency would subvert the press galleries' independence. The Standing Committee's "arm's length" policy continued until Voice reporters were finally admitted to the press galleries in 1981.[34]

A new breed of Voice of America correspondents resisted being defined as Cold War propagandists. Philomena Jurey called herself a reporter, "and that's all there was to it." The Voice made Jurey a well-known American journalist to everyone but Americans. She had come to the Voice of America after working as a "girl Friday" to the Washington correspondent of the *London Daily Telegraph,* which helped her see her own country from a non-American perspective. In 1961 she joined the VOA as a news writer, advancing to assignments editor and correspondent. The Voice tended not to put women on the air because, as they saw it, their voices lacked "broadcast quality" or sounded "too emotional," so Jurey took speech lessons to control her pitch. She also appreciated that a VOA broadcaster needed to speak slowly enough to be understood by listeners who were learning English from the programs. Her abilities gained her the plum assignment of covering the State Department, a critical post for the VOA. When President Richard Nixon traveled to China in 1972, the journalists in his entourage discovered that the Chinese did not know Walter Cronkite but they knew Philomena Jurey, the Washington press corps's most "famous unknown."[35]

U.S. leadership in the Cold War reconfirmed Washington's centrality in world news. Except for those who covered the financial markets and the United Nations, foreign correspondents in the United States shifted from New York to Washington—not without some grumbling that they were moving from "a huge and busy railroad terminal to a country church." Like their American counterparts, they struggled to establish sources to develop unique and original news stories rather than simply rehash news from the American media. Those who had previously reported from other world capitals expected the government to scrutinize their work closely, and to file angry protests over any signs of hostile reporting, but they met with indifference in Washington. With each administration fixated on reelecting the president, observed Richard Beeston of the *London Daily Telegraph,* "a reporter from the remotest regional rag rates higher than the grandest of correspondents from the overseas press."[36]

Stretched thin by the territory they had to cover, foreign correspondents sometimes filed erroneous and misleading reports. American officials blamed these mistakes on the "narrow physical orbit" in which the foreign reporters operated, complaining that they rarely saw much of America outside of Washington and New York City. Hapless reporting was not for lack of education or experience, as foreign correspondents in Cold War Washington tended to be college-educated, English-speaking, and well-versed journalists. Despite their abilities and credentials, foreign correspondents collectively had difficulty getting busy officials to grant them interviews. American officials were generally content to let the wire services transmit policy news overseas rather than cultivate the foreign press. Those State Department officials and congressional leaders who made themselves available usually showed a partiality toward European correspondents and English-language media. Wolf Blitzer corresponded for the English-language *Jerusalem Post,* not Israel's biggest paper but its best read among Washington diplomatic sources, who were usually willing to answer his questions. "These sources generally like to be able to read what they've said," Blitzer noted, "even if they are not identified by name." Reporters from developing nations complained of not receiving announcements of news conferences and of being excluded from background briefings. Despite intentions of doing first-hand reporting, foreign correspondents were often so overwhelmed by the mass of available information that they reverted to repackaging the news from the American media with their own commentary. Odd deadlines further complicated their lives—it was not unusual for overseas editors to awaken their Washington correspondents with telephone calls in the middle of the night.[37]

Never famous for giving straight answers, the State Department still provided the most fertile ground for foreign correspondents. It generated news of direct interest to overseas readers, and showed some sympathy for the needs of the foreign press. At State Department briefings, foreign correspondents could follow policy lines as they were being developed—not that they agreed with those policies. Foreign correspondents tended to look critically on American foreign policy from "a strong leftist bias," the libertarian F. A. Hayek commented. Hayek reasoned that in most countries the political right was more nationalistic and the left more internationalist, predisposing reporters from the left to foreign assignments. These foreign visitors found it easy "to get in touch with leftist circles" in the United States, who were opposed to Cold War policies. Regardless of ideological bent, foreign correspondents of all stripes were the "untouchables" of the Washington press corps caste system, denied seats on press planes, relegated to the back rows at press conference, and ignored when they tried to ask questions (unless a prominent official from their own country happened to be visiting).

Responding to the correspondents' complaints of being treated as "second-class citizens," in 1968 the U.S. Information Agency established the Washington Foreign Press Center first at the Department of State and then in the National Press Building, providing a reference library, photocopiers, and fax machines. USIA also arranged press briefings, wrote letters of introduction, and broadcast press briefings from the White House, State Department, and Pentagon. All this was a boon for the many one-person, low-budget foreign bureaus that honeycombed the National Press Building, but who often could not afford membership in the National Press Club upstairs. As crucial as these services were to correspondents from smaller nations, they were disdained by reporters from the major powers. The *Manchester Guardian*'s bureau chief Martin Walker instructed new staff that it was their job to make sure they were "not treated like the reporters at the eighth floor of the Foreign Press Center."[38]

Capitol Hill offered another haven for foreign correspondents. Some members of Congress were more cooperative than others, and their staffs would oblige with faxed copies of their remarks. They could be reached by phone for much-needed quotes, and often agreed to be interviewed on camera. Members of the Foreign Relations Committee had higher visibility abroad than most other senators and could knowledgeably discuss issues of interest to foreign readers, although the correspondents generally found it easier to arrange interviews with House members. Like the regional reporters on Capitol Hill, foreign correspondents tended to specialize. The Swiss covered banking legislation, while Saudi reporters followed oil issues. Those from government-sponsored news agencies, such as the Egyptians, could not get press passes, but C-SPAN allowed them to cover congressional debates at a distance. The sheer volume of activity in Congress and elsewhere in Washington made every day "a test of nerves," said a Turkish correspondent who called the Washington assignment a "high-hormone, high-voltage business."[39]

By the 1970s, with an ever-growing number of foreign correspondents operating out of Washington, National Public Radio broadcast a weekly program called *As Others See Us*. The program's moderator, John Anspacher, brought together panels of foreign correspondents to give insular Americans a better sense of how the rest of the world viewed their politics and society. The program's pilot featured Simon Winchester of the *Manchester Guardian*, Jacques Renard of *Le Figaro*, Ian Hicks of the *Sydney Morning Herald*, and Wolf Blitzer of the *Jerusalem Post*. In fact, most foreign correspondents commented on how little Americans seemed interested in how others saw them. "They don't seem to realize they are in the center of the world," puzzled Ludwina Joseph, a correspondent from India. Fritz Joubert represented the South African National Media during the congressional debates over the U.S. policy toward apartheid. He found American reporters less interested in the situation in South Africa than in their own government's political response to it. Though others in the press gallery treated him hospitably, they rarely consulted him as a source of information about South Africa. Foreign correspondents complained that their position held status within their own media, but in Washington they operated far down the pecking order. As what they reported significantly influenced America's image abroad, they were perplexed by American indifference—although they admitted that American journalists did not fare much better in *their* countries.[40]

Foreign broadcasters setting up television interviews commented that while voluble Americans were eager to talk at any time on any subject, those who knew what they were talking about were often the least cooperative. An interview for foreign television provided public officials with no appreciable return in promoting themselves or getting their points across. Some foreign television networks resorted to paying an "interview fee" to get informed commentary. Meanwhile, the advent of CNN and other satellite news channels reduced the need for foreign correspondents. Smaller news organizations cut costs and improved services by subscribing to CNN for their live coverage or by hiring American freelancers, rather than paying for their own correspondents and crew. CNN's live coverage of the Persian Gulf War made it clear to stations worldwide that they need not spend a fortune placing their own correspondents at the Pentagon. Many foreign news operations cut back on their expenses as soon as the war ended, and a few closed their Washington bureaus completely. The trend also disadvantaged American journalists who offered independent news reporting abroad. Connie Lawn, who freelanced for radio stations in New Zealand, had waited twenty years to get a booth at the White House for her broadcasts, only to lose it to a cable TV organization that had just arrived in the pressroom.[41]

Ultimately, foreign correspondents in Washington found that their greatest problem was not a shortage of sources but an overabundance of news. "This is obviously the news center of the world," commented the *Daily Telegraph*'s Richard Beeston, "but there is only so much space in a newspaper." Washington had become the ultimate goal of ambitious foreign correspondents, he mused, although it was "a much harder slog, less rewarding and a good deal less fun than the relatively carefree life of bumming around the Middle East and Africa." It had always been the job of the foreign correspondents to cull through the mountain of Washington news and reduce it to something meaningful and timely for home audiences. The veteran foreign correspondent Sir Willmott Lewis had described reporting from a nation other than one's own as looking at the reverse side of brocade, "all the threads are there but not the subtlety of color and designs." His successors at least have less need to function as quasi-diplomats or intelligence gatherers. They have enough trouble simply trying to explain Washington to baffled audiences around the world.[42]

6

Flash: The Wire Services

When the busload of reporters in the motorcade arrived at the Dallas Trade Mart, where President John F. Kennedy was due to deliver a luncheon address on November 22, 1963, the presidential party was nowhere in sight. Marianne Means of the Hearst Headline Service took advantage of the lull to call her bureau in Washington. "How's Kennedy?" the deskman immediately asked. He had just read a UPI dispatch that the president had been shot. Means shouted to the pack of reporters, who scrambled back on the bus and headed for the hospital. They were in Texas, covering the president, Means mused, "but we had less idea what had happened to him than those in Washington reading the wire services."[1]

The roundabout way that the reporters in Dallas learned of Kennedy's assassination showed what put the wire services at the core of Washington journalism. Out to "get the facts and move them fast," the wires were the first line of national media coverage. Wire reporters lived with constant deadlines. The pressures of the job encouraged speed over depth, yet the dispatches they filed often determined the way the rest of the press corps handled the same story. Other correspondents regularly asked wire reporters what they planned to make their lead, knowing that editors back home would question why their own versions deviated from what the wires reported. TV reporters would call their desk with a story angle only to be told, "Well, I haven't seen it on the wire yet. You can't go with it." Presidential press secretaries also paid close attention to the wire services, as Kennedy's press secretary, Pierre Salinger, explained, because "an unfavorable AP or UPI story can hurt you around the world."[2]

Many journalists considered experience as a wire service reporter the best preparation for any media reporting. Those who had mastered the quick story framing, short deadlines, and clear prose required by the wires could report anything under the most extreme conditions. The wire services had also literally defined objective reporting. During the Civil War, the Associated Press's first Washington correspondent, Lawrence Gobright, explained that because his stories went out to papers of all political leanings, he had to avoid opinion and include only "dry matters of fact and detail." By offering unadorned facts, the wire services paradoxically encouraged more interpretive reporting among the rest of the Washington correspondents. A century after Gobright, the communications director for Barry Goldwater's ill-fated 1964 presidential campaign commented, "The reporter for the *New York Times* or the *Chicago Tribune* dares not write the very same thing that AP and UPI does. He must be different. Enter 'interpretation.'"[3]

Founded as a news cooperative, the AP charged its member papers a fee to underwrite its reporting, and relied on them to supply most of its local news. An Associated Press franchise gave a paper a distinct advantage over its competitors in gathering national news. When Adolph Ochs bought the failing *New York Times* in 1896, its chief asset was an AP membership. Ochs depended almost entirely on AP reports until the *Times* could afford to field its own reporters. Protecting this advantage made AP members wary of admitting new papers into the cooperative. E. W. Scripps, whose chain of evening newspapers editorially sided with the labor movement, objected that his papers were denied AP franchises by the more business-oriented papers in the same cities. The people could never get "correct news" from an AP controlled by plutocrats, Scripps decided, and he set out to break the AP's monopoly. "I not only wanted to start a new paper if I chose," he declared, "but I wanted to make it possible for any other man to found a newspaper in any city in the Union." In 1907 Scripps created the United Press to provide news and features to afternoon newspapers, under the slogan "Today's News Today." To run the service, Scripps installed one of his star reporters, the energetic Roy Howard. (The chain eventually became Scripps-Howard.) Small in stature but forceful in bearing, Howard expanded the UP's services and put it into fierce competition with the AP. But Howard's obsession with scooping the rival news service led to a world-class blunder when the UP reported the Armistice ending the First World War in 1918 three days prematurely.[4]

William Randolph Hearst also bristled over the AP's exclusivity. While some of Hearst's papers held AP franchises, he failed repeatedly to get AP news for his flagship papers in New York and Chicago, so he created the International News Service. Originally intended only for his own papers, the INS later sold its features to those outside the chain on the assumption that other editors would appreciate the snappy features that had made Hearst's papers so successful. Reflecting the Hearst style, the INS mixed hard news with human interest, and was laced with outspoken columnists. A suspicion of unreliability clouded the INS's more attractive features, troubling prospective customers. Some publishers were also put off by a provision in the INS contract that permitted Hearst to cancel service to any paper within six months after he opened a competing paper in the same city. Hearst kept the struggling INS alive only by forcing his papers to buy its services, even if they also held AP franchises.[5]

The International News Service's resources never matched Hearst's aspirations, and its own director called it "one of the sickest cats that ever clung to the door-posts of metropolitan journalism." During the First World War, the

INS trailed so far behind the AP and UP in its battlefield coverage that INS editors in the United States clipped stories from foreign newspapers and re-printed them under phony bylines: John C. Foster in London, Brixton D. Allaire in Rome, and Franklin P. Merrick in Paris. *Harper's Weekly* exposed that cha-rade in 1915, much to Hearst's chagrin. Three years later, the news service suf-fered another blow when the Supreme Court ruled that the INS had pirated news from AP dispatches without attribution. Condescension from their col-leagues in the press spurred INS reporters to produce professional news re-porting and they took pride in single-handedly covering events to which half a dozen AP reporters had been assigned. The managers of the news service also realized that any overt attempts to impose Hearst's opinions in their dis-patches would alienate client papers outside the Hearst chain.[6]

The Associated Press, the largest of the news services, was under constant scrutiny from its member papers, and it pledged to provide comprehensive, nonpartisan news reports, swiftly and economically. Its mission was to tell the truth, said director Melville Stone—if not the whole truth, nothing but the truth. Stone noted that with member papers representing the political spectrum "from deep purple to infrared," AP reporters had to present the news straight, without speculation. Stone's successor, Kent Cooper, credited the Associated Press with "the finest moral concept developed in America and given the world. That is the concept that news must be truthful and unbiased."[7]

During the First World War, when European news services promoted their governments' positions, the AP resisted the U.S. State Department's efforts to turn it into a front to funnel money to editors in South America sympathetic to the Allied cause. In 1918 its Washington bureau manager boasted that the AP did not sit in judgment, nor did it "examine with the eye of criticism." It had no friends or enemies but simply aimed to report the facts. These lofty claims raised skeptical eyebrows among progressive reformers, who called the AP a "news trust" that colored the news to satisfy the businessmen who owned its member papers. The media critic Oswald Garrison Villard pointed out that the AP rarely took the lead in exposing government corruption, and that it generally accepted official statements at face value. Highlighting these accusa-tions was an incident in the 1920s when the State Department provided the wire service reporters with a not-for-attribution briefing that outlined Mexico's plot to seize Central America. The UP and the INS declined to publish the story because the State Department would not stand behind it, but the AP dutifully sent out the dispatch, which proved groundless. The AP's Washing-ton manager responded to critics that they had picked up the story "in the usual course of news" and had "no reason to doubt its accuracy."[8]

Technologically driven, the AP developed a reporting style that fit the re-quirements of telegraphy. Costs and limitations on how much copy could be transmitted per hour encouraged terseness. Differing needs and interests of member papers necessitated structuring stories so that a paper could use the entire text or just a few paragraphs to fit the available space. Consequently, wire reporters laid out the facts in their lead paragraph, with supporting material following in descending order of importance. Back when newspaper writers got paid by the word, they had learned to write verbosely. The cost of telegraph dispatches trained wire reporters to be concise. Telegraph tolls, leased wires, and telegraph operators were the greatest expenses of wire reporting until 1914, when the AP adopted "teletypewriters," or teletypes, electronic typesetters that could initially transmit sixty words a minute to the news bureaus of all its member papers. Operating over ordinary telegraph wires, teletypes used keyboards to write messages that were sent simultaneously to all member news bureaus, where teletype machines automatically printed them onto tape or rolls of paper, thereby eliminating the need for skilled telegraphers on either end.

The teletype's significant savings financed an employee benefit package of insurance, sick pay, and pensions, which in turn fostered staff loyalty. "An AP reporter was something like a letter carrier," scoffed the columnist (and one-time UP reporter) Westbrook Pegler. "If he didn't misbehave, he could stick around forever, and probably retire when he got old." Along with stability came stodginess. The AP resisted not only sensationalism but any form of human interest stories, which director Melville Stone dismissed as "tittle tattle," and banned the use of slang, even when covering sports. It took a while for the AP to stop referring to the New York American League Baseball Club and call the team the Yankees. Taking the opposite route, the UP and the INS adopted the punchy writing and lighter fare of the Scripps and Hearst papers. Their appealing features fit perfectly into the popular tabloids of the 1920s.[9]

Newspapers that subscribed to several wire services often pasted together stories by taking the facts from the AP and the colorful details from the UP or the INS. For many years, AP dispatches never carried a reporter's name, on the assumption that its news was so straightforward that anyone could have written it. A single AP dispatch, in fact, might be the product of several correspondents' writing, melded by rewrite editors and identified only as (AP). Because newspapers tended to run the first wire dispatch that came in on a breaking story, the AP emphasized speed and regarded stylish writing as a hindrance. The United Press and International News Service also stressed speed, but as they could better afford to offer praise than a raise they gave their reporters bylines and more freedom in developing their writing styles. The system tempted UP and the INS reporters "to strut our stuff and indulge in writing, instead of stating facts without embellishment or interpretation," Westbrook Pegler recalled. The AP could afford to throw so many reporters into a story "that they got in their own way," but the UP and the INS could compete only by compelling their thinner ranks to hustle. Wary of the competition, the AP hired the energetic Kent Cooper away from the UP to breathe new life into its stodgy operations. Entering the AP's New York City headquarters, Cooper decided that its Victorian furnishings resembled its reporting style. Both "reeked with old age." He imported many of the UP's practices, from bylines to interviews; created a sports department; and allowed the AP to mention Hollywood movie stars. But the AP's corporate mentality changed slowly. When Bess Furman interviewed for a job with AP's Washington bureau in 1928, she mentioned that the UP started some of its "feminine features" with a verse, and said that she could rhyme. Bureau chief Byron Price replied dryly that poetry was a talent the AP would never use.[10]

As the AP strained to enliven its style, the UP tried to improve its respectability. Moving away from the advocacy-oriented journalism of E. W. Scripps, the UP sought to strip opinion from its dispatches. As the wire services moved closer together in style, their intense competition entailed staggering costs, made worse by the Great Depression. The UP's Roy Howard complained about "the uselessness and waste of energy" in having all three news services chase the same stories. Howard approached William Randolph Hearst with a proposal to merge the UP and the INS into a single unit to better compete against the economically advantaged AP. Although the offer made sense financially, Hearst felt that Howard was questioning his competency to operate a news service. "The mother is always fondest of her sickest child," was how Hearst explained his rejection of the offer. With the depression continuing to drain revenues, the United Press made another bold gesture to the Associated Press by offering to stop all of its domestic reporting and concentrate on international news, if the AP would close all of its foreign bureaus. This assumed that all newspapers subscribed to both services, but because 80 percent of the AP's members did not take the UP, the offer went nowhere.[11]

In Washington, the three wires ran the largest, most all-encompassing news bureaus. Several smaller news services also operated out of the capital, among them the Federated Press (for labor papers), the Central News of America (for financial news), and the Associated Negro Press (for the black press). Each carried specialized news items that the wires either overlooked or underreported. Ubiquitous news service reporters gathered the bulk of Washington's routine news, from press releases, press conferences, public ceremonies, speeches, court rulings, and the latest federal regulations. Lower pay and irregular hours made these news service positions ideal for inexperienced reporters eager to break into the Washington press corps. Wire reporters might have had less status than the Washington correspondents, but they expressed great pride in their news product. They were jubilant whenever they beat a rival, by minutes or seconds. Burgeoning news of the federal government during the New Deal kept the wires well fed. In addition to blanket coverage of the government, in the 1930s the wires began charging extra fees to provide member papers with Washington stories tailored to their regional interests, about government decisions that directly affected their readers. The demand for specialized news grew so strong that in 1934 the Associated Press created a Washington Regional Service, dividing the nation into twenty-one regions, each with its own reporter, to generate regular supplies of Washington news. The arrangement multiplied the amount of wire service traffic, particularly from Capitol Hill.[12]

Byron Price headed the AP's Washington bureau throughout the New Deal years. An old hand who had worked his way up through the ranks reporting in Atlanta and New Orleans, Price wrote a weekly column, "Politics at Random," and supervised the largest news bureau in Washington. By the mid-1930s, the AP bureau employed sixty-eight reporters, editors, rewrite men, feature writers, and columnists. Price was the kind of manager willing to ignore the AP's myriad rules in order to get a big story, and he thrived on what he called the "nightly race for the front pages of America." Yet his Washington staff was by and large careful, cautious, and compliant. They covered stories in packs, often stationing as many reporters at an agency as the other news services combined. The AP promoted itself as "Caesar's wife," (a reference to Julius Caesar's insistence that his wife be "above reproach"), while the UP referred to it as "Grandma."[13]

The AP's Washington bureau occupied cramped quarters—noisy with the perpetual clatter of tickers and typewriters—in the *Evening Star* building on Pennsylvania Avenue. Byron Price wanted reporters to be out of the office on their beats, dictating their stories over the phone to typists at the bureau. Instead of assigning desks, he installed a shelf around the wall, with typewriters and chairs placed at intervals. A reporter would rush in and grab the nearest available typewriter. The arrangement left no space to keep files. Reporters were expected to research on their feet, mostly by interviewing. By contrast, the financially struggling United Press occupied swankier quarters in a new office building. During the boom years just before the depression, the UP had expanded its news service to include morning papers. As its first night manager in Washington, the UP appointed the veteran congressional and White House reporter Raymond Clapper, and gave him a budget to build a squad of reporters. His hires included such rising stars as Paul Mallon and Thomas L. Stokes, both of whom became syndicated columnists of distinction. Stokes started on the desk, with a small telephone switchboard where he took calls from reporters on direct lines from the White House, the Capitol, and the Supreme Court. Writing down whatever news reporters called in gave Stokes his education in the "names and places, the facts and geography of national politics." When the depression forced deep cutbacks in UP's staff, the wire service adopted a particularly ruthless policy of employing young reporters at the start of a congressional session and firing them as soon as Congress adjourned.[14]

As the UP's night manager, Ray Clapper continued to do his own reporting and published a hard-hitting series on nepotism, graft, and waste in the Hoover administration. In his off-hours, he expanded the series into a book, *Racketeering in Washington,* but by the time it appeared in print Franklin Roosevelt had replaced Herbert Hoover and the exposé had turned stale. Clapper got sixty-five dollars in royalties and a rebuke from UP's headquarters for writing on the side. Angry over the reprimand, and anguished over having to lay off correspondents with families, Clapper quit the UP to become national editor of the *Washington Post*. (Scripps-Howard later rehired him as a syndicated columnist.) He left the UP just as the New Deal was dramatically expanding the workload and the staff of the Washington bureau.[15]

The UP had a reputation for New Deal liberalism, showing more interest in labor and civil liberties, and friendlier toward Franklin Roosevelt, than the other wires. The INS headed in the opposite direction, following William Randolph Hearst's displeasure over Roosevelt's support for higher taxes and union organizing in the newspaper business. In its dispatches, the INS began substituting the term "raw deal" for New Deal. Some also suspected the impartial Associated Press of tilting against the New Deal. Left-leaning reporters found that there were stories that the AP would not touch, and described "feeling that if you told the story from the conservative slant you would never get into trouble, but if you gave the liberal slant you would." The young UP reporter Eric Sevareid attributed these complaints less to bias than to intense competition. The wires compiled weekly reports comparing their success in beating the opposition, and scoring how many papers had given their dispatches "top billing" in the headlines. Sevareid described the news services as "three competing merchants, each watching the other like a hawk and putting gaudier and gaudier displays in his window to attract passing customers."[16]

The Roosevelt administration entered the fray by challenging the AP's policy of denying membership to certain news organizations willing to pay for its services. "All the big national news-gathering organizations—like the Associated Press—should be declared public utilities," asserted Roosevelt's feisty interior secretary Harold Ickes, "and should be compelled to sell their services at a proper price to any responsible purchaser." In 1942 the Department of Justice filed an antitrust suit against the Associated Press, charging the cooperative with being a monopoly. For years the conservative publisher of the *Washington Times-Herald*, Cissy Patterson, had complained of being denied an AP franchise and had urged the Justice Department to file an antitrust suit. "You're not afraid of General Motors or the U.S. Steel," she taunted, "but you are afraid of the Associated Press." But it was not until Marshall Field launched the pro–New Deal *Chicago Sun* that the Justice Department stirred into action.

The anti–New Deal *Chicago Tribune* had vetoed sharing the AP's news with its upstart competitor. The *Sun* could purchase news from the UP and Reuters, but publisher Field asked the attorney general to look into whether the AP had operated in restraint of trade. The Justice Department cited the AP's own promotional materials—which stated that the AP spent more money on its operations and hired more personnel than any other news agency—in making a case that an AP franchise was essential in the highly competitive newspaper business. The AP countercharged that the next step would be for the government to regulate the wires like a public utility. A 1945 ruling by the Supreme Court ordered the AP to make its services accessible to any paper that could afford them. Much to the surprise of AP's management, "the earth did not tremble." Only three major newspapers applied for AP membership: Field's *Chicago Sun*, Patterson's *Washington Times-Herald*, and Hearst's *Detroit Times*. Unexpectedly, the court's ruling undermined the UP and the INS, which both lost customers that had previously been shut out of AP news.[17]

After the United States entered the Second World War, the federal government drafted Byron Price to direct wartime censorship. Paul Miller succeeded Price as the AP's Washington bureau chief. Miller came to the capital determined to change the AP's "old maidish and stilted and sissified" behavior. He prodded his reporters to "unbend," and exhorted them to write the way they talked. No matter how much the AP loosened its style, it retained faith in straight news. "There's no room in AP newswriting for your own opinions," said AP correspondent Walter Mears, "not even in copy labeled analysis."[18]

By 1950 the AP's Washington staff had increased to a hundred. The UP had seventy-five, and the INS trailed with thirty-seven. (By contrast, the *New York Times*'s bureau had a staff of twenty-four, and the *Chicago Tribune* had twelve.) Still, smaller papers often relied on one-man bureaus and specialized news services that could generate news-on-request more promptly than the wires. A *Denver Post* editor commented that it sometimes took the AP a week to respond to regional requests, while the paper's one-man Washington bureau could get the same story within twenty-four hours. Washington news took up a third of the ticker time each day, and the wire bureaus considered it a banner day whenever they could get out as many as thirty thousand words. Big breaking stories backed up everything else, and some lesser stories never got on the wires at all. The wire services vied for clients for whom a few minutes' head start or a jazzy lead decided what got into print or on the air. The UP warned reporters that the AP would knock them flat unless they scored a beat. The INS knew it could not compete with either rival in volume, but when a major story broke it would "gang up on the story" by sending the most prominent Hearst reporters and columnists to supplement the regular wire staff. "We just did it," is how one INS reporter, Al Spivak, described their uphill struggle. "We covered things sufficiently to satisfy our clients."[19]

The loss of client papers made it harder for the UP and the INS to handle the locally oriented coverage those papers had once provided. With expenses mounting, Scripps-Howard kept the United Press afloat on the returns from its United Features Syndicate, including the enormously profitable "Peanuts" comic strip. The INS had less of a financial base from which to draw than the other wires, especially after the death of its patron, William Randolph Hearst. Finally, in 1958, the INS merged into the UP to form United Press International. The antitrust division at the Justice Department raised no objection to this merger as it regarded the INS as a "failing corporation." The new UPI hardly represented an equitable amalgamation. Scripps-Howard held 95 percent of UPI stock, and all of UP's staff kept their jobs, while five hundred INS staffers were dismissed. On the day after the merger was announced, William Hutchinson, the brash, tough-talking, "lone-wolf reporter" who had headed the INS Washington bureau for twenty years, dropped dead of a heart attack.[20]

The combined UPI remained smaller than the Associated Press, but it boasted the most prominent wire service reporter in America, Albert Merriman Smith, known universally as Smitty. A Georgia native, Smitty had covered state politics before going to Washington in 1940—not long after Hollywood premiered *Mr. Smith Goes to Washington*. The UP soon posted him at the White House. Twenty years later, when John F. Kennedy toured the pressroom after his inauguration, he was still there. Kennedy introduced the reporter to his wife, saying, "This is Merriman Smith; he comes with the place."[21]

Belying wire service anonymity, Merriman Smith blossomed into a television celebrity. He added to his income with a string of best-selling books and popular magazine articles, and made regular appearances on *Meet the Press*, *Face the Nation*, *Reporter's Roundtable*, *Who Said That?* and the *Tonight Show*. *Cue* magazine described Smith as "literate, knowledgeable, well-spoken, amusing, and all other things TV guests should be." Those same qualities made him a star of the lecture circuit. Rumpled and intense, with a dour, pockmarked face, and a gruff voice, Smith could charm audiences with a repertoire of presidential anecdotes. The TV newsman David Brinkley noted that Smith filled his books with the type of humorous commentary that he could never put into his wire dispatches. Away from the lecture circuit, Merriman Smith embodied the on-the-spot, just-the-facts wire reporter who rushed out of press conferences clutching his notes, grabbed a phone and dictated one tightly-condensed story after another that went worldwide instantly. Smitty always knew where to find the nearest phone. He also loved gadgets that further enhanced his competitive edge. He was among the first Washington reporters to use a tape recorder, and once dictated a story from a tree using a walkie-talkie.[22]

When Merriman Smith joined the White House press as a green freshman, his United Press credentials gave him a spot in the front row with the senior men at FDR's crowded press conferences. The front-row regulars got to ask the most questions and spar most frequently with the quick-witted president. Smitty's irrepressible humor won Roosevelt's favor, although it did not spare him from occasional outbursts of presidential temper. When Roosevelt accused him of writing to curry favor with his bosses, Smitty parried that he would go back to Georgia on the day the United Press ordered him to slant a story. Before long, he became the senior wire service reporter, who by custom ended press conferences by saying "Thank you, Mr. President." He uttered that phrase for so many years that his colleagues thought he had originated the practice. Once he uttered those words, the doors burst open and the reporters bounded out in a full run to reach the phones in the pressroom. He had only seconds to organize his notes before dictating them, a process he described as a "nerve-wracking chore."[23]

Stationed full-time at the White House, Smitty spent his days in an eighteen-by-forty-foot pressroom, just off the lobby of the West Wing. The location seemed prestigious, but reporters compared covering the White House to covering police headquarters—for most of the day they just sat around waiting for something to happen. Shabby green leather couches and government-issued desks filled the room, along with a row of phone booths—one reserved for each wire service. The White House staff left the reporters alone in the pressroom, creating what Smith called a casual oasis in a desert of formality. From the pressroom, reporters kept an eye on the lobby and nabbed visitors leaving the Oval Office for interviews. The Secret Service prevented them from wandering too far beyond that. Reporters spent their days reading the papers, playing cards, and telling tales, which Smitty embroidered with each retelling. At lunchtime, the White House placed a "lid" on the news so that reporters could go out to eat, although wire reporters had to be prepared for the lid to pop open at any time, day or night, summoning them back like doctors making emergency calls.[24]

Merriman Smith was home with his family on Sunday, December 7, 1941, when his wife rushed to tell him of radio reports that the Japanese had bombed Hawaii. He nearly knocked her down getting to the phone. On his way to the White House, he flagged a motorcycle policeman for an escort through traffic. That afternoon the pressroom filled with the faces of unfamiliar reporters drawn by the big story. The AP, UP, and INS men had to post signs on their phone booths to keep the interlopers away. Wartime security gave President Roosevelt an excuse to withdraw from view and keep reporters at a distance. When he ordered them off his train on his travels, the press corps protested vehemently. Roosevelt reversed course and agreed to let representatives of the three wire services accompany him, so long as they held back their reports until each trip was over. Smitty stuck close to the president for the duration of the war, unable to tell either his bureau chief or his wife where he was going or for how long. So many of the trips turned out to be to Roosevelt's home in Hyde Park, New York, or his retreat at Warm Springs, Georgia, that the UP bureau chief Lyle Wilson accused Smith of making a career out of "going on another man's vacations." President Roosevelt likened the omnipresent wire reporters to "vultures waiting for something to happen to me." The UP reporter logged more than 125,000 miles with the president, a pace that left him "tired, wet, hungry, sick or completely exhausted," and kept him away from home for so long that he began referring to his wife as "the Widow Smith."[25]

The White House had agreed to the wire service pool in part to counter recurring rumors about Roosevelt's health. Traveling so constantly with Roosevelt, Merriman Smith witnessed the president's gradual physical decline, about which he kept his UP chiefs apprised, but not his readers. In the spring of 1945 he accompanied Roosevelt to Warm Springs, following the president's return from Yalta. The wire reporters were advised that Roosevelt intended to rest and that they should not expect any news. Smitty was out horseback riding on the afternoon when he last saw Franklin Roosevelt. As the president's car sped by, he heard a familiar voice boom out: "Heigh-O, Silver!" Two days later, as Smitty planned a barbecue for the presidential party, the assistant press secretary William Hassett unexpectedly summoned the three wire reporters to his cottage. They had no idea what the news might be, but Smith instinctively positioned himself next to the phone. Before Hassett had finished his announcement, the UP man was already dictating a flash to an editor in Washington: "Roosevelt died at 3:35, Warm Springs, this is Smith." He beat the AP and the INS men in Warm Springs, but had already been scooped from Washington, where Press Secretary Steve Early had made the same announcement at the White House.[26]

After an emotionally draining journey back to Washington on the funeral train, a haggard Merriman Smith turned coverage of the story over to the contingent of UP reporters waiting at Union Station. His wife begged him not to follow the funeral to Hyde Park. "I'm sorry," he said, "but I just came home for a nap." Phone calls from the United Press kept waking him, so he tried to "soak away some of the fatigue in the bathtub." After Roosevelt's funeral, he finally broke into tears from exhaustion and grief. Throughout the war he had offered to switch to combat reporting, but the UP defined the White House as "an important war front in itself." Now with a new president coming in, Smitty was ready to go. As Harry Truman left his apartment on his first morning as president, he spotted his poker-playing friend Tony Vaccaro, the AP's Senate reporter, standing out front on the sidewalk. "What are you doing here, Tony?" Truman greeted, and then gestured, "Get in the car." The sight of Truman arriving at the White House accompanied by an AP man signaled to Merriman Smith that it was time for him to leave. Once Vaccaro transferred to the White House, Smith had visions of being regularly outperformed. But his bureau chief ordered him back on the job and told him to "start learning to know the new boss." Fortunately, Truman did not play favorites among the press, but he dismayed them by taking early morning walks, for which Smitty had to get up a lot earlier than he liked. (He dubbed the excursions the "Independence Early Rising and Walking Society.")[27]

When Alice Dunnigan became the first African American woman to attend President Truman's press conferences, she was herded through the doorway to the Oval Office with other reporters, who elbowed their way to get nearest the president's desk. After half an hour of questions and answers, a "dapper, black-haired reporter" ended the proceedings with a brisk, "Thank you, Mr. President." She then watched in astonishment as Merriman Smith "dashed from the room practically running over everybody, sprinting through the lobby like a professional track star and into the pressroom on the opposite side where he immediately closed himself tightly into a tiny telephone booth." His exits were not always that graceful. On the day that Truman announced the end of the war in Europe, in May 1945, Smitty tore out of the Oval Office, tripped over a photographer's ladder, fell, scrambled to his feet, called in his story, and was rushed to the hospital with a badly dislocated shoulder.[28]

President Truman's penchant for talking at breakneck speed at press conferences made the wire reporters worry about misquotations and misinterpretations. Shorthand skills would not have helped, as they needed to condense stories while they took notes. But the reporters appreciated Truman's blunt style. Smith considered him the last president to engage in "truly head-to-head exchanges," and to actually originate news at his press conferences. Truman's staff went out of their way to accommodate the wire reporters. When a pressroom newcomer, Robert Donovan, took the front seat in the press car in one of Truman's motorcades, Smitty threw a fit and demanded that seat (by the car phone) as his absolute right of seniority. Donovan moved only after being politely prodded by a Secret Service agent. Merriman Smith had established such prominence within the Truman entourage that it raised eyebrows when he left to cover Governor Thomas E. Dewey's presidential campaign in 1948. (The UP wanted to give its White House correspondent some advance contact with the anticipated Dewey administration.) The Associated Press reporter Jack Bell whispered to Dewey's press secretary, James Hagerty, that Smith was a Roosevelt-Truman Democrat who would surely try to make the Republican candidate look bad. "Bell tried to cut me out every way he could," Smitty groused. Dewey lost in an upset, however, sending Bell back to cover Congress, and Smitty back to the Truman White House.[29]

After Truman retired from the presidency, Smitty picked up a rumor that the former president had fallen and injured his ribs, possibly while inebriated. The UP's bureau in Kansas City checked out the story, and the local reporter, Roy McGhee, reported back that Truman assured him there was nothing wrong with him. Smith indignantly replied that his source had been impeccable. McGhee again saw Truman, who again denied having fallen. The UP headquarters in New York advised McGhee that Merriman Smith complained that the Kansas City bureau had not properly followed up his request corroboration. McGhee returned for a third visit, and this time the former president stripped off his shirt and stood bare-chested to show that he had no bruises or bandages. The Kansas City bureau notified headquarters that Smith could print the story from his own sources, but they were "not verifying a damn word of this." Smitty finally dropped the story, concluding that it was not "cricket to ask even an ex-President to submit to that sort of disrobing cross-examination."[30]

Close identification with two Democratic presidents made Smith suspect to the incoming Republican administration in 1953. Dwight Eisenhower's press secretary, James Hagerty (inherited from the Dewey campaign), urged the UP to appoint someone else to the White House, but he backed down when the UP replied that no one told it whom to post on a beat. In deference to their mass audience and neutrality, Hagerty called Smith and the other wire reporters "the grand sachems" of the tribe of White House reporters, and treated them accordingly. "We were all buddies of his," recalled the INS's Robert Clark. Hagerty's assistance was essential for the reporters, given Eisenhower's intention of running a leak-free administration. After the comparably open Roosevelt and Truman administrations, Eisenhower's West Wing clamped down tightly. All interviews had to be arranged through Hagerty. Chief of Staff Sherman Adams even tried to convince congressional leaders not to talk to the press about their conversations with the president. Telling a member of Congress to remain quiet, snorted Merriman Smith, was like "trying to dam the Niagara with Kleenex." The gregarious Smith developed such a close friendship with Eisenhower's secretary, Ann Whitman, that the other wire reporters feared that if anything happened to Eisenhower, Whitman would tell him first.[31]

Eisenhower stayed aloof from the press corps and held his blood pressure down by reading few newspapers. Contrary to his warm public image, Ike treated reporters coolly. He regarded them as second lieutenants with whom a general did not fraternize. Before his election, Eisenhower had golfed with a few reporters, but those invitations ceased after his inauguration. All that meant, said Smitty, was that White House reporters played "stinking golf." Personally, he preferred Eisenhower's formality to the backslapping insincerity of so many headline-hungry politicians. Yet even Ike paid deference to Merriman Smith. He was the only member of the regular press corps whom the president regularly addressed by his first name, although he mangled it as "Mariam." Aside from his straight news reporting, Smitty also wrote a twice-a-week column for UP, "Backstairs at the White House." Usually light-hearted and inconsequential, these columns occasionally nettled Eisenhower by revealing such personal matters as the president's attempts to rid squirrels from the White House putting green. Eisenhower regarded most Washington journalists as "far from being as important as they themselves consider," but he held the wire reporters in high esteem for their fairness, accuracy, and objectivity.[32]

Despite James Hagerty's favoritism toward the wire reporters, he stunned them by opening Eisenhower's press conferences to television. Hagerty wanted the president to use the medium to speak directly to the people rather than through the liberal-leaning press corps. He believed that television appearances would make for "straighter and better reporting," as reporters could not slant their coverage of the president's position if their readers had already heard it for themselves. But it was not until the fall of 1954 that the television industry developed film fast enough to lower the lighting to tolerable levels for press conference coverage. Hagerty gave his approval for the networks to film the press conferences for later broadcasting—giving the White House an opportunity to delete any remarks it considered inappropriate for release. Hagerty hid the decision from other reporters until the last minute. Not until the print reporters noticed more television broadcasters than usual at his daily briefing on January 18, 1955, did he admit that he was allowing cameras into the next day's press conference. Merriman Smith asked what brand of beer would sponsor it. The wire service reporters complained so loudly that Hagerty reminded the television reporters that their networks were some of the wire services' biggest customers. "Why don't you let the wire services know?" That afternoon, Smitty returned waving the white flag. "Boy, you know how to hurt a guy, don't you?" he said. "In New York our main office has heard from ABC, NBC and CBS." He apologized and promised to shut up.[33]

In 1957, when CBS's television reporter Robert Pierpoint, a veteran foreign correspondent still in his thirties, rode in his first presidential motorcade, he sat on a jump seat opposite a groggy, hung-over Merriman Smith. "Why did CBS think a punk like you could cover the White House?" Smitty demanded. By the late fifties, the UP correspondent was drinking more heavily than usual. Neil MacNeil, a former UP reporter turned *Time* correspondent, remembered a harrowing drive from Gettysburg back to Washington with Smitty at the wheel finishing off a bottle of gin. One night at the Press Club bar, Smitty made an expansive gesture with his arms and struck the right-wing senator George "Molly" Malone, who happened to be passing by. After an investigation of the incident, the club exonerated the reporter of deliberately hitting the senator. For a time after his drinking increased, Smitty retained his reputation as an outstanding journalist, who avoided argumentative questions and kept probing for facts. By 1958, however, mounting reports of Smith's excessive drinking persuaded the United Press to pull him out of the White House and demote him to the Commerce Department beat, until he agreed to undergo rehabilitation. Smitty responded by tearing into the Commerce Department with a barrage of reports. Seven months later—after he had dried out—he regained his White House assignment. By then he was correspondent for the newly created United Press International, and he also gained a back-up reporter, Al Spivak, formerly of the INS.[34]

After the 1960 elections, a third colleague assigned herself to UPI's cramped cubicle in the White House pressroom. Helen Thomas covered Jacqueline Kennedy throughout the campaign and stayed around afterward to handle the "Jackie watch." Smitty resented her for the intrusion, but Al Spivak knew that covering the Kennedys would be an around-the-clock assignment and they needed all the help they could get. For the next three years, Mrs. Kennedy could not go anywhere without Thomas and her AP counterpart, Fran Lewine, trailing close behind. The women interviewed her hairdresser, the salespeople in stores where she shopped, and her children's diaper service. They were standing on the steps when she arrived at church. At night they interviewed her guests at social events, making the first lady wonder if they had any homes of their own. Despite Merriman Smith's crusty resistance to women reporters as a class, he begrudgingly admired Thomas's spunk and enterprise.[35]

Just four years older than the new young president, Merriman Smith was the dean of the White House press corps and a relic of the past. By the Kennedy era the wires had lost their primacy to television, and the president sealed that fate by permitting live television coverage of his news conferences. All the networks covered Kennedy's first press conference, at 6 p.m. on January 25, 1961, after which Smitty bolted instinctively for the phones before realizing that the nation had seen it, too. UPI's Washington bureau chief, Julius Frandsen, devised a more efficient way to cover press conferences. He positioned a television at the end of a long table in his office and summoned a group of reporters to watch. As each question was asked, Frandsen would point to a reporter who would take notes and then step into the newsroom to file the story. The AP waited for its reporter to emerge from the press conference and dictate his stories. UPI's strategy gave it the advantage until the AP figured out what was going on and copied it. UPI still needed reporting of the quality Smitty could produce, but the urgency on which he had thrived diminished.[36]

Ultimately, John Kennedy gave Merriman Smith his crowning moment as a wire reporter. On November 22, 1963, Smitty occupied his regular front seat in the pool car behind the presidential limousine as it slowly motored through Dallas. Jack Bell of the Associated Press sat behind him. As they entered Dealey Plaza, they heard three loud cracks that Bell mistook for cherry bombs, set off in celebration of the president's visit. Smitty, an avid gun collector, instantly identified the sound as gunfire. He grabbed the mobile radio-phone and called UPI's Dallas bureau. Before the president's limousine had reached the hospital, UPI had sent the first bulletin: "Three shots were fired at President Kennedy's motorcade in downtown Dallas." Teletypes alerted news bureaus around the world. "In those days, they had teletypes, and you'd hear *clack-clack-clack-clack-clack.* And when there was major news, it would go *ding-ding-ding*," recalled Mike Mosettig, who was just starting as a reporter in a small Washington bureau. "This time it was like *thump, thump, clang, clang,* loud enough that we could hear it all the way in the next office." The noise level of the machines increased with the urgency of the news in order to attract attention. Reporters called to a copyboy standing by the machine, who said that Kennedy had been shot. "Come on, stop joking around," they shouted. "And then he read us the bulletin. It was from Merriman Smith of UPI, that first bulletin." Meanwhile, the AP remained silent about the shooting, because Smitty still held the phone, despite Jack Bell's furious pounding on his back. By the time Bell wrestled away the phone, it had gone dead. Not until they reached the hospital could he call in a report. Smitty beat him again with a flash that went out nine minutes after the shooting: "Kennedy seriously wounded, perhaps fatally, by assassin's bullet." Walter Cronkite, a veteran of the United Press, immediately read Smith's reports on CBS. NBC hesitated while awaiting confirmation from the AP.[37]

Not being a regular White House reporter, Jack Bell went to the AP's Dallas bureau to write his story, while Smitty instinctively stayed with the press pool that followed the presidential entourage. In a crowded cabin on board Air Force One, he witnessed Lyndon Johnson take the oath as president. As the plane's door shut, he spotted an AP man running frantically toward them, too late to catch the plane. During the flight back to Washington, Smitty wrote a vivid account of the day's events, in which he coined the phrase "grassy knoll" that later became synonymous with assassination conspiracy theories. (Conspiracy theorists blamed Smith's instantaneous reporting for fixing in the collective memory such disputable facts as the number of shots fired.) At Andrews Air Force Base, he thrust his fistful of copy at Helen Thomas, who held an open telephone line. While she dictated his copy to the bureau, Smitty stayed with the presidential party. Later that night at UPI's offices at the National Press Building, he pulled up his shirt to reveal red welts where his rival had pounded on his back. The next day, Merriman Smith's byline dominated the front pages and UPI reprinted his story in its best-selling book *Four Days*. UPI rarely submitted entries for the Pulitzer Prize, believing that the judges were biased toward the AP, but Smitty's reporting on the Kennedy assassination won him the Pulitzer and an invitation to join the Gridiron Club, which had admitted the AP's Jack Bell a decade earlier.[38]

While basking in the spotlight, Smith found it grueling to report on Lyndon Johnson. "You help me and I'll help you," Johnson had promised. "I'll make you a big man in your profession." LBJ regularly invited the UP and AP correspondents for lunch and would continue talking while he undressed to take a nap. The wire reporters had to wait to slip out after the president had drifted off to sleep. Smitty regarded Johnson as "the most intriguing, frightening, contradictory and complicated" president whom he had ever covered. He lived in fear that some UPI story from elsewhere would rile the president and squeeze him out of Johnson's circle. Yet Smitty reported what he learned, regardless of whether it annoyed the president. A White House press aide once protested one of his dispatches, but the reporter stood by his anonymous source. "It looks as though somebody has filled Smitty in very well," the press aide concluded. "We do not know who it is, but Smitty is not the type of correspondent who writes this type of story without hard facts and a good source."[39]

Merriman Smith had stayed too long in his high-pressured post. When CBS sent Harry Reasoner to cover the White House in 1965, he observed that pressroom veterans had let the years go by until they were old fellows guarding their favorite chairs in the lounge and reminiscing "about the days when a press conference was Franklin Roosevelt calling a dozen people in for a friendly chat." The UPI correspondent best fit that description. At the same time he endured some painful episodes in his private life. His son, Albert Merriman Smith Jr., died in a helicopter crash in Vietnam in 1966. Smitty was in the midst of divorcing his wife of thirty years to marry the architect Gailey Johnson.

The birth of a daughter followed, and with two children by his first marriage in college, his expenses spiraled. "Hell, I don't have anything like the troubles you have," Lyndon Johnson once rebuked him, "—you lost your boy in Vietnam when you were going through a divorce from your first wife, behind in your taxes, poor-mouthing me on the Merv Griffin Show to make money for big tuition bills—I've got it a lot better than you have." Yet before Johnson left office, he awarded Smith the Presidential Medal of Freedom.[40]

The citation on that award celebrated the UPI correspondent's ability to retain his objectivity in a time of turmoil. While the civil rights and antiwar movements raised a conundrum about journalists' moral responsibility to take sides, Smitty clung to straight reporting. Despite losing a son in the Vietnam War, he could never bring himself to question the government's foreign policies. He told college audiences that Americans had to keep fighting in Asia because they had made a commitment to stop the spread of communism, and that anything less would mean a retreat into isolationism. He worried that the combined elements of dissent—black power, student power, and flower power—would trigger a backlash that would push the American middle class into the arms of the "repressive right." Johnson's "credibility gap" also troubled him. "The trouble starts when we refuse to accept as gospel some of the rubbish a government spews out in the name of news," he commented bitterly.[41]

Following the 1968 election, Smitty collapsed in Florida while covering the president-elect Richard Nixon. The doctor who treated him said that he had never seen anyone so fatigued. The job of a White House wire reporter "was simply not the kind of life in which a man took good care of himself," his son Timothy commented. Alcoholism sent Smitty in and out of rehabilitation. His personal expenses mounted, the Internal Revenue Service dogged him for back taxes, and he concocted all sorts of money-raising schemes such as dog breeding. Helen Thomas had witnessed many of her colleague's "down" moments. She got a call from him on the night of April 12, 1970, and "never heard him sound so low." The day marked the twenty-fifth anniversary of Franklin Roosevelt's death, and newspaper accounts of a reunion of Roosevelt's associates at Warm Springs did not help Smitty's depression. The next day he called in sick and stayed home to work on the script for the upcoming White House Correspondents Association dinner. That afternoon, he settled into the bathtub where he so often went to "soak away some of the fatigue" and shot himself. President Nixon had the flag over the White House lowered to half-staff and granted special permission for Merriman Smith to be buried beside his son at Arlington. His small marble tombstone stands in close proximity to the president whose assassination he covered so masterfully.[42]

The White House might have been the most prestigious beat, but Congress generated the largest amount of the wire services' Washington news, and employed far more wire reporters, such as Smitty's rival, Jack Bell. Whereas the UPI correspondent had stood almost as a lone sentry at the White House, Bell, as the AP's chief congressional correspondent, led an army of wire reporters who blanketed Capitol Hill. Having started as a reporter in Oklahoma, Bell came to Congress for the AP in 1937. "Way back there in the thirties," he later wrote, "you could cover the United States Senate with a half dozen members as your sources." He could go around to see a key Democratic senator, have a Scotch with him to get the administration's viewpoint, and then visit the Republican leader to get the other side. Between the two he could put together a balanced story. Bell found drama in the "everyday business of Congress." He insisted that good reporters needed to know a little bit about everything going on in the world as it was bound to come up sometime in the legislative halls. A morose man with an air of general dissatisfaction, Bell was regarded as the "commanding figure" in the press gallery. Other reporters commented that he looked and acted more like a senator than did some of the senators. Once when a Secret Service agent stopped Bell from leaving the Capitol until a dignitary had entered, the reporter demanded loudly, "Who in the hell are we waiting on?" When Vice President Nixon walked through the door, Bell muttered a curse that made it clear that he thought Nixon should have stepped aside for him.[43]

At the Capitol, the wires churned out "railroad timetable reporting," detailing where a bill was currently and what its next stop would likely be. When the legislation passed, wire reporters would call around for reactions from government officials and private interest groups. Squads of wire reporters "watched every rat hole," standing outside of closed committee rooms waiting for news to seep out. Each reporter would call back parts of the story, and writers at the bureau would mold them into a single story, known as the "big wrap." As a consequence, the non-wire correspondents could usually avoid hanging around the corridors, as they could read the wire reports before they filed their own stories. When these other reporters interviewed members of Congress, their editors would sometimes throw out much of what they had reported and run a wire service version of the story instead. (Their congressional sources would then be furious over having spent so much time talking about an issue and having gotten so little of what they said into the paper.) If a Washington correspondent's dispatch differed too much from what appeared on the wires, editors would invariably go with the wire report, a practice the correspondents called the "wire service syndrome." What appeared on the teletypes determined what would make the evening news programs and the next morning's front pages. This left the clear message: "If it isn't on the wire, it isn't news."[44]

The odd fact about the wire services, commented Larry Speakes, a press secretary on Capitol Hill and at the White House, was that they had "almost no influence in Washington," because they were looked on as practically "handout organizations" that accepted politicians' press releases at face value. The wires could not be ignored, however, because of their influence outside of Washington. Smaller papers across the country depended almost exclusively on the wires for their national and international news, as opposed to the major metropolitan papers that disdained running any AP bylines or UPI bylines on their front pages. Discerning this pattern, the White House sometimes released bad news directly to the wires to keep the *Washington Post* and *New York Times* from giving it front-page play. Members of Congress also appreciated the wires' links to their hometown papers. Anxious press secretaries (many of them former journalists) went to great lengths to ensure that the wires covered their bosses. They hand-carried fact sheets to the press galleries, provided summaries of bills, and wrote press releases that read like stories. Wire reporters in Washington regarded most of these offerings as "non-news," however, and paid little attention to it. Congressional offices often had better luck sending releases with a local angle directly to the wire bureaus in their home states.[45]

Regional reporting formed the backbone of the wire services' congressional coverage. Editors from member papers began to take it for granted that the wire reporters in Washington could get them anything from the census reports, to crop rotation data, to whether the town would get federal funding for a new sewer disposal plant. Regional reporting vastly expanded the volume of Washington news and provided the bulk of entry-level reporting jobs. Columnists such as William S. White and Robert Novak got started in Washington as regional reporters. White came to Washington to cover the Texas delegation for the AP, found the job a grind, and regarded it as "parole" when he was promoted to feature writer. Robert Novak began as a Midwestern regional reporter for the AP. To Novak's surprise, nearly all members of Congress "readily responded to telephone calls from a low-level AP reporter without an aide asking what he wanted." Novak parlayed his experience as a regional reporter into a job as a national news correspondent, covering the Senate for the *Wall Street Journal,* until he and Rowland Evans launched their long-running "Evans and Novak" column.[46]

After its merger, the United Press International established its own regional reporting service. Roy McGhee transferred to Washington to report on nine states in the southwestern congressional delegation, including Texas, which was represented by House Speaker Sam Rayburn and Senate Majority Leader Lyndon Johnson. McGhee's AP counterpart, L. T. "Tex" Easley Jr., covered only Texas, where he focused mostly on oil. "That's all he covered!" McGhee exclaimed. "Well, I covered everything." McGhee's advantage came from developing a wider range of sources. "I was never a lazy reporter, and frequently the AP guys were," said McGhee. "It was just the nature of our business to keep up and we had to work twice as hard as they did." Poker and drinking buddies, Easley and McGhee would do each other in on a story without hesitation. After getting a tip about an upcoming development in the deregulation of natural gas, McGhee prepared himself enough in advance that he could call in his bulletin while Easley was still reading the press release. "I got on the phone and I dictated that thing and I had it down cold," McGhee remembered, savoring the moment. "Front page in the *New York Times* the next morning—beat him, he didn't even get in the papers!" Regional reporters operated almost entirely out of the congressional press galleries. The UPI's Washington bureau provided no space at all for regional reporters. "They didn't want you there," McGhee noted. "They wanted you out getting the news."[47]

UPI boasted that its veteran House reporter, Frank Eleazer, "could out-write and out-report" his AP counterpart, William Arbogast. But Arbogast had the advantage of being a favorite of both Speaker Sam Rayburn and House Rules Committee chairman Howard Smith. Each day, the AP reporter drove Smith from their neighborhood in Virginia to the Capitol. "To some of us in the House press gallery—especially the younger reporters—the commuting arrangement was a matter of envy," recalled David Broder, then beginning his long career as a Washington correspondent. By the time Arbogast got to work, "he had a remarkably good idea of what the House would and would not do that day or that week." Broder called this symbolic of a "cozy, cliquish environment." Lou Cannon, who also did regional reporting before joining the national staff of the *Washington Post,* described such relationships as "based on mutual need and sometimes mutual laziness." The regional reporters' efforts to get the "local angle" publicized members who would otherwise have been overlooked by the national media. Members kept their doors open to the regional reporters, and provided timely tips. Occasionally, some member grew piqued over less than favorable coverage and barred the offending regional reporter from the office, but such embargoes burdened both sides, causing one or the other to back down. Doors would reopen, and the grateful reporter would reward the member with a glowing profile.[48]

By the 1960s, with some two-thirds of the AP and UPI wire reporters on Capitol Hill doing "local area news," the wire services began to reevaluate their regional reporting as overloaded with "self-serving stories on statements and handouts." The wires shifted reporters off of specific beats and had them follow a particular subject matter wherever it led. They sent out special teams to cover the civil rights movement, the antiwar movement, and the counterculture, and set up their first teams of investigative reporters. Among the AP's first investigative reporters was Seymour Hersh, who submitted a seven-part series on U.S. development of chemical and biological weapons that was hotter than anything the Associated Press had expected to handle. When cautious editors killed the series, Hersh quit the AP to freelance. Soon after, he won a Pulitzer Prize for exposing the My Lai massacre. UPI seemed equally leery of investigative dispatches. As a UPI reporter in Connecticut, the young Brit Hume wrote a three-part story on scandals surrounding Senator Thomas Dodd that his wire service killed. Hume then went to work for the columnist Jack Anderson, whose reporting led to Dodd's censure by the Senate. Still, the wire service's new system promoted greater expertise and depth of coverage, and allowed them to trim their staffs during the economic slump in 1970s. Regional reporting dwindled until it was folded into the general reporting staffs. Congressional coverage shrank accordingly, although the wires regularly produced more congressional news than the newspapers carried.[49]

Competition with the AP eventually pushed UPI into financial collapse. With expenses rising and income falling, UPI could not match the AP in worldwide outlets, technology, or reputation. Television absorbed much of the available advertising revenue and killed off the afternoon newspapers that had been UPI's stronghold. The surviving papers often had little competition in their markets and therefore worried less about being scooped. Newspapers were absorbed into chains that had their own news services. The *Los Angeles Times*, *Washington Post*, *New York Times*, and *Chicago Tribune* launched competing news services that offered greater in-depth reporting. Newspapers dropped UPI while keeping the AP, using the savings to purchase supplemental news services from the major metropolitan newspapers. Unable to pay competitive salaries, UPI suffered increased staff turnover that further diluted its reporting. UPI had an especially hard time keeping reporters on such critical beats as the Pentagon for any extended period.[50]

Scripps-Howard was anxious to unload UPI, but potential buyers, such as the British-based Reuters news agency, backed away. One suggestion had Scripps-Howard donating UPI to National Public Radio for a tax write-off. Instead, Scripps-Howard sold UPI in 1982 to a group associated with the Baha'i religious sect, which had no previous experience running a news service. The new owners hired CBS's former Washington bureau chief Bill Small as UPI's president, but his broadcasting background failed to translate to the wires. UPI stumbled from one unprofitable decision into another until it filed for bankruptcy. Over the next decade ownership passed to a Mexican publisher, a venture capitalist who was later convicted of bank fraud, and the brother-in-law of King Fahd of Saudi Arabia. During the 1990s, UPI's rolls shrank to a handful of employees and stringers who operated "virtual bureaus" that consisted of little more than computers in their home offices. UPI's largest staff worked out of its Washington bureau and mostly served foreign clients.[51]

One of the last UPI correspondents who still did original reporting was Helen Thomas, Merriman Smith's successor at the White House. She had been stationed there since 1961, and had become chief correspondent after Smith's death. She married the chief AP correspondent at the White House, Douglas Cornell, upon his retirement, when they were no longer rivals. Thomas broke gender barriers by becoming president of both the National Press Club and the Gridiron Club. Just before her fortieth anniversary at the White House, and her eightieth birthday, the news affiliate of the Reverend Sun Myung Moon's Unification Church, News World Communications, purchased the United Press International. Owned and subsidized by the conservative *Washington Times*, which was also the property of the Unification Church, News World Communications used what was left of UPI as an Internet service, designed in large part to distribute stories and features from the Washington paper outside the area. Finding the new employer's politics intolerable, Helen Thomas resigned from UPI, marking the end of an era.[52]

The collapse of UPI did not leave AP standing alone. In the 1990s the British news service Reuters expanded its American presence aggressively, and saw its best opportunity to do that on the Internet. Where the AP tried at first to limit its online services to member news organizations, Reuters provided news for hundreds of web sites, which provided the majority of its American revenues. That prompted AP to sell its news more openly on the Internet. The wire service went wireless, abandoning the old teletypes for digital electronic systems with greater speed and capacity for transmitting copy. With its war with radio long forgotten, the AP operated a radio news service, provided satellite transmission of news, and introduced a global television news service. AP reporters now carried cell phones and no longer raced for telephone booths; they sent text and photographs via computers. The AP closed the twentieth century with a staff of 3,500, and reached nearly every U.S. daily newspaper, along with thousands of radio and television clients. Its Washington bureau housed 160 reporters, editors, photographers, and other support staff. New competition continued to emerge from such specialized news organizations as Bloomberg News, a financial news service, and from the Internet. The AP's own web site paled beside more creative news outlets, largely because member papers did not want readers turning to the AP instead of to their own sites. Yet, most Internet news sites' desperate need for a steady supply of breaking news caused them to fill the screen with wire service dispatches. The old-fashioned wires came to dominate the content of digital news, turning personal computers into a new generation of teletypes—even as the original machines went on display as curiosities at the Smithsonian.[53]

7

The Business of Being Opinionated

Farthest from the neutral, fact-driven, straight-news wire services stand the syndicated columnists. *Time* dubbed them "pundits," from the Sanskrit word for "wise men." William Safire refined the definition to "an expert on nothing but an authority on everything." As news pages attempted to bury their partisanship, the columnists emerged as an elite within the profession, journalists licensed to express their own minds. From their prominent perches on the op-ed pages an assortment of Washington-based hawks, owls, eagles, and other harriers of power have exercised ample influence over policymaking, public opinion, and the rest of the press corps.[1]

By the time Lyndon B. Johnson came to the presidency in 1963, the top Washington columnists—Walter Lippmann, Joseph Alsop, Drew Pearson, David Lawrence, and Arthur Krock—had each been writing syndicated columns for thirty years. Politicians came and went, but the columnists remained in place, seemingly as fixed as the city's marble monuments. They made America's mind up for it, wrote the Washington correspondent and novelist Allen Drury, not meaning it as a compliment. Drury complained that idealistic young reporters came to Washington determined to tell the country the truth, but "almost without their knowing it they soon began to write, not for the country, but for each other," taking their cues from the eminent columnists.[2]

Lyndon Johnson considered himself the ultimate victim of the columnists' syndicated opinions. As president he took to heart some advice he received from the shrewd Washington operative James Rowe. Reporters might be "worse than a wolf pack when it comes to attacking public officials," Rowe counseled, but within their own profession they acted more like "a bunch of sheep" who always followed "the bellwether sheep"—the columnists. So long as columnists such as Walter Lippmann and James Reston supported Johnson, he would get good press. "You certainly have Lippmann and Reston in your pocket now," Rowe observed. "I hope you do not lose them."[3]

The columnists' clout had evolved over time. Nineteenth-century newspapers often ran columns of news, gossip, and political prognosis on their editorial pages under the headline "From Our Washington Correspondent." In 1921 the *New York World* swept the flotsam of book reviews, obituaries, and advertisements off the page opposite its editorials to make room for a broad range of specifically designated columns of opinion, and dubbed it the "Op-Ed Page." Convinced that "nothing is more interesting than opinion when opinion is interesting," the *World*'s editor, Herbert Bayard Swope, recruited a stable of regular columnists, including the sports reporters Heywood Broun and Ring Lardner and the theater critic Alexander Woolcott. They opined on politics and society as freely as they had second-guessed coaches and playwrights. Among the first generation of columnists, Clinton W. Gilbert struck it rich in 1921 by turning his "Man at the Keyhole" columns into a best-selling book, *The Mirrors of Washington.* Its inside stories from Washington inspired many imitators. The muckraking magazine writer Mark Sullivan started a syndicated Washington column for the *New York Tribune* in 1923, the same year that the *Washington Star* syndicated Frederic William Wile, and the *Baltimore Sun* began running Frank Kent's "The Great Game of Politics." In 1926 Kent became the first writer of the *New Republic*'s many "TRB" columns (named by reversing the initials of the subway he rode to the print shop, the Brooklyn Rapid Transit line).[4]

In their sociological study of a typical Midwestern town in the 1930s, Robert and Helen Lynd observed that through syndicated columns American newspaper readers were consuming large doses of "semi-editorialized information from the East." Some editors complained that the syndicated columnists were "boilerplating" newspapers by making everyone's editorial page sound alike, but the diversity of opinion provided by the columns balanced editorial single-mindedness and turned editorial pages more than ever before into public forums. When the Great Depression struck, the columnists also helped newspapers satisfy readers' insatiable appetite for Washington analysis. When relatively few papers could afford an exclusive Washington correspondent, for a minimum price they could share the costs of the syndicated columns.[5]

After the *New York World* folded in 1931, its editorial page editor, Walter Lippmann, turned to writing an erudite column entitled "Today & Tomorrow." Within a few years, his column was appearing in more than a hundred newspapers. Far more papers took Drew Pearson and Robert S. Allen's gossipy "Washington Merry-Go-Round," which first appeared in 1932. The following year, Adolph Ochs relaxed his opposition to editorializing in the *New York Times* and allowed Washington bureau chief Arthur Krock a signed column. Lippmann, Pearson, and Krock all lasted in the business for another three decades, while most of the other Washington columns that originated in the 1930s flared only briefly before vanishing.[6]

Because the United Press encouraged sprightly writing in contrast to the just-the-facts reporting of its rival, the Associated Press, its reporters had an advantage in making the transition to columnists. After a dispute with management in 1932, the UP's star Washington reporter Paul Mallon quit the wire service to start his "News behind the News" column. Combining his network of contacts inside the government with his explosive Irish temper, Mallon's investigative columns lit up the editorial pages.[7]

Another alumnus of the UP, Raymond Clapper, stressed reporting over opinions in his column. Despite its lack of "gossip and chitchat," Clapper's "Watching the World Go By" reached 180 newspapers through the Scripps-Howard syndicate. The Kansas-born Clapper tried to tell readers what he would like to have learned about what was going on in Washington if he was still living in Kansas. A 1936 poll of Washington correspondents picked Clapper's column as the "most significant, fair and reliable"—three times the vote given to Walter Lippmann. That judgment may have reflected Clapper's sympathies for the New Deal, which were more in line with the rest of the press corps than was Lippmann's skepticism. Although he appealed to his colleagues in the press corps, Clapper's liberal, internationalist perspective increasingly rankled his boss Roy Howard at Scripps-Howard. The syndicate censored some of Clapper's columns and complained about his nightly radio news broadcasts. Roy Howard thought that his syndicate should be "at least entitled to the *first* expression, if not the exclusive expression," of Clapper's views, and he worried that audiences who heard Clapper on the air the night before would regard his column the next day as a "re-hash." Howard also twitted the columnist for straying too far into the "I think" class. To restore his syndicate's confidence, and to inject more first-hand reporting to the column, Clapper traveled to the front lines during World War II. That decision cost him his radio sponsor, as he could not guarantee regular broadcasts from overseas. It also cost his life. While reporting from the Marshall Islands in February 1944, he died when his plane crashed into a lagoon. Having anticipated problems in transmitting messages from the war zone, Ray Clapper had built up a "cushion" of advance copy, so his column survived him for two weeks posthumously.[8]

Death did not deter some of Clapper's supporters from casting votes for him in the next ranking of Washington columnists. "It is deplorable that Raymond Clapper is not alive to be included in the poll," the writer Henry Pringle lamented. "Not improbably, he would have been declared the correspondent with the greatest influence both in Washington and in the nation." The honor went instead to Clapper's antithesis, Drew Pearson, whose muckraking had made him the most read—and most sued—Washington columnist. The press corps ranked Pearson as the columnist who exerted the most influence on the nation, and placed Walter Lippmann a distant second. Yet the same poll ranked Pearson among the lowest in accuracy. His peers regarded him as a keyhole journalist, "at once the least reliable but the best ratcatching reporter in town." Despite their mistrust of his accuracy, they acknowledged his unmatched national influence through his daily column in 620 newspapers and his weekly radio broadcasts.[9]

After a youth spent organizing parades to advertise Chautauqua meetings, Andrew Russell Pearson retained the flair of a carnival huckster. In the 1920s he had set out as a vagabond journalist, traveling around the world and paying his way through lectures and freelance reporting. He married Countess Felicia Gizycka of Poland and moved to Washington, where his mother-in-law, Eleanor "Cissy" Patterson, later became publisher of the *Washington Times-Herald*. In Washington, Pearson acquired what he called "a veneer of respectability" as the diplomatic correspondent for the *Baltimore Sun*. Tall and urbane, with a long horse-like face and a snort to match, Pearson confidently strode through the corridors of the State Department. He despised what he saw as the stuffy pretentiousness of the State Department's press corps and preferred to keep company with its iconoclasts, Laurence Todd of TASS and Robert S. Allen of the *Christian Science Monitor*. The short-fused Allen had written an exposé of Washington pomposity but his publisher prodded him to spice up the book with more gossip. Allen recruited Drew Pearson as a collaborator, and in 1931 the two anonymously published *Washington Merry-Go-Round*. The book's biting cynicism made it a runaway bestseller and generated handsome royalties. President Herbert Hoover saw little humor in its treatment of his administration, however, and ordered the Federal Bureau of Investigation to uncover the authors' identities. At Hoover's instigation, the *Christian Science Monitor* fired Allen. The *Baltimore Sun* stood behind Pearson for another year until he published a sequel, *More Merry-Go-Round*. This time Pearson's editor insisted that the *Sun* was "*not* a keyhole paper" that dealt in gossip. Given the option of resigning or being fired, Pearson chose dismissal, counting on the publicity to boost the "Washington Merry-Go-Round" column he planned to write with Robert Allen.[10]

The first "Merry-Go-Round" column in December 1932 attracted only six subscribers, requiring both men to hold day jobs. Pearson doubled as Washington correspondent for the French news agency Havas while Allen served as Washington bureau chief for the *Philadelphia Record*. By the end of their first year of teamwork, more than two hundred papers had subscribed, producing enough income for them to concentrate full time on the column. As they no longer worked for a single employer who might discipline them over some offensive item, they felt free to write as they pleased, and they did. Following the pattern of their books, the "Merry-Go-Round" peered behind closed doors and revealed the type of stories that circulated through the National Press Club without normally making it into print. They cultivated, cajoled, conned, and occasionally blackmailed sources for exclusives. Mirroring the style of Walter Winchell's popular gossip column, which turned "Broadway dirt and mud into gold," Pearson and Allen mined Pennsylvania Avenue.[11]

During World War II, Robert Allen joined the army and left the column in the hands of his noncombatant Quaker partner. Allen handled publicity for General George S. Patton, and he was offended when Pearson accused the general of having slapped a shell-shocked soldier in an army hospital. He impetuously dissolved their partnership, which left Pearson with sole possession not only of the column but of the radio show they had launched just before the war. On the air, as in his columns, Pearson imitated Walter Winchell's rapid-fire delivery and sensationalism. Pearson ended each broadcast with his "Predictions of Things to Come," often wildly off the mark but titillating for his listeners. Other journalists thought it hypocritical for a man who billed himself as a fighter for truth and honesty to broadcast half-truths and hyperbole, but Pearson felt reasonably certain about his deductions, and he delighted in stirring controversies, even where none existed. He could make trivial matters sound urgent, offer gossip as fact, and pick fights with prominent figures to draw attention to himself. Pearson also liked to twit the rest of the Washington press corps for not doing more exposés, and he broke the rules of the Gridiron Club (which never made him a member) by quoting from its off-the-record speeches.[12]

The success of Pearson and Allen inspired the North American Newspaper Alliance (NANA, a newspaper cooperative that generated columns and in-depth reporting in contrast to the breaking news provided by the wire services) to recruit its own pair of Washington insider columnists. NANA approached the Capitol Hill reporters Joseph Alsop and Turner Catledge, erstwhile rivals from the *New York Herald Tribune* and *New York Times* respectively, who had pooled their talents to write a series of magazine articles and a best-selling book on President Roosevelt's ill-fated plan to expand the Supreme Court. "I started a column because I needed the money," Alsop later admitted. Dependent on a stipend from his family to augment his modest paycheck as a reporter, he calculated that the syndicated column would triple his income. Catledge preferred reporting to punditry, and took a raise to stay with the *Times*. Because NANA insisted on a team, Alsop turned to Robert Kintner, a savvy, energetic, gnome-like colleague at the *Herald Tribune*'s Washington bureau. Their column, "Capital Parade," promised an intimate look at government. They intended to write their column as reporters, conducting interviews and doing the necessary legwork. Kintner wanted them to stick to uncovering the facts of what had happened. "But not Joe," he reflected. "Joe has always wanted to *make* things happen."[13]

Blue-blooded Joseph Wright Alsop V had been educated at Groton and Harvard and was a cousin to both Franklin and Eleanor Roosevelt. In 1935 the editors of the Republican *Herald Tribune* calculated that Alsop shared "that peculiar self-assurance, or brashness, which characterizes all Roosevelts," and that his family ties would open doors for him in the capital. Alsop arrived in Washington a portly young man, but an irregular heartbeat forced him to lose a great deal of weight. His new svelte appearance, together with his English suits and Italian silk shirts, set him visibly apart from the press gallery's rumpled members. He might have been discounted for his oddly baroque mannerisms, if it was not for his enviable connections and his gifts as a writer. He could get in to see the right people and then capture their personalities with vivid metaphors. Alsop's prose turned Senate Majority Leader Joe Robinson into an "Old

Reliable" elephant ready to trample the rajah's—Roosevelt's—opponents: "If a piece of legislation gets stuck in the clumsy machinery of Congress, Joe butts it through into law, and if the congressional populace shows signs of developing a mind of its own, Joe trumpets it into an appropriate submissiveness." Alsop's ability to unravel inside stories, such as the president's court-packing plan, made his articles and columns required reading among politicos and the press corps. On foreign policy, Alsop fell in with the isolationist crowd in Washington, until the Munich crisis of 1938 profoundly shook his assumptions. After Munich he came to believe that foreign aggression must be resisted, that neutrality laws alone could not protect the nation, and that the federal government should assume an active leadership in world affairs. Never again did he waver from those convictions.[14]

FDR's interior secretary Harold Ickes defined a columnist as someone who must speak with authority, must never be wrong, and must know everything. (After he left the government, Ickes became a columnist himself.) The self-assured Joe Alsop and his dogged partner Bob Kintner matched this profile and their "Capital Parade" reached 170 newspapers at its peak. As war approached, however, neither of them could bear to sit on the sidelines. In June 1941 they terminated the column and both joined the military, Kintner going into the army and Alsop into naval intelligence. Alsop had his heart set on going to England, and was furiously disappointed when the navy sent him instead to Asia, but his experiences there changed his perspective on the world. Taken prisoner of war after the Japanese conquered Hong Kong, Alsop said he was a journalist and won release in a prisoner exchange. He arranged for his release from the navy and spent the rest of the war in China, handling publicity for General Claire Chennault, a former U.S. aviator who organized American volunteer pilots, known as the "Flying Tigers," to defend Nationalist China from the Japanese. He returned home with an expansive vision of American responsibility in Asia.[15]

Alsop negotiated for a new postwar column with the *Herald Tribune*'s syndicate, but Kintner had been injured in a plane crash, taken an early medical discharge, and become news director for the American Broadcasting Company. Needing a new partner, Alsop turned his younger brother, Stewart, who was returning from service in Europe as an intelligence officer for the Office of Strategic Services. (In later years, whenever Stewart was asked about how to become a political columnist, he would reply, "Have a brother who already is one.") The Alsops called the new column "Matter of Fact," to emphasize reporting over opinion, but its tone of gloom and doom made critics suggest a new name, "For Whom the Bell Tolls." Their premier column appeared on the last day of 1945, as the wartime alliance with the Soviet Union was crumbling into Cold War. Troubled newspaper readers turned to Washington columnists for some rational explanation of their irrational times. The frequency with which people prefaced their remarks with something that Walter Lippmann or the Alsops had written indicated how much attention postwar readers paid to newspaper columnists. Editors often resented having these syndicated columnists contradict their own editorials, but they could neither control what the columnists wrote nor drop them without alienating readers. Some newspapers bought the exclusive rights in their market for columns that they rarely printed, just to keep their competitors from getting them. The Alsops' constant sounding of the alarm over Soviet expansion brought complaints from editors across the country, but the brothers took pride in having been among the first to alert the American public to the international Communist peril.[16]

In a Georgetown house that he had built, Joe Alsop worked and entertained in high style. Although his cousins had left the White House, Alsop had no trouble cultivating impeccable sources among a generation of like-minded government officials, men who shared his global perspective, Ivy League credentials, and a Georgetown address. In this clubby environment, he socialized with jurists, cabinet secretaries, and top officials from the State Department and Central Intelligence Agency. (His off-the-record dinners did not include Drew Pearson, one regular guest commented, because "nobody trusted him." Pearson claimed not to mind, reasoning that "the more you go out to dinner the more friends you make; and the more you diminish the number of people you can write about without qualms of conscience or rebukes from your wife." Pearson threw his own dinner parties.) Joe Alsop was always a better talker than a listener. He used social gatherings to confirm his preconceived ideas, pressing others around the table with "That's right, eh?" A connoisseur of food and wine, gardening, antiques, art, archaeology, and history, Alsop could be a charming but nettling host. He once apologized to Walter Lippmann for his "garrulous and heated" behavior by explaining: "In my family, no argument really *was* an argument unless everyone left the room at least twice, and this was bad training for the future."[17]

Early in the Cold War, Washington columnists quarreled over the seriousness of the Soviet threat and the nature of American responsibilities as a global leader. The first secretary of defense, James V. Forrestal, became a lightning rod for this debate. A hard-line anti-Communist, Forrestal pushed for greater defense spending at a time when President Harry Truman was trimming the budget. A rival for Forrestal's job, Louis Johnson, funneled damaging information about the defense secretary to Drew Pearson for his columns and radio programs. Pearson charged Forrestal with everything from disloyalty to the president to cheating on his income taxes. He portrayed the defense secretary as a coward who had once hid inside his Manhattan townhouse while his wife was being robbed at gunpoint at their front door. Even after Arthur Krock volunteered eyewitness testimony to exonerate Forrestal on that charge, Pearson refused to retract it. Under the relentless media assault, Forrestal grew disoriented. Truman requested his resignation and appointed Louis Johnson to replace him. Forrestal's paranoia deepened and his friends begged Pearson to hold his fire. The columnist agreed that there was "no use applying the whip to someone who is out of office." Yet when he heard that Forrestal had checked into the hospital, supposedly for a routine checkup, Pearson could not resist broadcasting a report that the former defense secretary had suffered a mental collapse and attempted suicide.[18]

Soon after that broadcast, in May 1949, James Forrestal jumped from a sixteenth-floor window at the Bethesda Naval Hospital. Forrestal's admirers held Pearson responsible. Arthur Krock devoted an angry column to those "in the press and on the air" who had slandered a man's character with malicious gossip that "followed him to the sick-room." *Time* magazine, which only months earlier had run a flattering cover story on Pearson, declared that the columnist had overstepped the bounds of decency. Pearson himself admitted lying awake at night wondering whether he had killed Forrestal. "Pearson has become a man of great power and special privilege," the iconoclastic columnist Westbrook Pegler blasted, "because other decent men like Forrestal go in fear of fantastic lies to be spread over the Nation by radio, all to stimulate the sale of a brand of hats or laxative." Pearson responded by filing libel charges against Pegler. So frequently had Pearson himself been sued that his syndicate made him financially responsible for his own courtroom battles. By contrast, Pegler's contract obligated the Hearst-owned King Features to pay all his legal fees. This protective cushion turned all decisions about Pegler's lawsuits over to his syndicate. Because Pegler had just lost a staggeringly expensive libel case, King Features cut its losses and reached an understanding with Pearson. To Pegler's annoyance, Pearson dropped his suit in return for having the entire Hearst chain carry the "Merry-Go-Round."[19]

In a morbid way, Secretary Forrestal's suicide had affirmed Drew Pearson's influence. Editors at the *Washington Post* regarded the "Merry-Go-Round" as distasteful and deleted some of its potentially libelous accusations. They dared not drop the column altogether because Pearson consistently ranked high in reader surveys, but they relegated him to the comic pages. Pearson brushed that aside, pointing out that a lot more people read the comics than the editorials. He ignored the disapproval of other journalists and over time restored his reputation by battling Joe McCarthy and by exposing scandals in Congress. A measure of his influence was the number of officials he drove out of office or sent to jail. In his later years, the aging Pearson appealed to the younger generation of the 1960s, who scorned conventional journalism and applauded investigative reporting. "His columns and broadcast were to him weapons in a just war," his partner Jack Anderson concluded. "Without the passion, the partisanship, the war-to-the-death zealotry, would there be a crusading spirit that makes the great muckraker?"[20]

An epilogue to the Forrestal story and the columnists' influence occurred when Louis Johnson, having used Pearson in his climb to the top, came under protracted attack from the Alsop brothers, who blamed him for America's unpreparedness at the start of the Korean War. When President Truman finally sacked Johnson as secretary of defense, Joe Alsop refrained from gloating and instead went to Korea, where his eyewitness reporting from the battlefront won him much notice. Alsop became recognized as one of Washington's best "descriptive reporters," at his finest when he wrote what he saw rather than what he thought. Yet preconceived notions too often molded his perceptions. He never flinched at taking sides, as he did to wage war in his column against the isolationism of Senator Robert Taft. When Taft made his bid for the presidency in 1952, Alsop avidly promoted General Eisenhower for the Republican nomination, and conservatives accused him of filling the column with pro-Eisenhower propaganda.[21]

Eisenhower failed to measure up to Joe Alsop's expectations. The columnist grew exasperated with the new president's apparent passivity. He pressed the administration to take stronger action against Joe McCarthy's anti-Communism at home and the spread of communism abroad. To Eisenhower's advisors, Alsop seemed to hold the president responsible for all the world's troubles. "Joe, you can't possibly mean that," protested Eisenhower's speechwriter, Arthur Larson. "Do you think the President of the United States is to blame for every depredation of some African tribal leader or Asian Communist rebel?" "Absolutely," Alsop replied. President Eisenhower, for his part, had no patience for the columnist's hectoring and bristled when he published classified information. Furious over Alsop's breaches of national security, Eisenhower referred to him as "the lowest form of animal life on earth."[22]

"Matter of Fact" derived much of its credibility from Alsop's personal ties with the men who ran the Central Intelligence Agency. Director Allen Dulles regularly invited Joe Alsop to breakfast, where he supplied him with classified information. Dulles leaked information that the Russians were outproducing the United States in bombers and intercontinental missiles—claims that the CIA did not know for sure and that would later prove specious. Alsop used it to warn the public of a "missile gap." The columnist justified his publication of government secrets on the grounds that the American public could not appropriately respond to international challenges without adequate information. He took pride that three presidential administrations considered him troublesome enough to tap his phones. Alsop's covert sources made "Matter of Fact" required reading among the rest of the Washington correspondents and made life difficult for the New York Times's Washington bureau. Because the Times did not subscribe to any syndicates, its Washington bureau established a "defensive arrangement" with editors from other noncompetitive papers who alerted it whenever columnists such as the Alsops were poised to break a story. This gave the bureau time to check the matter independently and rush its own version to the New York Times.[23]

The apocalyptic tone of the Alsops' column contributed to the public anxiety that fed the Red scare; but having helped unleash the beast, the brothers fought to corral it. In the McCarthy era, they rallied to defend prominent officials with whose policies they might disagree but whose loyalty they did not question. Predictably, Senator McCarthy responded by branding the Alsops as Communist sympathizers, an absurd charge given the stridently anti-Communist tone of their columns. McCarthy also made veiled allusions to Joe Alsop's homosexuality. While Alsop was in Moscow in 1957, Soviet intelligence agents photographed him in a sexual act and attempted to blackmail him. Alsop immediately reported the incident to the CIA and the FBI. A few years later, copies of the photos circulated around Washington sub rosa, but the press corps closed ranks and kept the story out of print. The Soviets dropped any further effort to expose Alsop when the CIA threatened to release comparable evidence about several KGB officers. Alsop defused the issue by marrying the widow of a close friend. But his partnership with his brother ended in divorce. The even-tempered Stewart Alsop exercised a moderating influence on the column. As the senior partner, Joe exerted his right to send him on assignments, needled him about his work, and claimed the larger share of their joint income. Their quarrels inevitably ended with Joe shouting and stamping his feet. Stewart dissolved what he called their "combative" collaboration in 1958 and began writing for the *Saturday Evening Post* and *Newsweek*. Joseph Alsop took "Matter of Fact" solo, after promising his syndicate that he would avoid an alarmist tone—a pledge that he was temperamentally incapable of upholding.[24]

In contrast to the mercurial Joe Alsop, who berated his guests for disagreeing with him, Walter Lippmann presided genially at his social gatherings, with an amiable tolerance for dissent. Alsop and Lippmann also differed in their prescriptions for world order. Lippmann opposed the use of military force as an extension of foreign policy, and advocated conflict resolution through diplomacy. Alsop insisted that diplomatic effectiveness required periodic saber rattling. "Joe considered Lippmann an appeaser," noted Henry Brandon, the Washington correspondent for *The Times* of London, who dined with them both. "Walter saw Joe as a warmonger." Their contrary views, expressed in newspapers nationwide, complicated life for a succession of presidents, as any policy that satisfied one would alienate the other. President Eisenhower dealt with them by not reading either columnist.[25]

Old enough to remember the public furor over the sinking of the U.S.S. *Maine*, Walter Lippmann had worked on government propaganda during World War I and had accompanied Woodrow Wilson to Paris during negotiation of the ill-fated Treaty of Versailles. Those incidents left him deeply distrustful of public opinion in forming public policy. Lippmann aimed his columns at the upper reaches of the reading public, who resided in the "power centers" along the Potomac, the Hudson, and the Charles. He reasoned that he needed to be read there, in order to be taken seriously by his sources. "He is a man of true intellectual independence, who thinks through a problem and refuses to avoid logical conclusions merely because they are unpopular," said Senate Majority Leader Lyndon Johnson, paying tribute to Lippmann in 1957. "He never seeks to curry favor with the mob." An unabashed elitist, Lippmann was not the most widely published Washington columnist, yet he won recognition as primus inter pares for his intelligent analysis, graceful prose, and influential devotees.[26]

Like Joe Alsop, Lippmann lived a complicated private life. Belying the restrained, contemplative tone of his columns, his domestic world underwent a turbulent upheaval in 1937 when he was caught having an affair with his best friend's wife. Divorce and remarriage made it socially awkward for Lippmann to remain in New York, so he moved to Washington to become the capital's "philosopher in residence." In fact, Lippmann disliked Washington. Finding its air and intellectual climate stifling, he sighed that it "drags upon you till you wilt and your head swims." Yet Lippmann appreciated that the New Deal had transferred power from New York to Washington, making it the best place for a political commentator to be located. He worried aloud about the corrupting effect of remaining in too close a proximity to those about whom he wrote, but no one had better sources than Lippmann among the highest-placed American officials and at Washington's leading embassies.[27]

While Walter Lippmann may not have had all the right answers, James Reston once wrote, he asked all the right questions. Cerebral, detached, and dispassionate, Lippmann projected the image of a public thinker who reflected on passing events through a fixed philosophy of life. In fact he did just the opposite. During his forty years of writing columns, Lippmann shifted ground whenever necessary. Unlike the one-note Joe Alsop, Lippmann produced a polyphony of opinions, and could argue both sides of an issue within the same column. His long intellectual odyssey took him from socialism to conservatism, so that he once defined the "truly civilized and enlightened American" as being "conservative and liberal and progressive." Having chosen a career that forced him to write on a deadline, Lippmann regretted that it never allowed him to pause long enough to be sure of what he really believed. Like Alsop, Lippmann had been badly shaken by the pre–World War II Munich crisis, which destroyed the illusion that the United States could afford to stand apart from world affairs. Unlike Alsop, however, Lippmann never let the Munich analogy or other common assumptions bind his thinking. During the Cold War, Lippmann warned that the United States could not police the entire world, and he predicted that the policy of containment of communism would send American troops to fight in the remotest regions of the world to defend corrupt client states on the grounds that they were fighting communism. He called for a realistic foreign policy that would balance the nation's commitments and its resources.[28]

On the home front, Lippmann reacted warily to McCarthyism. Although rabble-rousing distressed him, he devoted few columns to Senator McCarthy.

Lippmann trusted that Dwight Eisenhower's election would douse the anti-Communist crusade, but he, too, grew impatient with the new president's tepid responses. In a 1954 column, headlined "Nightmare in Washington," Lippmann condemned McCarthy's behavior and grieved that the government had "allowed itself it be intimidated by an ambitious and ruthless demagogue." He rebuked Eisenhower for not standing up for the executive branch and he assailed senators who thought "the cheapest and easiest way not to look red or pink was to be yellow." These were strong words from a man of Lippmann's stature and they resonated in the capital. They won little appreciation from the White House. "I haven't read Lippmann since I left Columbia," Eisenhower declared.[29]

Other world leaders treated Lippmann more deferentially. On one of his European tours, Lippmann scheduled a coveted interview with Soviet premier Nikita Khrushchev. As he boarded the plane to fly to Europe, the columnist was handed a message from Khrushchev asking to postpone their meeting for a week. "Impossible," Lippmann replied. By the time the plane had landed, word came that the Soviet leader had rearranged his own plans in order to accommodate the columnist. Such was the international influence of Walter Lippmann.[30]

For a man of worldly connections, Lippmann lived an oddly monastic life. He worked out of a spacious Tudor-style house across from the National Cathedral, where he had his upstairs office soundproofed to muffle the sound of the birds and the cathedral bells. A small staff of attentive secretaries and stenographers assisted with his columns and books. (During the Second World War, the Soviet government considered Lippmann so influential that it planted an agent in his home as his secretary.) He would emerge from this shelter to host dinners and cocktail parties that allowed him to make the kind of personal contact necessary to get "behind the communiqués and the handouts." Lippmann trafficked in political gossip at the highest altitudes.[31]

Max Frankel, while serving as a diplomatic correspondent at the *New York Times* Washington bureau, asked Lippmann's advice on becoming a columnist. There were only two kinds, Lippmann explained. "One of them is like Joe Alsop down the street. He lunges after every crumb of news at the dinner table and he's a reporter, he's a one-man news operation, competing with all of you guys at the *New York Times*. And then there's me." Lippmann explained that he wrote his column through his own "philosophy of life." In 1959 the National Press Club celebrated his seventieth birthday, and Lippmann took the opportunity to muse about "the business of being opinionated." He wondered aloud how anyone could have the audacity to pontificate in print several times a week. No columnist could know everything or have access to all the pertinent information, but he maintained that in any nation "governed with the consent of the governed" the governed needed all the help they could get. His job was "to infer, to deduce, to imagine, and to guess" what was going on inside the government for those who lacked the time or ability to inform themselves.[32]

It was a premature valediction. The 1960s reinvigorated Walter Lippmann's career and lifted him to greater prestige through his resolute opposition to the Vietnam War, which made him an icon to the young generation of antiwar protestors, and anathema to much of the Washington establishment. In his analysis of power in Washington, the *New Yorker*'s Washington correspondent Richard Rovere portrayed Washington columnists and correspondents as pillars of the capital's establishment, who shared the credentials, values, and lifestyles of the official elite. They all read the *New York Times*, Rovere noted, but they had to take at least one other paper to keep abreast of the pundits. Stewart Alsop celebrated Washington as "The Center," where only a small portion of Washingtonians either made policy or directly influenced it. He divided the press corps between its elite columnists and mass of reporters by their favored watering holes. The Alsops, Walter Lippmann, Arthur Krock, and James Reston dined at the exclusive, male-only Metropolitan Club, "the meeting place of the Washington Establishment," and Alsop disdained the National Press Club as a seedy place populated by public relations agents and lobbyists.[33]

When John F. Kennedy assumed the presidency in 1961, his press secretary, Pierre Salinger, found that the Washington press corps "had a code of tribal mores that would confuse a Nobel laureate in social anthropology." Out of twelve hundred reporters who held White House credentials, Salinger judged its "ruling establishment" consisted of no more than sixty journalists. The "sachems" of the tribe were the senior wire services reporters, such as Merriman Smith, followed by correspondents for the networks, newsmagazines, and newspapers. An even more "select fraternity" included the influential columnists, whose ranking members were, according to the White House staff, Reston, Lippmann, the Alsops, Marquis Childs, Doris Fleeson, William S. White, Evans and Novak, Joseph Kraft, and Drew Pearson. "A request from one of them to see the President personally was usually honored," Salinger recorded. Top White House staff made it standing operating procedure to contact these columnists and brief them during crises. With the Cold War at its height, the columnists became steady reading material at the White House, State Department, and Pentagon. They framed much of the public debate, and focused attention on certain issues and trouble spots to the exclusion of others, often aiming to provoke the government into action.[34]

Joe Alsop's stock within the fraternity rose along with the fortunes of his Georgetown neighbor, Senator John F. Kennedy, who had briefly been a reporter himself, having covered the British elections and the United Nations charter conference in 1945 as a special correspondent for William Randolph Hearst's *Chicago Herald Examiner*. Although Arthur Krock thought that he showed "great promise" in those assignments, Kennedy told friends that he decided to get out of the newspaper business because he "wanted to be in something more active" than just being an observer. Kennedy took from the experience an ability to deal with the press without a sense of awe or intimidation. He felt comfortable with reporters, and counted several of them as personal friends, from the conservative Hugh Sidey of *Time* to the liberal Ben Bradlee of *Newsweek*. Bradlee thought this was because he shared their craving "to know what was going on, and to know what people were like." In return, reporters liked him for being intelligent, charming, and uncommonly open with them. Joe Alsop enjoyed socializing with Kennedy, but initially found it hard to accept such an "incompletely tested" senator as a serious presidential contender. While standing on Kennedy's front stoop in 1958, Alsop had predicted that he could be the Democrats' next vice presidential nominee. The columnist nearly tumbled off the steps when Kennedy replied, "Well Joe, we don't want to talk too much about 'VP' until we're quite sure that we can't get just 'P.'" As he followed Kennedy on the campaign trail, however, he became mesmerized by his eloquent style. Alsop began to think that Kennedy could beat Vice President Richard Nixon, a prospect he "didn't exactly dislike."[35]

After Kennedy's victories in the primaries, Alsop and *Washington Post* publisher Philip Graham went to the Democratic convention in Los Angeles to convince the candidate to select Senate Majority Leader Lyndon Johnson as his running mate—and then helped persuade the skeptical Texas senator to accept the invitation. One of their arguments to Johnson was that Walter Lippmann had endorsed Kennedy because he considered Johnson ignorant about the world. "We're going to show him he's wrong," they insisted. Johnson's unexpected acceptance helped Kennedy carry Texas and win a narrow national victory in November. On the night of his inauguration, John Kennedy's much-publicized midnight visit to a party at Alsop's Georgetown home put Alsop squarely on the map as the new president's favorite columnist.[36]

At fifty-one, Joe Alsop marched in step with the young Kennedy administration, while Lippmann at seventy-one strolled more leisurely behind. Alsop freely offered advice to the president, encouraging intervention against Communist insurgencies in Southeast Asia. He dismissed British and French efforts to promote neutralization in the region (which Lippmann endorsed) as a polite form of appeasement. Kennedy deferentially sought Lippmann's counsel, but he shared Alsop's impatience with the older columnist's caution. "I know Khrushchev reads him," the president complained, "and he thinks that Walter Lippmann is representing American policy." Lippmann did not help matters by belittling Kennedy's Cold War instincts during a nationally televised interview. In earlier attempts at radio commentary, Lippmann had sounded dry to listeners, but he unexpectedly excelled in a series of television interviews for *CBS Reports*. Producer Fred Friendly commented that "Walter's frail voice, hardly audible in a living room, had, when amplified, an intensity

that was hypnotic." In the 1960s the media theorist Marshall McLuhan postu-
lated that radio was a "hot medium" that favored fervid presentations, while
television was a "cool medium" that worked best with understated perfor-
mances. The cooler medium captured Lippman's urbanity and intelligence. In
the second of his seven interviews for CBS, Lippmann responded to criticism
that he was advocating a "policy of appeasement" with the comment: "I don't
think that old men ought to promote wars for young men to fight." The program irked Kennedy and his national security advisor, McGeorge Bundy. "They
never protested to me," Lippmann commented, "but after that, it was over."[37]

More in tune with the administration, Joseph Alsop fixated on the communist challenge in Southeast Asia. His columns sounded the alarm on urgent
conditions in Laos. "It was principally some stories by Joseph Alsop that got
the managing editor all excited," *St. Louis Post-Dispatch* reporter Richard
Dudman wrote of his first assignment to Laos, a country he had trouble locat-
ing on a map. After the Laotian crisis faded, Alsop shifted his sense of alarm to
South Vietnam, traveling there personally. By 1963, American journalists in
Saigon were filing pessimistic reports about the South Vietnamese government's
struggle against the Communist insurgency. Joe Alsop took it upon himself to
lecture the young war correspondents on their lack of patriotism, at a time
when American "advisors" were trying to bolster South Vietnam's military resolve. Under a Saigon dateline, he condemned these "high-minded crusaders"
of the press corps who painted such a negative picture of the Vietnamese conflict. Among the correspondents whom he assailed, David Halberstam, who
covered Vietnam for the *New York Times,* dismissed Alsop as "wrong in almost
everything he said or wrote" about the war. UPI correspondent Neil Sheehan
added that Alsop "did not see those who disagreed with him as merely incor-
rect or misguided. He depicted them as stupid men who acted from petty or
selfish motives."[38]

President Kennedy's assassination in November devastated Joe Alsop. The
columnist fretted over how Lyndon Johnson would handle Vietnam. As much
as he admired Johnson's political skills, he suspected that the Texan lacked an
"internal compass" for foreign affairs. To Alsop's gratification, Johnson seemed
eager to hear his opinions. Thrust into the presidency, Johnson intended to
win support from the eastern, liberal "opinion makers" who had championed
Kennedy. He invited the columnists to the White House and visited their homes,
seeking their wisdom while he poured out his troubles to them. To Lippmann,
Johnson complained of having inherited a mess in Vietnam: "I don't like it,
but how can I pull out?" The president's reluctance to engage militarily in Vietnam reassured Lippmann, but it outraged Joe Alsop, who upbraided the White
House staff at every opportunity. "He thinks the column was good from your
standpoint and I am not sure that I convinced him otherwise," presidential
assistant Walter Jenkins reported to Johnson after protesting one of Alsop's

columns. Following another berating from Alsop in March 1964, National Security Advisor McGeorge Bundy told Johnson: "I think he really wants to
have a little old war out there." That May, Bundy reported that Alsop had returned from another trip to Saigon "breathing absolute fire and sulphur about
the need for war in South Vietnam."[39]

Johnson ran for election in 1964 as a peace candidate who would not send
American boys to fight an Asian war, but all the while he privately feared that
South Vietnam would fall to the Communists unless the United States intervened militarily. Publication of the Pentagon Papers in 1971 left the impression
that Johnson had simply talked peace while planning for war, but the release
of his tape-recorded telephone conversations in the 1990s revealed his lingering ambivalence over going to war. He desperately tried to keep his options
open for as long as possible, but he felt that those options were being progres-
sively narrowed by the highly public debate in the nation's op-ed pages. Joseph
Alsop and Walter Lippmann divided sharply on the Vietnam War, writing as
the most prominent hawk and dove respectively. Johnson saw neither Alsop's
strident militarism nor Lippmann's faith in a negotiated settlement as attractive alternatives. In his typical fashion, he tried to work both sides by assuring
each columnist that he stood with him. The closer that Johnson inched toward Alsop's military response, the more fulsomely he endorsed the diplomatic initiatives that Lippmann advocated. For a while, Johnson managed to
convince both columnists of his concurrence with their starkly contradictory
positions. The strategy marked Johnson's first steps into the "credibility gap"
that would erode his support within the Washington press corps and undermine his presidency.[40]

Alsop and his wife attended the president's wedding anniversary dinner at
the White House in June 1964. In her diary, Lady Bird Johnson described Alsop
as being "so amusing and articulate and so much fun" that night. But after the
other guests had departed, the columnist accompanied the president on a stroll
around the White House grounds, where he bluntly broke the evening's festive
mood by lecturing Johnson on his responsibility to honor the nation's commitment to South Vietnam. He warned the president that if he failed he would
bear responsibility for the first major military defeat in American history.
Johnson's aide Jack Valenti, who walked with them, felt that Johnson listened
carefully because he believed Alsop was expressing the majority opinion in the
nation. "The Alsop syndrome was the president's hairshirt," Valenti recorded.
"Its coarse covering could be felt by the president every time he ached to be rid
of Vietnam; it intruded into every presidential desire to cut losses and get out."
In a phone call with Defense Secretary Robert McNamara the next day, Johnson
mentioned that he had dinner with some folks who "think we're about to lose
the greatest race that the United States has ever lost." Johnson told McNamara,
"we're going to have to make a decision pretty promptly."[41]

In August, Johnson cited ambiguous evidence about an attack by North Vietnamese torpedo boats on American destroyers in the Gulf of Tonkin to win passage of a congressional resolution that authorized him to use "all necessary measures" to repel armed attacks on U.S. forces and prevent further aggression. The president intended the resolution to demonstrate American solidarity with South Vietnam to the North Vietnamese and at the same time protect his political flank from attack by his hawkish Republican challenger, Senator Barry Goldwater. Having passed the resolution, Johnson could then campaign safely against widening the war. Joe Alsop considered the president's dovish electioneering unwise and unnecessary, as Goldwater stood no chance of winning. When Johnson achieved his landslide, Alsop left him no time to savor it. Hearing reports that the president was seeking a way out of Vietnam "even if we have to set it up so that a withdrawal would have a better face," Alsop wrote a long post-election letter accusing the president of liquidating U.S. interests in the Pacific.

In a December column, under a Saigon dateline, Alsop dwelt on the fears of American advisors in Vietnam that the president was "consciously prepared to accept defeat." Repeating publicly what he had said privately, Alsop asserted that responsibility for "the greatest defeat in American history" would rest forever on Johnson's shoulders. Alsop played on Johnson's dread of appearing weak in comparison to his predecessor. The columnist equated the test that Vietnam posed for Johnson with John Kennedy's ordeal during the Cuban missile crisis. Would Johnson duck the challenge? Was he man enough to stand up to the Communists? Would he become the first American president to lose a war? Defeat in Vietnam, Alsop predicted, would lose all that Americans had fought for in the Pacific during the Second World War and in Korea. Reading these columns, Johnson stormed that he was "not going to take the advice of General Alsop." But, later, he traced the moment when he crossed the bridge for war to December 1964—a time when the Goldwater war hawks had been crushed and there was little political pressure for escalation.[42]

During a chance encounter with McGeorge Bundy at Washington's National Airport, early in 1965, Joe Alsop harangued the national security advisor over the administration's failure to pursue the war. Bundy refused to discuss Vietnam with him and stormed away. When he cooled down, Bundy apologized to the columnist and explained that anyone in his place had an obligation "to decide whom when and what in his dealings with reporters, even when they are very close friends." Lyndon Johnson thought his senior staff was entirely too close to the aggravating columnist. After the presidential aide Walter Jenkins resigned on a morals charge during the 1964 campaign, FBI director J. Edgar Hoover sent Alsop's FBI file to the president. "Walter Jenkins is just minor," Johnson assured members of his administration, urging them to read the file showing that Alsop had been involved in sexual misadventures "in practically every capital of the world."[43]

President Johnson withdrew from Joe Alsop and clasped hold of Walter Lippmann. In private, Johnson belittled Lippmann's insistence on negotiations. "If they came across the line from the other side and fired at our compound, he would want us to say, 'Thank you,'" Johnson ridiculed. In public, he groveled before the columnist. "I want you to meet Walter Lippmann," LBJ greeted his assistant, Eric Goldman. "He's smarter than all of us." Lippmann urged a negotiated withdrawal of American armed forces and the neutralization of South Vietnam, even if that meant accepting a Communist regime. Further expansion of the U.S. military presence could trigger a full-scale war, Lippmann warned, which "nobody in his right mind" thought the United States could win. Johnson found this advice unpalatable, but persisted in his efforts to keep the columnist in his camp. "Did you see Walter Lippmann last night? I thought he was wonderful," Johnson asked Georgia senator Richard Russell in a taped phone conversation, referring to the columnist's praise of the president during a television interview in April 1964. "I just wondered what it cost you," Russell laughed. That same year, Johnson awarded Lippmann the Presidential Medal of Freedom in recognition of his "measured reason and detached perspective." While lauding Lippmann, Johnson struck Joe Alsop's name from the White House guest list. Johnson's press secretary, Bill Moyers, confided to Alsop that the president felt his columns were narrowing his choices in Vietnam. "In his terms I suppose I was limiting his options," Alsop reflected, "because I was dragging the problem out from under the rug." Alsop continued to beat the drum loudly to make sure Johnson could not dodge the issue. "It was awfully funny in those days," said Alsop. "He was seeing Walter Lippmann all the time. And he wasn't seeing me at all."[44]

On Mondays, Wednesdays, and Fridays, Alsop's "Matter of Fact" pressed Johnson for a military solution in Vietnam. On most of the same editorial pages on Tuesdays and Thursdays, Lippmann's "Today & Tomorrow" railed against the folly of war. The unbroken thread running through all Alsop's columns was America's need to honor its commitments to preserve its credibility. Lippmann's columns had their own persistent theme, that America had no business sending ground troops to the Asian mainland. If the United States went to war in Vietnam, Lippmann commented, at least half the responsibility would be Alsop's, and he added: "If Joe Alsop can needle the President, so can I."[45]

In February 1965, Vietnamese Communists attacked a U.S. helicopter base and barracks at Pleiku, killing eight Americans. Johnson retaliated with bombing missions over North Vietnam. Administration officials worried that without a substantial military response, press hawks such as Alsop would assail them for craven inaction. Alsop dismissed the bombing as "tit-for-tattery" and a poor substitute for a full-scale expansion of the ground war. Writing for the doves, Lippmann rejected Alsop's advice as reckless and warned that getting into a land war in Asia "would be an act of supreme folly." They drew their battle lines in their columns and at their dinner tables. At a party at Lippmann's home shortly after Pleiku, he stimulated a debate between the senators George McGovern, Frank Church, and Gale McGee, all members of the Foreign Relations Committee. McGovern and Church took Lippmann's view that an over-extended America could not win a decisive victory in a jungle war, while McGee insisted that the nation needed to "stand tall in Vietnam" to hold back the communist advance in the Cold War. That debate spilled over onto the Senate floor, much to President Johnson's displeasure. Feeling trapped, Johnson tried to walk a line between all-out war and surrender, calculating that a limited war would get hawkish critics off his back, while American military superiority would force North Vietnam to the negotiating table at the earliest opportunity, and satisfy the doves."[46]

Lyndon Johnson disliked having the press analyze and classify him, James Reston surmised; he preferred to be loved. An obsessive consumer of newspapers, Johnson was easily irritated by what he read. He wanted to see the facts as he stated them, and he hated speculation of any kind. To keep the bellwether columnists on board, he assigned top White House staff to develop some "special relationships." McGeorge Bundy conspicuously consulted Lippmann "to plug his guns" and keep him in the president's camp. "Like the rest of us," Bundy explained, "Walter is always flattered when he is asked for his own opinion." Bundy assured Lippmann that Johnson was proceeding with cautious restraint. After meeting with Bundy at the White House, Lippmann taped a television interview for CBS, assuring viewers that the president was no war hawk. Johnson invited Lippmann back to the White House to preview an address he was planning to give at Johns Hopkins University that would hold out a carrot to North Vietnam in the form of massive economic aid for development. But Johnson disregarded Lippmann's advice to tie the aid to an unconditional cease-fire. Hanoi, which looked on negotiations as a tactic to be pursued only from a position of military strength, not while the United States was bolstering its forces in South Vietnam, ignored the overture.

Johnson returned to military solutions. He ordered a sustained bombing of North Vietnam, incrementally increased the number of American troops sent to South Vietnam, and authorized their engagement in direct combat. Yet, he resisted calling up the reserves and denied having changed his policies. Johnson's attempt to camouflage the war's escalation did not escape Lippmann's notice. It now seemed clear to him that the president was not honestly seeking a negotiated settlement. Lippmann found this revelation all the more embarrassing after Johnson's public show of visiting his home to seek his advice, all in violation of his own warnings to journalists against allowing politicians to get too close. "From Johnson's standpoint he thought he was being effective," commented the *Washington Post*'s diplomatic correspondent Chalmers Roberts, "but he was being counterproductive." After April 1965, Lippmann never returned to the White House, and his columns unrelentingly dissented from the war.[47]

As Vietnam boiled, Joe Alsop stoked the fire. He nagged others journalists to go and see things for themselves, especially James Reston, who for the past dozen years had been writing a column called "Washington" for the *New York Times*. Reston finally visited Vietnam during the summer of 1965, but rather than accepting the military's rosy scenarios, his eyewitness accounts squared with those of the *Times*'s skeptical young war correspondents. Reston returned to Washington dubious about the chances of victory, which made him persona non grata at the Johnson White House. A generation older than Reston, Walter Lippmann had never visited Southeast Asia, and declined an invitation from the U.S. ambassador to Vietnam. "If I were 25 years younger, I would be tempted to accept, if only to say when I got home that I had been there," he replied. "But I would not expect to find out anything more than the stream of visiting journalists and VIPs bring back with them." Lippmann relied instead on the reporting of others such as the *St. Louis Post-Dispatch*'s Richard Dudman. During repeated visits, Dudman rejected American military press releases for trying to "make bad news sound less bad." He followed the troops into the field and concluded that the Viet Cong had won the countryside. Nor did he believe that bombing North Vietnam would bring a quick end to the conflict. Lippmann's sources inside the U.S. intelligence community confirmed Dudman's reports. "Nobody denies it, and nobody has issued a statement saying he is wrong about it," Lippmann pointed out. Although he cited the reporter in his own columns, he regretted that newspapers in Washington and New York were not reprinting Dudman's articles, which meant they would not be widely read by those setting policy.[48]

With his thin skin easily penetrated, Johnson made it clear that he detested the "Georgetown columnists." He complained to the TV news broadcaster Nancy Dickerson that the "Georgetown press" in their "candle-lit drawing rooms" joked about the size of his ears, the cut of his clothes, and his Texas origins. Drew Pearson fed Johnson's suspicions that other Washington journalists were laughing at him behind his back. Pearson, whose fulsome support for Johnson won him jeers as "Lyndon's lackey," used his column to return fire on the president's critics. He twitted Joe Alsop's inability to arrange interviews with Secretary of State Dean Rusk and CIA Director William Raborn. An indignant Alsop attributed the attack directly to the president, and believed that Johnson was tapping his phones. Johnson dismissed this complaint by commenting that Alsop was paranoid and "going through menopause," although the president took the precaution of checking with the Justice and Defense Departments to make sure that no one had Alsop under surveillance. Johnson interpreted Alsop's criticism as "pure blackmail," designed to pressure the administration into giving him "some secrets that he's not getting."[49]

A puzzled Johnson watched his public relations deteriorate. Drew Pearson advised that his problem was that he saw "too many newspapermen," and that familiarity bred contempt. Johnson had been too eager, too friendly, and too self-serving in his attempts to influence the Washington press corps. Early in his administration, on one flight back to Washington from Texas, Johnson had gathered the pool reporters on Air Force One and advised them that if they cooperated with him, he would see that they got their stories. Such blatancy caused the reporters to recoil. Excessive intimacy with the president, said *Newsweek* correspondent Charles Roberts, would require them to "sacrifice their objectivity or their independence or their integrity." Journalists wanted to get close enough to be first-hand observers, but not cheerleaders. Before long, the same reporters whom Johnson sought to cultivate were writing about his "credibility gap." Such "whoppers" as his persistent denials of escalating the war in Vietnam devalued his word.[50]

To revive his sinking image, Johnson appointed the president of NBC, Robert Kintner, as a special assistant to do "missionary work" among the critics in the press corps. An experienced Washington correspondent, columnist, and radio and television news executive, Kintner met with the leading columnists, magazine writers, and news broadcasters. He heard plenty of grievances about Johnson's excessive sensitivity to press reporting, and collected anecdotes about reporters being cut off from White House sources for taking issue with some policy. Kintner coaxed the president into lifting past restrictions. He also wrote Johnson a memo asking for permission to have lunch with Walter Lippmann. Not that he had any chance of converting Lippmann, but Kintner hoped to do "a little something" to improve relations with him. On the memo, Johnson checked his approval and added, "I'm sorry he disagrees with some of my policies and decisions as I'm sorry that Lady Bird does. The lunch will be good you & him & me." When Lippmann and Kintner met they merely reminisced about the past, however, and both steered clear of mentioning either Johnson or Vietnam.[51]

Kintner had better results with his former partner Joe Alsop, who had been isolated from Johnson since the "incident" at the president's wedding anniversary. After a few lunches and dinners, Kintner detected signs of a more positive attitude toward the administration in Alsop's columns. "I talked with Joe Alsop on the telephone yesterday, to urge on him as much support as possible for the President's Vietnam policy," Kintner reported to Johnson that summer. "As the President knows, Alsop is a strong supporter of the President's Vietnam policy and a strong derider of Senator Fulbright, Walter Lippmann and Scotty Reston." When Alsop planned his next trip abroad, he expressed interest in seeing Johnson for an off-the-record talk before the trip, so long as Johnson invited him. But Johnson would meet only at Alsop's request. The resourceful Kintner invited Alsop to visit *him* at the White House, and by prearrangement the two men dropped by uninvited to see Johnson. The president graciously picked up their conversation without mentioning the long interregnum, and Alsop came away (as Kintner reported) "feeling very warm and friendly toward the President." Thereafter, Johnson saw the columnist for other off-the-record interviews, leaked information to him, and invited him to formal White House functions. He personally added Alsop to the guest list for a reception for presidential scholars while deleting Lippmann and Reston. But there were no more invitations to social occasions at the White House. Lyndon Johnson, Alsop decided, was "not a likable man."[52]

No one waved the flag more fervently during the Vietnam War than did Joseph Alsop. His columns were always seeing "a little light at the end of the tunnel," and exhorting that "the war can be won." When a quick victory was not forthcoming, Alsop admitted to being "over-optimistic about the war's timeframes," but excused it as a reaction to so much negative reporting by others. He felt sure that he had been right to press Johnson into the war "against all his own political and other inclinations," but he believed the president had blundered by escalating the conflict so gradually. Johnson should have rallied national patriotism, Alsop suggested, but his obsession with secrecy and flexibility had kept the public so ill informed that it barely realized it was fighting a major war. "You can't be a good political leader if you're secretive," Alsop judged. As the Johnson administration sank into a public relations quagmire, even McGeorge Bundy acknowledged their credibility gap. What they needed, Bundy advised, was to make the press see the progress in South Vietnam for themselves. A single prominent journalist such as Joe Alsop, writing favorably but independently, Bundy assured Johnson, "was worth ten official spokesmen." As a consequence, when Alsop periodically descended on Vietnam, he got better treatment than most congressional delegations. The U.S. ambassador offered him accommodations at the embassy and he had access to helicopters normally reserved for the top brass. The army provided stacks of captured enemy documents that reinforced Alsop's certainty about the Viet Cong's imminent collapse. These officials did not mislead Alsop; he was fully capable of deceiving himself. The *Washington Post* war correspondent David Hoffman commented that Alsop "might just as well have been back home in Washington," as he saw only what he wanted to see.[53]

Alsop's strident columns on the war steadily eroded his standing in his profession. Prominent journalists pegged his column as propaganda. New Leftists ignored Alsop's long commitment to civil rights, civil liberties, and social reform, and dismissed him as a right-wing militarist. The *New Republic* blasted his imperious tours of Vietnam, and the humor columnist Art Buchwald wrote a satirical play about a megalomaniac columnist, "Joe Mayflower," who provokes a needless war. The *Washington Post*'s editor Ben Bradlee observed that Alsop began measuring people "on a scale that was calibrated solely to his feelings on Vietnam," which contracted his social circle. With more people turning against the interminable war, Alsop was stunned to find himself "suddenly out of fashion."[54]

Joe Alsop withered while the aged Walter Lippmann regenerated, due to the new relevance he gained with the youthful antiwar movement. Lyndon Johnson complained that the columnist was actually a "neo-isolationist" whose writing was inspiring domestic dissent and hardening North Vietnam's resistance. Johnson had Robert Kintner lead a White House "Lippmann Project" that read back through thirty years of the columnist's writings in search of errors and inconsistencies. What they found, they slipped to prominent hawks such as the *New York Times* columnist C. L. Sulzberger, who wrote how badly Lippmann had underestimated Hitler in 1933, and categorized him with "our Know-Nothings" and "our Know-It-Alls." Former secretary of state Dean Acheson added that it was a good thing the reading public's memory rarely lasted longer than three days, "or Lippmann would have been out of business long ago." The Washington writer Allen Drury devoted his fourth novel, *Capable of Honor*, to mocking the self-importance of a columnist he named (over the objections of his publisher's lawyers) Walter Dobius, a man who thought he had "a mandate from the Lord to run the White House, the country, and the world."[55]

By 1967, Lippmann had decided to give up both his column and the capital. "I simply can't stand Washington," he stated. "It's impossible to breathe or think in this town." One factor in Lippmann's retirement was the demise of the outlet for his column in New York, first by the closure of the *New York Herald Tribune* and then by the failure of its short-lived successor, the *World-Journal-Tribune*. Lippmann tentatively approached the *New York Times*, but managing editor Turner Catledge made it clear that the *Times* "is not now and never has been interested in publishing syndicated columns." "Today & Tomorrow" instead appeared in the dovish *New York Post*, where it preached to the choir. Lippmann finally discontinued his newspaper column and devoted himself instead to a weekly column in *Newsweek*. "More and more," he told his readers, "I have come to wish to get rid of the necessity of knowing, day in and day out, what the blood pressure is at the White House and who said what and who saw who and who is listened to and who is not listened to." As he prepared to move to New York, Lippmann privately blamed his decision to leave on Johnson's having misled him. Johnson publicly retaliated with snide remarks about the departure of "a prominent commentator of yesteryear." His verbal sniping prompted the *Washington Post* cartoonist Herblock to sketch the Zeus-like president hurling lightning bolts at the benign columnist seated at his typewriter. "Thank goodness Walter Lippmann never learned to draw," Johnson said when he saw it. White House aide Robert Kintner warned Johnson that his comments were giving the columnist "undue prominence," and Press Secretary George Christian told White House speechwriters to "lay off" Lippmann, before they made a martyr out of him. Still, in Johnson's farewell remarks to the National Press Club he told reporters that after he left the White House he planned to sit in the rocking chair on his front porch for about ten minutes. "Then I am going to put on my hat and go out and find Walter Lippmann."[56]

When asked about the best Washington columnists, Lippmann graciously included Joe Alsop—"when he is not writing about Vietnam." Like Lippmann,

Alsop had lost New York's critical market by the implosion of that city's newspapers following a devastating newspaper strike and a shift in advertising revenue from afternoon newspapers to television. The dovish *New York Post* would have been an entirely unsatisfactory venue for Alsop, and the hawkish *New York Daily News* decided against publishing his column. Robert Kintner dismally informed the president that he now had "no strong columnist support except for Drew Pearson in New York City itself on the Vietnam operation." But even Pearson bailed out. After North Vietnam's unexpected Tet offensive, in January 1968, Pearson notified Johnson "that your policies in the Far East are taking us down a perilous road which can end only in disaster for you personally and for the nation; and that I must leave you." Joe Alsop would not break ranks over Vietnam. "I rather enjoy being alone—so long as one is right in the end," he insisted. Yet isolation from his peers took its toll, and Alsop told an interviewer that he felt he had been around "since before the Flood." He had come to Washington at twenty-five, younger than most everyone around him, and by fifty-eight he described himself as "the dean of the columnists." "What about Walter Lippmann?" asked the interviewer. "He's retired," Alsop replied peevishly, "and, anyway, I was here first."[57]

Lyndon Johnson's withdrawal from the presidential race in 1968 disheartened Alsop. The columnist supported Hubert Humphrey and worried that a victory for Richard Nixon would have "about the same effect as the defeat of Lincoln by McClellan would have had in 1864." For opposite reasons, Walter Lippmann endorsed Nixon in 1968 as "the only one" capable of extracting the nation from Vietnam. "I think Nixon's whole future will be staked on getting a cease-fire and a self-respecting withdrawal of our land forces," Lippmann wrote in an influential column late in the campaign that enticed antiwar votes to that unlikely peace candidate. The instincts of both columnists were wrong. Nixon would end up impressing Alsop and disappointing Lippmann.[58]

To his surprise, Alsop discovered that President Nixon shared his conviction that the United States would sink to second-rate status if it lost in Vietnam. Alsop praised the "cool courage" of Nixon's stand on Southeast Asia, in columns that the White House press office excitedly circulated. When Nixon telephoned Alsop at home to discuss the planned invasion of Laos, word of the call spread around town. Rather than confirm Alsop's insider status, however, the call only solidified his reputation as "an Administration flack." A 1970 survey of the press corps placed Joe Alsop in the "Worst Columnist" list for being "hung up on Vietnam," and "getting stale." Unrepentant, Alsop declared: "We'll see who was over-optimistic about Viet Nam when the war is over. If we win, I shall have been a lot more right than most people." But the retired *New York Times* columnist Arthur Krock told colleagues that if a war crimes tribunal should follow Vietnam, then Joseph Alsop should stand in the dock for having talked Kennedy and Johnson into going to war. As Alsop's professional isolation continued his personal life also faltered, his fabled dinner parties degenerated into his rude diatribes over the war, his wife left him, and his brother Stewart died of leukemia in 1974. After that, Joe Alsop said he lost "the zest and gusto and eagerness to know what will happen next." He announced plans to end his column, a decision that others in the press corps regarded as long overdue. "Matter of Fact" last ran in December 1974, the same month that Alsop's distinguished rival, Walter Lippmann, died in New York at eighty-five.[59]

Walter Lippmann had left Washington, D.C., just as the last miles of concrete were being poured to complete a highway that encircled the city and provided it with a new metaphor. "Inside the Beltway" had a pejorative connotation suggesting that those who trafficked in knowledge at the highest-levels of government had lost touch with what the rest of the country outside the Beltway was thinking. During the Beltway's construction, an *Esquire* profile of the "Washington Press Establishment" drew attention to the remarkable longevity of columnists David Lawrence, Walter Lippmann, Drew Pearson, Arthur Krock, and Joseph Alsop. "Administrations may come and go," *Esquire* remarked, "but Arthur Krock is there forever." Shortly afterward, in 1966, the eighty-year-old Arthur Krock formally retired as a columnist for the *New York Times*. Assured that the *Times*'s editors welcomed his future contributions, Krock was chagrined when they deleted some of his opinions. "We third floor editors," managing editor Clifton Daniel informed him, "feel we have the right and duty to eliminate words that have an emotional content or editorial slant." Krock rarely submitted anything else to the *Times*. Only in retirement did he fully appreciate the extraordinary latitude with which he had written as a Washington columnist. He died in 1974, the same year as Stewart Alsop and Walter Lippmann. Drew Pearson and David Lawrence had predeceased them.[60]

"Every red-blooded Washington reporter wants to grow up to be a syndicated columnist," asserted the *Washington Post*'s Julius Duscha in 1970. Reporters admired the columnists' intellectual freedom and higher salaries, and their longer lunch hours and larger readerships. Within the new breed of Washington columnists, some such as Joseph Kraft modeled their style after Walter Lippmann. Others such as Rowland Evans and Robert Novak emulated the Alsop brothers' style of mixing reporting and opinion. Carl Rowan and William Raspberry were among the first African American columnists to break into the mainstream press; while Mary McGrory, Shana Alexander, and Elizabeth Drew covered politics unsentimentally from a woman's perspective. Conservatives and neoconservatives, from James J. Kilpatrick to George F. Will and Charles Krauthammer, claimed significant portions of the editorial pages. The *New York Times* began syndicating columns by James Reston, Tom Wicker, and Russell Baker as part of its news service to subscribing papers. As the columnists proliferated, Arthur Krock predicted that their individual impact would be diluted by the "glut of the product."[61]

With the number of newspapers shrinking, some columnists gravitated toward television. Jack Germond admitted that income from his appearances on TV panel shows allowed him to continue reporting and writing his newspaper column "rather than becoming an editor." Robert Novak observed that for every person who stopped him at an airport to talk about his column, a hundred others said, "I see you on television." Appearing on television expanded the audience for the columnists, but it also flattened some of their status by placing them on a par with many other eager "talking heads." The *Washington Post*'s social arbiter Sally Quinn observed that previously only a few columnists with the stature of Alsop, Lippmann, and Reston had played leading roles in the Washington social scene, while "the rest of the journalists were considered hacks, sort of not worthy." Television now turned a broader selection of Washington correspondents into national celebrities.[62]

The new breed of columnists continued to inform, irritate, and influence public opinion, although none dominated the national discourse as thoroughly as Lippmann and Alsop did in their prime. Nor did any subsequent president match Lyndon Johnson's fixation on the columnists. Joseph Alsop did not precipitate American involvement in the Vietnam War—that decision belonged to Lyndon Johnson and his military and diplomatic advisors—but Alsop fostered the sense of urgency under which Johnson made his decision. Walter Lippmann's diplomatic appeals offered some counterbalance, but both columnists traveled far past their roles as detached commentators on global matters of war and peace. In his forced retirement at his ranch in Texas, Johnson railed against the columnists. To Doris Kearns, his assistant in writing his memoirs, Johnson repeated practically verbatim the advice Jim Rowe had offered at the beginning of his presidency: "The Washington press are like a wolf pack when it comes to attacking public officials, but they're like a bunch of sheep in their own profession and they will always follow the bellwether sheep, the leaders of their profession." As long as the columnists stayed with him, he asserted, so had the rest of the press corps. "But once they left me in pursuit of their fancy prizes, everyone else left me as well."[63]

8

Off the Women's Page

Reporting on politics and governance was men's work—at least in the opinion of those who did the hiring for much of the twentieth century. Women who aspired to Washington reporting were directed to the women's pages, to cover embassy parties, social receptions, and other soft-news features. Mary McGrory had inched her way up from book reviewer for the *Washington Evening Star* to writing light editorials about squirrels and dogs, to doing a series of Capitol Hill profiles for the Sunday paper. One day in 1954, when she was thirty-five, the *Star's* national editor, Newbold Noyes, stopped at her desk to ask, "Say, Mary, aren't you ever going to get married?" If not, he had in mind expanding her assignments by sending her to cover the Army-McCarthy hearings. Noyes suggested that she could add some color and humor to their news accounts by reviewing the hearings in the style of a drama critic. Indeed, Joe McCarthy cast himself perfectly as the villain of the script and her barbed commentary on the proceedings drew favorable notice from the press corps. The *New York Times* bureau chief James Reston was sufficiently impressed with McGrory's writing to offer her a job as a reporter on his prestigious staff, as long as she did not mind also working part-time at the bureau's telephone switchboard. Chagrined, McGrory passed up the offer and remained at the *Star,* where her columns later earned her a Pulitzer Prize.[1]

Reston's switchboard bargain epitomized the second-class status that women journalists in Washington long endured. The predominantly male press corps saw Washington as "a man's town" and ran press operations like men's clubs. A survey of the press corps in the 1960s reported that its "twin fortresses" were the Gridiron and the National Press Club, noting that the Gridiron was the more exclusive while at the Press Club "almost anyone, providing he is a male, can get in." Neither club admitted women as a matter of policy. Women could join and pay dues to the White House Correspondents Association, but could not attend its annual dinners. The few Washington bureaus that employed women reporters invariably assigned them to cover the capital from the "women's angle." Hard news belonged to the men. When Bess Furman went to Washington for the Associated Press in 1929, she learned that "the AP men on Capitol Hill kept it as holy ground on which I was not supposed to step foot without explicit orders."[2]

Men defended their fraternal clubs and stag dinners as harmless social escapes from mixed company. For men, the National Press Club served as a convenient watering hole, especially as so many Washington reporters worked out of news bureaus on the lower floors of the National Press Building. They could take the elevator up to the club for a drink, a meal, and a little camaraderie. At the Gridiron Club's white-tie dinners, reporters socialized with prominent guests and performed a little political song and dance as a relief from the serious side of the news. Excluded as a class, women naturally saw these institutions differently, arguing that they combined social and professional activities. The National Press Club let men gather at teletype machines to read wire service reports, or look over the handout table where the stacks of press releases eliminated the need to make the rounds of the agencies. The Press Club bar provided a place to pick up the latest gossip or learn which bureaus were hiring. Press Club luncheons headlined prominent visitors whose responses to questions from the audience generated countless news stories. Membership in the Press Club made the workday easier; membership in the Gridiron Club conferred prestige.[3]

Women reporters found it difficult to overcome their newspapers' traditions and their editors' stereotypes. "For reasons I will never understand," presidential press secretary Pierre Salinger commented in the 1960s, the *New York Times* and *Washington Post* maintained policies of "printing news off the women's beat only in the women's section, regardless of its importance." In Washington, the women's pages provided employment for a small squad of society reporters, who claimed an advantage in collecting news over cocktails rather than outside of closed committee room doors. They argued that social receptions at the capital served as extensions of the political process, and pointed out that Washingtonians read the society news closely to determine who was in and who was out. Another cluster of women reported for the local Washington newspapers, usually covering the neighborhoods rather than the national news. They occasionally crossed paths with reporters on federal beats but led an essentially separate existence. "The political writers see Washington solely in terms of Capitol Hill, the White House, and the complex machinery of government," explained Ishbel Ross of the *New York Herald Tribune*. "They work in an exhilarating atmosphere of national drama. Once bitten with it, they rarely want to do anything else."[4]

Historically, the predominance of men in the Washington press corps had less to do with natural selection than with genetic engineering. Before 1880, twenty women had held congressional press gallery passes. After 1880, almost none sat in the press galleries for decades. A series of scandals had revealed that lobbyists were posing as journalists and reporters were moonlighting as lobbyists. To reform the system, the leading newspaper correspondents of the era persuaded Congress to give them control over press gallery accreditation. The reporters elected a Standing Committee of Correspondents to judge credentials, and they set rules that limited press gallery membership to those who filed dispatches for daily newspapers via telegraph. The rules eliminated the lobbyists but also excluded the women reporters, whose papers paid telegraph tolls only for breaking political news, and instructed them to mail in their society news. In the nineteenth century, graduates of a host of new women's colleges were entering journalism, but only an occasional woman could get into the congressional press galleries. The first to gain a seat after the rules change was Margaret Sullivan Burke, who published under the gender-neutral byline of M. S. Burke. She briefly held a press pass in 1887. The next, Isabel Worrell Ball, said that when she arrived as a correspondent for the *Lawrence (Kansas) Journal* and *Arkansas City Traveler* in 1891, the men of the press gallery admitted her "with the enthusiasm of a case of smallpox."[5]

Marie Manning reported for the *New York World* and wrote an advice column as "Beatrice Fairfax" for the *New York Journal* before retiring after her marriage in 1905. The stock market crash of 1929 forced her back into the job market and she resumed writing columns out of Washington. She rated the new women journalists she encountered as far more aggressive than those of her youth. "Who of us, in those days, would have dreamed of tackling a political figure on a political subject?" Manning wondered. In the interval, the Nineteenth Amendment had granted women the right to vote, and some of the activists who generated national publicity for the suffrage movement went on to pursue careers in journalism. In 1918 the former suffragist Cora Rigby scored a notable breakthrough by becoming Washington bureau chief for the *Christian Science Monitor*. Feminists such as Rigby resisted being "herded off" on the women's pages. "There is no more reason for this feature than there is for a men's page," declared Janet Stewart of the *Philadelphia North American*. "News belongs to the people, not to a sex."[6]

The generation of women journalists emerging from the suffrage movement founded the Women's National Press Club in 1919. Lacking the resources to buy or rent a permanent headquarters, club members met for lunch at different restaurants. Meanwhile, the all-male National Press Club constructed an imposing fourteen-story headquarters in 1927 on the site of Washington's old "Newspaper Row." Unlike the men's club, which rarely invited a woman to speak, the women invited prominent men to address their luncheons, although some of their guest speakers treated them like "debutantes to be flattered" instead of working journalists, leaving the women deflated and resentful.[7]

During the Jazz Age of the 1920s when women exerted a greater degree of economic independence and social liberation than before, newspapers opened more jobs for women in their editorial and marketing departments and also as reporters. Winifred Mallon, a State Department cable clerk, had written part-time for the Washington bureau of the *Chicago Tribune* since 1902. The *Tribune* gave her a byline whenever she dealt with women's issues, but anything else she wrote appeared as an anonymous "special." In 1913, Mallon started a column for the *Tribune* on the campaign for woman suffrage. During the First World War she earned a place on the Washington bureau's regular staff, writing a column on legislation pending in Congress. She mastered immigration legislation so thoroughly that a House committee called her as an expert witness. Mallon fell out with the *Tribune*'s management in 1925 and left the paper to handle publicity for the National Women's Party. At the 1928 political conventions, she freelanced for the *New York Times*, interviewing women delegates and wives of the candidates. That led the *Times* to hire her as the first woman member of its Washington staff, to cover the social side of the White House, weddings, the Red Cross, and similar assignments. A small woman who carried an oversized handbag that trailed along the ground, Mallon appeared eccentric, but colleagues recognized that she held her job because she possessed "a lively mind and the ability to think clearly and to write clearly." She reported for the *Times* until 1949, although years before her retirement the bureau turned over most of her beat to Bess Furman, a veteran of the Associated Press. Even after bureau chief Arthur Krock considered the aged Winifred Mallon "virtually no use," he kept her on the payroll because she was single and lacked a pension.[8]

Family connections drew May Craig and Mary Hornaday to Washington journalism. Trained as a nurse, Elisabeth May Craig got into the news business when her husband, the columnist Don Craig, was seriously injured in a car crash while on assignment in 1923. During his convalescence, she helped him put together his syndicated column, "On the Inside in Washington," for the Gannett newspapers in Maine. When her husband died in 1936, never having fully recovered, May Craig took over the column. Mixing political and social news, she presented Washington as "a regular sewing circle" where high level officials engaged in "chit-chat and gossip and little digs and humorous incidents." Craig alternately irritated and amused the men in the press corps and became something of a "hair shirt" to women reporters for her unrelenting advocacy of equal rights in the press galleries and press clubs. Although her column ran in only a few papers, her feisty style later gained her celebrity status on national radio and television news programs. Mary Hornaday, the daughter of a prominent Washington correspondent, joined the *Christian Science Monitor* after her graduation from Swarthmore. Bureau chief Cora Rigby assigned her to cover general political and economic news. The night that Hornaday turned in her first story in 1927, the bureau's telegraph operator complimented it by saying, "You write like a man." She remained a mainstay of her paper's Washington reporting for the next forty years.[9]

Ruby Black and Genevieve Forbes Herrick were reporters in their own right when they accompanied their journalist spouses to Washington. Scripps-Howard transferred Black's husband, Herbert Little, to Washington in 1924. Although she was also an experienced reporter and had taught journalism at the University of Wisconsin, Black had to take short-term assignments at one

Washington news office after another, until 1928 when she founded her own Ruby A. Black News Bureau, doing regional news reporting for a half dozen newspapers from Maine to Wisconsin. Genevieve Forbes Herrick had spent a decade as a star reporter for the *Chicago Tribune* before moving with her husband to Washington in 1931. Her publisher, Colonel Robert R. McCormick, employed women mostly as decoration for his paper. He preferred them to write "sob stories" or do stunt reporting where their daring deeds and disguises became part of the story. "Geno" Forbes, for instance, had gone through Ellis Island in 1921 disguised as an Irish immigrant. Later she won regular bylines for her interviews with everyone from Al Capone to Lady Astor, and spent so much time covering the Leopold-Loeb murder trial with her fellow *Tribune* reporter John Herrick that she married him. The judge postponed the sentencing over the weekend to avoid interfering with their wedding. When John became White House correspondent for the *Chicago Tribune,* Geno reported on the social side of the capital. Not until he accepted a government post in the Roosevelt administration did she get a chance to move into political reporting.[10]

In 1928 the Associated Press decided to hire some women reporters for its Washington bureau and "see how it worked." Barely twenty-one, Marguerite Young approached the bureau with a letter of introduction from her editor at the *New Orleans Item-Tribune.* A vivacious redhead, she became instantly popular with the young bachelors in the press corps. Her colleague Bess Furman complained that whenever a good story came along, Marguerite Young got the assignment because she had been "out dancing with the man 'on desk' the night before." Young dated New York Democratic senator Robert Wagner, but declined his offer of marriage because it would jeopardize her future in journalism. The investigative reporter Paul Y. Anderson admired Young's intensity and urged her to quit the anonymity of the AP to write under a byline. She took a job with the *New York World-Telegram,* a paper that proved far too orthodox for her radical politics. In the press gallery, Ruby Black teased about her new employment, "Marguerite, you don't *look* like a reactionary!" In fact, Young took classes on Marxism and accepted an offer to report on Washington for the Communist Party newspaper, the *Daily Worker.* Editor Clarence Hathaway sought to enlist professional journalists to make the *Worker* more readable—although its jargon-laden prose, as Whittaker Chambers later pointed out, made that "practically impossible." Hathaway assured Young that she need not join the Communist Party, so long as she wrote with an "iron hand in a silk glove." As an inducement, he hired her unemployed lover, Seymour Waldman, for another job at the Washington bureau.[11]

In 1934 Marguerite Young resigned from "the service of the capitalist press" and denounced the *World-Telegram* for the "uncounted reams of woman-story piffle" it published. She announced that she would set up "a really honest radical labor news bureau in Washington." Her transformation puzzled her old contacts in Congress. "How did a nice girl like you get mixed up with such people?" asked Representative Martin Dies, who later chaired the House Un-American Activities Committee. Being the Washington correspondent for the *Daily Worker* lost her few friends in the press galleries, where sentiments had shifted noticeably to the left during the depression. Finding no trouble in tapping her old sources on Capitol Hill, Young got an exclusive interview with Senator Wagner. She paid little attention to the party line, however, and was mortified when the *Worker* published a front-page retraction of one of her stories. The *Daily Worker* fired both Young and Waldman in 1936. The Communists dumped her "like an old shoe," she complained, "because they thought I no longer fitted into their strategy and tactics." But past association with the *Daily Worker* proved no impediment for Marguerite Young, who landed her next job with the rock-ribbed Republican *New York Herald Tribune*.[12]

The depression worked against women's career aspirations. Cutbacks and job losses deepened men's prejudices against any women who worked after marriage, and pregnancy invariably terminated a reporter's employment. Washington bureaus expected their staff to work odd hours and to travel on assignment anywhere at any time, and they made few concessions to family demands. Bess Furman, Beth Campbell, and Ruth Cowan all lost their jobs with the AP's Washington bureau because of marriage or childbirth. AP correspondent Flora Lewis secretly married *New York Times* correspondent Sydney Gruson in a civil ceremony over her lunch hour to hide it from her management. The Associated Press set its retirement age for women at fifty-five, while letting men work until sixty-five. The United Press had an even poorer record in dealing with women reporters. Texas-born Ruth Cowan told how she had covered the 1928 Democratic National Convention in Houston for the UP under the byline R. Baldwin Cowan. A UP executive called from Austin asking for Baldwin Cowan. "You're speaking to her," she replied. "No, no, I want to talk to him," the man insisted. "There ain't no 'him' here," she explained. "Look, United Press does not hire a woman," said the executive, who promptly fired her.[13]

In these hard times, women reporters gained a welcomed patron in Eleanor Roosevelt. After covering the election of 1932, Associated Press reporter Lorena Hickok urged the new first lady to hold her own press conferences. Insecure and uncertain about how the press would treat her, Roosevelt got further encouragement from her husband, who saw value in the additional publicity. Roosevelt's own past experience in Washington had shown her how women reporters picked up most of their information informally via the back stairs, and she saw no reason not to provide them news directly. She also reasoned that by limiting attendance at her conference to women, she could protect their jobs. In her first meeting with the press, Roosevelt nervously passed a box of chocolates around to break the tension and make it more informal. Later she told Hickok, "Well, the girls were so friendly and nice, I really think I'll have another conference." Over the next dozen years, Eleanor Roosevelt held 348 news conferences, the last one just a few hours before Franklin

Roosevelt's death. They evolved from announcements of her daily calendar and reports on various social functions into a regular channel for promoting her crusades for social welfare.[14]

The White House required no special press passes at first. Aides simply recorded the names of the reporters as they passed a desk in the front hall. The women congregated downstairs until an usher opened a gate to the stairway leading up to the family quarters. Ann Cottrell, who was in her early twenties when she began covering the White House for *Newsweek,* was amazed at the spryness of the older women reporters who sprinted ahead of her to claim the front seats. Roosevelt's conferences attracted many visiting society reporters for smaller newspapers, whom the regular Washington reporters considered "frivolous," but all the women benefited from the rule that barred men. The United Press bent its all-male employment practices to hire Ruby Black specifically to cover Mrs. Roosevelt's conferences.[15]

The women found Eleanor Roosevelt inexhaustible. To keep up with her pace, Bess Furman had to switch to low-heeled shoes. Yet much of what the women filed about her never got past their editors, who preferred such human interest stories as the first lady's participation in the White House Easter egg roll or her tumble from a horse to her opinions on social and economic issues. Frances Lide of the *Washington Star* conceded that she and other novice reporters were learning the ropes and submitted a lot of items that did not warrant publication. From time to time, however, the conferences got the women's bylines onto the front pages, beginning with Roosevelt's announcement that beer and wine would once again be served in the White House following the repeal of Prohibition. Typically, Roosevelt opened her press conferences by outlining her upcoming schedule, after which she might raise a specific issue or introduce a woman official from the administration to give a report, and then took questions. They could quote her remarks, except when one of her "inner circle," such as Bess Furman or Ruby Black, protectively interjected, "Oh, Mrs. Roosevelt, you'd better put that off the record."[16]

If more women showed up than there were chairs, the overflow would seat themselves informally on the floor. A photograph of an early conference, showing some of the women sitting at the first lady's feet, caused newsmen to scoff at "Mrs. Roosevelt's willing slaves." Viewing this image with disdain, Mrs. George F. Richards, a columnist for Republican papers in New England, vowed never to attend another press conference. Even Bess Furman, who had arranged for the photo to be taken, felt that it made the women look like "a bunch of tourists who never saw a President's wife before."[17]

On the same night that the president attended the all-male Gridiron Cub dinner, Eleanor Roosevelt invited the women reporters to a "Gridiron Widows" dinner at the White House. Among the guests was Secretary of Labor Frances Perkins, the sole member of the president's cabinet not invited to the Gridiron in 1933—nor to any of the other annual dinners during her twelve years in office. At the White House dinner, the women performed their own satirical skits and songs to parallel the entertainment at the men's dinners. Beth Campbell recalled that as soon as she stepped off the train at Union Station to start her new job with the AP, the newswoman who met her asked if she knew "Silent Night." She was to sing it that night for the "Gridiron Widows."[18]

Eleanor Roosevelt became one of them by publishing her own newspaper column, "My Day," and joining the Women's National Press Club in 1936. The women reporters developed such a deep affection for her that it influenced their reporting. A male reporter complained that Ruby Black's dispatches had "deteriorated into sweetmeats for the White House." Genevieve Forbes Herrick's anti–New Deal publisher, Colonel Robert R. McCormick, accused her of letting herself become "socially subsidized" by Mrs. Roosevelt. That prompted Herrick to quit the *Tribune* and write features for the North American Newspaper Alliance (NANA). Another of Roosevelt's admirers, Doris Fleeson, wrote a "Capital Stuff" column jointly with her husband, John O'Donnell. Fleeson remained a liberal internationalist while her husband and their newspaper, the *New York Daily News,* turned increasingly conservative and isolationist. After a bitter divorce, he took custody of the Washington column and she was demoted to writing radio news reports.[19]

Women reporters wanted to cover Franklin as well as Eleanor Roosevelt, but when too many reporters showed up for the president's press conferences, as Mary Hornaday recalled, "I was always the one to get cut off." Ishbel Ross's book, *Ladies of the Press,* published in 1936, had celebrated the advances of women reporters in Washington, but Bett Hooper of the *Washington Post* dissented. "The fact is that newspaper women are still regarded as a class apart," she wrote. "The male reporter has never believed that the bit of fluff bent over the typewriter next to his didn't enter the field . . . because of the glamour attached to it."[20]

Conditions and attitudes changed rapidly after the United States entered the Second World War. As the press galleries emptied of men who joined the military or went overseas as war correspondents, women took their places. A few women also left Washington to report on the war from abroad. Doris Fleeson escaped from radio writing by reporting from Europe for the *Woman's Home Companion.* Flora Lewis's scoops at the State Department convinced the AP to send her to London. May Craig advanced to the front lines in France and Germany despite rules that barred women from military planes and naval vessels because they lacked "facilities" for women. Craig bristled whenever the military used "facilities" as an excuse to prevent her "from doing what men reporters could do." While trying to join an expedition to Greenland, she told the officer in charge that all she needed was a bush. "Mrs. Craig," the officer replied, "in the Arctic there are no bushes."[21]

The former Washington reporter Jane Eads had taken an advertising job in New York but was drawn back into journalism by the war. As she listened to

President Roosevelt's radio address following the attack on Pearl Harbor, she made up her mind to return to Washington, "if they'll take me." Eads was hired by the Associated Press. The war finally enabled the veteran Winifred Mallon to cover some non-women's news for the *New York Times,* which ran her bylines on front-page stories about wartime coal strikes. Recent college graduates who had no prior experience in journalism also found work in Washington. "At the bottom of the manpower barrel," wrote *Time* magazine, newspapers recruited "more & more women." Thirty women had been accredited to the House and Senate press galleries in 1938, a number that more than tripled by 1944. Women handled every major beat until the familiar opening greeting at Washington press conferences, "Good morning, gentlemen," seemed inappropriate.[22]

A generation of women reporters who would become familiar faces in the press corps arrived at the capital during the war. Newcomer Helen Thomas left Detroit for Washington in 1942, working as a restaurant hostess until the *Washington Daily News* hired her as a copygirl. Then she knocked on doors at the National Press Building until she found a job with the United Press writing radio news. Sarah McClendon came to the Pentagon to handle publicity for the Women's Auxiliary Army Corps (WAACs). A fleeting wartime marriage left her pregnant, ending her military service. Nine days after giving birth in 1944, McClendon visited her fellow Texan, Bascom Timmons, at his regional news bureau in the National Press Building. Short of staff, Timmons hired her on the spot. His office manager disapproved of women reporters, however, and McClendon spent several fruitless days tracking down members of Congress before she realized that the press galleries could have helped her. "Why didn't you tell me there was a press gallery?" she confronted the office manager. "Well, I figured you wouldn't be here but a few days," he replied.[23]

Ruby Black had been the sole woman in the United Press Washington bureau for years. After she left to take a wartime government job, the UP hired eleven women for wartime reporting and another eight to handle editorial and office work. Among them was Eileen Shanahan, a District of Columbia native and former copygirl at the *Washington Post.* At the UP, Shanahan started on dictation and moved up to the radio desk. The AP similarly replaced the departing men with women. A recent college graduate, Virginia Van Der Veer, typed stories that reporters dictated to her. She jumped at the chance to take a reporting job on the "lowest rung" of the ladder. As a southerner, Van Der Veer was assigned to cover Alabama, Louisiana, and Mississippi on Capitol Hill, which she called "almost as routine as covering the PTA." The news she collected dealt mostly with the appointment of postmasters and the awarding of war contracts. If someone in her delegation happened to make big news, the AP would give the story to one of the men.[24]

The war also prompted Eleanor Roosevelt's only coed press conference. On her return from the Pacific Theater in 1943, she thought her battlefront report might interest men well as women, and she opened her press conference accordingly. So many reporters attended that the venue had to be shifted to the Green Room, where they all stood. Twenty men shifted uneasily among the fifty women reporters, "like little boys at their first dance," and they deferred to the women in asking questions. "I never realized before that a big group of women could be so terrifying to the male of the species," Roosevelt observed.[25]

Wartime security forced the "professionalization" of the women's press corps. The open nature of Eleanor Roosevelt's press conferences had haphazardly admitted freelancers and sporadic social reporters, but now the Secret Service insisted on a formal system of accreditation. The regular reporters seized the opportunity to set rules that paralleled those of the White House Correspondents Association and would winnow out the amateurs. They issued passes in the name of the "Mrs. Roosevelt's Press Conference Association." The day that these rules went into effect in 1942, Winifred Mallon was stranded outside the White House, having neglected to submit an application. "You can't do this to the *New York Times!*" Mallon protested. The rules limited access to full-time reporters for daily papers, but as they referred only to "persons," two men applied: Gordon Cole of the leftist tabloid *PM* and Frederick Othman, a Washington humor columnist. If women believed in equality, May Craig insisted, they ought to admit both sexes. The equally feminist Ruby Black argued against her, and the accrediting board sided with Black. "Some members seemed to feel it is up to us to end the discrimination against men," board chair Mary Hornaday explained to Eleanor Roosevelt; "others felt that women have so many strikes against them in this business that is wise to keep this one advantage." Roosevelt was inclined to let the decision rest with the reporters, but she warned that if admitting men changed the press conferences drastically, she might discontinue them. The women remained divided until Roosevelt "saved" them by announcing that she still wanted only women at her conferences.[26]

Eleanor Roosevelt held her last White House press conference on April 12, 1945. That day the questioning centered around Drew Pearson's "Washington Merry-Go-Round" column, which had described a chill in the relations between the first lady and the "press girls" after the White House accused a woman reporter of misquoting her. Roosevelt's defenders deftly shifted the issue from an attack on the White House to an attack on themselves. Bess Furman stopped the first lady from answering and suggested that the association would take up the matter the next day. But Franklin Roosevelt's death that afternoon altered everything. The association had to struggle for the inclusion of a single woman in the pool of ten reporters who covered the president's White House funeral. Before leaving Washington, Eleanor Roosevelt held a farewell meeting with the women journalists but permitted no quotes for publication.[27]

Having grown accustomed to Eleanor Roosevelt's press conferences, women reporters were "really caught short when we didn't have regular access to the First Lady," commented Malvina Stephenson, who ran a one-woman news bureau. They urged Bess Truman to continue the official organization, promising to change its name if she did. More reticent in public than her predecessor, the new president's wife had no intention of holding press conferences and let the association dissolve. Her social secretary talked with reporters, but she dismissed routine personal inquiries by insisting she "wouldn't think of asking Mrs. Truman such a question!"[28]

The men returned from the war to reclaim their old jobs or take better ones. Helen Thomas managed to keep her spot at the UP's radio desk only because the salary was so low and the hours so unappealing that no man wanted it. Eileen Shanahan also stuck to the UP's radio desk until she left to have her first child in 1947. Bascom Timmons had to let Sarah McClendon go, but he helped her set up her own McClendon News Service, turning over a few of his own accounts. Virginia Van Der Veer, who had been promoted to the AP's national staff, was advised that she "need no longer worry about complicated subjects like freight rates." Her future reporting would be confined to what outfit the first lady planned to wear at public events. The ultimate Washington career woman, Representative Clare Booth Luce, advised young women to get married, and Van Der Veer did just that six months later, abandoning Washington reporting.[29]

The end of the war sent women reporters back to the women's pages. Judy Mann, who wrote for the *Washington Daily News* and later for the *Washington Post,* described the newspapers of that era as being "in the grip of white men whose wives had stayed at home." It took another two decades for Washington women reporters to regain the level they achieved during the war. As jobs disappeared and assignments turned mundane, veteran women reporters stood in employment lines ahead of newly-arrived aspirants. Although many women wanted to keep doing straight news reporting, they accepted the prevailing attitudes and exchanged their feminism for femininity. Symbolic of the shift was the Women's National Press Club publication in 1955 of a cookbook, *Who Says We Can't Cook!*[30]

The postwar era revived the "Queen Bees" who did social reporting for the women's pages. Betty Beale promoted her society column for the *Washington Star* as "politics after six." Maxine Cheshire, who had cut her teeth as a reporter in Harlan County, Kentucky, came to Washington in 1954 with no taste for "tea-party journalism," but the only job she could get was as a society reporter for the *Washington Post.* Her editor, Marie Sauer, aspired to transform the paper's For and about Women section into something more substantial (although she failed in her attempt to rename the section For and about People). Sauer hired women with hard-news experience and insisted that they be fully aware of current political issues before venturing out to cover social functions. "See what the Secretary of Defense thinks about this," she instructed reporters. Judith Martin learned that it was easier to "talk my way into someplace I didn't belong, grab the president of the United States and ask him some awful question no one else would dare to" than to explain to Sauer why she had not.[31]

Some of the women fiercely resisted returning to the women's pages. Those who had gone through exhilarating wartime assignments were outraged as men muscled them out of choice assignments. Georgie Anne Geyer, who entered journalism in 1959, thought that her predecessors' quest for professionalism had caused them to detach themselves from other women. "They were responding to the demands of a very hard time," Geyer reasoned. "But the fact was that they hated women and hated being women. They were always (Good God!) parachuting here and walking around in Marines' clothing there." Doris Fleeson came back from the war to start her own hard-hitting Washington column, for which she roamed the Capitol like "a tiger in white gloves" stalking her prey. Marguerite Higgins breezed into Washington after winning a Pulitzer Prize for her Korean War reporting for the New York *Herald Tribune*. She defied both her male colleagues and the military brass to accompany troops into combat and sent back dramatic eyewitness accounts. Korea had made Higgins a national celebrity, and advertisers sought her endorsement. In 1957 she shocked the Washington press corps by appearing in ads for Crest toothpaste and Camel cigarettes. Because the rules of the press galleries specifically prohibited its members from doing paid promotional work, the Standing Committee of Correspondents called Higgins to account. She gave up her accreditation rather than the ads, commenting that she rarely went to the press galleries or to a press conference. "I depend upon personal contact for news," she asserted.[32]

Joining Fleeson and Higgins as Washington political columnists in the 1960s were Marianne Means for Hearst's King Features and Mary McGrory for the *Washington Star*. Means found that editors had "a hard time taking a young woman seriously," and put the top stories off-limits to her. She also suffered from the absence of a Hearst paper in Washington, which meant that Washington officials rarely read her pieces. She hoped that the *Washington Post* would pick up the column, but concluded that it wanted no women on its editorial pages. While Means saw the small number of women political columnists and reporters as a sign of discrimination, Mary McGrory argued that it was up to each woman individually to prove herself a good journalist. McGrory credited newsmen with having helped get her established, but she complained that male politicians talked to women reporters more about their personal lives than their politics. "I've heard more than I care to know about unhappy wives and wayward children," she groaned.[33]

At televised presidential press conferences, the few women journalists stood out from an otherwise all-male press corps. Tiny May Craig sported distinctive hats to get herself noticed in the crowd. The men regarded her as a comic figure, but her fiery questioning made her a popular panelist on the television news program *Meet the Press*. Sarah McClendon had learned to shout her questions to be heard. Other reporters shook their heads at her bellowing Texas twang and called her a "buzz saw" who harassed successive presidents. The two African American women reporters, Alice Dunnigan and Ethel Payne, also stood out, either to be called on or to be ignored depending on whether a president wanted to deal with questions on civil rights. But for most women reporters a White House assignment still meant covering the first lady.[34]

"She's such a good reporter everyone forgets she's a woman," ABC news broadcaster John Scali once said of Associated Press correspondent Fran Lewine. The prejudice embedded in that statement testified to the persistent obstacles facing female journalists, even as more opportunities opened. In 1961 the *New York Times* hired Marjorie Hunter, an experienced legislative reporter, to take over its coverage of the social side of Washington news. The next year the *Times* bureau added Eileen Shanahan on economics, and the following year Nan Robertson on politics—over the objections of bureau chief James Reston, who believed that any more women would disrupt the office. The women were the lowest-paid members of the *Times* bureau, and the most excluded. "It was the men Scotty called to his councils in his office," Robertson fumed. Once Reston invited the bureau staff to lunch with the *Times*'s new publisher, Arthur "Punch" Sulzberger, at the male-only Metropolitan Club, so the women reporters stayed back at their desks.[35]

As journalists, women confronted situations that men never faced. When Susan Jacoby applied to the *Washington Post* in 1962, she was required to write an essay on how she planned to combine motherhood with reporting. "I poured all of my childless 21-year-old wisdom into several paragraphs insisting that the combination of work with parenthood would pose *absolutely no problem,*" she recalled. "If the personnel head had told me to produce an essay on my method of birth control, I probably would have done that too." Newsmen, by contrast, were hardly known for domesticity. They worked late, slept late, missed meals, and left their wives to raise the children while they were off on assignment. Newswomen balanced deadlines with school schedules, illnesses, and other parental crises. Isabelle Shelton, writing for the women's pages of the *Washington Star,* once got an exclusive interview with President Lyndon Johnson on the same day as her daughter's fourteenth birthday. Before going to the Oval Office, she phoned instructions to her family and placed a grocery order for the birthday party. During the interview, Johnson suddenly announced that he was going to a wedding in Maryland, and invited Shelton to ride along in his limousine. After the wedding she tried to slip away unobtrusively, but Johnson corralled her into his limousine to finish the interview while they sped back to the White House. As the motorcade approached her neighborhood, Shelton confessed her predicament and begged to be let out. The rest of the press corps called her "the only reporter in history who voluntarily broke off an interview with the President."[36]

Job pressures created agonizing self-doubts. Maralee Schwartz, a researcher at the *Washington Post*, got promoted to reporting on politics just before the 1964 Republican convention in San Francisco. After filing one of her first dispatches, she suffered a bout of anxiety over what the editors would think of it. Schwartz was waiting anxiously at the convention hall when her publisher, Katharine Graham, walked in, noticed her expression, and asked what was the matter. "Aren't we women just like that?" said Graham, who had just succeeded her late husband as publisher. "We're our own worst enemies. We grew up thinking that only men could do the big important jobs. We always worry that we're not good enough. Do you think there is even one man out there who is worrying about what he wrote? Not one. We're our own hardest critics."[37]

In renovating the *Washington Post*, Graham's new managing editor, Ben Bradlee, had combined the women's pages with theater and music reviews into a new section called Style, and had appointed a man as its editor. Where previously Marie Sauer had to fight to get a photographer for a story or to make the composing room listen to her ideas about layout for the women's pages, the section's new editor got what he wanted in terms of graphics and a mix of political and social commentary. On the other hand, he showed little interest in the women's movement. For and about Women had been systematically following federal policy on the status of women, but Style largely abandoned that coverage, just as it jettisoned the traditional women's reporting on parties, fashions, and interiors. These were the "frothy" items that Katharine Graham had especially enjoyed. When she complained to Bradlee about some of the snide material appearing in Style, he snapped back, "I can't edit this section unless you get your finger out of my eye." Thinking twice, Bradlee decided to mollify his publisher by restoring some of the society news, but the reporters he had just liberated from the women's pages now considered it sexist to be stereotyped as party reporters.[38]

Bradlee solved his problem by hiring Sally Quinn, whose background in public relations and party giving had not included writing a single word as a journalist. Quinn's inexperience made her copy bright and biting. Unwilling to flatter her hosts with what she called the typical type of "sycophantic, fawning" social reporting of the past, she produced profiles that managed to offend her subjects as much as they amused her readers. Embassies and nervous socialites banned her from their gatherings. "It became obvious that it was dangerous to invite reporters, no longer harmless, and one's guests began to resent it when they arrived to find a society reporter and photographer on hand," Quinn observed. If word got out that reporters were going to cover a party, "no one who was anyone" would attend, which defeated the purpose of the reporters being there. Outside of White House social events, Washington's antiquated party reporting largely passed into history.[39]

When it came to their own social functions, newsmen wanted to keep their distance from women reporters. The prestigious Nieman Fellowships—which gave promising journalists a year of study at Harvard, taking any classes they desired—at first went only to men. The program's director, Louis Lyons, recommended admitting women reporters, but Harvard president James B. Conant objected. "Why, you serve whiskey at these Nieman dinners, don't you?" Conant asked. "Let's not complicate it." In Washington, May Craig protested that dues-paying women members of the White House Correspondents Association were barred from its annual dinner for the president. The head of the association, the United Press's White House correspondent Merriman Smith, advised Craig that the men kept women out because the entertainment was "too dirty." They liked it bawdy, Smith explained, and had no intention of changing "the kind of dinner it is." When the women sent checks for tickets anyway, the association returned their money and tried to hide the date of the next year's dinner. "It hurts women professionally to be barred," Craig complained, "and it makes the Association unrepresentative." The singular exception to the social ban on women reporters was the annual dinner given by the Radio Correspondents Association. Accustomed to being treated like second-class journalists by the print reporters, radio correspondents formally declared that female colleagues were "fully entitled and will be expected to attend any social functions sponsored by the association." However, the radio newsmen worried about inviting women guests when their wives were not also included.[40]

It especially vexed women reporters that the National Press Club refused to admit them as either members or guests. An oil painting of a nude "Phyrne the Courtesan," prominently displayed in its lounge, reinforced its men's club image. Membership in the National Press Club was a prerequisite for most newsmen. The day that Roy McGhee joined the Washington bureau of United Press in 1958, his bureau chief told him, "Well, the very first thing we have to do is get you to join the National Press Club." For newswomen operating out of the same bureaus, the club remained forbidden territory. They could not walk ten feet inside it to read the teletypes, contact co-workers in the bar, or take a meal there, regardless of how late they worked in the bureaus downstairs, or what the weather was outside. In 1946 a room used to store broken furniture was converted into the Ladies Dining Room for the members' wives. So long as a woman reporter was married to a member, or was invited as a member's guest, she could use this small dining room in the evening, provided that she did not venture into the rest of the club. During the 1950s the wives successfully extended their privileges to the main dining room, but went too far when they requested access to the bar. "I can tell you that anguish prevailed in the board room," wrote columnist Frederick Othman. He recorded that some club members threatened to resign "if a female ever stuck her powdered nose past the swinging door." The men struck a compromise by opening a Ladies' Cocktail Lounge and affixing a brass plate on the door to the members' bar: "Accompanied Male Guests Only."[41]

The women ran their own press club but resented being treated as a class apart. "I had always felt that it was important to be on a newspaper as a reporter," said Beth Campbell, "just like a man reporter." When her husband, Joe Short, became president of the National Press Club in 1948, he proposed admitting women, but the motion lost. "I don't want to drink at their bar," said the Hearst columnist Marianne Means, "but the problem is that sometimes they close off easy access to sources that others, my competitors, have." Once when Sarah McClendon tried to attend a Texas Senate candidate's press conference at the National Press Club, attendants stopped her at the front desk because the meeting was taking place in the bar. She beat furiously on the counter and raised a ruckus until the candidate emerged, begged ignorance of the rules, and moved his press conference to another room where she could attend. "The men don't want us in here, so we're just going to have to push our way in," McClendon advised a young intern. "I believe in being aggressive," she asserted. "How else could a woman from east Texas get anywhere in Washington?"[42]

For women reporters, the worst part of the exclusion was being shut out whenever the National Press Club held luncheons for visiting dignitaries. The Cold War made Washington a powerful draw for world leaders, who sought to reach American audiences, and the State Department obliged by scheduling them to speak at the Press Club. As an AP reporter, Jane Eads said she could usually interview the leading personalities away from the Press Club, "unless it was some diplomat or somebody coming from a foreign country and only there for a day." But women from smaller news organizations rarely stood a chance of obtaining an exclusive interview.[43]

When the National Press Club admitted Louis Lautier as its first African American member in 1955, the women hoped that their turn would soon follow. Sarah McClendon submitted a formal application, which the board denied receiving. Other women made their own efforts, but division within the Women's National Press Club on the issue hindered collective action. Some women preferred having their own club instead of joining with the men. Others suspected that southerners at the National Press Club were promoting women for membership as a tactic for keeping black men out. Liz Carpenter, the *Houston Post* correspondent who headed the Women's National Press Club, explained that women reporters "don't like being used by the Dixiecrats" when she rejected their proffered alliance. Finally, in 1956, the men who ran the National Press Club proposed a compromise that invited all members of the "working press," including women, to attend their "newsmaker" luncheons, so long as nonmembers agreed to listen to the proceedings from the balcony above the ballroom.[44]

On the floor below, the men dined with visiting editors, publishers, lobbyists, and friends. In the balcony above, women stood in a narrow space alongside television cameras and crews, hot lights and coils of electrical wiring, and any overflow of men. Women in the balcony could not question the speakers, and had to enter and leave via a back door. They were expected to vacate the premises as soon as the programs ended. For Nan Robertson, "it couldn't have been meaner." After Marjorie Hunter stood on a rolled-up carpet at the back of the balcony in order to see, and even then could barely hear what was being said, she stormed back to the *Times* office and told her bureau chief, "Scotty, don't you ever send me to that damned National Press Club again." Reston appeared perplexed by her attitude.[45]

Dissatisfied with their perch, the newswomen petitioned scheduled speakers not to address the Press Club unless women could sit in the dining room as guests. One of the few to comply was Soviet premier Nikita Khrushchev, who in 1959 gladly seized the opportunity to publicize an American injustice. Thanks to Khrushchev, thirty-three women broke bread with the men—for that luncheon only. Molly Thayer of the *Washington Post* wandered into the members' bar that day and was hurriedly escorted out. Club president Bill Lawrence gruffly admonished her to "try to act like a lady if you can while we must have you in here." Lawrence, the top political correspondent for the *New York Times*, took a leave of absence from the paper to devote himself to his presidency of the National Press Club, and he particularly relished the opportunity of introducing its distinguished luncheon speakers. This amused his younger colleagues at the *Times* such as Russell Baker, who rated the club presidency "as just two notches above total dreariness." Lawrence was so outraged over the women's efforts to disrupt his presidency that President Dwight Eisenhower's press secretary, James Hagerty, impishly proposed holding a summit meeting between Lawrence and Women's National Press Club president Helen Thomas to settle their differences. "With all the trouble in the world today, involving the White House, I would think that Hagerty could successfully devote his time to affairs other than those which concern the National Press Club," Lawrence griped. The women had their own club, and he was sure that "none of our members would want to join theirs." Helen Thomas replied that her club members wanted only their professional right "to cover any head of state who comes to Washington." Editors should not have to decide against sending someone on assignment because the host institution discriminated against them.[46]

Politicians took flak in the crossfire. Candidates for the 1960 presidential election spoke at the National Press Club at their own risk. Vice President Richard Nixon compensated by bringing his wife, Pat, to a club luncheon, while Massachusetts senator John F. Kennedy looked up at the women reporters in the balcony and said, "My mother is in Chicago and wasn't able to be with us today so I invited May Craig to come along." Craig took a bow from the balcony.[47]

Women reporters counted on Kennedy to support their bid for equal access, and they felt betrayed when his State Department continued to schedule visiting dignitaries at the Press Club. At a press conference in 1961, Sarah McClendon pointed out that Kennedy did not visit clubs that were racially segregated, and asked why he allowed members of his administration to participate "in functions where women newspaper reporters are barred." Kennedy replied that as an honorary member of the Press Club he thought the luncheons were professional events to which "all working reporters" should be permitted on a basis of equality. But the new club president John Cosgrove of *Broadcasting* magazine called it ridiculous to have the issue brought up at a presidential press conference. He advised the women reporters to "mind their own business." On Air Force One, Kennedy privately lobbied reporters in the press pool in favor of giving women full privileges at the Press Club. The UPI's Merriman Smith reminded the president that feelings ran high against the idea and advised him to stick to "things you understand, like the Congo." When Kennedy persisted, Bill Lawrence responded with exasperation, "Look, Mr. President, I might sleep with them, but I'll be damned if I'll eat lunch with them."[48]

When Martin Luther King Jr. led the March on Washington in 1963, he spoke at the National Press Club over the women's protests. Feeling an urgent need to reach the mainstream press, the civil rights leader was willing to address an audience segregated by gender rather than by race. The humor columnist Art Buchwald caught the irony by insisting that "our women were happy to sit in the balcony until outside agitators from the North came down here and started trouble." If the men let the women reporters eat with them, he predicted, "pretty soon they'll want to dance with us and neck with us, and before you know it all the barriers will be down and they'll be wanting to play poker with us."[49]

At the same time, the *Washington Post* took Susanna McBee off a civil rights story that year because she could not attend male-only press conferences at the National Press Club. The edict infuriated *Post* reporter Elsie Carper, the new president of the Women's National Press Club, and she escalated its campaign to keep speakers away. Carper cabled women members of the British Parliament to ask them to dissuade Labor Party leader Harold Wilson from speaking at the Press Club. Wilson got the message and addressed the press at the British embassy. After Lyndon Johnson assumed the presidency in 1963, reporter Liz Carpenter became press secretary to Lady Bird Johnson and worked from inside the White House to discourage Johnson administration officials from appearing at Press Club luncheons unless women journalists sat beside the men.[50]

The National Press Club lost ground on all fronts. Younger men regarded the ban as antediluvian. The *Washington Post* columnist Nicholas von Hoffman dismissed the club as "a dull place with all the attractive contemporaneous spirit of a 1927 dining car." Its membership further dwindled as the larger news bureaus moved out of the Press Building into newer offices. Getting to the club at Fourteenth and F Streets grew less convenient after Washington dismantled its streetcar system in 1963. The middle class spread into the suburbs of Maryland and Virginia and changed patterns of commuting that reduced the nightly crowd at the members' bar. The 1968 riots further devastated much of the capital's downtown and the long-delayed plans to renovate Pennsylvania Avenue left the vicinity of the National Press Club looking dilapidated and dangerous.[51]

Don Larrabee, who reported for newspapers in Maine, had not campaigned as a reformer when he won the National Press Club presidency, since he noted that it was "impossible . . . to seek office in the Club if you favored admission of women members." Although he did not consider himself a champion of women's rights, Larrabee realized that the club had to admit women "or go down the drain." Other board members agreed and during a mid-summer meeting, when attendance was low, they adopted a resolution to put the admission of women to a vote of the entire membership. They hoped that most members "would be too embarrassed to reject the ladies of the press in a public referendum." Among those who opposed the initiative was the syndicated columnist Ralph de Toledano, who warned, "First it's the tap room. Then the billiard room. Then the card room. And eventually it'll be the men's room." The first vote, by mail ballot, fell short of the two-thirds requirement to change the constitution. A second vote, by a show of hands at the annual membership meeting, carried 227 to 56. A last-ditch proposal to reserve the bar and card room for the men lost in a sea of hands. Some senior members of the club never spoke to Larrabee again.[52]

Twenty-four women members entered the National Press Club in February 1971. "You don't know what this means to me," said a tearful Sarah McClendon. "I've worked 25 years on the 10th floor—it's taken me a quarter of a century to travel three floors." Some of the men felt misty-eyed as well. *New York Daily News* Washington correspondent Paul Healy lamented that the men's bar, "the safest haven from wives and girl friends in town," had passed into memory. On the day that women were admitted, UPI reporter Roy McGhee grabbed Judith Martin of the *Washington Post* and said, "Come with me, we're going to integrate the men's bar." The bartender served her a beer and expressed his hope that she would choke on it.[53]

The Women's National Press Club now renamed itself the Washington Press Club and voted to admit men. But the club's inability to obtain a liquor license complicated efforts to hold social events at the townhouse it used for its headquarters. Meanwhile, the National Press Club still faced pressing financial problems. One president of the club had to pay for beer delivery himself to keep the bar open, and the aging building required extensive renovation. Rather than perpetuate the competition, the National Press Club proposed a merger with the women's club in 1985. The women sold their townhouse and used the proceeds to establish a separate Washington Press Club Foundation. Fittingly, the merger cleared the way to renovate the ballroom and the hated balcony.[54]

Integration of the National Press Club left the Gridiron as the last male bastion of the Washington press corps. When Bess Furman first went to the

House press gallery for the AP, she noticed "the old grads, the gentlemen who wear the little gold pins of the Gridiron Club on their coat lapels." The Gridiron's fifty members represented the most prominent members of the Washington press corps. Since its founding in 1885, the Gridiron had claimed recognition as "the most celebrated dining organization in the country, if not the world." At its dinners, the Gridiron had two fixed rules: Ladies were always present; reporters never were. Both were figures of speech. Women did not attend, but speakers had to avoid off-color and offensive humor as if they did. Journalists packed the hall, but all remarks were off-the-record. Back in 1907 the club's more progressive members had passed a motion to invite female guests to the dinners, but stand-patters voted to delay the invitations for another fifty years. It took longer.[55]

The Gridiron's limited membership also excluded most men in the press corps, which generated some scorn. The *New York Times* correspondent Harrison E. Salisbury regarded the club as "an assembly of troglodytes," and recommended that women celebrate their exclusion rather than protest it. Still, the Gridiron's unbending resistance rankled women reporters, particularly when they heard about skits that belittled women. Columnist Doris Fleeson furiously confronted *New York Herald Tribune* correspondent Robert Donovan for dressing up as Eleanor Roosevelt in a Gridiron parody. "Although Doris was a good friend of mine, I was unaware that she was a red-hot feminist," Donovan later commented. "In fact, like most members of the Gridiron Club in the 1950s, I was under the impression that feminism had passed into history with the women's suffrage movement."[56]

The octogenarian Arthur Krock revered the Gridiron as a "men's night on the town." *Washington Post* columnist Nicholas von Hoffman noted that his boss, Katharine Graham, "would be arrested if she tried to crash the stud party Saturday night, but her competitors, male newspaper owners, will be allowed to come and make contact with the highest government officials." At the 1971 Gridiron dinner, President Nixon and Vice President Spiro Agnew performed a skit at two pianos, with Agnew playing "Dixie" to drown out any tune Nixon attempted—a musical reference to the administration's "Southern Strategy." Outside on the street, a twenty-two-year-old freelance writer on environmental issues, Rachel Scott, had organized a protest against the discriminatory dinner. About thirty women reporters, influenced by the women's movement they were covering, walked the picket line. They were joined by Carl Bernstein of the *Washington Post* and a few other men. The picketers held open the doors of the club to embarrass "all those nice liberal editors and publishers" going in until the Washington police moved them away from the hotel's main entrance under the pretext that they were picketing within five hundred feet of the Soviet embassy down the block. Most of the picketers complied, although Rachel Scott, carrying a protest sign that read "Gridiron Studs are Sexist Bigots," was arrested for disorderly conduct.[57]

At the *Washington Post* and *Washington Star*, signs posted in the women's restrooms invited staff to evening meetings to discuss existing job inequities and the media's reinforcement of gender stereotypes: "An awareness of women as people must start here." After several meetings the women staff presented petitions demanding better salaries and more women in managerial positions. Unfortunately, their story was overshadowed that day when the National Guard killed four students at Kent State University. In response to the women's demands, the *Washington Post* editor Ben Bradlee pledged to expand the role of women in the newsroom "as fast as possible, consistent with quality and opportunity." Bradlee did not move fast enough to stop the women at the *Post* from filing a formal complaint with the Equal Employment Opportunity Commission. In 1974 the EEOC concluded that the *Post* concentrated women reporters in its Style and Metro sections, had no women editors or assistant editors, and paid women less than men doing comparable work.[58]

The Gridiron members meanwhile attempted to defuse the women's demands by hosting a special dinner for their wives and prominent Washington women. Club president Jack Steele welcomed "Members of the Women's Lib" to the event and assured them that the Gridiron members "would be happy to have women admitted to membership—in the National Press Club." The empty gesture calmed no tempers. By then, the *New York Daily News* correspondent Ann Wood and other reporters had organized the ad hoc Journalists for Professional Equality and sent a request to everyone on the Gridiron's high-level guest list for the special dinner: "The Gridiron Club, which has always represented its members as the most distinguished journalists in the Washington press corps, gives a dinner each year for government leaders. Women journalists are barred from membership and from attending this prestigious event for our profession. . . . If you are invited, we urge you to register your disapproval of such professional discrimination by declining to attend and by making your reasons known."[59]

As a private club, the Gridiron men felt under no more obligation to invite women to their dinner than to have them "sit in on the Saturday night poker game," but Gridiron members hated being roasted by their critics. They were irked when presidential aspirant George McGovern withdrew his acceptance of an invitation to the dinner. Invited officials who ignored the boycott included such prominent liberals as Senator Hubert Humphrey and Supreme Court justice William O. Douglas. They entered the hotel to cries of "shame, shame" and "go home." Senator Bob Dole, whose Gridiron speech that night admittedly fell flat, later quipped, "Frankly, after my poor performance, I had the feeling I should not have 'crossed the picket line.'"[60]

The protests inspired some Gridiron members to lobby for change internally. Alan Otten of the *Wall Street Journal* and Grant Dillman of UPI proposed inviting women officials to the annual dinners as guests and opening membership to "otherwise qualified newspaperwomen." The opposition, led by club president Jack Bell, the AP's chief political correspondent, responded that a poll of the membership showed a preference for stag affairs. The dissidents, who also included reporters Jack Germond, Peter Lisagor, Richard Dudman, and the cartoonist Herblock, rebutted with their own poll showing wide support for admitting women. Unless the club acted, these dissidents intended to invite women as their guests to the next dinner. Gridiron members split largely along generational lines. Older members mostly clung to the social traditions of the club; younger members saw it as a professional organization that should not discriminate. Finally, Gridiron president Jack Bell became convinced that "the Club must move ahead and recognize the importance of women's role in government and in our society." Members voted 24 to 17 to permit women as guests, but not as members. In 1972 invitations went out to Mrs. Nixon, members of Congress, Katharine Graham, and Coretta Scott King. "The sex barrier in the all-male Gridiron Club has been breached," wrote *Washington Star* reporter Isabelle Shelton, "but only slightly."[61]

The Gridiron dinner of April 1972 featured representatives Martha Griffiths and Margaret Heckler as speakers. However, most of the invited women, including Coretta Scott King, Senator Margaret Chase Smith, and anthropologist Margaret Mead, declined to attend. Katharine Graham had wanted to go after years of exclusion, but reluctantly declined her invitation at the urging of women reporters at the *Post*. Instead, Graham and editor Meg Greenfield drove around the hotel that night to observe the guests run the gauntlet of picketers carrying placards that read: "This is the Last Supper." Representative Shirley Chisholm, the first African American woman to serve in Congress, made headlines by declining the Gridiron's invitation with a statement, "Guess who's not coming to dinner!" She charged that the Gridiron's lack of women and minority members was "symbolic of the racism and sexism which pervades the news industry." In the parking garage entrance to the hotel, Sarah McClendon ambushed Hubert Humphrey, who assured her, "I'll battle for you, I'll work inside." True to his word, Humphrey concluded his after dinner remarks by proposing a Humphrey amendment to add "and women" to the club's constitution. The proposal was "pure Humphrey," Gridiron member Richard Wilson responded in his column, because "his solution was larger than the problem." Another guest at the dinner, Senator Barry Goldwater, added that he could accept Humphrey's amendment "and women" for "most anything but hunting trips, fishing trips . . . and the Gridiron Club"[62]

In November 1972 the Gridiron rectified another long-standing exclusion by admitting the columnist Carl T. Rowan as its first black member. Feeling nostalgic for the days when "parodies in the Negro dialect were very popular and not subject to protest," Arthur Krock opposed the nomination on the grounds that Rowan had held appointed posts under two Democratic presidents and because the Gridiron had never before admitted anyone who was strictly a columnist. Walter Lippmann and Joseph Alsop had never been members, and Krock saw no reason to change that policy "for the purpose of making a gesture to one of the 'minority' groups that are being championed by the 'liberals' for political motivation." With Rowan as a member, Shirley Chisholm agreed to attend the next dinner, but other women planned further protests. When Vice President Gerald Ford addressed the Gridiron's winter dinner in December 1973, he commented that he had spent his first few days as vice president "taking phone calls from ladies of the press demanding that I boycott this male chauvinist affair." The Washington bureau chief of the *Boston Globe* publicly resigned from the Gridiron in protest of its ban on women members.[63]

As picketing had stopped few guests from attending the dinners, the protestors shrewdly adjusted their tactics. The Journalists for Professional Equality held a Counter-Gridiron party at Mount Vernon College's gymnasium on the same evening as the next dinner in April 1974, attracting presidential candidates, members of Congress, prominent television broadcasters, and a larger crowd than the Gridiron dinner itself. Conceding that the women had thrown a better party, the men of the Gridiron Club capitulated. Gridiron president Walter Ridder, of the Knight Ridder chain, proposed expanding active membership from fifty to sixty to provide vacancies to admit women (an increase that also reflected the vast growth of the Washington press corps over the past century). His proposals passed by a vote of 39 to 4. Arthur Krock, who had begged new members not to vote to admit women while he was alive, did not live to see the dreaded outcome. He died that spring at eighty-seven, hating all the changes in his way of life.[64]

As the Gridiron's first female member, Helen Thomas professed not to mind being a token, as someone had to be first over the threshold. Her membership did not end the Gridiron's "woman problem," however, and the Counter-Gridiron continued for another year to put the club on notice that one woman was not enough. One button proclaimed: "Tokens Are for Subways." By 1977 the Gridiron had admitted five women members, although when the Associated Press announced that its own reporter Frances Lewine had been inducted, it spelled her name "Francis."[65]

Once the formal barriers to Washington's women journalists fell, Helen Thomas held the presidency of both the National Press Club and the Gridiron Club, and also headed the White House Correspondents Association. The feisty Sarah McClendon attended a Gridiron dinner and won election to fill a short term as vice president of the Press Club. True to form, McClendon devoted her four months in office to investigating the club's operations and issued press releases warning of unsanitary conditions in its kitchen. The board censured her for blowing the whistle. "I think I was a fine vice president," McClendon insisted. "It seems to me that raising a little hell when it's called for is part of the job description."[66]

More important, women had achieved greater parity in political reporting. In 1970, when the UPI's longtime chief White House correspondent Merriman

Smith died, UPI's Washington bureau chief Grant Dillman persuaded the wire service to give the post to Helen Thomas. That position made her one of the most recognizable journalists on the national scene. On Capitol Hill, Helen Dewar became a regular congressional correspondent for the *Washington Post*. Mary McGrory won a Pulitzer Prize for her political commentary in 1975, and after the *Washington Star* closed she continued her column in the *Post*. In the press galleries the number of women increased noticeably. Young women found new entry-level jobs in the proliferating specialized publications, trade magazines, newsletters, and online news services. Newswomen also made strides in radio and television, where their presence was most obvious to audiences. Some of the veterans, like Eileen Shanahan and Elsie Carper, moved from reporting into management.[67]

The opening of political reporting to women journalists especially benefited women politicians. Representative Martha Griffiths, a Michigan Democrat, complained that for years after she came to the House in 1955 "the press never gave women any coverage." The quality of reporting on the Equal Rights Amendment that Griffiths sponsored deeply disappointed her, except for Eileen Shanahan's articles in the *New York Times*, as Shanahan had "ardently" favored the amendment. Women in Congress noticed that newsmen rarely questioned them about anything other than women's issues, and one male reporter told Griffiths, "This town is so completely controlled by men that you forget that there are women who are running some of these committees or subcommittees and that they do have ability." By the century's end, record numbers of women were serving in Congress and in the press galleries. When First Lady Hillary Rodham Clinton ran for the U.S. Senate in 2000, a reporter counted heads among the press contingent that was following her and decided that the "boys on the bus" had been replaced by the "girls in the van."[68]

9

The Camera's Eye

For years, print reporters discounted television news as little more than a headline service. Television executives conceded that the full text of a half-hour news broadcast would barely fill three-quarters of the columns on the front page of the *New York Times*. To compensate for the sparseness of its story, television news necessarily relied on visuals. In the early days of the industry, CBS pioneered a double-projector system that enabled on-camera broadcasters to narrate silent film footage projected behind them, but when that device grew stale producers sought to inject some "style and character" through ambient noise and filmed interviews. Those efforts evolved just as CBS's Washington bureau completed construction of a newsroom flanked by a row of windowless cubicles that resembled display cases rather than offices. The odd arrangement had been designed to allow the cameras to roll up to the correspondents who would report from their desks, but that plan was scrapped after management in New York decreed that only anchorman Walter Cronkite and commentator Eric Sevareid would be filmed sitting down. Other Washington correspondents were to report standing up in front of the agencies they covered or anywhere else outside. In a pinch, they could use the traffic island across from the bureau. These "stand-ups" would vary the look of the program at a reasonable cost. To further reinforce the "CBS news image," management instructed correspondents to identify themselves, their network, and their location when they signed off, as in: "This is CBS News correspondent Roger Mudd on Capitol Hill."[1]

In the glory days of network news, the Washington bureau handled the bulk of CBS's national news coverage, and was the network's largest news operation outside of New York. Even though Walter Cronkite had a preference for Washington reports, the bureau generated more stories than Cronkite had time to air on any given night. Among the bureau's correspondents, this created a jockeying for airtime and a "don't tread on me" attitude. Fred Graham, who covered legal issues, found the CBS Washington bureau a noticeably less congenial place than the *New York Times*'s bureau, where he had worked previously, with this lack of camaraderie further aggravated by the correspondents' need to spend so much time away from the bureau on assignment. Television correspondents labored to encapsulate complex issues in a few well-chosen words and with enough visual appeal to avoid being bumped from the evening news program by some late-breaking item with more spectacular pictures.[2]

Newspapers were slow to appreciate television's news value. On the eve of the 1952 national conventions, the Washington bureau of the *New York Times* requisitioned a television set to monitor the proceedings. In New York, managing editor Turner Catledge balked. "We would hate to spend money on an expensive set unless you really need it," he advised, and asked what possible use the bureau would have for a television after the conventions had adjourned? "TV is a necessity whether or not you personally like the medium," the bureau's office manager replied. The correspondents watched the Sunday news shows to write their Monday morning stories, and they had rented a set when there were not enough available seats in the press gallery for General Douglas MacArthur's "Old Soldiers Never Die" address to Congress. Reporters who left the bureau to watch television elsewhere ran the risk of running late and missing deadlines. New York finally relented, although it advised the Washington bureau to wait until it could get them a set wholesale.[3]

Before long, no one questioned the presence of television sets in newsrooms. As more Americans turned on the evening news, they caused a shift in advertising revenue that would drive once-profitable afternoon newspapers and glossy magazines into extinction. By 1963, TV broadcasters proclaimed themselves "the #1 news medium." The lure of television's higher salaries and visibility drew skilled reporters away from newspapers and wire services. Television drew the newsmakers as well. It influenced who ran for office, how they spoke, and how they governed. "The power of television news," said the TV news producer Av Westin, "astonishes even those of us who work for it."[4]

Television's most enthusiastic boosters predicted that it would produce a better-informed society. They trusted the camera's eye to give voters a truer picture of government than anything that newspapers could publish, turning everyone into an eyewitness. Television did leave durable images on viewers' minds, but those images could also be manipulated. CBS's first television news chief, Sig Mickelson, lamented that the camera's eye gradually developed astigmatism, a condition he blamed on the limited airtime allotted to national news. In its toddler years, TV presented news in fifteen-minute installments. As it matured, national news went to half an hour (less seven to eight minutes for commercials). Fierce resistance from the networks' affiliates to expanding the news to an hour-long format, however, stunted its growth. Network affiliates were business operations for whom news constituted only a fraction of their business. In TV's early years, evening news programs generated little revenue, so the affiliates tolerated them essentially as a public service price paid to renew their federal broadcasting licenses. They balked at giving up additional time that would cut into their more profitable programming.[5]

If time constraints reduced the chance of in-depth news coverage, television could still give audiences the vicarious thrill of "being there." TV producers insisted that ideas came first in putting news programs together, pictures second. But TV correspondents knew that compelling film footage improved their chances of getting on the air. There was no shortage of dramatic images to keep mass audiences tuned in, as TV news reached its apex during decades of war, protests, riots, and political scandals. The apocalyptic reports during the Cold War era made it a civic responsibility to be well informed, and watching television news evolved from a novelty to a ritual. "Do you remember when people who wished to consider themselves informed watched the network evening broadcast news every day?" the Washington columnist Michael Kelly asked nostalgically as the century ended.[6]

Coaxial cable linked TV's hub in New York with Washington in January 1947, just in time for CBS-TV to broadcast live from the Capitol steps at the opening of the 80th Congress. Correspondent Bill Henry interviewed several members of Congress and a few Federal Communications commissioners "with their pants pressed, throats sprayed and hair parted, ready to give their all." The newly installed House Speaker, Joseph Martin, arrived at the broadcast out of breath after presiding over the opening of the session. Speaker Martin announced on the air that he would permit television to film President Truman's State of the Union message in the House chamber. CBS got the scoop, but NBC had the initial advantage in covering Washington, having invested in several portable cameras (purchased from the defunct Office of War Information) and multiple camera crews. CBS's lone cameraman in Washington was often reduced to following NBC's cables through government corridors to catch up with its crews and do his own filming. A former AP correspondent, Ted Koop, took over CBS's Washington television bureau in January 1948, and found that he had to educate government officials about the time that television camera crews needed to set up equipment before press conferences. Until then, officials had dealt with photographers who simply arrived and snapped.[7]

Both parties held their national conventions in Philadelphia in 1948 on the pledge that TV would broadcast the proceedings live on the East Coast and on kinescope (made by filming broadcasts off of television screens) to the rest of the nation. Covering his last convention, the aging H. L. Mencken watched a test of television's klieg lights. The sensation reminded him of sunning on a Florida beach: "In a few minutes I began to wilt and go blind." The glare of the lights wilted the delegates as well, and made the networks' air-conditioned broadcast booths popular places to visit. Network executives pressured reluctant radio commentators to handle both radio and television reporting at the conventions. At ABC, producers asked their sole female broadcaster, Pauline Frederick, why she had not signed up for TV duty. "Maybe if enough of you men go on television, there will be a chance for me around here," she quipped. Frederick feared that appearing on television would typecast her as a performer rather than a serious journalist, but the network ordered her on camera to interview the candidates' wives and women delegates. She alternated with Elmer

Davis, who interviewed the men. For the next decade, Frederick was national television's sole woman news correspondent.[8]

The networks at first loved political conventions for their theatrical nature, filled with showmanship, suspense, and spontaneity. The attention they lavished on the conventions revealed broadcast journalism's show business roots. CBS News's Sig Mickelson also saw evidence of this heritage in TV's designation of its news editors as "directors" and "producers." Unlike entertainment programs, which the networks bought prepackaged, they produced their own news shows to meet the Federal Communications Commission's requirements for public affairs programming. CBS news producer Don Hewitt felt that network executives "believed we were in the news business only because of the FCC." Beyond appeasing the government, daily news programs gave the stations a distinctive identity and authoritative newscasters literally became the face of the network. News programs also drew more complains from irate viewers than entertainment shows, suggesting how seriously audiences took them.[9]

Drawing on a generation trained in radio, TV news initially adopted a radio format, with a single announcer reading headlines in short installments. NBC premiered the first national television news program in 1948, the ten-minute *Camel Newsreel Theatre.* It was narrated off-camera by the radio announcer John Cameron Swayze—who worried that "the real money was in radio." The next year, NBC put Swayze's face on the screen in a revised fifteen-minute *Camel News Caravan.* CBS coaxed radio announcer Douglas Edwards into doing TV news and dubbed him news "anchor," a title that sounded more prestigious than "announcer" but less opinionated than "commentator." At the time, CBS was putting more money into Edward R. Murrow's weekly documentary series *See It Now* than into its nightly TV news broadcasts, a factor that reinforced Murrow's indifference to anchoring television news. The talented "Murrow Boys," radio broadcasters he had recruited during the Second World War, collectively considered radio better suited for news reporting. They suspected that pictures would dominate television news, and that film editors would control the script. Eric Sevareid, a Murrow protégé who had developed his radio essays into "a kind of literary form," resisted television at first but experienced a change of heart after his first appearance on camera. The realization that his image and words would impact millions of households left Sevareid with a feeling of immense power that he compared to "controlling the throttle on a locomotive."[10]

The fusion of pictures with words also appealed to advertisers. Calculating that men who smoked would watch the news, R. J. Reynolds Tobacco sponsored the *Camel News Caravan.* Nonsmoker John Cameron Swayze placed an ashtray prominently on his desk. The tobacco company prohibited them from showing any film footage that contained a "No Smoking" sign or anyone other than Winston Churchill holding a cigar. NBC acquiesced because the tobacco company's advertising underwrote its entire news operations. "One reason

Fulton Lewis Jr., the "voice with a snarl," delivering his commentary on the Mutual radio network. *Broadcasting Archives, University of Maryland*

An American Marxist who never joined the Communist Party, Laurence Todd served as TASS's Washington correspondent from 1927 to 1952. *Ollie Atkins*

Elmer Davis checks the wire service tickers at the Office of War Information during World War II. *Broadcasting Archives, University of Maryland*

Prime Minister Winston Churchill joins President Franklin D. Roosevelt for a press conference in the Oval Office in December 1941. *Franklin D. Roosevelt Library*

Contrary to the warm inscription he wrote in 1943, *New York Times* Washington bureau chief Arthur Krock was not eager for James "Scotty" Reston to report from his office. *James Reston*

President Franklin D. Roosevelt shares a cordial moment with Raymond Brandt of the *St. Louis Post-Dispatch* (center) and Merriman Smith of United Press (right) at the White House Correspondents Association dinner in 1944. *Franklin D. Roosevelt Library*

House Speaker Sam Rayburn meets with reporters in the House chamber before the opening of the day's session. *Arthur E. Scott, Senate Historical Office*

The *Washington Evening Star*'s Clifford Berryman lampooned the women reporters at Eleanor Roosevelt's press conferences as "one of the penalties of being the First Lady." *Franklin D. Roosevelt Library*

Women replaced men in the congressional press galleries during World War II. Seen here in the front row of the House gallery are (left to right): Elizabeth Donahue of *PM*, Virginia Pasley of the *New York Daily News*, Ann Hagner of the *Washington Post*, May Craig of the *Portland Press Herald*, Mary Spargo (standing) of the *Washington Post*, Beatrice Heiman of TASS, Ann Cottrell of the *New York Herald Tribune*, and Nancy MacLennan of the *New York Times*. Seated behind them are Jo Tompson and Lyn Crost of the Associated Press. *National Press Club Archives*

Reporters crowd into a press conference by the future Speaker of the House, Joe Martin (standing on the left), following the Republican victory in the congressional elections of 1946. To Martin's right are I. F. Stone (bespectacled, standing) and Sarah McClendon (seated). *Arthur E. Scott, Senate Historical Office*

Illinois senator C. Wayland Brooks (right) welcomes Louis Lautier and Alice Dunnigan as the first African American correspondents accredited to the Senate press gallery. Standing between Lautier and Dunnigan is Griffing Bancroft, Washington correspondent for the *Chicago Sun-Times*, who chaired the Standing Committee of Correspondents. *Senate Historical Office*

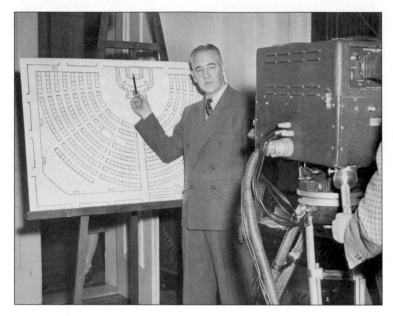

CBS correspondent Bill Henry diagrams the U.S. House of Representatives chamber for television audiences in anticipation of the first televised State of the Union message, which President Harry Truman delivered in 1947. *Broadcasting Archives, University of Maryland*

Reporters gather in the Senate press gallery, which in the late 1940s still resembled a men's club. *National Press Club Archives*

Former UPI reporter Walter Cronkite started in television news at a local Washington, D.C., station before advancing to the national news. Here, he hosts the CBS *Morning Show* in 1954. *Library of Congress*

The dapper David Schoenbrun, who reluctantly returned from the Paris bureau to head the CBS Washington bureau, delivers a radio report. *Broadcasting Archives, University of Maryland*

Senator Joseph R. McCarthy (far left) rides last in the National Press Club's "Freakness" race at the Charles Town, West Virginia, track on June 25, 1949, a few months before he went to Wheeling to accuse the State Department of harboring "known Communists." *Dan Frankforter, National Press Club Archives*

Joseph Alsop (right) works with his brother Stewart (standing) at his Georgetown home, where they wrote their syndicated column. *Library of Congress*

On election night 1954, James "Scotty" Reston (right) along with Bill Lawrence (left) and Bill Blair prepare the lead story for the *New York Times*. *New York Herald Tribune*

CBS correspondent Nancy Dickerson visits John F. Kennedy in the Oval Office, shortly after his inauguration in January 1961. *Broadcasting Archives, University of Maryland*

DAVID BRINKLEY
WASHINGTON

Chet Huntley, who usually broadcast from New York, visits David Brinkley (right) on the Washington set of the *Huntley-Brinkley News Report*. *Broadcasting Archives, University of Maryland*

A former Washington correspondent and columnist, Robert Kintner oversaw television news broadcasting on ABC and NBC before he joined the White House staff to try to salvage Lyndon Johnson's press relations. *Broadcasting Archives, University of Maryland*

South Vietnam's Madame Ngo Dinh Nhu speaks to the National Press Club on October 19, 1963, as women reporters watch from the balcony above. *Harris & Ewing, National Press Club*

CBS's Roger Mudd interviews Kentucky senator Thurston Morton during the filibuster against the Civil Rights Act of 1964. *Arthur E. Scott, Senate Historical Office*

Eric Sevareid interviews Walter Lippmann (seated on the couch) in one of a series conducted in the 1960s. Although Lippmann had been unsuccessful on the radio, television perfectly captured the urbanity and intelligence of the columnist. *Broadcasting Archives, University of Maryland*

Republican senators Carl Curtis and Jacob Javits face the press in the mid-1970s. *Arthur E. Scott, Senate Historical Office*

Colleagues at the *Washington Star* present Mary McGrory with a cake in 1974 to celebrate the Pulitzer Prize for her Watergate columns. *National Press Club Archives*

Both Howard K. Smith and Harry Reasoner left CBS to anchor the news on ABC. *Broadcasting Archives, University of Maryland*

Reporters join in a champagne toast for Helen Thomas's election as the first woman officer of the National Press Club in 1971. *Walter Fisk (U.S. News Service), National Press Club Archives*

Metro reporters Carl Bernstein (left) and Bob Woodward took on the Watergate story when the national press corps failed to pursue it. *Martin Luther King Jr. Library, Washington, D.C.*

Doug Harbrecht, president of the National Press Club, welcomes Matt Drudge, wearing his trademark fedora, as he steps out of the Internet to address the press corps on June 2, 1998. *Art Garrison, National Press Club*

Camel picked NBC was that we emphasized pictures more than CBS," explained news producer Reuven Frank, "and one reason we continued to do this was that Camel wanted them." With a primmer sense of decorum, CBS tried to shield its news personnel from advertising, but sponsors prevailed on the network to allow Douglas Edwards to introduce their commercials. Ad revenues depended on ratings, which encouraged the networks to produce the most visually appealing package they could devise. They started with newsreels, but chronically late delivery complicated the nightly effort to coordinate pictures with the news. Television turned to producing its own film footage, most of it silent for technological and budgetary reasons. Announcers read a text in a voice-over. Only NBC's Washington bureau initially filmed with sound, on the reasonable assumption that "Washington stories were all talk, anyway."[11]

An unlimited supply of people with something meaningful to say gave Washington its first television niche in the form of Sunday talk shows. Aired on an otherwise quiet news day, Sunday programs generated stories for the newspapers, whose Monday editions gave the networks free publicity. In 1947, NBC shifted its radio program *Meet the Press* to television. Advertised as "America's press conference of the air," it featured a panel of reporters quizzing prominent officials. Producers allowed a little show business to creep into *Meet the Press* by encouraging Washington correspondents to add more bite to their tone as panelists, because "the public enjoys it." CBS correspondent Eric Sevareid disliked the NBC program's deliberate needling of guests, and encouraged his own network's competing Sunday program, *Face the Nation*, not to "stage a battle." With Washington bureau chief Ted Koop acting as moderator, *Face the Nation* originally intended to have average citizens around the country ask questions of Washington power brokers. Producers scratched that format after deciding that "you almost have to be a news reporter to be able to do the kind of interrogation that will elicit the responses that will interest the audience." The revised version in 1954 resembled *Meet the Press,* with a panel of Washington correspondents questioning newsmakers, beginning with their first guest, the obligingly belligerent Senator Joe McCarthy.[12]

As a measure of the status of the press corps, the Sunday talk shows recruited newspaper reporters to serve as interviewers, and paid the print journalists more than broadcasters received for these appearances. The quest for status likewise prompted the Sunday shows to pass over most reporters for the local Washington, D.C., newspapers, and tap the national press instead. Sunday news shows drew small but significant audiences, particularly among the capital's officialdom. Members of Congress could gain greater attention from their colleagues by speaking on television than in the House or Senate chambers. Reporters for papers not widely read in Washington found that by appearing on TV they acquired name recognition that helped get their phone calls returned. Because that was less of a problem for *New York Times* correspondents, their paper resolutely refused to allow them to go on a competing media (the *Times* also had a longstanding policy of discouraging the development of a star system among its writers). In 1953, *New York Times* political correspondent Bill Lawrence asked permission to join the regulars on a news show being planned by Edward R. Murrow. *Times* editor Turner Catledge replied that he held Murrow in high regard but would not allow him to turn a prominent byline writer into a television "actor." A decade later, Lawrence quit the *Times* to become Washington correspondent for ABC-TV.[13]

Because the same networks dominated both radio and television, the congressional radio gallery shifted seamlessly into the radio-TV gallery. During its early years, television was better represented in the galleries by camera crews than reporters. When lights and cameras rolled into committee rooms and press conferences, they blocked the view of the newspaper reporters, who also objected that broadcasters took up space at already crowded press tables. Print reporters complained about the "hectic, noisy, movie-set atmosphere" that TV created, but politicians fluttered to the lights. President Harry Truman, then facing an uphill battle for reelection, welcomed television into the White House, although his first broadcast opened inauspiciously with a view of the backside of NBC newscaster Bryson Rash as he bent over to adjust the president's tie. TV broadcast a congressional hearing as early as 1947, but senators did not grasp its potential until televised lightning struck a freshman senator from Tennessee.[14]

The gangly, bespectacled Estes Kefauver chaired a special Senate committee to investigate organized crime. In 1950 the committee launched a national tour, holding hearings in different cities where crime syndicates flourished. In January 1951, six months into the hearings, the committee reached New Orleans, where station WDSU televised an hour of the testimony. At the next stop, a station in Detroit preempted the children's program *Howdy Doody* to broadcast the senators grilling local mobsters. Stations in St. Louis and Los Angeles followed suit. Like a theater company performing previews on the road, the Kefauver committee gained rave reviews as it headed for Broadway. There the *New York Daily News*'s station, WPIX, provided live feed to the networks for national broadcast. One witness at the New York hearings, the gambler Frank Costello, objected to appearing on camera, and the committee ordered TV not to show his face. The cameras instead focused on the mobster's agitated hands, which made riveting viewing. Fascinated by the drama, people gathered around office television sets at work and housewives threw "Kefauver parties" at home. "Something big, unbelievably big and emphatic, smashed into the homes of millions of Americans last week," the Associated Press reported, "when television cameras, cold-eyed and relentless, were trained on the Kefauver Crime Committee hearings."[15]

Senator Kefauver exploited his video celebrity by appearing on the game show *What's My Line?* and narrating episodes of the TV series called *Crime Syndicated*. Kefauver went on to win improbable victories in a string of the presidential primaries in 1952. Although he missed getting the Democratic Party's nomination, his successes testified to the power of television exposure. Troubled by the notoriety that TV had bestowed on the crime investigations, Senator Alexander Wiley, the ranking Republican on Kefauver's committee, urged the adoption of rules to prevent future hearings from degenerating "into a three-ring circus, a fourth-rate stage production with hamming and phony theatrics or an unjust inquisition of people under klieg lights." Senator Kefauver had treated witnesses judiciously, critics agreed, but what would stop a less scrupulous politician from making indiscriminate accusations on national television? Attorney Thurmond Arnold, who had defended clients charged with disloyalty at congressional inquiries, speculated that if someone like Joe McCarthy ever chaired a committee, Kefauver's efforts would "look like the work of inept amateurs."[16]

On the House side, TV coverage of a raucous session of the House Un-American Activities Committee in 1952 convinced Speaker Sam Rayburn to ban television cameras from all House committees. The "Rayburn Rule" prevailed for the next two decades, for both committees and House floor debates. "Televise sessions of the House?" Rayburn snorted. "Hell, no! Not while I'm around here are they going to do that televising." Politically ambitious representatives regretted the missed opportunities for national TV exposure, but some expressed relief at not having to face television cameras in their committee rooms. Mississippi democrat Thomas Abernathy described himself as a stump speaker who could not translate his folksy style to television, a medium that "shows up your—well, your deficiencies."[17]

House members joked about colleagues who got elected to the Senate: "Right away they get all cleaned up in a Brooks Brothers suit and start combing their hair more neatly because they are going to be on TV." The cameras could make political careers, and could destroy them just as readily. In 1953, when Senator McCarthy became chairman of the Permanent Subcommittee on Investigations, he wallowed in live television coverage of his anti-Communist hearings. He made frequent appearances on the Sunday talk shows, and demanded equal time to respond to any criticism from anyone else on television. Television tended to report on McCarthy uncritically, with the notable exception of Edward R. Murrow's withering portrait of the senator on the popular CBS program *See It Now*. Surprised at the furor it created, Murrow commented that he been saying the same things on radio. "I imagine it was McCarthy's words and McCarthy's picture that made the impact." In a more sustained manner, McCarthy's unruly behavior before the cameras during the Army-McCarthy hearings in 1954 finally discredited him in the public's eyes.

All three major networks had planned to cover the hearings gavel to gavel, but the committeee forbade any interruptions for commercials. With no end in sight after ten days CBS and NBC returned to their profitable daytime soap operas and game shows and broadcast filmed segments of the hearings later in the evening. Only ABC's news president Robert Kintner pledged to televise all the hearings live—for what turned out to be six more weeks. This was less of a financial sacrifice for ABC, which had few sponsored daytime programs, but by forfeiting even its meager daytime advertising the network had to slash the rest of its budget by 20 percent to cover its losses. The sustained broadcasting of the Army-McCarthy hearings boosted the viewership of the third-place ABC network, quickened the sale of television sets, and paved the way for Joe McCarthy's censure. It also established television as a serious source of news, although even the broadcasters recognized that they had triumphed more through technology than journalism.[18]

The U.S. Capitol, which was constructed in the eighteenth and nineteenth centuries, did not lend itself easily to television technology. Television personnel packed into the cramped radio galleries and used makeshift studios. Wiring was complicated by an antiquated electrical system, which as late as 1960 still used direct current. When the Senate authorized construction of a second office building, the Radio and Television Correspondents Association appointed a watchdog committee to ensure that the new committee rooms were able to accommodate cameras and lights. In the new building, TV cameras operated behind recessed panels, and committee members no longer sat at the same table with witnesses. For better TV visibility, senators were perched upon an elevated dais facing the witness table. Microphones also facilitated broadcasting, although the first sound system screeched so loudly that committees had to adjourn until technicians repaired the system. On the House side, the new office building named for Speaker Sam Rayburn came fully wired for broadcasting, even though the Rayburn Rule continued to ban radio and television from House hearings.[19]

In the Capitol's basement, a government-sponsored recording studio allowed senators to tape their own television programs. The facilities enabled Blair Moody, who reported for the *Detroit News* until his appointment to the Senate as a Democrat from Michigan in 1951, to keep on doing the same *Meet Your Congress* programs as a senator that he had done as a journalist. South Dakota Republican senator Karl Mundt produced *Your Washington and You on the Air,* in which he answered prearranged questions from a "Washington Correspondent"—actually the superintendent of the Senate recording studio. The House Republican Congressional Committee arranged for its members to tape prepared questions to be spliced into prerecorded answers by members of President Eisenhower's cabinet, making it appear that the member had conducted the interview personally. Print reporters called these antics "Every Congressman a Television Star."[20]

Washington correspondents blamed television for encouraging government public relations officers to stage "scripted events" for the cameras' benefit. The print reporters similarly dismissed the first TV news broadcasts as shallow and fragmentary, and regarded TV correspondents as performers. NBC's Washington correspondent Ray Scherer commented that the "writing gentry" made TV reporters feel like "fugitives from show business." Old-time radio broadcasters such as H. V. Kaltenborn shared the same prejudices. In covering the 1952 presidential conventions for NBC, Kaltenborn loathed the lights, makeup, and posing for the cameras. His low ratings confirmed that the new medium was not for him.[21]

At the same conventions where Kaltenborn's sun set, TV audiences met Walter Cronkite, who was on his way to becoming the nation's "most trusted" television newsman. A former United Press correspondent, Cronkite had run a small Washington bureau for several Midwestern radio stations, lugging around a heavy tape recorder for his interviews. CBS hired him in 1950 to do radio coverage of the war in Korea, but before he could leave, the local CBS affiliate in Washington, WTOP, asked for help in starting a late night television news program. "Well, Cronkite's the newest man here and therefore has the least to do," said bureau chief Ted Koop. As he did not yet own a television set (until his sponsor gave him one) Cronkite had no role models to go by. He wrote and memorized his own scripts so he could look straight at the camera and talk informally. He used a chalkboard to map troop movements in Korea. The head of CBS News, Sig Mickelson, traveled to Washington frequently at the time and found Cronkite's video persona appealing. Cronkite bemoaned his bad luck at having been stuck at "a lousy local TV station" instead of going to Korea, but he also contributed Washington reports for the national evening news and hosted a Sunday morning talk show, *Capitol Cloakroom*. When other radio commentators were cool toward anchoring television coverage of the political conventions, CBS tapped Cronkite. His success at it got him transferred to New York. Once he perceived that he was entering "show business," Cronkite promptly hired an agent.[22]

Four years later, the 1956 conventions elevated another Washington broadcaster, David Brinkley. NBC executives had lost patience with John Cameron Swayze, who could read a script but could not ad-lib during the long lulls between convention business. The network's higher-ups leaned toward replacing Swayze with a craggy, somber-looking reporter named Chet Huntley, although some of them worried that "audiences would not sit still for the serious stuff unless we gave them something entertaining as well." NBC's Washington bureau chief urged them to consider Brinkley, the network's puckish Washington correspondent, but the network's vice president for news, Davidson Taylor, strongly resisted him. "After all, I was from Washington," Brinkley later commented. "In his silly view, I was halfway down there in the South toward the corn-pone belt, living and working in a city full of verbose, tiresome politicians and, worst of all, *I was not in New York*." Unable to decide between the two, NBC used them both.[23]

During the slow moments of the conventions, Huntley and Brinkley chatted on camera. The blend of Huntley's gravity and Brinkley's relaxed detachment impressed the critics and won high ratings. "This convention marks the first time that the Columbia Broadcasting System, with such established stars as Edward R. Murrow and Eric Sevareid, has had real competition from NBC in the matter of news personalities," rated the *New York Times*'s TV reviewer Jack Gould. After the conventions, NBC swiftly replaced Swayze's broadcast with the *Huntley-Brinkley News Report*. Each night, Huntley reported from New York and cued technicians to switch the feed at the end of his segments by saying "David." In Washington, Brinkley reversed the procedure by saying "Chet." Although both regarded their closing lines of "Good night, Chet" and "Good night, David" as hokey, it became a memorable and much-quoted signature. Belying their friendly patter, the two anchors worked out of different cities and rarely saw each other off the air. Huntley handled the bulk of each program, but NBC reserved at least a third of the airtime for Brinkley, whose wry humor pin-pricked Washington's "pretension and folly." By relieving much of the grimness of the news, he accounted for a good share of the program's ratings. The arrangement also gave Washington stories precedence, regardless of whether the capital had produced much news that day. "The one function that TV news performs very well is that when there is no news, we give it to you with the same emphasis as if there were," Brinkley commented. By highlighting Brinkley, however, NBC limited the on-camera appearances of its other Washington correspondents.[24]

Behind Huntley-Brinkley stood NBC's president, Robert Kintner, previously a Washington correspondent, columnist, and ABC news director. Kintner set out to make NBC News superior to CBS, and because he had charge of both the news and entertainment divisions, he always gave news the right of way. Before Kintner, NBC's news producers complained that they could not get much news on the air. After he arrived, they could not keep up with his demands for more news programs. "We compete for prestige, for public attention, and for public acceptance," Kintner exhorted. When he tripled the news budget, speculation had it that Kintner poured so much money into news to compensate for the drivel in the rest of the network's schedule. Although Kintner spent lavishly, he expected that Huntley and Brinkley's healthy ad revenues would make the news deficits manageable. He also negotiated a hefty subsidy from the Gulf Oil Corporation to underwrite the cost of preempting commercial programming with late-breaking news and to produce news specials. "I like to think we would do it even if CBS weren't breathing down our necks," he said.[25]

At first, CBS producers dismissed the Huntley-Brinkley format as a gimmick, but had to scramble to determine why the team shot past them in the ratings. News analyst Eric Sevareid—hoping to win some dispensation for his own commentary—suggested that what worked best for Huntley and Brinkley was their "apparent freedom to speak their own minds." But *CBS Evening News* producer Don Hewitt concluded that the network's format of having the news read by a single anchorman was too static for television and needed to be enlivened by putting more reporters on the program. For correspondent Harry Reasoner, CBS's decision to send out reporters rather than just camera operators to cover stories finally distinguished television news from movie theater newsreels. Instead of simply narrating pictures, TV reporters would generate the stories and determine their content. CBS still paid a bigger salary to its radio news anchor, Lowell Thomas, than to its TV anchor, Douglas Edwards, so many of the veterans stuck to radio. Instead, CBS began adding some "unknown young men" to its reporting staff. Soon they would be some of the nation's most familiar faces.[26]

It did not take the new crop of broadcasters long to discover that "television news was not news unless you could prove it on film," as NBC White House correspondent Ray Scherer put it. Some of the television correspondents' weaker interviews got on the evening news just because they had them on film. Almost any presidential appearance made good television—and good public relations for the federally regulated broadcasters. The networks implored President Dwight Eisenhower to use their medium creatively. CBS president Frank Stanton arranged to televise one of Eisenhower's cabinet meetings, although that staged event, with one cabinet member after another delivering canned remarks, was so excruciatingly dull that the network never repeated it. By 1955, Eisenhower had let television cameras into his press conferences, but not for live broadcasts. The networks could play excerpts on the evening news or show the entire conference at a later hour. David Brinkley regarded Eisenhower's news conferences as an affliction. The president's convoluted syntax caused Brinkley and his producer to run the film back and forth, desperately seeking "a few sentences that started with a thought and moved coherently through it and came to a clear end," as Brinkley recalled. "There weren't any." They had to splice phrases and sentences together until they produced something reasonably coherent.[27]

Five years later, when the *New York Times* correspondent Russell Baker covered the first Kennedy-Nixon debate in Chicago, he took notes while listening to a studio monitor at which he barely glanced. Like most of the print reporters in the audience that night, Baker rated the debate a tie, so he was surprised to hear Kennedy's campaign staff cheerfully proclaim that their man had won. The reporters had not appreciated Kennedy's visual advantage, but the rest of the country "had been looking, not listening." Baker doubted whether many people bothered to read his story in the next morning's *Times*, having watched the debate for themselves. He marked it as the moment when television passed newspapers as the primary communications medium. With 85 percent of American households owning televisions, John F. Kennedy became the nation's first made-for-television president. Eric Sevareid noted that Kennedy had "hit the TV screens with his manly charm at the peak viewing session of the 1956 convention." From then on he held the cameras' attention as a member of the Senate's televised labor-racketeering investigations, and by his appearances on such programs as Jack Paar's *Tonight Show*. Senior senators did not take Kennedy's presidential ambitions seriously until they began to notice the coils of TV cable outside his Senate office. Writing in *TV Guide* in 1959, Senator Kennedy predicted that television would shift the focus of campaigning from issues to image, but he expressed confidence that the impression the public received from the televised images would be "uncannily correct." Kennedy met his prediction by appearing cool and unflappable during the first debate, in vivid contrast to his pale and perspiring opponent. Don Hewitt supervised the first debate and came away troubled. "We may have made the right choice, but it worried me that it might have been for the wrong reason," he commented. "We were electing a matinee idol."[28]

Like the politicians, TV newscasters also achieved stardom. *Newsweek* correspondent Ben Bradlee had been in Europe for a decade before he lunched with his old friend David Brinkley at the 1960 Democratic convention. Bradlee was taken by surprise when delegates and tourists kept interrupting them to have their pictures taken with Brinkley. The broadcaster seemed to be drawing larger crowds than some of the candidates. Envious of their TV colleagues, newspaper reporters began preening for the cameras. When President Kennedy agreed to live coverage of his press conferences, the UPI's cantankerous Merriman Smith grumbled that the cameras turned the conference into a sideshow. Knowing that their editors would be watching, reporters jockeyed to ask questions on national TV—and took longer to ask them. Those reporters, such as Smith, who sat in the front row now had to remember to get their hair cut and not to chew gum.[29]

During the Kennedy era, Walter Cronkite succeeded Douglas Edwards as anchor, but the *CBS Evening News* continued to trail the *Huntley-Brinkley Report*. Desperate for a breakthrough, CBS persuaded its affiliates to allow the national news to expand to a half hour. The expanded format would double the time for news, and double the advertisements. Color television sets were just becoming affordable, and color TV ads gave the networks a competitive edge against full-color advertisements in news magazines. *Time* magazine correspondent Neil MacNeil blamed his magazine's decline on the end of "gray beer" on TV. Adding a quarter hour to the nightly news boosted CBS's Washington bureau, but tensions persisted with New York. From Manhattan, producers viewed Washington as too insular and its news "too portentous and full of politicians." Correspondent Harry Reasoner fantasized that if he ran the network he would close the Washington bureau down and send crews down there only when necessary. While they were limited to fifteen minutes, correspondents in Washington had complained that Cronkite was summarizing too much of the news himself. The extra fifteen minutes opened time for all of the principal CBS Washington correspondents to appear on the nightly news several times a week (more airtime than their counterparts at NBC, where Brinkley dominated the Washington reports).[30]

Over the Labor Day weekend in 1963, CBS inaugurated its expanded format. The first half-hour evening news program featured Walter Cronkite interviewing President Kennedy at Hyannisport. Labor Day being a traditionally slow news day, CBS assumed that the longer program would attract extensive notice in the newspapers, but NBC's wily president Robert Kintner countered with a three-hour news documentary on the civil rights movement. Glowing reviews for NBC's "The American Revolution of '63" overshadowed Cronkite's half hour. Kintner meanwhile used CBS's initiative to overcome resistance from NBC's affiliates to also expand the *Huntley-Brinkley Report* to half an hour. Surveys now showed that more Americans relied on TV than newspapers as their chief source of news.[31]

Two months later, President Kennedy's assassination confirmed television's primacy in news. From Cronkite's reading of the first UPI flash that Friday afternoon until the funeral on Tuesday morning, the three networks stayed exclusively with the story. NBC's Robert Kintner suspended all commercial programming, with CBS and ABC following his lead. The coverage was both protracted and restrained. CBS's Washington bureau chief instructed all his correspondents to talk only if there was something they needed to say, and to otherwise let the picture tell the story. Television gave a grieving nation a front-row view of Kennedy's funeral and broadcast live the murder of his assassin. TV coverage touched a nerve, brought the nation together, and seared some iconic moments into people's memories—from a parade of foreign dignitaries to a son's salute. It also made the rest of the media finally take television news seriously.[32]

In the next quarter century after the evening news went to thirty minutes, Washington reports averaged eight of the twenty-three minutes allotted to news (with seven minutes for commercials). To fill those eight minutes, CBS budgeted millions of dollars annually for a Washington bureau that at its peak housed a staff of two hundred employees, including producers, technicians, lawyers, lobbyists, news correspondents, and camera crews. The *CBS Evening News with Walter Cronkite* established its primacy in the ratings through an avuncular anchor and a powerful Washington bench. CBS's seasoned, serious-minded correspondents managed to convey the news of the day in short segments framed by the capital's most familiar landmarks. Correspondent David Shoemaker explained that CBS saw itself as the network of record. "At CBS you are very much aware of the tradition, and it goes back all the way to the radio days and Ed Murrow," he said. "You have a view of your self that is not much different than the feeling of a *New York Timesman* . . . that you are better than anyone else."[33]

To run its growing Washington operations, CBS experimented with a number of bureau chiefs. In the 1950s Eric Sevareid had served as CBS's chief Washington correspondent and commentator, until a collapsing marriage and boredom with the Eisenhower administration prompted his transfer to London. As his replacement, CBS brought its foreign correspondent, Howard K. Smith, back to Washington, where he delivered occasional analysis for the evening news, appeared on *Face the Nation*, and did weekly radio commentary. A liberal southerner whose worldview had been profoundly shaped by the struggle against European fascism, Smith sympathized with the struggle for racial equality. His blunt reports on civil rights infuriated CBS's southern affiliates, who protested that expressions of personal opinion on the air ran contrary to network policy. Smith shrugged off the charges, pointing out that analysis required making judgments. When CBS trimmed his editorial license, he suspended his television commentaries entirely. That reduced Smith's appearances on the evening news, so CBS compensated by naming him Washington bureau manager as well as chief correspondent. At the height of his prestige, Smith moderated the first Kennedy-Nixon debate. In 1961, CBS blue-penciled portions of Smith's text for a documentary on the civil rights struggle in Birmingham, Alabama. Smith allowed the deletions from his television report, feeling that powerful film footage would make the point more effectively than anything he said. But he delivered the unexpurgated text as a radio commentary. CBS chairman William Paley summoned Smith to his office in New York and angrily dressed him down, provoking Smith to walk away from an "unbreakable" five-year contract with the network.[34]

CBS called back another foreign correspondent, David Schoenbrun, to take over the Washington bureau. The dapper, erudite, but easily ruffled Schoenbrun liked living in Paris, but CBS News president Richard Salant assured him that John Kennedy's presidency made Washington "the center of the world." Schoenbrun complained that he would be the only bureau chief and chief correspondent in Washington without his own program or column, and he reminded network news executives in New York that "Washington is an elitist town and quickly rates the men and women who come there." If he did not deliver his own commentary he worried that he would be "far down in the pecking order." CBS preferred that Schoenbrun stick to straight reporting and concentrate on beating NBC's Brinkley, but he fussed until the network awarded him a news show, *Washington Report*, at the dead-end slot of Sunday noon. Making the best of it, Schoenbrun lined up consequential guests, starting with John F. Kennedy. The president later confirmed that he was a regular viewer by sending Schoenbrun a message on the air during the Cuban missile crisis. Kennedy wanted the crisis described as a victory for humanity rather than an American triumph—to keep Khrushchev from changing his mind. Schoenbrun not only obliged but called this bit of presidential news management a "coup for television news" as it proved the viability of midday Sunday news programs.[35]

Schoenbrun's bureau chief status did not stop producers in New York from overruling his stories. He was furious when they dropped one of his Washington reports to run film of a fire near the homes of movie stars in Beverly Hills. The diminutive Schoenbrun (who perched on a box while doing his stand-up reports) complained of being "surrounded by pygmies." His petulance convinced CBS news president Richard Salant that it had been a mistake to appoint a correspondent as bureau chief, "particularly when the person has an insatiable appetite for power, for airtime, and for visibility." Protective of their anchor's prerogatives, New York producers insisted that Walter Cronkite interview some of the newsmakers whom Schoenbrun had scheduled for his Sunday show. When CBS expanded its evening news to half an hour, the network compensated its affiliates by returning other time slots to entertainment programming. Schoenbrun would make regular appearances as chief Washington correspondent and analyst on the enlarged nightly program, but he had to give up his Sunday *Washington Report*. Feeling betrayed, Schoenbrun resigned, signed on with Metromedia, and to CBS's satisfaction "just faded away."[36]

CBS brought Eric Sevareid back to Washington as a news analyst but abolished his earlier title as chief correspondent. To head the bureau they elevated Schoenbrun's deputy manager, William Small, formerly a local news director in Chicago and Louisville. The stocky, square-jawed, no-nonsense Bill Small ran the bureau for a dozen years. Like the *New York Times* correspondents who could never call Arthur Krock anything but "Mr. Krock," CBS correspondents called their chief "Mr. Small." The bureau chief put correspondents out on regular beats to develop subject expertise and cultivate sources: Roger Mudd on Capitol Hill, Marvin Kalb at the State Department, Dan Rather at the White House, Ike Pappas at the Pentagon, Fred Graham at the Supreme Court, and Daniel Schorr doing investigative reporting. Working for Small was no easy task. "He's a hard-nosed boss," said correspondent Robert Pierpoint. "With him, your job and CBS must be absolutely above everything." Small's willingness to fight New York for assignments and airtime helped the Washington correspondents achieve considerable independence, as did their expertise. "Once a man carves out a little niche on the air," Roger Mudd reflected, "it's very difficult for people to get at you." Criticism from producers tended to be muted. "The power is in the box," said Mudd, "not with the credits at the end."[37]

Newspaper reporter Douglas Kiker turned down an offer to join CBS's Washington bureau after he looked over its lineup of correspondents. "If I went to work for them, and the first string was wiped out in an airplane crash, and the second string died of heart failure," said Kiker, "I'd still have trouble getting to be first string." By contrast, Bob Schieffer was determined to join CBS because it was the best in the capital. On his first day at the bureau, Schieffer felt like "a little leaguer stepping out onto the field at Yankee Stadium to play for the first time." After Bill Small pointed out the offices where all the prominent correspondents worked, Schieffer asked where he would sit. "You won't,"

Small replied, "if you want to stay." The newer staff—"reporters," not yet "correspondents"—made do with a few chairs in a narrow back corridor.[38]

When Schieffer first looked around the newsroom, he saw only two women in non-secretarial jobs—a reporter and an editor. The face of CBS news had remained resolutely male until Nancy Hanschman stepped before the cameras in 1960 as its first woman correspondent. Although women delivered the news on European television, American network executives considered their voices too thin and high-pitched for "hard-core news." The husky-voiced Pauline Frederick, first on ABC and later on NBC, had avoided women's stories by covering the United Nations. She studiously resisted suggestions that she dress more femininely, change her hairstyle, or take off her glasses. Nancy Hanschman proved more compliant in matters of appearance but just as resistant to being typecast as a "woman's news" reporter. Willowy, stylish, and single, she had started as a clerk-typist for the Senate Foreign Relations Committee where she dated several senators, among them John F. Kennedy. Fascinated by the deference that powerful senators paid to reporters, she applied to CBS in 1954 when she heard the network was looking for "a man who knew Capitol Hill." She was hired to co-produce the new television show *Face the Nation,* and began lining up her senatorial friends as guests.[39]

Anxious to get out from behind the cameras, Hanschman felt the need to act quickly as she turned thirty. She signed up for speech classes and proposed unique stories to report, but ran into opposition from the men. Under CBS's fee system, correspondents were paid for each appearance on camera. The men resented any intrusion into their airtime, especially from a woman without a family to support. Looking for her break, Hanschman persuaded the notoriously camera-shy House Speaker Sam Rayburn to let her interview him on his seventy-eighth birthday. Not realizing that she meant it to be on television, Rayburn "literally roared" when he found his Capitol Hill office cluttered with equipment and crew, she recalled. "Then he tripped over a cable." Her profuse apologies softened the Speaker and he gave the interview. After CBS broadcast it, the network immediately hired her to do general political news on television and a daily radio show, *One Woman's Washington.* When she went on her old program, *Face the Nation,* however, a dubious CBS news executive warned her not to giggle.[40]

Two of Hanschman's closest senatorial friends, John Kennedy and Lyndon Johnson, won election as president and vice president in 1960. In the Capitol rotunda, as Kennedy waited to go to his inauguration, he stopped to chat with her, an event that CBS reported proudly on the air. Rumors floated that the new president's attention had little to do with her journalism. "Some of Kennedy's favorite reporters were women," huffed Sarah McClendon. "I knew Kennedy liked women and so, it seemed, did the networks." Nancy Hanschman's elegant appearance prompted other women reporters to alter their own hair and dress styles. "The broadcast girls gave a new look to the press," said reporter Liz Carpenter, "but I don't know that they improved its quality." One advantage to being stylish was getting noticed in a crowd. The *Washington Post*'s Eve Edstrom found that President Kennedy called on her more frequently at news conferences after she began wearing a hot pink suit.[41]

CBS's first woman correspondent dismayed network executives in 1962 when she married the businessman C. Wyatt Dickerson and took his surname. For six months on the air the network identified her as Nancy Hanschman Dickerson to get viewers accustomed to her new name. The Dickersons purchased a sprawling estate in Virginia and a spacious townhouse in Washington, and entertained regally. "There's no one in Washington who doesn't know Nancy, and there are very few people she doesn't see socially," gushed a magazine account that dubbed her the "princess of the press corps." Sarah McClendon regarded this type of political entertaining as "an occupational disease of journalists who can afford it," and complained that it gave Dickerson an unfair advantage, allowing her to use social contacts to get stories. But Dickerson's son John, who later became a Washington correspondent himself, defended her socializing as a means of overcoming the "locker-room atmosphere" of Washington politics that favored her male colleagues. "Nancy's very industrious and highly intelligent," Arthur Krock confirmed paternally. "She's a good objective reporter with the additional gifts of being a very lovely, effective and charming woman." For all that, she found it hard to compete for airtime on CBS. In 1963 she switched to NBC, being promised regular appearances on the *Huntley-Brinkley Report* and the morning *Today Show*, together with her own daily five-minute afternoon news report. She thrived at NBC during Lyndon Johnson's presidency. (Johnson especially appreciated her ability to get members of his administration on *Today*, because "every damned afternoon newspaper" quoted from that morning program.)[42]

Intent on overcoming NBC's lead in the ratings, CBS made Fred Friendly president of its news division in 1964. A big bear of a man who had once been Edward R. Murrow's producer, Friendly took Washington news seriously and championed Bill Small's efforts to gain more exposure for the Washington bureau on the evening news. The intense and volatile Friendly pushed CBS News to be bold but responsible, to inform viewers but also make them take notice, in essence a revival of the Murrow era. Yet anchorman Walter Cronkite was no Edward R. Murrow. Cronkite preferred a straightforward wire-service style of objective reporting. He resisted the temptation to take stands on the air, demurring that the "difficulty visually of separating fact from opinion" made television different from newspapers that had separate editorial pages. For a news broadcaster to deliver editorials, he felt, "would only confuse the viewing public and embarrass his position as an unbiased, impartial newsman." The *Evening News*'s sole commentator, Eric Sevareid, gave such balanced presentations that some viewers called him "Eric Severalsides." Friendly encouraged Sevareid to become more outspoken, and assured him, "Your job in Washington is to keep me in trouble."[43]

Fred Friendly resented the ban on cameras in the Senate and House chambers, and in House committee hearings. He predicted that it was "going to be easier to telecast a program from the surface of the moon than from the Senate floor." (He was correct. TV got to the moon seventeen years before it began broadcasting Senate debates.) If CBS correspondents had to stay outside, he determined to make the most of it. When southerners opened a filibuster against the Civil Rights Act of 1964 Friendly pulled correspondent Roger Mudd off the Goldwater campaign to do regular reports from the Capitol steps. Born and raised in Washington, Mudd had graduated from Washington and Lee University and earned a master's degree in history from the University of North Carolina at Chapel Hill in 1951. He wrote a master's thesis about Franklin Roosevelt and the press, and took a summer job with the *Richmond News Leader* to get a look inside journalism. The paper sent him across the street to handle news reports at its radio station, and he never went back to his graduate studies. In 1956, Mudd joined CBS's Washington affiliate, WTOP, and five years later stepped up to the network news (a move that broke CBS's pledge not to raid its affiliates' news operations). The year before the filibuster, Mudd had won plaudits for anchoring CBS's coverage at the Lincoln Memorial during Martin Luther King Jr.'s March on Washington, and for doing voice-over commentary during John F. Kennedy's state funeral. On Capitol Hill, he took high marks for knowing the issues and respecting the institution. Calm in delivery and fairly serious in demeanor, he let it be known that his filibuster coverage would be "straight reporting with all sides being heard." Still, NBC's correspondent at the Capitol disparaged the experiment. "I can't imagine who'd be listening to the stuff," Mudd overheard him say.[44]

When the CBS remote transmission truck arrived at the Capitol on March 30, 1964, snow was falling and there was no cover for outside filming. The first senator whom Mudd interviewed, Hubert Humphrey, came out without an overcoat and had to slip into Bill Small's ill-fitting raincoat. Every day that the filibuster continued, Mudd made at least five TV spots. "I did the morning news, which was then Mike Wallace at 9 o'clock," he recalled. "I did a piece for the 12:24 news, the 3:25 news, the Cronkite news, and then I did a feed for the 11 o'clock affiliates." Another seven reports went out over the radio. By definition, filibusters are stalling tactics that rely on long-winded speeches and tedious procedural delays. Other reporters wondered how Mudd could keep finding something new to report. "What the hell are you going to say today?" they would ask. "I'll find something," he replied. Viewers saw Mudd standing out in the snow, rain, and blazing sun, for a dozen weeks. Some people called their stations to express concern about his health. CBS superimposed a clock on his reports to show how much time the debate had consumed, and the longer the filibuster dragged on the more it grated on public opinion. Although Mudd gave equal time to the southern senators, they came to realize that his vigil was working against them by highlighting their obstructionism. They complained that he had become such a tourist attraction that crowds of curious onlookers were blocking their entrance into the Capitol. By May, the southerners prevailed on the Capitol police to move him off the steps and over to the sidewalk on the opposite side of the plaza.[45]

Finally on June 10, 1964, the Senate voted for cloture and shut off the filibuster. Outside, in temperatures that hit a hundred degrees, Roger Mudd announced each vote as it was reported by telephone from the Senate press gallery to the CBS control room, which relayed it to his earpiece. Passage of the Civil Rights Act followed swiftly after cloture, profoundly altering America's social landscape. For injecting such a large dose of reality back into television, Mudd won high praise from his network and even from the newspapers. Unique in a media that measured stories in minutes or less, his sustained reporting may well have contributed to the outcome of the debate by heightening the public's attention on the issue and its pressure on the senators. The *New York Herald Tribune*'s television critic John Horn wrote that Mudd's "continued presence at the scene of Washington inaction has personalized and dramatized the halting process of our Government to the average viewer in a way no amount of words or secondary reports could have." Warren Weaver, who covered Congress for the *New York Times,* concluded that Mudd's commentary "could have been delivered on radio, or even printed in the newspapers, without losing much impact," but if CBS had actually been able to film the debate, newspapers "would have been hard pressed to compete." The extended airtime brought financial reward as well under CBS's fee system. All those appearances on the air during the filibuster enabled Mudd to enlarge his home.[46]

Fred Friendly was so taken with Mudd's ability that he teamed him with Robert Trout—a broadcasting warhorse since the 1930s—to cover the 1964 Democratic National Convention. Friendly counted on the chemistry between Mudd and Trout to cut into Huntley and Brinkley's lead in the convention ratings, but the demotion of the regular anchorman Walter Cronkite offended viewers. When the ratings for CBS's convention coverage sank, Cronkite resumed his primacy. Afterward, Mudd detected signs of retaliation from New York. For a while the *CBS Evening News* used less of his Capitol Hill reporting, and some New York producers began referring to him as a "Washington provincial." Mudd might have overcome that image by taking assignments elsewhere, but he loved covering politics and government, and he was raising four children in the Washington area. By comparison, CBS's White House correspondent, Dan Rather, transferred from Washington to London and volunteered to go to Vietnam. Washington correspondent Bob Schieffer accepted a promotion to host the *CBS Morning Show* before informing his family that they would have to move to New York. He was stunned by their negative reaction. "I had been gone so much their lives no longer really included me," Schieffer belatedly realized.[47]

Yet Washington in the 1960s offered an abundance of major stories to put Roger Mudd and others in the Washington bureau on the air regularly. "In terms of news coverage by television, there is more activity in Washington than anywhere else in the world," bureau chief Bill Small boasted. By 1965, with Great Society legislation roaring through Congress and more American troops going to Vietnam, stellar reporting from Washington helped the *CBS Evening News with Walter Cronkite* finally surpass the *Huntley-Brinkley Report*. Cronkite never relinquished that lead. NBC newscasters mocked his wire-service approach as "no style" and dismissed his show's writing as pedestrian, yet NBC remained dependent on its two popular anchors while CBS was building its evening news program around a team of skilled correspondents. Roger Mudd suspected that some of his NBC counterparts "rather enjoyed being second." It was easier, he speculated "not having to be up and running at the crack of dawn; not having to explain why you got beat again by CBS." The *CBS Evening News* opened with an announcer reading the names and locations of the correspondents who would appear that night. NBC correspondent Garrett Utley thought that sent a clear message to the viewers: "If they wanted style and wit with the news, they could turn to NBC. If they wanted straight news, CBS was the place to be."[48]

The political and social turmoil of the decade produced compelling images for television news, but there were disturbing signs that the politicians and protestors alike were learning how to stage events to attract television news cameras. Government thought it held the upper hand, being able to command the airwaves for presidential press conferences and important announcements, but youthful protestors, having grown up in the television era, grasped the medium's addiction to dramatic moments and organized their demonstrations accordingly. The spectacle of protestors playing to television cameras began raising questions about whether the cameras filmed reality or distorted it.[49]

As American involvement in South Vietnam escalated into full-fledged combat, the Johnson administration portrayed it as an idealistic mission to protect democracy against the spread of international communism. Pentagon officials lectured American reporters about their patriotic duty of being "on the team" and urged them to "get out and cover the war." While following the marines on a search-and-destroy mission, CBS correspondent Morley Safer and his cameraman recorded them using cigarette lighters to torch Vietnamese huts. These disturbing TV images clashed with the Johnson administration's optimistic assessments of the war's progress. Television had developed sufficient mobility to follow troops into combat and to broadcast in color. "The goriness of the battle wasn't quite the same without the redness of blood," Cronkite reflected. CBS executives bore the brunt of presidential ire and felt vulnerable to federal regulation. To appease President Johnson, CBS dropped its live daytime coverage of the Senate Foreign Relations Committee hearings on the war to return to scheduled reruns of *I Love Lucy*. In protest, Fred Friendly resigned from CBS News.[50]

NBC correspondent Sander Vanocur returned from Vietnam convinced that government officials had lied to him about the war. "But in the name of objectivity, or more accurately stated, in the name of staying on the air," he ruminated, "I could not scream: 'Liars.'" Reluctant to be used as propaganda tools, the correspondents adopted an ever more skeptical attitude toward government pronouncements. The Johnson administration viewed this shift in television coverage with a "horrible fascination," Press Secretary George Christian later wrote. The administration cynically attributed the networks' attention to antiwar demonstrators to their competition for ratings. Lyndon Johnson began to complain that a handful of men determined everything Americans saw on television, and he accused news broadcasters of injecting editorial comments into their reports—meaning that they questioned his policies. For Johnson, the nadir occurred in February 1968, when Water Cronkite, on tour in Vietnam following the Tet offensive, delivered a rare editorial assessment that the war had mired in stalemate. Watching the broadcast, Johnson turned to an aide and said it was all over. If he had lost Cronkite, he had lost the country.[51]

Johnson's surprise decision not to run for reelection boosted the chances of the Republican candidate, Richard Nixon, a man who viewed himself as cool, confident, and commanding, but who most of the Washington correspondents saw as tense, suspicious, and insecure. They had been courted by Nixon, and had felt his contempt. Since he rescued his vice-presidential candidacy in 1952 with his nationally televised "Checkers" speech, Nixon had prided himself on his mastery of the media. Abnormally introverted for a politician, he admitted that he felt more comfortable speaking to millions on television than to small groups in person. He also appreciated that TV enabled him to reach the public without going through the filter of a hostile press corps. Then in 1960 his disastrous first televised debate with Kennedy sabotaged his presidential hopes. Two years later, Nixon lost his race for governor of California and promised reporters that they would not have him to "kick around any more." He blasted the newspapers but thanked television for keeping the record straight.[52]

Six years after this seemingly terminal outburst, a savvy team of media advisors repackaged the candidate as a "New Nixon," more confident but also more cautious of debates, press conferences, and any other spontaneous, unscripted moments. Nixon campaigned in 1968 via a series of carefully staged televised events. When TV correspondents questioned these tactics and his undefined plan to end the war, he became convinced that the networks were tilted against him. After his narrow election, Nixon ordered his staff to monitor the network news broadcasts for signs of bias. His lists of "enemies" included some of Washington's most prominent names in television. Nixon enjoyed a brief presidential honeymoon, until peace negotiations in Vietnam stalled and the antiwar movement revived. Massive protests against the war were scheduled for October and November 1969.

As president, Nixon could command television time almost at will, without giving his critics in Congress equal time for rebuttal. (The networks preferred analysis from their own correspondents rather than from politicians.) Midway between the antiwar protests, Nixon delivered a televised address on Vietnam aimed at the nation's "silent majority," in which he laid out plans to withdraw American forces and turn the fighting over to the South Vietnamese. (Walter Lippmann called this the first time any nation had expected to prevail by withdrawing its troops from combat.)[53] With his staff monitoring the network commentators' responses, Nixon provoked a confrontation with the networks by speaking for thirty-two minutes. Because programs were scheduled in half-hour blocks, he could have minimized any commentary by keeping his remarks to less than thirty minutes. Once he went over, he left nearly half an hour of airtime for the network correspondents. "How else on short notice, or no notice, could we fill network airtime?" David Brinkley asked. "Organ music?" The day after, the White House spread the word that the president and his family had been "livid with rage" over the correspondents' "instant analysis." Dean Burch, chairman of the Federal Communications Commission and a former chairman of the Republican Party, ominously telephoned the networks to request transcripts of the commentaries.[54]

Vice President Spiro Agnew was then dispatched to poke a finger in the media's eye. Upon first reading the draft prepared by the White House staff, Agnew worried that the speech sounded "a bit abrasive," but agreed to deliver it before a Republican meeting in Des Moines, Iowa, ten days after Nixon's televised address. "Why can't the President of the United States make a speech without the networks following it with instant analysis and querulous criticism?" Agnew demanded. The network evening news that millions watched, he continued, was the work of just a dozen anchormen, commentators, and producers, "a concentration of power over American public opinion unknown in history." This "unelected elite" lived and worked in New York City and Washington, read the same papers, and shared the same viewpoints. Their monopolistic grip on television news had produced "a distorted picture of American life." Agnew called on the American people to let the networks know that they wanted their news "straight and objective." The White House had distributed advance copies of the vice president's speech to the networks to avoid any appearance of a "sneak attack." The advance text created panic among networks executives, who rushed to disprove Agnew by broadcasting his speech live, moving their own evening news programs half an hour earlier to accommodate him. They wound up giving his inflammatory remarks a prime-time audience. Agnew's speech adroitly shifted blame for the "credibility gap" from the government onto the networks. Polls, along with the letters and phone calls that flooded the networks, showed that a majority of Americans agreed with the vice president.[55]

The day after Agnew's speech, sociologist Herbert Gans visited NBC News and found its correspondents baffled and resentful over the assertion of their "immense power." David Brinkley, who aimed his sardonic remarks at liberal and conservative politicians alike, felt proud that the vice president had singled him out as the worst offender, but CBS commentator Eric Sevareid, who balanced his liberal political leanings with a conservative temperament, felt as if "a pail of garbage" had been dumped on him. Adding to the insult were threats from the networks' affiliates to black out any future analyses of presidential addresses. Meetings with the networks' affiliates turned into impassioned attacks on the national news programs, with station owners accusing the correspondents of favoring protestors against the president. These clashes triggered a sudden surge of attribution on the evening news programs, as reporters strained to make clear they were quoting others rather than speaking their own minds.[56]

Agnew had echoed antinetwork themes previously sounded by Lyndon Johnson and the New Left, but the vice president's conservative following blamed the problem on the media's liberal bias. A *TV Guide* staff writer, Edith Efron, produced a detailed content analysis of prime-time national news during Nixon's campaign for the presidency, offering statistics that showed a pattern of disparagement of conservative candidates. As a student, Efron had sold copies of the *Daily Worker* in Harlem, until the day she sat down on a park bench to read the paper, and threw the stack away in embarrassment. Having moved from left to right, Efron accused the television networks of deliberately twisting the news for ideological reasons. John Corry, the conservative television critic for the *New York Times*, thought the liberal bias was more systemic, noting that television reflected the "dominant culture." Even though news broadcasters tried to get their facts right and allowed different sides in any issue to respond, the medium preferred conflict to calm and, as a result, portrayed a disintegrating society desperately in need of restructuring. "This was a message from the left," Corry charged, "and to the extent that television allowed the message to capture its news agenda, television was a captive of the left."[57]

The newscasters rejected such accusations of bias, especially when leveled by a *TV Guide* writer. Eric Sevareid dismissed the magazine as "dedicated to the propagation of extreme right wing ideology." Anyone who stood that far to the right, he said, would naturally find most of the media well to their left. Yet most of the correspondents agreed that they shared similar world outlooks, and their jobs required them to live in proximity to each other, making it natural for them to intermingle socially and professionally. "Too many of us interview the people we have had dinner with the night before," commented Harry Reasoner. Eric Sevareid thought it was too bad that television news had never developed a means of airing viewers' complaints, like the "letters to the editor" column in a newspaper. If disaffected viewers had been able to talk back, Sevareid speculated, "the gas of resentment could have escaped the boiler in a normal way" rather than waiting for someone like Agnew to ignite it. Speaking at Washington and Lee University in December 1970, Roger Mudd added his own condemnation of television's tendency "to strike at the emotions rather than the intellect." Mudd regretted that television news concentrated "on happenings rather than issues; on shock rather than explanation; on personalization rather than ideas." Coming as it did in the wake of Agnew's criticism, Mudd's speech struck some CBS executives as an act of disloyalty, and they dropped him as a substitute anchor for Walter Cronkite. When he considered quitting, the network reversed itself, offered him a new contract as CBS's national affairs correspondent, and restored him as Cronkite's regular replacement.[58]

In short order, Mudd became embroiled in another flap when he narrated a documentary for CBS called *The Selling of the Pentagon*. The program charged American military leaders with having conducted elaborate publicity campaigns to bolster their appropriations. Pentagon officials accused CBS of editing its interviews to twist their meanings, and Vice President Agnew deemed the program a "propaganda attempt to discredit the defense establishment." On Capitol Hill, the Pentagon's supporters opened what Mudd called "a full-bore barrage." A House subcommittee demanded the documentary's unedited outtakes, but CBS president Frank Stanton refused to comply, citing the First Amendment. The subcommittee voted to hold him in contempt of Congress. The full House split almost evenly. "CBS won by just four votes," Mudd said of the narrowness of their escape. Sensing the network's vulnerability, President Nixon's special assistant Charles Colson worked with the CBS lobbyists to defeat the contempt motion, and took credit for the victory. Colson then tapped the lobbyists as conduits for complaints about unfair reporting.[59]

Not surprisingly, in this ominous atmosphere, the badgered networks were slow to grasp the political implications of the Watergate burglary. Nixon's staff regarded CBS's contentious White House correspondent Dan Rather as an implacable foe out to embarrass the president at every turn, but Rather left the Watergate story alone at first, sure that it would fade like "a puff of talcum powder." CBS bureau chief Bill Small instead assigned Watergate to his greenest reporter, Lesley Stahl. She happened to be dating the *Washington Post* reporter Bob Woodward at the time, and he convinced her of the story's merits. Stahl had a tougher time persuading CBS, as her bureau "tended to rely more on *The New York Times* than on the new kid." As the story gained plausibility, CBS hired Fred Graham, a lawyer, to serve as its legal correspondent. The bureau divided its Watergate coverage between Graham at the courts, Dan Rather at the White House, and Daniel Schorr in Congress, leaving Stahl to do the "clean-up" of whatever fell in between those beats. All of them found Watergate a hard story to capture on film. Schorr's first breakthrough came when his crew filmed the indicted conspirator E. Howard Hunt frantically trying to elude their camera. That night's *CBS Evening News* devoted almost as much time to Hunt's mad dash as it did to the president's press conference, and producers were ecstatic at having beaten the other networks with such a "visual" story, even if it had provided no news. Thereafter, Schorr took over the Watergate story from Stahl. "When Lesley started out, she had some things to learn," he said, dismissing her complaints.[60]

Finding it difficult to narrate Watergate coherently in occasional segments, CBS aired a retrospect of the scandal on the evening news in October 1972— four months after the burglary and a few weeks before the election. The first installment consumed half of one evening's program, with a second install- ment scheduled to fill an equal time slot the next program. This marked a noticeable departure from the show's normal format. CBS reporters gathered at a monitor in the studio to watch the first installment "with a tingling sense," in Schorr's words, "of seeing the Edward R. Murrow era reborn." The feature did little more than summarize the *Washington Post*'s running accounts, and even used a montage of *Post* headlines as its backdrop. Yet while it added little original news, the report synthesized the complex Watergate story to a vast audience. From the Nixon White House, Charles Colson angrily telephoned CBS chairman William Paley and threatened retaliation via the FCC. Deeply shaken by the call, Paley instructed the news division to scale back the planned second installment. "Instant analysis" had survived Spiro Agnew's earlier as- sault, but word came down that there would be no more commentary follow- ing any future presidential addresses. At the Washington bureau, Roger Mudd drafted a letter of protest to CBS News president Dick Salant, signed by him- self, Marvin Kalb, Daniel Schorr, and George Herman. Dan Rather declined to sign the letter, concerned that it might further strain his toxic relations with the White House. It was not, Rather conceded, "one of my heroic moments." Salant sided with the correspondents, and Paley rescinded his ban on instant analysis. In the end, CBS's controversial Watergate reports served chiefly to validate the *Washington Post*'s reporting. From that point on, the networks took more of their cues from the *Post*'s reporting. "We read the *Post* bulldog edition every night, as we have ever since Watergate," a CBS bureau chief con- firmed a decade later.[61]

By December 1972 the CBS Washington bureau was holding a daily meeting about the Watergate story. Producers and correspondents heard rumors about the administration's pressure on their network's leaders, and felt the need for extra caution. Fred Graham recalled feeling "a little intimidated about being critical of the president." When Nixon publicly declared he was "not a crook," none of the team of CBS correspondents mentioned that demeaning assertion in their instant analysis. Yet Nixon's supporters accused the correspondents of bias—like the motorist who stopped his car near the bureau one day and rolled down his window to shout, "Fred Graham, I hate you." Equally upsetting to the correspondents were the viewers who congratulated them on their supposed campaign to "get Nixon." Still, the television correspondents recognized that they were not just reporting events, they were shaping them. Their nightly reports exposed inconsistencies in Nixon's self-defense and forced regular reactions from the administration. As a news story, Watergate gained solid traction when it became evident that the Watergate burglars had been paid to keep silent. The cover-up unraveled swiftly and unpredictably. By the time that Nixon fired Special Prosecutor Archibald Cox, anything seemed possible, a situation that gave the correspondents a sense of exhilaration that matched no other Washington story they had covered.[62]

The mounting disclosures of the Watergate cover-up derailed the administration's campaign against the press and also eliminated the president's chief hatchet man. Nixon had used Spiro Agnew to "soften the press," although he had rarely consulted with his vice president and considered dropping him from the ticket in 1972, until aides convinced him that the antimedia campaign had made the vice president "almost a folk hero." Less than a year into their second term, Agnew resigned in disgrace, when he pleaded no contest to charges of bribery and tax evasion. Television news covered the downfall of its loudest critic with considerable restraint. At the same time, President Nixon was being investigated by a special prosecutor and a special Senate committee. The three networks broadcast the Senate Watergate Committee's proceedings live, but to minimize advertising losses, they rotated it among themselves. The new Public Broadcasting Service had no commercial sponsorship to lose, so it devoted most of its schedule to the hearings, which helped build its audience. The House of Representatives had repealed the Rayburn Rule in time to broadcast the House Judiciary Committee's hearings on Nixon's impeachment in 1974, the first televised House hearings in twenty years. "We've been waiting for a long time for this to open up," CBS bureau chief Bill Small exulted. Richard Nixon's fall prompted the Senate to install the first TV cameras in its chamber in anticipation of an impeachment trial. But Nixon's resignation made the issue moot, and Senate debates remained out of camera range for another decade.[63]

The unfurling Watergate story gave the Washington correspondents abundant airtime and promoted the bureau chief to vice president of CBS News. The New York headquarters had given Bill Small responsibility for the bureau and, as Bob Schieffer commented, "the authority to back up that responsibility." Small consistently fought the correspondents' battles with New York. By contrast, his successor, Sandy Socolow, appeared to have been sent from New York to bring the bureau to heel. That August, when Nixon announced his resignation, CBS executives worried that he might personally attack television in general, and their network in particular, for driving him from office. Bureau chief Socolow advised correspondents to "take it easy tonight" and not sound vindictive. Standing among a celebrating throng in Washington's Lafayette Square, Dan Rather described the mood of the crowd as "somber," and later proclaimed Nixon's voluntary departure to be his "finest hour." Roger Mudd had spent the day on Capitol Hill and had missed Socolow's warning. Mudd pointed out that Nixon had ignored the main reasons why he was leaving, and judged his speech an unsatisfactory performance, "just from a pure congressional point of view." The discrepancy in tone between Mudd and Rather drew notice at a time when both were seen as potential replacements for Cronkite as news anchor.[64]

As Walter Cronkite neared retirement age, Washington journalists rated the competition to succeed him a "national event" more avidly followed than some political battles. The network contemplated teaming Mudd and Rather, a partnership that Mudd refused to consider. "Dan Rather did not make Roger Mudd's short list of beloved colleagues," CBS News president Bill Leonard remarked. In 1980, ABC forced its rival's hand by attempting to recruit Rather as its news anchor. CBS hastily made him a multimillion-dollar counteroffer to succeed Cronkite. Once Rather's selection was announced, Mudd demanded immediate release from his contract. CBS instead gave him a paid leave of absence for the remainder of his contract, to fend off the other networks. Mudd walked out of the Washington bureau and never returned. "I have regarded myself as a news reporter, not as a newsmaker or a celebrity," he said. The other networks naturally bid for his services. He declined an offer to anchor the ABC evening news, which would have meant relocating to New York, and went instead to NBC, where his old bureau chief Bill Small had become president of the news division.[65]

Small imported several other prominent refugees from the CBS Washington bureau—and irritated NBC veterans by touting their superiority. Mudd became NBC's chief Washington correspondent, and his contract stipulated that he would eventually anchor the evening news. But to prevent ABC from raiding another rising star, former White House correspondent and *Today* show host Tom Brokaw, NBC chose to team Mudd in Washington with Brokaw in New York. The network intended to recapture the Huntley-Brinkley allure, but this pairing failed to coalesce. Mudd and Brokaw gave the impression they were conducting two separate programs. When NBC dropped Mudd as co-anchor, he returned to his familiar beat at chief congressional correspondent, this time for PBS's *MacNeil/Lehrer News Hour*. The three commercial networks had run out of places for the man widely regarded as television's best political reporter. Looking back over his long career, Roger Mudd most regretted his departure from CBS, which he equated with having played for the New York Yankees, because "there wasn't anybody any better."[66]

On the night of Spiro Agnew's Des Moines speech, the CBS Washington bureau's roster stood at twenty-one correspondents; thirty years later it had shrunk to nine. Without noticing it, network news peaked around 1980, when the three networks attracted 120 million viewers nightly, and had no appreciable competition on the air. Lesley Stahl bragged that "our deadline at 6:30 Eastern Time became the deadline of the entire federal government." Overconfident news executives snickered when Ted Turner launched the twenty-four-hour-a-day Cable News Network, deriding its low-budgeted productions as the "Chicken Noodle Network" and excluding its reporters from press pools. CNN pioneered cable news in 1980, at a time when the diminished scale of world events seemed to have drained much of the news's compelling nature. The end of the Vietnam War and the disbanding of the antiwar movement took much of the punch out of the nightly news, observed NBC correspondent Garrett Utley, and the civil rights movement and Watergate scandal were hard to follow with images of Jimmy Carter in a cardigan sweater, admonishing folks to turn down their thermostats. Reacting to charges of elitism, TV journalists also struggled to relate the news more directly to their viewers. They framed national stories such as the energy crisis in terms of how it affected average people, and did stand-ups in front of corner gas stations rather than on the Capitol lawn, turning the camera's eye from politics and government to human interest.[67]

Even at the height of network domination, half of all television owners never bothered to watch the evening news, and only one in fifty watched the news every night. News shows drew their viewers from older, better-educated, middle- and upper-income professionals, who were disproportionately white and male. If the networks had any hope of expanding the audience for news, they had to attract more women, blue-collar workers, and racial minorities. A shift in focus began at the local news level, where marketing consultants convinced station managers that some lightening of local news programs could attract larger numbers of women and young adults—the consumers whom advertisers most wanted to reach. Hard-news reporters despaired that the new formats turned local news into "nightly vaudeville," with heavy doses of crime, disaster, scandal, and celebrity features. Yet ratings and revenue boomed. As local shows became moneymakers they expanded to fill several hours of airtime, and trumped the networks' attempts to extend the national news to one hour.[68]

Having long languished in third place in the ratings, ABC News appointed sports producer Roone Arledge to head the news division in 1977. From *Wide World of Sports* to *Monday Night Football,* Arledge had moved sports coverage into prime time by highlighting the athletes' individual sagas and letting viewers share "the thrill of victory, the agony of defeat." He transplanted the same concepts to the news, demanding that it tell a story rather than simply record events. Arledge's broadcasting style—along with his safari suits and gold chains—so clashed with the news division's traditional values that the ABC correspondents Peter Jennings and Ted Koppel personally appealed to network executives to keep him away from the news. Despite their doubts, he wound up advancing the careers of both men, making Jennings anchor for the network's *World News Tonight* and installing Koppel as host of *Nightline* (after using the Iranian hostage crisis in 1980 to wrestle half an hour of late-night airtime from the affiliates). Arledge launched a prime-time news program, *20/20*, and enticed David Brinkley away from NBC to host an expanded Sunday morning news show. ABC's use of multimillion-dollar contracts to procure news "stars" away from the other networks gave Walter Cronkite a sickening sensation "that all of our efforts to hold network television news aloof from show business had failed." The profusion of snappy graphics and the abridgment of news stories at ABC inspired Garry Trudeau to spoof Arledge's product as the "ABC Wide World of News" in his comic strip *Doonesbury*.[69]

Elvis Presley died on August 16, 1977, and ABC's *World News Tonight* led with the story. The *CBS Evening News* opened instead with a report on the current status of the Panama Canal treaties. A network that discouraged its correspondents from excessive smiling and expected them to deliver the news in serious tones, CBS was not about to pander to Presley's fans. Walter Cronkite's steadily high ratings had discouraged much experimentation. CBS had increased its news budget sixfold since the early 1960s, and doubled its personnel. It spent more money to cover the news than any other news organization in the world. After Cronkite retired in 1981, the evening news program's ratings began to slide. In its scramble to modernize, CBS put Van Gordon Sauter in charge of the news. Having worked his way through local TV news in Chicago and Los Angeles (and headed CBS Sports), he brought the local news ethos with him. Sauter rejected the old issue-laden approach to the news, and regarded much of what was reported from Washington as boring. He announced that he intended to make the *CBS Evening News* less like the *New York Times* and more like a tabloid. Depressed by this notion, the Washington bureau's seasoned correspondents were thrown further off balance by Sauter's demand that TV news grab the viewers' hearts and emotions, and his insistence that their stories contain "moments" that would "*touch* people."[70]

Finding few "moments" to report at government offices, the Washington correspondents argued that they should not have to be entertaining to get on the *Evening News*. More reports from the Washington bureau were being boiled down for the news anchor to read, but when the correspondents protested, network officials would retort that their reporting had been "done in a way that no one could care about it." CBS cut back on stand-ups outside government buildings and sent correspondents out "in the field," on the assumption that those inside the Beltway had lost touch with the rest of the country. The new policy favored general assignment reporters over those on fixed beats, causing familiar Washington faces to fade from nightly view. "Thank God they picked Rather," Roger Mudd later commented, grateful that he did not have to anchor the reversal of network news priorities.[71]

As CBS reduced its Washington staff, it literally elevated its anchorman in New York. The network's original anchor, Douglas Edwards, came back to tour the impressive new set that had been designed for Dan Rather. He described it as "cathedral-like with its galleries and its anchor desk as a high altar." Visitors whispered in reverence. But the "cathedral mentality" waned as new technology freed news broadcasting from the studio and dispatched anchormen to the scene of breaking news. The spiraling cost of the new technology came just as the television networks were encountering cable competition.[72]

CBS and the other networks looked down on CNN, said one news executive, "just about the way General Motors regards Harley Davidson." Former CBS correspondent Bernard Shaw—the Washington bureau's first African American correspondent—took a gamble by agreeing to anchor for "a network that didn't exist." Shaw moved into CNN's small office in Washington, linked by satellite to its headquarters in Atlanta. During one broadcast, a cleaning woman walked in front of him and emptied his wastebasket while he was delivering the news. As cable reached more cities, CNN expanded its audience and upgraded its facilities in Washington and Atlanta. It repackaged its material into headline news, international news, and airport news broadcasts, and sold film to the other networks' affiliates for their local news shows. The requirements of broadcasting for twenty-four hours each day stretched resources thin but gave CNN the advantage in reporting breaking news. CNN broadcast President Reagan's speech at the Washington Hilton in March 1981, and Shaw was summarizing the president's remarks when a commotion arose at the assignment desk behind him. The deskman had been monitoring police radios and advised him that shots had been fired at the president's motorcade. With a few shreds of information, Shaw became the first television news broadcaster to report the shooting of the president. Reagan later rewarded the upstart cable network by inviting Bernard Shaw to join "all four networks" in a group interview in the Oval Office.[73]

A different type of competition emerged with the Cable-Satellite Public Affairs Network. C-SPAN broadcast congressional debates gavel-to-gavel, and filled the congressional recesses with live coverage of press conferences, ceremonies, and speeches. Ever since Roger Mudd stood on the Capitol steps during the civil rights filibuster, the networks had anticipated installing cameras in the Senate and House chambers. Without pictures, the drive for "moments" had made it harder to broadcast congressional stories. CBS Senate correspondent Phil Jones grumbled that he could get the senators on the air more frequently if they would just ride in a fire truck. By the time that the House and Senate allowed their proceedings to be televised, the networks had lost interest in the debates and were content to show occasional clips. The nation's cable stations took the initiative instead and pooled their resources to finance broadcasting of congressional debates live and in their entirety.[74]

C-SPAN's founder, Brian Lamb, had served in the Johnson White House and then in Nixon's Office of Telecommunications Policy. The director of that office, Clay Whitehead, complained that "You just have to turn on the television set and watch the evening news, or the local news, you watch practically anything and you see things you don't agree with." Whitehead had a vision of breaking the networks' monopoly by fostering competition via cable and communications satellites. But his efforts to promote deregulation collapsed when the Watergate scandal forced the release of Nixon's secret tapes, which captured the president plotting to use broadcasting license renewals against his critics in the media, particularly the TV stations owned by the *Washington Post*. "Watergate pervades everything," Whitehead despaired. "How could I say with credibility that we didn't want to control the press in the wake of those memos and that stupid conversation in the Oval Office about the *Post* stations?" Whitehead resigned shortly before Nixon did, regretting that the president's vendetta against the news media had overshadowed efforts to democratize broadcasting. But Nixon's appointees at the FCC had managed to reverse earlier policies that limited cable TV to local programming.[75]

Brian Lamb also left the government in 1974. While Jimmy Carter's appointees to the FCC continued to deregulate cable television, Lamb approached cable executives with a plan for them collectively to fund a public-affairs channel that would add stature to the nascent cable channels. In 1979, C-SPAN opened in a one-room office in Arlington, Virginia. Its first programs alternated with wrestling from a sports channel. When the House of Representatives turned on its cameras that year, C-SPAN was prepared to broadcast the proceedings live. The networks "didn't think we were a bona fide news organization," recalled C-SPAN executive Mike Michaelson. They froze the upstart out of the presidential debates and tried to charge it for using pool camera feed—common film footage available to all networks—at hearings. C-SPAN's "video vérité" approach seemed a refreshing contrast for viewers who just wanted to see what was going on, without graphics, sound bites, and the babble of news commentators filling airtime. "Just as Detroit didn't see the Hondas and the Subarus and the Toyotas crowding them off the road," admitted CBS's Don Hewitt, "we didn't see the CNNs and the C-SPANs, and the ESPNs crowding us off the road."[76]

Belatedly awakened to the challenge, the networks sought their own alliances with the newly emerging media. CBS misread the market and launched a highbrow fine arts cable channel that it soon wrote off as a loss. ABC's parent company, Capital Cities Communications, invested more profitably in the sports cable network ESPN, and other ventures. NBC formed a partnership with the Consumer News and Business Channel, CNBC, and later joined with the software giant Microsoft to form the cable channel MSNBC, hoping that the mix of network news, cable, and the Internet would attract younger audiences. NBC News was therefore best able to spread news costs between its network and cable outlets, and offer news whenever audiences wanted it. For all its advantages of a major network, twenty-four-hour broadcasting ability, and a fabulously prosperous software designer, MSNBC struggled to define itself and lagged behind the hard-news CNN and the opinion-driven Fox News. Other channels repackaged everything from local news to the BBC and other international news shows. Cable news offered more choices, but like the expansion of professional baseball, it diluted the talent.[77]

Television's transformation happened under the watch of a president who was a former television star. Unlike the confrontational Richard Nixon, who had stormed ineffectively against the networks, a sunny Ronald Reagan basked in deregulation. Reagan's appointees to the FCC lifted restrictions on broadcasting licenses in 1987, allowing more time for commercials, dropping requirements for public service broadcasts, and abolishing the "fairness doctrine" that required networks to give equal time to all sides. "When I was growing up in television, there was nothing the networks wanted more than to get the FCC off their backs," said Don Hewitt. "What they dreamed of was a television world in which they would be free to regulate themselves. What they woke up to, when they finally got what they wanted, was a television world in which nobody regulates anything and everybody bumps into everyone else." Deregulation ended the networks' monopoly status and also made them more vulnerable to corporate takeovers on Wall Street.[78]

In their rush to give the news a fresher look and generate higher ratings the networks' news budgets had ballooned, making them prime targets for corporate downsizing. During the 1980s, financier Laurence Tisch assumed control of CBS; the Walt Disney Corporation took over ABC; and General Electric acquired NBC. The new corporate proprietors identified their news departments as financial drains. Previously, news directors had not had to worry about profits and advertising so long as they satisfied FCC requirements. But once public service was no longer an issue for licensing, the red ink seemed less tolerable. To balance the books, the new management wanted higher ad revenues and smaller staffs. Network accountants pointed to the ratings and revenues of news magazine shows such as *60 Minutes* as something for the evening news programs to match. At ABC, where Roone Arledge had spent prodigiously to build a premier news organization, the network trimmed jobs from the news department. At NBC, a senior news producer charged that General Electric had put the news division under "relentless pressure to cut costs and make profits, just as GE's light bulb factories do." NBC News's president resigned rather than decimate his department. His successor swiftly swung the axe.[79]

At CBS, Washington correspondents suspected Van Gordon Sauter of putting a damper on any critical reporting of Ronald Reagan, not wanting to rile the public with attacks on the affable president. Yet Sauter's quest for "moments" coincided with a deep economic recession during Reagan's first term. By shifting the focus of the news from Washington to the plight of average citizens, the *CBS Evening News* appeared to be playing the liberal critic to a conservative president. Lingering resentment of Dan Rather's reporting during the Nixon years surfaced when North Carolina's Republican senator Jesse Helms joined with conservative media watchdog groups to encourage their supporters to buy CBS stock and "become Dan Rather's boss." CNN's Ted Turner also expressed interest in buying control of CBS. Anxious to halt these efforts, the CBS board of directors turned in 1985 to Laurence Tisch, president of the Lowe's Corporation, as a more attractive alternative. Tisch saw TV as strictly a business, not a public trust. Once in control, he set about maximizing profits through draconian cost cutting.[80]

To CBS's Washington bureau, Tisch offered his personal assurances that he wanted the network's news to remain the best. Despite that promise, successive waves of downsizing thinned the ranks of correspondents, producers, directors, writers, and camera crews (events that provided the backdrop for the movie *Broadcast News*). The Washington bureau cut Pentagon reporter Ike Pappas, Supreme Court correspondent Fred Graham, and Marlene Sanders, who had anchored its prime-time newsbreaks and appeared regularly on *Sunday Morning*. Sanders bitterly observed that none of her professional contributions mattered if she did not meet producers' standards of "charisma, looks, or age." On Capitol Hill, where CBS had traditionally assigned a full-time correspondent to the Senate and another to the House, only Bob Schieffer remained, and his title as "chief political correspondent" frequently took him away from Congress. When Schieffer left the assignment, CBS no longer regularly posted a correspondent at the Capitol, simply sending someone when needed. Tighter budgets meant that network correspondents could go to fewer places, witness fewer events, and cover less news, all while facing round-the-clock competition from cable news channels.[81]

Network news also lost viewers. Just as television had once enticed the public out of movie theaters and drained advertising revenue away from newspapers and magazines, cable poached viewers and advertisers from the networks. The networks' audience share slid from 98 percent in the 1960s to 50 percent by the 1990s. All that saved network news, Dan Rather speculated, was its centrality in establishing a network's identity, as "without news, it's pretty hard to get and hold affiliates over a long period of time." Critics pined for the content-driven news programs and documentaries of TV's "Golden Age," but accountants reminded them that memorable documentaries by Edward R. Murrow and Howard K. Smith had attracted comparatively small audiences. "Very few people watched," agreed ABC Washington correspondent Sam Donaldson, "didn't matter, didn't have to make money." Donaldson noted that corporate executives now expected news programs to raise their ratings and their revenues by making the news "fascinating, interesting, dynamic, dramatic, maybe even slightly titillating." If some viewers felt alienated by the new approach, they could turn to CNN or to PBS's *NewsHour*—which aimed to "slow down, take its time and pick its way a little more coherently through the complexities of the day."[82]

The downsized networks took a further hit during the Persian Gulf War in 1991, when American planes bombed the television station in Baghdad where they broadcast. CNN had set up a separate link. By chance, CNN's Washington anchor Bernard Shaw was in Baghdad to interview the Iraqi dictator Saddam Hussein. By remaining in the war zone, Shaw and CNN correspondents Peter Arnett and John Holliman gave CNN hours of exclusive commentary on the allied bombing campaign. Although CNN's ratings dropped as soon as the war ended, its Iraqi coverage made the round-the-clock news network a fixture in every newsroom. So pervasively did CNN influence press corps perceptions that when a federal office building in Oklahoma City was bombed in 1995, most of the media followed CNN's initial speculations about Islamic terrorists. A small Middle Eastern news service in Washington challenged this notion and suggested that American militia groups might have been responsible, noting that the bombing occurred on the anniversary of the FBI's fatal raid in Waco, Texas. "We don't have CNN on in our office during the day," said an editor of that news service, explaining its deviation from the news consensus. "It is much too distracting when you're trying to think."[83]

In 1988 when he returned, after a nine-year absence, to cover the White House, ABC correspondent Sam Donaldson was stunned that he was not called upon at his first press conference back. None of the network correspondents were recognized that day. "WHAT'S THIS?!" Donaldson thundered. "I was ALWAYS called on!" Donaldson realized that his competition was no longer CBS and NBC, but CNN, MSNBC, and Fox News. He could no longer hold an exclusive news item to report on the evening news program, because cable news correspondents could scoop him at any moment. In addition to breaking news, cable appealed to younger viewers by encouraging its commentators to dress more casually and to express their feelings more openly than was customary on the networks.

Cable's ratings shot up with each big news story, from overseas military action to President Bill Clinton's "inappropriate relationship" with a White House intern, and then flattened when the sensation subsided. (The business-oriented CNBC's fortunes fluctuated more with the stock markets, surging with the bull market of the 1990s, and slipping with the bears.) Trying for more consistent ratings, and to avoid the tedium of repeating the same news every hour, cable news punctuated its schedule with crossfire dialogues and celebrity interviews. Its attempt to generate news features caused some missteps, most notably when CNN's *NewsStand* had to retract its claim that U.S. military forces had used a lethal nerve gas on American defectors in Laos.

Conservatives blamed the error on CNN's liberal bias, and Fox News director Roger Ailes twitted his rival as the "Clinton News Network." Once a media advisor to Richard Nixon, Ailes built healthy ratings for Rupert Murdoch's Fox News Channel through aggressive reporting and brash commentary. Although critics charged Fox with tilting to the right, the network insisted that it was simply giving conservatives an equal voice denied to them on other channels.[84]

In the days when the networks still dreamed of hour-long evening news programs they had planned a half hour of hard news to be followed by lighter features. Perpetually confined to the half-hour format, network news began to condense hard news into the opening segments of the programs and inflate feature stories through the rest. NBC drastically revamped its *Nightly News* to devote more airtime to health and consumer issues. "These are not the traditional stories we've all grown up with, subcommittee hearings and whatever the political development of the day is," admitted anchorman Tom Brokaw. He pointed out that the old format had been put together by white, middle-aged men and it was through their prism that television viewers saw the world. Brokaw cited his daughters as more typical modern viewers, who wanted news that related to marriage, families, and jobs rather than anything that happened in a congressional committee room. NBC promoted the new format as a populist approach, but dissenters on its Washington news staff dubbed it "News Lite." NBC's chief congressional reporter, Gwen Ifill, had increasing trouble getting her stories on the air. "If a hurricane was a story of the day, maybe something important was happening on the Hill—maybe there was a campaign finance vote—but that will never get reported," she commented, judging that the network had grown "bored by Washington." Ifill quit NBC for public broadcasting.[85]

"Get ready to be outraged," said CBS news anchor Dan Rather one night, as he encouraged his viewers to stay tuned through the commercial. Veteran newscasters disdained the hyping of network news. They blamed television news for shifting political attention away from getting things done to "telling people that you were up here doing what you were supposed to do," as Roger Mudd put it. Walter Cronkite regretted that so many of the proliferating cable channels had allowed sober news analysis to give way to "polarizing diatribe." At the same time, television news contributed to improvements in the print media. TV's speed in delivering the news forced newspapers to adjust or be rendered obsolete. Newspapers responded by putting greater emphasis on the kind of in-depth news that the half-hour broadcasts could not match. They developed Internet web sites that they could update throughout the day. From *USA Today* to the "gray" *New York Times,* newspapers adopted color images and splashy graphics, expanded social features, and gave reporters greater rein to interpret the news. Where CBS had once aspired to become the *New York Times* of the air, the *New York Times* had absorbed television's visual style.[86]

10

Washington, Deceit

On a quiet Saturday afternoon in August 1963 John Corry was working the desk at the Washington bureau of the *New York Times* when word came that the *Washington Post*'s publisher, Philip L. Graham, had committed suicide. Having recently transferred from New York, Corry was surprised when the reporter to whom he had assigned the story demurred, saying that he could not bring himself to call the bereaved family for details. Then call the police, said Corry. The nonplused reporter replied that he had never before had to contact the Washington police, leading Corry to wonder whether anyone on the Washington staff could find the nearest police station. The only courts that reporters at the *Times*'s bureau covered were federal, and not much had changed by June 1972, when police arrested five men inside the Democratic National Committee headquarters at the Watergate. To Fred Graham, who covered the Supreme Court for the *Times*, the burglary seemed like the sort of local police story that "the nation's leading newspaper did not normally pursue." The next day's *New York Times* ran a short unsigned piece deep inside the paper, in contrast to the *Washington Post*'s first Watergate story, which made the front page.[1]

For months, the national press corps neglected the political story of the century. Washington's most accomplished reporters followed the presidential campaign and the peace negotiations in Vietnam rather than the brewing Watergate scandal. Their fumbling of the story would long haunt reporters as a nightmare of missed opportunities. Top political columnists and correspondents later admitted that they did little to help readers understand what Watergate meant in the months leading up to the election of 1972. Those who reported on the White House and Capitol, and even those on the national news desk at the *Washington Post*, considered presidential involvement in the Watergate burglary highly implausible. Most Washington correspondents did not like Richard Nixon, but they respected his intelligence. It seemed unfathomable to them that he would jeopardize his presidency by bugging his faltering opposition.[2]

By the time the press corps finally connected smoke to fire, two green reporters on the *Post*'s Metro section had practically copyrighted the Watergate story. Bob Woodward and Carl Bernstein were so far ahead of the press corps in assembling the murky facts and establishing sources that other reporters had trouble finding ways to advance the story independently. The UPI's Washington desk called reporter Roy McGhee one morning and told him to develop his own version of yet another *Post* exclusive. McGhee protested that there was no way that he could replicate in a few hours what the *Post* reporters must have worked on for weeks. He advised UPI to swallow its pride and cite the *Post.* Yet the wire services, and newspapers such as the *New York Times,* hesitated to accept the *Post*'s allegations unless they could confirm the evidence, and the television networks took their cues from the *Times* rather than the *Post.* "If this is such a hell of a story," wondered the *Post*'s beleaguered publisher, Katharine Graham, "then where is everybody else?"[3]

The Watergate story, like all investigative reporting, inverted the impulses of objective journalism, which set investigative reporters apart from the rest of the press corps. Objectivity forbid reporters from taking sides, while investigative reporting operated on the assumption that one side was in the wrong. Investigative reporters hungered to uncover whatever the authorities wanted to suppress. Their instincts ran contrary to the herd-like mentality that often prevailed among other reporters who were driven by daily deadlines, editors' demands, and conventional wisdom. "They ran in packs," observed Alan Ehrenhalt, describing the days when he covered Congress for the Associated Press, "more concerned about missing out on news a competitor had than about learning something fresh." The pack attended the same press conferences, read the same releases, interviewed the same types of officials, and produced variations on the same themes. "What's the lead?" correspondents asked, knowing that editors would be suspicious of anything that strayed too far from what the wires and the rest of the pack reported.[4]

Both traditional and investigative reporters gathered significant amounts of news from sources who demanded anonymity. Unofficial rules had developed to determine how reporters would attribute such information and protect their sources' confidentiality. During the Truman administration, *Newsweek* correspondent Ernest K. Lindley had proposed the "Lindley Rule" by which government officials gave reporters briefings "on background" with the assurance that nothing would be attributed to them by name. Stories on background could refer to the source's sphere of operations, such as "a senior White House official," those "on deep background" could not be identified in any manner. Being able to credit information to someone by name and title added authenticity to a news story, but as the *Washington Post* reminded its readers, "We cannot always expect named sources to contradict the official line or policy of the officials, agencies or companies for which they work." Backgrounders and other off-the-record sources permitted authoritative discussions of delicate matters, and an informality of access that fostered greater trust between officials and the press corps. (When presidential administrations began using backgrounders to deliver glowing accounts of their accomplishments, the *Washington*

Post also speculated that backgrounders helped shield officials "from embarrassment for sounding like cheerleaders.")[5]

Trust lulled reporters into complacency, but the press corps was jolted awake in 1960, when the State Department spokesman Lincoln White admitted that the Eisenhower administration had flatly lied to the press about the true nature of U-2 flights over the Soviet Union. What the government had tried to pass off as a weather plane that strayed off course had been a high-altitude spy plane. The government admitted the deception only after the Soviet Union announced that it had shot down the plane and recovered the pilot alive. Roger Mudd, who had just begun covering presidential press conferences as a television reporter, watched the reaction of such veterans as Raymond Brandt of the *St. Louis Post-Dispatch*, Richard Wilson of the *Des Moines Register*, James Reston of the *New York Times*, and May Craig of the *Portland Press-Herald*. "Those old hands—Brandt and Wilson and Reston and Craig—who had been through campaigns and wars and everything else you could think of—were furious, were incredulous that a spokesman of their government would deliberately lie," Mudd recalled. The confessed falsehood shocked the Washington press corps, Mudd believed, "because most journalists at that time were trusting and uncritical of the government; they tended to be unquestioning consumers and purveyors of official information."[6]

The next shock wave occurred in 1962, when President Kennedy's Pentagon spokesman, Arthur Sylvester, publicly asserted that the government had an "inherent right" to lie to the press and the public about matters of national security. Then Lyndon Johnson deepened the government's credibility gap by denying his gradual escalation of the Vietnam War. Editors began to question the validity of the official versions of events that came out of off-the-record and not-for-attribution sessions, and demanded that the Washington bureaus scrutinize the information more carefully and name more of their sources in their stories. "We won't send any more reporters to backgrounders," decreed Jim Bellows, when he became editor of the *New York Herald Tribune* in 1963. "If government officials don't have the courage to speak on the record, they won't be in the *Herald Tribune*." His Washington bureau chief agreed that it was a deplorable practice, but pointed out that the next time the AP or the *New York Times* reported on information from a backgrounder, Bellows would likely be on the phone demanding to know why his bureau had not gotten the same story. The *Washington Post* editor Ben Bradlee went a step further and on one occasion broke the ground rules to identify National Security Advisor Henry Kissinger as the Nixon administration's most flagrant practitioner of "deep backgrounders." Bradlee denounced the practice as a conspiracy to restrain public truth, and he demanded that *Post* reporters seek specific attribution. Despite their editors' objections, Washington correspondents saw backgrounders and other off-the-record sources as often the only feasible way of getting dependable information. "Your time is taken up by the large, regular flow of presidential news announcements, the campaign, summit meetings," explained Robert Donovan, Washington bureau chief of the *Los Angeles Times*. "There's almost always something going on that deprives one of the time to dig underneath."[7]

"Every government is run by liars, and nothing they say should be believed," warned the leftist gadfly I. F. Stone. On the right, the *Chicago Tribune*'s Walter Trohan agreed that modern presidential administrations had "subtly bribed and coerced" the Washington press corps away from its role as watchdog. Both the New Left and the Goldwater Right regarded the mainstream media with distrust, and the initial coverage of the Vietnam War and the Watergate scandal seemed to validate their skepticism. Reporters themselves developed doubts. "You can't go through something like the Vietnam War as a reporter, either here or there, and have any faith that you are being told the truth at any given time," said Ben Bradlee. A creeping suspicion that government was peddling lies and half-truths helped revive the largely dormant practice of investigative reporting. Claiming a bias toward truth, investigative reporters questioned authority in order to expose falsehood. For Jack Anderson, for instance, this meant operating as a "reporter-advocate." Tenacious and abrasive as a breed, investigative reporters tended to work apart from others in their newsroom and avoided the events and places where the pack gathered its material. They searched for what the government had no intention of releasing among an underground of whistle blowers, disgruntled employees, and other leakers. Watergate made investigative reporters national heroes, although the critic Joseph Epstein found it ironic that anyone could win fame and fortune from society by "telling it how rotten it was."[8]

Many a politician complained of unprecedented media scrutiny, but the *Washington Post* correspondent Chalmers Roberts called this "simply the reflex of a man who has felt the muckraker's barb for the first time." The muckrakers who exposed corruption during the first decade of the twentieth century set precedents for latter day investigative reporting. Addressing themselves to the "beaten and the bewildered" of society, muckraking magazine writers confirmed people's worst suspicions about those who held power—to the dismay of both the politicians and their allies in the Washington press corps. Newspaper correspondents had cheered President Theodore Roosevelt for coining the label "muckrakers" to describe their magazine competitors. The magazine writers operated mostly out of New York and passed through Washington only in search of a story. They had less need to cultivate sources and therefore avoided succumbing to the "Washington point of view."[9]

The reporter credited with injecting muckraking into Washington journalism was Paul Y. Anderson, the sardonic correspondent for the *St. Louis Post-Dispatch*. From a childhood of poverty, Anderson always identified with the underdog. His father had died in an industrial accident and his mother taught school to provide for her children. When the uncle for whom he was named turned him down for a job, the hot-tempered young Anderson retaliated by changing his middle initial to an enigmatic "Y." At seventeen, he became a cub reporter for the *Knoxville Journal,* and then moved on to work for the *St. Louis Post-Dispatch.* Anderson covered the East St. Louis race riot of 1917, returning to the newsroom in blood-splattered clothes to file a vivid account of how the police had abandoned African Americans to the mercy of the mob. These stories got him barred from the police stations in East St. Louis, but sent twenty men to prison. They also won commendation from a congressional investigating committee: "He saw everything; reported what he saw without fear of consequences; defied the indignant officials whom he charged with criminal neglect of duty; ran a daily risk of assassination, and rendered an invaluable public service by his exposures."[10]

Unable to persuade the *Post-Dispatch* to send him to Washington, Anderson quit and went east as a freelancer. At the Capitol, he picked up rumors that something had been irregular in the sale of naval oil reserves at Teapot Dome, Wyoming, to a private oil company. The Senate had appointed a special committee to investigate, headed by Montana senator Thomas Walsh, but the Washington press corps dismissed his hearings as a publicity stunt. The regular White House correspondents, wrote the United Press reporter Tom Stokes, "sat, all the time, at the outer gate, so to speak, and had known nothing." Anderson, however, sensed the "rottenness" of Warren G. Harding's administration and began writing investigative reports about Teapot Dome for such liberal publications as the *New York World*, the *Nation,* and the *New Republic.* Anderson also shared his findings with Senator Walsh, suggested witnesses to call, and drafted questions for the senator to ask. Walsh's probe steadily uncovered evidence that revealed that Interior Secretary Albert Fall had taken a bribe from the oil industry, news that generated banner headlines. So many reporters showed up to cover the hearings that the committee had to move to a larger room. Anderson recorded that "larger press tables were hastily drafted in, and Senators, after introducing themselves to the chairman as members of the committee, took their seats at the table for the first time, wearing an air of stern resolve." Anderson's reporting on Teapot Dome got him the job he had wanted at the *St. Louis Post-Dispatch*'s Washington bureau, and won him a Pulitzer Prize.[11]

The scrappy Anderson mocked the "journalistic statesmen" of the Washington press corps. His gloves-off style of news reporting forced a federal judge to resign and sparked a congressional investigation into the Ku Klux Klan's political influence. Anderson's slash-and-burn methods flourished in the Harding, Coolidge, and Hoover era; but in the 1930s his sympathy for the New Deal hobbled him. Finding less to uncover in an administration he supported, and questioning whether any of his past investigations had actually improved social conditions, Anderson grew melancholy. His provocative and incisive writing turned belligerent and irreverent. His drinking bouts caused him to miss so many deadlines that the *Post-Dispatch* fired him in 1938. Although the rival *St. Louis Star-Times* promptly picked him up, Anderson found it harder to write anything. Instead of finishing a planned article on the House Un-American Activities Committee, he gave it as a radio address that sharply rebuked the committee's tactics. HUAC's chairman, Martin Dies, countered by producing evidence that the publicity director of the Democratic National Committee had arranged Anderson's radio address, making the reporter appear more like a political flack than an independent journalist. Drinking heavily at the National Press Club bar one night, Anderson revealed the name of the Supreme Court justice who had been an anonymous source for his former *Post-Dispatch* colleague, Marquis Childs. Then Anderson fell out with columnist Westbrook Pegler, who had stood as the best man at his third wedding. The vituperative Pegler fired off a letter to the *Star-Times* urging the paper to fire Anderson as an "irresponsible drunk." After seeing that letter, Anderson took an overdose of sleeping pills, saying that he felt his usefulness had ended. He died at the hospital, at age forty-five. "Drunk or sober," said the columnist Heywood Broun at his funeral, Paul Anderson was "the finest journalist of his day."[12]

The press corps hailed Anderson as "the last of the muckrakers," an apt description considering how few of them followed his lead. Editors expected their Washington correspondents to grapple with national issues, not play police reporters. Anderson's influence could be seen, however, in the reporting of Drew Pearson and Robert S. Allen, who cited him as an inspiration for their *Washington Merry-Go-Round* column. The *Washington Post* reporter Kenneth Crawford dedicated his exposé of lobbying practices, *The Pressure Boys*, to Anderson. "Like most of my colleagues in the Washington press corps, I have the job of watching day by day and reporting edition by edition what our statesmen, their bosses and their minions do for the weal and woe of the people of the United States," Crawford explained in his book. "Being a reporter, not a columnist, I am circumscribed by the rules of my craft, one of which forbids expression of the writer's opinions in the news columns. I am cramped, too, by the exigencies of daily journalism which often make it impossible to get the whole story until the event is no longer headline news."[13]

A generation later, Clark R. Mollenhoff also listed Paul Y. Anderson as his inspiration for taking up investigative reporting. A huge, imposing man, Mollenhoff could "strike terror in a government department merely by walking in and asking if Joe Blow is on the payroll," said the UPI's Merriman Smith. At six foot four, Mollenhoff had played college football and had been drafted by the New York Giants. Instead of turning pro, he attended law school and became a journalist. Mollenhoff made politicians squirm, and his hulking presence and booming voice grated on his fellow reporters as well. He fixed on a topic relentlessly, bringing the same issue up at one press conference after another until officials responded to his satisfaction. Colleagues shook their heads and said that he could see neither the forest nor the trees. But James Reston counted it "good to have a fellow like Clark Mollenhoff roaring around Washington," because he kept people honest. For years, Mollenhoff battled the bureaucracy from the outside while harboring a desire to reform it from the inside. He repeatedly crossed the line between observer and participant, working the back rooms of congressional investigations, tendering advice to candidates, and going on the White House payroll.[14]

A Neiman fellowship to spend a year at Harvard in 1949 led to Mollenhoff's promotion from statehouse reporter for *Des Moines Register* to the Washington bureau of Cowles Publications. Once in Washington, he became swept up in Senator Estes Kefauver's investigation of organized crime and began his own research into corruption within the Teamsters Union. Mollenhoff persuaded Senator John McClellan, the chairman of the Permanent Subcommittee on Investigations, and his chief counsel, Robert F. Kennedy, to launch a formal Senate investigation into labor racketeering. He volunteered his services and put Kennedy in contact with other investigative reporters, among them Ed Guthman of the *Seattle Times,* John Seigenthaler of the *Nashville Tennesseean,* and Pierre Salinger of the *San Francisco Chronicle,* who joined the investigation's staff. Mollenhoff had a key to Kennedy's office so he could enter at night and look over documents without anyone "leaking" them to him. His reporting on Kennedy's chief target, Teamster leader Jimmy Hoffa, grew so intense that Hoffa took him aside during the hearings and said, "Everyone has his price. What's yours?" Mollenhoff's exposés of the Teamsters won a Pulitzer Prize for investigative reporting.[15]

Despite being a registered Republican, Mollenhoff clashed with the Eisenhower administration when it unjustly branded an Agriculture Department employee, Wolf Ladejinsky, as a security risk. His investigation led to Ladejinsky's exoneration, but other reporters groaned when he brought up the issue over and over again at press conferences. Mollenhoff was also offended when President Eisenhower invoked executive privilege to deny information to Senator Joe McCarthy. Although Mollenhoff had no sympathy for McCarthy, he viewed government secrecy as a threat to democracy. He lambasted others in the press corps for their shortsightedness in not protesting executive privilege, "as long as the only victims appeared to be Senator McCarthy and his little knot of followers." At one of Eisenhower's press conferences, Mollenhoff grew so argumentative that the president told him to sit down. In 1960 the Republican Mollenhoff praised the Democratic platform's promise to tear down the wall of secrecy between the executive and legislative branches and encourage the free flow of information. He urged John F. Kennedy to appoint a special investigator as watchdog for the administration (seeing himself as the natural candidate). Instead, Kennedy appointed him to the U.S. Advisory Commission on Information Policy.[16]

Having worked with congressional Democrats against Eisenhower, Mollenhoff shifted to the side of congressional Republicans during the Kennedy and Johnson administrations. The reporter slipped Republican members of Congress information about irregularities and possible scandals in the administration. His allies inserted this material into the *Congressional Record*, which enabled him to cite it in his newspaper articles. His congressional connections helped push his issues to the national forefront, otherwise Mollenhoff complained that no one paid attention to anything he exposed until the *New York Times* took up the story. It rankled him that much of the press corps automatically sided with the president against Congress. Mollenhoff railed against the government's attempts to manipulate the press and crusaded for passage of the Freedom of Information Act.[17]

His detractors in the press corps took pleasure in defeating Mollenhoff's bid to become president of the National Press Club in 1964. They resented that he hectored them about being tools of the government when he was frequently dabbling in politics himself. Mollenhoff, for instance, offered campaign strategy suggestions to Republican candidates Barry Goldwater and Richard Nixon. Notoriously suspicious of the press corps, the Nixon camp regarded Mollenhoff as one of the few friendly reporters, and awarded him a seat next to the candidate on long campaign flights. Mollenhoff used the opportunity to dust off his proposal for an administration ombudsman, to which Nixon responded positively. When Nixon won, Mollenhoff resigned from his news bureau to join the White House staff, ignoring warnings from friends and family that he would never fit into such a tightly managed political operation. "After spending twenty-five years exposing government corruption and mismanagement," Mollenhoff rationalized, "I wanted to test some of my theories on preventive efforts."[18]

President Nixon had less lofty intentions for him. The White House gave Mollenhoff access to income tax returns, ostensibly to avoid any scandal among its own appointees, but actually in hope of using the confidential information as political fodder. Mollenhoff's job was to investigate Nixon's enemies rather than to police his administration. Nixon mused to his chief of staff, H. R. Haldeman, that he had been slow to use the power of the White House "to reward and punish," but that he planned to play tougher in the future. The president authorized Haldeman to set up a "dirty tricks" squad, and Nixon named Clark Mollenhoff as its possible head. Nixon's staff also compiled an "enemies list" of critical journalists for Mollenhoff to keep an eye on.[19]

No matter how hard he tried, the reporter never became part of Nixon's inner circle. Haldeman, the chief of staff, and John Ehrlichman, the chief domestic advisor, intercepted Mollenhoff's memos to the president, and made sure that one of them was present whenever he went to the Oval Office. They looked askance at his internal investigations and were angered when he tried to derail a planned presidential pardon for Jimmy Hoffa. When Mollenhoff reminisced about how Hoffa had once told him that everyone had his price, Ehrlichman retorted, "We know your price—a White House title and $35,500 a year." Realizing the futility of being the "muckraker in residence" at the White House, Mollenhoff resigned in 1970. As a parting insult, Haldeman and Ehrlichman reminded him that executive privilege, which he so passionately hated, forbade him from revealing anything in which he had participated. Rather than appoint a successor, the administration turned over most of his ombudsman's functions to the president's counsel, John Dean.[20]

The *Des Moines Register* rehired Mollenhoff to be its Washington bureau chief and syndicated columnist. Other members of the press corps by then had grown so estranged from the Nixon administration that they doubted whether anyone "with honest motives" could have worked for the president. Reporters suspected that Nixon was still using Mollenhoff for dirty work. Indeed, in August 1972, when rumors spread about a scandal involving a former Democratic cabinet officer, President Nixon told John Ehrlichman, "Isn't it about time we called in Clark Mollenhoff to do something and give him the whole file?" Mollenhoff by then had concluded that Nixon's administration had become corroded by the "poison of secrecy." After the Watergate burglary, his columns urged the president to appoint a bipartisan investigative commission, advice that Nixon ignored. Mollenhoff's own reporting on the scandal went nowhere as his panicked former associates in the administration refused to return his calls.[21]

Mollenhoff was at work in his bureau in October 1972 when the wire service tickers reported that Nixon was giving an impromptu news conference. The reporter raced four blocks to the White House but was barred from entering the already ongoing meeting. Mollenhoff cornered Press Secretary Ron Ziegler to protest his exclusion, and during the give-and-take he extracted an admission from Ziegler that he assumed the hush money for the Watergate burglars must have come from the Committee to Reelect the President. When Mollenhoff published this revelation, Ziegler called it a misinterpretation. At Ziegler's next press conference, Mollenhoff irately raised the issue again. Timothy Crouse happened to be there while researching his book on campaign reporters, *The Boys on the Bus*, and watched Ziegler dodge Mollenhoff's questions. Another reporter whispered to Crouse, "There is the male Sarah McClendon." Mollenhoff insisted that the Nixon administration had never controlled him, but in 1975 revelations about how he had gotten access to the income tax returns of prominent Democrats severed his relations with his paper. Still looking for a horse to ride back into power, Mollenoff supported Senator Henry "Scoop" Jackson for the Democratic presidential nomination in 1976, and then switched to Jimmy Carter. Inevitably, Carter disillusioned him too, as the title of his last book—*The President Who Failed*—indicates. In declining health, Mollenhoff finally abandoned the capital to teach journalism at Washington and Lee University.[22]

Even before he left, a new generation of investigative reporters had already replaced him. During the 1970s, Pulitzer Prizes went to Seymour Hersh for his exposure of the My Lai massacre, to columnist Jack Anderson for revealing the Nixon administration's tilt toward Pakistan against India, and to the *New York Times*, for which reporter Neil Sheehan acquired the secret Pentagon Papers that revealed the beginnings of the Vietnam War. Those prizes were awarded "for exposing Government secrets," Jack Anderson pointed out. "The Pulitzer board therefore has recognized the right of the people to know what goes on in the back rooms of government." There were not enough Jack Andersons and Neil Sheehans, declared James Reston in April 1972. Two months later, a "third-rate burglary" gave investigative reporters their greatest triumph.[23]

After the *New York Times* published the Pentagon Papers, President Nixon reminisced about how reluctant the Justice Department had been to make a strong perjury case against Alger Hiss. As a congressman he had prodded the department. "I played it in the press like a mask," Nixon boasted. "I leaked out the papers. I leaked everything, I mean, everything that I could. I leaked out the testimony. I had Hiss convicted before he ever got to the grand jury." All presidents had ambiguous attitudes toward leaks. They cursed them when unauthorized, but leaked freely when it was to their advantage. During Lyndon Johnson's administration, the American ambassador to South Vietnam, Henry Cabot Lodge, had asserted that leaking was a "presidential prerogative." Lodge described other officials as "usurping" the president's right when they leaked. "What bugs a president is not leaks, but leaks from people who may disagree with him," reasoned the *Washington Post* columnist David Broder. Washington was a "Leak City" where members of Congress and friends and enemies of the administration all slipped information to reporters under the cloak of anonymity.[24]

The leak was the flip side of a press release: an unofficial, unattributable source of information intended to generate news. Stories ascribed to named experts carried an authenticity that made editors and readers more comfortable, but government officials spoke more candidly off the record. Reporters grew used to dealing with officials who leaked trial balloons to test public opinion, with congressional staff who passed along tips to generate some interest for an upcoming hearing, and with civil servants who blew the whistle on mismanagement and corruption. "I engaged in a lot of leaks," explained the social activist and attorney Joseph Rauh, "because I believe that the only way you ever get anything done in the government is to get the problem out in the open." Sources knew that reporters would fiercely guard their confidentiality, to ensure their continued access and to gain the confidence of others. So long as the information was accurate, commented reporter William Lambert, "Who cares whether the lead came from a disgruntled bureaucrat, a self-serving politician, or an anonymous phone caller?" Reliance on anonymity, however, left lingering questions about the leakers' motives.[25]

"Deep Throat," Washington's best-known anonymous source, first surfaced in the best-selling book *All the President's Men*. The *Washington Post* reporters Bob Woodward and Carl Bernstein had intended to write an account from the conspirators' point of view, until the actor Robert Redford—envisioning a movie version—persuaded them to tell it from their own perspective, more like a detective story. Posters later advertised the movie as "the most devastating detective story of this century." Although journalists usually kept themselves out of their own reporting, they agreed to cast themselves as the protagonists. Woodward's furtive encounters with a shadowy tipster supplied much of the drama. Clark Mollenhoff later dismissed Deep Throat as a gimmick to sell the book. He insisted that the young reporters' real strength had been their diligent search for records and tireless pursuit of witnesses. Reliance on the uncorroborated evidence of a single unnamed source would have been irresponsible, Mollenhoff declared, "unless the editors knew more about that mystery figure than we have been told."[26]

A couple of Metro reporters were not likely to have access to the president's inner circle, nor get their phone calls returned from the officials the White House press corps cultivated. Their source was not the average Washington leaker, Richard Nixon reasoned as he pondered the steady barrage of Watergate coverage by the *Washington Post*; this was an informer, someone who could never come out from under wraps. Woodward and Bernstein themselves conceded that Deep Throat had not been "a traditional news source." He did not so much leak as he confirmed, guided, and explained. Even before Watergate, Woodward's source had helped him develop leads on other stories, and the accuracy of his information had impressed editors at the *Washington Post*. They never demanded his name, but the *Post* reporter James Mann, who covered the burglars' trial during the summer of 1972, claimed that before anyone had named the leaker Deep Throat (after the hard-core sex film showing in downtown Washington at the time), Woodward had talked instead about his "friend at the FBI."[27]

Identifying Bob Woodward's source as having a connection to the Federal Bureau of Investigations suggests a motive for the leaker. The cover-up that eventually caused Nixon to resign the presidency had been aimed at keeping the FBI from conducting a full investigation of the Watergate burglary or from following the political money trail back to the White House. For months, Woodward's source helped generate news accounts that kept the investigation on track. The source seemed to know everything that the FBI had uncovered, but revealed nothing that cast the bureau in a poor light. Deep Throat, for instance, did not mention the former FBI agent Alfred Baldwin, who had monitored the wiretaps for the Watergate burglars. Baldwin had handled previous "black bag" jobs that the bureau did not want disclosed. It was the *Los Angeles Times* not the *Washington Post* that eventually broke Baldwin's story. "Sometimes people accuse us of bringing down the president, which of course we didn't do and shouldn't have done," publisher Katharine Graham commented. "What the *Post* did . . . was to keep the story alive."[28]

Master bureaucrat J. Edgar Hoover had spent half a century preventing presidents of the United States from turning the FBI into their "personal goon squad." He capped his career by frustrating Richard Nixon's efforts to use the FBI for his own political purposes, and dragged his feet on investigating the leaking of the Pentagon Papers. "If the FBI was not going to pursue the case, then we would have to do it ourselves," Nixon wrote in his memoirs, justifying his formation of a team of "plumbers" to stem the leaks. Hoover also successfully outmaneuvered all of Nixon's attempts to ease him into retirement, until the director's unexpected death in May 1972 left the FBI politically vulnerable.[29]

On the day that Nixon named the FBI building for the late director, he stunned the bureau by selecting an acting director from outside its hierarchy. Assistant Attorney General L. Patrick Gray III had previously served on Nixon's vice-presidential staff and was considered a Nixon loyalist. Clark Mollenhoff labeled Gray "totally susceptible to the dictates of the White House." FBI veterans regarded the acting director and his personal staff as rank amateurs. Gray initiated some long-overdue reforms, among them loosening the FBI's dress code and encouraging the recruitment of women and minorities as agents, but he announced these decisions to the media without first consulting with the senior staff. "Gray was moving into the Director's office, surrounded by reporters and photographers," deputy director W. Mark Felt complained, while "the rest of us were reading the newspapers in shocked disbelief." Hoover's closest assistants spirited away the late director's "secret files" from headquarters to deny Gray access. "The record amply demonstrates that President Nixon made Pat Gray the Acting Director of the FBI because he wanted a politician in J. Edgar Hoover's position who would convert the Bureau into an adjunct of the White House machine," Felt insisted. "What Mr. Nixon did not foresee was that the Bureau's professional staff would fight this tooth and nail."[30]

Two weeks after Hoover died, presidential candidate George Wallace was shot while speaking at a shopping mall in a Washington suburb. On hearing this news, President Nixon and his top aides considered planting Democratic campaign literature in the gunman's apartment, until they found that the FBI had already sealed it off. "You got Pat Gray," Nixon advised his aides (recorded on his secret taping system). "He will be an accomplice. Use him." In the same frenzied hours that followed the shooting, the *Washington Post* was anxious to learn the shooter's name. Metro reporter Bob Woodward advised his editor that he had a high-placed friend who might know. Another reporter got the name first, but over the next few days Woodward filed several stories that cited "a reliable federal source close to the investigation." The son of an Illinois judge, Bob Woodward had served as a navy communications liaison officer between the Pentagon and the White House during the Johnson administration. After returning to civilian life, he applied for a job at the *Washington Post,* but the

Post's editors thought he needed some "aging in the bottle" and arranged for him to try out at the suburban *Montgomery County Sentinel*. He skipped the usual tree-planting reporting in favor of stories rooting out local corruption. (Otherwise reluctant officials agreed to talk with Woodward in part because he had "the disarming voice and manner of a Boy Scout offering to help an old lady cross the street," Colin Powell later certified.) Woodward bombarded editors at the *Post* with his clippings until they hired him for the night police beat. Then he produced more front-page bylines than any other Metro reporter, assisted occasionally by his reliable anonymous source.[31]

L. Patrick Gray was touring FBI field offices in California when police arrested five men inside the Democratic National Committee's offices at the Watergate complex, early in the morning of June 17, 1972. Under a mistaken assumption that the men had been attempting to plant a bomb, the police called in the FBI. The FBI agents quickly determined that the confiscated equipment was for wiretapping, and because that was a federal offense they launched a formal investigation. By the time Gray returned to Washington, four days later, assistant FBI director Charles W. Bates had made Watergate a top priority for the Washington field office as well as for the rest of the bureau. On June 19, the *Washington Post* ran the first joint byline of Bob Woodward and Carl Bernstein. The two Metro reporters got the assignment because the paper treated it as a police report, not a political story. None of the *Post*'s national reporters saw a credible link between the break-in and the White House. But Woodward questioned his anonymous source about Watergate that day and learned that the FBI had connected a former White House aide, E. Howard Hunt, to the case. The next morning, Woodward's front-page story on Hunt cited "federal sources close to the investigation." Another Woodward story on June 21 advised that "sources in the FBI" revealed that agents had been ordered to question Hunt. These stories caused White House staff to demand that Acting Director Gray plug the leak at the FBI. Gray later testified that top White House aides "were obviously concerned about the fact that apparently FBI information, at least attributed to the FBI, was ending up in news stories." Rumors spread that Gray planned to "collapse the investigation" and would block FBI agents from subpoenaing the telephone records of presidential aides, suggesting that the White House had "neutralized the FBI."[32]

With no need for inside sources, the *Washington Post*'s editorial cartoonist Herblock instinctively linked the Watergate burglary to Richard Nixon. Herblock's cartoon on June 23, 1972, depicted footsteps from the "bugging case" and other scandals leading straight to the White House. That same day, Chief of Staff H. R. Haldeman warned the president that the FBI was "not under control, because Gray doesn't exactly know how to control them," and that the investigation was moving "in some directions we don't want it to go." Gray informed the White House that the FBI had traced the Watergate burglars' funds to a Mexican bank and was attempting to pursue the "money chain" back to its source. On hearing this, Nixon sanctioned Haldeman's plan to have the CIA advise the FBI that the Watergate incident had been part of a CIA operation. This would give Gray an excuse to "put the hold on this." (Tape recordings of this conversation provided the "smoking gun" that linked Nixon irrefutably to the cover-up.) Although CIA director Richard Helms had repeatedly told Gray that the CIA had nothing to do with the Watergate break-in, deputy CIA director Vernon Walters followed the White House script and asked the FBI to close its investigation "south of the border," based on their mutual agreement not to interfere with each other's operations.[33]

The White House compromised the FBI's investigation in every possible way. Presidential counsel John Dean received copies of all FBI reports on Watergate and participated in all FBI interviews with White House staff. Dean's presence had a chilling effect on these inquires, and he hindered the agents' efforts to obtain the contents of Howard Hunt's safe. (The agents did not know that Dean had given the most damaging contents of the safe to L. Patrick Gray, who later burned them.) At a tense meeting on June 24, Gray castigated the FBI's Washington field staff for the leaks appearing in the *Post,* and he ordered that each of them be interrogated as the possible source. When top FBI officials protested these restrictions placed on their inquiry, Gray sought written confirmation that the CIA wanted the investigation contained. By then, however, the CIA had turned down a White House request that it pay the bail money for the burglars, and Vernon Walters felt tired of being used. Walters refused to sign a written authorization and warned Gray that both of their agencies were in danger of being implicated in a cover-up. A shaken Gray had to let the FBI investigation proceed.[34]

The Watergate burglar James McCord later speculated that, had it not been inhibited, the FBI should have been able to break the Watergate case during the summer of 1972. "The FBI was boxed in," wrote McCord, "—blamed on the one hand because it didn't develop the facts of the Watergate case, but unable on the other hand to act on the leads its senior supervisory personnel proposed and knew to be necessary to develop the full story." The conspirators had good reason to feel satisfied that summer. Opinion polls showed that half the American public had never heard of Watergate, and that the rest cared very little about it. Most of the media had dismissed the burglary as a political prank. "We were way ahead of the FBI," John Dean concluded. "We were even further ahead of the press."[35]

After an initial flurry of reporting on Watergate, the press corps's interest waned and left the story almost exclusively to the *Post.* Woodward and Bernstein's bylines appeared regularly throughout the summer of 1972, and FBI agents were impressed with the authority of their reporting. One agent told Carl Bernstein, "I don't know how you guys are doing it, but you've got access to the 302s, and some people think you're getting them from us." (FD-302s were the raw files that tracked an FBI investigation). The *Post* reporters published some details of the investigation only hours after the bureau itself had learned of them.[36]

On September 15 a grand jury limited indictments to the five burglars and their two handlers, E. Howard Hunt and G. Gordon Liddy. President Nixon and his advisors felt confident that they had succeeded in keeping the inquiry from spreading up the chain of command. That day, the president instructed his staff to keep "comprehensive notes on all those who tried to do us in." He had not yet used the FBI against his opponents, he mused, "but things are going to change now." His Democratic opponent, Senator George McGovern, expressed frustration over the limited investigation and accused the FBI of conducting a whitewash. The Justice Department countered that more than three hundred agents in fifty-one field offices had conducted more than fifteen hundred Watergate-related interviews. In fact, having so many agents so deeply involved had fueled resentment within the FBI over the continued curbs on its investigation. Deep Throat chose that moment to fuel the *Washington Post*'s coverage by confirming that money from the Committee to Reelect the President (CRP) had financed not only the Watergate burglary but "other intelligence-gathering activities" as well. "I just talked to my friend at the FBI," Woodward told his colleague Jim Mann on the day of the indictments. "I think we're on to a whole new level on this thing." Three days later, Woodward and Bernstein reported that Gordon Liddy had received payments from a secret fund at the Committee to Reelect the President. Ten days after that, they quoted from "reliable sources" that former Attorney General John Mitchell had authorized payments from the fund.[37]

At a clandestine meeting with Woodward on Sunday night, October 8, his source complained that "politics had infiltrated every corner of government," that "junior White House aides" were issuing orders to the highest levels of the bureaucracy, and that they were determined "to fight dirty and for keeps." The source recommended that the reporters could "untie the Watergate knot," by following other administration-sponsored acts of political espionage, sabotage, and dirty tricks. "Remember you don't do those 1,500 interviews and not have something on your hands other than a single break-in," Deep Throat advised. He alleged that fifty people had been working for the White House and CRP on dirty tricks, spying, and sabotage. This turned out to be a trumped-up claim, but it encouraged the *Washington Post* reporters to connect the Watergate burglary to a wider pattern of political sabotage. *Post* editors described the story that ran on October 10—under the headline "FBI Finds Nixon Aides Sabotaged Democrats"—as the centerpiece of their pre-election Watergate coverage. Yet this story was such an overstatement that John Dean seriously considered recommending that the administration admit to having deployed only a single saboteur, Donald Segretti. Because any confession risked revealing more damaging financial dealings, the White House simply denounced the *Post*'s story as "hearsay, innuendo and guilt by association."[38]

"I've always felt the leak is at the FBI," Nixon ruminated at Camp David on October 15. An attorney for the *Washington Post* had privately identified Mark Felt as the leaker, but the president could not take action because Felt knew "everything that's to be known in the FBI," and might go on network television to tell it. Instead, the White House sent word to Pat Gray not to place any further confidence in his deputy. Confronted with these suspicions, Felt protested, "Pat, I haven't leaked anything to anybody. They are wrong!" From that point on, Deep Throat refused to allow Woodward to use him as a source on any "Haldeman story." Heedlessly, on October 25 Woodward and Bernstein reported that grand jury testimony had implicated Haldeman as the controller of the secret funds, despite Deep Throat's refusal to confirm or deny that story. When the accusation was proven erroneous, it called into question the rest of their reporting. The reporters had moved too swiftly in the right direction; Haldeman had controlled the funds indirectly through subordinates. "At one point as the day progressed," the journalist David Halberstam wrote of the botched story, "Woodward became so frustrated that he wanted to blow the name of a source at the FBI." Woodward's source angrily let him know that the blunder had set back the investigation, "It puts everyone on the defensive—editors, FBI agents, everybody has to go into a crouch after this."[39]

The *Washington Post*'s reliance on Woodward's source ran contrary to Ben Bradlee's pronouncement against using sources without attribution. That policy had lasted, as David Broder noted, "about as long as Bradlee's attention span did." Republican National Committee chairman Robert Dole charged that the *Post* had violated its anti-anonymity rule "almost every day for the past week, in blatant contradiction of its own policy." The *Post* had invested so much of its credibility in the Watergate story that failure could have broken the paper, yet Bradlee claimed never to have asked the identity of Woodward's secret source. What he demanded was that the reporters find a second source for every accusation, and that they assure him that none of those sources had a "big ax to grind on the front page of the *Washington Post*."[40]

The intensity of the *Post*'s Watergate coverage enabled the FBI to pursue its investigation. So deeply had Bob Woodward been immersed in Watergate that he was stunned when Richard Nixon won a landslide reelection. Nixon's lopsided margin indicated how little their reporting had influenced public opinion. John Dean later asserted that *"not one story* written by Woodward and Bernstein for *The Washington Post*, from the time of the arrest on June 17, 1972, until the election in November 1972, gave anyone in the Nixon White House or the reelection campaign the slightest concern that 'Woodstein' was on to the real story of Watergate." White House special counsel Charles Colson chuckled that Watergate had diverted the Democrats' attention during the campaign, "Dumb bastards were on an issue that the public couldn't care less about."[41]

Once into his second term, President Nixon nominated L. Patrick Gray as permanent director of the FBI. By then the Federal Communications Commission was threatening the *Washington Post*'s broadcast licenses. "So the White House wants to eat the *Washington Post*, so what?" Deep Throat consoled Woodward. He promised that the end was in sight. "It's building and they see it and they know they can't stop the real story from coming out." Gray had gotten his nomination, the source asserted, because he threatened "that all hell could break loose" if he did not stay at the bureau to keep the lid on. But during his confirmation hearings, senators on the Judiciary Committee forced Gray to admit that John Dean had "probably lied" to the FBI agents when he denied knowing whether Hunt had an office at the White House. Deep Throat then confirmed that Gray himself had destroyed evidence from Hunt's safe. Once that story broke, Gray withdrew his name from consideration, and Deep Throat provided little further information.[42]

The media critic Edward J. Epstein ridiculed the notion that Woodward and Bernstein had "solved" the Watergate puzzle. All they had done, he argued, was to serve as conduits for leaks from government investigators. Epstein pointed to the crucial evidence the reporters had failed to uncover, which came out in court proceedings or in the testimony before the Senate Watergate Committee. Clark Mollenhoff similarly dismissed Woodward and Bernstein's fame as so much myth making. Investigative reporters almost always had to have "the right committee chairman, the right judge, and the right political climate," he insisted, to have an impact. Still, the pair's dogged hunt for evidence, and the *Washington Post*'s willingness to make Watergate a running daily story, had bolstered the official investigations. Their reporting tied together enough seemingly unconnected threads to convince enough people that Herblock had been right about all the footsteps leading back to the White House. FBI field agents called Woodward and Bernstein "thieves" who had stolen their hard work, but the agents appreciated that the glare of publicity opened doors for their inquiry and caused events to unfold "in the light of day."[43]

The bulk of the Washington press corps missed the mark badly during the first months of the Watergate story, and none more embarrassingly than the *New York Times*. Because the five burglars were Cuban Americans, the *Times*'s Washington bureau had initially assigned the story to Tad Szulc, who a decade earlier had broken a story about the planned Bay of Pigs invasion. To great relief at the White House, Szulc led the *Times* down a diversionary path that depicted the burglary as a renegade Cuban American scheme to keep George McGovern out of the White House. Max Frankel, at the time nearing the end of his tenure as Washington bureau chief, had discouraged other *Times* correspondents from pursuing Watergate. "Not even my most cynical view of Nixon had allowed for his stupid behavior," Frankel later confessed. Further clouding the bureau's judgment was its condescending attitude toward the *Washington Post*. Dismissing the *Post*'s continual coverage during the summer of 1972,

Frankel insisted that Woodward and Bernstein's reporting failed to measure up to his standards of credibility.[44]

Months after the Watergate break-in, the *New York Times* hired the investigative reporter Seymour Hersh. A journalist who wanted "to change things," Hersh reported first for the Dispatch News Service, which supplied the alternative press. After he went to the Pentagon in the 1960s as an AP correspondent, a mid-level officer chastised him for believing what the top brass said at a press conference. Hersh took that advice to heart and began avoiding press conferences. He started prowling the Pentagon's rings in search of other dissenters. His exposés discomforted the AP, however, and he left the wire service to freelance. Another Pentagon tip led to his revelation of the My Lai massacre, which won a Pulitzer Prize. At the *Times,* Hersh felt no pressure from his editors to follow the Watergate trail, so he pursued other stories. When he finally turned his attention to Watergate early in 1973, Hersh scooped even Woodward and Bernstein by documenting how White House hush money had gone to the Watergate burglars. "This story hit home!" John Dean affirmed. By then, other reporters such as Jack Nelson of the *Los Angeles Times* were developing their own leads, and the rest of the pack began piling on top. Press Secretary Ron Ziegler assured President Nixon that the press corps was more intent on getting the story than on driving him from office. None of the reporters at his daily briefings had done an "ounce of investigative reporting" on Watergate, said Ziegler, but as a group they had gotten swept up in the story's emotional momentum.[45]

Watergate dominated the news until Nixon's resignation in August 1974. No story had ever grabbed Washington the way Watergate did. Ben Bradlee exulted that he could walk for blocks without missing a word of the Senate hearings, because every radio and television was tuned in. The *Post* published more than three hundred stories related to the scandal, but its readers were so hungry for more that some called contacts at the paper for advance notice on what might appear the next day. The frenzied finish contrasted so starkly with the scandal's languid beginning that journalists engaged in much self-examination of why they had missed the story for so long. The White House press corps came in for the harshest criticism, accused of having become "prisoners" of the presidency. Former presidential press secretary Bill Moyers described them as "sheep with short attention spans." They spent more time looking for authorities to quote than in drawing their own conclusions, and they had grown too dependent on the very people they needed to scrutinize. "Police reporters do not often uncover police graft," UPI correspondent Thomas Powers asserted, "just as White House reporters do not often uncover White House scandals."[46]

Those attracted to investigative reporting after Watergate talked of restoring a moral connection to journalism, and grew more emotionally involved in their stories. An outgrowth of the "new journalism" of the 1960s and 1970s, it was part of a trend in which journalists consciously revealed themselves and their sentiments in their writing. Some might call this bias, but as the *St. Louis Post-Dispatch* correspondent James Deakin pointed out, "without bias there would be few investigative stories." Otherwise, reporters would accept everything at face value. Assuming the worst from politicians was often a safe proposition, but that mind-set also left investigators susceptible to innuendo, circumstantial evidence, and questionable sources. A fine line separated conspiracy from conspiracy theory. Theories were easier to postulate than to prove. Having invested extensive time and emotional commitment in a story, investigators were sometimes tempted to interpret any evidence—or lack of evidence—as confirmation of their suspicions. They were susceptible to magnifying mistakes into deliberate behavior and vague answers into evasiveness. The threat of a libel suit had restrained such reporting in the past, and had subjected controversial charges to line-by-line review by a newspaper's attorneys, but the Supreme Court's ruling in *New York Times* v. *Sullivan* in 1964 made it nearly impossible for public figures to sue successfully for libel. (A Montgomery, Alabama, city commissioner, L. B. Sullivan, had sued the *Times* for publishing a paid advertisement that accused him of repressing civil rights activists. The Supreme Court overturned a jury decision in Sullivan's favor and decreed that in order to establish libel a public official had to prove that the defendant acted with "actual malice.") That eased the worries of publishers and reduced the pressures on investigative reporters.[47]

Two best-selling books and a major motion picture made Woodward and Bernstein the most famous of all Washington reporters. After Watergate, Carl Bernstein left the *Washington Post* to head the ABC News Washington bureau and then to freelance. Bob Woodward remained with the paper. He was assistant managing editor of the Metro section in 1979 when he heard rumors that the president of Mobil Oil had awarded millions of dollars of company contracts to his own son's shipping line. Woodward encouraged another of the *Post*'s investigative reporters, Patrick Tyler, to pursue the story. Tyler acquired confidential documents from a congressional subcommittee and dug further. When the *Post* published his charges, the father and son sued for libel and in a stunning decision were awarded more than two million dollars in damages. Years of appellate litigation and a small fortune in lawyers' fees followed until the U.S. Court of Appeals—in a decision written by Judge Kenneth Starr—found in favor of the *Post*. Woodward cited that ruling as an even greater watershed for investigative reporting than Watergate. Despite the paper's ultimate victory, in the aftermath of the protracted case the *Post* grew more cautious about its investigations.[48]

In the post-Watergate flush of investigative reporting, reliance on anonymous sources grew into an occupational hazard that eventually exploded on the front-page of the *Washington Post*. In 1981 a promising young reporter, Janet Cooke, fabricated sources for a story about an eight-year-old drug addict. Cooke claimed to have invented pseudonyms to protect the boy and his family, and Metro editor Bob Woodward did not challenge her to divulge their identities. Cooke won a Pulitzer Prize for "Jimmy's World," but when her account proved entirely fictitious the *Post* returned the award and accepted her resignation. The embarrassing incident derailed Woodward's rise within the *Post*'s management and he returned to investigative reporting. Questions arose as to why the paper was allowing its sources to evade responsibility through anonymity. "What we call the record often tends to be the precise opposite of a record," wrote the *Post*'s editorial page editor, Meg Greenfield. "It is, rather, the artifice, the cooked-up part, the image that the politician, with our connivance, hopes to convey and generally does." Were investigative reporters fearless outsiders whittling away at the establishment? Or were they the ultimate insiders, who so protected their sources that they were subject to manipulation by them?[49]

If reliance on confidentiality sometimes blinded investigative reporters to their sources' motives, conventional wisdom too often obscured the view of the rest of the press corps. The same attitudes that had caused the *New York Times* to discount presidential involvement in Watergate slowed its response to the Iran-Contra scandal a decade later. While riding the bus to work one morning, *Times* correspondent Stephen Engelberg read Jack Anderson's column charging that the Reagan administration had sold arms to Iran to win the release of American hostages. Engelberg and his colleague Leslie Gelb attempted to verify the facts but all their high-level contacts dismissed Anderson's assertions as farfetched. They dropped the story, convinced that President Reagan would "never *do that*." Later, when a cargo plane crashed near Nicaragua, Engelberg's Washington bureau chief, Bill Kovach, speculated that it might be a CIA operation and put him on the story. Another *Times* reporter, James LeMoyne heard reports that the CIA had been ferrying supplies to the Nicaraguan Contras from an air base in El Salvador, but once again the reporters considered it inconceivable that the CIA would operate so openly. "Nobody," LeMoyne scoffed, "could be that stupid." A strong sense of implausibility kept the *New York Times* from connecting the pieces of the Iran-Contra puzzle that had sat in front of it for months.[50]

Some reporters adopted cynicism as a defense mechanism. The *Washington Post*'s diplomatic correspondent Don Oberdorfer reflected that when he first came to the capital in the 1950s, national affairs reporters had been "trusting and uncritical of the ways of government," but after the U-2 incident, Vietnam, Watergate, and Iran-Contra, many had gone to the opposite extreme. They became automatically suspicious of official statements. Fear of being deceived or manipulated by officials created a corrosive climate that raised suspicions of impropriety. "Without at least a modicum of trust on both sides," Oberdorfer commented, "it is difficult to see how reporters and officials can relate effectively." Increasingly scandal-oriented reporters made politicians less inclined to speak honestly in private. "I was raised on issues; I was not raised on scandal," said the editor Arnaud de Borchgrave. "That's where I drifted apart from my younger reporters at the *Washington Times*. What was going on in somebody's basement was never of interest to me."[51]

Investigative reporting had started on the political left, but by the 1980s the right had joined the hunt. For forty years, Democrats had held the majority in the House of Representatives, so long that representatives and reporters alike had accepted it as the natural order. Washington correspondents staked out willing sources among committee and subcommittee chairs on the majority side, and hesitated to impugn them. Their complacency gave reporters for conservative publications an advantage in chronicling violations of congressional ethics. Drawing on sources in the minority, Paul Rodriguez of the *Washington Times* published incriminating evidence against House Speaker Jim Wright, and against the senators who made up the "Keating Five." Rodriguez broke the story of the House bank scandal in 1992 and forced disclosure of which members had written excessive overdrafts on their accounts. Then he uncovered embezzlement in the House post office, where powerful members of Congress had abused their franking privileges. His aggressive reporting prompted the resignation of the House postmaster, and the indictment of the chairman of the House Ways and Means Committee. It also fed the anti-incumbency mood that helped Republicans recapture the majority in 1994.[52]

Simultaneously, Bill Clinton's embattled presidency unleashed a frenzy of investigative reporting. When Clinton ran for president in 1992, the *New York Times* reporter Jeff Gerth began inquiring into a failed real estate venture called Whitewater, in which Clinton had been suspected of using his governorship to bail out his bad investment. The candidate's reluctance to provide information raised the suspicions of the *Times*'s editor Joseph Lelyveld, who put Gerth's accounts on the paper's front page. Taking their cue from the *Times*, other papers followed doggedly along the same twisting trail. The *Wall Street Journal's* unrelenting pursuit of Whitewater and other perceived scandals triggered the suicide of a White House legal counsel, Vincent Foster, who left behind shreds of a note that decried the "spotlight of public life in Washington," where "ruining people is considered sport." The polarized atmosphere of the Clinton era renewed editors' tolerance for anonymous sources, while the multiplicity of media outlets, from cable television to the Internet, allowed leakers to shop their stories around town until someone agreed to publish them. If one media outlet broke a story, the rest gained license to repeat it, with or without substantiation.[53]

The reporter who most aggressively rode the Clinton scandals was Michael Isikoff, of the *Washington Post* and *Newsweek*. Isikoff had graduated from journalism school in the afterglow of Watergate, and had made his mark exposing a congressman he covered as a regional reporter. Illinois representative George Shipley had managed to miss every vote on a farm bill critical to his district, but he assured Isikoff that a bad back had kept him in bed throughout the voting. After Isikoff published that version of the story, a political rival of Shipley's informed the reporter that the congressman had played in a golf tournament on the day he missed the votes. Furious over having swallowed the lie, Isikoff ran an exposé that ended Shipley's ten-term career. He moved on to a job with Ralph Nader's Capitol Hill News Service, then went to the *Washington Star,* and wound up at the *Washington Post,* where he covered the Justice Department, until he began his pursuit of Bill Clinton.[54]

During the 1992 campaign, stories of Clinton's extramarital affairs had been the stuff of supermarket tabloids. The *New York Times* and *Washington Post* both felt more comfortable looking into financial scandals such as Whitewater than into sexual allegations, but Isikoff conjectured that Clinton's personal behavior revealed larger patterns of political deception. Despite a lack of enthusiasm among his editors at the *Washington Post,* he pursued charges of sexual harassment made by a former Arkansas state employee, Paula Jones. A shouting match with one editor cost Isikoff a two-week suspension, during which time he sought another job. The *Post* sat on the story until President Clinton hired a prominent Washington attorney to defend him against Paula Jones's accusations, which the *Post* felt compelled to explain to its readers. By the time that Isikoff's story finally made the front page, he had negotiated a position with *Newsweek* (which although owned by the Washington Post Corporation was operated separately from the newspaper). Isikoff devoted himself so thoroughly to the brewing scandal that *Time* magazine's Washington bureau chief described Paula Jones as "practically a subsidiary of *Newsweek.*" The Jones story introduced Isikoff to the literary agent Lucianne Goldberg and her client, Linda Tripp, a disgruntled former Clinton White House staffer who intended to write a tell-all book under the pseudonym "Joan Dean." The women saw Isikoff as a friendly vehicle for another brewing story about a former White House intern, Monica Lewinsky.[55]

As a weekly newsmagazine, *Newsweek* developed its stories by consensus at editorial meetings, a style that clashed with the independent style of investigative reporting. At one meeting, *Newsweek*'s chief of correspondents, Ann McDaniel, stunned Isikoff by asserting that there were times when "it's just not worth being first." As a result, the magazine held back his reporting on Lewinsky's relations with the president pending verification. Isikoff informed Lucianne Goldberg that his editors were sitting on the story, and soon afterward that news reached the Internet gossip columnist Matt Drudge. By revealing the magazine's indecision, the online *Drudge Report* scooped Isikoff on his own story. *Newsweek* responded by rushing Isikoff's version online in advance of its next issue, and the rest of the press corps came tumbling after, turning the Lewinsky affair into what Isikoff called "the most over-covered story in the universe." Accusations that the president had lied about his "inappropriate relationship" during his grand jury testimony in the Jones case led to his impeachment by the House of Representatives and his trial and acquittal in the

Senate. For all that, the saga never measured up to Watergate nor amassed for Isikoff the plaudits lavished on Woodward and Bernstein.[56]

The Clinton-Lewinsky story lingered in the news for months, thanks in large part to reporters' ready access to information from the office of the special prosecutor Kenneth Starr. Accused of conducting a trial by leaks, Starr insisted that he was simply countering the misinformation about his investigations being spread by the White House. Through such "deep background" avenues, reporters for the *Washington Post* gained access to the president's sealed court deposition in Paula Jones's sexual harassment suit, headlining its account without even veiled attribution. The president's press secretary condemned this "sourceless" news, but the *Post* editor Leonard Downie Jr. replied that it was an occasion "when this is the only way we can publish something that is really important." Without such unauthorized disclosures, the *Post* would be dependent "on government's self-presentation—which is to say its propaganda." But anonymity put reporters in a bind as the president and special prosecutor traded accusations about each other's leaking. Those who knew the truth of the matter could not report it without violating their sources' confidences.[57]

The perils of leaking played out in the indictment of the special prosecutor's own press spokesman. During Clinton's impeachment trial, the *New York Times* ran a front-page article quoting Starr's "associates," who said that the special prosecutor believed that he had the constitutional power to indict the president while in office. FBI inquiries into this leak disclosed that Charles Bakaly III had met repeatedly with the *Times* reporter who wrote the article and faxed him internal documents, contrary to Bakaly's claims in his deposition to the grand jury. Although found not guilty of intentionally lying, Bakaly admitted that he had provided the reporter with information in order to send "a message to the public." The original article had quoted Bakaly as saying, "We will not discuss the plans of this office or the plans of the grand jury in any way, shape or form." The reporter perpetuated the deceit to get the story. It served as a reminder that leaks were, as Richard Harwood of the *Washington Post* called them, "rarely innocent of purpose."[58]

11

Company Town Papers

Rumors rolled through the Capitol in February 1981, from the reporters in the press galleries to the elevator operators and the pages. Shots had been fired at the vice president of the United States as he left a woman friend's Capitol Hill townhouse at dawn. The Secret Service had rushed him to safety but it was uncertain whether he had been wounded. Countless people passed along some version of the shooting story—all of them untrue. A few weeks later, the *Washington Post* deftly dissected it all in a front-page account, "Anatomy of a Washington Rumor." The article traced how the rumor originated, how it circulated, and how it lacked the slightest substance. Sharing a byline for the story was Janet Cooke, a promising young reporter whose name had been appearing with marked frequency in the *Post*. Not long afterward, Cooke received a Pulitzer Prize for her story about an eight-year-old heroin addict. The prize revived newsroom suspicions about her work—and those rumors proved true. She had invented the story entirely, and her editors had accepted it blindly. The incident exposed serious flaws in Washington's preeminent local newspaper less than a decade after its triumph with Watergate.[1]

The Cooke affair provoked serious self-reflection at the *Washington Post,* just as the paper was adjusting to the Reagan Revolution. From the McCarthy era through Watergate, the *Post* had built a reputation for liberalism that made it anathema among conservative politicians, who were now firmly in power. National desk editor Peter Milius sensed that Ronald Reagan's election in 1980 had not been an aberration but a watershed in American politics, and he urged the staff to report on the new administration objectively, not from an adversarial attitude. *Post* reporters credited his policy with giving their coverage of Reagan more insight and coherence. Further breaking the liberal mold, publisher Katharine Graham hosted several private luncheons for First Lady Nancy Reagan where the only other guest was Graham's close friend and editorial page editor Meg Greenfield. It was mostly the visual impact of Herblock's cartoons that preserved a liberal appearance for the *Post*'s increasingly ambivalent editorial pages, as Greenfield opened more of its columns to conservatives and neoconservatives. Never a "cause person," she considered it healthy for the editorial pages to reflect the national "swing back from certain leftward political excesses of the recent past."[2]

Despite conservatives' charges of a liberal bias in the media, President Reagan's press secretary, Marlin Fitzwater, claimed not to have known which White House reporters were Republicans or Democrats, liberals or conservatives. The *Washington Post* political analyst David Broder measured the ideology of the average Washington reporter as the equivalent of vermouth in a good martini, "Not much." Since the New Deal, most of the press corps had sympathized with the goals of liberal, activist presidents, and had shared in the broad Cold War consensus on foreign policy. Yet in spite of the liberal sentiment within the press corps, voters had drifted to the right. To Sidney Blumenthal, who covered the 1984 presidential campaign for the *New Republic*, the liberal media itself bore responsibility for the conservative triumph. Blumenthal charged that the post-Watergate impulse toward investigative reporting had shocked the public with constant exposés of the government. As public faith in government officials eroded, ideologues had rushed in to fill the political vacuum.[3]

Shifts in national political trends had long been problematic for the newspapers that operated in a company town whose major product was politics. In the 1920s the media critic Oswald Garrison Villard had lamented the absence of any newspapers of consequence in the nation's capital. Washington lacked the commercial base to sustain a major paper with advertising, and its citizens could not vote, which cost the press political ads as well. Dependent on sources and subscribers whose own lives were directly affected by shifting political winds, Washington newspapers tended to take on "a faint tinge of the color" of whatever administration happened to be in power, Villard assessed. That caused the national politicians to not take the local Washington press all that seriously, so "the Washington correspondents, not the local newspaper men, are the journalists who have influenced the political life of the capital." Discriminating readers chiefly scanned the Washington papers while waiting for the trains to bring in better papers from New York, Philadelphia, and Baltimore. For Warren G. Harding's inauguration in 1921 the *New York Times* advertised that delivery "by SPECIAL AIRPLANES" would have the paper at Washington newsstands by 8:00 a.m.[4]

The *Evening Star* had long dominated Washington's newspaper scene by its extensive coverage of local events, by stripping its prose of partisan adjectives, and by not publishing anything that might offend anyone. Typical *Star* editorials, a *Chicago Tribune* correspondent commented, "called on the citizens to save its beautiful dogwood trees and advised all who could to leave town in July and August in order to escape the sultry heat." As an afternoon paper, the *Star* reaped the bulk of the city's advertising from merchants who wanted to attract the bureaucrats on their way home from work; but the profits discouraged innovation. For reporters, a job on the *Star* was equivalent to a civil service post, as the paper rarely fired anyone. The *Star*'s two unprofitable afternoon competitors owed their existence essentially to their publishers' egos. William Randolph Hearst underwrote the afternoon *Washington Times,* with its snappy news style, colorful features, and eccentric editorials. E. W. Scripps's *Washington Daily News* championed his liberal, prolabor policies. Neither paper turned a profit and the heavily subsidized *Daily News* at first carried no advertising at all.[5]

The morning *Washington Post* had little more than an AP franchise to offer its readers. The paper reflected the passions of its right-wing publisher Ned McLean for gossip, society, and sports. The *Post*'s inflammatory reporting had been blamed for provoking a race riot in the District in 1919. Then McLean managed to get personally entangled in the scandals of Warren Harding's administration—being forced to testify during the Teapot Dome investigation. All of this earned the contempt of the Washington press corps. "They despise, dislike, and distrust it," Oswald Garrison Villard asserted, describing reporters' attitude toward the *Washington Post*; "to them it is not only a poison sheet—it is also a contemptible one and they question its moral integrity." The *Post* competed against Hearst's morning paper, the *Washington Herald*. The flamboyant Eleanor "Cissy" Patterson took over its editorial helm in 1930 and turned the *Herald* into a bright and breezy paper, doubling its circulation. By 1939, Patterson had merged both Hearst papers into the *Times-Herald*, with morning and afternoon editions.[6]

Ned McLean stumbled into alcoholism and a difficult divorce, and the *Washington Post* sank along with him. In 1929, McLean turned down an offer of five million dollars for the paper from the New York financier Eugene Meyer. The banks eventually forced the dissolute McLean out—he spent the rest of his life in a sanatorium—and auctioned off the *Post* to settle creditors' claims. On June 1, 1933, a crowd gathered for the bankruptcy sale on the steps of the paper's headquarters near Pennsylvania Avenue. The publisher's former wife Evelyn Walsh McLean attended, wearing the Hope diamond that she had contemplated selling in order to buy the paper back for her sons. William Randolph Hearst sent an agent to bid up to $800,000. Cissy Patterson, also in the crowd, had failed to convince Hearst to go any higher. An attorney made the winning bid of $825,000 for his anonymous client, later identified as Eugene Meyer. He had snatched up the paper for a fraction of his initial offer, and for less than half of what he had been prepared to pay.[7]

Eugene Meyer intended to make himself useful to the nation "at a critical time." As an investment banker, he had specialized in buying undervalued stocks and holding them until everyone else started buying them back. He went to Washington during World War I to serve on the War Industries Board, and stayed to hold posts in the Harding, Coolidge, and Hoover administrations, culminating with his appointment as chairman of the Federal Reserve Board. An independent-minded Republican, Meyer disagreed with his party's "hard-money crowd," whose deflationary policies he blamed for worsening the depression. Washingtonians viewed him as a rich Republican banker and assumed that he would use the *Post* to batter Franklin Roosevelt's newly installed Democratic administration. Instead, Meyer designated the *Post* an independent newspaper. He insisted that he had purchased it on his own, not for his party. (He also declined to chair the Republican National Committee.) Despite this avowal, dubious *Post* reporters turned out the kinds of stories they thought a Republican publisher would want, and the news columns displayed considerable skepticism of the New Deal. The *Daily Worker*'s Washington correspondent, Marguerite Young, branded Meyer's paper a "banker's organ."[8]

Eugene Meyer admitted that he knew next to nothing about newspapers when he bought the *Washington Post*. "I had no information on circulation, costs, losses, profits, advertising, people," he later mused. What he had was money, and he intended to spend whatever it took to build a prestigious paper. Meyer raided other newspapers for staff, among them the *Baltimore Sun*'s foreign correspondent Felix Morley, whom he made editorial page editor. The new publisher became a familiar figure as he roamed throughout the *Post* headquarters, from the newsrooms to the pressrooms. He argued with his editors and reporters but refrained from imposing his opinions on them. In 1936, when the anti-Roosevelt Liberty League held a glittery dinner in Washington, the *Post*'s chief political reporter lost patience with its antics. Franklyn Waltman wrote a straightforward news account of the event under his byline, along with an unsigned commentary that mocked the tipsy, cavorting guests, "tailcoat to tailcoat, fluttery bouffant taffeta to sleek black velvet dress." Meyer sighed when he read the next day's *Post*. "It might have been possible to offend more of my friends," he said, "but I don't know how."[9]

To maximize the *Post*'s influence among government officials, Felix Morley convinced Meyer to concentrate his resources on the editorial rather than the news side—running against the received wisdom that reporting made or broke a newspaper. Morley envisioned a dynamic, self-contained editorial page that would not rely on syndicated columns. The publisher's ample checkbook paid for a stable of editorial writers that included political analysts Raymond Clapper and Franklyn Waltman, economic authority Anna Youngman, and foreign affairs specialist Barnet Nover. But the strategy left the paper with a national news staff smaller than the Washington bureau of the *New York Times*. Subscribers not surprisingly rated the editorial pages the best part of the paper. Meyer intended to avoid labels and live up to the assertion in its editorial page of being "An Independent Paper." Both the editor and publisher shared a distrust for Franklin Roosevelt's New Deal, but they agreed not to level criticism merely along partisan lines. Their lofty aspirations were rewarded in 1938 with a Pulitzer Prize for Morley's editorials.[10]

Although paternalistic, Eugene Meyer did not consider the *Post* a charitable institution. He and his wife Agnes owned the paper as a partnership and deducted its losses from their taxes. While Meyer's personal fortune kept the paper afloat, the depression hampered his efforts to make it run profitably.

Eventually, it dawned on Meyer that his earlier spending spree had made him look like a dilettante. Determined to prove himself a serious, hard-boiled publisher, he instituted a general retrenchment policy in 1935. He turned salary decisions over to the paper's business manager, much to the dismay of the managing editor, Bill Haggard, who threatened to quit unless he regained some say over salaries. Several of the staff promised to walk out with him. Within the paper, Felix Morley, Raymond Clapper, and Franklyn Waltman organized the opposition to the threatened strike. The paper continued to publish, but it lost a dozen members of the staff, including Haggard. The most lasting result of the abortive strike was the formation of the *Post*'s first Newspaper Guild chapter. Meyer did not help morale when he addressed a meeting of *Post* employees and described his own personal sacrifices, "You should realize that I have made no additions to my collection of French Impressionists since I bought the *Post*." With budgets tight and salaries low, some of Meyer's talented acquisitions followed the money elsewhere.[11]

Although no match for the *New York Times*'s coverage of the battle over President Roosevelt's plan to enlarge the Supreme Court in 1937, Franklyn Waltman's reporting and Felix Morley's editorials against the "court packing" plan gave the *Washington Post* national prominence. Meyer was delighted that other newspapers reprinted so much of the *Post*'s output. At the same time, he also hired the pro–New Deal correspondent Ernest K. Lindley. For all its opposition to Roosevelt on domestic issues, the *Post* was moving closer to supporting the president's foreign policy. As international tensions mounted, Meyer and Morley traveled together to Europe during the summer of 1937. They returned with vastly different impressions of how the United States should prepare for the gathering storm. Morley had absorbed Quaker pacifism at Haverford College, where his father was a professor. He believed that the United States must remain isolated to preserve itself as a "trustee for what remains of Western Civilization." His publisher, a nonpracticing Jew, had been too shocked by Nazi Germany to maintain such a detached attitude. Morley's isolationism also clashed with columnist Barnet Nover's militancy, giving the editorial page a split personality. To Morley's chagrin, the *Post*'s news columns attacked congressional isolationists in a slashing investigative series on pro-Nazi activities in the United States. Nor was Morley pleased in 1938 when Meyer signed the *Post* onto the *New York Herald Tribune*'s syndicate service, putting the internationalist columns of Walter Lippmann and Dorothy Thompson on his editorial pages. Morley's gloom deepened further when his publisher asked him to find room on the staff for his "New Dealish" daughter Katharine, a University of Chicago graduate who had been working as a labor reporter for the *San Francisco News*. Morley felt certain that Kay was being groomed for succession. When she married the mercurial lawyer Philip Graham in 1940, the situation grew even more unpredictable, and Morley resigned to become president of Haverford. To replace him, Meyer tried to hire the radio commentator Elmer

Davis but could not match the broadcaster's salary, gasping, "Why, that fellow makes more than $50,000 a year!"[12]

The *Post*'s capital location, together with its pitiful salaries and puny staff, made it an easy entryway into journalism for green reporters. Meyer hired the Oxford-educated Hedley Donovan (later editor in chief of Time Inc.) as a cub reporter and asked if he thought he would be worth his salary. "It would be hard not to be," the young Donovan brazenly replied. Writing general assignment stories for the city desk gave novice reporters a chance at "the bigger stuff" as local and national news mingled at every level in Washington. Once they learned the ropes, most of the bright young hires left for better-paying publications, although not everyone was so transient. Robert C. Albright stayed for decades as the *Post*'s Capitol Hill correspondent. Edward T. Folliard covered the White House from Roosevelt to Kennedy. And Alfred E. Lewis, who started as the *Post*'s night police reporter in 1933, held the same job long enough to file the paper's first byline on the Watergate burglary. Chalmers Roberts joined the *Post* as a cub reporter in 1933. Unable to get even a small raise, he took a more remunerative job with the Associated Press, but later returned to spend a long career as a diplomatic correspondent for the *Post*.[13]

World War II allowed the *Washington Post* to eke out a profit. By the 1940s the *Post*'s endorsement of Roosevelt's foreign policies had made it his staunchest supporter among Washington papers. Isolationists regarded the paper as a propaganda sheet for Meyer's internationalist views, but none could accuse him of the kind of deference to authority that made the *Evening Star* so bland. "Average Washington folks read the *Star* most of all," wrote William Kiplinger, sorting out the city's readers. "Intellectuals and internationalists dote on the *Post*. Sensation lovers find the *Times-Herald* most satisfying." The *Washington Post* had ranked fifty-seventh among the nation's morning newspapers in national advertising in 1932, but had climbed to fourth place a decade later as its wartime circulation tripled. On the tenth anniversary of Meyer's purchase of the *Post*, *Time* magazine saluted it as "one of the world's 10 greatest newspapers," and *Fortune* ranked it "among the first half-dozen newspapers in the United States." Such accolades were still premature.[14]

The wartime rationing of newsprint convinced Meyer to sacrifice news columns for ad space, hoping to build loyalty among advertisers who were unable to place ads in the crowded pages of Meyer's competitors that would outlast the global conflict. Once peace returned and the ration was lifted, however, fickle advertisers switched back to the higher-circulation *Star* and *Times-Herald*, and the *Post*'s profits evaporated. By contrast, the *New York Times* did not publish all the ads it was offered and used its newsprint allotment to print more copies rather than fatter editions, thereby expanding its reader base. At the war's end, Meyer turned seventy and was eager to turn the paper over to his son-in-law, Phil Graham, once he returned from military service in the Pacific. The thirty-year-old Graham planned to pursue a political career in Florida, but Meyer persuaded him to join the *Post* in January 1946. Six months later, Eugene Meyer became the first president of the World Bank. The Hoover Republican handed full responsibility as publisher to his liberal Democratic son-in-law.[15]

Charming, brilliant, and ambitious, Phil Graham had grown up in hard times while his father struggled as a mining engineer, sugarcane planter, dairy farmer, and politician. At the University of Florida, Graham edited the campus newspaper, the *Alligator,* although he planned a career in law. His fraternity brother, George Smathers, regarded Graham as a "wild guy," smart enough to score top grades without much study, which left too much free time for partying. "In our fraternity we had a lot of whiskey drinkers," Smathers recalled, and "they didn't drink socially." One afternoon, Graham's father arrived at the fraternity house and found his son drunk. He brought him home to drive a milk truck until he returned to college the next year. Graham went on to Harvard Law School, became president of the *Harvard Law Review*, and immensely impressed Professor Felix Frankfurter, for whom he later clerked on the Supreme Court. In Washington, Graham lived in a group house filled with young New Deal lawyers. He seemed poised for a political career until he met and swiftly married Katharine Meyer.[16]

As the *Post*'s new publisher, Phil Graham held a majority of the voting stock but not his father-in-law's deep pockets. He had to convince Meyer to pay for any improvements and innovations, a teeth-grinding chore for a man with his vision. Graham compensated for his own inexperience by recruiting Russell Wiggins, a former Washington correspondent and editor of the *Saint Paul Dispatch-Pioneer Press,* to be managing editor, and John Sweeterman, from the *Dayton Journal & Herald,* as general manager. Wiggins built up the news reporting, while Sweeterman devised ways to make the paper profitable. They created the Sunday package of comics, magazines, television guide, and classified ads to appeal to Washington's blossoming suburbs. The *Post*'s headquarters also housed WINX, a local AM radio station with no network affiliation. Certain that the future lay in television, Graham sold the station to purchase a majority interest in the local CBS radio affiliate, WTOP, with an understanding that it would lead to the acquisition of the CBS-TV affiliate in Washington. He made similar investments in TV stations in Florida (including a Miami station that was later renamed WPLG for Philip L. Graham). Broadening the company's financial base enabled Graham to boost salaries at the *Post*.[17]

What ultimately solidified the *Washington Post* was its acquisition of the *Washington Times-Herald*. Cissy Patterson had repeatedly turned down Eugene Meyer's overtures to buy her paper, knowing that it would inevitably disappear in a merger. At her death in 1948, she willed the *Times-Herald* to seven of her top staff (collectively known as the seven dwarfs) but without any operating capital. "She left us a gold mine," said one of the dwarfs, but "forgot to give us a shovel." The Washington lobbyist Thomas "Tommy the Cork"

Corcoran tried to persuade the financier Joseph Kennedy to buy the *Times-Herald*. "See what a principality Eugene Meyer built out of the *Post*—he turned it into the 49th state," Corcoran enthused. "Why don't you be the 50th and let me be part of the shadow?" Kennedy declined the opportunity and the paper instead went to Cissy's cousin, Colonel Robert R. McCormick. The publisher of the *Chicago Tribune* disliked equally Washington and the *Washington Post*. McCormick installed his niece, Ruth "Bazy" Miller, to run the paper, and she promptly made it an enthusiastic booster of Senator Joseph McCarthy's anti-Communist crusade. But Miller alienated her uncle by carrying on an affair with her managing editor. Ill and aging, Colonel McCormick washed his hands of the mess in 1954 by selling the *Times-Herald* to its competitor, Meyer and Graham's *Post*. (The rivalry between the papers had been such that when Miller's daughter dated Graham's son, Joe Alsop pronounced them "the Montagues and the Capulets.") The deal folded Washington's most conservative paper into its most liberal. The *Post* kept its former competitor's popular features, from comics to columnists, as a way of preventing the *Times-Herald*'s readers and advertisers from migrating to the *Star*. Meanwhile, management at the *Star* felt so confident of its commanding lead in advertising, and so reluctant to reinvest revenues in the paper, that they failed to bid for the *Times-Herald*—an ultimately fatal mistake. Soon after the *Post* became Washington's sole morning paper, it surpassed the *Star* in readers and within four years established a lead in advertising that it never relinquished. Unexpectedly, the merger also turned the *Post* into more of a local paper. While Graham held national ambitions for the paper, he felt he first had to "win in Washington."[18]

The *Washington Post* extinguished the capital's only pro-McCarthy paper during its own war against "McCarthyism"—a term coined by the *Post*'s gifted editorial cartoonist, Herblock. Eugene Meyer hired Herbert L. Block as he mustered out of the army after World War II. Herblock, as the cartoonist signed himself, had already won a Pulitzer Prize for his liberal, internationalist drawings for Scripps-Howard's Newspaper Enterprise Association, but that syndicate's shift to the right made him anxious to work somewhere more compatible. Herblock viewed the *Post* as a weak paper with a strong editorial page, but he reasoned that a move to Washington would let him examine his subjects up close—and have some assurance that his subjects would see what he drew. As the *Post*'s staff cartoonist he started out doing seven cartoons a week and special sketches on demand. Herblock commenced at the paper the same week as the hard-charging Phil Graham, who actively injected himself into editorial decisions. Graham never told the cartoonist what to draw. But in 1952, when the *Washington Post* endorsed Dwight D. Eisenhower for president, Herblock could not abide Ike's running mate, California senator Richard Nixon, and his image of a benign Ike mildly chastising Nixon and Joe McCarthy as two ruffians holding smear brushes disconcerted Graham. Refusing to alter his opinions to fit the paper's editorials, Herblock suggested that the *Post* not run his cartoons for the rest of the campaign. When they appeared else-where in syndication, however, their publication gave the impression that he had been censored at home. Never again would the *Post* suppress Herblock's cartoons.[19]

Widely distributed, Herblock's anti-McCarthy cartoons gave the *Post* greater national visibility. The paper earned further credit for Alan Barth's civil liber-tarian editorials. Some of Barth's editorials were so tough on Senator McCarthy that Phil Graham toned them down to avoid frightening off advertisers. The senator responded in his fashion by calling the *Washington Post* "the local *Daily Worker.*" *Post* editors set aside a disproportionately large number of news col-umns to scrutinize McCarthy's charges, on the grounds that they could con-ceive of "no other way to provide coverage of a sort that let the reader decide the truth for himself." For two years, reporter Murrey Marder handled the McCarthy beat full time, writing both straight news and analysis of the senator's charges of conspiracy, subversion, and espionage within the government. When Eisenhower won the presidency in 1952, Phil Graham assumed that the general would rein in the marauding senator. "This is the end of the McCarthy pe-riod," Graham congratulated Murrey Marder. "We'll have to find something else for you to do." Marder corrected him, saying, "You're going to have to put two men on McCarthy now."[20]

In its zeal to discredit McCarthy, the *Washington Post* fell prey to a con artist named Paul Hughes. Having been rejected for a job on the senator's staff, Hughes peddled himself as a disillusioned McCarthyite who had evidence of the senator's illegal activities. Phil Graham snapped up the bait and offered Hughes "expense money" for the exclusive rights to his story. Just before the twelve-part series was set to run, however, Murrey Marder's fact-checking dis-proved most of Hughes's evidence. The documents Hughes offered turned out to be forgeries and the people who had supposedly given him affidavits were nowhere to be found. The series never appeared in print, but word of the scam surfaced anyway. In its sole editorial on the subject, the *Post* defended itself by insisting that "The time it takes to prove a story false will be as well spent as the time it takes to prove a story true."[21]

Phil Graham had wrung enough money from his father-in-law to construct a modern, air-conditioned headquarters for the *Post* on L Street in 1950. He tried to acquire the *New York Times*'s Washington bureau as a tenant, and at the same time he sought to convince the *Times*'s top Washington correspon-dent, James Reston, to take over the *Post*'s editorial page. Graham confided to Reston that he intended to make the *Post* a "miniature *New York Times.*" But in 1953 the *Times* Washington bureau chief, Arthur Krock, agreed to step aside in Reston's favor rather than lose his star reporter to "the locals." For all its ambi-tion, the *Washington Post* still relied excessively on the wire services for its news as it had no foreign correspondents and only nine reporters on its na-tional desk—compared with twenty-four at the *New York Times* Washington bureau. *Times* reporters, such as Max Frankel, boasted that their bureau "had serious journalism in Washington all to itself." Struggling to compete, the *Post* decreed that all new staff members should be college graduates. Its managing editor and most of his veteran reporters had not gone past high school, but the GI Bill was producing a bumper crop of college graduates to populate the staff. Among the new hires was the Harvard-educated Benjamin Crowning-shield Bradlee, who hoped to cover the White House or Capitol but got sent instead to the municipal courts. To further improve morale and reward loyalty, the *Post* launched a profit-sharing plan and in 1955 Eugene Meyer awarded half a million dollars worth of nonvoting stock to be divided among all *Post* employees with at least five years' service. The *Post*'s White House correspondent, Edward Folliard, reported that his counterpart from the *New York Times*, Bill Lawrence, "clipped out the story and sent it to Mr. Sulzberger."[22]

A *Time* magazine cover story in 1956 featured a beaming Phil Graham ringed by Herblock cartoons. At the height of his prestige, Graham nevertheless showed signs of strain. Unsatisfied with reporting the news, he wanted to shape its outcome, and he so immersed himself in civil rights battles from Capitol Hill to Little Rock, Arkansas, that he suffered a nervous breakdown. For the next half dozen years, Graham alternated between bursts of energy and immobility. In his upbeat moods, he divided his attention between the *Washington Post*, its broadcasting subsidiaries, and his political activism, creating a tension that he said caused him "at times almost unbearable difficulty." Katharine Graham commented that "When Phil was politicking, there was always a little bit of a tear between being a newspaperman and being a politician." He brushed aside rhetoric about the separation of news reporting and editorials as having "a strong smell of pure baloney." On Capitol Hill, Graham developed a close friendship with Senate Majority Leader Lyndon Johnson, and at the Democratic National Convention in 1960, the publisher lobbied John Kennedy for Johnson's nomination as vice president. When the ticket won, *Washington Post* staff appreciated the inside news that his connections harvested, but they worried that he was undermining their independence. *Post* reporters blamed their paper's failure to investigate leads about the planned Bay of Pigs invasion on Graham's support for the Kennedy administration, and rated the *Post*'s handling of that story "extremely poor." The *Post* was not alone in this lapse. The *New York Times* also suppressed the story at the personal request of President Kennedy.[23]

Eager to prove that he had done more than marry the boss's daughter, Graham seemed happiest when acquiring new property. In 1961 he added *Newsweek* to the Washington Post Company's holdings. "Ozzie baby, I know where the smart money is," Ben Bradlee, who had left the *Post* to become *Newsweek*'s Washington correspondent, told his managing editor, Osborn Elliot. "It's in Phil Graham's pocket." Bradlee convinced Graham that *Newsweek* was the right property to help the *Post* "move toward national and international stature."

Bradlee's reward came as a promotion to *Newsweek*'s Washington bureau chief. Oz Elliot judged his new publisher to be witty, graceful, brilliant, impossible, and "hungry to be the best, the biggest, the most powerful publisher in America." By diverting funds from the *Post*, Graham enabled *Newsweek* to open new bureaus and expand its corps of correspondents. The New York staff praised their new publisher for not interfering in editorial decisions, but Bradlee admitted that Graham "meddled beyond endurance" with the Washington bureau, forcing them to tone down any criticism of his friends in the Kennedy administration and the CIA.[24]

Between uplifting business deals, Phil Graham's depressions turned him alcoholic, abrasive, and abusive. In 1963 he left his wife, carried on a flagrant affair with an employee, and delivered a drunken harangue before an audience of publishers, until he finally had himself confined to a psychiatric hospital. That August, Graham checked out of the hospital and committed suicide at the family's retreat in Virginia. President Kennedy, members of Congress, justices of the Supreme Court, and a sea of journalists attended his funeral at Washington's National Cathedral. Katharine Graham reassured the board of the Washington Post Company that the paper was not for sale. "This is a family company," she asserted, "and there is a new generation coming along." Oz Elliott told his staff that what Graham had brought to *Newsweek* "was what he brought to everything he touched—a marvelously invigorating gust of fresh air." *Time* magazine editor Hedley Donovan similarly acknowledged that Graham had vastly improved *Newsweek*. Critics were less charitable when they assessed the *Washington Post* to be "a political hack paper," for all of its publisher's brilliance and energy. The *Post* remained understaffed, inconsistent in its news coverage, and overly dependent on wire service reports. Even so, editor Russell Wiggins credited Eugene Meyer and Phil Graham with turning a bankrupt sheet into "a solid property" and laying the foundation for a truly great newspaper.[25]

Katharine Graham succeeded her late husband as publisher, more certain of her paper than of herself. She was therefore startled when James Reston asked her, "Don't you want to leave a better paper for the next generation than the one you inherited?" Until then she had never considered that the *Washington Post* "wasn't good enough." Afterward, she began to notice the indecision among its management and the "lack of adrenaline" in its newsroom. She appealed to Reston to revitalize the *Post*, but once again he declined to leave the *Times*. Ben Bradlee, by comparison, made it clear that he wanted to edit the *Post*, and he kept pushing, as Henry Brandon of *The Times* of London recalled, "like a terrier who had smelled prime beef." Her husband had expended his energy and capital on the company, with its broadcasting and magazine subsidiaries, but by appointing Bradlee as managing editor in 1965, Katharine Graham put her prime focus on the *Washington Post*. Bradlee later reflected that he came to the *Post* at the right moment, "when its financial position was secure and at a time when the new owner, Katharine, had convinced herself you have to spend some money to get better." Worn down by Phil Graham's long illness, the *Post*'s management had adopted a "bunker mentality," Bradlee observed, and that attitude was not likely to incite "great leaps forward."[26]

Bradlee coaxed the business managers into doubling his news budget, which allowed him to hire Haynes Johnson away from the *Washington Star*, Ward Just from *Newsweek*, Stanley Karnow from the *Saturday Evening Post*, Nicholas von Hoffman from the *Chicago Daily News*, Richard Harwood from the *Louisville Courier-Journal*, Don Oberdorfer from the Knight News Service, and David Broder from the *New York Times* (whose editors were stunned that such a promising political reporter would leave them for a paper like the *Post*). Added to these pros, Bradlee also recruited young writers straight from the best universities. He encouraged them to tackle stories with the kind of impact that would shock people into thinking and talking about what they had read. For the most part, Bradlee kept his hands off and let them do their jobs. He rarely intervened until the final stages of a story, when he reserved the right to declare something unready to print. In that way he turned the *Washington Post* into a reporter's paper, where ideas came up from the staff rather than down from the editors. Reporters competed with each for space on the front pages, in a system known as "creative tension," which encouraged them to follow a story wherever it led, even if that meant crossing over into someone else's beat. By 1968, Bradlee had replaced Russell Wiggins as executive editor. The *Post* split away the responsibility Wiggins held for the editorial pages and entrusted them to Philip Geyelin, a former *Wall Street Journal* correspondent, to ensure a sharper division between the news and editorial departments. Eugene Patterson of the *Atlanta Constitution* became managing editor, and Ben Bagdikian from the *Saturday Evening Post* was recruited as national editor. Bagdikian got his job after writing an article that described the *Washington Post* as a paper that "nobody edits."[27]

The dozen years that Bradlee had spent at *Newsweek* inspired him to convert the *Washington Post* into a "daily newsmagazine." He started by dismantling the For and about Women section and replacing it with Style, designed to blend cultural reporting, gossip, and social commentary. Reporter Nicholas von Hoffman became a regular columnist for Style after demonstrating his inability to write a normal news story. When Bradlee read von Hoffman's reporting on James Meredith's march through Mississippi in 1966, he thought it reeked of "local sociology" and barely mentioned Meredith's name. Editors had to add leads to von Hoffman's articles to let readers know what they were about. But Bradlee admired his unconventional style and gave him a column where he could tweak the powerful at will. A New Leftist in politics, the columnist judged that his editor lacked any strong political leanings. Bradlee stood open to "any idea, regardless of its ideological hue," von Hoffman observed, and his neutralism gave the *Post* a "screwy, unpredictable catholicity." Bradlee could create electricity in the newsroom, von Hoffman recalled, just by tossing a football or wandering around talking to reporters about their work, and he made journalism "the adventure people go into the work hoping it will be."[28]

At the Pentagon, the *Washington Post* had relied for too long on a correspondent whose habit of borrowing the carbon copies of other reporters' stories earned him the nickname "Black Sheet Jack." At the height of the Vietnam War, Bradlee replaced him with an ex-police reporter from the *Washington Star*, George C. Wilson, who treated the military like a police beat. The *Post* encouraged Wilson to cultivate his own sources instead of duplicating what the wires reported. His stories exposed military cost overruns, and unpreparedness and job dissatisfaction among officers. The *New York Times*'s Pentagon correspondent especially admired Wilson's writing on the U.S.S. *Pueblo* incident in 1968, when North Koreans seized an American naval vessel, although he doubted that the *Times* would have accepted the same style. Wilson explained his dramatic writing by saying, "The *Post*, frankly, is a little more free-swinging." As a Washington paper, the *Post* could also bombard the Pentagon from multiple directions. Its Metro staff interviewed military families about the high cost of being stationed in the capital; its economic reporter examined defense contracting overruns; its White House correspondent followed the latest policy dispute; its federal columnist raised problems with health benefits for Department of Defense employees; and Style pounced on military-related cultural issues. No other paper, not even the *New York Times*, could match that diversity. "For defense officials," noted one press officer, "reading the *Washington Post* can be as unpleasant as having a collision at sea—it can ruin your whole day."[29]

The *Post*'s new strength shook assumptions at the *New York Times*. Traditionally, the *Times* viewed the *New York Herald Tribune* as its chief rival. Situated in the same market and aimed at the same upscale readership, the *Herald Tribune* compensated in style for its inability to match the *Times* in depth. A protracted printers' strike in 1963 fatally wounded the *Herald Tribune*, but just as the *New York Times* was left standing even more alone in New York City, the Washington bureau reported that it had fallen into a "wholly new competitive situation" with the *Washington Post*. From New York, editor (and former Washington correspondent) Turner Catledge lectured the Washington bureau not to write in "Washington terms—political maneuvers, procedures, and the struggle for power." They should tell the news instead in human terms, reporting less about the passage of a bill than about its potential effect on everyday lives. "I hope that the congressional staff will not forget that the *New York Times* is written for the voters and not the legislators," Catledge instructed. "We have a very sizeable circulation in Washington, but it is a very small percentage of the total."[30]

Accustomed to regarding the *Washington Post* as little more than a provincial paper in a government town—perhaps a step or two above Albany—editors and reporters at the *New York Times* were startled by the Washington paper's sudden competitiveness. The *Times* correspondent and editor Harrison Salisbury marveled that "hardly a day goes by without the *Post* having a good secondary exclusive story or angle on Page 1." In 1970, after a protracted internal debate, the *Times* finally decided to revamp its editorial pages into more of a "forum for intellectual exchange," only to have the *Post* unveil an op-ed page days earlier in order to steal the *Times*'s thunder. Compounding problems for the *Times* was the demoralization of its Washington bureau resulting from the New York managers' attempts to exert more control over this notoriously independent outpost. Two men, Arthur Krock and James Reston, had run the Washington bureau with much independence for three decades; it then went through five chiefs over the next fifteen years. Rivalries from aggressive regional news bureaus such as the *Los Angeles Times, Boston Globe, Wall Street Journal,* and *Chicago Tribune* forced the *Times* bureau to scramble to retain its premier position.[31]

In this combative atmosphere, the *New York Times*'s Washington bureau pounced on what bureau chief Max Frankel called one "helluva big story" that came its way in March 1971. Neil Sheehan, a former Saigon correspondent who had become strongly opposed to American policies in Southeast Asia, handed Frankel a large bag of classified documents detailing how the United States had gotten into the Vietnam War. Some of the more wary *Times* editors would have preferred to run a story about the Pentagon Papers without actually reprinting them, but James Reston insisted that the "paper of record" should publish the text of the documents, despite their being stamped "top secret." The *Washington Post* reporter Chalmers Roberts picked up rumors about a *Times* story so big that it "could end the war," but the paper was unable to penetrate its rival's secrecy. Not until the *Times* appeared on Sunday, June 13, 1971, did those at the *Post* learn about the Pentagon Papers. All that the *Post* could do was to run condensations of the revelations, rewritten by Roberts and Murrey Marder.[32]

The *Washington Post* desperately sought its own set of the classified papers, and national news editor Ben Bagdikian snared the prize via the *Times*'s original source, a disgruntled former Pentagon aide, Daniel Ellsberg. The *Post*'s managing editor quietly sent his top diplomatic correspondents, Roberts, Marder, and Don Oberdorfer, on a clandestine mission to Bradlee's home in Georgetown. There, Bagdikian dumped onto the floor two bulky cardboard boxes filled with thousands of pages in no particular order. Ellsberg had asked that the *Post* start with something earlier than the Johnson administration, to show that the dissembling had been part of a larger pattern, and Chalmers Roberts spotted something about Eisenhower's role in canceling the Vietnamese elections of 1954. He thought he could put a story together for the next day's paper, but cautioned that it would hardly be earthshaking. "Write it, write it, write it," Bradlee implored.[33]

As the reporters sifted through the documents in Bradlee's sunroom, the paper's attorneys and editors argued in his living room. The lawyers warned that the court order against the *New York Times* had forbidden "any agent" of that paper from printing the classified material. The editors rebutted that they were competing, not conspiring, with the *Times*. Bagdikian had gotten nothing from anyone at the *Times*, nor had his source been an agent of the *Times*. Frederick "Fritz" Beebe, chairman of the Washington Post Company's board of directors, reminded them that government prosecution could undermine its first public stock offering and that the Nixon administration might use a conviction as grounds for stripping away the company's broadcast licenses. The lawyers proposed a compromise by which the *Post* would notify the Justice Department that it had the Pentagon Papers but wait a day before publishing anything. To Chalmers Roberts, who was getting ready to retire, this seemed such an obvious invitation for a government injunction that he threatened to resign in protest. With the news and business sides of the paper deadlocked, the decision rested with publisher Katharine Graham. Called at her home while hosting a party, she listened to both sides. Graham understood the grave threat to her paper but she also appreciated Bradlee's determination to put the *Post* on an equal level with the *Times*, and she recognized how losing the story would demoralize the newsroom. "I say we print," she consented. Ben Bagdikian assumed that Graham must have been aware of the patronizing attitude of the nation's predominantly male newspaper publishers, and how they bandied tales of her inadequacies. With one decision she proved them wrong.[34]

The Pentagon Papers put the *Washington Post* on the world map. Foreign correspondents stationed in Washington were astonished over the confrontation between the American government and its leading newspapers over divulging official secrets. The British journalist Henry Brandon called the newspapers' initiative "unthinkable in any other country." The episode completed the *Post*'s turnabout on the Vietnam War. In the 1950s, while U.S. policy was unfurling in Vietnam, the *Post* had not a single correspondent in Southeast Asia. The paper gathered its news and its assumptions about the region at the White House, the State Department, and the Pentagon. By the time the first *Post* reporter arrived in Saigon, the paper's editorial policies had been "pretty well fixed," according to national editor Richard Harwood. The *Post*'s editor Russell Wiggins so ardently endorsed the official line on the war that President Johnson declared him worth "two American divisions," and rewarded him with appointment as UN ambassador. Wiggins's departure opened the way for the far more skeptical Philip Geyelin to shift the *Post*'s editorial page into the antiwar camp (for which Geyelin won a Pulitzer Prize in 1970). Publishing the Pentagon Papers made Bradlee feel assured that people would at last talk about the *Post* and the *New York Times* "in the same breath." But the newsroom's collective sense of achievement verged on hubris. When Stanley Karnow returned to the *Post* in 1971 after having lived abroad as a foreign correspondent, he was appalled to hear the national editor say, "There are 25 members of the *Post* national staff and 25 members of the *New York Times* Washington bureau and we are the most powerful people in America."[35]

Management and staff at the *New York Times* were furious over having lost their exclusive to "a small-town newspaper." "I was jumping up and down in here like a madman," said *Times*'s editor Abe Rosenthal. Even so, the *Post*'s entry into the fray aided the *Times* in court. Their attorneys could argue that prior restraint had failed, as other papers were publishing the same classified material. (The *Boston Globe* had also obtained and printed portions of the Pentagon Papers.) The Nixon administration moved to stop them all with another court order. The federal judge hearing the case ordered the government to pick the "ten worst cases" of classified documents whose publication would endanger the national security. Bradlee had arranged for the *Post*'s Pentagon reporter, George Wilson, to attend the closed session in the judge's chambers. When the government's attorneys produced their first document, Wilson felt certain that he had read it before. He rifled through his briefcase and produced a published volume of the Senate Foreign Relations Committee hearings that contained the same item. Max Frankel of the *Times* dismissed this as a "dumb coincidence," but the *Washington Post* reporter had demonstrated his breadth of knowledge about his beat. One by one, the remaining "secrets" turned out to have been published elsewhere. The papers won favorable verdicts and the government appealed. On the day that Chalmers Roberts formally retired from the *Washington Post*, the Supreme Court ruled six to three that the government had failed to justify prior restraint of the newspapers. "The press was to serve the governed, not the governors," wrote Justice Hugo Black for the majority. Publication of the Pentagon Papers helped "stiffen the spines of all journalists," cheered Fred Friendly, who had resigned as president of CBS News five years earlier over media timidity.[36]

President Richard Nixon reacted indifferently at first to the Pentagon Papers—taking some sly pleasure at seeing his predecessors' reputations taken down a notch—until National Security Advisor Henry Kissinger convinced him that a leak of such magnitude made his administration look weak. Finding the FBI uncooperative, the White House recruited its own operatives to investigate and plug the leaks. While the Nixon White House hunkered down in an atmosphere of closed-door secrecy and intrigue, the *Washington Post* occupied its new wide-open newsroom on Fifteenth Street. Ben Bradlee disliked having reporters working alone in cubicles where they might hang autographed photos of the politicians they covered. He preferred that they work out of a common newsroom where he could wander, pausing here and there for quick conversations. "If he stopped to talk to you," recalled reporter David Remnick, "you were golden; if not, you were meat." Bradlee had a glass wall installed in his own office so he could see and be seen. "We work on an adversary basis here," Bradlee explained to the architects. However Richard Nixon might have interpreted that remark, Bradlee referred to the internal competition he instilled within the *Post*.[37]

Given its close ties to the Kennedy and Johnson administrations, while continuing to maintain that it was an "independent newspaper," the *Post* had refrained from automatically opposing the Nixon administration. During the 1968 campaign Bradlee had hired Don Oberdorfer from the Knight News Service to cover the Republican candidate because he was uncertain whether there were any resident *Post* reporters who did not hate Nixon. Facing the likelihood of a Nixon victory, the *Post* had to build some reliable sources within the incoming administration. "Our readers are not typical," Bradlee once commented. "They have better résumés than most newspaper readers." Even Nixon's insular staff could not ignore the paper. *Post* reporters noted that high-level officials had previously read the *New York Times* first and then looked to see if the *Washington Post* had something the *Times* had missed. By the time of the Nixon administration, officials were reading the *Post* first and then going to the *Times*. Part of the problem for the *Times* was logistics. It was still shipping early editions of its papers from New York, so the locally produced *Post* could always beat it on late-breaking news. *Post* reporters now had confidence that "everybody read the *Post*" and that what they wrote would reach those who set policy.[38]

Bradlee's creative tension system continued to pit reporters against each other. When antiwar activists staged a massive moratorium in Washington in 1970, the *Post*'s National and Metro desks both claimed the primary coverage. "The capital is in Washington—how is that a metropolitan story?" roared national editor Ben Bagdikian. But the Metro section called for the lead on the grounds that its younger reporters could get closer to the demonstrators. Competitiveness stimulated first-rate reporting, but also an undercurrent of insecurity. The fittest survived, while others wound up in dead-end jobs or left. The newsroom's intensity contrasted with the collegiality that prevailed at the *Evening Star* and *Washington Daily News*. Those papers might be going down, but they gave their staff "that great lifeboat feeling," columnist Mary McGrory recalled, with "people pulling for each other and sticking together." Congeniality could not save a paper, however, and in 1972 the *Daily News* "died happy" by merging with the *Star*.[39]

That year, creative tension fueled the *Washington Post*'s coverage of the Watergate scandal. The ambitious self-starter Bob Woodward was called to cover the arraignment of the Watergate burglars because he was divorced, had no family obligations, and never complained about Saturday assignments. Woodward resented the intrusion of Carl Bernstein into the story, but the shaggy, undisciplined, college drop-out had more experience as a reporter and was a better writer. (Frustrated with low-level assignments at the *Post*, Bernstein had just applied for a job as a political writer for *Rolling Stone*.) Somehow the two suppressed their competitiveness to forge so close a team that the newsroom tagged them "Woodstein." The two Metro reporters rode Watergate to a national political story because the *Post*'s top political reporters discounted it. The national desk vigorously protested that the *Post* was taking too much of a risk on the work of such novices. White House correspondent Carroll Kilpatrick suffered the administration's retaliation for Woodward and Bernstein's exposés, which even he found questionable. National news editor Richard Harwood similarly dismissed the Watergate story until it grew so compelling that he tried to wrestle back control for his own reporters.[40]

Ben Bradlee kept close watch on Woodward and Bernstein, rejecting some of their early drafts and sending them in search of more evidence. Bradlee never let his reporters rest on yesterday's laurels; he wanted to know what they planned to deliver for tomorrow's edition. He exulted whenever one of their Watergate exclusives forced the *New York Times* to quote the *Post* on its front page. Bradlee's worst nightmare was that the Watergate story would "peter out" inconclusively. But his confidence in his reporters comforted Katharine Graham throughout the long months when the *Post* stood alone. The editor and publisher could often be seen huddled in conversation, with Graham appearing troubled and Bradlee looking determined. Observers noted that by the end of each encounter, he had made her laugh. Bradlee retained Graham's full confidence in his judgment. Nor did she press the reporters about their anonymous sources. Instead she put the full resources of her paper behind them (and passed along whatever information she could glean from social gatherings with her powerful friends).[41]

In 1973 the *Washington Post* received a Pulitzer Prize for its Watergate coverage, along with worldwide prestige for standing up against a corrupt administration. Woodward and Bernstein had been offended when Bradlee entered the paper in the Pulitzer's category for meritorious public service rather than singling them out for their reporting, but Bradlee called it the most prestigious category, the "Big Casino." (The *New York Times* had won the public service award the previous year for publishing the Pentagon Papers.) He assured them that it would hardly detract from their fame. In fact, members of the public service jury had remained so skeptical of the Watergate story that they had not included the *Post* among the finalists. The Pulitzer advisory board, which at that time included Newbold Noyes, editor of the *Washington Star*, and James Reston of the *New York Times*, overruled the jury to recognize the *Post*'s stellar achievement. The price of victory, Bradlee later learned, was a parallel decision to overrule two other jury recommendations that would have awarded *Post* reporters prizes in those categories.[42]

In the *Washington Post* editorial room they hung up the hot type from the paper's August 9, 1974, headline: NIXON RESIGNS. Beyond the prestige of that trophy, the paper gained financial rewards by selling transcripts of Nixon's tapes and a book of its Watergate reporting, *The Fall of a President*. The Washington premiere of the Hollywood film *All the President's Men* brought further renown, although it stirred resentment among those in the newsroom whose contributions the film version slighted. In the wake of Watergate, Washington reporters assumed that a better-informed public would become more involved in government and politics. To the contrary, the percentage of Americans who voted dropped by alarming rates. Politics seemed to mean less to people, suggesting that the intense Watergate coverage had drained public faith in the government, along with interest in Washington news.[43]

Labor problems further tempered the mood at the *Post*. Women on the staff filed charges of discrimination against the paper and won a cash settlement for all the women who worked there between 1972 and 1974 (even Katharine Graham got a share). Reporters in the Newspaper Guild conducted a sixteen-day strike in 1974, but management worried less about the newsroom than the composing room and pressroom. There, the printers' unions determined who would be hired, what shifts they would work, and how many employees would work each press. The union's intransigence forced the *Post* to use ancient, labor-intensive, hot-type Linotype machines, rather than install the latest photo-composition equipment. The paper's first scanner, for instance, sat in storage. Featherbedding practices blocked the acquisition of technology that could replace dozens of keypunch operators. Union agreements also required the *Post* to employ those printers laid off by the defunct *Washington News*, which swelled the pressroom staff even further. Control rather than job security was the issue— the *Post* offered lifetime employment to the pressmen if they dropped their opposition to automation. Gearing up for a confrontation, the *Post* secretly trained its management and nonunion employees to produce the paper on their own. When the pressmen staged a brief walkout in November 1973, they returned from the picket line sooner than expected and discovered that replacements had already set up the nightly run.[44]

Once their contracts expired, the pressmen walked out again in October 1975. Despite their employment at a newspaper, they lacked any sense of public relations. To prevent management from publishing without them, the strikers smashed the presses with crowbars and sledgehammers, and bloodied a foreman who tried to stop them. The pressmen regarded the vandalism as an act of self-defense, but few others accepted their justification for the damage. The *Washington Star* ran photos of the destruction on its front page, and the *Post*'s management escorted groups of reporters to see it for themselves. "As far as I was concerned, those were my presses, our presses," said correspondent Don Oberdorfer. He considered it the union's privilege to go out on strike, but he would not stand "behind these guys who tried to destroy the newspaper." At a Newspaper Guild meeting in a nearby church, union officials called on the reporters to walk out in support of the pressmen, but several of the paper's leading correspondents emotionally denounced the violence and the unit voted

not to honor the picket line (some reporters joined the picketers independently). Helicopters flew copy to print shops in Virginia, and the *Washington
Post* missed only a single day of publication. Home deliveries of a slimmed-
down version of the paper continued uninterrupted, because the paper had
always relied on nonunion drivers. After three months, the *Post* began hiring
replacements for the strikers. Graham insisted that she had not set out to break
the union, although that was the result. The seventeen printers who had operated each press before the strike were now reduced to nine. The workforce for
the first time included sizeable numbers of women and minorities. Other newspaper publishers were ecstatic that the liberal *Post* had taken such a militant
stand against its union. Afterward the *Post*'s pressroom stayed nonunion and
the number of strikes against newspapers nationwide declined markedly. Rather
than damage the paper's financial standing, the strike improved it. Strike insurance gave the *Washington Post* a better fourth quarter in 1975 than the previous year. Its stock soared more than 400 percent during the decade following
the strike.[45]

During these years, the *Post* vied for national prominence with the *New
York Times*, and also competed in its local market with the *Washington Star-
News* (so named after the 1972 merger). The *Star-News* fell behind the *Post* in
the first months of Watergate reporting but it reaped the benefits of Richard
Nixon's reelection in 1972. The president intended to punish the *Post* by be-
stowing favors on its hometown rival, starting with an exclusive post-election
interview with the *Star-News*. "He didn't say a damn thing in the interview,"
Ben Bradlee noted, "but we could identify a shot across our bow when we saw
one." Nixon's aides banned the *Post*'s society reporter Dorothy McCardle from
covering White House social events. In a rare show of solidarity, the *Star-News*'s
society reporter Isabelle Shelton boycotted any event from which McCardle
was excluded, until the White House rescinded its ban.[46]

The old *Evening Star* had been too set in its routines to convert itself into a
morning paper, ignoring clear signs that television was steadily draining advertising and audiences away from the afternoon dailies. In 1974 the Kauffmann
and Noyes families sold the *Star-News* to Joe Allbritton, a Houston lawyer who
had made his fortune investing in banking, real estate, and funeral parlors. For
his managing editor, Allbritton imported Jim Bellows, promoter of the stylish
"new journalism" at the late *New York Herald Tribune*. "I redefined news," Bellows boasted, proud of having pushed aside traditional reporting for whatever
was new and unusual. The *Star-News*'s redesign emphasized interpretive reporting and soft news on the assumption that readers would already have gotten their hard news from television and that morning's *Post*. Bellows shortened
the paper's name to the *Washington Star,* changed its typeface, hired the pungent editorial cartoonist Pat Oliphant, and launched a brassy gossip column
called "The Ear" (which delighted in prying into Ben Bradlee's personal affairs). The second paper in a market had to take aim at the first, Bellows rea-

soned. "You have to be sassy and irreverent, and you have to get people talk-ing." Joe Allbritton also missed no opportunity to remind Washington busi-ness leaders of their interest in the *Star*'s economic survival, as without it, the *Post* would have "unbridled power."[47]

Allbritton relished attending Gridiron dinners and other social functions where he could mingle with political luminaries, but he seemed out of his element in his own noisy, casual newsroom, filled with "sloppy, gabby, cheeky" reporters. That informality appealed to reporters and sustained their morale after the boss cut their salaries by 20 percent. Allbritton also grew tired of having his editor take all the credit for the paper's transformation. "People talk like I hired Michelangelo to paint a barn," he complained. After losing thirty million dollars in four years, Allbritton fired Bellows and sold the *Star* to Time Inc., for twenty million dollars. He recouped his losses by holding onto the *Star*'s radio and television stations (as Allbritton Communications). Executives at Time Inc. failed to calculate that the broadcasting units' profits had kept the *Star* alive.[48]

Reporters at the *Star* looked forward to an infusion of funds from Time Inc., and to sharing its many foreign correspondents, as by then the *Star* no longer had regular correspondents overseas. Time Inc.'s president James Shepley had once headed the UP's Washington bureau, and editor in chief Hedley Donovan had reported for the *Washington Post*. Both men were ambitious to establish a newspaper presence in the national capital, and they felt sure that they had bought a first-rate paper for a fair price, despite its brisk loss of money. Murray Gart, *Time* magazine's chief of correspondents, took over as editor, recruited prominent writers, and put out a morning edition of the *Star* to go head-to-head with the *Post*. Nothing worked as expected. Gart switched the paper back from soft-news features to hard-news coverage of national and international affairs. His insistence on short, simple, highly focused articles squeezed out the creative writing that Bellows had nurtured. With less than half the *Post*'s staff and editorial budget, the *Star* had little hope of displacing its rival as the capital's number one paper, but it aimed for a strong second place. Instead, its circulation and advertising plummeted. Without the televi-sion revenue that had sustained the *Star* in the past, losses exceeded $85 mil-lion until *Time* abruptly extinguished the *Star* in 1981.[49]

Katharine Graham heard the news on her car radio, as did many *Star* em-ployees. Editors from afar "swooped down" to acquire the *Star*'s staff, recalled the reporter Philip Gailey, who moved on to edit the opinion page of the *St. Petersburg Times*. Among the general news staff, Robert Pear went to the *New York Times*, as did Maureen Dowd (via *Time* magazine), Gloria Borger to *U.S. News & World Report*, Fred Barnes to the *Baltimore Sun,* and Lisa Meyers to NBC News. The largest contingent—including the columnist Mary McGrory, the book reviewer Jonathan Yardley, and reporters Michael Isikoff and Howard Kurtz—headed across town to the *Washington Post*. McGrory compared it to traveling from Rome to Paris. The *Star* was Rome, "untidy, raucous, funny, non-judgmental, and warm," while the *Post* was Paris, "very elegant, very well laid out, a little bit chilly."[50]

In the *Star*'s farewell edition, President Ronald Reagan deplored its loss as a "setback for the cause of diversity in the press." Conservatives lamented that there would be no Washington daily sympathetic to Reagan's cause. "I think it's just an unhealthy situation," said the mass-mailing fund-raiser Richard Viguerie, "to have only one source for daily news in the most important city in the free world." Senator Gordon Humphrey, a conservative Republican from New Hampshire, regretted that "the *Washington Post* will have even greater influence than it has today." Ben Bradlee himself felt troubled that the lack of competition for the *Post* would "bland the paper out." Nevertheless, the *Post* purchased the *Star*'s offices and printing presses, to preempt a potential competitor from using them to start a new paper.[51]

Within months, an alternative to the *Washington Post* emerged when the Unification Church announced that it planned to underwrite a new paper, the *Washington Times*. The Reverend Sun Myung Moon proclaimed that he "established the *Washington Times* to fulfill God's desperate desire to save this world." He made the decision in response "to Heaven's direction" at the time of his conviction for income tax evasion. The Unification Church's media arm, News World Communications, spent one hundred million dollars to convert a warehouse into newsrooms and printing facilities, and hired many of the *Star*'s stranded staff. Identification with his church hobbled the *Washington Times* from its start. News sources asked *Times* reporters whether they were "Moonies," and suspiciously regarded the paper as a propaganda sheet. But Ronald Reagan hailed the *Washington Times* as his favorite newspaper and Republicans in Congress cited it as "the best source for Republican thinking." The paper gained exclusive interviews and inside tips from Republican officeholders, although editor Wesley Pruden denied any partisanship. He insisted that the *Times* was a conservative paper "with a small c." It ran stories that would "resonate with the average Joe," and its populist attitude was aimed at the region's African Americans and blue-collar workers.[52]

The *Washington Times* made the most of its limitations. With few overseas bureaus, it drew its international news largely from the wire services, and eventually News World Communications bought the remains of United Press International. Reliance on the wires made its foreign coverage at times more comprehensive than at the *Post*, where editors gave preference to reports from their own foreign correspondents. When journalists for the *Washington Times* traveled abroad, they acted as if they had a mission. When two of its editors visited Nelson Mandela in a South African prison, he commented that "They seemed less intent on finding out my views that on proving that I was a Communist and a terrorist. All of their questions were slanted in that direction." On the home front, the *Washington Times* knew that it could not match the

Post in staff resources, so it urged reporters to devote their attention to items that the other paper overlooked. That policy generated a fair number of scoops. Counting them up one week, the *Post*'s own ombudsman commented that the *Washington Times* was administering a "water-torture treatment" to its rival. Liberals began to read the *Times* to find out what conservatives were planning. "I know that we're hitting people beyond the choir," chortled editor Wes Pruden, "because we're getting angry mail now."[53]

"Get it Right," the *Times* advertised with double meaning. *Washington Times* reporters did not regard themselves as ideological, although they learned to submit the kind of copy their editors expected. Some reporters chafed when the editorial staff chose stories that promoted particular policies or revised copy to make it fit the editorial line. Headline writers at the *Times* wrote to appeal to their editors even more than to their readers. Reporter Peggy Weyrich quit the *Times* when one of her articles on the Clarence Thomas hearings was rewritten to portray Thomas's accuser, Anita Hill, as a "fantasizer." Periodically, reporters resigned over charges of ideological meddling, despite the *Times*'s steadfast denials that the Unification Church interfered in its news columns. Yet opinion spilled freely into the news pages. A front-page banner headline story on the Kyoto fossil fuel agreement in 1997 read like an editorial: "Under the deal, the use of coal, oil and other fossil fuel in the United States would be cut by more than one-third by 2002, resulting in lower standards of living for consumers and a long-term reduction in economic growth." Reporters around Washington admitted that they enjoyed the *Washington Times*'s audacious approach to the news, although they did not feel the need to read it regularly.[54]

Across the Potomac in Virginia, another daily paper operated within the Beltway, but deliberately avoided a local focus. In 1982 the Gannett chain transported its corporate headquarters from New York City to Arlington, Virginia, on Chairman Allen Neuharth's assumption that "the action center for the world in the field of news and information is Washington." For its flagship, Gannett created a national newspaper, *USA Today*. Abbreviated stories and a light and upbeat style won it the nickname "McPaper," and its staff joked about establishing a Pulitzer Prize for the best investigative paragraph. Profuse with color graphics, *USA Today* appealed to television-era readers, and inspired the rest of the press to adopt their own eye-catching devices. Determined to retain an "outsider" status, Gannett editors shunned the National Press Club and sent their reporters out of town whenever possible to avoid filing under Washington datelines. *USA Today*'s news coverage expanded over time, as did its national audience, although it provided little competition in the *Washington Post*'s home base. As a neighbor, Gannett provided fodder for the *Post*'s business pages, and Al Neuharth responded by flailing the *Post* as arrogant and overrated. He accused it of publishing "unprovable, unanswerable, and unethical stories" based on anonymous sources—a practice he tried to ban at *USA Today*, but that crept back into the paper when reporters felt pressured to compete for scoops with the *Washington Post* and the *New York Times*.[55]

The post-Watergate *Washington Post* garnered an international reputation, an enviable financial standing, and a host of critics. Just as Sidney Blumenthal had blamed the conservative revival of the 1980s on the liberal press, some analysts traced the roots directly back to the *Post*'s exposure of Richard Nixon. E. J. Dionne Jr., a political correspondent and columnist for the *Post*, concluded that Watergate had reinvigorated the political right by driving a centrist president from office and weakening the moderate wing of his party. The media rather than liberal Democrats had gotten the lion's share of the credit for bringing Nixon down, and the wave of adversarial journalism that followed Watergate had eroded public confidence in big government. As the country drifted rightward, so did the *Post*. Reporter William Greider traced the shift to the collapse of the *Star*. Without a creditable competitor to contrast its version of the truth, the *Post* had lowered its tone. The *Post* also boasted the best circulation among households of its region of any major metropolitan newspaper, reaching every neighborhood from the inner city to the affluent suburbs, but this diversity restrained it from taking up any single constituency's point of view. Affluence further affected the newsroom. Greider had joined the staff during the *Post*'s leaner years and had watched its reporters become "upwardly mobile in spite of ourselves." The scruffy, long-haired, counterculture phase of the newsroom made way for journalists who toted briefcases. Personnel practices favored applicants from the Ivy League, producing a generation of secular, socially tolerant journalists, whose attitudes inevitably infiltrated their work.[56]

What some perceived as a liberal bias could also be defined as a "social distance" growing between Washington reporters and large segments of their readers. Richard Harwood, who had grown up during the Great Depression, ridden the rails, and fought in the marines before joining the *Washington Post* as a reporter, editor, and columnist, expressed irritation with the young, upwardly mobile professionals who had taken over the newsroom and were remaking journalism in their image. Because of them, papers such as the *Post* now dealt with average folks only "in some Archie Bunker way," Harwood complained. "The poor, the blacks, the people in trouble, we don't tell our readers much about the world they live in." Washington journalists enjoyed lifestyles consistent with their incomes. They lived in the best neighborhoods, vacationed abroad, drove expensive cars, and took sabbaticals to write books. "Yes, we're snobs," agreed Alex Johnson, an editor in the *Post*'s Metro section. He pointed out that few reporters of his generation had served in the military, raised a family on the minimum wage, or ridden the bus to work. The rest of the Washington press corps had undergone a similar social and economic transformation, but *Washington Post* reporters lived where their paper was published, which magnified their social distance from much of their readership.[57]

The *Washington Post* was both a national paper and a local paper in a city with a majority African American population. The *Post* did not hire a black general news reporter until 1952, and that experiment in integration had failed when the reporter, Simeon Booker, resigned after a year of feeling harassed and isolated. Nor did the *Post* attract many black readers until 1954, when it absorbed the *Times-Herald,* the white paper with the highest circulation in black neighborhoods. In 1957 the *Post* hired Wallace Terry, an African American graduate of Brown University who as a student had managed to interview Arkansas governor Orville Faubus during his resistance to school integration. William Raspberry joined the *Post* in 1962 as a teletype operator, having previously reported for the *Indianapolis Recorder,* a black weekly. Raspberry moved up to library assistant, police reporter, and copy editor. Reporter Leon Dash commented that blacks were still an "oddity" in the newsroom and had to prove themselves to skeptical white colleagues. While a student at Howard University, Dash came to the *Post* as a copyboy and took umbrage when reporters summoned him with the cry "Boy!" Judith Martin, who had suffered the indignity herself as a copygirl, recalled watching one day when a white reporter called "Boy!" A copyboy who looked "ten feet tall with Afro and dashiki" arrived and asked what he had called him. "Sir," the reporter replied meekly.[58]

As the civil rights saga developed, the *Post* sent interracial teams to cover racially oriented stories. The paper paired Wallace Terry with a white reporter to cover civil rights in the South, and sent a white man and a black woman to cover James Meredith's entry into the University of Mississippi. Bill Chapman covered the white campus, while Dorothy Gilliam wrote about the black community's reaction. He stayed at a motel, but the only accommodation she could find was at a black funeral home. When rioting broke out in the Watts area of Los Angeles in 1965, the *Post* pulled William Raspberry off copyediting and sent him to Los Angeles, teamed with veteran reporter Chalmers Roberts. That experience won Raspberry a promotion to general assignment reporter, and soon after that he became the *Post*'s first black columnist. By April 1968, when rioting and looting broke out in downtown Washington following the assassination of Martin Luther King Jr., the *Post*'s newsroom could send fourteen black reporters and photographers to cover the turmoil, in a way that the capital's many all-white bureaus could not match. Black reporters were later outraged to find that whites got all the front-page bylines. Because every available black reporter had been on the streets, whites had worked the phones in the newsroom when they called in their stories. The *Post* normally gave credit to the rewriters. The outcry prompted a change in policy to add a box containing the names of all reporters who contributed to a story.[59]

The *Post*'s first full-time African American woman reporter, Dorothy Butler Gilliam, had written for the black press and attended the Columbia School of Journalism, but when she interviewed for a job in 1961 she was advised to "go off in the boondocks for a couple of years and get some experience, and maybe you'll be good enough for the *Post*." Instead, Gilliam went to Kenya with Operation Crossroads (a forerunner of the Peace Corps) and sent some pieces about Africa back to the *Post*. They struck a spark and got her hired. She entered a newsroom that consisted almost entirely of white men. City editor Ben Gilbert went out of his way to help her adjust. He agreed not to stereotype Gilliam by assigning her only to write about poverty, welfare, and civil rights (although it took her a while to realize that those were precisely the news stories that would give her "page-one play"). When Gilliam had children, she requested part-time work but was rejected on the grounds that it would ruin the morale of the men who wanted time off to write their novels. She left to freelance, and later returned to the *Post* in 1972, when black staff members were protesting their exclusion from editorial positions. She became the first African American assistant editor at Style.[60]

Working under a sympathetic editor, Gilliam fielded a group of black reporters who wanted to capture modern black culture. They soon began to hear rumblings that white reporters "looked at the Style section and thought it was the *Afro-American*." A new editor reshuffled assignments and placed Gilliam in charge of anything but black culture. She proposed that she edit the *Post*'s Sunday magazine *Potomac*. (The *Post* also distributed the nationally syndicated *Parade* each Sunday, because, as Bradlee explained, "Mrs. Graham wanted a magazine for people who moved their lips when they read.") Bradlee intended to revamp the dowdy magazine but was not yet sure what he wanted. He countered by offering her a column in Metro, reasoning that she could move around town "in circles where no one else moved." The column assured Gilliam space in the paper on a regular basis without having to run story ideas past anyone. Her editors encouraged her to do people-oriented profiles, but she preferred writing more point-of-view columns that reflected her growing racial consciousness. In a column about a Ku Klux Klan march in Washington, she defended a minor rampage staged by Klan opponents as justifiable—a stand that brought "tons of letters" in protest. One thing she learned about white culture, Gilliam commented, was that "you don't ever condone any damage to personal property." Although never censored, she had lost the confidence of her editors. When Gilliam took a sabbatical to write a book, the *Post* replaced her with a younger black columnist with a less confrontational style.[61]

For both whites and blacks the *Post* was a demanding place to work. Creative tension fostered competition but not much guidance for newcomers. The paper hired graduates from the best universities, after intense screening, and then assigned them to beats in the far suburbs. Black reporters could never feel sure whether editors singled them out for their race or whether they treated everyone so poorly. They suspected that white reporters regarded them as in-terlopers rather than colleagues. Assigned to a three-man team, Nathan McCall doubted that the two white reporters ever backed him up. He observed them whispering with their white editor, who made excuses for them while showing impatience toward McCall. He wondered if this was "racist, merely competi-tive, or both."[62]

The specter of Janet Cooke also haunted the *Washington Post*. She had come to the *Post* with an impressive but inflated resumé, and had worked her way from the back-of-the-paper District Weekly to the front pages. When her block-buster story "Jimmy's World" appeared, editors at the *Post* protected her from city officials who demanded the boy's identity so he could get medical treat-ment. The editors belatedly examined her notes and the tale did not hold up. After a lengthy investigation, the *Post*'s ombudsman, Bill Green, concluded that the newsroom culture led newcomers such as Cooke to assume that ad-vancement came only through writing "big-splash" stories. Green faulted the *Post*'s editorial system for wanting Cooke's story so badly that it never verified her claims. Ben Bradlee's instinct for eyebrow-raising articles bore a lot of the burden for the debacle. Bradlee remained with the *Post* for another decade, until he turned seventy, but the newsroom turned more cautious.[63]

The *Washington Post* stepped up its drive to diversify both its newsroom and its news coverage. Eventually it led every major metropolitan newspaper, including the *New York Times,* in its percentage of black readers. Yet its black reporters remained dissatisfied. Dorothy Gilliam and Jill Nelson organized a black woman's caucus to improve the status and salaries of women at the *Post*. Nelson became an officer of the Baltimore-Washington Newspaper Guild, which filed complaints with the Office of Human Rights charging the *Post* with discrimination by age, race, and sex. A comparison of salaries showed that black women at the *Post* received smaller salaries than any other employ-ees. Black reporters made an effort to obtain overtime pay, which the *Post* op-posed on the grounds that federal labor law exempted professionals from such requirements. In defining the reporters' trade, the *Post*'s attorney explained that reporting involved gathering facts rather than expressing opinion, which caused federal judge Gerhard Gesell, who was hearing the case, to quip, "I've been reading that rag for a long time," the judge quipped. "There is consider-able editorializing on the front page."[64]

Racial protests erupted over the premiere issue of the Sunday *Washington Post Magazine* in 1986. An editor imported from *People* magazine had set out to deal with serious issues and not to pander to the "Georgetown set," but had unwisely run the first cover story on a black rap singer charged with murder. The same issue carried a column by Richard Cohen sympathizing with white jewelers who locked black youths out of their stores. A local radio broadcaster invited irate citizens to dump piles of the magazine outside the *Post*. "Years ago we wrote things with impunity because it was white males writing for other white males," Cohen conceded. "We didn't give much thought to people who weren't like us." The fiasco encouraged the *Post* to set goals for hiring minority staff, after which African Americans became more visible in the newsroom. That policy was thrown back at the paper by a *New Republic* cover story claiming a racial backlash within the *Post*. Writer Ruth Shalit quoted anonymous white staffers who complained that minorities were receiving special treatment in recruitment, assignments, and promotions. Stung by the quotes, black reporters circulated a memo denouncing their "gutless colleagues" who disparaged them anonymously. Those cited by name accused Shalit of misrepresenting them, and the *Post* reminded readers that serious charges had been raised against Shalit's work (causing her soon after to resign from the *New Republic*). *Post* editors denounced her charges as "maliciously hurtful," although conceding that the paper had "surfaced those tensions" itself by confronting racial issues so openly.[65]

Donald Graham succeeded his mother as publisher in 1979, and Leonard Downie Jr. followed Ben Bradlee as executive editor in 1991. No Ivy Leaguer, Downie had attended Ohio State University on a journalism scholarship and was dubbed in the newsroom "Land Grant Len." He came to the *Post* as a summer intern in 1964 and never worked for another paper. Downie and Donald Graham adopted a more low-key manner than their stylish predecessors. "We're the dull guys," Downie jested. Yet between them the *Washington Post* became what Eugene Meyer had hoped for, no matter how implausible that seemed when he purchased the bankrupt shell of a paper. The *Post* entered the twenty-first century with a news staff of almost nine hundred, operating out of its Washington headquarters, a dozen suburban bureaus, a half dozen national bureaus, and twenty-two foreign bureaus. It also established an extensive Internet presence. For all that, some reporters looked back nostalgically to the days when Bradlee gave the *Post* its flair and "breaking-news mentality."[66]

Downie's strict standards of objectivity kept him from voting in order to maintain his neutrality. Earlier he had done investigative reporting and had seen journalism as a means of awakening an "indifferent public" to action. But after Watergate, Downie concluded that the *Post* had overreached and needed to be more modest. "The paper is so big, our concerns are so high," he wrote, "that we may have missed ordinary people." Under his editorship the *Post* accelerated its efforts to broaden its local audience. He encouraged more analyses of race, religion, and poverty. Each section of the *Post* had set amounts of column space, but the "news hole"—the space available for news stories—did not depend on the amount of advertising coming in, as was the case with most other papers. When a major story broke, extra pages could accommodate anything from a presidential impeachment to a terrorist attack. The *Post* could afford it: the company's annual revenues of $84 million when Katharine Graham took over in 1963 had spiraled to $1.4 billion. The *Post*'s news budget, which stood at \$4 million when Bradlee took over, reached \$100 million by the century's end.[67]

Once known as a tough town for newspapers, Washington, D.C., had blossomed into one of the best newspaper markets in the country. A city hungry for news had a paper shrewd enough to tailor itself not only to those who ran the government, "but also for the people who clean their offices." Donald Graham deliberately held the *Post*'s newsstand price low to keep its circulation among minorities high, calculating that every price increase would "whiten the readership another shade." If some readers and reporters lamented that the paper lacked its earlier flair, Katharine Graham explained that it had been easier to produce a sparkling paper when they were still building it up. "When you get full grown, so to speak, it makes it harder to take the risks that Ben and, I guess, I took. Size and success make you more cautious." By the time that Donald Graham stepped aside as publisher to devote himself to the company's business side in 2000, the *Post* rested on a rock solid financial and readership base. If not equal to the *New York Times* nationally, it had achieved primacy in the national capital. Or as the Washington editor for *USA Today*, Don Campbell, advised aspiring journalists, "If you want to be considered a serious reporter, act like one. Don't even pick up the phone in the morning until you've read the *Washington Post*."[68]

12

Anyone with a Modem

Watching a rerun of *All the President's Men* a quarter century after Watergate, *Washington Post* music critic Joseph McLellan marveled at how little the newsroom it portrayed had changed since then, until he caught sight of the actor Dustin Hoffman, playing Carl Bernstein, inserting a sheet of six–ply paper into his typewriter. That brought back memories of the thick sheaves of carbons and the pneumatic tubes that carried them to the composing room. He also recalled that "to file a story from outside the office, you had to find a telephone and call the dictation department," practices that already seemed quaint. By the time he retired in 2001, everything about the news—writing, editing, and disseminating it—had gone digital.[1]

For the news business, the digital revolution happened with breathtaking speed. Until the 1980s, newspapers had invested more in computers for their pressrooms than for their newsrooms. Just as the introduction of advanced technology triggered labor unrest among the printers, it met with resistance from reporters. A natural distaste for any disruption of their work habits was heightened by the relentless expansion of newspaper chains and media conglomerates that had eroded reporters' sense of autonomy and job security. Moreover, "digitized" newsrooms involved not just new tools for the workplace but the possibility of an entirely new form of electronic media. Washington correspondents had traditionally resented any new media, belittling its ability to report the news while anguishing over its potential competition, and the Internet was no exception. Responding to this intransigence in 1993, Michael Crichton, the author of *Jurassic Park*, warned journalists at the National Press Club that they must evolve with the new technology or risk becoming fossils. "To my mind, it is likely that what we now understand as the mass media will be gone within ten years—vanished without a trace," Crichton forecast. He envisioned a future that appeared on computer screens linked by the World Wide Web. Advocates believed that the Internet would empower users by providing them "unfiltered news," from verbatim transcripts to videos, and turn audiences from passive recipients into interactive participants.[2]

The first computers installed in newsrooms were cumbersome, slow, and unreliable, and there were never enough terminals to go around. The *New York Times* spent millions to make its back clippings electronically accessible during the 1970s, but produced a system that was so complicated that staff continued to use the paper's antiquated morgue. Some reporters found it challenging just to use electronic mail. "Once you've mastered sending and receiving messages outside of your interoffice system, jumping around the computer systems may seem a bit less foreboding," an instructional manual assured the fainthearted. The new equipment muscled out longtime traditions of the trade. In the press galleries, reporters had been used to yanking a story from the typewriter and shouting "Copy!" A Western Union copy aide would run by, grab it, and rush it to an operator to telegraph it to the newspaper. Once reporters could send dispatches to their papers electronically, by the mid-1990s, the telegraph was entirely removed from the Capitol, where Samuel Morse had first demonstrated it 150 years earlier. The wire services also disposed of the bulky teletype machines when they could send reports online. At the same time, reporters began using the Internet for research, some perhaps too much. Editor Howell Raines was astonished to learn that a *New York Times* reporter declined to go on reporting trips because he felt he could get whatever information he needed from the Internet. But readers had access to the same sources, which troubled print journalists such as the *Washington Post*'s Richard Leiby. "It used to be that editors and writers like me were in charge of the news," Leiby wrote. "We filed the stories or scrolled through the wire service reports exclusively available to us, and decided (arrogantly, perhaps) what you should read the next morning. Then along came the Internet, and suddenly John and Jane Doe were able to download the wire feeds and access all the White House briefing transcripts they cared to."[3]

Hope and fear drew newspapers and networks online. News organizations felt that they could not simply fight the kind of rearguard action that they had once waged against broadcasters. Polls showed that people in their twenties were less likely than their parents to read a newspaper and would be more attracted to the availability of news on demand. If the Internet was indeed going to open a portal to the future of global communications, publishers felt they had to leap through before any rivals beat them to it. Troubled by the prospect of competition for advertising from Microsoft and America Online, *Washington Post* publisher Donald Graham summed up his paper's need to succeed online in three words: "classifieds, classifieds, classifieds." The first newspapers to foray into cyberspace simply replicated themselves electronically, with scant awareness that the digital audience expected more graphics, interactivity, and attitude—without having to pay for it. Attempts to charge subscriptions for online news services met with failure generally, and assumptions that the Internet would require no change in reporting style proved equally wrong. Michael Kinsley left the old world of print and broadcast media to edit Microsoft's Internet journal *Slate*, fully intending to inject some serious journalism into it. Web realities quickly forced him to cut stories down in size, overcome his suspicion of interactive bulletin boards, add links to other sites, and give up trying to charge fees. Kinsley's readers surfed from site to site. "If they really like a particular site, they may visit it often," he commented, "but they are unlikely to devote a continuous half-hour or more to any one site the way you might read a traditional paper or magazine in one sitting."[4]

Feeling their way through the web, the established media encountered a brash new world of virtual journalists. Internet news sites constituted an alternative media that in many ways mirrored the alternative press that the counterculture had spawned in the 1960s and 1970s. Both appealed to the young and the alienated. Both operated with limited budgets and tapped affordable systems of distribution. Sold cheaply on street corners, the counterculture's "seedier media" had thumbed their collective noses at big government, big business, and big universities. In 1969 more than a hundred papers were signed onto the politically oriented Liberation News Service, while hundreds more got their news from the Underground Press Syndicate, which showed less interest in politics than in sex, drugs, and music (making it far more attractive to advertisers). Harassment from the FBI and the Internal Revenue Service, and apathy among activists following the abolition of the military draft, caused so many of these papers to fold that even the term "underground" disappeared: the Underground Press Syndicate renamed itself the Alternative Press Syndicate. By the 1970s the alternative press provided entry for aspiring reporters who considered the mainstream media too aloof and stodgy for their political inclinations. By the 1990s, the Internet produced its own jumble of magazines, online news sites, and one-person web logs. These venues offered independent entrepreneurs an opportunity to circulate their commentary without the nuisance of editors and fact-checkers. Smaller sites aimed at niche audiences defined the Internet more than did the established media, despite all its resources. For all the commonality in their methods, the two alternative media were separated by an ideological gap. The counterculture's alternative press had leaned to the left, while a preponderance of Internet news sites tilted to the right. The conservative commentator Ann Coulter called the Internet a "samizdat media," comparing it to the Russian underground press that had once challenged authorities in the Soviet Union.[5]

More skeptically, the blue-ribbon Committee of Concerned Journalists concluded from a series of studies in 1998 that rapid technological change had thrown American journalism into "a state of disorientation." The proliferation of cable television, talk radio, and Internet news outlets had caused a scramble for audiences and revenues that pushed reporting toward sensationalism and untempered opinion. Round-the-clock deadlines made it harder for reporters to sort out the substantive from the speculative and spurious. The copious presentation of information in "real time"—live as it happened—created more chance for error and distortion, and gave news reporting, in the eyes of the concerned journalists, "a more chaotic, unsettled, and even numbing quality." Mounting competition between media also enhanced the bargaining position of the reporters' sources, who could shop a story from one news outlet to another, until someone agreed to release it on their terms—leaving the rest of the media to stampede after it. The clash of cultures between the established media and its innovative alternatives produced a pungent atmosphere that would cloud most of Bill Clinton's presidency. It would also embroil his closest ally in the Washington press corps in a protracted legal battle with an Internet antagonist.[6]

As a force in the news, the Internet broke into Washington's political consciousness through an assault on an alumnus of the older alternative media. Sidney Blumenthal, a former alternative press reporter, had made his way into the mainstream as a prominent correspondent and news analyst. On the night before he was due to join the White House staff as a special assistant to President Clinton, in August 1997, he clicked onto the *Drudge Report* and read: "New White House Recruit Sidney Blumenthal Has Spousal Abuse Past." Matt Drudge, an Internet gossip purveyor nearly twenty years Blumenthal's junior, reported that "top GOP operatives" were spreading word of his history of wife beating. Drudge also quoted a "White House source" who dismissed the charge as fallacious, and added that he had been unable to reach Blumenthal for comment. Blumenthal's wife Jacqueline, who headed the White House fellows' program, had warned her husband when he accepted the presidential appointment, "The day you have to hire a lawyer is the day you're out of there." As it turned out, Blumenthal hired a lawyer on his first day on the job. With the president's approval, the former Washington correspondent sued the Internet gossip columnist for libel and demanded that he reveal his anonymous sources.[7]

Chicago-born Sidney Blumenthal got his start in politics as a twelve-year-old "runner," paid by a local Democratic precinct captain to round up votes during the 1960 election. He attended a campaign rally where John Kennedy spoke, and when he learned that Kennedy read the *New York Times,* Blumenthal began reading that paper religiously. "To me growing up in the Midwest," he reflected, "newspapers were the opening up of the world." At Brandeis University during the turbulent 1960s, he joined Students for a Democratic Society, the radical student organization that vied against militarism abroad and injustice and inequality at home. Upon graduating in 1969, Blumenthal found work as a reporter for a Boston underground newspaper, the *Phoenix.* "It was only partly about journalism," a colleague defined the paper. "It was about politics and counterculture." Alternative journalism served as an extension of New Left politics, taking on the establishment through edgy, adversarial, and investigative reporting. It never occurred to them, Blumenthal later commented, "that we should toil in backwater small-town newspapers and work our way up the chain until we arrived at a big-city daily." Anything but neutral, the generation of New Left journalists felt less restrained by the boundaries of "objective journalism," because they intended to take sides and shake things up.[8]

First at the *Phoenix* and then at the *Real Paper,* Blumenthal reported on Boston politics, chronicling the disintegration of the New Deal Democratic coalition as it confronted such socially explosive issues as abortion and school busing. In 1980 he organized his columns into a discerning book, *The Permanent Campaign,* in which he charted the rise of new-style pollsters and consultants who intended to run government like a political campaign. Blumenthal attributed Ronald Reagan's victory that year to shrewd media politics, and he blamed liberal journalists' insistence on professional detachment and neutrality for failing to prevent the conservative resurgence. In his view, the left needed the media's help to restore its public appeal.[9]

During the 1984 presidential election, Blumenthal became national political correspondent for the *New Republic* and covered Colorado senator Gary Hart's challenge to Vice President Walter Mondale for the Democratic nomination. Despite its modest circulation, the *New Republic* exerted a substantial pull within the Washington press corps. It offered writers modest salaries but high profiles, and served as a springboard to advancement. Blumenthal supplemented his income by providing campaign commentary for the *Today* show, where his appearances caught the attention of Katharine Graham. *Washington Post* editors hired him in 1985, hoping to use him to stir up its national reporting during the second Reagan administration.[10]

No sooner had Blumenthal joined the paper than another *Post* reporter, Martin Schram, published a campaign history that credited him with transforming Gary Hart from "a lackluster campaigner and pedantic speaker" into "a forceful and thematic and effective one." The turning point in Hart's campaign had been his "New Generation of Leadership" speech at Brandeis University, where he offered himself as an alternative between "the outworn positions of the Reagan Republicans, who care only for a few, and the outmoded ideas of those Democrats who promise everything to everybody." A Hart campaign aide told Schram that Sidney Blumenthal had crafted the speech and afterward had written a glowing cover story for the *New Republic* about Hart's new ideas. Blumenthal explained this conflict of interest by describing the *New Republic* as a journal of opinion with "a long history of involvement in campaigns." But this analytical approach to journalism involved more polemics than news reporting generally permitted, and because the *Washington Post*'s national staff already viewed him suspiciously for not having paid his dues as a working reporter, the paper shifted Blumenthal to its Style section.[11]

Calling Style "a daily alternative newspaper within the paper," Blumenthal created a "conservative beat" there, producing a stream of articles that documented the rise of a new right-wing establishment. Some conservatives appreciated getting serious attention from a prominent newspaper such as the *Post,* but Blumenthal's criticism grated on most of them. Particularly offended were those former New Leftists turned neoconservatives, whom he depicted as suffering from "multiple forms of alienation—personal, professional, and political." One of his articles mocked David Horowitz and Peter Collier for shifting to Reaganites after being editors of *Ramparts* (the audacious New Left monthly that challenged the establishment from 1962 to 1975). Horowitz read it as an effort to isolate them and resented being portrayed as having abandoned his principles and his family for a hedonistic life. After protesting to the *Post,* Horowitz got the offending article dropped from its weekly edition, but Blumenthal compounded the insult by reprinting it in one of his books.[12]

An extramarital affair evicted Gary Hart from his second run for president in 1988, and left Blumenthal in search of another New Democrat with new ideas. When he boosted the candidacy of Massachusetts governor Michael Dukakis, the Washington writer Christopher Hitchens marveled at Blumenthal's "ability to put a radical shine on the most wretched Democratic nominees." Even before Dukakis lost that election, the reporter had met a more charismatic contender, Arkansas governor Bill Clinton. By 1992, Blumenthal had returned to the *New Republic,* this time writing a cover story that anointed Clinton as the front-runner for the next Democratic nomination. Blumenthal berated other reporters who lacked his enthusiasm for Clinton. They regarded Blumenthal as a campaign insider. To tap his Clinton connections, the *New Yorker's* trendy editor Tina Brown hired Blumenthal as the magazine's Washington editor to write its prestigious "Letter from Washington."[13]

As the press corps began to dig into Bill Clinton's personal life, Blumenthal steadfastly refused to join the pack. His reluctance to write about President Clinton's involvement in the failed Whitewater real estate deal caused the *New Yorker* to assign the story to someone else, and that reporter came to suspect that Blumenthal was warning Clinton's team not to talk to him. Before long, the *New Yorker* replaced Blumenthal as Washington editor with his polar opposite, Michael Kelly. Born into a family of Washington journalists, Kelly still managed to write as an angry outsider. He had come to regret having voted for Clinton in 1992, and had moved to the political right, disparaging liberals and blasting the new president with spiraling stridency. Kelly called Clinton a liar and an opportunist, and saw Blumenthal as the president's shill. Although Blumenthal remained a special political correspondent for the *New Yorker*, animosities ran so high that the new Washington editor barred his predecessor from entering the magazine's Washington office. Blumenthal defined himself more charitably as a "cross between a reporter and an analyst and a columnist," who was carrying on the tradition of "access journalism" once practiced by Walter Lippmann and Joseph Alsop. He lamented that the old practice of according Washington correspondents status based on their high-level sources had been "flipped on its head in the post-Watergate era." Reporters now set out to demolish public officials rather than to cultivate them. Blumenthal wrote a play on the subject, *This Town*, which he staged at the National Press Club, twitting the press corps as scandal-crazed.[14]

Few Washington journalists were therefore surprised when Blumenthal quit their ranks to join Clinton's administration at the start of its second term in 1997. As assistant to the president he would work on communications strategy, review material for press briefings, prep the president for his press conferences, and analyze what the talk shows and news programs reported. His job would not involve speaking on the record or appearing on camera as an official spokesman. The former alternative press outsider had made the leap to ultimate Washington insider, with an office in the West Wing. He denied it had been that much of a leap, however, as he had gone into journalism to "help make a difference."[15]

What did seem surprising was that Blumenthal had bothered at all to click on the *Drudge Report*, which the liberal columnist Joe Conason labeled the "favorite web page of the credulous right wing." Yet even those who deplored Drudge's politics found guilty pleasure in reading his mix of Hollywood and Washington gossip. Matt Drudge grew up as a self-described "aimless teen" in the Washington suburbs. Drudge delivered the afternoon *Washington Star* and spent his nights listening to a police scanner he called his "unconditional best friend." Poor grades kept him out of college, and he wound up working the swing shift at the local 7-Eleven. There at least he could read the newspapers during the early morning hours. At other times he wandered through downtown Washington, gazing enviously at the news bureaus where he knew he stood no chance of being hired.[16]

Escaping from a dead end in Washington, Drudge headed to Los Angeles and found work at the CBS gift shop. In 1994 his father bought him a Radio Shack computer to help him find some direction in life, and Drudge began posting items on the Internet. Within a year he started the *Drudge Report*, replete with recycled material from the trashcans at CBS, anything from the Nielsen ratings to the scuttlebutt about TV stars. A sociologist who studied the effects of the virtual world found that Internet users often imagined themselves at the "center of the universe," and used computers "as a portal to a different world of experiences" beyond the pedestrian communities around them. Drudge felt exhilarated in the virtual world, where for practically no cost he could send "any*thing* from any*where* out to *everyone*." The Internet made him a journalist without credentials—or editors, as his sloppy copy plainly indicated. Drudge's father ran his own Internet reference site with handy online access to dictionaries and encyclopedias. The *Drudge Report* instead linked to news services, columnists, and commentators. It stood among a crowd of sites that made the Internet's vast store of information more accessible by serving as convenient intermediaries between producers and consumers. In his case the product he gathered was news that others had reported or discarded.[17]

Adopting Walter Winchell's trademark fedora, Drudge patterned himself after the gossip columnist who had turned mud into gold. Gossip had been an element of national news since George Washington's administration, but for years the press corps clung to a reluctance to reveal private behavior unless it infringed on public business. In print, reporters cleaned up politicians' language and ignored many of their indiscretions. Even writing about the posthumous revelations of John F. Kennedy's extramarital affairs made some Washington correspondents feel as if they were smearing themselves with mud. Coming on the heels of Watergate, however, suppressing the Kennedy affairs seemed like self-induced blindness. Columnist Lewis Lapham compared Kennedy's sexual appetite to Richard Nixon's neuroses and blamed journalists' unwillingness to report on personal character for the election of "damaged politicians." To Lapham, the traditional code of protecting privacy had encouraged politicians to tell partial truths and construct misleading images, which too often had resulted in public disillusionment. In the following years, the explosion of new media, from talk radio to cable television and the Internet steadily reversed attitudes about privacy and eroded media tolerance for indiscretion.[18]

Despite a lack of experience or resources, Matt Drudge styled himself an "Internet Reporter." He collected news by scanning newspapers online, watching cable television, and picking up tips via e-mail. His unadorned web page was accessible at no charge and initially without advertisements. He derived a modest income from fees he charged his e-mail subscribers, and kept costs down by working out of his apartment. Impressed by Drudge's resourcefulness and bravado, the Internet writer Scott Shuger wrote a flattering profile of him in 1996. The *New Yorker* turned it down—Drudge at the time did not generate sufficient "buzz"—and the story ran instead in *Los Angeles Magazine*. Instead of dismissing Drudge as someone who simply sat in his apartment and read e-mail, Shuger asked, "What does a newsman do at *The New York Times*? He gets on the phone with people. What's the difference?" The Internet was a democratic phenomenon, where any citizen could be a reporter, and where any "computer geek" could have an equal voice with prominent journalists and politicians. Less tolerant reviewers thought the *Drudge Report* showed what could be done if one lacked taste and restraint. The Washington correspondent Jules Witcover dismissed Drudge as "a reckless trader in rumor and gossip," who passed along reports he could not verify. Even the admiring Scott Shuger admitted that Drudge too often operated "without adult supervision." Drudge's creeping obsession with Bill Clinton made him a magnet for undigested gossip about members of Clinton's administration—such as the spousal abuse allegations against Blumenthal. As Shuger noted, "He didn't go look in court papers—which is sort of Journalism 101."[19]

The Internet fostered large quantities of sarcasm, suspicion, and conspiracy theories, for which the Clinton presidency provided an irresistible target. Clinton came to office assuming that talk shows and cable television represented the wave of the future, which would free him from wasting time on such "old modes" of communication as televised press conferences. Sidney Blumenthal wrote in the *New Yorker* that Clinton's staff attempted to tap "every media outlet except the Washington correspondents." The media had truly changed in the dozen years since the Democrats last occupied the White House, but the alteration had not been in their favor. After the Federal Communications Commissions abolished the "fairness doctrine," the new media, from cable to talk radio to the Internet, abandoned balance for bombast. Overtly ideological commentators fixed on everything from Whitewater to the suicide of a White House aide, rather than the administration's agenda. By chance, Clinton was appearing on *Larry King Live* when word came of Vincent Foster's suicide. Unlike the congenial King, other talk show hosts relished conspiracy theories and sensational accusations that disparaged the president and his wife.[20]

An anti-Clinton undercurrent swept through the Internet well before Matt Drudge turned his attention to national politics. His first political scoop came in 1996, when a Republican insider tipped him off that Bob Dole planned to select Jack Kemp for his vice presidential running mate. The *Drudge Report*, supplied by no end of anonymous sources, soon fixed its sights on Bill Clinton. On July 4, 1997, Drudge reported that *Newsweek*'s investigative reporter Michael Isikoff was "hot on the trail" of a woman who claimed that the president had sexually propositioned her. Two weeks after that report appeared, America Online announced that it had hired the "Runaway Gossip Success" because Drudge fit AOL's "style and demographic" with his "instant, edgy information." By that time, the *Drudge Report* was going to 85,000 e-mail subscribers, with thousands more visiting the site gratis. Later that month, Drudge identified the president's accuser, Kathleen Willey, and mocked *Newsweek* for lacking the nerve to run the story. His reports nudged *Newsweek* and other mainstream publications into reporting the sordid accusations. Isikoff angrily regarded Drudge as a scavenger who spread bits of raw reporting. "This is not harmless fun; it's reckless and ought to be condemned," the reporter protested. "He ought not to be treated as an impish character." Sidney Blumenthal soon after encountered Isikoff at a Washington party and commented, "We have a common enemy."[21]

In August, when the spousal abuse charge appeared, Blumenthal hired an attorney and threatened Drudge with legal action for maliciously spreading falsehoods. Drudge belatedly attempted to verify the story—the kind of journalistic drudgery he should have done before publishing it. "This is a case of using me to broadcast dirty laundry," he admitted. "I think I've been had." Drudge issued an online retraction, but couched it by insisting that he had reported the story "in good faith." He also refused to identify his sources. Sidney and Jacqueline Blumenthal went ahead and filed suit, seeking $10 million in compensatory damages and $20 million in punitive damages. They intended to make the point that the laws of libel applied online as in print, and that Internet sites could not "spread false stories, even about a public figure." Only three years earlier the first Internet libel suit had been filed by Benjamin Suarez against the breezy online newsletter, *Cyberwire Dispatch,* that had accused him of spamming (or blanket e-mailing to promote products). In an out-of-court settlement, Suarez received $64 in court costs. The proliferation of Internet "clipping services" that culled news from elsewhere provoked another suit in 1997 when six media organizations, including the *Washington Post,* sued a "virtual newsstand," TotalNEWS, for "framing" their sites. (Framing was the practice of a web site copying someone else's copyrighted material and pasting it within its own identifying frame on the screen.) TotalNEWS agreed to link to the other media sites rather than framing them.[22]

Matt Drudge was hardly in a position to pay $30 million, but Blumenthal's lawsuit made America Online a codefendant for paying Drudge a salary, promoting his web site, and not immediately removing the slanderous material. In its defense, AOL defined itself as a "news-packaging" not a "news-gathering" operation. It had no more control over the *Drudge Report,* AOL insisted, than a bookstore did over the publications it sold. *USA Today* columnist Susan Estrich wrote about the First Amendment aspects of Blumenthal's suit and was surprised to receive a phone call from a White House deputy press secretary, who complained that she was "under contract" to AOL: Her newspaper column was also carried on the AOL web site *The Great Debate.* If this was a private lawsuit, Estrich asked, why had a White House official registered the complaint? The issue became moot when a federal judge dropped AOL from the suit on the grounds that Congress had granted Internet providers statutory immunity. Federal law treated AOL as a newsstand, not a publisher.[23]

Liberals in the media generally sided with Blumenthal against Drudge's recklessness. They rejected the notion that the Internet's speed in any way voided the old journalistic requirement of fact-checking. Conservatives responded that the lawsuit endangered freedom of expression. They portrayed Drudge as "a modern Tom Paine." Michael Ledeen, a former Reagan administration official who wrote for the *American Spectator,* had been a target of what he called Blumenthal's "mean-spirited" reporting during the Iran-Contra scandal. Ledeen's wife contacted the writer David Horowitz for help in Drudge's defense. As director of the Los Angeles-based Individual Rights Foundation, Horowitz rallied to the cause by setting up a legal fund for the "Internet David" against the "White House Goliath." He arranged for an attorney to handle Drudge's defense, and posted an online "Matt Drudge Information Center." Horowitz called on reporters to put aside their "snobbish disdain for cyberspace journalism" and consider the potential consequences of Blumenthal's lawsuit.[24]

Any expectation Sidney Blumenthal might have had about his lawsuit restraining the *Drudge Report* was seriously mistaken. On January 17, 1998, Drudge posted a "World Exclusive" that *Newsweek* had killed another story by Michael Isikoff, this time about the president's affair with a former White House intern. As he pressed the enter button, Drudge felt a thrill from "taking on the most powerful man in the free world from a Hollywood apartment using the Internet." Presidential press secretary Michael McCurry dismissed the charge as just "more sludge from Drudge." The story remained Drudge's questionable exclusive for four days, until the *Washington Post* gave it credence with its own front-page version. Not until then did the rest of the media and the public pay much attention. Drudge declared it his "Paul Revere moment," crowing that all those thousands of reporters in Washington had missed the story.[25]

New York Times editor Joseph Lelyveld later called it disgraceful that an Internet gossip columnist had "set the agenda for mainstream news organizations," including his own. The scandal transformed Drudge into a much-sought-after guest on television news shows and the subject of glossy magazine profiles. Shaken members of the Washington press corps reasoned that Drudge might be irresponsible, but he was reporting on a personally irresponsible president. "We're in a new world in terms of the way information flows to the nation," said James O'Shea, an editor at the *Chicago Tribune.* "The days when you can decide not to print a story because it's not well enough sourced are long gone." When the *Drudge Report* and others broke stories on their web sites that they could not substantiate, the mainstream media felt compelled to tell readers about the charges they made. The Monica Lewinsky scandal did for the Internet what the Kennedy assassination had done for network television, its boosters insisted, making the web the first place to turn for news.[26]

The *Washington Post*'s star investigator Bob Woodward dismissed Drudge as someone who "got lucky" when the Lewinsky rumors turned out to be true. Drudge snapped back that he had gotten the scoop because *Newsweek,* which was owned by the Washington Post Company, had failed to publish it. He boasted of having been "First to report that Lewinsky had signed an affidavit denying a relationship with the president. . . . First to report that there were tapes. . . . First to report the dirty dress. . . . First to report that the president had invoked executive privilege. . . . First to report the cigar, the sex before church on Sundays. . . . First with over 20 exclusive stories later confirmed in the Starr impeachment referral. . . . First to report that Bob Woodward looks great in green."[27]

When reporters asked about the Lewinsky allegations, Sidney Blumenthal responded, "I don't put much stock in the *Drudge Report* because, among other reasons, I'm suing him for defamation." From the White House, Blumenthal fought back against Drudge's allegations and against a steady stream of leaks from the staff of special prosecutor Kenneth Starr by faxing stories critical of Starr to various Washington reporters. He also wielded the lawsuit as a weapon. Blumenthal's attorney responded to Drudge's appearance on NBC's *Meet the Press* by criticizing moderator Tim Russert for having treated Drudge like "a reputable journalist." If Russert intended to testify on behalf of Drudge, "to vouch for his credentials as a journalist," the lawyer wrote, then "we wish to take your deposition." This idle threat seems to have been aimed at denying the Internet reporter a mainstream forum.[28]

Blumenthal demanded that Drudge turn over his subscription list and disclose the "top GOP operatives" he had quoted in the wife-beating accusation. Drudge responded with a report that Kenneth Starr's staff believed that Blumenthal was leaking "misinformation" about them to the press, a potential obstruction of justice. Indeed, the special prosecutor's office subpoenaed Blumenthal before the grand jury and questioned him about whether he had encouraged the Internet magazine *Salon* to look into the background of Starr's staff. As Blumenthal left the courthouse, he stepped up to a row of microphones to denounce the prosecutor's tactics. "I never imagined that in America I would be hauled before a grand jury to answer questions about my conversations with members of the media," he said. Insisting that they had failed to intimidate him, he hung a framed copy of his subpoena in his White House office. "It would take an awful lot to get the honest press to rally around Sid Blumenthal, but if anybody can pull it off, Ken Starr can," his old antagonist Michael Kelly mused. Starr and his staff retaliated by releasing portions of the closed-door testimony revealing that Blumenthal had named the news media outlets he dealt with voluntarily.[29]

In September 1998 the special prosecutor handed to the House Judiciary Committee 119,059 pages, some with luridly graphic findings, which the House of Representatives immediately posted on the web, on the same day that another congressional committee was holding hearings about pornography on the Internet. Broadcasters who read the Starr report on the air had to skip over its steamier passages. CBS correspondent Bob Schieffer advised his viewers that they could go online to read whatever he could not say. Some 25 million people logged on to read the Starr report during its first two days online, swamping any previous volume of Internet use. The rush to distribute the report electronically proved a tactical blunder. So single-mindedly stacked against the president was the report that it actually boosted Clinton's public standing. Unlike the months of patient inquiry by the Watergate committee in 1973, the Starr report had been dumped on the public too abruptly for digestion.[30]

Among the peculiarities of the investigations was the special prosecutor's obsession with Sidney Blumenthal. The man who sued Matt Drudge was himself suspected of rumormongering. As the lawsuit proceeded, Drudge gave a deposition at the same federal courthouse where Starr's grand jury was meeting. He provoked scornful laughter from reporters by describing himself as "a working reporter who has written thousands of stories and driven dozens of news cycles." Drudge defended his spousal abuse story as an "an accurate report of an inaccurate rumor," and he portrayed himself as a solitary fighter for the First Amendment. Oddly enough, Blumenthal had a harder time testifying in his own lawsuit. As a presidential advisor he had to invoke executive privilege and decline to answer questions that might reveal his conversations with the president.[31]

In Washington to testify, Drudge stopped by the U.S. House of Representatives to watch it debate launching an impeachment inquiry against the president. At the same time, in venues other than the *Drudge Report*, stories surfaced about the personal indiscretions of Clinton's congressional opponents, ranging from extramarital affairs to illegitimate children. Republicans suspected Blumenthal of being behind this mudslinging as a ploy to distract public attention from the Lewinsky scandal. The conservative web site *No Holds Barred* charged that his "alleged smear campaign against perceived foes of the president and his use of the defamation suit to silence Drudge may have collided explosively—exposing the former and undermining the latter." Speculation arose that Blumenthal's deposition in the Drudge case, in which he denied under oath having talked to reporters about sex scandals involving members of Congress, could bring perjury charges against him.[32]

Basking in the publicity, Drudge accepted an invitation to address the National Press Club. "So why is Matt Drudge here?" asked club president Doug Harbrecht, *Business Week*'s editor. "He's on the cutting edge of a revolution in our business and everybody in our business knows it. And like it or not, he's a newsmaker." Harbrecht's own teenage children could identify Drudge, whereas they had no idea who David Broder and Helen Thomas were. "Thank you, Sidney Blumenthal," Drudge intoned. In August 1998, Drudge stepped into the media mainstream himself with his own radio show on WABC in New York. The *Drudge Report* began carrying advertising, and Fox News offered him his own television program, with a commensurate salary. His program on Fox opened with an announcer intoning, "He's the mod muckraker, the Internet informer, citizen journalist, and everyone's dying to know what he'll say next." Unaccustomed to editorial supervision, however, Drudge walked off his television show after Fox barred his use of some graphic anti-abortion material. When he protested that the network's restrictions mocked its own motto, "We report, you decide," Fox released him from his contract. Drudge announced that if he could not speak his mind, he would "just go to a medium where I can." Then ABC canceled his Sunday night radio programs, which Drudge interpreted as punishment for his criticism of ABC's parent company, Walt Disney. "I guess I was a bad Mouseketeer," he shrugged. "The air we breathe is free, the airwaves are not."[33]

In Congress, the House members responsible for managing the president's impeachment inserted into the official record the original *Drudge Report* that broke the intern story. One of the three witnesses from whom the House managers chose to take video depositions was Sidney Blumenthal. Why should the prosecution call the president's staunchest defender? "All he can do is prove beyond a shadow of a doubt that Clinton is a cad," which was hardly an impeachable offense, wrote the columnist Mary McGrory. Instead, House managers repeatedly asked if Blumenthal had been the source of stories that depicted Lewinsky as a "stalker." Blumenthal genially deflected the inquiry and won commendation from his interrogators for behaving like a gentleman. Harsher treatment came from one of Blumenthal's friends, the writer Christopher Hitchens, who signed an affidavit that Blumenthal had told him the "stalker" story at lunch in March 1998. The press corps seemed more uncomfortable with Hitchens's breach of professional and personal confidence than with his accusation. The incident demolished the friendship but produced no indictment. After the White House Correspondents Association's annual dinners, Hitchens hosted *Vanity Fair*'s exclusive "hip alternative" parties. Speaking at the dinner in May 1999, Clinton drew a laugh when he commented, "Last year, Sidney Blumenthal swore he could get me into the *Vanity Fair* party. What a difference a year makes."[34]

President Clinton could afford to banter after winning acquittal in the Senate, but Blumenthal still had a pending lawsuit. Drudge was content to let the publicity-laden case continue forever. His refusal to disclose his confidential sources prompted Blumenthal to petition the court to uncover those sources by subpoenaing twenty-five journalists, a veritable who's who of conservative writers. The list got leaked to the *Washington Post*'s gossip column, "The Reliable Source," where it ran under the headline: "Free the Blumenthal 25!" Following this fiasco, Blumenthal admitted defeat. He conceded that he had unwittingly given Drudge "the oxygen of publicity that he thrived on" and had to cut it off.[35]

On May Day, 2001, Blumenthal signed settlement papers at the federal courthouse in Washington. Drudge participated virtually, by fax and conference call. The plaintiff agreed to drop his $30 million lawsuit and to pay $2,500 to cover some of the defendant's legal expenses. Although Blumenthal presumed that Drudge had unlimited legal defense funds, the money David Horowitz raised for Drudge had barely covered the expenses for depositions, court costs, and travel to Washington. Blumenthal agreed to make up the difference. He had sued to "make absolutely clear that his story was a malicious and reckless lie," but he concluded that Drudge lacked any incentive to settle as "bad publicity for him is good for his kind of business." The online operation of the *Wall Street Journal* called Blumenthal the first litigant to complain "of being victimized by his own lawsuit."[36]

Drudge declared total victory, except for his disappointment over how little press attention the settlement received. "Big Media Silent on Blumenthal's Cash Settlement," the *Drudge Report* headlined. The media had grown weary over the endless Clinton wars, including *Blumenthal v. Drudge*. The *National Journal*'s media analyst William Powers called the two men "weird mirror images of each other," describing them as "journalists second and ideological warriors first." For the rest of the press corps, the abortive lawsuit stood as an embarrassing reminder of their own frenzied scandal reporting. Nor did the suit seem as relevant to the Internet now that the major media operations were gaining a firmer online presence. "One day you'll look at Matt Drudge and remember when he was so hot back at the turn of the century," he said, projecting his eclipse. As for Sidney Blumenthal, after the Clinton presidency came to an end he returned to journalism, writing a column and heading the Washington bureau of the Internet magazine *Salon.* The *Drudge Report* hot linked his column.[37]

The media's fixation on President Clinton's morality had conspicuously clashed with the public's seeming indifference. The mainstream Washington press corps regarded the president's tawdry behavior as personally offensive. "He came here and he trashed the place," said the *Washington Post* columnist David Broder, "and it's not his place." The media justified its fixation on scandal as an obligation to uncover the truth, no matter how sordid. To the *New Republic* editor Charles Lane, the disconnect between the press and the public suggested that average citizens saw truth more as "a relative value" than did the reporters. Lane encouraged journalists not to become disheartened. They had to be willing to "depart from, or even offend, public sensibilities." His pronouncements were soon overshadowed by the *New Republic*'s own crisis of confidence when Lane had to fire a promising young staff writer caught fabricating stories.

Writer Stephen Glass had a knack for being able to "get into rooms other reporters couldn't get into, and come away with quotes and anecdotes that others couldn't get." Glass's article on "Hack Heaven" described how a fifteen-year-old computer genius had been hired by the software company Jukt Micronomics after he hacked into the company's web site. Absolutely none of it was true. Drawing from his imagination, Glass had managed to fool the magazine's fact-checkers. Adam Penenberg, an editor at the online magazine *Forbes Digital Tool,* could not believe that an opinion magazine could have scooped them on a hacker story. His digging found no evidence that any such company as Jukt existed. Confronted with this revelation, Charles Lane reviewed all of Glass's articles in the magazine and found that they blended substantial amounts of fiction into fact. The *New Republic* dismissed Glass and obliterated all traces of him on its Internet site, *TNR Online.* "When an article appears in print. . . it cannot be erased," the editors commented. "But 'publishing' online is different."[38]

For Internet advocates, the sorry episode proved that reporting on paper was no more trustworthy than reporting on a computer screen. "If media traditionalists are going to point to Matt Drudge as the embodiment of online journalism," wrote Pete Denko in the magazine *Wired,* "can't online folks point to 'Hack Heaven,' and say, 'People who print Glass articles shouldn't throw stones?'" Adam Penenberg took particular pride that an Internet journalist like himself had exposed the fraud. "I feel strongly that we've been dissed by traditional media so often," he commented, "maybe this whole incident will show that we deserve some respect."[39]

The traditional media had developed sufficient respect to claim the Internet for itself. After several false starts, major newspapers and networks established web sites that attracted regular readers. Office workers logged on from their desks during the workday, and newspapers rediscovered the afternoon markets by bringing out a "PM Extra." Newspaper sites generally reproduced the bulk of their daily news and features, along with special reports from regular reporters, wire dispatches, and additional news stories from staff who wrote especially for the web—although most online news staff collected and collated news from other sources rather than covering events themselves. The Internet spilled over into the regular newsroom and changed its rhythms. Newspapers with web sites encouraged reporters to file multiple versions of developing news stories, so they could update the online edition every few hours. Some reporters worried that this meant sacrificing depth of coverage for instant reporting, and complained that Internet sites were turning their news organizations into "mini APs." But others thought the new arrangement resembled the old "rewrite bank" that had once been a staple of newspaper reporting, with editors in the bureau fashioning the bits and pieces of a reporter's phoned-in account into a coherent account. The Internet made reporters relearn what they had once known how to do, said the *New York Times* Washington bureau chief Michael Oreskes, "Write and distribute reports quickly." Yet he warned that the mass media could not afford to sacrifice the reliability of its news for the sake of speed. "To put it as bluntly as I know how," Oreskes asserted, "Matt Drudge and I are not in the same profession."[40]

The Internet gave many newcomers an opportunity to break into journalism at online operations, and offered some grizzled veterans a second chance. After CNN dropped reporter Peter Arnett, for instance, he joined foreigntv.com. So long as Internet stocks soared with irrational exuberance during the 1990s, online news operations could also lure talented writers with attractive stock options. Even those who stuck with the print and broadcast media discovered that the Internet offered stunning capabilities as a reportorial tool. "It's changed the whole drill," exclaimed J. Robert Port at the Associated Press. "I can find out if a person has been sued, or divorced, or whether he or she has a criminal record. I can locate within five minutes any person in the United States who uses a credit card or has a bank account, and I can probably locate his or her family members and address history in less than thirty minutes." Online databases gave reporters the phone numbers of people in the vicinity of some breaking news. They could put together a detailed story by making a few calls before any reporter made it to the scene. The advent of wireless technology further allowed them to maintain unbroken contact with their newsrooms. Rather than run for the nearest phone booth, reporters would head to nearest Starbucks offering wireless Internet access.[41]

For the mainstream media, the multitude of independent Internet news gatherers served as an early-warning system for gossip that might evolve into something substantive. Objective news sites hot linked themselves to ideologically bent material, to the dismay of traditionalists who labeled the Internet as "synonymous with confusion, clutter, gossip and sensationalism." Disdainful reporters rarely missed an opportunity to highlight Internet errors, and churned out stories on Internet pornography, hackers, viruses, and the perennial bad example, Matt Drudge. Some of these reporters looked down on the Internet operations of their own news organizations. The print side complained that news sites were usually too long on technical personnel and too short on reporters, and claimed that their operating expenses dug deeply into the editorial budget without producing sufficient advertising revenue.[42]

To meet the fluid needs of the Internet, print reporters had to readjust their deadlines and file updates on their work throughout the day. Editors called this "owning the story." Reporters called it "continuous work." Early postings often contained errors, and not everyone caught the later corrections. During the Lewinsky scandal, highly reputable reporters filed some very wrong reports, NBC's Tom Brokaw commented, "and that gave us migraine headaches all along." Some journalists also felt ill at ease with the Internet's interactivity and regarded "message boards" and "chat rooms" as unproductive. The *Washington Post* decided against becoming "a common carrier for anybody who wants to say anything," and opted instead to invite readers to participate in "live chats" online with *Post* staff. The paper attempted to differentiate its product from the sleazier aspects of the Internet, but the *Post*'s editors were chagrined to discover that more Internet users were being routed to their web site via the *Drudge Report* than any other source. Drudge proudly posted their sheepish admission.[43]

A compulsion to stay up to the moment with breaking news caused online news operations to rely heavily on the most traditional of news sources, the wire services. More Reuters and Associated Press stories appeared on newspapers' web sites than in their printed editions. Disheartened Internet enthusiasts felt that over reliance on wire dispatches was diluting the individuality of many news and information sites and making them indistinguishable from each other. Even Matt Drudge repeatedly tapped the wires for his "headline stories." In fact, it was only through the wires and other news services that the myriad of smaller web sites had any chance of offering timely news. Meanwhile the tradition-bound AP hesitated until 2000 before it began regularly carrying reports from Internet sites, and even then its members accepted the decision with "some queasiness."[44]

Corporate conglomerates further blurred the distinctions between the old and new media. When America Online merged with Time Warner, it promoted the event as the dawn of the "Internet Century." The biggest media companies owned the majority of the most popular Internet web sites. NBC and the *Washington Post* entered a content-sharing arrangement for MSNBC. ABCNews.com became a partner with *New York Times*. CNBC reached an accord with the

Wall Street Journal. The Chicago Tribune Company bought the Times Mirror Company for the express purpose of using its print journalists to supplement its broadcasting and web news services. All these alliances anticipated the advent of high-speed broadband Internet service that would permit speedier downloading of video. The fusion of television and the Internet was expected to encourage far more consumers to seek news online. News organizations calculated that the ready accessibility of broadband at the work place accounted for greater use of Internet news services during working hours. Although home markets proved slow to embrace broadband, the assumption of its inevitability spurred newspaper web sites to acquire video components to stay competitive. As Internet news sites grew more expensive to maintain, it appeared that they would require higher financing than single operators could afford. "The Internet's about independence," Matt Drudge continued to insist. He disdained broadband and accused the corporate takeover of "bastardizing the Internet."[45]

Internet news faltered when the stock market bubble burst at the century's end. In 2000 stock in NBC Internet tumbled 89 percent, forcing the network to pull the plug. MSNBC.com survived thanks to its partnership with the enormously affluent Microsoft. Other than the *Wall Street Journal*, which managed to collect subscriptions for its stock reports, most web sites still found it difficult to charge for their content. Advertising revenue remained well below expectations. As it became clearer that Internet news sites would not return the millions invested in them, investors turned away, forcing online news operations to reduce budgets and staff. Facing annual losses of $60 million, Rupert Murdoch's News Corp. dismantled its online division, laid off half of its employees, and distributed the rest among its television networks. The *New York Times* and Knight Ridder similarly cut hundreds of jobs at their Internet operations. Looking over the ruins, just before resigning as editor of *Slate,* Michael Kinsley concluded, "The novelty has worn off." As larger operations stumbled, however, one-person news sites flourished anew. Prominent Washington writers competed to replicate Matt Drudge's success by setting up their own web logs—or blogs—essentially self-syndicated columnists. Andrew Sullivan, a former editor of the *New Republic*, found it liberating to be rid of editors and advertisers—"all the things that can constrain you"—although doing a blog required "venting on a daily or hourly basis." Further spurring the blogs were central web sites that simplified access to the "online diary community" and turned the Internet into a vast soapbox.[46]

Some self-appointed commentators applied for formal press accreditation in Washington, and faced the same resistance encountered earlier by reporters for new technologies that did not fit the prevailing definitions of journalism. During the Clinton impeachment trial in 1999, the Senate press galleries filled to capacity. Internet writers who had never before set foot on Capitol Hill applied for day passes to compete with regular correspondents for the limited space. Normally, the press galleries sat empty as reporters watched congressional speeches on C-SPAN, but everyone wanted to be inside the chamber for the trial. Internet reporters for mainstream news organizations gained access, but most of the independents failed to meet the necessary requirements that they sold their news to subscribers or made a profit. These were questionable criteria, as even the largest Internet news sites often lacked formal subscription lists and lost rather than earned money. Yet the Standing Committee of Correspondents puzzled over how else to define Internet reporting without opening the press galleries to anyone with a modem.

The Capitol's periodical press gallery, which housed reporters for magazines and newsletters, rejected the application of Vigdor Schreibman, despite his formerly having been accredited as a reporter for Epin Publications. During the 1990s, Schreibman had demonstrated the Internet's endless possibilities to his skeptical friends in the press gallery, who "thought it was terrible." After his retirement, he launched a web site called the Federal Information News Syndicate out of his home on Capitol Hill. He served as its editor, publisher, and sole reporter. The Standing Committee rejected its legitimacy, finding that the web site carried "dense monographs" on the information age rather than news reporting. The committee ruled that Schreibman was not a full-time journalist because he lived off his retirement income. "What are you charging and what is your client base?" the superintendent of the House Press Gallery asked. "That has always been important for the Standing Committee." Schreibman charged a token annual rate for subscribers for twice-monthly reports by e-mail, although the same reports could be viewed on his web site for free. "Vigdor is the first of those with a home page or who just post their work on mailing lists," said Richard Durham, the *Business Week* reporter who chaired the Standing Committee that turned down his application.[47]

Schreibman filed a lawsuit against the Standing Committee and failed, but his action prompted the members of the committee to reevaluate their treatment of Internet correspondents. The old media signaled a tentative willingness to accept their new online colleagues when the radio-TV gallery awarded technical membership to the Washington-based HearingRoom.com, which provided text and audio from congressional hearings to other news organizations. Newspaper reporters in the press gallery, and magazine and newsletter writers in the periodical press gallery, formally recognized "the emergence of electronic publications as a legitimate extension of the print tradition" by specifying that web news services must publish original news and charge market rates through subscription sales or advertising. Vigdor Schreibman protested that his First Amendment rights were the issue, not his income. The Standing Committee was keeping out the "little people" who had gotten their say on the Internet, he insisted. "This is new, this is revolutionary."[48]

Even the well-funded Bloomberg news service encountered resistance when it applied for press passes. As a business news operation, Bloomberg sought accreditation to get its Washington reporters into the government agencies that released such economic indicators as the Gross Domestic Product and Consumer Price Index. These were distributed in closed sessions (known as lockups), to prevent any reporters from trading on the information in advance. The chairman of the Standing Committee, a *Wall Street Journal* correspondent, seemed perplexed about Bloomberg's nonprint distribution. "What are you?" he asked. "We don't have criteria for you." The news service finally cleared the hurdle of the "journalists' commissar committee" as Michael Bloomberg called them. Within a few years one of Bloomberg's own reporters, William Roberts, was elected to the Standing Committee, and he chaired it when the news site *WorldNetDaily* applied for a press pass in 2001. Increasingly tightened security in government buildings made a press pass essential for its sole Washington reporter, Paul Sperry, to gain reasonable access. But the Standing Committee unanimously rejected Sperry's application because of *WorldNetDaily*'s connection to a conservative advocacy group, the Western Journalism Center, which violated the gallery's antilobbying rules.[49]

The founder of *WorldNetDaily*, Joseph Farah, took the rejection as an insult. His web site was a freedom fighter to "restore real freedom to America," he insisted, and it had separated entirely from the Western Journalism Center. As an alternative source of news, *WorldNetDaily* aimed to "champion the watchdog role of the press—exposing corruption, fraud, waste and abuse in government and setting its own aggressive editorial agenda," said Farah. He blamed "Stalinists" on the Standing Committee for rejecting him while it accredited state-sponsored reporters from China's Xinhua News Agency to Egypt's *Al-Ahram*. Bloomberg's William Roberts, as chairman of the Standing Committee of Correspondents, countered that the committee could find very little original reporting on *WorldNetDaily*, which "looks a lot like Drudge." Farah conceded that his site mostly offered wire reports and links to other news outlets, but countered that "the majority of newspapers are packed with Associated Press." Losing its appeal, *WorldNetDaily* served notice that it intended to sue, and posted vitriolic attacks on the reporters who served on the Standing Committee. Concerned that the committee's vague definitions might prove "legally problematic" in court, three committee members, including the chairman, reversed their positions and voted to accredit *WorldNetDaily*. "Lo and behold, the rules don't say anything about credentialing Internet publications," said chairman Roberts as the press galleries struggled with their first major revision of the rules in half a century. Once again a major change in communications had shaken the settled world of the Washington press corps and forced it to adjust to a new order.[50]

Epilogue

Washington, D.C., 2001

"I don't want to alarm anybody right now, but apparently, there—it felt, just a few moments ago, like there was an explosion of some kind here at the Pentagon," NBC correspondent Jim Miklawzewski reported live on the *Today Show* on September 11, 2001. The pressroom on the Pentagon's outer ring faced the Potomac River, on the far side of that massive building from where a hijacked passenger airliner had just struck. "I hear no sirens going off in the building," Miklaszewski said. "I see no smoke, but the building shook for just a couple of seconds." Looking into the hallway, he saw security personnel hurriedly clearing people from the building. It was the program's anchor in New York, Katie Couric, who told him, "We're looking at live pictures of the Pentagon, where there is billowing smoke." Miklaszewski responded that an army officer running by had said that it might have been a bomb detonated at the adjacent heliport. Couric contradicted him with unconfirmed reports that a plane crash, like those that had just occurred at the World Trade Towers, had caused the Pentagon explosion. "I have no idea, Katie," Miklaszewski responded. He mentioned that no one had ordered the reporters to leave the pressroom, but that the hallway outside it had become a scene of pandemonium. "And you're in your office in the Pentagon right now, Mik, reporting to us?" Couric asked. "I am in the office, but I'm at the opposite side of where this crash occurred," he replied, beginning to piece the events together and realizing that the network in New York had a better view of what had happened at the Pentagon than he did from inside the building.[1]

After a decade of seeming indifference, when hard news steadily lost space and airtime to soft features, the terrorist attack on September 11 jolted the nation's civic consciousness. Fiery images of destruction sent Americans to every form of news media available to learn what had happened and what it meant. Television news viewing surged. Newspapers doubled their print runs. Newsmagazines rushed out special editions. Online news sites were overloaded with the demand. With the audiences came a rebounding of journalists' standing in the opinion polls. As the media turned red, white, and blue, commented the *Washington Post* columnist E. J. Dionne Jr., many of those who had been hostile in the past "saw us in a different light."[2]

The end of the Cold War had appeared to drain American leadership of a sense of national purpose, what President George H. W. Bush called "the vision thing." Reporters who covered the first President Bush liked him personally but felt that he squandered his presidency by articulating few clear objectives. Press Secretary Marlin Fitzwater defended the president's minimalist style and suggested that the fault lay with the press corps for paying excessive attention to the White House. He advised them to "back off." The public backed off as well, demonstrating a waning of interest in national affairs that persuaded news management to reorient reporting toward more human-interest issues and upbeat lifestyle stories. Not much seemed to distinguish hard from "lite" news in a decade when the top stories were a presidential extramarital affair, a celebrity murder trial, and the death of a princess, but journalists shrugged that it was their job to offer what seemed most relevant to the largest audiences. The "new news" gave less emphasis to reports from Washington because its advocates believed it was a misplaced priority to put news about the Pentagon ahead of news about the supermarket.[3]

Washington news bureaus dismantled the conventional beats at government agencies. Instead of "building coverage"—for example, being posted regularly at the Capitol or the Pentagon—reporters were assigned to follow broad issues of education, health, and consumer safety that cut across agency lines. For the routine news from the federal agencies, news bureaus simply relied on the wire services. Young reporters believed they could gather news via e-mail, fax, and web sites rather than spending their time at press conferences or lingering in the halls of the bureaucracy. Veteran reporters complained that such a remote approach to the job missed the personal observations, inside tips, and general expertise that they had developed in the past. But editors responded that the changes in coverage reflected the general loss of public interest in the type of news that Washington had generated for so long.[4]

For the generation of Americans who had lived through the Great Depression and the Second World War, national news had a compelling, life-or-death quality that sent them to daily newspapers and news broadcasts. Their children, who grew up in the atomic age, inherited the notion that following what the government was doing, even when they disagreed with it, was a civic responsibility. Vietnam and Watergate shook that collective civic faith. Increasingly disengaged Americans attended fewer public meetings, drifted away from the polling booths, and read newspapers and watched network news less regularly than before. Demographically, those who took their news from newspapers and the major networks grew older, while younger audiences gravitated to the newer technology, from the cable networks to the Internet.[5]

A growing sense of disconnection separated the Washington correspondents from their audiences, leading them to question the value of the stories they reported. Two years into Bill Clinton's presidency he failed to win enactment of a sweeping health care reform and the Democrats lost their majorities in Congress. Thereafter, Clinton approached social issues incrementally, in small steps that lacked much media appeal. "Our key stories in the late '90s—when we weren't being interrupted by scandals—were the economy, health care, education, the quality of American life, family issues," commented Doyle McManus, Washington bureau chief for the *Los Angeles Times*. Sex scandals got the most attention. "We were covering it the way tabloid television was," McManus observed, "but still it did not feel like the kind of story most of us came to Washington to work on." Jack Smith, who followed his father Howard K. Smith into television news broadcasting as a White House and State Department correspondent, abandoned network news because Washington had "lost its allure" since the end of the Cold War. "I now have the front seat to the stains on Monica's dress," he said despairingly.[6]

The yawning gap between the public's indifference to Clinton's impeachment trial and the media frenzy over it symbolized the press corps's isolation. The columnist Robert Samuelson saw this gap as the defining trend during his three decades as a Washington reporter. "Over this period, Washington has grown more insular," wrote Samuelson. Average citizens no longer believed that government could solve social problems, and had consequently become alienated from the "inside the Beltway crowd." Voter distrust kept either party from gaining effective control of the national government, and years of gridlock turned political dialogue strident. During these decades, the media had blurred the boundaries between news and opinion. "In 1969, when I started as a newspaper reporter, news mainly meant 'hard news,'" Samuelson reflected. "It focused on crime, politics, government, disasters, scandals and sports. Since then, 'soft news' has mushroomed." As news writing turned more personal, analysis and advocacy invaded the former quest for objectivity. Multiple news outlets competed for shrinking audiences by descending into gossip, slander, and scandal.[7]

The mishandling of the election of 2000 by television news further shook public confidence. As CBS anchorman Dan Rather acknowledged, the election coverage took "a chunk out of our credibility." Before the polls had closed in Florida, NBC had rushed to declare that Vice President Al Gore had carried the state, making his victory in the presidential election likely. Within minutes, CBS, ABC, CNN, and Fox made the same call. Two hours later, CNN recanted and declared Florida "too close to call." The other networks quickly followed. At 2:26 a.m., Fox reported that Texas governor George W. Bush, although trailing in the popular vote, had taken a narrow lead in Florida and therefore had won the electoral college. The other networks soon after reached the same conclusion. The Associated Press hesitated to make the assessment unanimous, however, as "the numbers weren't adding up." The Florida vote was so close that it would trigger an automatic recount. Once he got word of this, Vice President Gore retracted his concession, and a month-long political and legal battle ensued. Republicans charged the networks with bias against their candidate, but the root of the problem had been budgetary. Financial cutbacks had caused the networks to pool their polling services. They created the Voter News Service (VNS) to tabulate unofficial vote counts, conduct exit polls, provide analysis, and project winners. As most of the media depended on the same source for election data, if it failed, they all would.[8]

Television news compounded the miscalled election by overdramatizing the subsequent recounting of the ballots. "Isolated by their narrow Washington perspective and whipped up by the need to fill so much air time," wrote the media critic Caryn James in the New York Times, "they projected hysteria onto a postelection scene that never called for it." Robert Bianco of USA Today lamented the obsession with speed over accuracy as television news correspondents rushed breathlessly to report on the Supreme Court's decision in Bush v. Gore before they had a chance to read it. When NBC anchor Tom Brokaw was asked why his network had not waited a few minutes to allow its Washington correspondent to digest the decision, he replied, "Are you kidding?" Had they hesitated, they would have lost their audience to other networks.[9]

In January 2001 the U.S. Commission on National Security issued a report that predicted terrorist attacks on American soil. The Bush administration, Congress, and the news media all gave the report minimal attention. Not one reporter from the New York Times Washington bureau covered the report's release and the "paper of record" failed to publish the commission's recommendations. Except for reporters for the Los Angeles Times, most of the Washington press corps filed perfunctory accounts, without further pursuit of the issues that the report had raised. Former senators Warren Rudman and Gary Hart, who chaired the board, attributed the conspicuous lack of attention it received to the general indifference toward Washington news. Rudman and Hart suspected that so many years of political candidates running "against Washington" had created the impression that the government could not meet serious challenges. "The anti-Washington bias may play well at home," said Senator Warren Rudman, "but it is self-defeating." Nine months later the commission's predictions proved appallingly accurate.[10]

Shortly before 9:00 a.m. on September 11, the morning news shows reported that a plane had hit one of the 110-story World Trade Towers. Television began showing live video of the scene even before correspondents reached the scene, and the broadcasters narrating the video images could not determine whether the incident had been accidental or deliberate. Then, recorded live on the air, another plane hit the second tower. A third airliner struck the Pentagon in Washington, and a fourth crashed in a Pennsylvania field before it could reach its intended target. "We were immersed in confusion," said ABC's news anchor Peter Jennings, who spent seventeen hours broadcasting that day, "suffocated by chaos."[11]

Horrific images of the burning World Trade Towers dominated the news. When the towers collapsed and clouds of smoke and debris rolled over the streets below, scores of reporters were caught in the melee. The *World Street Journal* had to evacuate its offices at the World Financial Center, shifting responsibility for compiling the story to the *Journal*'s Washington bureau. There, editor Bryan Gruley handled dispatches from fifty reporters and blended them into the paper's Pulitzer Prize–winning front-page account. "What that story did, what good newspapering does," wrote *Journal* staff member Daniel Henninger, "is take the chaos that is the Information Highway and submit it to an organizing intelligence—first the reporters and after them a series of editors and copy editors who have the skills, in a few hours, to make that chaos coherent."[12]

"Get to New York," CNN instructed Washington-based correspondent Bob Franken. By the time Franken stopped at the Washington newsroom, however, his assignment had changed. "Forget New York, get out to the Pentagon," they told him. On the road, Franken and his camera crew pulled over to the side to film smoke rising from the Pentagon, staff streaming out its doors, military jets circling overhead, and ambulances speeding past. A police officer told them to move on. "We have to be here," Franken held his ground. "This is history." It was a day when the images were sharp and indelible, and yet at the same time things seemed a blur, the correspondent commented. With everything going on at once, reporters "reacted in an instinctive way." They took down the facts and tried to keep their heads in order to provide accurate information to a stunned nation.[13]

From downtown Washington, reporters could see a smoke plume rising across the Potomac. Driving along the highway, Mike Walter, a television correspondent for *USA Today Live*, watched a hijacked passenger aircraft fly at full throttle into the western side of the Pentagon. Among the passengers was Barbara Olson, a familiar face on cable television as a conservative commentator during the Clinton era. The plane left a gaping hole and destroyed several corridors of offices in the Pentagon, providentially in an area that had just undergone renovation and was not fully occupied. Reporters inside the building felt a jolt and heard an explosion. Loudspeakers ordered them to evacuate. ABC News correspondent John McWelty made his way around to the crash site, where he interviewed eyewitnesses and pieced the story together. Unable to use his cell phone, he ran to a nearby gas station to use the pay phone. A police officer shouted at him to leave the area, warning that a fourth plane might be approaching, but McWelty refused to surrender the phone. "Look, I'm a reporter," he exclaimed. "I have to report to my network. Shoot me."[14]

CBS's Pentagon correspondent David Martin was crossing Memorial Bridge over the Potomac when he saw smoke that made him assume that a tanker truck had exploded on the highway alongside the Pentagon. By the time Martin got to the press parking lot—on the farthest side from the crash site—he heard radio reports that it might have been a plane. As he rushed around the building, thick smoke prevented him from seeing what had happened, "but there were all these bodies everywhere." Determined not to jump to conclusions, Martin hesitated reporting that a plane had hit until he tripped on a piece of the fuselage. He was able to call in confirmation of a plane crash before his cell phone went dead.[15]

Newsday correspondent Elaine Povitch had heard radio reports of planes hitting the World Trade Towers but went to the Senate press gallery without connecting the events in New York to her own safety in Washington. No sooner had she settled at her desk than Capitol Police rushed into the press gallery, pointing up and shouting: "Get out of the building. RUN!" There were reports that a fourth plane had been hijacked and was headed toward Washington where the imposing Capitol dome made a likely target. As reporters, legislators, staff, and visitors poured out onto the plaza, they were startled to see a large plane approaching from the north, and were relieved when it turned out to be a military jet sent for interception. Crowds gathered on the Capitol lawn, where the Senate chaplain led a prayer service and the nearby Taft memorial carillon was by chance playing "God Bless America."[16]

Senators were talking with reporters on the Capitol lawn when they were jolted by another explosion, perhaps a sonic boom from the military jets overhead. Following the blast, Washington radio and television stations were inundated with calls erroneously reporting car bombs at the State Department, the FBI, and on the Mall. Without verification, some of the stations repeated these stories on the air, adding to the confusion and turning an orderly evacuation at the Capitol into near chaos. "Don't go to the Capitol!" was the phone message CBS correspondent Bob Schieffer got from his Washington bureau as he drove into the city. Schieffer diverted to the White House, which was also under evacuation. He broadcast from the roof of the Chamber of Commerce Building across Lafayette Square.[17]

In Florida, most White House correspondents who had accompanied President Bush to a second grade class at an elementary school on September 11 were stranded there when the presidential entourage hastily departed and all other air traffic was grounded. The few pool reporters aboard Air Force One would spend the day being whisked from one secure location to the next, not told where they were going, and forbidden to use cell phones or pagers to contact their news organizations to prevent any disclosure of the president's whereabouts. Those reporters who had remained behind at the White House were herded out of the pressroom by guards shouting at them to run. Reporters tumbled into a mob of presidential aides and tourists, and congregated in Lafayette Park across Pennsylvania Avenue, until the Secret Service warned them of the location's extreme vulnerability in the event of an aerial attack on the White House. Even the White House's fabled telephone operators were evacuated. When the *New York Times* columnist Maureen Dowd called the switchboard, a recording told her to hold for an operator, and then the line went dead. "Washington had the silence of the grave," Dowd reported. "Downtown you could smell smoke and see the plume rising from the Pentagon full of carnage and fire and see the flag over the emptied White House flying at half-staff." Another *Times* correspondent, Francis X. Clines, described the white and orange smoke rising from "the supposedly impregnable Pentagon, staining the western horizon of the national capital with evidence of some eerie battle on a brilliantly sunny day." Television cameras recorded the scene from the roof of the Hay-Adams Hotel across from the White House. The silvermaned historian David McCullough, who was staying at the hotel, stepped out onto the street and encountered a young reporter with his notebook in hand, who asked, "Well, with all your experience, what do you make of this, Mr. Cronkite?"[18]

Police closed the streets around the White House and shut down the bridges over the Potomac. Downtown traffic gridlocked. Washington's Metro subway system closed its station at the Pentagon, forcing people to walk to get away from the area. In his Capitol Hill neighborhood, Courtland Milloy of the *Washington Post* stood in disbelief, "watching people stream through the nation's capital like refugees." Parents rushed to retrieve school children as the schools closed early. "If I had been sleepwalking through the reality of global terrorism," Milloy wrote, "I sure as hell was awake now." Many reporters were parents, too, and had to balance the urgent demands of their jobs with worry about their frightened children. The story had hit home like no other. "Days like this have only one alleged use for people like me," wrote Tish Durkin of the *National Journal*, "and that use is for us to dive into the reality at hand and swim open-eyed through it all, with the aim of seeing *something* that can be pulled up and cleaned off for you all to see, too."[19]

The plane that hit the Pentagon "dragged the capital from the complacent calm of a sunny September morning into an eerie world of destruction, tension and terror," reported a Washington correspondent for the British weekly magazine the *Economist*. Government leaders were whisked off to safety, buildings emptied out, and stores closed. Groups of people huddled around transistor radios. Everyone appeared somber and scared. "And within a couple of hours they had all gone," the *Economist* correspondent reported. "The streets were deserted, save for emergency vehicles and snipers on roofs. Washington had emptied, and with all roads into the city closed, the capital—like America itself—seemed sealed off."[20]

The news bureaus stayed open while the government shut down. "A newsroom gets up on its toes very quickly when something like this happens," said ABC News anchor Peter Jennings. The *Washington Post* put its entire staff on the story. Even retired editor Ben Bradlee went to the office when he heard the first reports that morning. "I haven't got anything to do," Bradlee admitted, "but there was no way of not coming down." The paper's lead article on the day's events listed 149 staff writers and researchers as contributors. Media critic

William Powers judged that the terrorist attacks brought out the *Washington Post*'s most evocative writing, highlighting a style that had steadily transformed it and other American newspapers. Feature writing migrated out of the Style section and into the front section, which had formerly been reserved for hard news. Powers dubbed this the "feminization" of the news, reflective of the fact that newspapers were no longer run exclusively by men. Among the women who now served as senior editors, Mary Hadar oversaw features on the *Post*'s front page.[21]

The crisis reaffirmed television's primacy for reporting breaking news. TV showed the attacks as they happened and sustained the video images by re-running them endlessly. Television commentary, for the most part, remained shocked and subdued, and news broadcasters refrained from drawing premature conclusions. They watched the pictures along with their audiences, without much more knowledge of what was happening than what they could see on the screen. "Oh, my goodness. Oh, my goodness," said one voice-over. "We're looking at a live picture from Washington, and there is smoke pouring out of the Pentagon." The astonishing pictures of the World Trade Towers tilted the story to New York, CNN correspondent Judy Woodruff noted. Although she operated out of a studio close enough to the Capitol to worry about her own personal safety, Woodruff attributed the New York focus to the graphic images of two very tall buildings collapsing. "We didn't have that picture at the Pentagon," she said. "We just had the aftermath."[22]

The networks suspended regular programming and devoted blanket coverage to the events of the day. They shifted additional news to their entertainment cable channels: CBS on the music channel MTV, ABC on the sports network ESPN, and Fox on its commercial entertainment channel FX. The national news desks handled most of the coverage, but stations in New York and Washington cut away frequently to broadcast local reports. Washington television stations dedicated more attention to the Pentagon than did the New York–based networks, and made frequent announcements of school closings. This infuriated the *Washington Post*'s television critic Tom Shales, who found it inexplicable that local stations would "chose to view this, incredibly enough, as a local story and reported it initially as if it were a winter snow day and school closings were of the utmost importance."[23]

"If you are looking for news, you will find the most current information on TV or radio," the Internet search engine Google advised users on September 11. "Most online news sites are not available, because of extremely high demand." During the crisis, reporters needed no reminders to file regular reports with their papers' web sites, but users found familiar sites spare that day. As the surge in user traffic overwhelmed them, Internet news operations stripped out the graphics, audio and video components, and advertisements—the *New York Times* even dropped its masthead. "We're just promoting bare bones, stripped down news reporting," said an MSNBC official. Subscribers who received e-mail alerts of breaking news encountered long delays. The *New York Times Direct* took more than an hour to alert its list that the first plane had hit the World Trade Tower. With the Internet lagging behind television's live, shocking pictures, surveys showed that 81 percent of Americans got most of their news from television that day, and only 2 percent from Internet. People also returned to newsprint, with the *Washington Post, Chicago Tribune, Los Angeles Times,* and *New York Post* among the papers that went to rare afternoon "extras."[24]

In spite of the overload, electronic communications did not go down. For reporters trying to reach their newsrooms, e-mail became their salvation after cell phone service shut down. "Here at *The Hill,* it was how we received our reporting, how we sent our information to the printer, how we got the images from our photographers," reported David Silverberg. The reliability of the system during the crisis validated its original intention, when the Defense Department's Advanced Research Projects Agency created ARPANET as a communications medium that could withstand a nuclear attack. Beyond news, the Internet also offered virtual human contact, allowing users to reach their families and vent their emotions. "Suddenly it was a lifeline for loved ones and a public forum for those who needed a place to yell their cries for vengeance or simply wanted answers," the *Washington Post* observed. Champions called the Internet "a first-person news network," where citizens could provide personal journalism through eyewitness accounts—although in fact most users simply responded to what they had seen on television. A national appetite developed to be part of "The Conversation," commented Matt Welsh of the online magazine *Reason.* Amateurs generated news sites such as the "World Trade Center Attack" and compiled copious data on the victims, donation centers, and memorials. But along with such positive gestures came an abundance of online rumors, hoaxes, and conspiracy theories.[25]

September 11 reanimated national news reporting. Washington news bureaus that had abolished beat reporting suddenly felt the need to station correspondents at the State Department, the Pentagon, the White House, and the Capitol. Some of the reporters they sent were so unfamiliar with the territory that they had trouble finding the right doors to enter these buildings. The scramble for hard news expanded bureau staffs and refocused attention on government activities, written off so recently as yesterday's news. The *Chicago Tribune* sent three more reporters to augment its staff of thirteen at its Washington bureau, and shifted some coverage back to Chicago to relieve the mounting burden. Washington reporters called themselves "instant war correspondents." The *Boston Globe* had hired Glen Johnson to cover the Massachusetts delegation in Congress, but when the news broke on September 11 it tapped Johnson's previous experience as an aviation reporter and assigned him to write about the vulnerabilities in the nation's air traffic system. Sabrina Eaton, a *Cleveland Plain Dealer* correspondent who covered the Pentagon attack, complained about the stress she felt to a friend who replied that her father, a government official, had been stuck in a bunker since the attacks. Eaton picked up on the tip and wrote the first story about the shadow government that was operating away from the capital in the event of another terrorist attack.[26]

Within a month, anthrax-filled letters addressed to government officials and to the news media added to the capital's anxiety. News bureaus issued notices of evacuation drills and handed out the antibiotic Cipro to staff who might have been exposed to anthrax. "I don't want Cipro," said Helen Kennedy, who reported for the *New York Daily News*. "I want antidepressants." Yet many found themselves reinvigorated by the tension. "Not since Watergate have journalists felt such a strong sense of mission and responsibility," observed the former Washington correspondent Ted Gup. Government news was on top again. "Washington reporters, once stereotyped as caught up in the minutiae of the capital," wrote Gup, "now find themselves increasingly covering subjects that know no boundaries and that integrate the foreign and domestic into a seamless story."[27]

The terrorist attacks restored the imperative to Washington reporting. "Before September 11, it was easy to feel that one was an extra in a political environment where the key players were David Letterman, Jay Leno, and Oprah," wrote Walter Shapiro in *USA Today*. "They were really the only ones who got to interview Gore and Bush in the waning weeks of the 2000 campaign." Shapiro had once lamented that Walter Lippmann had been able to write about World War II, the Cold War, and Vietnam, while he had been dealt Newt Gingrich and Bill Clinton. But the terrorist attacks recharged Shapiro's feeling of being part of history in the making. PBS news commentator Gwen Ifill sensed that after September 11 Americans paid closer attention to the news, "so that people like me, who make a living trying to explain to people why Washington matters, don't have to make that case quite so strongly any more."[28]

In a wartime atmosphere, Washington reporters discarded some of their professional distance to rally around the flag and the president. The dean of the press corps, David Broder, whose seventy-second birthday had fallen on September 11, 2001, now perceived qualities of Lincoln in George W. Bush, whose public approval ratings shot up to the stratosphere. Neutrality was no longer an option. Reuters news service came under harsh criticism for declining to use the word terrorist, on the grounds that "one man's terrorist is another man's freedom fighter." The slightest hint of unfavorable reporting about the president brought angry protests. When *USA Today* reporter Susan Page quoted a historian who had criticized the president for not returning to Washington immediately following the attacks, she was swamped with irate mail. The media put aside lingering references to the electoral dispute and the faltering economy. Reporters felt grateful that the firm response of the Bush administration to the terrorist attacks had made Washington once again "the place to be in terms of the news," even as they struggled with a tightly controlled White House and intense security at government buildings. The reporters' deference to those in authority surprised even themselves. "I wasn't around during World War II and in Vietnam, everybody was against the war," commented Sally Quinn. "So I had never seen a situation where journalists basically sided with the administration."[29]

Conservatives expressed skepticism about the durability of these trends and remained attentive to signs of defeatism. Fred Barnes, who wrote for the Washington-based *Weekly Standard,* called patriotism "not exactly a staple of the liberal media." A month after the terrorist attacks, David Westin, the president of ABC News, spoke at the Columbia School of Journalism, where he was asked whether the Pentagon had been a legitimate "enemy" target for terrorists to attack. Westin replied that "as a journalist I feel strongly that's something I should not be taking a position on." His textbook definition of objectivity sounded callous under the circumstances, although it did not gain notice until a C-SPAN broadcast of his remarks fired up critics from Fox News to the *Drudge Report.* Impartiality was unacceptable in a struggle perceived to be between good and evil. Westin apologized and declared that under any interpretation, the attack on the Pentagon had been without justification. The liberal columnist Michael Kinsley found it ironic that conservatives blamed the news media for excessive objectivity.[30]

If television dominated news coverage on September 11, newspapers claimed that the following day belonged to them. Americans hungered for information when their interests were at stake, and newspapers offered greater depth of coverage than did television. Newspapers generated most of the original reporting on the events and provided the most credible information. Circulation soared, returning newspapers back to an upward track for the first time in forty years. On September 12 the *Washington Post* sold 150,000 more copies than usual, and could have sold more if it had printed them. Thereafter, its daily print-run increased by ten thousand copies. Smaller papers that had been concentrating on local news now expanded their national and international coverage.[31]

In meeting the surging demand for news, publishers pleaded with government for more openness in the flow of information. Investigative reporters, rebounding from a decade of sordidness, began delving into issues of intelligence failures, international terrorism, government infringement on civil liberties, nuclear proliferation, and the hunt for weapons of mass destruction. Foreign correspondents coped in their own way with the impact of the terrorist attacks. Hafez Al-Mirazi, the Washington bureau chief for the Arabic-language TV news network al Jazeera, had been negotiating to lease space in an office building near the Potomac. After September 11 the deal collapsed because other tenants feared that his agency might become a target for anti-Arab reprisals. European correspondents puzzled over the deferential attitude that the Washington press was showing those in power. "In Europe, interviewers are adversarial," the BBC Washington correspondent Nick Bryant asserted. "Over here they try to end an interview on good terms." As the United States waged war in Afghanistan and Iraq, Europeans faulted American news organizations for not reporting the human cost of war, and the widespread antiwar demonstrations, although the BBC's Bryant acknowledged, "We watched 9-11 live on TV but it hasn't touched our lives in the same way."[32]

The terrorist attack on the American home front helped restore the demand for serious news. Even if September 11 did not permanently alter public news consumption—as many Americans would soon tune out again until something else of a spectacular nature occurred—the episode reaffirmed journalists' own sense of the significance of their work. Members of the Washington press corps shook off a suspicion that competition from new technology, corporate cost cutting, and public distraction had devalued their product. Reporters shared a collective sense of pride in having responded to the utmost challenge in a professional manner. Keeping the nation informed that day reminded them once again why they went into journalism, and why reporting the news from Washington still mattered.[33]

A Note on Sources

Individually and collectively, those who reported from Washington served as the chief sources for this history of the press corps. They documented their careers abundantly through their reporting, personal papers, interviews and oral histories, memoirs, and a mountain of books.

At the Library of Congress, I consulted the personal papers of Joseph and Stewart Alsop, Raymond Clapper, Elisabeth May Craig, Elmer Davis, Richard Dudman, Bess Furman, Eugene Meyer, Ethel Payne, Eric Sevareid, and the Gridiron Club. The papers of Arthur Krock are at Princeton University; Blair Moody at the Bentley Library of the University of Michigan; Turner Catledge at Mississippi State University; Walter Cronkite and Sig Mickelson at the University of Texas's Institute for News Media History; Claude Barnett at the Chicago Historical Society; and John M. Anspacher, Mary Hornaday, and the Overseas Press Club at the American Heritage Center in Laramie, Wyoming. Alden Todd and Ann Wood made available papers from their private collections. Thomas C. Reeves deposited his research notes and interviews for his biography of Joseph McCarthy at the State Historical Society of Wisconsin. The records of the Federated Press are at Columbia University.

The Broadcast Archives at the University of Maryland in College Park holds manuscripts, books, and periodicals on the development of radio and television. I also made use of their interviews with Martin Agronsky, Nancy Dickerson, Theodore F. Koop, Sig Mickelson, and Bryson Rash. The Eric Freidheim Library and News Information Center contains the records of the National Press Club. At the U.S. Capitol, the Standing Committees of Correspondents for the press gallery and radio-TV gallery maintain their historical minutes.

At the presidential libraries, I used the papers of Richard Oulahan at the Herbert Hoover Library; Stephen T. Early, Harry L. Hopkins, James Rowe Jr., and Samuel I. Rosenman at the Franklin D. Roosevelt Library; and Drew Pearson and Robert Kintner at the Lyndon B. Johnson Library. Presidential libraries have also been diligent in collecting media-related oral histories. Among these, I used the interviews with Jonathan Daniels at the Roosevelt Library; Willard Edwards and Joseph Rauh at the Harry S. Truman Library; Robert E. Clark, James C. Hagerty, and Ann Whitman at the Dwight D.

Eisenhower Library; George Aiken, Joseph Alsop, Henry Bragdon, and a press panel group interview at the John F. Kennedy Library; and Joseph Alsop, Nancy Dickerson, Katharine Graham, Drew Pearson, Charles Roberts, Chalmers Roberts, and William S. White at the Johnson Library.

Additional oral histories with H. V. Kaltenborn, Arthur Krock, Eugene Meyer, and Abel A. Schechter are located at the Columbia Oral History Research Office in New York. Alice Dunnigan's oral history is in the Schlesinger Library at Harvard University. The U.S. Senate Historical Office has related interviews with Pat Holt, Roy McGhee, Floyd Riddick, Dorothye Scott, Darrell St. Claire, Howard Shuman, George Smathers, George Tames, Rein Van Der Zee, Ruth Young Watt, and Francis Wilcox, which are deposited in the Library of Congress and the National Archives. Also at the Library of Congress are interviews done by the Former Members of Congress with Thomas B. Abernathy and Martha Griffiths. The Women in Journalism oral history project at the National Press Club includes interviews with Jane Eads Bancroft, Dorothy Gilliam, Flora Lewis, Sarah McClendon, Mary McGrory, Ruth Cowan Nash, Ethel Payne, Isabelle Shelton, Beth Campbell Short, and the Eleanor Roosevelt Press Conferences, a joint interview with Ann Cottrell Free, Frances Lide, Ruth Montgomery, and Malvina Stephenson. I relied extensively on the transcripts of interviews with journalists on C-SPAN's *Booknotes*, at http://www.booknotes.org.

Among the print reporters, the most useful autobiographies were Holmes Alexander, *Never Lose a War: Memoirs and Observations of a National Columnist* (Greenwich, Conn.: Devin-Adair, 1984), and *Pen and Politics: The Autobiography of a Working Writer* (Morgantown: West Virginia University Library, 1970); Joseph Alsop with Adam Platt, *"I've Seen the Best of It": Memoirs* (New York: W.W. Norton, 1992); Stewart Alsop, *Stay of Execution: A Sort of Memoir* (Philadelphia: J.B. Lippincott, 1973); Jack Anderson, *Confessions of a Muckraker: The Inside Story of Life in Washington during the Truman, Eisenhower, Kennedy, and Johnson Years* (New York: Random House, 1979), and *Peace, War, and Politics: An Eyewitness Account* (New York: Forge, 1998); Russell Baker, *The Good Times* (New York: William Morrow, 1989); Herbert Block, *Herblock: A Cartoonist's Life* (New York: Macmillan, 1993); Simeon Booker, *Black Man's America* (Englewood Cliffs, N.J.: Prentice-Hall, 1964); Ben Bradlee, *A Good Life: Newspapering and Other Adventures* (New York: Simon & Schuster, 1995); Lou Cannon, *Reporting: An Inside View* (Sacramento: California Journal Press, 1977); Liz Carpenter, *Ruffles and Flourishes* (College Station: Texas A&M University Press, 1993); Turner Catledge, *My Life and the Times* (New York: Saturday Review Press, 1972); John Chamberlain, *A Life with the Printed Word* (Chicago: Regnery Gateway, 1982); Marquis Childs, *Witness to Power* (New York: McGraw-Hill, 1975); Raymond Clapper, *Watching the World* (New York: McGraw-Hill, 1944); John Corry, *My Times: Adventures in the News Trade* (New York: Grosset/Putnam, 1993); Hedley Donovan, *Right Place, Right Times; Forty*

Years in Journalism Not Counting My Paper Route (New York: Henry Holt, 1989);
Alice Allison Dunnigan, *A Black Woman's Experience—From Schoolhouse to
White House* (Philadelphia: Dorrance & Company, 1974); Max Frankel, *The
Times of My Life and My Life with the* Times (New York: Random House, 1999);
Bess Furman, *Washington By-Line: The Personal History of a Newspaperwoman*
(New York: Knopf, 1949); Jack W. Germond, *Fat Man in a Middle Seat: Forty
Years of Covering Politics* (New York: Random House, 1999); Virginia Van Der
Veer Hamilton, *Looking for Clark Gable and Other 20th-Century Pursuits: Col-
lected Writings* (Tuscaloosa: University of Alabama Press, 1996); William F.
Kerby, *A Proud Profession: Memoirs of a* Wall Street Journal *Reporter, Editor,
and Publisher* (Homewood, Ill.: Dow Jones-Irwin, 1981); Arthur Krock, *Mem-
oirs: Sixty Years on the Firing Line* (New York: Funk & Wagnalls, 1968); Don
Larrabee, *It's News to Me: A Maine Yankee Reports from Washington* (Washing-
ton: privately published, 1989); Bill Lawrence, *Six Presidents, Too Many Wars*
(New York: Saturday Review Press, 1972); Judy Mann, *Mann for All Seasons:
Wit and Wisdom from the* Washington Post's *Judy Mann* (New York:
MasterMedia, 1990); Nathan McCall, *Makes Me Wanna Holler: A Young Black
Man in America* (New York: Random House, 1994); Sarah McClendon, *Mr.
President! Mr. President! My Fifty Years of Covering the White House* (Santa
Monica, Calif.: General Publishing Group, 1996), and *My Eight Presidents* (New
York: Wyden Books, 1978); Felix Morley, *For the Record* (South Bend, Ind.:
Regnery/Gateway, 1979); Jill Nelson, *Volunteer Slavery: My Authentic Negro
Experience* (Chicago: Noble Press, 1993); James Reston, *Deadline: A Memoir*
(New York: Times Books, 1992); Chalmers M. Roberts, *First Rough Draft: A
Journalist's Journal of Our Times* (New York: Praeger, 1973); Nan Robertson,
The Girls in the Balcony: Women, Men, and the New York Times (New York:
Random House, 1992); Richard H. Rovere, *Arrivals and Departures: A Journalist's
Memoirs* (New York: Macmillan, 1976); Harrison E. Salisbury, *A Time of Change:
A Reporter's Tale of Our Time* (New York: Harper & Row, 1988); Samuel Shaffer,
On and off the Floor: Thirty Years as a Correspondent on Capitol Hill (New
York: Newsweek Books, 1980); Thomas L. Stokes, *Chip off My Shoulder*
(Princeton, N.J.: Princeton University Press, 1940); Helen Thomas, *Dateline:
White House* (New York: Macmillan, 1975), and *Front Row at the White House:
My Life and Times* (New York: Scribner, 1999); Ralph de Toledano, *Lament for
a Generation* (New York: Farrar, Straus, and Cudahy, 1960); Laurence Todd,
Correspondent on the Left: The Memoirs of Laurence Todd, 1882–1957 (Anchor-
age: privately printed, 1996); Walter Trohan, *Political Animals: Memoirs of a
Sentimental Cynic* (Garden City, N.Y.: Doubleday, 1975); William S. White, *The
Making of a Journalist* (Lexington: University Press of Kentucky, 1986); Roger
Wilkins, *A Man's Life: An Autobiography* (Woodbridge, Conn.: Ox Bow, 1982);
and Marguerite Young, *Nothing but the Truth* (New York: Carlton, 1993).

Radio and televison news broadcasters' memoirs included Forrest Boyd,
Instant Analysis: Confessions of a White House Correspondent (Atlanta: John

Knox, 1974); David Brinkley, *Brinkley's Beat: People, Places, and Events That Shaped My Time* (New York: Knopf, 2003) and *11 Presidents, 4 Wars, 22 Political Conventions, 1 Moon Landing, 3 Assassinations, 2,000 Weeks of News and Other Stuff on Television, and 18 Years of Growing Up in North Carolina* (New York: Knopf, 1996); Walter Cronkite, *A Reporter's Life* (New York: Knopf, 1996); Nancy Dickerson, *Among Those Present: A Reporter's View of Twenty-Five Years in Washington* (New York: Random House, 1976); Fred Graham, *Happy Talk: Confessions of a TV Newsman* (New York: W.W. Norton, 1990); H. V. Kaltenborn, *Fifty Fabulous Years, 1900–1950: A Personal Review* (New York: Putnam, 1950); Edward P. Morgan, *Clearing the Air* (Washington: Robert B. Luce, 1963); Robert Pierpoint, *At the White House: Assignment to Six Presidents* (New York: Putnam, 1981); Dan Rather with Mickey Herskowitz, *The Camera Never Blinks: Adventures of a TV Journalist* (New York: William Morrow, 1977); Harry Reasoner, *Before the Colors Fade* (New York: Knopf, 1981); Bob Schieffer, *This Just In: What I Couldn't Tell You on TV* (New York: Putnam, 2003); David Schoenbrun, *On and off the Air: An Informal History of CBS News* (New York: Dutton, 1989); Howard K. Smith, *Events Leading Up to My Death: The Life of a Twentieth-Century Reporter* (New York: St. Martin's, 1996); Lesley Stahl, *Reporting Live* (New York: Simon & Schuster, 1999); Daniel Schorr, *Clearing the Air* (Boston: Houghton Mifflin, 1977) and *Staying Tuned: A Life in Journalism* (New York: Pocket, 2001); Raymond Swing, *"Good Evening!" A Professional Memoir* (New York: Harcourt, Brace, 1964); Frederic William Wile, *News Is Where You Find It: Forty Years' Reporting at Home and Abroad* (Indianapolis: Bobbs-Merrill, 1939); and Judy Woodruff, *"This Is Judy Woodruff at the White House"* (Reading, Mass.: Addison-Wesley, 1982).

Among the foreign correspondents who wrote memoirs were Richard Beeston, *Looking for Trouble: The Life and Times of a Foreign Correspondent* (London: Brassey's, 1997); Henry Brandon, *Special Relationships: A Foreign Correspondent's Memoirs from Roosevelt to Reagan* (New York: Atheneum, 1988); Philomena Jurey, *A Basement Seat to History: Tales of Covering Presidents Nixon, Ford, Carter, and Reagan for the Voice of America* (Washington: Linus, 1995); Masuo Kato, *The Lost War: A Japanese Reporter's Story* (New York: Knopf, 1946); Connie Lawn, *Voice from America: Off the Air with Radio New Zealand's Washington Correspondent* (Auckland: HarperCollins, 1994); and Arthur Willert, *Washington and Other Memories* (Boston: Houghton Mifflin, 1972).

Reporters examined their own profession in such books as Joseph and Stewart Alsop, *The Reporter's Trade* (New York: Reynal & Company, 1959); Bert Andrews and Peter Andrews, *A Tragedy of History: A Journalist's Confidential Role in the Hiss-Chambers Case* (Washington: Robert B. Luce, 1962); James Aronson, *The Press and the Cold War* (Boston: Beacon, 1970); Edward Bliss, *Now the News: The Story of Broadcast Journalism* (New York: Columbia University Press, 1991); Harold Brayman, *The President Speaks Off-the-Record: Historic Evenings with America's Leaders, the Press, and Other Men of Power at*

Washington's Exclusive Gridiron Club (Princeton: Dow Jones Books, 1976); David Broder, *Behind the Front Page: A Candid Look at How the News Is Made* (New York: Simon and Schuster, 1987); Douglass Cater, *The Fourth Branch of Government* (Boston: Houghton Mifflin, 1959); Delbert Clark, *Washington Dateline* (New York: Frederick A. Stokes, 1941); Elias Cose, *The Press* (New York: William Morrow, 1989); [John P. Cosgrove], *shrdlu: An Affectionate Chronicle* (Washington: National Press Club, 1958); Timothy Crouse, *The Boys on the Bus* (New York: Random House, 1973); Elmer Davis, *But We Were Born Free* (Indianapolis: Bobbs-Merrill, 1954); James Deakin, *Straight Stuff: The Reporters, the White House and the Truth* (New York: William Morrow, 1984); Leonard Downie Jr., *The New Muckrakers* (Washington: New Republic Book Company, 1976); James H. Dygert, *The Investigative Journalist: Folk Heroes of a New Era* (Englewood Cliffs, N.J.: Prentice-Hall, 1976); J. Frederick Essary, *Covering Washington: Government Reflected to the Public in the Press, 1822–1926* (Boston: Houghton Mifflin, 1927); James Free, *The First 100 Years! A Casual Chronicle of the Gridiron Club* (Washington: The Gridiron Club, 1985); David Halberstam, *The Powers That Be* (New York: Knopf, 1979); Ray Eldon Hiebert, ed., *The Press in Washington* (New York: Dodd, Mead, 1966); Marvin Kalb, *One Scandalous Story: Clinton, Lewinsky, and Thirteen Days That Tarnished American Journalism* (New York: Free Press, 2001); Tom Kelly, *The Imperial Post: The Meyers, the Grahams, and the Paper That Rules Washington* (New York: William Morrow, 1983); Howard Kurtz, *Hot Air: All Talk, All the Time* (New York: Times Books, 1996); A. Maurice Low, *America at Home* (New York: Arno, 1974 [1908]); A. Kent MacDougall, ed., *The Press: A Critical Look from the Inside* (Princeton, N.J.: Dow Jones Books, 1972); Clark R. Mollenhoff, *Investigative Reporting: From Courthouse to White House* (New York: Macmillan, 1981); Joe Alex Morris, *Deadline Every Minute: The Story of the United Press* (Garden City, N.Y.: Doubleday, 1957); Cabell Phillips, et al., *Dateline: Washington: The Story of National Affairs Journalism in the Life and Times of the National Press Club* (Garden City, N.Y.: Doubleday, 1949); James Reston, *The Artillery of the Press: Its Influence on American Foreign Policy* (New York: Harper & Row, 1967); Ishbel Ross, *Ladies of the Press: The Story of Women in Journalism by an Insider* (New York: Harper & Brothers, 1936); Harrison E. Salisbury, *Without Fear or Favor: The New York Times and Its Times* (New York: Random House, 1980); Marlene Sanders and Marcia Rock, *Waiting for Prime Time: The Women of Television News* (New York: Harper & Row, 1988); Kenneth Stewart, *News Is What We Make It: A Running Story of the Working Press* (Boston: Houghton Mifflin Company, 1943); Tom Wicker, *On Press* (New York: Viking, 1978); and [Wythe Williams] The Man at the Microphone, *Washington Broadcast* (Garden City, N.Y.: Doubleday, Doran, 1944).

Reporters also reflected on Washington life and politics in Stewart Alsop, *The Center: People and Power in Political Washington* (New York: Harper & Row, 1968); Jack Bell, *The Splendid Misery: The Story of the Presidency and*

Power Politics at Close Range (Garden City, N.Y.: Doubleday, 1960); Sidney Blumenthal, *Our Long National Daydream: A Political Pageant of the Reagan Era* (New York: Harper & Row, 1988) and *The Rise of the Counter-Establishment: From Conservative Ideology to Political Power* (New York: Times Books, 1986); David Brinkley, *Washington Goes to War* (New York: Knopf, 1988); Meg Greenfield, *Washington* (New York: Public Affairs, 2001); Marquis Childs, *I Write from Washington* (New York: Harper & Brothers, 1942); Charles Hurd, *When the New Deal Was Young and Gay* (New York: Hawthorne, 1965); Michael Isikoff, *Uncovering Clinton: A Reporter's Story* (New York: Crown, 1999); Judith Martin, *The Name on the White House Floor, and Other Anxieties of Our Times* (New York: Coward, McCann & Geoghean, 1972); Clark R. Mollenhoff, *Washington Cover-Up* (Garden City, N.Y.: Doubleday, 1962) and *Despoilers of Democracy: The Real Story of What Washington Propagandists, Arrogant Bureaucrats, Mismanagers, Influence Peddlers, and Outright Corrupters are Doing to Our Federal Government* (Garden City, N.Y.: Doubleday, 1965); [Drew Pearson and Robert S. Allen] *Washington Merry-Go-Round* (New York: Horace Liveright, 1931); William Small, *To Kill a Messenger: Television News and the Real World* (New York: Hastings House, 1970); Merriman Smith, *The Good New Days: A Not Entirely Reverent Study of Native Habits and Customs in Modern Washington* (Indianapolis: Bobbs-Merrill, 1962) and *Thank You, Mr. President* (New York: Harper & Brothers, 1946); Timothy G. Smith, ed., *Merriman Smith's Book of Presidents: A White House Memoir* (New York: W.W. Norton, 1972); and Ralph de Toledano and Victor Lasky, *Seeds of Treason: The True Story of the Hiss-Chambers Tragedy* (New York: Funk & Wagnalls, 1950).

Finally, my own interaction with hundreds of Washington correspondents furthered my understanding of their profession. As thanked by name in the preface, many of these journalists agreed to personal interviews or provided information during various encounters on the phone, visits to the office, in the Capitol's corridors and galleries, at press conferences, in radio and television studios, and at receptions and formal dinners. Some of them quoted me in their news stories, and for the most part treated me fairly, with a professional objectivity that I have tried to emulate in reporting about them.

Notes

Preface

1. See Douglass Cater, *The Fourth Branch of Government* (Boston: Houghton Mifflin, 1959); and Timothy E. Cook, *Governing with the News: The News Media as a Political Institution* (Chicago: University of Chicago Press, 1998).

2. *Examining Our Credibility*, a report for the American Society of Newspaper Editors, 1998; Daniel Sutter, "Can the Media Be So Liberal? The Economics of Media Bias," *Cato Journal*, 20 (Winter 2001), 431–51; L. Brent Bozell III and Brent H. Baker, eds., *And That's the Way It Is(n't): A Reference Guide to Media Bias* (Alexandria, Va.: Media Research Center, 1990), ix; Sarah Chayes, "Breaking Ranks: A Reporter Dons the Wings of Advocacy," *Columbia Journalism Review* (November/December 2003), 66–67; Norman Solomon and Jeff Cohen, *Wizards of Media Oz: Behind the Curtain of Mainstream News* (Monroe, Maine: Common Courage, 1997), 75, 131; Jay Rosen, *Getting the Connections Right: Public Journalism and the Troubles in the Press* (New York: Twentieth Century Fund, 1996), 2.

3. William A. Rusher, *The Coming Battle for the Media: Curbing the Power of the Media Elite* (New York: William Morrow, 1988), 16; Stanley E. Flink, *Sentinel under Siege: The Triumphs and Troubles of America's Free Press* (Boulder, Col.: Westview, 1997), 5–17.

4. Elmer Davis, *But We Were Born Free* (Indianapolis: Bobbs-Merrill, 1952), 175; Donald A. Ritchie, *American Journalists: Getting the Story* (New York: Oxford University Press, 1997), 94–98, 142–47; Lincoln Steffens, *The Autobiography of Lincoln Steffens* (New York: Harcourt, Brace, 1931), vol. 1: 179; see also Gerald J. Baldasty, *The Commericalization of News in the Nineteenth Century* (Madison: University of Wisconsin Press, 1992); Dan Shiller, *Objectivity and the News: The Public and the Rise of Commercial Journalism* (Philadelphia: University of Pennsylvania Press, 1981); Michael Schudson, *Origins of the Ideal of Objectivity in the Professions: Studies in the History of American Journalism and American Law, 1830–1940* (New York: Garland, 1990); and Richard L. Kaplan, *Politics and the American Press: The Rise of Objectivity, 1865–1920* (New York: Cambridge University Press, 2002).

5. James Reston to Turner Catledge, June 13, 1963, Turner Catledge papers, Mississippi State University.

6. Louis M. Lyons, ed., *Reporting the News: Selections from Nieman Reports* (New York: Atheneum, 1968), 296; *Washington Post*, March 24, December 18, 28, 2002.

7. Stanley Walker, "Our Bloviating Journalists," *The Freeman*, 3 (November 17, 1952), 131; Walter Trohan, *Political Animals: Memoirs of a Sentimental Cynic* (Garden City, N.Y.: Doubleday, 1975), 388–95; panel discussion on press coverage of Congress, National Press Club, November 9, 1998; Ray Eldon Hiebert, ed., *The Press in Washington* (New York: Dodd, Mead, 1966), 60–63; Fred Inglis, *People's Witness: The Journalist in Modern Politics* (New Haven, Conn.: Yale University Press, 2002), 207–10; Howard K. Smith, *Events Leading Up to My Death: The Life of a Twentieth-Century Reporter* (New York: St. Martin's, 1996), 265–76; Kristina Borjesson, ed., *Into the Buzzsaw: Leading Journalists Expose the Myth of a Free Press* (Amherst, N.Y.: Prometheus, 2002), 205; *Washington Post*, March 15, June 10, 2002.

8. S. Robert Lichter, Stanley Rothman, and Linda S. Lichter, *The Media Elite* (Bethesda, Md.: Adler & Adler, 1986), 33, 56–57; *New York Times*, November 25, 1959; Jonathan Schell, *The*

Time of Illusion (New York: Knopf, 1976), 110; Jonathan Chait, "Victim Politics: The Contradictions of Conservative Media Criticism," *New Republic*, 226 (March 18, 2002), 22–25; Eric Alterman, *What Liberal Media? The Truth about Bias and the News* (New York: Basic, 2003); Gary Rosen, "Fire-Breather," *Commentary*, 114 (November 2002), 82–84; Russell Baker letter, *New York Review of Books*, 50 (December 18, 2003), 100.

9. Adam Smith, *An Inquiry into the Nature and Causes of the Wealth of Nations* (Chicago: Encyclopedia Britannica, 1952), 13; Delbert Clark, *Washington Dateline* (New York: Frederick A. Stokes, 1941), 103–6.

10. Donald A. Ritchie, *Press Gallery: Congress and the Washington Correspondents* (Cambridge: Harvard University Press, 1991), 27–29, 90–91; H. L. Mencken, *Prejudices: A Selection* (New York: Vintage, 1958), 227.

11. Bruce Catton, *The Warlords of Washington* (New York: Harcourt, Brace, 1948), 86–87; Cabell Phillips, et al., *Dateline: Washington: The Story of National Affairs Journalism in the Life and Times of the National Press Club* (Garden City, N.Y.: Doubleday, 1949), 289–90; *The Hill*, September 9, 2003.

12. Tom Wicker, *On Press* (New York: Viking, 1978), 95; Lyons, ed., *Reporting the News*, 154, 251; Elaine S. Povitch, *Partners & Adversaries: The Contentious Connection between Congress and the Media* (Arlington, Va.: The Freedom Forum, 1996), 15; *The Hill*, February 19, 2003, August 13, 2003; Jon Katz, "No News Is Good News," *HotWired* (October 9, 1996), 1, 9; Daniel C. Hallin, *We Keep America on Top of the World: Television Journalism and the Public Sphere* (New York: Routledge, 1994), 18–39, 170–80.

13. Allen Drury, *Advise and Consent* (Garden City, N.Y.: Doubleday, 1959); Drury letter to the author, July 1993.

14. Jonathan Yardley, "Lights, Camera, Career," *Washington Post Book World* (January 24, 1999), 3; Yardley letter to the author, March 6, 1999.

Prologue

1. Eugene A. Kelly, "Distorting the News," *American Mercury*, 34 (March 1935), 308; William F. Kerby, *A Proud Profession: Memoirs of a* Wall Street Journal *Reporter, Editor, and Publisher* (Homewood, Ill.: Dow Jones-Irwin, 1981), 52–53.

2. Delbert Clark, *Washington Dateline* (New York: Frederick A. Stokes, 1941), 114; *Editor & Publisher* (May 8, 1919), 16; James Bryce, *The American Commonwealth* (New York: Macmillan, 1888), vol. 3, 585–94; Luther Huston, "World's Top News City," *The Quill*, 47 (November 1959), 53.

3. Theodore G. Joslin, *Hoover Off the Record* (Freeport, N.Y.: Books for Libraries, 1971 [1934]), 68–69; Willard Grosvenor Bleyer, ed., *The Profession of Journalism* (Boston: Atlantic Monthly Press, 1918), 243–63; Marguerite Young, "Ignoble Journalism in the Nation's Capital," *American Mercury*, 34 (February 1935), 239; Richard F. Shepard, *The Paper's Papers: A Reporter's Journey through the Archives of the* New York Times (New York: Times Books, 1996), 200; Walter Trohan, *Political Animals: Memoirs of a Sentimental Cynic* (Garden City, N.Y.: Doubleday, 1975), 50.

4. Silas Bent, *Ballyhoo: The Voice of the Press* (New York: Boni and Liveright, 1927), 42, 181–98; Cabell Phillips, et al., *Dateline: Washington: The Story of National Affairs Journalism in the Life and Times of the National Press Club* (Garden City, N.Y.: Doubleday, 1949), 63; Marion Elizabeth Rodgers, ed., *The Impossible H. L. Mencken: A Selection of His Best Newspaper Stories* (New York: Doubleday, 1991), 15–16, 135–36, 497; Theo Lippmann, Jr., ed., *A Gang of Pecksniffs and Other Comments on Newspaper Publishers, Editors and Reporters by H. L. Mencken* (New Rochelle, N.Y.: Arlington House, 1975), 135–36; Clark, *Washington Dateline*, 62–63; [John P. Cosgrove], *shrdlu: An Affectionate Chronicle* (Washington: National Press Club, 1958), 55–56; Frank R. Kent, "Mr. Coolidge," *American Mercury*, 11 (August 1924), 385–90.

5. [Drew Pearson and Robert S. Allen], *Washington Merry-Go-Round* (New York: Horace Liveright, 1931), 51–77; Clark, *Washington Dateline*, 66–71; Irwin Hood (Ike) Hoover, *Forty-*

Two Years in the White House (Boston: Houghton Mifflin, 1934), 209–10; Louis W. Liebovich, *Bylines in Despair: Herbert Hoover, the Great Depression, and the U.S. News Media* (Westport, Conn.: Praeger, 1994), 83–97, 143–47.

6. Ruth Young Watt oral history, Senate Historical Office, 18; Phillips, et al., *Dateline: Washington*, 61–64; [Cosgrove], *shrdlu*, 59–71; Will Irvin, *Propaganda and the News, or What Makes You Think So?* (New York: Whittlesey House, 1936), 308–9; Donald J. Lisio, *The President and Protest: Hoover, MacArthur, and the Bonus Riot* (New York: Fordham University Press, 1994 [1974]), 61; Oswald Garrison Villard, *Some Newspapers and Newspaper-Men* (New York: Knopf, 1923), 173–74, 184–87, 191; Lawrence Sullivan, *All about Washington* (New York: John Day, 1932), 185–86. *Washington Post*, December 7, 1931.

7. Bess Furman, *Washington By-Line: The Personal History of a Newspaperwoman* (New York: Knopf, 1949), 108; Paul Y. Anderson, "Some Sweet-Smelling Politics," *The Nation*, 135 (August 3, 1932), 102; Kerby, *A Proud Profession*, 50–52; Young, "Ignoble Journalism in the Nation's Capital," 242.

8. John D. Weaver, "Bonus March," *American Heritage*, 14 (June 1963), 23; Herbert Hoover, *The Memoirs of Herbert Hoover: The Cabinet and the Presidency, 1920–1933* (New York: Macmillan, 1952), 285; Joe Alex Morris, *Deadline Every Minute: The Story of the United Press* (Garden City, N.Y.: Doubleday, 1957), 179–81; Furman, *Washington By-Line*, 107–8, 123; Lisio, *The President and Protest*, x, 76–82, 104–7, 143, 156–57, 171, 177.

9. Lisio, *The President and Protest*, 190–225; Laurence Todd, *Correspondent on the Left: The Memoirs of Laurence Todd, 1882–1957* (Anchorage, Alaska: privately printed, 1996), 272–94; Paul Y. Anderson, "Tear-Gas, Bayonets, and Votes," *The Nation*, 135 (August 17, 1932), 139; Kerby, *A Proud Profession*, 55; Clark, *Washington Dateline*, 116; George Manning, "News Men in Thick of B.E.F. Fighting," *Editor & Publisher*, 65 (August 6, 1932), 9.

10. Anderson, "Tear-Gas, Bayonets, and Votes," 139–40; Anderson, "Republican Handsprings," *The Nation*, 135 (August 31, 1932), 188–89; Anderson, "Mourning Becomes Herbert," *The Nation*, 135 (September 28, 1932), 280; Laurence Todd, "Hoover Stamps on Veterans with an Iron Heel," July 29, 1932, Federated Press papers, Columbia University.

11. Joslin, *Hoover Off the Record*, 276; Lisio, *The President and Protest*, 242; Liebovich, *Bylines in Despair*, 168; Todd, *Correspondent on the Left*, 276–77; *Washington Post*, July 30, 1932; *New York Times*, July 31, 1932.

12. Phillips, et al., *Dateline: Washington*, 81–82.

13. London *Times*, July 30, 1932; Clark, *Washington Dateline*, 114–17; Thomas L. Stokes, *Chip off My Shoulder* (Princeton, N.J.: Princeton University Press, 1940), 301–4; Chalmers M. Roberts, *The Washington Post: The First 100 Years* (Boston: Houghton Mifflin, 1977), 189; *Washington Post*, July 3, 1932.

14. "Washington, D.C.," *Fortune*, 10 (March 1934), 59; Richard W. Steele, *Propaganda in an Open Society: The Roosevelt Administration and the Media, 1933–1941* (Westport, Conn.: Greenwood, 1985), 25–31; Charles Hurd, *When the New Deal Was Young and Gay* (New York: Hawthorne, 1965), 247; Turner Catledge, *My Life and the Times* (New York: Saturday Review, 1972), 81–82.

15. For the Washington reporters' political leanings in the 1930s, see the surveys conducted by the sociologist Leo C. Rosten in *The Washington Correspondents* (New York: Harcourt Brace, 1937), 188–218.

Chapter One

1. Grace Tully, *F.D.R. My Boss* (New York: Charles Scribner's Sons, 1949), 76; Graham J. White, *FDR and the Press* (Chicago: University of Chicago Press, 1979), 113–16; Leo C. Rosten, *The Washington Correspondents* (New York: Harcourt Brace, 1937), 71; *Detroit News*, March 3, 1935, and an undated clipping in the Blair Moody Papers, Bentley Library, University of Michigan.

2. Collectively, the Hearst papers ranked even lower than the *Chicago Tribune* in the Washington correspondents' estimate. Rosten, *The Washington Correspondents*, 195–96, 274; Delbert Clark, *Washington Dateline* (New York: Frederick A. Stokes, 1941), 313.

3. Harold L. Ickes, *America's House of Lords: An Inquiry into the Freedom of the Press* (New York: Harcourt, Brace, 1939), 55, 83; Richard Norton Smith, *The Colonel: The Life and Legend of Robert R. McCormick* (Boston: Houghton Mifflin, 1997), 277; Joseph Freeman, *An American Testament: A Narrative of Rebels and Romantics* (New York: Farrar & Rinehart, 1936), 210–11; Willard Edwards interview, Thomas C. Reeves Collection, State Historical Society of Wisconsin; Walter Trohan, *Political Animals: Memoirs of a Sentimental Cynic* (Garden City, N.Y.: Doubleday, 1975), 28; John Tebbel, *An American Dynasty: The Story of the McCormicks, Medills, and Pattersons* (Garden City, N.Y.: Doubleday, 1947), 221; [Drew Pearson and Robert S. Allen], *Washington Merry-Go-Round* (New York: Horace Liveright, 1931), 356–57.

4. Willard A. Edwards oral history, 48, Harry S. Truman Library, Independence, Missouri; *Chicago Tribune*, May 1721, 1953, January 2, 1954. Arthur Sears Henning's reminiscences appeared in sixty-five installments in the *Chicago Tribune* between 1953 and 1957.

5. *Chicago Tribune*, January 2, 1954, January 8, 1956; Trohan, *Political Animals*, 31–33.

6. Elisabeth May Craig, unpublished memoir, Craig papers, Library of Congress; Joseph Gies, *The Colonel of Chicago* (New York: Dutton, 1979), 126–28; *Chicago Tribune*, April 2, 1955; see also Fred W. Friendly, *Minnesota Rag: The Dramatic Story of the Landmark Supreme Court Case That Gave New Meaning to Freedom of the Press* (New York: Random House, 1981).

7. Lloyd Wendt, Chicago Tribune: *The Rise of a Great American Newspaper* (Chicago: Rand McNally, 1979), 562; Harold L. Ickes, *The Secret Diary of Harold L. Ickes: The First Thousand Days, 1933–1936* (New York: Simon & Schuster, 1953), 204; Trohan, *Political Animals*, 31.

8. Edwards oral history, 1–9, 25, 28, 38–40; Wendt, Chicago Tribune, 562.

9. Rudolph M. Under, ed., *The* Chicago Tribune *News Staff, 1920s–1960s* (Chicago: privately published, 1991), 52; Chesly Manly, *The Twenty-Year Revolution from Roosevelt to Eisenhower* (Chicago: Henry Regnery, 1954), 32–46; Wendt, Chicago Tribune, 562; Trohan, *Political Animals* 22–25, 33–35, 54, 61–62, 66, 130, 157.

10. Michael Reilly, *Reilly of the White House* (New York: Simon & Schuster, 1947), 87–90; Smith, *The Colonel*, 360–64; Trohan, *Political Animals*, 62.

11. "All Swell on the Potomac," *Times Talk*, 1 (November 1947), 6–7, Turner Catledge papers, Mississippi State University; Richard Oulahan, "Washington Bureau Covers a Wide Field," *The Little Times* (August 17, 1929), Richard V. Oulahan papers, Herbert Hoover Library, West Branch, Iowa; Lippmann to Krock, March 25, 1932, Arthur Krock papers, Princeton University; Rosten, *The Washington Correspondents*, 169–72, 195–98.

12. Krock, "My Life with Turner Catledge," manuscript for *Times Talk*, personal memorandum, May 5, 1927, Krock papers; Arthur Krock, *Memoirs: Sixty Years on the Firing Line* (New York: Funk & Wagnalls, 1968), 13–32, 67, 79.

13. James Sayler, "Window on an Age: Arthur Krock and the New Deal Era, 1929–1941" (Ph.D. diss., Rutgers, 1978), 103–4; Hanson W. Baldwin and Shepard Stone, eds., *We Saw It Happen: The News behind the News That's Fit to Print* (New York: Simon and Schuster, 1938), 27–28; Arthur Krock, "Krock Tells of Ochs' 'Cautious Daring' in Planning Paper," *Editor and Publisher* 67 (April 13, 1935), 6; Lester Markel, *What You Don't Know Can Hurt You: A Study of Public Opinion and Public Emotion* (Washington: Public Affairs Press, 1972), 233, 236.

14. Richard F. Shepard, *The Paper's Papers: A Reporter's Journey through the Archives of the New York Times* (New York: Times Books, 1996), 200.

15. Krock, *Memoirs*, 80–81; Turner Catledge, *My Life and the Times* (New York: Harper & Row, 1971), 59–60, 77–78; Sayler, "Window on an Age," 134, 137–43, 150; *New York Times*, April 13, 1974; Krock, "My Life with Turner Catledge," Krock to Mark Ethridge, March 31, 1960, Krock papers; Shepard, *The Paper's Papers*, 200; Neil MacNeil letter to author, March 31, 2001.

16. See Richard Kluger, *The Paper: The Life and Death of the* New York Herald Tribune (New York: Knopf, 1986); Arthur Krock, *The Consent of the Governed and Other Deceits* (Boston: Little, Brown, 1971), 233–34; James B. Reston, "The Job of the Reporter," in Robert Edward

Garst, ed., *The Newspaper: Its Making and Its Meaning* (New York: Charles Scribner's Sons, 1945), 106–7; Richard Burritt to Catledge, 15 June 1953, Catledge papers.

17.   Bess Furman, *Washington By-Line: The Personal History of a Newspaperwoman* (New York: Knopf, 1949), 348; Catledge to Luther Huston, February 14, 1947, Huston to Catledge, March 13, May 13, July 29, 1947, and May 24, 1949, Huston Memorandum, December 23, 1950, Lewis Wood to Catledge, March 13, 1947, Theodore M. Bernstein to Catledge, December 19, 1963, Catledge papers; Catledge, *My Life and the* Times, 167; Catledge to Krock, January 23, 1950, Krock papers; Reston, "The Job of the Reporter," 107; *New York Times*, April 13, 1974; *Washington Post*, April 13, 1974; Shepard, *The Paper's Papers*, 327. The verse is John 15:4.

18.   *Washington Post*, April 13, 1974; Elmer Davis, *History of the* New York Times, *1851–1921* (New York: Greenwood, 1969 [1921]), vii–xxii, 197–202; Lester Markel, "Interpretation of the News and the Sunday Newspaper," in Garst, ed., *The Newspaper*, 25–29; Markel, *What You Don't Know Can Hurt You*, 238; Krock, *In the Nation, 1932–1966* (New York: McGraw Hill, 1966), 3–9.

19.   "The Troubled Press," *Fortune*, 45 (February 1952), 176; School of Public and International Affairs, Princeton University, *Conference on the Press, April 23–25, 1931* (Washington: Printing Corporation of America, 1931), 20; Kenneth Stewart, *News Is What We Make It: A Running Story of the Working Press* (Boston: Houghton Mifflin Company, 1943), 217–18; *New York Times*, April 13, 1974; Tom Wicker introduction to Krock, *In The Nation*, xiv.

20.   Neil MacNeil letter to the author, March 13, 2001; *New York Times*, April 13, 1974; *Washington Post*, April 13, 1974; Josephson, "The Talleyrand of the *Times*," in John E. Drewry, ed., *More Post Biographies: Articles of Enduring Interest about Famous Journalists and Journals and Other Subjects Journalistic* (Athens: University of Georgia Press, 1947), 139–40, 150–51; Harrison E. Salisbury, *Without Fear or Favor: The* New York Times *and Its Times* (New York: Random House, 1980), 419.

21.   Krock, *Memoirs*, 146–47, 151, 159; "The Reminiscences of Arthur Krock," 12–13, 15, 140, Oral History Research Office, Columbia University, 41; Sayler, "Window on an Age," 213–21; Turner Catledge to Gay Talese, July 14, 1968, Catledge papers.

22.   *New York Times*, March 3, 25, 1933; Gary Dean Best, *The Critical Press and the New Deal: The Press versus Presidential Power, 1933–1938* (Westport, Conn.: Praeger, 1993), 47; Merriman Smith, *The Good New Days: A Not Entirely Reverent Study of Native Habits and Customs in Modern Washington* (Indianapolis: Bobbs-Merrill, 1962), 19.

23.   M. E. McIntyre memorandum for Early, April 2, 1933, Krock to Marguerite LeHand, May 2, 1933, LeHand to Krock, May 3, 1933, Stephen Early papers, Franklin D. Roosevelt Library; Rosten, *The Washington Correspondents*, 41; Tully, *F.D.R. My Boss*, 200.

24.   Krock, *Memoirs*, 144–45, 153–54, 169–70; "Reminiscences of Arthur Krock," 24, 28; *New York Times*, April 13, 1933; James E. Sargent, *Roosevelt and the Hundred Days: Struggle for the Early New Deal* (New York: Garland, 1981), 124–25; Josephson, "The Talleyrand of the *Times*," 155; Baldwin and Stone, eds., *We Saw It Happen*, 11–13; Best, *The Critical Press and the New Deal*, 14; Krock, *The Consent of the Governed and Other Deceits*, 55; "Reminiscences of Arthur Krock," 23–24, 31; Charles Hurd, *When the New Deal was Young and Gay* (New York: Hawthorne, 1965), 179.

25.   Timothy G. Smith, ed., *Merriman Smith's Book of Presidents: A White House Memoir* (New York: W.W. Norton, 1972), 240; White, *FDR and the Press*, 5–24; Neil MacNeil, *Without Fear of Favor* (New York: Harcourt Brace, 1940), 154; Hurd, *When the New Deal was Young and Gay*, 230; H. V. Kaltenborn, *Fifty Fabulous Years, 1900–1950: A Personal Review* (New York: Putnam's, 1950), 173; Laurence Todd, *Correspondent on the Left: The Memoirs of Laurence Todd, 1882–1957* (Anchorage, Alaska: privately printed, 1996), 298.

26.   *New York Times*, February 2, 1934; Krock, *Memoirs*, 172; Harrison E. Salisbury, *A Journey for Our Times: A Memoir* (New York: Harper & Row, 1983), 127; Reilly, *Reilly of the White House*, 91; Betty Houchin Winfield, *FDR and the New Media* (Urbana: University of Illinois Press, 1990), 36; Josephson, "The Talleyrand of the *Times*," 146; Sayler, "Window on an Age," 65.

27. Catledge, *My Life and the* Times, 77–78; Shepard, *The Paper's Papers*, 200, 215; Sayler, "Window on an Age," 66, 296–99; Krock *Memoirs*, 82, 89, 175, 178; *New York Times*, November 25, 1934.

28. Krock to Stephen Early, December 26, 1934, Early papers.

29. *New York Times*, February 2, 1934; Krock, *Memoirs*, 172; Salisbury, *A Journey for Our Times*, 127; Reilly, *Reilly of the White House*, 91; Winfield, *FDR and the News Media*, 6.

30. Raymond Clapper, "Why Reporters Like Roosevelt," *Literary Digest*, 14 (June 1934), 89–90; Hurd, *When the New Deal was Young and Gay*, 12, 240–42, 267; Markel, *What You Don't Know Can Hurt You*, 74; Salisbury, *A Journey for Our Times*, 127.

31. Rosten, *The Washington Correspondents*, 53–54; Best, *The Critical Press and the New Deal*, 16–18, 31–32, 46; Clark, *Washington Dateline*, 83–86; Arthur M. Schlesinger, *The Coming of the New Deal*, 1933–1935 (Boston: Houghton Mifflin, 1959), 565; Stephen Skowronek, *The Politics Presidents Make: Leadership from John Adams to Bill Clinton* (Cambridge, Mass.: Belknap, 1997), 288–95, 305–13; John Orman, "Covering the American Presidency: Valanced Reporting in the Periodical Press, 1900–1982," *Presidential Studies Quarterly*, 14 (Summer 1984), 385.

32. Gay Talese, *The Kingdom and the Power* (New York: World, 1969), 52–53; Turner Catledge to Talese, July 14, 1968, Catledge papers; *New York Times*, May 7, 1935.

33. Baldwin and Stone, eds., *We Saw It Happen*, 6, 11, 20, 27; *New York Times*, July 4, 1934; Michael R. Beschloss, *Kennedy and Roosevelt: The Uneasy Alliance* (New York: W.W. Norton, 1980), 79, 110, 126; Richard J. Whalen, *The Founding Father: The Story of Joseph P. Kennedy* (New York: New American Library, 1964), 145–46; Nigel Hamilton, *JFK, Reckless Youth* (New York: Random House, 1992), 154, 162, 212; see the exchange between Richard Harwood and James Sayler in the *Washington Post*, April 24 and June 3, 1993.

34. Krock, *Memoirs*, 145, 162–65; Krock to Catledge, January 14, 1971, Krock papers; Catledge, *My Life and the* Times, 86; White, *FDR and the Press*, 71–72.

35. Catledge to Krock, February 3, 1955, Krock papers; Catledge to Talese, July 14, 1968, Catledge papers; Catledge, *My Life and the* Times, 86–88; Krock, *Memoirs*, 86, 175–77; Josephson, "The Talleyrand of the *Times*," 157–58; Sayler, "Window on an Age," 66; "Reminiscences of Arthur Krock," 39, 41, 44–45, 89; see also Joseph P. Lash, *Eleanor and Franklin* (New York: W.W. Norton, 1971), 564–65.

36. Harold L. Ickes, *The Secret Diary of Harold L. Ickes: The Inside Struggle, 1936–1939* (New York: Simon & Schuster, 1954), 66; MacNeil, *Without Fear of Favor*, 154–55.

37. Krock to Early, February 16, 23, 1937, Early Papers; Krock, *Memoirs*, 173; "Reminiscences of Arthur Krock," 51–53; *New York Times*, February 6, 28, 1937. Sayler, "Window on an Age," 326–28; Arthur Krock, *In the Nation, 1932–1966* (New York: McGraw-Hill, 1966), 47.

38. Winfield, *FDR and the New Media*, 62–63; Krock to Early, March 1, 1937, Early Papers; Josephson, "The Talleyrand of the *Times*," 156; Hurd, *When the New Deal was Young and Gay*, 229–30; Krock memorandum December 23, 1937, Joseph P. Kennedy to Krock, March 8, 1938, Krock papers; *New York Times*, April 13, 1974; Krock, *Memoirs*, 310–11; Josephson, "The Talleyrand of the *Times*," 142–43; David E. Koskoff, *Joseph P. Kennedy: A Life and Times* (Englewood Cliffs, N.J.: Prentice-Hall, 1974), 140–41, Trohan, *Political Animals*, 113–15; Smith, *The Colonel*, 379; Baldwin and Stone, eds., *We Saw It Happen*, 3–5.

39. A. W. Noyes to Krock, February 7, 1938, Krock papers; Sayler, "Window on an Age," 382, 390; Krock, *Memoirs*, 205–7; "Reminiscences of Arthur Krock," 58–61, 65–66; U.S. Senate, Committee on Commerce, *Nomination of Harry L. Hopkins to Be Secretary of Commerce*, 76th Cong., 1st sess., (1939), 11–12, 54–57.

40. Berger, *The Story of the* New York Times, 423–24, 430; Josephson, "The Talleyrand of the *Times*," 163; Krock, *Memoirs*, 82–83, 86; Susan E. Tifft and Alex S. Jones, *The Trust: The Private and Powerful Families behind the* New York Times (Boston: Little, Brown, 1999), 175–76; Krock, "My Life with Turner Catledge," Krock papers; Eric Alterman, *Sound and Fury: The Washington Punditocracy and the Collapse of American Politics* (New York: HarperCollins, 1992), 54; Edwin Diamond, *Behind the* Times: *Inside the* New York Times (New York: Villard, 1994), 43.

41. Krock, *Memoirs*, 175–77; "Reminiscences of Arthur Krock," 44–45; *New York Times*, November 6, 1940; Sayler, "Window on an Age," 369–72; Winfield, *FDR and the New Media*, 128, 144; Shepard, *The Paper's Papers*, 215; Hurd, *When the New Deal was Young and Gay*, 239; "President & Press," *Time* (July 24, 1939), 35–36; David Bulman, ed., *Molders of Opinion*, (Milwaukee, Wis.: Bruce, 1945), 1–12; F. B. Marbut, *News from the Capital: The Story of Washington Reporting* (Carbondale: Southern Illinois University Press, 1971), 178–79; Richard V. Steele, *Propaganda in an Open Society: The Roosevelt Administration and the Media, 1933–1941* (Westport, Conn.: Greenwood, 1985), 60–61, Trohan, *Political Animals*, 157–58.

42. Wendt, Chicago Tribune, 615, 618–20; Smith, *The Colonel*, 415–19; Burton K. Wheeler with Paul F. Healy, *Yankee from the West* (Garden City, N.Y.: Doubleday, 1962), 32–36.

43. Wendt, Chicago Tribune, 617; Wheeler, *Yankee from the West*, 36; Wayne S. Cole, *Roosevelt and the Isolationists, 1932–1945* (Lincoln: University of Nebraska Press, 1983), 478–79; David M. Kennedy, *Freedom from Fear: The American People in Depression and War, 1929–1945* (New York: Oxford University Press, 1999), 485–88; Trohan, *Political Animals*, 169–70; Thomas Fleming, "The Big Leak," *American Heritage*, 38 (December 1987), 65–71.

44. Gies, *The Colonel of Chicago*, 165–69, 206–11; Trohan, *Political Animals*, 165–80.

45. Krock, *Memoirs*, 177; Krock to Edwin L. James, November 17, 1943, Krock to Walter Lippmann, November 1943, Krock papers.

46. John F. Stacks, *Scotty: James B. Reston and the Rise and Fall of American Journalism* (Boston: Little, Brown, 2002), 162–63; Bill Lawrence, *Six Presidents, Too Many Wars* (New York: Saturday Review Press, 1972), 47–51; Catledge, *My Life and the* Times, 132, 159; James Reston, *Deadline: A Memoir* (New York: Times Books, 1992), 101–2; Krock, *Memoirs*, 92; Shepard, *The Paper's Papers*, 202; author interview with Neil MacNeil.

47. Reston, *Deadline*, 104–5, 110–11, 130–33, 137–39; Reston, "The Job of the Reporter," 104–7; Shepard, *The Paper's Papers*, 202; "Man of Influence," *Time*, 75 (February 15, 1960), 74–76; Clifton Daniel to Krock, December 8, 1966, Krock papers.

48. Reston, *Deadline*, 141–43; Reston, "The Job of the Reporter," 97; "Reminiscences of Arthur Krock," 93; author interview with Neil MacNeil; Stacks, *Scotty*, 112; Arthur Hays Sulzberger to Reston, April 14, 1947, Reston to Sulzberger, April 15, 1947, Edwin L. James to Krock, April 28, 1947, Krock to James, May 12, 1947, Krock papers.

49. Reston, *Deadline*, 138; Krock, *Memoirs*, 83–84; Shepard, *The Paper's Papers*, 215.

50. Josephson, "The Talleyrand of the *Times*," 164; James MacGregor Burns, *Roosevelt: The Soldier of Freedom* (New York: Harcourt Brace, 1970), 201; Krock, *Memoirs*, 141; "Reminiscences of Arthur Krock," 10, 29, 45, 89; Reston, *Deadline*, 144; Krock, "The Gathering of the News," in Garst, ed., *The Newspaper*, 43–44; "All Swell on the Potomac," *Times Talk*, 1 (November 1947), 6–7.

51. Catledge, *My Life and the* Times, 144; Krock, *Memoirs*, 208; Berger, *The Story of the* New York Times, 507; *New York Times*, April 13, 1945.

52. Charles Puckette to Arthur H. Sulzberger, March 20, 1952, Catledge papers; Reston, *Deadline*, 139.

53. Trohan, *Political Animals*, 184, 242–44; Edwards oral history, 25; Smith, *The Colonel*, 483–85.

54. *The Hill*, August 4, 2003; Neil Hickey, "Converge Me Up, Scottie: Tribune Beams toward a Multimedia Future," *Columbia Journalism Review* (May/June 2000), 18–22; Paul Starobin, "Mr. Warren Goes to Washington," *Columbia Journalism Review* (November/December 1994), 13.

55. Diamond, *Behind the* Times, 63, 236–37; Robert Sam Anson, "The Best of Times, the Words of Times," *Esquire* 119 (March 1993), 103–10, 181–82, 184, 186–88; *Washington Post*, November 6, 1993.

Chapter Two

1. See Harvard Sitkoff, *A New Deal for Blacks: The Emergence of Civil Rights as a National Issue* (New York: Oxford University Press, 1978) and Nancy J. Weiss, *Farewell to the Party of Lincoln: Black Politics in the Age of FDR* (Princeton, N.J.: Princeton University Press, 1983).

2. Enoch P. Waters, *American Diary: A Personal History of the Black Press* (Chicago: Path Press, 1987), 302; see also Kathleen A. Hake, *Ted Poston: Pioneer American Journalist* (Athens: University of Georgia Press, 1998), 89–109.

3. Mary Church Terrell, *A Colored Woman in a White World* (New York: Arno, 1980 [1940]), 383–96; Constance McLaughlin Green, *The Secret City: A History of Race Relations in the Nation's Capital* (Princeton, N.J.: Princeton University Press, 1967), 184–214; David L. Lewis, *District of Columbia: A Bicentennial History* (New York: W.W. Norton, 1976), 57–80; Gunnar Myrdal, *An American Dilemma: The Negro Problem and Modern Democracy* (New York: Harper, 1944), 631–32; Louis Lautier, "Jim Crow in the Nation's Capital," *The Crisis*, 47 (April 1940), 107, 125; Elliott M. Rudwick, "Oscar De Priest and the Jim Crow Restaurant in the U.S. House of Representatives," *Journal of Negro Education*, 35 (Winter 1966), 77–82; Simeon Booker, *Black Man's America* (Englewood Cliffs, N.J.: Prentice-Hall, 1964), 145–46.

4. Booker, *Black Man's America*, 153; *Baltimore Afro-American*, April 19, 1947; Waters, *American Diary*, 135, 141–42; "Fortune Press Analysis: Negroes," *Fortune* (May 1945), 233, 235; *Chicago Defender*, August 6, 1955; Myrdal, *An American Dilemma*, 908–17. Some southern white papers published "black star" editions for African Americans by omitting the financial page and replacing it with news and features from the black community, while a few white papers ran regular columns on "Colored Activities." Maxwell R. Brooks, *The Negro Press Re-Examined* (Boston: Christopher Publishing House, 1959), 63.

5. Vishnu V. Oak, *The Negro Newspaper* (Yellow Springs, Ohio: Antioch Press, 1948), 69, 85–86; see also Lee Finkle, *Forum for Protest: The Black Press during World War II* (Cranbury, N.J.: Associated University Presses, 1975); Roland E. Wolseley, *The Black Press, U.S.A.* (Ames: Iowa State University Press, 1980); Jannett L. Dates and William Barlow, eds., *Split Image: African Americans in the Mass Media* (Washington: Howard University Press, 1990).

6. Waters, *American Diary*, 235, 419, 424; Lawrence D. Hogan, *A Black National News Service: The Associated Negro Press and Claude Barnett, 1919–1945* (Rutherford, N.J.: Dickinson University Press, 1984), 45–48, 60–69.

7. Claude Barnett to Alvin White, March 9, April 11, 1939, and January 9, 1940, White to Barnett, February 12, 1939, Claude Barnett papers, Chicago Historical Society; Trezzvant W. Anderson to Stephen Early, October 23, 1933, Frederick S. Weaver to Early, October 22, 1933, Weaver to Franklin D. Roosevelt, November 6, 1933, Early to Weaver, November 15, 1933, Frieda Kirschway to Franklin D. Roosevelt, March 1, 1941, Stephen T. Early papers, Franklin D. Roosevelt Library; Jonathan Daniel oral history, 19–20, 24, Roosevelt Library; Graham J. White, *FDR and the Press* (Chicago: University of Chicago Press, 1979), 18–19; Betty Hochin Winfield, *FDR and the News Media* (Urbana: University of Illinois Press, 1990), 55–56.

8. Jonathan Daniels, *White House Witness, 1942–1945* (Garden City, N.Y.: Doubleday, 1975), 11–13; Eleanor Roosevelt, *This I Remember* (New York: Harper, 1949), 164; Joseph P. Lash, *Eleanor and Franklin* (New York: W.W. Norton, 1971), 521, 531–32; Maurine H. Beasley, *Eleanor Roosevelt and the Media: A Quest for Self-Fulfillment* (Urbana: University of Illinois Press, 1987), ix, 102, 142–43; Stephen Early memoranda for Malvina Thompson Scheider, August 5, September 11, 1935, Early memorandum for Mrs. Roosevelt, March 20, 1936, Early papers.

9. Walter White to Franklin D. Roosevelt, November 27, 1939, James Rowe Jr. memorandum for Roosevelt, December 27, 1939, October 23, 25, 1940, James Rowe Jr. papers, Roosevelt Library; Steve Early press conference, statements by Bruce Pinter, John Henry, Walter Trohan, and George Duro, October 30, 1940, Blair Moody to the editor of *Time* magazine, November 14, 1940, James M. Sloan to Early, November 22, 1940, Early papers; "White House Corps Defend 'Steve' Early," *Editor & Publisher* (November 16, 1940), 4.

10. Frederick S. Weaver to editors, November 26, 1940, Claude Barnett to Alvin White, December 7, 11, 1940, White to Barnett, December 1940, Barnett to Paul J. McGahan and Alfred J. Flynn, December 19, 1940, Robert L. Vann to Barnett, April 6, 1939, P. B. Young to Barnett, April 7, 1939, Barnett to White, March 9, April 11, 1939, January 9, 1940, Barnett

papers; Claude Barnett to Stephen Early, December 7, 1940, James Allen memorandum to William D. Hassett, December 10, 1940, Early papers; Louis Lautier to C. A. Franklin, January 22, 1941, FDR Official Files, Roosevelt Library.

11. A. S. Scott to Early, May 7, 1941, Early to Scott, May 13, 1941, Ruthjane Rumelt to Hassett, May 15, 1941, Paul Wooten to A. S. Scott, May 28, 1941, Early memorandum to William D. Hassett, May 31, 1941, Early to Eleanor Roosevelt, February 10, 1941, Early papers; author interview with William Gordon (former editor of the *Atlanta Daily World*).

12. Claude Barnett to Ulrie Bell, February 15, 1942, Barnett to Alvin White, January 15, February 18, 1942, Barnett Papers; Hogan, *A Black National News Service*, 107; Waters, *American Diary*, 304.

13. Alvin White to Claude Barnett, May 10, August 8, 1942, Barnett papers; Hogan, *A Black National News Service*, 215–29; Waters, *American Diary*, 83, 303–4; Carlton B. Goodlett, "50 Years of NNPA and Its Future Service Role," *National Black Monitor* (June 1990), reprinted in the *Congressional Record*, 101st Cong., 2nd sess., E 2241–43.

14. Patrick S. Washburn, *A Question of Sedition: The Federal Government's Investigation of the Black Press during World War II* (New York: Oxford University Press, 1986), 89–91; *Chicago Defender*, June 26, 1948; Waters, *American Diary*, 24, 70; J. Edgar Hoover to Edwin M. Watson, September 24, 1943, with FBI report, "Survey of Racial Conditions in the United States," Official Files, Roosevelt Library.

15. John Sengstacke to Early, January 18, 1944, Jonathan Daniels memorandum to Early, February 4, 1944, Early papers; Washburn, *A Question of Sedition*, 199–200, 265.

16. McAlpin's byline identified him as representing the "Washington bureau of the *Atlanta Daily World* and NNPA," *Atlanta Daily World*, February 9, 1944; *Atlanta Daily World* to John Sengstacke, November 1943, Sengstacke to Early, February 1, 9, 1944, John T. Sherwood to Frank J. Wilson, February 4, 1944, C. A. Scott to Early, February 4, 1944, Aurelius S. Scott, et al., telegram to Roosevelt, February 9, 1944, Early papers.

17. *Washington Tribune*, April 21, 1945.

18. U.S. Congress, Senate, Committee on Rules and Administration, unpublished "Hearing on the Application of Louis R. Lautier for Admission to Senate Press Gallery and Hearing on Reports of Discrimination in Admission to Senate Restaurants and Cafeterias," 80th Cong., 1st sess., March 18, 1947, pp. 24–26, R.G. 46, National Archives and Records Administration.

19. Alvin White to Claude Barnett, January 26, 1943, Barnett to White, February 12, 1943, Frederick C. McMillen to ANP, March 9, 1943, Ernest S. Johnson to A. Philip Randolph, August 1, 1941, Johnson to Barnett, February 8, May 13, 23, June 16, 19, 1943, April 5, 30, 1945, Barnett to Johnson, February 9, 16, 1943, March 15, 1943, June 19, 1945, Johnson to William Hassett, June 30, 1943, Barnett papers.

20. Ernest S. Johnson to Claude Barnett, May 9, October 10, 1944, January 14, 1945, Johnson to Sam Rayburn, July 31, 1943, Johnson to Harold Beckley, March 24, 1944, Barnett to Johnson, July 17, 1943, January 12, 1945, Barnett papers.

21. Alvin White to Claude Barnett, January 3, 1946, Ernest S. Johnson to Barnett, September 11, 22, October 16, 1945, January 29, 1946, Barnett to Johnson, August 30, 1944, January 23, 1945, Barnett papers; Hogan, *A Black National News Service*, 228–29.

22. "Hearing on the Application of Louis Lautier," 10–12, 14, 34–35, 57, 61–73; *Baltimore Afro-American*, March 25, 1947; *Chicago Daily News*, March 12, 1947; *New York Times*, March 9, 1947; *Chicago Bee*, March 16, 1947; *Washington Evening Star*, March 12, 1947; *Washington Post*, March 7, 20, 1947; *New York Herald Tribune*, March 7, 20, 1947; *Baltimore Afro-American*, March 15, 22, 29, 1947.

23. Author interview with Griffing Bancroft; "Hearing on the Application of Louis Lautier," 29–43, 54–55, 58.

24. "Hearing on the Application of Louis Lautier," 59; *Newsweek*, March 31, 1947; *Washington Post*, March 30, 1947; *New York Times*, March 27, 1947.

25. "Hearing on the Application of Louis Lautier," 40; Allice Allison Dunnigan, *A Black Woman's Experience: From Schoolhouse to White House* (Philadelphia: Dorrance, 1974), 187, 189–212;

Alice Dunnigan to Claude Barnett, January 2, 1947, Dunnigan to Franklin Davis, March 21, 1947, Davis to Dunnigan, April 29, 1947, Davis to William Theis, April 2, 1947, Barnett to Dunnigan February 5, 1947, January 26, 1948, Barnett papers.

26.   Dunnigan, *A Black Woman's Experience*, 211.

27.   *Washington Evening Star*, May 7, 1962; *New York Times*, May 8, 1962; *Washington Post*, May 8, 1962; Lautier, "Jim Crow in the Nation's Capital," 107, 125; Andrew Buni, *Robert L. Vann of the* Pittsburgh Courier*: Politics and Black Journalism* (Pittsburgh: University of Pittsburgh Press, 1974), 145, 311.

28.   Author interview with Bob Barr; *Washington Post*, May 8, 1962; Booker, *Black Man's America*, 207–8; *New York Times*, May 8, 1962.

29.   Waters, *American Diary*, 425; Ruth Edmonds Hill, ed., *The Black Women Oral History Project*, vol. 3 (Westport, Conn.: Meckler, 1991), 96–97.

30.   Dunnigan, *A Black Woman's Experience*, 163–64, 182; Hill, ed., *The Black Women Oral History Project*, 72–94; see also Rodger Streitmatter, "Alice Allison Dunnigan: Champion of the Decline of Jim Crow," in *Raising Her Voice: African-American Women Journalists Who Changed History* (Lexington: University Press of Kentucky, 1994), 107–17.

31.   Dunnigan, *A Black Woman's Experience*, 169–72.

32.   Ibid., 174, 184–87, 194–201.

33.   Ibid., 199–205; Carlton Goodlett to Alice Dunnigan, 1943, Dunnigan to Claude Barnett, November 21, 1946, Barnett to Dunnigan, November 27, 1946, January 27, 1947, February 5, 1947, April 29, 1947, January 26, 1948, Barnett papers.

34.   Dunnigan, *A Black Woman's Experience*, 220–21, 298; F. M. Davis to Dunnigan, June 25, 1947, Barnett papers.

35.   Dunnigan, *A Black Woman's Experience*, 228–33.

36.   Ibid., 233–36; on pooling, see Beth Campbell Short oral history, Washington Press Club Foundation, Archives of the National Press Club, 54.

37.   Dunnigan, *A Black Woman's Experience*, 253–55, 294–95, 301–2, 334–35.

38.   Dunnigan to Barnett, c. May 1947, c. August 1947, August 26, 1947, January 30, 1948, Dunnigan to ANP, August 4, 1947, Barnett papers; Dunnigan, *A Black Woman's Experience*, 338.

39.   Ethel Payne oral history, Washington Press Club Foundation; see also Rodger Streitmatter, "No Taste for Fluff: Ethel L. Payne, African-American Journalist," *Journalism Quarterly*, 68 (Fall 1991), 528–40; Streitmatter, "Ethel L. Payne: Agent for Change in the Civil Rights Movement, in *Raising Her Voice*, 118–28; and Donald A. Ritchie, *American Journalists: Getting the Story* (New York: Oxford University Press, 1997), 264–67.

40.   Dunnigan, *A Black Woman's Experience*, 339–40, 350; Ethel Payne, "A Tribute to Sherman Briscoe," November 17, 1979, Ethel L. Payne papers, Library of Congress; see also Ethel L. Payne, "Loneliness in the Capital: The Black National Correspondent," in Henry G. LaBrie III, ed., *Perspectives of the Black Press: 1974* (Kennebunkport, Maine: Mercer, 1974), 153–61.

41.   Denton L. Watson, *Lion in the Lobby: Clarence Mitchell Jr.'s Struggle for the Passage of Civil Rights Laws* (New York: William Morrow, 1990), 228, 244, 255–56; Payne oral history, 45–50, 153; Dunnigan, *A Black Woman's Experience*, 374–76; Public Papers of the Presidents of the United States, *Dwight D. Eisenhower, 1953* (Washington: Government Printing Office, 1960), 205; Public Papers of the Presidents of the United States, *Dwight D. Eisenhower, 1954* (Washington: Government Printing Office, 1960), 435–36, 623–24.

42.   Dunnigan, *A Black Woman's Experience*, 384–86; Streitmatter, "Ethel L. Payne," 123–24; *Washington Evening Star*, July 7, 1954; *Baltimore Afro-American*, May 25, 1954; Payne, "A Tribune to Sherman Briscoe," Payne papers.

43.   Rodger Streitmatter, "After the Barriers Fell: How Racism and Sexism Plagued the First Two African-American Journalists Accredited to Cover the Untied States Congress," paper presented to the Organization of American Historians, April 2, 1992; Dunnigan, *A Black Woman's Experience*, 380–81; Payne oral history, 125.

44.   *Washington Evening Star*, May 7, 1962; *Washington Post*, May 8, 1962; [John P. Cosgrove] *shrdlu: An Affectionate Chronicle* (Washington: National Press Club, 1958), 103–4, 151; Rob-

ert C. Cottrell, *Izzy: A Biography of I. F. Stone* (New Brunswick, N.J.: Rutgers University Press, 1993), 217–18; Tyler Abell, ed., *Drew Pearson Diaries, 1949–1959* (New York: Holt, Rinehart and Winston, 1974), 321; author interviews with Bob Barr and Alden Todd.

45. *Washington Evening Star*, March 7, 1955; Streitmatter, "After the Barriers Fell"; Dunnigan, *A Black Woman's Experience*, 478–79.

46. Alice Fox Pitts, *Read All About It! 50 Years of ASNE* (Eaton, Penn.: American Society of Newspaper Editor, 1974), 23; Booker, *Black Man's America*, 145–46; Ben Gilbert, "Toward a Color-Blind Newspaper: Race Relations and the *Washington Post*," *Washington History*, 5 (Fall/Winter, 1993–94), 5–27; Howard Bray, *The Pillars of the Post: The Making of a News Empire in Washington* (New York: W.W. Norton, 1980), 160–63; Chalmers M. Roberts, *The Washington Post: The First 100 Years* (Boston: Houghton Mifflin, 1977), 292–94.

47. Booker, *Black Man's America*, 208–9; E. Frederick Morrow, *Black Man in the White House: A Diary of the Eisenhower Years by the Administrative Officer for Special Projects, The White House, 1955–1961* (New York: Coward-McCann, 1963), 47–48, 63–64, 114–15, 158, 218.

48. Booker, *Black Man's America*, 210.

49. Stewart Alsop, *The Center: People and Power in Political Washington* (New York: Harper & Row, 1968), ix, 15, 26; Dunnigan, *A Black Woman's Experience*, 382–83; author interview with George Tames.

50. Author interview with Clay Claiborne; *New York Times*, May 8, 1962; *Washington Post*, May 8, 1962; Dunnigan, *A Black Woman's Experience*, 301, 567–84. The state of Kentucky erected a historical highway marker in Dunnigan's honor at City Park in Russellville.

51. In 2001, after a thirty-year hiatus, the NNPA appointed another Washington correspondent, Hazel Trice Edney. *New York Amsterdam News*, March 22, 2001; Dunnigan, *A Black Woman's Experience*, 301–2; Waters, *American Diary*, 424; see also Jeremy Zilber and David Niven, *Racialized Coverage of Congress: The News in Black and White* (Westport, Conn.: Praeger, 2000).

Chapter Three

1. Cabell Phillips, et al., *Dateline: Washington: The Story of National Affairs Journalism in the Life and Times of the National Press Club* (Garden City, N.Y.: Doubleday, 1949), 82; School of Public and International Affairs, *Conference on the Press held at Princeton University, April 23–25, 1931* (Washington: Printing Corporation of America, 1931), 32–36.

2. Lee de Forest, *Father of Radio: The Autobiography of Lee de Forest* (Chicago: Wilcox & Follett, 1950), 338–39; Moses Koenigsberg, *King News: An Autobiography* (Philadelphia: F.A. Stokes, 1941), 469.

3. Minutes of the Radio and Television Correspondents Association, August 4, 1954; Phillips, et al., *Dateline: Washington*, 76–92.

4. David Brinkley, *11 Presidents, 4 Wars, 22 Political Conventions, 1 Moon Landing, 3 Assassinations, 2,000 Weeks of News and Other Stuff on Television and 18 Years of Growing Up in North Carolina* (New York: Knopf, 1996), 21, 42–43; Ronald Reagan with Richard G. Hubler, *Where's the Rest of Me?* (New York: Duell, Sloan and Pearce, 1965), 47, 56; Edward P. Morgan, *Clearing the Air* (Washington: Robert B. Luce, 1963), xii–xiii.

5. *Commercial Radio Advertising: Letter from the Chairman of the Federal Radio Commission in Response to Senate Resolution No. 129, A Report Relative to the Use of Radio Facilities for Commercial-Advertising Purposes, Together with a List Showing the Educational Institutions Which Have Been Licensed*, S. Doc. 137, 72nd Cong., 1st sess. (Washington: Government Printing Office, 1932), 2–14; Thomas Streeter, *Selling the Air: A Critique of the Policy of Commercial Broadcasting in the United States* (Chicago: University of Chicago Press, 1996), 59–110.

6. Erik Barnouw, *A Tower in Babel: A History of Broadcasting in the United States*, vol. 1 (New York: Oxford University Press, 1966), 105–85; Philip T. Rosen, *The Modern Stentors: Radio Broadcasters and the Federal Government, 1920–1934* (Westport, Conn.: Greenwood, 1980), 64–68, 88–89; Tom Lewis, *Empire of the Air: The Men Who Made Radio* (New York:

HarperCollins, 1991), 176–77; Susan Smulyan, *Selling Radio: The Commercialization of American Broadcasting, 1920–1934* (Washington: Smithsonian Institution Press, 1994) 37–64.

7.　　H. V. Kaltenborn, *Fifty Fabulous Years, 1900–1950: A Personal Review* (New York: Putnam, 1950), 111–13; "The Reminiscences of H. V. Kaltenborn," 1950, Columbia University Oral History Research Office, 106; H. V. Kaltenborn, "Kaltenborn Looks Back on Early Days of Radio News," *The Quill*, 47 (November 1959), 36–37; Douglas B. Craig, *Fireside Politics: Radio and Political Culture in the United States, 1920–1940* (Baltimore: Johns Hopkins University Press, 2000), 216–23.

8.　　Rosen, *The Modern Stentors*, 89; Lewis, *Empire of the Air*, 177; *New York Times*, January 9, 1929; Robert Sobel, *The Manipulators: America in the Media Age* (Garden City, N.Y.: Anchor Press, 1976), 169; Craig, *Fireside Politics*, 18–35.

9.　　Gwenyth L. Jackaway, *Media at War: Radio's Challenge to the Newspapers, 1924–1939* (Westport, Conn.: Praeger, 1995), 14–18; "The Reminiscences of H. V. Kaltenborn," 186–89; Joe Alex Morris, *Deadline Every Minute: The Story of the United Press* (Garden City, N.Y.: Doubleday, 1957), 192–94.

10.　　*Commercial Radio Advertising*, 92–94; *New York Times*, January 24, 1930; Murray Katzman, "News Broadcasting in the United States, 1920–1941," (Ph.D. diss., New York University, 1968), 162–63; George H. Douglas, *The Early Days of Radio Broadcasting* (Jefferson, N.C.: McFarland, 1987), 108–9; Ray Poindexter, *Golden Throats and Silver Tongues: The Radio Announcers* (Conway, Ark.: River Road, 1978), 79–81; Lowell Thomas, *Good Evening Everybody: From Cripple Creek to Samarkand* (New York: William Morrow, 1976), 289–96.

11.　　William S. Paley, *As It Happened: A Memoir* (Garden City, N.Y.: Doubleday, 1979), 119, 122; Sally Bedell Smith, *In All His Glory: The Life of William S. Paley, The Legendary Tycoon and His Brilliant Circle* (New York: Simon and Schuster, 1990), 117–18; Lewis J. Paper, *Empire: William S. Paley and the Making of CBS* (New York: St. Martin's, 1987), 43–45; Edward L. Bernays, *Biography of an Idea: Memoirs of Public Relations Counsel Edward L, Bernays* (New York: Simon and Schuster, 1965), 426–34; Gene Fowler, *Skyline: A Reporter's Reminiscence of the 1920s* (New York: Viking, 1961), 178; David Holbrook Culbert, *News for Everyman: Radio and Foreign Affairs in Thirties America* (Westport, Conn.: Greenwood, 1976), 23; Zoe Becker to Eric Sevareid, January 22, 1947, Eric Sevareid papers, Library of Congress.

12.　　*Conference on the Press*, 84; Frederic William Wile, *News Is Where You Find It: Forty Years' Reporting at Home and Abroad* (Indianapolis: Bobbs-Merrill, 1939) 19; [Drew Pearson and Robert S. Allen], *Washington-Merry-Go-Round* (New York: Horace Liveright, 1931), 360.

13.　　Eugene A. Kelly, "Distorting the News," *American Mercury*, 34 (March 1935), 322; Wile, *News Is Where You Find It*, 434–49; *Washington Evening Star*, July 16, 1932, April 7, 8, 1941; *Broadcasting*, 3 (August 1, 1932), 18; David H. Hosley, *As Good As Any: Foreign Correspondence on American Radio, 1930–1940* (Westport, Conn.: Greenwood, 1984), 10; "The Reminiscences of H. V. Kaltenborn," 170–71.

14.　　Lawrence W. Lichty and Malachi C. Topping, eds., *American Broadcasting: A Source Book on the History of Radio and Television* (New York: Hastings, 1975), 576–80; Silas Bent, *Ballyhoo: The Voice of the Press* (New York: Boni and Liveright, 1927), 295–99; Howard Henderson, "Changes in Advertising Media, 1929–1932," *Broadcasting*, 4 (January 15, 1933), 5–6; "Politicians Warned Not to Expect Press to Print Radio Talks," *Editor & Publisher*, 65 (August 20, 1932), 14; *Conference on the Press*, 39, 43–46, 54; Anne O'Hare McCormick, "Radio's Audience: Huge, Unprecedented," *New York Times Magazine* (April 3, 1932), 4; Paul W. White, *News on the Air* (New York: Harcourt, Brace, 1947), 33–36; Jackaway, *Media at War*, 21–22.

15.　　"A.P. and A.N.P.A. Declare War on Radio," *Broadcasting*, 4 (May 1, 1933), 5–6; "The Reminiscences of A. A. Schechter," Columbia Oral History Research Office, 5–13; A. A. Schechter with Edward Anthony, *I Live on the Air* (New York: Frederick A. Stokes, 1941), 4–6; Thomas, *Good Evening Everybody*, 297–98; William J. Small, "Radio News Has Matured Since World War II," *The Quill*, 47 (November 1959), 50–51.

16. Katzman, "News Broadcasting in the United States," 64, 86; "Eric Sevareid: He Was There," *Broadcasting* (September 12, 1977), 36; Robert Metz, *CBS: Reflections in a Bloodshot Eye* (New York: Signet, 1976), 3–6, 37–38, 46; "The Reminiscences of H. V. Kaltenborn," 167–71, 188; White, *News on the Air*, 38–39.

17. "CBS News Bureau Serving Net Sponsors, Commentators," *Broadcasting*, 5 (October 1, 1933), 10; "Columbia News Service Asks Admission of Reporters to Capitol Press Galleries," *Broadcasting*, 5 (November 15, 1933), 11; Katzman, "News Broadcasting in the United States," 191–92; Phillips, et al., *Dateline: Washington*, 75–76.

18. "The Reminiscences of A. A. Schechter," 13–15; Phillips, et al., *Dateline: Washington*, 82–86; Jackaway, *Media at War*, 28–33; White, *News on the Air*, 41; Martin Codel, "New Plan to End Radio-Press War," *Broadcasting*, 6 (January 1, 1934), 10, 30; Martin Mayer, *Making News* (Boston: Harvard Business School Press, 1993), 169; Will Irvin, *Propaganda and the News, Or What Makes You Think So?* (New York: Whittlesey, 1936), 252–53.

19. David Bulman, ed., *Molders of Opinion* (Milwaukee: Bruce Publishing, 1945), 58; Arthur Robb, "New Radio Regulation Basis Urged before New York Publishers," *Editor & Publisher*, 65 (September 17, 1932), 10; "Roosevelt Praises Radio, Raps Press," *Broadcasting*, 16 (May 15, 1939), 9; Martin Codel, "Radio Plays Major Role in Banking Crisis," *Broadcasting*, 4 (March 15, 1933), 5–7; Charles Hurd, *When the New Deal Was Young and Gay* (New York: Hawthorn, 1965), 247–50; Craig, *Fireside Politics*, 140–66; See also Russell D. Buhite and David W. Levy, *FDR's Fireside Chats* (Norman: University of Oklahoma Press, 1992).

20. Phillips, et al., *Dateline: Washington*, 84.

21. *New York Times*, February 17, 1929; *Washington Evening Star*, March 23, 27, 1932; U.S. Senate Committee on Rules, *Broadcasting of Senate Proceedings* (Washington: Government Printing Office, 1932), 2, 5, 7, 12–13; Stephen T. Early, "White House Secretary Lauds Industry," *Broadcasting*, 17 (July 15, 1939), 19, 40, 41; Kaltenborn, *Fifty Fabulous Years*, 172; "The Reminiscences of H. V. Kaltenborn," 71, 178.

22. *New York Times*, September 6, 1936; Sol Taishoff, "Election Augers Well for American Radio," *Broadcasting*, 11 (November 11, 1936), 1; James A. Farley, *Behind the Ballots: The Personal History of a Politician* (New York: Harcourt, Brace, 1938), 318–19.

23. "The Reminiscences of H. V. Kaltenborn," 71, 178; Neal Gabler, *Winchell: Gossip, Power, and the Culture of Celebrity* (New York: Random House, 1994), 110–16, 171–72, 199–202, 213–15; Schechter, *I Live on the Air*, 8; "Reminiscences of A. A. Schecter," 16–17; Sammy Danna, "The Rise of Radio News," in Lichty and Topping, eds., *American Broadcasting*, 342; White, *News on the Air*, 48.

24. Bourke Carter broadcast, *The American Forum of the Air*, 2 (October 29, 1939), 12–13; Bernays, *Biography of an Idea*, 571–81 647–48; White, *News on the Air*, 33; Culbert, *News for Everyman*, 34, 39, 44, 47–48, 54–55; Poindexter, *Golden Throats and Silver Tongues*, 8, 161–62; Paper, *Empire*, 72–73.

25. *New York Times*, May 7, 30, 1935; James Sayler, "Window on an Age: Arthur Krock and the New Deal Era, 1929–1941 (Ph.D. diss., Rutgers, 1978), 346; Meyer Berger, *The Story of the New York Times: The First 100 Years, 1851–1951* (New York: Arno, 1970 [1951]), 495; Leo C. Rosten, *The Washington Correspondents* (New York: Harcourt, Brace, 1937), 186; Walter Trohan, *Political Animals: Memoirs of a Sentimental Cynic* (Garden City, N.Y.: Doubleday, 1975), 31; Arthur H. Sulzberger to Arthur Krock, April 30, 1947, Arthur Krock papers, Princeton University.

26. John William Thompson Jr. oral history, 1–4, "History of WTOP and WTOP-TV" typescript, Broadcast Archives, University of Maryland; *Washington Post*, September 23, 1979; Katharine Graham, *Personal History* (New York: Knopf, 1997), 177–78.

27. James L. Baughman, *Henry R. Luce and the Rise of the American News Media* (Boston: Twayne, 1987), 74–81; Edward Bliss Jr., *Now the News: The Story of Broadcast Journalism* (New York: Columbia University Press, 1991), 36–38; "The Reminiscences of A. A. Schechter," 25.

28. *Washington Post*, April 21, 1940; Bulman, ed., *Molders of Opinion*, 48–49; White, *News on the Air*, 46–47; "The Reminiscences of A. A. Schecter," 23; Culbert, *News for Everyman*, 73–74;

Paper, *Empire*, 64; "The Reminiscences of H. V. Kaltenborn," 206–7; Kaltenborn, "Kaltenborn Looks Back on Early Days of Radio News," 37.

29. *New York Herald Tribune*, September 14, 1939; John Luskin, *Lippmann, Liberty, and the Press* (Tuscaloosa: University of Alabama Press, 1972), 109; *New York Times*, August 22, 1966; Booton Herndon, *Praised and Damned: The Story of Fulton Lewis Jr.* (New York: Duell, Sloan and Pearce, 1954), 1–2, 5; [Wythe Williams], The Man at the Microphone, *Washington Broadcast* (Garden City, N.Y.: Doubleday, Doran, 1944), 249.

30. *New York Times*, August 22, 1966; Kenneth G. Crawford and Hobart Rowen, "Voice with a Snarl," *Saturday Evening Post*, 220 (August 30, 1947), 23; Herndon, *Praised and Damned*, 16–25; Irving E. Fang, *Those Radio Commentators!* (Ames: Iowa State University Press, 1977), 201; Bulman, ed., *Molders of Opinion*, 79–80.

31. *Broadcasting*, 16 (May 15, 1939), 48; Herndon, *Praised and Damned*, 12, 41–42; [Williams], *Washington Broadcast*, 249; Fang, *Those Radio Commentators!* 203; Poindexter, *Golden Throats and Silver Tongues*, 65.

32. "Washington Is Here To Stay, WOL Washington, DC," promotional booklet, 1945, Broadcast Archives, University of Maryland; Bliss, *Now the News*, 29–30; Marya Mannes, "The Commentators," *The Reporter*, 9 (August 4, 1953), 31.

33. Robert E. Kintner, "Broadcasting and the News," *Harper's*, 230 (April 1965), 49–50; *Broadcasting*, 16 (May 15, 1939), 45, 48; "Galleries Opened in House, Senate," *Broadcasting*, 17 (August 1, 1939); Phillips, et al., *Dateline: Washington*, 84.

34. "Congress Formally Recognizes Radio with Gallery Facilities," *Broadcasting*, 16 (May 1, 1939), 13; *Broadcasting*, 16 (May 15, 1939), 45; *Congressional Record*, 84th Cong., 2nd sess., July 17, 1956, 12,992–93; Bryson Rash oral history, 36–37, Broadcast Archives, University of Maryland.

35. *Congressional Record*, 84th Cong., 2nd sess., July 17, 1956, 12,992–93; Richard Langham Riedel, *Halls of the Mighty: My 47 Years at the Senate* (Washington: Robert B. Luce, 1969), 60–61; Phillips, et al., *Dateline: Washington*, 85–86; White, *News on the Air*, 248; Fang, *Those Radio Commentators!* 203.

36. Eric Sevareid, *Not So Wild a Dream* (New York: Atheneum, 1976 [1946]), 196; Brinkley, *11 Presidents*, 49–53; Culbert, *News for Everyman*, 170; Delbert Clark, *Washington Dateline* (New York: Frederick A. Stokes, 1941), 158; Bulman, ed., *Molders of Opinion*, 72; Fang, *Those Radio Commentators!* 210.

37. Wayne S. Cole, *Charles A. Lindbergh and the Battle against American Intervention in World War II* (New York: Harcourt Brace, 1974), 71–74, 172–73; Herndon, *Praised and Damned*, 10, 42–48, 78; Culbert, *News for Everyman*, 164–65; Fang, *Those Radio Commentators!* 203–5; Ed Nellor interview, Thomas C. Reeves Collection, State Historical Society of Wisconsin.

38. Bulman, ed., *Molders of Opinion*, 71–81; Fang, *Those Radio Commentators!* 201–9.

39. "The Reminiscences of A.A. Schechter," 22–24; Eric Sevareid to Edwin Newman, September 28, 1949, Sevareid papers; William L. Rivers, *The Mass Media: Reporting, Writing, Editing* (New York: Harper & Row, 1964), 424; *Washington Post*, July 14, 1940.

40. Robert Lloyd Davis, ed., *By Elmer Davis* (Freeport, N.Y.: Books for Libraries Press, 1970), x–xi; Elam H. Davis to Elmer Davis, March 15, 1910, October 26, 1912, Carl Van Anda to Davis, July 12, 1920, Charles Willis Thompson to Davis, August 5, 1925, Elmer H. Davis papers, Library of Congress; John Chamberlain, *A Life with the Printed Word* (Chicago: Regnery Gateway, 1982), 20.

41. Fang, *Those Radio Commentators!* 182, 189; Mayer, *Making News*, 166; Roger Burlingame, *Don't Let Them Scare You: The Life and Times of Elmer Davis* (Philadelphia: Lippincott, 1961), 154, 168–69; Culbert, *News for Everyman*, 125, 132; "Elmer Davis, 1890–1958," *Harper's*, 217 (July 1958), 67.

42. Culbert, *News for Everyman*, 146; Metz, *CBS*, 88; Fang, *Those Radio Commentators!* 186; Davis, ed., *By Elmer Davis*, 179; Burlingame, *Don't Let Them Scare You*, 169–70; Paper, *Empire*, 65–66.

43. Edward R. Murrow to Elmer Davis, September 15, 1940, Davis papers; Burlingame, *Don't Let Them Scare You*, 158, 167; Kintner, "Broadcasting and the News," 52.

44. Elmer Davis to Harry L. Hopkins, March 25, April 3, 1942, Harry L. Hopkins papers, Franklin D. Roosevelt Library; *New York Times*, May 19, 1958; Culbert, *News for Everyman*, 142–44; Burlingame, *Don't Let Them Scare You*, 182–83, 186–87; Richard Lauterbach, "Elmer Davis and the News," *Liberty*, 20 (October 23, 1943), 13; H. W. Ross to Elmer Davis, June 16, 1942, Davis papers.

45. [Williams], *Washington Broadcast*, 242–54; Jonathan Daniels to Samuel Rosenman, March 16, 1944, Samuel I. Rosenman papers, Franklin D. Roosevelt Library; Phillips, et al., *Dateline: Washington*, 220–26; Davis, "Role of Information in World War II," The United States Naval War College, November 16, 1951, George Creel to Elmer Davis, August 4, 1942, Davis papers; Chamberlain, *A Life with the Printed Word*, 91; Bess Furman, *Washington By-Line: The Personal History of a Newspaperwoman* (New York: Knopf, 1949), 298–99; Chesly Manly, *The Twenty-Year Revolution from Roosevelt to Eisenhower* (Chicago: Henry Regnery, 1954), 112; Sydney Weinberg, "What to Tell America: The Writers' Quarrel in the Office of War Information," *Journal of American History*, 55 (June 1968), 73–89.

46. Bruce Catton, *The Warlords of Washington* (New York; Harcourt, Brace, 1948), 188–90, 221–25; John W. Henderson, *The United States Information Agency* (New York: Praeger, 1969), 34; Howard Fast, *Being Red* (Boston: Houghton Mifflin, 1990), 4–28; *Congressional Record*, 83rd Congress, 1st sess., A1271; Herbert Brucker, *Freedom of Information* (New York: Macmillan, 1949), 152.

47. Edward Klauber to Elmer Davis, August 16, 1943, Davis to Herbert Brownell Jr., chairman of the Republican National Committee, October 3, 1944, Davis to Robert Kintner, June 24, 1947, Davis papers; Furman, *Washington By-Line*, 304–5; Allan M. Winkler, *The Politics of Propaganda: The Office of War Information, 1942–1945* (New Haven, Conn.: Yale University Press, 1978), 31–32, 150, 157; Holly Cowan Shulman, *The Voice of America: Propaganda and Democracy, 1941–1945* (Madison: University of Wisconsin Press, 1990), 36–37.

48. Catton, *The Warlords of Washington*, 186–87; David F. Krugler, *The Voice of America and the Domestic Propaganda Battles, 1945–1953* (Columbia: University of Missouri Press, 2000), 32–24; "The Reminiscences of A. A. Schechter," 25–27; Phillips, et al., *Dateline: Washington*, 88–90.

49. Paley, *As It Happened*, 136; Paper, *Empire*, 107–8; Smith, *In All His Glory*, 233–34; Kintner, "Broadcasting and the News," 51; Raymond Swing, *"Good Evening!" A Professional Memoir* (New York: Harcourt, Brace, 1964), 250–51; Burlingame, *Don't Let Them Scare You*, 265; Elmer Davis, *But We Were Born Free* (Indianapolis: Bobbs-Merrill, 1954), 148; Fang, *Those Radio Commentators!* 192; Robert E. Kintner to Joseph Alsop, January 20, February 20, 1947, Alsop to Kintner, March 26, 1947, Jane Adams to Joseph Alsop, March 20, 1947, Nellie Allen to Joseph Alsop, March 24, 1947, Joseph Alsop to Thomas L. Stix Jr., April 10, May 2, August 21, 1947, Stix to Joseph Alsop, April 14, 1947, Stix to Stewart Alsop, September 19, 1947, Joseph and Stewart Alsop papers, Library of Congress.

50. Robert Kintner to Elmer Davis, June 23, 1947, Davis to Kintner, June 24, 1947, Davis papers; Burlingame, *Don't Let Them Scare You*, 276; *Washington Evening Star*, March 9, 1949.

51. Mannes, "The Commentators," 32; Davis, *But We Were Born Free*, 15–27, 159–64, 173–74; Bernard Roshco, "A Giant Named Elmer," *Washington Journalism Review*, 13 (December 1991), 35–37.

52. Martha MacGregor to Eric Sevareid, January 11, 1955, Sevareid papers; James Reston, *Sketches in the Sand* (New York: Knopf, 1967), 206–8; Burlingame, *Don't Let Them Scare You*, 253–54; Fang, *Those Radio Commentators!* 209; Arthur I. Boreman to Elmer Davis, July 13, 1950, Davis to Boreman, July 21, 1950, Davis papers.

53. Walter Goodman, *The Committee: The Extraordinary Career of the House Committee on Un-American Activities* (New York: Farrar, Straus, and Giroux, 1968), 279–82; *Washington Times-Herald*, December 3, 1949; Herndon, *Praised and Damned*, 88–92; Giraud Chester,

"What Constitutes Irresponsibility on the Air? A Case Study," *Public Opinion Quarterly*, 13 (Spring 1949), 73–83; Eric Sevareid to John Osborne, January 9, 1950, Sevareid papers; see also Eduard Mark, "Venona's Source *19* and the 'Trident' Conference of May 1943: Diplomacy or Espionage?" *Intelligence and National Security*, 13 (Summer 1998), 1–31.

54. Nellor interview, Thomas C. Reeves Collection, Wisconsin Historical Society; Senate Subcommittee on Privileges and Elections, Committee on Rules and Administration, *Maryland Senatorial Election of 1950*, 82nd Cong., 1st sess. (Washington: Government Printing Office, 1951), 20–26, 579–93; Elmer Davis, *Must We Mislead the Public?* (Minneapolis: University of Minnesota School of Journalism, 1951), 10.

55. Sidney Reisberg, "Fulton Lewis Jr.: An Analysis of His News Commentary" (Ph.D. diss., New York University, 1952), 33–34; Herndon, *Praised and Damned*, 11, 95, 98–103, 107; *New York Times*, August 22, 1966; Adlai Stevenson to Elmer Davis, December 1, 1952, K. Bagwell to Davis, November 17, 1952, Davis papers; Gilbert Seldes, "Mr. Elmer Davis," *The Nation* (April 4, 1953), 44.

56. J. B. Matthews, "Elmer Davis Runs Scared," *American Mercury* (December 1954), 57–65; Fang, *Those Radio Commentators!* 194–95; Mrs. M. J. Durkin to Elmer Davis, April 20, 1951, Davis to George E. Stringfellow, April 11, 1952, Frank B. Best, to Davis, May 6, 1953, Davis to Best, May 13, 1953, Groucho Marx to Davis, June 13, 1951, Davis to Simeon H. F.Goldstein, March 1, 1954, Davis papers; Martin Agronsky to Davis, November 27, 1953, Minutes of the Radio and Television Correspondents Association, U.S. Capitol; Burlingame, *Don't Let Them Scare You*, 334, 337; *New York Times*, May 19, 1958, November 27, 1977.

57. A. J. Liebling, *The Press* (New York: Ballantine, 1975 [1961]), 455, 514–20; Fang, *Those Radio Commentators!* 208–9, 211; Paper, *Empire*, 171; Culbert, *News for Everyman*, 163; Nellor interview, Reeves Collection; Marya Mannes, "News Heard, News Seen," *The Reporter*, 9 (July 7, 1953), 40; *New York Times*, August 22, 1966.

58. Statement of William A. Costello to the Senate Rules Committee, August 4, 1954, Minutes of the Radio and Television Correspondents' Association; Leigh Plummer, "Griffing Bancroft," *Biography News* 2 (September 1975), 933; author interview with Griffing Bancroft.

59. *New York Times*, December 28, 1930; Erik Barnouw, *Tube of Plenty: The Evolution of American Television* (New York: Oxford University Press, 1975), 77–100; Eugene Lyons, *David Sarnoff: A Biography* (New York: Harper & Row, 1966), 276–78; James L. Baughman, *Television's Guardian: The FCC and the Politics of Programming* (Knoxville: University of Tennessee Press, 1985), 3–19,

60. *Washington Evening Star*, January 3, 1947; "Effect of Television on Specific Types of Nighttime Radio Programs," (January 1949), WOR Research Department, Broadcast Archives, University of Maryland; Brinkley, *11 Presidents*, 65; Morgan, *Clearing the Air*, xiv; Swing, *"Good Evening!"* 227; "The Reminiscences of H. V. Kaltenborn," 240–41.

61. Fred W. Friendly, *Due to Circumstances beyond Our Control. . .* (New York: Vintage, 1967), 162–63, 204–6; Rivers, *The Mass Media*, 40; Paley, *As It Happened*, 221, 228; Bliss, *Now the News*, 190–91, 197; Lou Adler, "Off the Air," *Media Studies Quarterly*, 10 (Spring/Summer 1996), 119–22; Kaltenborn, "Kaltenborn Looks Back on Early Days of Radio News," 37; James L. Baughman, *The Republic of Mass Communications: Journalism, Filmmaking, and Broadcasting in America since 1941* (Baltimore: Johns Hopkins University Press, 1997), 65–69.

62. Howard Kurtz, *Hot Air: All Talk, All the Time* (New York: Times Books, 1996), 228–55; Ken Adelman, "Voice in the Box," *Washingtonian*, 35 (March 2000), 31–34; Bob Edwards, "I'm Bob Edwards," *Southern Living, 36* (February 23, 2001); *Washington Post*, March 25, 2004; *Boston Globe*, February 11, 1999.

Chapter Four

1. "The Troubled Press," *Fortune*, 45 (February 1952), 174, 176; *New York Times*, November 25, 1959; Richard Nixon, *In the Arena: A Memoir of Victory, Defeat, and Renewal* (New York: Simon and Schuster, 1990), 255.

2. John Hoving, "My Friend McCarthy," *The Reporter*, 2 (April 25, 1950), 31; George Dixon, *Leaning on a Column* (Philadelphia: J.B. Lippincott, 1961), 84; Ed Nellor interview, Willard Edwards to Thomas C. Reeves, December 22, 1978, Thomas C. Reeves Collection, State Historical Society of Wisconsin; *Washington Times-Herald*, May 14, 1948; *Washington Evening Star*, December 30, 1961; *Washington Post*, December 31, 1961.

3. *Washington Post*, June 23, 1966; Edwin R. Bayley, *Joe McCarthy and the Press* (New York: Pantheon, 1981), 151–58; David Halberstam, *The Powers That Be* (New York: Knopf, 1979), 197; John G. Adams, *Without Precedent: The Story of the Death of McCarthyism* (New York: W.W. Norton, 1983), 62.

4. Dixon, *Leaning on a Column*, 85–88; Samuel Shaffer, *On and off the Floor: Thirty Years as a Correspondent on Capitol Hill* (New York: Newsweek Books, 1980), 28; Nellor and Edwards interviews, Reeves Collection; Roy Cohn, *McCarthy* (New York: New American Library, 1968), 1–3; William F. Buckley Jr. and L. Brent Bozell, *McCarthy and His Enemies: The Record and Its Meaning* (Chicago: Henry Regnery, 1954), 44–51.

5. *Wheeling Intelligencer* article, February 10, 1950, reprinted in Subcommittee of the Committee on Foreign Relations, *State Department Employee Loyalty Investigation*, 81st Cong., 2nd sess. (Washington: Government Printing Office, 1950), part 2, 1,756–57; Bayley, *Joe McCarthy and the Press*, 17–26.

6. George Water's tenure in McCarthy's office from January 25 to March 7, 1950, is recorded in *Report of the Secretary of the Senate, July 1, 1949, to June 30, 1950*, 82nd Cong., 1st sess., S. Doc. 1 (Washington: Government Printing Office, 1951), 8. He returned to the senator's payroll briefly from January 18 to February 8, 1952; *Report of the Secretary of the Senate, July 1, 1951, to June 30, 1952*, 83rd Cong., 1st sess., S. Doc. 2 (Washington: Government Printing Office, 1953), 81; David Brinkley, *11 Presidents, 4 Wars, 22 Political Conventions, 1 Moon Landing, 3 Assassinations, 2,000 Weeks of News and Other Stuff on Television and 18 Years of Growing Up in North Carolina* (New York: Knopf, 1996), 113–14; Bayley, *Joe McCarthy and the Press*, 26–38; Nellor interview, Reeves Collection; Thomas C. Reeves, *The Life and Times of Joe McCarthy* (New York: Stein & Day, 1982), 247–50; Lindsey Chaney and Michael Cieply, *The Hearsts: Family and Empire—The Later Years* (New York: Simon and Schuster, 1981), 128–29; Robert Griffith, *The Politics of Fear: Joseph R. McCarthy and the Senate* (Lexington: University Press of Kentucky, 1970), 62–65, 85–86; *New York Times*, December 31, 1961.

7. McCarthy and his supporters attributed the label "McCarthyism" to Owen Lattimore's statement to the Tydings Committee on May 4, 1950, reinforced in a *Daily Worker* headline the next day, but Herblock had already used "McCarthyism" in an editorial cartoon in the *Washington Post* on March 29, 1950. *The Freeman*, 4 (December 14, 1953), 185; Herbert Block, *Herblock: A Cartoonist's Life* (New York: Macmillan, 1993), 133–34.

8. Martin Dies, *Martin Dies' Story* (New York: Bookmailer, 1963), 133–34; Raymond Clapper, *Watching the World* (New York: McGraw-Hill, 1944), 38–40; Marquis W. Childs, *I Write from Washington* (New York: Harper & Brothers, 1942), 92–93; Eleanor Roosevelt, *This I Remember* (New York: Harper & Brothers, 1949), 202–3; Maurice Isserman, *Which Side Were You On? The American Communist Party during the Second World War* (Middletown, Conn.: Wesleyan University Press, 1982), 88–102, 161–66, 208–13; Michael E. Brown, et al., eds., *New Studies in the Politics and Culture of U.S. Communism* (New York: Monthly Review Press, 1993), 45–73.

9. David K. Niles to D. E. Krauss, September 10, 1943, Harry Hopkins papers, Franklin D. Roosevelt Library; see also A. C. Rosander, *Washington Story: Behind the Scenes in the Federal Government* (Boulder, Colo.: Johnson, 1985), 28; and Earl Latham, *The Communist Controversy in Washington, From the New Deal to McCarthy* (Cambridge, Mass.: Harvard University Press, 1966), 137–50.

10. Vivian Gornick, *The Romance of American Communism* (New York: Basic, 1977); Harvey Klehr, John Earl Haynes, and Fridrikh Igorevich Firsov, *The Secret World of American Communism* (New Haven, Conn.: Yale University Press, 1995), 71–118; Robert Louis Benson

and Michael Warner, eds., *Venona: Soviet Espionage and the American Response, 1939–1957* (Washington: National Security Agency and Central Intelligence Agency, 1996), 123; Ralph de Toledano and Victor Lasky, *Seeds of Treason: The True Story of the Hiss-Chambers Tragedy* (New York: Funk & Wagnalls, 1950), 87–90; Whittaker Chambers, *Witness* (New York: Random House, 1952), 12–13.

11. Sam Tanenhaus, *Whittaker Chambers: A Biography* (New York: Random House, 1997), 169–70, 206–7; Richard Helms with William Hood, *A Look over My Shoulder: A Life in the Central Intelligence Agency* (New York: Random House, 2003), 141–60; see also John Earl Haynes and Harvey Klehr, *Venona: Decoding Soviet Espionage in America* (New Haven, Conn.: Yale University Press, 1999).

12. Allen Weinstein and Alexander Vassiliev, *The Haunted Wood: Soviet Espionage in America— The Stalin Era* (New York: Random House, 1999), 102–9.

13. Murray Kempton, "The Limits of Irony," *New Republic*, 158 (April 13, 1968), 28–34; Daniel Patrick Moynihan, *Secrecy: The American Experience* (New Haven, Conn.: Yale University Press, 1998,) 70–73; de Toledano and Lasky, *Seeds of Treason*, 136–39, 145, 155; Stanley M. Brand, "Alger Hiss: How Not to Be a Congressional Witness," *The Hill* (November 27, 1996), 11; Ralph de Toledano, *One Man Alone: Richard Nixon* (New York: Funk & Wagnalls, 1969), 80–81; Irwin F. Gellman, *The Contender: Richard Nixon: The Congress Years, 1946– 1952* (New York: Free Press, 1999), 196–224.

14. Felix Morley, *For the Record* (South Bend, Ind.: Regnery/Gateway, 1979), 429–31; Bert Andrews and Peter Andrews, *A Tragedy of History: A Journalist's Confidential Role in the Hiss-Chambers Case* (Washington: Robert B. Luce, 1962), 74, 226–27; Roger Morris, *Richard Milhous Nixon: The Rise of an American Politician* (New York: Henry Holt, 1990), 418– 20, 440, 449; Richard Nixon, *RN: The Memoirs of Richard Nixon* (New York: Grosset & Dunlap, 1978), 68; *Washington Post*, September 21, 1952; Richard Kluger, *The Paper: The Life and Death of the* New York Herald Tribune (New York: Knopf, 1986), 406–10; James Reston, *Deadline: A Memoir* (New York: Times Books, 1991), 215.

15. Ralph de Toledano, "The Liberal Disintegration: A Conservative View," *The Freeman*, 1 (November 13, 1950), 109–11; Ralph de Toledano, *Lament for a Generation* (New York: Farrar, Straus, and Cudahy, 1960), 43, 106, 113–14, 122; Dale Kramer, "The American Communists," *Harper's*, 180 (May 1940), 594; Robert Lloyd Davis, ed., *By Elmer Davis* (Indianapolis: Bobbs-Merrill, 1964), 102–6; Murray Kempton, *Part of Our Time: Some Ruins and Monuments of the Thirties* (New York: Simon and Schuster, 1955), 176.

16. de Toledano, *Lament for a Generation*, 206–7; de Toledano, "The Hiss Case," in William F. Buckley Jr., ed., *The Committee and Its Critics: A Calm Review of the House Committee on Un-American Activities* (New York: Putnam, 1962), 174; see also George H. Nash, *The Conservative Intellectual Movement in America since 1945* (Wilmington: Intercollegiate Studies Institute, 1996 [1976]), 74–117.

17. Max Ascoli, "The G.O.P.'s Choice," *The Reporter*, 2 (June 6, 1950), 4; Jack Bell, *The Splendid Misery: The Story of the Presidency and Power Politics at Close Range* (Garden City, N.Y.: Doubleday, 1960), 25.

18. Jack Alexander, "The Senate's Remarkable Upstart," *Saturday Evening Post*, 220 (August 9, 1947), 15, 57; Jack Anderson with Ronald W. May. *McCarthy: The Man, the Senator, the "Ism"* (Boston: Beacon, 1952), 123–24; Allen Drury, *Three Kids in a Cart: A Visit to Ike, and Other Diversions* (Garden City, N.Y.: Doubleday, 1965), 123–24.

19. Alexander, "The Senate's Remarkable Upstart," 57; author interview with Neil MacNeil; George Tames oral history, Senate Historical Office, 31; *Washington Star*, June 26, 1949, April 11, 1954.

20. Pat Holt oral history, Senate Historical Office, 24–26; Richard H. Rovere, *Arrivals and Departures: A Journalist's Memoirs* (New York: Macmillan, 1976), 97–102; Gridiron Skit, 1952, Blair Moody papers, Bentley Library, Ann Arbor, Michigan.

21. Hoving, "My Friend McCarthy," 28; Bill Lawrence, *Six Presidents, Too Many Wars* (New York: Saturday Review Press, 1972), 199; Memo, Sen. Joseph McCarthy–Drew Pearson Col-

umn References, [1951], Drew Pearson papers, Lyndon B. Johnson Presidential Library; Jack Anderson with James Boyd, *Confessions of a Muckraker: The Inside Story of Life in Washington during the Truman, Eisenhower, Kennedy, and Johnson Years* (New York: Random House, 1979), 6–14, 102, 107–9, 116–18, 174–79, 188–89, 194–202; Jack Anderson with Daryl Gibson, *Peace, War, and Politics: An Eyewitness Account* (New York: Forge, 1998), 70–71.

22. Author interview with Neil MacNeil; Arthur Krock, *Memoirs: Sixty Years on the Firing Line* (New York: Funk and Wagnalls, 1968), 222, 319; Krock, *In the Nation, 1932–1966* (New York: McGraw-Hill, 1966), 168–69; Nathaniel Weyl, *The Battle against Disloyalty* (New York: Thomas Y. Crowell, 1951), 248; see also Robert P. Newman, *Owen Lattimore and the "Loss" of China* (Berkeley: University of California Press, 1992).

23. *Washington Post*, April 21, 1950; *New York Times*, April 23, 1950.

24. "The Necessity of 'Red-Baiting,'" *The Freeman*, 3 (June 1, 1953), 619–20; John Chamberlain, *A Life with the Printed Word* (Chicago: Regnery/Gateway, 1982), 141; Douglass Cater, "The Captive Press," *The Reporter*, 2 (June 6, 1950), 17; Elmer Davis and Granville Hicks, "Lattimore and the Liberals," *The New Leader*, 33 (May 27, 1950), 16–18; see also Arthur Herman, *Joseph McCarthy: Reexamining the Life and Legacy of America's Most Hated Senator* (New York: Free Press, 2000), 120–28.

25. William F. Buckley Jr., "Senator McCarthy's Model?" *The Freeman*, 1 (May 21, 1951), 533; Willard Edwards, "McCarthy's Record," *Human Events* (November 10, 1954) reprinted in the *Congressional Record*, 83rd Cong., 2nd sess., 16,109; Daniel J. Boorstin, *The Image: A Guide to Pseudo-Events in America* (New York: Atheneum, 1987 [1961]), 21–23; Jim Tuck, *McCarthyism and New York's Hearst Press: A Study of Roles in the Witch Hunt* (Lanham, Md.: University Press of America, 1995), 73–74; Chaney and Cieply, *The Hearsts*, 79–82; see also Finis Farr, *Fair Enough: The Life of Westbrook Pegler* (New Rochelle, N.Y.: Arlington House, 1975).

26. JMH [John M. Henshaw] to Drew Pearson, 1951, Pearson papers; David M. Oshinsky, *A Conspiracy So Immense: The World of Joe McCarthy* (New York: The Free Press, 1983), 108, 182; Edwards interview, Reeves Collection; *Chicago Tribune*, February 21, 1950; Cater, "The Captive Press," 18; Bayley, *Joe McCarthy and the Press*, 19, 155; Holmes Alexander, *Never Lose a War: Memoirs and Observations of a National Columnist* (Greenwich, Conn.: Devin-Adair, 1984), 100; Roy McGhee oral history, Senate Historical Office, 1992, 69–70.

27. Edwards interview, Reeves Collection; Bayley, *Joe McCarthy and the Press*, 156; Richard Norton Smith, *The Colonel: The Life and Legend of Robert R. McCormick, 1880–1955* (Boston: Houghton Mifflin, 1997), 498; *Chicago Tribune*, March 31, 1950; Newman, *Owen Lattimore and the "Loss" of China*, 225, 231, 304.

28. Alexander, *Never Lose a War*, 106–11.

29. Willard Edwards oral history, 31–32, Harry S. Truman Presidential Library; Edwards interview, Reeves Collection; Reeves, *The Life and Times of Joe McCarthy*, 247–49, 296, 327, 349; Smith, *The Colonel*, 503–4; Senate Committee on Rules and Administration, *Report on the Maryland Senatorial Election of 1950*. S. Rep. 647, 82nd Cong., 1st sess. (Washington: Government Printing Office, 1951), 23–31, 36–43.

30. *Chicago Tribune*, November 8, 1950; Bayley, *Joe McCarthy and the Press*, 96–97; Reeves, *The Life and Times of Joe McCarthy*, 373–74; Earl T. Barnes, "Forrest Davis," *Biography News* (September/October 1975), 973–75; John Chamberlain, "Forrest Davis, RIP," *National Review*, 12 (May 22, 1962), 357; Chamberlain, *A Life with the Printed Word*, 141–42.

31. Alexander, *Never Lose a War*, 59–60, 72–73, 85–86, 99–100, 115; Holmes Alexander, *Pen and Politics: The Autobiography of a Working Writer* (Morgantown: West Virginia University Library, 1970), 36, 147–48, 152, 155–59, 196.

32. Anderson and May, *McCarthy*, 389–91; Cohn, *McCarthy*, 243, 268–69; Richard Langham Riedel, *Halls of the Mighty: My 47 Years at the Senate* (Washington: Robert B. Luce, 1969), 227–28; McCarthy testimony in Subcommittee on Rules, Senate Rules and Administration Committee, *Rules of Procedure for Senate Investigating Committees* (Washington: Government Printing Office, 1954), 461.

33.   Edwards interview, Reeves Collection; Floyd Riddick oral history, Senate Historical Office, 359–60; de Toledano, *One Man Alone*, 118, 176–77; de Toledano, *Lament for a Generation*, 181; Lee Edwards, *Goldwater: The Man Who Made a Revolution* (Washington: Regnery, 1995), 219.

34.   "The Troubled Press," *Fortune*, 45 (February 1952), 124–26; Anderson and May, *McCarthy*, 270, 283; Reeves, *The Life and Times of Joe McCarthy*, 717–18; Oshinsky, *A Conspiracy So Immense*, 182–83; Bayley, *Joe McCarthy and the Press*, 67–68, 72, 80; John L. Steele, "The News Magazines in Washington," in Ray Eldon Hiebert, ed., *The Press in Washington* (New York: Dodd, Mead, 1966), 61; Memo, "Associated Press Managing Editors Assn. meeting— Atlanta, 1950," Pearson papers; author interview with Al Spivak.

35.   Marquis Childs, *Witness to Power* (New York: McGraw-Hill, 1975), 66; William S. White, *The Making of a Journalist* (Lexington: University Press of Kentucky, 1986), 17–18; Martin Agronsky oral history, 20, Broadcast Archives, University of Maryland.

36.   White, *The Making of a Journalist*, 14; Bell, *The Splendid Misery*, 25–26; Joseph W. Alsop, *"I've Seen the Best of It": Memoirs* (New York: W.W. Norton, 1992), 334–35; Jeff Broadwater, *Eisenhower and the Anti-Communist Crusade* (Chapel Hill: University of North Carolina Press, 1992), 26–53.

37.   de Toledano, *Lament for a Generation*, 182, 186, 210; Nellor interview, Reeves Collection; Ruth Young Watt oral history, Senate Historical Office, 106, 109, 129.

38.   Senate Governmental Affairs Committee, *Executive Sessions of the Senate Permanent Subcommittee on Investigations, 83rd Congress, 1st and 2nd Sessions* (Washington: Government Printing Office, 2003), five volumes; Senate Government Operations Committee, *Special Senate Investigation on Charges and Countercharges Involving Secretary of the Army Robert T. Stevens, John G. Adams, H. Struve Hensel, and Senator Joe McCarthy, Roy M. Cohn, and Francis P. Carr*, part 27 (Washington: Government Printing Office, 1954), 987; Weyl, *The Battle against Democracy*, 242.

39.   *Chicago Tribune*, February 13, 1953; Philip Horton, "Voices within the Voice," *The Reporter*, 9 (July 21, 1953), 25–29; Senate Permanent Subcommittee on Investigations, *Annual Report*, Senate Report 881, 83rd Cong., 2nd sess. (Washington: Government Printing Office, 1954), 18; Martin Merson, *The Private Diary of a Public Servant* (New York: Macmillan, 1953), 11–41; *New York Times*, March 7, 1953.

40.   Richard H. Rovere, "The Adventures of Cohn and Schine," *The Reporter*, 9 (July 1953), 9–16; James Burnham, "Editor Meets Senator," *The Freeman*, 3 (June 15, 1953), 659–62; Horton, "Voices within the Voice," 28–29; de Toledano, *Lament for a Generation*, 185–86; James A. Wechsler, *The Age of Suspicion* (New York: Random House, 1953), 266–325; see also Permanent Subcommittee on Investigations, *Executive Sessions of the Senate Permanent Subcommittee on Investigations of the Committee on Government Operations, Eighty-Third Congress, 1953–1954* (Washington: Government Printing Office, 2003), 5 volumes.

41.   McCarthy, *McCarthyism*, 89; Reeves, *The Life and Times of Joe McCarthy*, 480; Freda Utley, "Facing Both Ways in Germany," *The Freeman*, 3 (December 15, 1952), 191–93; Buckley and Bozell, *McCarthy and His Enemies*, 297; James Aronson, *The Press and the Cold War* (Boston: Beacon, 1970), 96–99.

42.   *Washington Post*, May 3, 1957; *Chicago Tribune*, October 17, 1953, February 25, 1954; Telford Taylor, *Grand Inquest: The Story of Congressional Investigations* (New York: Simon and Schuster, 1955), 114–15, 120; Reeves, *The Life and Times of Joe McCarthy*, 547; Oshinsky, *A Conspiracy So Immense*, 355–71.

43.   Senate Government Operations Committee, *Special Senate Investigation in Charges and Countercharges Involving: Secretary of the Army Robert T. Stevens, John G. Adams, H. Struve Hensel and Senator Joe McCarthy, Roy M. Cohn, and Francis P Carr*, 83rd Cong, 2nd sess., Part 10 (Washington: Government Printing Office, 1954), 377.

44.   Edwards oral history, 51–53; Reeves, *The Life and Times of Joe McCarthy*, 558; Oshinsky, *A Conspiracy So Immense*, 390–93; Arthur V. Watkins, *Enough Rope* (Englewood Cliffs, N.J.: Prentice-Hall, 1969), 23.

45. Drury, *Three Kids in a Cart*, 137–38.

46. Michael D. Murray, "Television's Desperate Moment: A Conversation with Fred W. Friendly," *Journalism History*, 1 (Summer 1974), 69; Cohn, *McCarthy*, 120, 125–29, 141, 185–87, 207; commentary by Daniel Schorr and George Herman, American Film Institute, April 22, 2004.

47. Nellor and Edwards interviews, Reeves Collection; Walter Trohan, *Political Animals: Memoirs of a Sentimental Cynic* (Garden City, N.Y.: Doubleday, 1975), 248–49; Lloyd Wendt, *Chicago Tribune: The Rise of a Great American Newspaper* (Chicago: Rand McNally, 1979), 703–4; Edwards oral history, 47–48, Truman Library.

48. William F. Buckley Jr., ed., *Odyssey of a Friend: Whittaker Chambers' Letters to William F. Buckley, Jr., 1954–1961* (New York: privately printed, 1970), 48–52, 176–77; Nash, *The Conservative Intellectual Movement in America*, 110.

49. *New York Times*, January 4, 5, 1958; *Chicago Tribune*, January 5, 1958; *New York Daily News*, February 26, 2001; *New York World-Telegram & Sun*, July 12–16, 1954; Bayley, *Joe McCarthy and the Press*, 174–75.

50. Murray Kempton, *America Comes of Middle Age: Columns 1950–1962* (Boston: Little, Brown, 1963), 301–2; George Reedy, *Lyndon B. Johnson, A Memoir* (New York: Andrews and McMeel, 1982), 102, 105–6; Bell, *The Splendid Misery*, 28–30; *Washington Post*, May 3, 1957.

51. Dwight D. Eisenhower, *Mandate for Change, 1953–1956* (Garden City, N.Y.: Doubleday, 1963), 388–89; Edwards interview, Reeves Collection; Francis Wilcox oral history, Senate Historical Office, 25, 106–7; pamphlet, "A Service to the Public by Cortland Herbst, 2425 Foxhall Road, N.W., Washington 7, D.C.: Foreign Policy Speech of Senator Joe McCarthy, United States Senate—June 16, 1955," Pearson papers; Ruth Watt oral history, 148–50; Fred I. Greenstein, *The Hidden-Hand Presidency: Eisenhower as Leader* (New York: Basic, 1982), 218; Sherman Adams, *Firsthand Report: The Story of the Eisenhower Administration* (New York: Harper & Brothers, 1961), 152.

52. May Craig, "Inside in Washington" columns, October 4, 1951, March 5, 1953, November 15, 1954, Elisabeth May Craig papers, Library of Congress; Margaret Chase Smith, *Declaration of Conscience* (Garden City, N.Y.: Doubleday, 1972), 3–8, 12; Patricia Ward Wallace, *Politics of Conscience: A Biography of Margaret Chase Smith* (Westport, Conn.: Praeger, 1995), 56–57, 108, 168–69; Janann Sherman, *No Place for a Woman: A Life of Senator Margaret Chase Smith* (New Brunswick, N.J.: Rutgers University Press, 2000), 168.

53. *New York Times*, August 22, 1966; Walter Winchell, *Winchell Exclusive* (Englewood Cliffs, N.J.: Prentice-Hall, 1975), 252–57; Neal Gabler, *Winchell: Gossip, Power, and the Culture of Celebrity* (New York: Vintage, 1995), 477–80; de Toledano, *Lament for a Generation*, 148, 211–12, 262.

54. Wendt, Chicago Tribune, 703; Reeves, *The Life and Times of Joe McCarthy*, 768; Bayley, *Joe McCarthy and the Press*, 151–52, 156; Edwards oral history, 49.

55. Roy M. Cohn, *McCarthy* (New York: New American Library, 1968), 225; Medford Evans, *The Assassination of Joe McCarthy* (Boston: Western Islands, 1970), 270; William F. Buckley Jr., "A New Look at a Controversial Committee," *National Review*, 12 (January 16, 1962), 15; Herman, *Joseph McCarthy*, 296; Alexander, *Pen and Politics*, 152, 168, 171–72, 177, 196–202, 205; Alexander, *Never Lose a War*, 119; M. J. Heale, *American Anticommunism: Combating the Enemy Within, 1830–1970* (Baltimore: Johns Hopkins University Press, 1990), 191–202.

56. Bayley, *Joe McCarthy and the Press*, 75–87; Douglass Cater, *The Fourth Branch of Government* (Boston: Houghton Mifflin, 1959), 106–7; William S. White, *The Making of a Journalist* (Lexington: University Press of Kentucky, 1986), 16; White, "Trying to Find the Shape—If Any—of the News in Washington," *Harper's Magazine*, 217 (August 1958), 111; Herbert Block, *Herblock's Here and Now* (New York: Simon and Schuster, 1955), 111; Philip L. Graham to Elmer Davis, August 13, 1952, Elmer H. Davis papers, Library of Congress.

57. de Toledano, *One Man Alone*, 118, 176–77; Edwards interview, Reeves Collection; Ronald Radosh, John Earl Haynes, and Harvey Klehr, "Spy Stories," *New Republic*, 219 (November

16, 1998), 15–16; see also "McCarthy's Ghost," in Peter Collier and David Horowitz, *Destructive Generation: Second Thoughts about the Sixties* (New York: Free Press, 1996), 192–210.

Chapter Five

1. TASS is the acronym for the Telegraphnoye Agentstvo Sovyetskovo Soyuza or Telegraph Agency of the Soviet Union. Merle Miller, "Washington, the World, and Joseph Alsop," *Harper's*, 236 (June 1968), 55; [Drew Pearson and Robert S. Allen], *Washington Merry-Go-Round* (New York: Horace Liveright, 1932), 359; Walter Trohan, *Political Animals: Memoirs of a Sentimental Cynic* (Garden City, N.Y.: Doubleday, 1975), 37; James Reston, *The Artillery of the Press: Its Influence on American Foreign Policy* (New York: Harper & Row, 1967), 75.

2. Reston, *The Artillery of the Press*, 74–75; George Christian, *The President Steps Down: A Personal Memoir of the Transfer of Power* (New York: Macmillan, 1970), 194.

3. John Hohenberg, *Foreign Correspondence: The Great Reporters and Their Times* (New York: Columbia University Press, 1964), 62–66, 76; Kent Cooper, *Barriers Down: The Story of the New Agency Epoch* (New York: Farrar & Rinehart, 1942), 6–8, 11–12, 17; Jonathan Fenby, *The International News Services* (New York: Schocken, 1986), 23–42.

4. James Bryce, *The American Commonwealth*, vol. 3 (London: Macmillan, 1888), 585–94; Edward Chalfant, *Better in Darkness: A Biography of Henry Adams: His Second Life, 1862–1898* (Hamden, Conn.: Archon, 1994), 192; Arthur Willert, *Washington and Other Memories* (Boston: Houghton Mifflin, 1972), 89; James Sayler, "Window on an Age: Arthur Krock and the New Deal Era, 1929–1941" (Ph.D. diss. Rutgers University, 1978), 100.

5. A. Maurice Low, *America at Home* (New York: Arno, 1974 [1908]), 19–24, 86, 90, 92, 206, 219–23, 228; see also J. Frederick Essary, *Covering Washington: Government Reflected to the Public in the Press, 1822–1926* (Boston: Houghton Mifflin, 1927), 146–47.

6. George Boyne, James Curran, and Pauline Wingate, eds., *Newspaper History from the Seventeenth Century to the Present Day* (Beverly Hills, Calif.: Sage, 1978), 205; Martin Walker, *Powers of the Press: Twelve of the World's Influential Newspapers* (New York: Adama, 1983), 29–40; *The History of* The Times: *The 150th Anniversary and Beyond, 1912–1948* (London: The Times, 1952), 15–16; Joel H. Wiener, *Papers for the Millions: The New Journalism in Britain, 1850 to 1914* (New York: Greenwood, 1988), 277–78, 281; Kenneth E. Olson, *The History Makers: The Press of Europe from Its Beginning through 1955* (Baton Rouge: Louisiana State University Press, 1966), 18; Willert, *Washington and Other Memories*, 32, 39–40.

7. Willert, *Washington and Other Memories*, 49, 52–53, 60, 75, 99–101, 145; David H. Burton, *Cecil Spring Rice* (Rutherford, N.J.: Fairleigh Dickinson University Press, 1990), 152–80, 197–200; *The History of* The Times, 418, 424–26, 439; Essary, *Covering Washington*, 156–58; *The Times*, April 4, 1917; Susan A. Brewer, *To Win the Peace: British Propaganda in the United States during World War II* (Ithaca, N.Y.: Cornell University Press, 1997), 18, 23.

8. U.S. Committee on Public Information, *The Creel Report: Complete Report of the Chairman of the Committee on Public Information, 1917, 1918, 1919* (New York: Da Capo, 1972 [1920]), 106–8; [John P. Cosgrove], *shrdlu: An Affectionate Chronicle* (Washington: National Press Club, 1958), 51–52;

9. Percy Bullen, "The Association's History," *The Foreign Press Association, Directory of Members, 1944*, 7–12, Steven Early papers, Franklin D. Roosevelt Library; *The History of* The Times, 566, 1,106, 1,123; Essary, *Covering Washington*, 154; Oliver Pilat, *Drew Pearson: An Unauthorized Biography*, 112–13.

10. Maxine Davis, "Britain's Ambassador Incognito," *Saturday Evening Post*, 213 (January 25, 1941), 50, 52–53; *Washington Post*, January 5, 1950, January 5, 2001; [Cosgrove], *Shrdlu*, 51–52; invitation for the dinner on January 30, 1931, Laurence Todd papers, in the possession of Alden Todd, Anchorage, Alaska.

11. Davis, "Britain's Ambassador Incognito," 50; Brewer, *To Win the Peace*, 29; *Washington Post*, July 16, 1939; Nicholas John Cull, *Selling War: The British Propaganda Campaign against*

American "Neutrality" in World War II (New York: Oxford University Press, 1995), 19–20; John Chamberlain, *A Life with the Printed Word* (Chicago: Regnery/Gateway, 1982), 120; Henry Brandon interview, *Booknotes*, April 30, 1989, C-SPAN; Henry Brandon, *Special Relationships: A Foreign Correspondent's Memoirs from Roosevelt to Reagan* (New York: Atheneum, 1988), viii, 4–5, 8–9.

12. Laurence Todd, *Correspondent on the Left: The Memoirs of Laurence Todd, 1882–1957* (Anchorage: privately printed, 1996), 299; Davis, "Britain's Ambassador Incognito," 27, 53; Bullen, "The Association's History," 12–16; Hohenberg, *Foreign Correspondence*, 387; *Time*, 35 (April 1, 1940), 44; *Time*, 49 (January 20, 1947), 71–72; *Foreign Correspondence*, 6 (April 18, 1945), 1 (May 2, 1945), 2.

13. Raymond Swing, *"Good Evening!" A Professional Memoir* (New York: Harcourt, Brace, 1964), 191; Cull, *Selling War*, 12–13, 44; Alistair Cooke, *America Observed: From the 1940s to the 1980s* (New York: Knopf, 1988), xi–xiv, 4–10; *New York Times*, March 8, 2004.

14. Cabell Phillips, et al., *Dateline: Washington: The Story of National Affairs Journalism in the Life and Times of the National Press Club* (Garden City, N.Y.: Doubleday, 1949), 74; Todd, *Correspondent on the Left*, 221–22, 285–88, 291; *New York Times*, July 9, 1934, December 11, 1941; *Washington Post*, July 16, 1939, December 10, 1941; John Roy Carlson, *Under Cover: My Four Years in the Nazi Underworld of America* (New York: Dutton, 1943), 208, 447; U.S. Congress, House of Represenatives, Special Committee on Un-American Activities, *Investigation of Nazi Propaganda Activities,* October 16–17, 1934 (Washington: Government Printing Office, 1934), 95–138; Delbert Clark, *Washington Dateline* (New York: Frederick A. Stokes, 1941), 224–25; Michael F. Reilly, *Reilly of the White House* (New York: Simon & Schuster, 1947), 83; Arthur T. Weil, "Freedom of the Press: Is It Being Abused by Foreign Correspondents in the United States?" *The American Hebrew* 7 (January 10, 1941), 9.

15. U.S. Congress, House of Representatives, Committee on Un-American Activities, *Investigation of Un-American Propaganda Activities in the United States,* Appendix—Part 2 (Washington: Government Printing Office, 1940), 969–1,113; Weil, "Freedom of the Press," 9, 16; Brett Gary, *The Nervous Liberals: Propaganda Anxieties from World War I to the Cold War* (New York: Columbia University Press, 1999), 214–15; Saul Friedländer, *Prelude to Downfall: Hitler and the United States, 1939–1941* (New York: Knopf, 1967), 49–56, 242–46, 298–303; Manfred Zapp, *Zwischen Wallstreet Und Kapitol* (Berlin: Wilhelm Limpert-Verlag, 1943), 142–43; *New York Herald Tribune*, April 25, 1947; *Congressional Record*, 81st Cong., 2nd sess., 10,138–41.

16. Masuo Kato, *The Lost War: A Japanese Reporter's Story* (New York: Knopf, 1946), 18–25, 57–81, 259–60.

17. Joseph E. Davies, *Mission to Moscow* (New York: Simon and Schuster, 1941), 46–50; *New York Times*, June 2, 1934, January 27, 1937.

18. Daily mail service sheets, Federated Press papers, Columbia University; Todd, *Correspondent on the Left*, 1–29, 168–69, 192–93, 291; Laurence Todd to Vera Todd, December 16, 1924, and to Irving Stone, February 10, 1945, Todd papers; Laurence Todd testimony, House of Representatives, Special Committee to Investigate Communist Activities in the United States, *Investigation of Communist Propaganda*, 71st Cong, 2nd sess. (Washington: Government Printing Office, 1930), 423–25; Alfred McClung Lee, *The Daily Newspaper in America: The Evolution of a Social Instrument* (New York: Macmillan, 1937), 541–42; *Washington Star*, December 1, 1957; *New York Times*, August 18, 1949.

19. Laurence Todd to Vera Todd, October 3, 1927, Todd papers; Chambers, *Witness*, 242–43; Marguerite Young, *Nothing but the Truth* (New York: Carlton, 1993), 133; James R. Mock and Cedric Larson, *Words That Won the War: The Story of the Committee on Public Information, 1917–1919* (Princeton, N.J.: Princeton University Press, 1939), 90; Paul F. Healy, "Stalin's American Snoops," *Saturday Evening Post,* 223 (January 20, 1951), 52; *Washington Post*, July 16, 1939.

20. Todd to Walter Todd, March 5, and November 12, 1933, Todd papers; author interview with Alden Todd; Healy, "Stalin's American Snoops," 44; Todd, *Correspondent on the Left*,

193–94, 245, 329; Senate Subcommittee to Investigate the Administration of the Internal Security Act, Committee on the Judiciary, *Scope of Soviet Activity in the United States* (Washington: Government Printing Office, 1956), 27; Young, *Nothing but the Truth*, 133.

21.   Todd to Walter Todd, December 14, 1934, Todd papers; Todd, *Correspondent on the Left*, 310, 320–24; Trohan: *Political Animals*, 37–38; Arthur M. Schlesinger Jr., *The Coming of the New Deal* (Boston: Houghton Mifflin, 1959), 457–61.

22.   Joseph P. Lash, *Dealers and Dreamers: A New Look at the New Deal* (New York: Doubleday, 1988), 175–77; J. B. Matthews, "Communists and the New Deal," reprinted in *Congressional Record*, 83rd Cong., 1st sess., A4457–60.

23.   British Security Coordination, *The Secret History of British Intelligence in the Americas, 1940–45* (New York: Fromm, 1999), 112; Todd, *Correspondent on the Left*, 195, 342–45; Healy, "Stalin's American Snoops," 47; Senate Subcommittee to Investigate the Administration of the Internal Security Act, Committee on the Judiciary, *Scope of Soviet Activity in the United States* (Washington: Government Printing Office, 1956), 18–19, 67, 413–15.

24.   Alice Fox Pitts, *Read All About It! 50 Years of ASNE* (Easton, Penn.: American Society of Newspaper Editors, 1974), 178–79.

25.   [Cosgrove], *shrdlu*, 157; Todd, *Correspondent on the Left*, 194–95, 378, 393; Healy, "Stalin's American Snoops," 22–23; Blair Moody, "A Reporter-Senator Reports on the Senate," *New York Times Magazine* (August 5, 1951), 10; Chambers, *Witness*, 546–47.

26.   *New York Times*, February 5, 1947, September 4, 7, 15, 19, 21, 29, 1951; Healy, "Stalin's American Snoops," 44, 47; Todd, *Correspondent on the Left*, 194–95.

27.   Allen Weinstein and Alexander Vassiliev, *The Haunted Wood: Soviet Espionage in America—the Stalin Era* (New York: Random House, 1999), 68; John Earl Haynes and Harvey Klehr, *Venona: Decoding Soviet Espionage in America* (New Haven, Conn.: Yale University Press, 1999), 242–43; Todd, *Correspondent on the Left*, 194; Healy, "Stalin's American Snoops," 47; *New York Times*, July 8, 1953; *Washington Post*, December 1, 1957; Howard Fast, *Being Red* (Boston: Houghton Mifflin, 1990), 319–20.

28.   Author interview with Alden Todd; Senate Subcommittee to Investigate the Administration of the Internal Security Act, Committee on the Judiciary, *Scope of Soviet Activity in the United States* 84th Cong., 2nd sess. (Washington: Government Printing Office, 1956), 845–51.

29.   Author interview with Alden Todd; *Washington Star*, December 1, 1957; *Washington Post*, December 1, 1957.

30.   *Washington Post*, February 21, 1993; Jack Anderson with Daryl Gibson, *Peace, War, and Politics: An Eyewitness Account* (New York: Forge, 1999), 373; Mark D. Alleyne and Janet Wagner, "Stability and Change at the 'Big Five' News Agencies," *Journalism Quarterly*, 70 (Spring 1993), 40–50.

31.   John W. Henderson, *The United States Information Agency* (New York: Praeger, 1969), 30–31, 163; Holly Cowan Shulman, *The Voice of America: Propaganda and Democracy, 1941–1945* (Madison: University of Wisconsin, 1990), 26–28, 38, 53, 79–82, 90–99, 101, 150–51, 170, 178, 183–89; *Washington Post*, March 23, 2003; *New York Times*, July 28, 1943; Kenneth Stewart, *News Is What We Make It: A Running Story of the Working Press* (Boston: Houghton Mifflin, 1943), 286; Lewis L. Gould, ed., *Watching Television Come of Age: The New York Times Reviews by Jack Gould* (Austin: University of Texas Press, 2002), 8.

32.   *USIA: New Directions for a New Era* (Washington: Institute for the Study of Diplomacy, Georgetown University, 1993), 38–41; *Congressional Record*, 103rd Cong., 1st sess., 1,289–90; Shulman, *The Voice of America*, 192, 245; Philip Horton, "Voices within the Voice," *The Reporter*, 9 (July 21, 1953), 25–29; Raymond Swing, "VOA—A Survey of the Wreckage," *The Reporter*, 9 (July 21, 1953), 30–33; Edwin R. Bayley, *Joe McCarthy and the Press* (New York: Pantheon, 1981), 180–82; Henderson, *The United States Information Agency*, 49, 163–68.

33.   United States Senate, Committee on Foreign Relations, *Nominations of Edward R. Murrow and Donald M. Wilson (United States Information Agency), Hearings,* 87th Cong., 1st sess. (Washington: Government Printing Office, 1961), 13–19, 26–28.

34. Eric Sevareid to Willard F. Shadel, October 3, 1951, Shadel to Sevareid, January 6, 1952, Frank Stanton to Rep. William S. Hill, August 2, 1951, Eric Sevareid papers, Library of Congress; David F. Krugler, *The Voice of America and the Domestic Propaganda Battles, 1945–1953* (Columbia: University of Missouri Press, 2000), 2; "Include AP Out," *Newsweek*, 27 (January 28, 1946), 74–75; *New York Times*, February 14, 1950; John M. Anspacher to Charles B. Seib, September 26, 1977, Seib to Anspacher, September 27, 1977, Anspacher papers, American Heritage Center, University of Wyoming; *Washington Post*, September 16, 1977.

35. Philomena Jurey, *A Basement Seat to History: Tales of Covering Presidents Nixon, Ford, Carter, and Reagan for the Voice of America* (Washington: Linus, 1995), 1–9, 13–20, 25–27, 99, 354–56.

36. Walter Gong to Eric Sevareid, August 18, 1954, Sevareid papers; Brandon, *Special Relationships*, 56–59, 65–66; Henry Brandon, *Booknotes* interview, C-SPAN, April 30, 1989; Richard Beeston, *Looking for Trouble: The Life and Times of a Foreign Correspondent* (London: Brassey's, 1997), 121.

37. Alfred Balk and James Boylan, eds., *Our Troubled Press: Ten Years of the* Columbia Journalism Review (Boston: Little, Brown, 1971), 108; Raymond Moley and Raymond Moley Jr., "British Reporters and U.S. Politics," *The Freeman*, 3 (January 25, 1953), 307–10; John C. W. Suh, "126 Foreign Correspondents Talk about Work in America," *Editor & Publisher*, 105 (April 29, 1972), 27–30; Wolf Blitzer, *Between Washington and Jerusalem: A Reporter's Notebook* (New York: Oxford University Press, 1985), ix; Shailendra Ghorpade, "Sources and Access: How Foreign Correspondents Rate Washington, D.C." *Journal of Communications*, 34 (Spring 1988), 34; John Hohenberg, *Between Two Worlds: Policy, Press, and Public Opinion in Asian-American Relations* (New York: Praeger, 1967), 57–59, 71; Ian McDougall, *Foreign Correspondence* (London: Frederick Muller, 1980), 40–41.

38. Christina Ianzito, "Strangers in a Strange Land: Foreign Correspondents Translate Washington's Weirdness," *Capital Style*, 2 (April 1999), 21; Todd, *Correspondent on the Left*, 195; F. A. Hayek, "Leftist Foreign Correspondents," *The Freeman*, 3 (January 12, 1953), 275; Coates Lear, "The Outside Scoop," *Washington Monthly*, 23 (November 1991), 22–23; Hohenberg, *Between Two Worlds*, 60; *The Hill*, April 16, 1997; David Finkel, "They've All Come to Look for America," *Washington Post Magazine* (June 16, 1991), 13–14.

39. *The Hill*, June 28, 1995, April 16, 1997.

40. John M. Anspacher, proposal for *As Others See Us*, October 1, 1974, Anspacher to John E. Reinhardt, June 2, 1975, Simon Winchester to Susan Harmon, May 3, 1976, Anspacher papers; author interview with Fritz Joubert; Finkel, "They've All Come to Look for America," 12–14, 24; Suh, "126 Foreign Correspondents Talk about Work in America," 30; Ianzito, "Strangers in a Strange Land," 18–21; see also "The Culture of Foreign Correspondence," in Stephen Hess, *International News & Foreign Correspondents* (Washington: Brookings Institution, 1996), 47–59; and "From Our Correspondent in Harry's Bar," in Jean-Louis Servan-Schreiber, *The Power to Inform: Media: The Information Business* (New York: McGraw-Hill, 1974), 151–62.

41. Hohenberg, *Foreign Correspondence*, 412; "The Foreign Press in the U.S.A.," *Editor & Publisher* (June 11, 1960), 15; Ianzito, "Strangers in a Strange Land," 18–21; *The Hill*, April 16, 1997; *Washington Post*, November 14, 1992; Connie Lawn, *Voice from America: Off the Air with Radio New Zealand's Washington Correspondent* (Auckland, New Zealand: HarperCollins, 1994), 84–85, 183–85, 210.

42. Dom Bonafede, "Foreign Correspondents: 'We Try to Cover Almost Everything about America,'" *National Journal* 14 (April 17, 1982), 666–67; Beeston, *Looking for Trouble*, 112–36; *Washington Post*, April 21, 1936.

Chapter Six

1. Ken Hoyt and Frances Spatz Leighton, *Drunk before Noon: The Behind-the-Scenes Story of the Washington Press Corps* (Englewood Cliffs, N.J.: Prentice-Hall, 1979), 198.

2. "Accuracy, Speed 'Musts' for Wires," *Staff* [Committee on House Administration] (May/ June 1980), 2–5; Lou Cannon, *Reporting: An Inside View* (Sacramento: California Journal Press, 1977), 114; Delbert Clark, *Washington Dateline* (New York: Frederick A. Stokes, 1941), 94; William L. Rivers, *The Opinionmakers* (Boston; Beacon, 1967), 22, 44; Stephen Hess, *The Washington Reporters* (Washington: Brookings Institution, 1981), 35; panel discussion on press coverage of Congress, National Press Club, November 9, 1998; Walter Mears, *Booknotes* interview, January 11, 2004, C-SPAN; Pierre Salinger, *With Kennedy* (Garden City, N.Y.: Doubleday, 1966), 112.

3. Donald A. Ritchie, *Press Gallery: Congress and the Washington Correspondents* (Cambridge, Mass.: Harvard University Press, 1991), 65; Lee Edwards, *You Can Make a Difference* (Westport, Conn.: Arlington House, 1980), 25.

4. Kent Cooper, *Kent Cooper and the Associated Press: An Autobiography* (New York: Random House, 1959), 191; Milton A. McRae, *Forty Years in Newspaperdom: The Autobiography of a Newspaper Man* (New York: Brentano's, 1924), 120–24, 146; Oliver Knight, ed., *I Protest: Selected Disquisitions of E. W. Scripps* (Madison: University of Wisconsin Press, 1966), 296–300; Joe Alex Morris, *Deadline Every Minute: The Story of the United Press* (Garden City, N.Y.: Doubleday, 1957), 20–23, 77; Will Irwin, *Propaganda and the News, or What Makes You Think So?* (New York: Whittlesey House, 1936), 100; A. Kent MacDougall, ed., *The Press: A Critical Look from the Inside* (Princeton, N.J.: Dow Jones Books, 1972), 109.

5. Moses Koenigsberg, *King News: An Autobiography* (Philadelphia: F.A. Stokes, 1941), 440–41; Jonathan Fenby, *The International News Services* (New York: Schocken, 1986), 58.

6. H. D. Wheeler, "At the Front with Willie Hearst," *Harper's Weekly*, 61 (October 9, 1915), 340–42; Koenigsberg, *King News*, 454–56; Lindsay Chaney and Michael Chaney, *The Hearsts: Family and Empire–the Later Years* (New York: Simon and Schuster, 1981), 197–98.

7. Walter Mears, *Booknotes* interview, January 11, 2004, C-SPAN; Ritchie, *Press Gallery*, 65; *Congressional Record*, 63rd Cong., 1st sess, 1,511; Willard Grosvenor Bleyer, *The Profession of Journalism* (Boston: Atlantic Monthly Press, 1918), 127; Edmond D. Coblentz, ed., *Newsmen Speak: Journalists on Their Craft* (Freeport, N.Y.: Books for Libraries Press, 1954), 161; Kent Cooper, *Barriers Down: The Story of the News Agency Epoch* (New York: Farrar & Rinehart, 1942), 18.

8. Cooper, *Barriers Down*, 45–51; Calvin Woodward and Deborah Mesce, *Washington (AP): Witness to Power and Politics* (Washington: Associated Press, 1998), 2; Bleyer, *The Profession of Journalism*, 112; Oswald Garrison Villard, *The Disappearing Daily: Chapters in American Newspaper Evolution* (New York: Knopf, 1944), 40–44; Silas Bent, *Ballyhoo: The Voice of the Press* (New York: Boni and Liveright, 1927), 82.

9. Vincent Alabiso, Kelly Smith Tunney, and Chuck Zoeller, eds., *Flash! The Associated Press Covers the World* (New York: Associated Press, 1998), 175–76; Cooper, *Kent Cooper and the Associated Press*, 45, 61–62, 97–98, 152–53, 176; *Washington Times-Herald*, July 28, 1953.

10. Cooper, *Kent Cooper and the Associated Press*, 35–38; Alabiso, Tunney, and Zoeller, eds. *Flash!* 178–79; Irwin, *Propaganda and the News*, 100–1; Richard A. Schwarzloze, *The Nation's Newsbrokers: The Rush to Institution, from 1865 to 1920* (Evanston, Ill.: Northwestern University Press, 1990), 224–25; *Washington Times-Herald*, July 28, 1953; Bess Furman, *Washington By-Line: The Personal History of a Newspaperwoman* (New York: Knopf, 1949), 13–14.

11. [Drew Pearson and Robert S. Allen], *Washington Merry-Go-Round* (New York: Horace Liveright, 1931), 341–43; Irwin, *Propaganda and the News*, 243; Cooper, *Kent Cooper and the Associated Press*, 69, 168–70; Koenigsberg, *King News*, 464–65; Gregory Gordon and Ronald E. Cohen, *Down to the Wire: UPI's Fight for Survival* (New York: McGraw-Hill, 1990), 19.

12. Cooper, *Kent Cooper and the Associated Press*, 163; Leo C. Rosten, *The Washington Correspondents* (New York: Harcourt Brace, 1937), 119–20; Hess, *The Washington Reporters*, 35.

13. Oliver Grambling, *AP, The Story of News* (New York: Farrar and Rinehart, 1940), 419; Rosten, *The Washington Correspondents*, 119; William S. White, *The Making of a Journalist* (Lexington: University Press of Kentucky, 1986), 63–64; William Lawrence, *Six Presidents, Too Many*

Wars (New York: Saturday Review Press, 1972), 24–25; Coblentz, ed., *Newsmen Speak,* 157–63; Sarah McClendon, *My Eight Presidents* (New York: Wyden, 1978), 206.

14. MacDougall, ed., *The Press,* 112–13; Furman, *Washington By-Line,* 91; Raymond Clapper, *Watching the World* (New York: Whittlesey House, 1944), 13; Morris, *Deadline Every Minute,* 181; Thomas L. Stokes, *Chip off My Shoulder* (Princeton, N.J.: Princeton University Press, 1940), 68–70, 217, 292.

15. Clapper, *Watching the World,* 13–14, 21–23; Rosten, *The Washington Correspondents,* 122.

16. Kenneth Stewart, *News Is What We Make It* (Boston: Houghton, Mifflin, 1943), 295–97; Rosten, *The Washington Correspondents,* 124; Eric Sevareid, *Not So Wild a Dream* (New York: Atheneum, 1976 [1946]), 106–7.

17. Harold L. Ickes, *Freedom of the Press Today* (New York: Vanguard, 1941), 34, 151; Cooper, *Kent Cooper and the Associated Press,* 277, 282; Margaret A. Blanchard, "The Associated Press Antitrust Suit: A Philosophical Clash over Ownership of First Amendment Rights," *Business History Review,* 61 (Spring 1987), 44–70; *New York Times,* April 20, 1943.

18. Associated Press, "In Their Words: Letters, Testimony, and Observations from AP Washington's Past," typescript, 1998, 32; Woodward and Mesce, *Washington (AP),* 106–7; John Chancellor and Walter R. Mears, *The News Business* (New York: Harper & Row, 1983), 80.

19. Ray Eldon Hiebert, ed., *The Press in Washington* (New York: Dodd, Mead, 1966), 42; Rosten, *The Washington Correspondents,* 122; "The Troubled Press," *Fortune,* 45 (February 1952), 126, 164; Coblentz, ed., *Newsmen Speak,* 152–56; author interview with Alvin A. Spivak.

20. Gordon and Cohen, *Down to the Wire,* 16–24; Chaney and Chaney, *The Hearsts,* 194–99; Richard Langham Riedel, *Halls of the Mighty: My 47 Years at the Senate* (Washington: Robert B. Luce, 1969), 43; MacDougall, ed., *The Press,* 108–9; *Washington Post,* May 26, 1958; *Washington Star,* May 26, 1958; *New York Times,* May 24, 26, 1958.

21. Salinger, *With Kennedy,* 53; Sander Vanocur, "The President and the Media," Heritage Foundation public forum, March 16, 2000.

22. "Merriman Smith," *Current Biography,* 1964, 429–31; Timothy G. Smith, ed., *Merriman Smith's Book of Presidents: A White House Memoir* (New York: W.W. Norton, 1972), 16, 22–25; *Washington Star,* April 14, 1970; *Washington Post,* April 14, 1970; *New York Times,* April 14, 1970; Helen Thomas, *Front Row at the White House: My Life and Times* (New York: Scribner, 1999), 227.

23. Merriman Smith, *Thank You, Mr. President* (New York: Harper & Brothers, 1946), 16–21, 24–25, 78; MacDougall, ed., *The Press,* 108–9.

24. Smith, *Thank You, Mr. President,* 4–5, 7–8, 10–11, 274; Harry Reasoner, *Before the Colors Fade* (New York: Knopf, 1981), 123–24; Thomas, *Front Row at the White House,* 230–31; Alvin A. Spivak remarks at the Eisenhower Seminar, Gettysburg, October 28, 2000.

25. Smith, *Thank You, Mr. President,* 2–3, 25, 46, 49–53, 112–18.

26. Ibid., 56–64, 183–86, 203; Edward Bliss Jr., *Now the News: The Story of Broadcast Journalism* (New York: Columbia University Press, 1991), 165; William D. Hassett, *Off the Record with FDR* (New Brunswick, N.J.: Rutgers University Press, 1958), 337.

27. Smith, *Thank You, Mr. President,* 20–21, 197–99, 208–9; Frank Holeman oral history, Harry S. Truman Library.

28. Alice Allison Dunnigan, *A Black Woman's Experience: From Schoolhouse to White House* (Philadelphia: Dorrance, 1974), 6; Smith, *Thank You, Mr. President,* 215–17.

29. Smith, *Thank You, Mr. President,* 26–29, 41; Smith, ed., *Merriman Smith's Book of Presidents,* 240; Patrick J. Sloyan, "Total Domination," *American Journalism Review,* 20 (May 1998), 52.

30. Roy L. McGhee oral history, Senate Historical Office, 5–6; Merriman Smith, *Meet Mister Eisenhower* (New York: Harper & Brothers, 1955), 113.

31. Neil MacNeil letter to author, March 13, 2001; Robert E. Clark oral history, Dwight D. Eisenhower Library, 8; Robert Clark comments at Eisenhower Seminar, Gettysburg, October 28, 2000; Salinger, *With Kennedy,* 58; James C. Hagerty oral history, Eisenhower Library, 450; Ruth

Adler, ed., *The Working Press: Special to the* New York Times (New York: Putnam, 1966), 51. Smith, *Meet Mister Eisenhower,* 269, 277; Smith, ed., *Merriman Smith's Book of Presidents,* 97, 243; Ann Whitman oral history, Eisenhower Library.

32. Russell Baker, *The Good Times* (New York: William Morrow, 1989), 265; Robert H. Ferrell, ed., *The Eisenhower Diaries* (New York: W.W. Norton, 1981), 270–71; Merriman Smith, *A President Is Many Men* (New York: Harper & Brothers, 1948), 15, 40; Liz Carpenter, *Ruffles and Flourishes* (College Station: Texas A&M University Press, 1993), 38–39, 100; Smith, ed., *Merriman Smith's Book of Presidents,* 68.

33. *Washington Star,* January 26, 1953; Kenneth W. Thomson, ed., *Ten Presidents and the Press* (Washington: University Press of America, 1983), 50–55; Hagerty oral history, 57, 62–63, 79–81, 175–79.

34. Robert Pierpoint, *At the White House: Assignment to Six Presidents* (New York: Putnam, 1981), 29–35, 53, 57; Neil MacNeil letter to author, March 13, 2001; McGhee oral history, 175–76; panel discussion on press coverage of Congress, National Press Club, November 9, 1998; Sloyan, "Total Domination," 55; *New York Times,* April 14, 1970.

35. Helen Thomas, *Dateline: White House* (New York: Macmillan, 1975), 7–16; Thomas, *Front Row at the White House,* 55–57, 65–66; Neil MacNeil letter to author, March 13, 2001; author interviews with Helen Thomas and Alvin A. Spivak.

36. Smith, *A President Is Many Men,* 93; Baker, *The Good Times,* 326; Smith, ed., *Merriman Smith's Book of Presidents,* 240–41; McGhee oral history, 175; see also Merriman Smith, *The Good New Days: A Not Entirely Reverent Study of Native Habits and Customs in Modern Washington* (New York: Bobbs-Merrill, 1962).

37. Sloyan, "Total Domination," 52–53; Jack Bell, *The Johnson Treatment: How Lyndon B. Johnson Took Over the Presidency and Made It His Own* (New York: Harper & Row, 1965), 7; Mike Mosettig interview on "Covering the Kennedy Assassination," PBS NewsHour, November 22, 2003; William Manchester, *The Death of a President: November 20–November 25, 1963* (New York: Harper & Row, 1967), 134, 167–68, 190.

38. Barbie Zelizer, *Covering the Body: The Kennedy Assassination, the Media, and the Shaping of Collective Memory* (Chicago: University of Chicago Press, 1992), 51–55, 83, 108; Thomas, *Front Row at the White House,* 68–70; Thomas, *Dateline,* 35, 42–43; Nancy Collins, "Helen Thomas: Hot Off the Press," *George,* 6 (March 2001), 118; Harrison E. Salisbury, *A Time of Change: A Reporter's Tale of Our Time* (New York; Harper & Row, 1988), 85.

39. Thomas, *Dateline,* 60; Smith, ed., *Merriman Smith's Book of Presidents,* 35, 45; McGhee oral history, 61; Justin A. Nelson, "Drafting Lyndon Johnson: The President's Secret Role in the 1968 Democratic Convention," *Presidential Studies Quarterly,* 30 (December 2000), 688–713.

40. Reasoner, *Before the Colors Fade,* 124; Sloyan, "Total Domination," 55; author interview with Alvin A. Spivak.

41. Festys Justin Viser, ed., *The News Media—A Service and a Force* (Memphis: Memphis State University Press, 1970), ix, 34–44; *New York Times,* April 14, 1970.

42. The White House Correspondents Association presents an annual Merriman Smith Award for excellence in presidential news coverage. *Washington Post,* April 14, 1970; *Washington Star,* April 14, 1970; Smith, *Merriman Smith's Book of Presidents,* 22–25; Sloyan, "Total Domination," 55; Thomas, *Front Row at the White House,* 70; Smith, *Thank You, Mr. President,* 199.

43. McGhee oral history, 58–59; author interview with Bob Barr; Riedel, *Halls of the Mighty,* 53; Hiebert, ed., *The Press in Washington,* 144–56; *New York Times,* September 16, 1975.

44. Author interview with Jim Talbert; David Broder, *Behind the Front Page: A Candid Look at How the News Is Made* (New York: Simon and Schuster, 1987), 224; William L. Rivers, *The Other Government: Power and the Washington Media* (New York: Universe, 1982), 149–51; Hiebert, ed., *The Press in Washington,* 42, 46–47, 272–73; Forrest Boyd, *Instant Analysis: Confessions of a White House Correspondent* (Atlanta: John Knox Press, 1974), 49, 52.

45. Larry Speakes, *Speaking Out: The Reagan Presidency from inside the White House* (New York: Scribner's, 1988), 230; Lanny J. Davis, "Scandal Management 101," *Washington Monthly,* 23 (May 1999), 39; "Accuracy, Speed 'Musts' for Wires," 2–5.

46. Thomas L. Adkinson, "Sears U. Establishes Campus in Capitol for J-Students," *Editor & Publisher*, 105 (May 13, 1972), 14; Smith, *Thank You, Mr. President*, 9; Grambling, *AP*, 378–79; White, *The Making of a Journalist*, 51; Robert Novak, Booknotes interview, C-SPAN, January 30, 2000; *Washington Post*, May 12, 1997.

47. McGhee oral history, 16–25, 55–57, 87–88.

48. Broder, *Behind the Front Page*, 217; Lou Cannon, *Reporting: An Inside View* (Sacramento: California Journal Press, 1977), 178–95; A. Robert Smith, *Tiger in the Senate: The Biography of Wayne Morse* (Garden City, N.Y.: Doubleday, 1962), 187–201.

49. Hiebert, ed., *The Press in Washington*, 43–46; Rivers, *The Other Government*, 146–49; Bob Thompson, "The Hersh Alternative," *Washington Post Magazine* (January 28, 2001), 9–11; Brit Hume, *Inside Story* (Garden City, N.Y.: Doubleday, 1974), 16; David Ranii, "The Bureau," *Washington Journalism Review*, 3 (April 1981), 33; Len Allen, "Makeup of the Senate Press," in Commission on the Operation of the Senate, *Senate Communications with the Public*, 94th Cong., 2nd sess. (Washington: Government Printing Office, 1977), 24–40; "Accuracy, Speed 'Musts' for Wires," 2; Woodward and Mesce, *Washington (AP)*, 60–63; Broder, *Behind the Front Page*, 223; Chancellor and Mears, *The News Business*, 28.

50. MacDougall, ed., *The Press*, 108–9; Gordon and Cohen, *Down to the Wire*, 24, 28, 37–39, 47–49, 87, 145, 242, 369; Fenby, *The International News Services*, 72–73; Richard A. Schwarzlose, "The Associated Press and United Press International," in Philip S. Cook, Douglas Gomery, and Lawrence W. Lichty, eds., *The Future of News: Television-Newspapers-Wire Services-Newsmagazines* (Baltimore: Johns Hopkins University Press, 1992), 147–66; Robert B. Sims, *The Pentagon Reporters* (Washington: National Defense University Press, 1983), 12.

51. "UPI Costs Rise to $57 Million," *Editor & Publisher*, 105 (April 22, 1972), *New York Times*, December 28, 1998; 18.

52. Gordon and Cohen, *Down to the Wire*, 203; *New York Times*, August 7, 1999; *Washington Post*, May 17, 2000; Cheryl Arvidson, "Helen Thomas Quits UPI over Sale," *Free! The Freedom Forum Online*, May 16, 2000.

53. John Motavalli, *Bamboozled at the Revolution: How Big Media Lost Billions in the Battle for the Internet* (New York: Viking, 2002), 130–38; Alabiso, Tunney, and Zoeller, eds. *Flash!* 183–85; Charlotte Grimes, "Rewired," *American Journalism Review*, 19 (October 1997), 28–35; Brent Cunningham, "The AP Now," *Columbia Journalism Review*, 39 (November/December 2000), 30–61; Woodward and Mesce, *Washington (AP)*, 4; Mark D. Alleyne and Janet Wagner, "Stability and Change at the 'Big Five' News Agencies," *Journalism Quarterly*, 70 (Spring 1993), 40–50; William Powers, "Hello, World," *National Journal*, 33 (June 30, 2001), 2,082–85.

Chapter Seven

1. William Safire, "Pundit-Bashing," *New York Times Magazine* (May 27, 1990), 10; see also Sam G. Riley, *The American Newspaper Columnist* (Westport, Conn.: Praeger, 1998).

2. Karl E. Meyer, "The Washington Press Establishment," *Esquire*, 61 (April 1964), 73; Allen Drury, *Capable of Honor* (Garden City, N.Y.: Doubleday, 1966), 26–28.

3. George Christian, *The President Steps Down: A Personal Memoir of the Transfer of Power* (New York: Macmillan, 1970), 186; James Rowe to Lyndon B. Johnson, April 9, 1964, White House Central Files, Lyndon B. Johnson Library.

4. Karl E. Meyer, ed., *Pundits, Poets, and Wits: An Omnibus of American Newspaper Columns* (New York: Oxford University Press, 1990), xxxvii–viii; E. J. Kahn Jr., *The World of Swope* (New York: Simon and Schuster, 1965), 260–74; Bruce Bliven, *Five Million Words Later: An Autobiography* (New York: John Day, 1970), 170–71; Charles Fisher, *The Columnists* (New York: Howell, Soskin, 1944), 11, 214.

5. Robert S. Lynd and Helen Merrill Lynd, *Middletown in Transition: A Study of Cultural Conflicts* (New York: Harcourt, Brace, 1937), 375–76; Alice Fox Pitts, *Read All About It! 50*

Years of ASNE (Easton, Pa.: American Society of Newspaper Editors, 1974), 56; James Reston, *Sketches in the Sand* (New York: Knopf, 1967), xii–xiii.

6. Ronald Steel, *Walter Lippmann and the American Century* (Boston: Little, Brown, 1980), 279–82; Arthur Krock, *In the Nation: 1932–1966* (New York: McGraw-Hill, 1966), 4–5; Cabell Phillips, et al., *Dateline: Washington: The Story of National Affairs Journalism in the Life and Times of the National Press Club* (Garden City, N.Y.: Doubleday, 1949), 176–78.

7. David Bulman, ed., *Molders of Opinion* (Milwaukee: Bruce Publishing, 1945), 1–12.

8. Raymond Clapper to George A. Carlin, February 3, 1939, Clapper to John Mead, March 6, 1939, Roy Howard to Clapper, April 29, May 8, 1939, Clapper to Howard, May 2, 1939, Raymond Clapper papers, Library of Congress; *Washington Post*, February 4, 1944; John E. Drewry, ed., *More Post Biographies* (Athens: University of Georgia Press, 1947), 77–83; Raymond Clapper, *Watching the World* (New York: Whittlesey House, 1944), 11–13, 21, 28–29, 36–37, 47, 57; Olive Ewing Clapper, *Washington Tapestry* (New York: Whittlesey House, 1946), 41, 23–32; Leo C. Rosten, *The Washington Correspondents* (New York: Harcourt Brace, 1937), 95, 348.

9. Henry F. Pringle, "SRL Washington Poll: Surveying the Capital Correspondents," *Saturday Review of Literature*, 27 (October 14, 1944), 17–19; *Congressional Record*, 78th Cong., 2nd sess., 1,903–4, 3,683–84; James Reston to Turner Catledge, September 9, 1953, Catledge papers, Mississippi State University; "Man of Influence," *Time*, 75 (February 15, 1960), 75.

10. Drew Pearson oral history, 1–2, Johnson Library; Pearson, "Confessions of an S.O.B.," *Saturday Evening Post*, 229 (November 2, 1956), 23–24, (November 10, 1956), 72 (November 24, 1956), 36; H. Montgomery Hyde, *Room 3603: The Story of the British Intelligence Center in New York during World War II* (New York: Farrar, Straus, 1963), 204; Oliver Pilat, *Drew Pearson: An Unauthorized Biography* (New York: Harper's Magazine Press, 1973), 80–84, 94–95, 114–16, 131; Fisher, *The Columnists*, 107–8; [Drew Pearson and Robert S. Allen], *Washington Merry-Go-Round* (New York: Horace Liveright, 1931), 321–66; *New York Times*, September 13, 1931; Drewry, ed., *More Post Biographies*, 230; Robert S. Allen, "My Pal, Drew Pearson," *Collier's*, 124 (July 30, 1949), 56; Tyler Abell, ed., *Drew Pearson, Diaries, 1949–1959* (New York: Holt, Rinehart, 1974), 469–70; George H. Manning, "'More Merry-Go-Round' Last Straw from *Baltimore Sun* and Pearson," *Editor & Publisher*, 65 (September 10, 1932), 9.

11. Allen, "My Pal, Drew Pearson," 14; Bulman, ed., *Molders of Opinion*, 107–8; Drewry, ed., *More Post Biographies*, 223–25; Fisher, *The Columnists*, 214–15, 243; Neal Gabler, *Winchell: Gossip, Power, and the Culture of Celebrity* (New York: Knopf, 1994), 111.

12. Jack Anderson with Daryl Gibson, *Peace, War, and Politics: An Eyewitness Account* (New York: Forge, 1999), 61; Robert E. Kintner, "Broadcasting and the News," *Harper's*, 230 (April 1965), 61; Pearson, "Confessions of an S.O.B." (November 10, 1956), 74; Drewry, ed., *More Post Biographies*, 221–22; Brit Hume, *Inside Story* (Garden City, N.Y.: Doubleday, 1974), 8–9, 23; Krock to Arthur Hays Sulzberger, December 16, 1948, Arthur Krock papers, Princeton University.

13. Joseph Alsop with Adam Platt, *"I've Seen the Best of It": Memoirs* (New York: W.W. Norton, 1992), 119–20, 128; Merle Miller, "Washington, the World, and Joseph Alsop," *Harper's*, 236 (June 1968), 45; Turner Catledge, *My Life and the Times* (New York: Harper & Row, 1971), 98–100; Delbert Clark, *Dateline Washington* (New York: Frederick A. Stokes, 1941), 199; Bernard Law Collier, "The Joe Alsop Story," *New York Times Magazine* (May 23, 1971), 73.

14. Robert W. Merry, *Taking on the World: Joseph and Stewart Alsop: Guardians of the American Century* (New York: Viking, 1996), 93–104, 123–45; Joseph Alsop Jr. and Turner Catledge, "Joe Robinson, The New Deal's Old Reliable," *Saturday Evening Post*, 209 (September 26, 1936), 5; Miller, "Washington, the World, and Joseph Alsop," 49; Joseph W. Alsop Jr., *Reporting Politics* (Minneapolis: University of Minnesota, 1960), 8.

15. Harold Ickes, *America's House of Lords: An Inquiry into the Freedom of the Press* (New York: Harcourt Brace Jovanovich, 1939), 98–99; Marquis W. Childs, *I Write from Washington* (New York: Harper & Brothers, 1932), 258–59.

16. Alsop, *"I've Seen the Best of It,"* 262–65; Joseph and Stewart Alsop, *The Reporter's Trade* (New York: Reynal & Company, 1959), 6–9, 79; Stewart Alsop, *Stay of Execution: A Sort of Memoir* (Philadelphia: J.B. Lippincott, 1973), 96; A. J. Liebling, *The Press* (New York: Ballantine, 1975), 222, 299, 311; Edwin M. Yoder Jr., *Joe Alsop's Cold War: A Study of Journalistic Influence and Intrigue* (Chapel Hill: University of North Carolina Press, 1995), 19, 187–88; Clark, *Washington Dateline,* 137, 187–88, 191.

17. Joseph and Stewart Alsop, "Why Has Washington Gone Crazy?" *Saturday Evening Post,* 215 (July 29, 1950), 20–21, 59; Kai Bird, *The Color of Truth: McGeorge Bundy and William Bundy: Brothers in Arms: A Biography* (New York: Simon & Schuster, 1998), 179–80; Sidney Blumenthal, "The Ruins of Georgetown," *New Yorker,* 72 (October 21 & 28, 1996), 223; Pearson, "Confessions of an S.O.B." (November 3, 1956), 87; Walter Isaacson and Evan Thomas, *The Wise Men: Six Friends and the World They Made: Acheson, Bohlen, Harriman, Kennan, Lovett, McCloy* (New York: Simon and Schuster, 1986), 409, 431–32; Joseph Alsop to Walter Lippmann, February 16, 1950, Alsop papers.

18. John T. Connor, "Impressions of the Secretary," October 23, 1961, Felix Belair to Luther Huston, January 30, 1946, Krock memorandum, 1948, Krock to Drew Pearson, January 16, 21, 1949, Krock memorandum, May 6, 1949, Ferdinand Eberstadt to Krock, May 26, 1949, Krock papers; Frank Kluckhohn and Jay Franklin, *The Drew Pearson Story* (Chicago: Charles Hallberg, 1967), 51–52, 59; Jack Anderson with James Boyd, *Confessions of a Muckraker: The Inside Story of a Life in Washington during the Truman, Eisenhower, Kennedy, and Johnson Years* (New York: Random House, 1979), 123, 126–27; *Congressional Record,* 81st Cong., 1st sess., A3220; Arthur Krock, *Memoirs: Sixty Years on the Firing Line* (New York: Funk and Wagnalls, 1968), 237; Abell, ed., *Drew Pearson, Diaries,* 35, 38–39, 42.

19. *New York Times,* May 24, 29, 1949; *Time,* 55 (June 6, 1949), 43; "Press Is Criticized Sharply for Attacks on Forrestal," *Editor & Publisher,* 82 (May 28, 1949), 5, 52; Abell, ed., *Drew Pearson, Diaries,* 50, 52, 55–57; Pearson, "Confessions of an S.O.B." (November 3, 1956), 24, 91; Anderson, *Confessions of a Muckraker,* 141–44; *Washington Times-Herald,* May 24, 1949; *New York Journal-American,* July 20, 1949; Douglas A. Anderson, *A "Washington Merry-Go-Round" of Libel Actions* (Chicago: Nelson-Hall, 1980), 227–32; Oliver Pilat, *Pegler: Angry Man of the Press* (Boston: Beacon, 1963), 204, 217–18, 236–39; Finis Farr, *Fair Enough: The Life of Westbrook Pegler* (New Rochelle, N.Y.: Arlington House, 1975), 119–20, 193.

20. Eugene Meyer to Philip L. Graham, February 13, 1954, Eugene Meyer papers, Library of Congress; Pearson, "Confessions of an S.O.B." (November 24, 1956), 148, 150; Jack Anderson memo to Pearson, October 23, 1953, Drew Pearson papers, Lyndon B. Johnson Library; Chalmers M. Roberts, *The Washington Post: The First 100 Years* (Boston: Houghton Mifflin, 1977), 243–44; William L. Rivers, *The Opinionmakers* (Boston: Beacon, 1970), 110–28; William Rivers, *The Adversaries: Politics and the Press* (Boston: Beacon, 1970), 251; Peter Edson, "Interpretation and Analysis of Washington News," in Ray Eldon Hiebert, ed., *The Press in Washington* (New York: Dodd, Mead, 1966), 40; Anderson, *Confessions of a Muckraker,* 145.

21. Krock memorandum, September 27, 1950, Krock papers; Yoder, *Joe Alsop's Cold War,* 23–26, 47; "Man of Influence," 75; Liebling, *The Press,* 222, 299, 311; Stewart Alsop to Richard Nixon, March 12, 1958, Alsop papers; Merry, *Taking on the World,* 82, 227–29; Alsop, *The Reporter's Trade,* 136; Alsop, *"I've Seen the Best of It,"* 334–35.

22. Sherman Adams, *First Hand Report: The Story of the Eisenhower Administration* (New York: Harper & Brothers, 1961), 413; Arthur Larson, *Eisenhower: The President Nobody Knew* (New York: Charles Scribner's Sons, 1968), ix; Craig Allen, *Eisenhower and the Mass Media: Peace, Prosperity, and Prime-Time TV* (Chapel Hill: University of North Carolina Press, 1993), 187.

23. Stewart Alsop, *The Center: People and Power in Political Washington* (New York: Harper & Row, 1968), 229, 233; Marquis Childs, *Witness to Power* (New York: McGraw-Hill, 1975), 2; Chalmers M. Roberts; *First Rough Draft: A Journalist's Journal of Our Times* (New York: Praeger, 1973), 147–48; *New York Herald Tribune,* December 23, 1963; Yoder, *Joe Alsop's Cold*

War, 164–75; Joseph Alsop testimony, House Government Operations Committee, *Hearings on the Availability of Information from Federal Departments and Agencies* (Washington: Government Printing Office, 1956), 22–23; Alsop, *The Reporter's Trade*, 66; Reston, *Deadline*, 216–17.

24. Alsop, *The Reporter's Trade*, 27–31; Alsop, "I've Seen the Best of It," 326–43; Yoder, *Joe Alsop's Cold War*, 152–58; Merry, *Taking on the World*, 329, 360–65; Richard Helms with William Hood, *A Look over My Shoulder: A Life in the Central Intelligence Agency* (New York: Random House, 2003), 150–51; Eric Alterman, *Sound and Fury: The Washington Punditry and the Collapse of American Politics* (New York: HarperCollins, 1992), 41–42; Stewart Alsop, *Stay of Execution*, 97; *New York Herald Tribune*, March 12, 1958.

25. Henry Brandon, *Special Relationships: A Foreign Correspondent's Memoirs from Roosevelt to Reagan* (New York: Atheneum, 1988), 60–62.

26. Marquis Childs and James Reston, eds., *Walter Lippmann and His Times* (New York: Harcourt, Brace & World, 1959), 1–20, 159, 226–38; David Elliott Weingast, *Walter Lippmann: A Study in Personal Journalism* (New Brunswick, N.J.: Rutgers University Press, 1949), 22–32; Theodore H. White, *In Search of History: A Personal Adventure* (New York: Harper & Row, 1978), 440; *Congressional Record*, 85th Cong., 1st sess., 11,307.

27. Steel, *Walter Lippmann and the American Century*, 342–66; Walter Trohan, *Political Animals: Memoirs of a Sentimental Cynic* (Garden City, N.Y.: Doubleday, 1975), 393; *Congressional Record*, 90th Cong., 1st sess., 7,210.

28. James Reston, *Booknotes* interview, December 8, 1991, C-SPAN; Childs and Reston, eds., *Walter Lippmann and His Times*, 126–46; Bulman, ed., *Molders of Opinion*, 9–10, 37–38; *Congressional Record*, 90th Cong., 1st sess., 7,210, 93rd Cong., 2nd sess., 39,998; Weingast, *Walter Lippmann*, 47–60, 78–92; John Luskin, *Lippmann, Liberty, and the Press* (Tuscaloosa: University of Alabama Press, 1972), 118–20; Walter Lippmann, *U.S. Foreign Policy: Shield of the Republic* (Boston: Little, Brown, 1943), x–xii.

29. David M. Oshinsky, *A Conspiracy So Immense: The World of Joe McCarthy* (New York: Free Press, 1983), 187; Steel, *Walter Lippmann and the American Century*, 484–85; *Congressional Record*, 83rd Cong., 2nd sess., 6,214–15; Allen, *Eisenhower and the Mass Media*, 49.

30. Steel, *Walter Lippmann and the American Century*, 526.

31. Luskin, *Lippmann, Liberty, and the Press*, 145–46, 153; Reston, *Deadline*, 145–51; John Earl Haynes and Harvey Klehr, *Venona: Decoding Soviet Espionage in America* (New Haven, Conn.: Yale University Press, 1999), 99–100.

32. Max Frankel, *Booknotes* interview, April 18, 1999, C-SPAN; Max Frankel, *The Times of My Life and My Life with the Times* (New York: Random House, 1999), 260–61; William H. Lawrence to Krock, September 15, 1959, Krock papers; Walter Lippmann, "The Job of the Washington Correspondent," *Atlantic Monthly*, 205 (January 1960), 47–49.

33. William S. White, "Trying to Find the Shape—if Any—of the News in Washington," *Harper's*, 217 (August 1958), 78; Douglass Cater, *The Fourth Branch of Government* (Boston: Houghton Mifflin, 1959); Richard H. Rovere, *The American Establishment and Other Reports, Opinions, and Speculations* (New York: Harcourt, Brace, 1962), 3–21; Stewart Alsop, *The Center*, ix–x, 15, 23, 25, 171–73.

34. Pierre Salinger, *With Kennedy* (Garden City, N.Y.: Doubleday, 1966), 111–12, 120; Christian, *The President Steps Down*, 188; Paul Martin to Jack Valenti, May 13, 1964, White House Central Files, Johnson Library; see also Bernard C. Cohen, *The Press and Foreign Policy* (Princeton, N.J.: Princeton University Press, 1963).

35. Krock, *Memoirs*, 326–27; Thomas J. Whalen, *Kennedy versus Lodge: The 1952 Massachusetts Senate Race* (Boston: Northeastern University Press, 2000), 21; Ben Bradlee, *A Good Life: Newspapering and Other Adventures* (New York: Simon & Schuster, 1995), 23; Press panel oral history, 16–20, Joseph Alsop oral history, 9–12, John F. Kennedy Presidential Library.

36. *Washington Post*, April 13, 1959; Alsop, *The Reporter's Trade*, 258; Theodore H. White, *The Making of the President, 1964* (New York: Atheneum, 1965), 407–15; Joseph Alsop oral history, Johnson Library, 1, 5–7.

37. Joseph Alsop, second interview, Kennedy Library, 71; *Newsweek*, 58 (December 18, 1961), 65; Fred W. Friendly, *Due to Circumstances beyond Our Control . . .* (New York: Vintage, 1967), 117–19; *Washington Post*, June 17, 1961; Montague Kern, Patricia W. Levering, and Ralph B. Levering, *The Kennedy Crises: The Press, the Presidency, and Foreign Policy* (Chapel Hill: University of North Carolina Press, 1983), 28–29, 71–72; Bird, *The Color of Truth*, 216–17; Marshall McLuhan, *Understanding Media: The Extensions of Man* (New York: McGraw-Hill, 1964), 36–45.

38. Kern, Levering, and Levering, *The Kennedy Crises*, 27–29, 35, 174–75; Alsop, *The Reporter's Trade*, 43; Daniel C. Hallin, *The "Uncensored War": The Media and Vietnam* (New York: Oxford University Press, 1986), 48, 72–74; 360; Alsop, *"I've Seen the Best of It,"* 459; *Washington Post*, September 23, 1963; Stanley Karnow, "The Newsmen's War in Vietnam," [December 1963] in Louis M., Lyons, ed., *Reporting the News: Selections from Nieman Reports* (New York: Atheneum, 1968), 356–57; David Halberstam, *The Powers That Be* (New York: Knopf, 1979), 449–50, 530; Neil Sheehan, *A Bright Shining Lie: John Paul Vann and America in Vietnam* (New York: Random House, 1988), 10, 347–48.

39. William S. White oral history, interview #2, 4, Joseph Alsop oral history, 1–3, Johnson Library; Brian VanDeMark, *Into the Quagmire: Lyndon Johnson and the Escalation of the Vietnam War* (New York: Oxford University Press, 1991), 47; Walter Jenkins to Johnson, January 15, 1964, White House Central Files, Johnson Library; Michael Beschloss, ed., *Taking Charge: The Johnson White House Tapes, 1963–1964* (New York: Simon & Schuster, 1997), 262–63, 357.

40. See Neil Sheehan, et al., *The Pentagon Papers: As Published by the* New York Times (New York: Bantam, 1971); Beschloss, ed., *Taking Charge* and *Reaching for Glory: Lyndon Johnson's Secret White House Tapes, 1964–1965* (New York: Simon & Schuster, 2001); and William Gaffin and Erwin Knoll, *Anything but the Truth: The Credibility Gap—How News Is Managed in Washington* (New York: Putnam, 1968).

41. Lady Bird Johnson, *A White House Diary* (New York: Holt, Rinehart, and Winston, 1970), 167–68; Jack Valenti, *A Very Human President* (New York: W.W. Norton, 1975), 299–301; Beschloss, ed., *Taking Charge*, 410.

42. George C. Herring, *America's Longest War: The United States and Vietnam, 1950–1975* (New York: Knopf, 1986), 119–23; Turner Catledge, memo on a conversation with President Johnson, December 15, 1964, Krock papers; Joseph Alsop oral history, Johnson Library, 4, 8–13; Joseph Alsop to Robert Kennedy, November 1964, and to Melvin J. Lasky, October 11, 1965, Alsop papers; *New York Herald Tribune*, December 23, 28, 30, 1964; Beschloss, ed., *Reaching for Glory*, 150; Committee on Foreign Relations, [William Conrad Gibbons], *The U.S. Government and the Vietnam War: Executive and Legislative Roles and Relationships*, Part III (Washington: Government Printing Office, 1988), 156; Fredrik Logevall, *Choosing War: The Lost Chance for Peace and the Escalation of the War in Vietnam* (Berkeley: University of California Press, 1999), 287–89, 298–99, 389–95.

43. Bird, *The Color of Truth*, 272–73, 328–29; McGeorge Bundy to Johnson, December 16, 1964. White House Central Files, Lyndon B. Johnson Library; Helms, *A Look over My Shoulder*, 292–93; Beschloss, ed., *Reaching for Glory*, 145, 150, 185.

44. Eric F. Goldman, *The Tragedy of Lyndon Johnson* (New York: Knopf, 1969), 94; Beschloss, ed., *Taking Charge*, 313; *Washington Post*, February 11, 1961; Robert Dallek, *Flawed Giant: Lyndon Johnson and His Times, 1961–1973* (New York: Oxford University Press, 1998), 243–44; Alsop oral history, Johnson Library, 9–10.

45. *Washington Post*, February 15, 18, 1965; Steel, *Walter Lippmann and the American Century*, 557–58.

46. Daniel Ellsberg, *Secrets: A Memoir of Vietnam and the Pentagon Papers* (New York: Viking, 2002), 71; David Halberstam, *The Best and the Brightest* (New York: Random House, 1972), 499–500; Melvin Small, *Johnson, Nixon, and the Doves* (New Brunswick, N.J.: Rutgers University Press, 1988), 40–41; [Gibbons], *The U.S. Government and the Vietnam War*, part III,

131–41; Joseph A. Califano Jr., *The Triumph & Tragedy of Lyndon Johnson: The White House Years* (New York: Simon & Schuster, 1991), 338–41;

47.   James Reston, "Portrait of a President," *New York Times Magazine* (January 17, 1965), xx; Bird, *The Color of Truth*, 314–17; Bill Moyers to Horace Busby, Jack Valenti, and Douglass Cater, April 19, 1965, Bundy to Lippmann, April 20, 28, 1965, White House Central Files, Johnson Library; Chalmers Roberts oral history, 32, Johnson Library.

48.   Reston, *Deadline*, 323–29; Ruth Adler, ed., *The Working Press: Special to the New York Times* (New York: Putnam, 1966), 101–9; David M. Barrett, *Lyndon B. Johnson's Vietnam Papers: A Documentary Collection* (College Station: Texas A&M University Press, 1997), 23–24, 79, 271; Robert Kintner to Johnson, May 19, 1966, Kintner Office Files, Johnson Library; Committee on Foreign Relations [William Conrad Gibbons], *The U.S. Government and the Vietnam War: Executive and Legislative Roles and Relationships* (Washington: Government Printing Office, 1994), Part IV: 230; transcript of a dialogue between Walter Lippmann and members of the Massachusetts Historical Society, April 8, 1965, Marquis Childs to Richard Dudman, March 5, 1965, Dudman to Childs, March 12, 1965, Dudman to Roger Hillsman, October 26, 1965, Richard Dudman papers, Library of Congress; *Washington Post*, March 30, 1965.

49.   Nancy Dickerson oral history, 16, Alsop oral history, 9–13, Lyndon Johnson phone conversation with McGeorge Bundy, March 30, 1965, Johnson Library; Henry Brandon, *Special Relationships: A Foreign Correspondent's Memoirs from Roosevelt to Reagan* (New York: Atheneum, 1988), 205; Barrett, *Lyndon B. Johnson's Vietnam Papers*, 253; Rivers, *The Opinionmakers*, 168; Alsop to Drew Pearson, July 20, 1965, Pearson to Alsop, July 26, 1965, Alsop papers; *Washington Post*, June 14, 1974; Kathleen J. Turner, *Lyndon Johnson's Dual War: Vietnam and the Press* (Chicago: University of Chicago Press, 1985), 180; Miller, "Washington, the World, and Joseph Alsop," 54; Beschloss, ed., *Reaching for Glory*, 252–53; 259–61, 368.

50.   Drew Pearson oral history, 5–7; Drew Pearson to Bill Moyers, July 9, 1965, White House Central Files, Johnson Library; Charles Roberts oral history, 39–44, Johnson Library; Charles Roberts, "LBJ's Credibility Gap," *Newsweek*, 68 (December 19, 1966), 24–26; see also James Deakin, *Lyndon Johnson's Credibility Gap* (Washington: Public Affairs Press, 1968).

51.   Robert Kintner to LBJ, April 21, 27, July 6, 1966, Kintner to Bill Moyers, April 20, June 6, 1966, Kintner Office Files, Johnson Library; John Anthony Maltese, *Spin Control: The White House Office of Communications and the Management of Presidential News* (Chapel Hill: University of North Carolina Press, 1992), 10–11.

52.   Kintner to Johnson, May 4, July 13, 25, 1966: Kintner to Moyers, June 3, 1966, Kintner to Joseph Califano, July 13, 1966, Kintner Office Files, Johnson Library; Kintner to Johnson, May 10, 1966, Kintner to Marvin Watson, July 20, 1966, P. Siemien [office of Eric F. Goldman] memo for the files, May 17, 1966, White House Central Files, Johnson Library; *Washington Post*, May 9, 1966; Alsop oral history, Johnson Library, 9–13; Miller, "Washington, the World, and Joseph Alsop," 54.

53.   Alsop's most militant columns were collected in Clyde Edwin Pettit, *The Experts* (Secaucus, N.J.: Lyle Stuart, 1975); *Washington Post*, May 12, 1968; Reston, *Sketches in the Sand*, 275–77; William M. Hammond, *Public Affairs: The Military and the Media, 1962–1968* (Washington: Center of Military History, 1988), 328–29; Alsop, oral history, Johnson Library 14–17; Alsop to Joe B. Frantz, appendium to his oral history, August 17, 1972, Alsop papers; Yoder, *Joe Alsop's Cold War*, 114–15; Merry, *Taking on the World*, 423–30; Miller, "Washington, the World, and Joseph Alsop," 46; Hugh C. Sherwood, *The Journalistic Interview* (New York: Harper & Row, 1972), 18.

54.   Clifton Daniel to Frederick Hunter Klein, November 13, 1967, Alsop papers; Zailin B. Grant, "Alsop Lets His Friends Down," *New Republic*, 158 (May 18, 1968), 9–10, and Alsop's response, (May 25, 1968), 43; letters to the editor by Alsop and Ward Just, *Harper's*, 237 (August 1968), 4; "Aiming at Joe," *Time*, 91 (June 14, 1968), 80–81; Bradlee, *A Good Life*, 196, 301–2; Merry, *Taking on the World*, 431.

55. Kintner memo to Johnson, August 12, 1966, Kintner Office Files, Johnson Library; Fredrik Logevall, "First among Critics: Walter Lippmann and the Vietnam War," *Journal of American-East Asian Relations*, 4 (Winter 1995), 351–75; Halberstam, *The Powers That Be*, 546–48; *New York Times*, February 25, 1966; Trohan, *Political Animals*, 393; Allen Drury to Krock, March 14, 1966, Krock papers.

56. *Washington Post*, May 7, 25, 1967; Kintner memo to Johnson, May 8, 1967, George Christian memo to John Roche, May 12, 1967, White House Central Files, Johnson Library; Steel, *Walter Lippmann and the American Century*, 539, 576, 580–81; Luskin, *Lippmann, Liberty, and the Press*, 153–54; *Congressional Record*, 90th Cong., 1st sess., 7,210; *Public Papers of Lyndon B. Johnson, 1968–69* (Washington: Government Printing Office, 1970), 622, 1,351.

57. "Lippmann in New Form," *Newsweek*, 69 (June 5, 1969), 64; Alsop to Kintner, January 5, 1968, Alsop papers; Turner, *Lyndon Johnson's Dual War*, 117, 186; Barrett, *Lyndon B. Johnson's Vietnam Papers*, 663–64; Miller, "Washington, the World, and Joseph Alsop," 47, 55.

58. Alsop to Lee Lescaze, July 3, August 2, 1968, and to Andrew Kopkind, August 20, 1968, Alsop papers; *Washington Post*, October 6, 1968.

59. Collier, "The Joe Alsop Story," 23, 64, 71, 74–75; Julius Duscha, "Washington Columnists," *Washingtonian*, 5 (July 1970), 35–37, 61–62; Ken Hoyt and Frances Spatz Leighton, *Drunk before Noon: The Behind-the-Scenes Story of the Washington Press Corps* (Englewood Cliffs, N.J.: Prentice Hall, 1973), 184–85; "Aiming at Joe," *Time*, 91 (June 14, 1968), 14; Harrison E. Salisbury, *Without Fear or Favor: The New York Times and Its Times* (New York: Ballantine, 1980), 86–87; Alsop, "*I've Seen the Best of It*," 467–70; Alsop, *Stay of Execution*, 298; Howard Bray, *The Pillars of the Post: The Making of a News Empire in Washington* (New York: Norton, 1980), 51–53; *New York Times*, September 30, 1974.

60. Meyer, "The Washington Press Establishment," 73; Krock to Edwin L. James, July 26, 1950, Krock to Catledge, December 16, 1963, December 14, 1966, and April 2, 1968, Catledge to Krock, December 12, 1966, Krock to E. C. Daniel, December 7, 12, 1966, Daniel to Krock, December 8, 1966, Krock papers.

61. Richard Harwood, "The Fourth Estate," in Laura Longley Babb, ed., *The Washington Post Guide to Washington* (New York: McGraw-Hill, 1975), 80–87; Duscha, "Washington Columnists," 34–37, 60–64; Childs and Reston, eds., *Walter Lippmann and His Times*, 109.

62. Jack W. Germond, *Fat Man in a Middle Seat: Forty Years of Covering Politics* (New York: Random House, 1999), xi; Robert Novak, *Booknotes* interview, January 30, 2000, C-SPAN; *The Hill* (March 15, 2000), 29; *Washington Post*, March 29, 2001.

63. Doris Kearns, *Lyndon Johnson and the American Dream* (New York: Harper & Row, 1976), 313–14.

Chapter Eight

1. Mary McGrory oral history, Washington Press Club Foundation, 1–18; Winzola McLendon and Scottie Smith, *Don't Quote Me! Washington Newswomen and the Power Society* (New York: Dutton, 1970), 32–36; Nan Robertson, *The Girls in the Balcony: Women, Men, and the New York Times* (New York: Random House, 1992), 102–3.

2. Meg Greenfield, *Washington* (New York: Public Affairs, 2001), 112; Karl E. Meyer, "The Washington Press Establishment," *Esquire*, 61 (April 1964), 73; Bess Furman, *Washington By-Line: The Personal History of a Newspaperwoman* (New York: Knopf, 1949), 36–37.

3. Sarah McClendon oral history, Washington Press Foundation, 56; Leo C. Rosten, *The Washington Correspondents* (New York: Harcourt, Brace, 1937), 213, 263; Cabell Phillips, et al., *Dateline: Washington: The Story of National Affairs Journalism in the Life and Times of the National Press Club* (Garden City, N.Y.: Doubleday, 1949), 166; see also [John P. Cosgrove], *shrdlu: An Affectionate Chronicle* (Washington: National Press Club, 1958) and James Free, *The First 100 Years! A Casual Chronicle of the Gridiron Club* (Washington: Gridiron Club, 1985).

4. Pierre Salinger, *With Kennedy* (Garden City, N.Y.: Doubleday, 1966), 120; Ishbel Ross, *Ladies of the Press: The Story of Women in Journalism by an Insider* (New York: Harper & Brothers, 1936), 510.

5. Donald A. Ritchie, *Press Gallery: Congress and the Washington Correspondents* (Cambridge, Mass.: Harvard University Press, 1991), 120–21, 145–62; Gerda Lerner, *The Woman in American History* (Menlo Park, Calif.: Addison-Wesley, 1971), 106–17; Richard Langham Riedel, *Halls of the Mighty: My Forty-Seven Years at the Senate* (New York: Robert B. Luce, 1969), 48–49.

6. Marie Manning, *Ladies Now and Then* (New York: Dutton, 1944), 206; "Marie Manning," *Notable American Women,* vol. 2 (Cambridge, Mass.: Belknap, 1971), 491–92; Ross, *Ladies of the Press,* 79–84, 332–35; Frances Parkinson Keyes, *Capital Kaleidoscope: The Story of a Washington Hostess* (New York: Harper & Brothers, 1937), 281–82; Maurine H. Beasley and Sheila J. Gibbons, *Taking Their Place: A Documentary History of Women in Journalism* (State College, Penn.: Strata, 2003), 142.

7. Maurine Beasley. "The Women's National Press Club: Case Study of Professional Aspirations," *Journalism History, 15* (Winter 1988), 112–21.

8. Sara M. Evans, *Born for Liberty: A History of Women in America* (New York: Free Press, 1989), 175–96; Silas Bent, *Ballyhoo: The Voice of the Press* (New York: Boni and Liveright, 1927) 114–17; *New York Times,* April 5, 1954; *Washington Star,* April 5, 1954; profile of Winifred Mallon by Violet Libby, Washington Press Foundation papers, National Press Club; TB [Tiffany Blake] to Arthur Sears Henning, telegram, October 7, 1918, Winifred Mallon to Richard Oulahan, November 19, 1928, from Mallon's scrapbooks in the Bess Furman papers, Library of Congress; Furman, *Washington By-Line,* 36–37; Arthur Krock to Samuel A. Tower, August 25, 1948, Turner Catledge papers, Mississippi State University.

9. May Craig, "Inside in Washington," *Portland Press,* June 7, 1943; unpublished memoir, Elisabeth May Craig papers, Library of Congress; Jane L. Twomey, "May Craig: Journalist and Liberal Feminist," *Journalism History,* 27 (Fall 2001), 129–38; Ross, *Ladies of the Press,* 335–36; Margaret Chase Smith, *Declaration of Conscience* (Garden City, N.Y.: Doubleday, 1972), 3; David Brinkley, *Brinkley's Beat: People, Places, and Events That Shaped My Time* (New York: Knopf, 2003), 32–36; Biographical sketch, Mary Hornaday Collection, American Heritage Center, University of Wyoming, Laramie.

10. Rosten, *The Washington Correspondents,* 166, 307–23; Ross, *Ladies of the Press,* 347–49, 539–43; Keyes, *Capital Kaleidoscope,* 294–97; *Washington Star,* December 16, 1957; Genevieve Forbes Herrick to Bess Furman, September 16, 1952, Furman papers; Lloyd Wendt, *Chicago Tribune: The Rise of a Great American Newspaper* (Chicago: Rand McNally, 1979), 481, 613; Kay Mills, *A Place in the News: From the Women's Page to the Front Page* (New York: Dodd, Mead, 1988), 30–31; Linda Steiner and Susanne Gray, "Genevieve Forbes Herrick: A Front Page Reporter 'Pleased to Write about Women,'" *Journalism History, 12* (Spring 1985), 8–16.

11. Marguerite Young, *Nothing but the Truth* (New York: Carlton, 1993), 15, 25, 61–63, 99–106, 121, 124–28, 270–71, 278; Furman, *Washington By-Line,* 55; Freda Kirchwey, et al., *Where Is There Another? A Memorial to Paul Y. Anderson* (Norman, Okla.: Cooperative Books, 1939), 17, 20; Paul Y. Anderson, "A Washington Honor Roll," *The Nation,* 132 (January 28, 1931), 94; Kenneth Stewart, *News Is What We Make It: A Running Story of the Working Press* (Boston: Houghton Mifflin, 1943), 107; Whittaker Chambers, *Witness* (New York: Random House, 1952), 219–20.

12. *Daily Worker,* January 6, 7, 1934; Young, *Nothing but the Truth,* 140–41, 170–75; Ross, *Ladies of the Press,* 352–54.

13. Flora Lewis oral history, Ruth Cowan Nash oral history, 5, Washington Press Club Foundation.

14. "The Eleanor Roosevelt Press Conferences" (joint interview with Ann Cottrell Free, Frances Lide, Ruth Montgomery, and Malvina Stephenson), 4, Washington Press Club Foundation; Eleanor Roosevelt, "Our Ladies of the Press," *Newspaperman* (April 1945), 9; Maurine

H. Beasley, *Eleanor Roosevelt and the Media: A Public Quest for Self-Fulfillment* (Urbana: University of Illinois Press, 1987), 35–39; Eleanor Roosevelt, *This I Remember* (New York: Harper & Brothers, 1949), 102–4; Barbara Belford, *Brilliant Bylines: A Biographical Anthology of Notable Newspaperwomen in America* (New York: Columbia University Press, 1986), 186.

15. "The Eleanor Roosevelt Press Conferences," 1–5; Ruth Cowan Nash oral history, 5, Washington Press Club Foundation.

16. Furman, *Washington By-Line*, 191; "The Eleanor Roosevelt Press Conferences," 10–13; Beasley, *Eleanor Roosevelt and the Media*, 52–53, 63; Manning, *Ladies Now and Then*, 206–12.

17. "The Eleanor Roosevelt Press Conferences," 26; Dorothy Dunbar Bromley, "The Future of Eleanor Roosevelt," *American Mercury*, 180 (January 1940), 134; Ross, *Ladies of the Press*, 309, 316; Furman, *Washington By-Line*, 153.

18. Free, *The First 100 Years!* 125; Beth Campbell Short oral history, 62, Washington Press Club Foundation; Beasley, "The Women's National Press Club," 116.

19. Eugene A. Kelly, "Distorting the News," *American Mercury*, 34 (March 1935), 313; Ross, *Ladies of the Press*, 350–52, 539–43; Mills, *A Place in the News*, 30–31; Belford, *Brilliant Bylines*, 258–64; Doris Fleeson, *An Art to Be Practiced* (Minneapolis: University of Minnesota School of Journalism, 1957), 5–6; Mary McGrory, "Doris Fleeson," *Notable American Women*, vol. 4, 239–41; McGrory oral history, 30–32.

20. Kathleen L. Endres, "Capitol Hill Newswomen: A Descriptive Study," *Journalism Quarterly*, 53 (Spring 1976), 133; *Washington Post*, September 20, 1936.

21. Unpublished memoir, Craig papers; *Women Come to the Front: Journalists, Photographers, and Broadcasters during World War II* (Washington: Library of Congress, 1998), 13.

22. Author interview with Jane Eads Bancroft; Jane Eads Bancroft oral history, 59–60, 68, Washington Press Club Foundation; Scott Hart, *Washington at War, 1941–1945* (Englewood Cliffs, N.J.: Prentice-Hall, 1970), 94–95; W. M. Kiplinger, *Washington Is Like That* (New York: Harper & Brothers, 1942), 176–77; *Time*, (March 13, 1944), 83.

23. *New York Times*, October 23, 1943; Helen Thomas, *Dateline: White House* (New York: Macmillan, 1975), xii; Shirley Biagi, ed., *NewsTalk I: State-of-the-Art Conversations with Today's Print Journalists* (Belmont, Calif.: Wadsworth, 1987), 181–84; Sarah McClendon, *My Eight Presidents* (New York: Wyden, 1978), 3–23; Sarah McClendon with Jules Minton, *Mr. President! Mr. President! My Fifty Years of Covering the White House* (Santa Monica, Calif.: General Publishing Group, 1996), 12–25, 42–45, 123–28; McClendon oral history, 47–50; Evan Smith, "The Watchdog," *Texas Monthly*, 21 (December 1993), 79–81; *Washington Post*, June 8, 1987, January 24, 1996.

24. *Washington Star*, December 16, 1957; Mills, *A Place in the News*, 52–54; Virginia Van Der Veer Hamilton, *Looking for Clark Gable and Other 20th-Century Pursuits: Collected Writings* (Tuscaloosa: University of Alabama Press, 1996), 90–103.

25. Roosevelt, "Our Ladies of the Press," 9; "Coed Conference," *Newsweek* (October 11, 1943), 88, 90,

26. Fred Pasley, "Five Women Writers Barred at White House by New Order," *New York Daily News* clipping, Craig unpublished memoir, Craig memorandum, Mrs. Roosevelt's Press Conference Association news release, December 11, 1942, Craig papers; "The Eleanor Roosevelt Press Conferences," 7–8; Beasley, *Eleanor Roosevelt and the Media*, 142–43, 149; Roosevelt, *This I Remember*, 104–5.

27. *Washington Post*, April 8, 1945; "The Eleanor Roosevelt Press Conferences," 19, 29; Beasley, *Eleanor Roosevelt and the Media*, 163–64.

28. Mrs. Roosevelt's Press Conference Association open letter to members, April 16, 1945, Craig papers; "The Eleanor Roosevelt Press Conferences," 30–31, 41; Furman, *Washington By-Line*, 324–25; see also Franklin D. Mitchell, *Harry S. Truman and the News Media: Contentious Relations, Belated Respect* (Columbia: University of Missouri Press, 1998), 130–51.

29. Marion Marzolf, *Up from the Footnote: A History of Women Journalists* (New York: Hasting House, 1977), 72; Thomas, *Dateline: White House*, xii; Biagi, *News Talk 1*, 184; McClendon oral history, 47–50; Van Der Veer, *Looking for Clark Gable*, 103–5.

30. Judy Mann, *Mann for All Seasons: Wit and Wisdom from the* Washington Post's *Judy Mann* (New York: MasterMedia, 1990), 6; Beasley, "The Women's National Press Club," 119; Women's National Press Club, *Who Says We Can't Cook!* (Washington: McIver Art and Publications, 1955).

31. Betty Beale, *Power at Play: A Memoir of Parties, Politicians, and the Presidents in My Bedroom* (Washington: Regnery Gateway, 1993), 27–31; McLendon and Smith, *Don't Quote Me!* 16–20; Marzolf, *Up from the Footnote*, 109; Maxine Cheshire with John Greenya, *Maxine Cheshire, Reporter* (Boston: Houghton Mifflin, 1978), 21–31; Judith Martin, "Too Much a Lady?" *New York Times Book Review* (August 29, 1999), 34; *Washington Post*, October 9, 2001.

32. Georgie Anne Geyer, "Women in Journalism," *Dateline: 1976, Journalism in the United States, The First 200 Years*, 40–41 in the files of the Overseas Press Club, American Heritage Center; Doris Fleeson to Arthur Krock, August 7, 1961, Arthur Krock papers, Princeton University; McGrory, "Doris Fleeson," 239–41; *Washington Post*, March 14, 1971; *The Hill*, June 7, 1995; Tom Wicker, *On Press* (New York: Viking, 1978), 189–90; "Miss Higgins Dropped from Press Gallery," *Editor & Publisher*, 90 (November 16, 1957), 12; "Tempest in Toothpaste," *Newsweek*, 50 (November 25, 1957) 81; see also Antoinette May, *Witness to War: A Biography of Marguerite Higgins* (New York: Penguin, 1985).

33. McLendon and Smith, *Don't Quote Me!* 23–38.

34. Greenfield, *Washington*, 121; Roberta Oster Sachs, "Role Model: Sarah McClendon," *Columbia Journalism Review*, 42 (May/June 2003), 12; *Washington Post*, March 14, 1971; Rodger Streitmatter, *Raising Her Voice: African-American Women Journalists Who Changed History* (Lexington: University of Kentucky Press, 1994), 107–28.

35. William L. Rivers, *The Opinionmakers* (Boston: Beacon, 1967), 33–34; Max Frankel, *The Times of My Life and My Life with the* Times (New York: Random House, 1999), 322; Robertson, *The Girls in the Balcony*, 103; *Washington Post*, November 3, 2001.

36. *Washington Post Book World*, May 16, 1993; Isabelle Shelton, "A Mad Day with LBJ," *U.S. News & World Report* (May 2, 1964), 46–47; see also Isabelle Shelton oral history, Washington Press Club Foundation.

37. *Washington Post*, July 18, 2001.

38. Carol Williams and Irwin Touster, *The* Washington Post: *Views from the Inside* (Englewood Cliffs, N.J.: Prentice-Hall, 1976), 120–23; Peggy A. Simson, "Covering the Women's Movement," *Nieman Reports*, 53–54 (Winter 1999–Spring 2000), 40–45; *Washington Post*, July 18, 2001.

39. Sally Quinn, *We're Going to Make You a Star* (New York: Simon and Schuster, 1975), 50–61.

40. Louis M. Lyons, ed., *Reporting the News: Selections from Nieman Reports* (New York: Atheneum, 1968), 1–13; May Craig to Franklin D. Roosevelt, March 5, 12 1944, Stephen Early papers, FDR Library; *Time* (March 13, 1944), 83; Radio Correspondents Annual Meeting, March 6, 1945, minutes of the Radio and Television Correspondents Association, Senate Radio and Television Gallery, U.S. Capitol.

41. Roy McGhee oral history, 146, Senate Historical Office; [Cosgrove], *shrdlu*, 95; Phillips, et al., *Dateline: Washington*, 255–56; Greenfield, *Washington*, 123–24; Ruth Cowan Nash oral history, 32, Washington Press Club Foundation.

42. Short oral history, 78–79; McClendon, *My Eight Presidents*, 230; Sachs, "Role Model: Sarah McClendon," 12; *Washington Post*, March 13, 1970.

43. Bancroft oral history, 77–78; Helen Thomas, "Memories from the National Press Club," April 19, 2002, column for the Hearst newspapers.

44. McClendon oral history; Beasley, "The Women's National Press Club," 119; "Mary Hornaday Protests Bars to Newswomen," undated clipping, Hornaday papers; *Washington Post*, February 23, 1955.

45. Robertson, *The Girls in the Balcony*, 99–102.

46. Bill Lawrence, *Six Presidents, Too Many Wars* (New York: Saturday Review Press, 1972), 227–28; Russell Baker, *The Good Years* (New York: William Morrow, 1989), 308, 317; *Reli-*

able Sources: The National Press Club in the American Century (Washington: National Press Club, 1998), 111; *Washington Post*, October 30, 1959; Thomas, *Dateline*, xviii; author interview with Helen Thomas.

47.   [Cosgrove], *shrdlu*, 144, 148; Don Larrabee, *It's News to Me; A Maine Yankee Reports from Washington* (Washington: privately published, 1989), 80.

48.   Author interview with Helen Thomas; Harold W. Chase and Allen H. Lerman, eds., *Kennedy and the Press: The News Conferences* (New York: Thomas Y. Crowell, 1965), 141–42; *Washington Post*, November 30, 1961; Thomas, *Dateline: White House*, 23; Lawrence, *Six Presidents, Too Many Wars*, 227–28.

49.   Civil rights activist Pauli Murray condemned the civil rights leaders for disregarding the Press Club's "notorious policy of segregation and discrimination against qualified newspaper women," adding, "Frankly, if I were a newspaper woman . . . I would picket you." Pauli Murray to A. Philip Randolph, August 21, 1963, Ethel L. Payne papers, Library of Congress; Robertson, *The Girls in the Balcony*, 99–102; *Washington Post*, August 22, 26, 29, 1963.

50.   Beasley, "The Women's National Press Club," 119.

51.   *Washington Post*, March 13, 1970; McGhee oral history, 156–57.

52.   Author interview with Don Larrabee; Larrabee, *It's News to Me*, 80; *Reliable Sources*, 118; Beasley, "The Women's National Press Club," 119; *National Press Club Record*, 21 (January 21, 1971).

53.   *Washington Daily News*, February 22, 1971; *Philadelphia Inquirer*, March 21, 1971; *New York Daily News*, March 1971, clippings in Gridiron Club Records; McGhee oral history, 156.

54.   *Washington Post*, June 10, 1985; author interviews with Nan Robertson and Mary Kay Quinlan.

55.   Furman, *Washington By-Line*, 83–84, 160–65; J. Fred Essary, *Covering Washington: Government Reflected to the Public in the Press, 1822–1926* (Boston: Houghton Mifflin, 1927), 234–36; Ritchie, *Press Gallery*, 127–28; Free, *The First 100 Years!* 125.

56.   Harrison E. Salisbury, *Without Fear or Favor: The New York Times and Its Times* (New York: Ballantine, 1981), 94–95; Robert J. Donovan, "White Tie and Hallowed Nonsense: The Gridiron Club Turns 100," *Washington Journalism Review*, 7 (April 1985), 43–47.

57.   Arthur Krock memorandum, April 19, 1972, Krock papers; *Washington Post*, March 5, 13, 16, 1970; *Washington Star*, March 15, 1970; Robert Sherrill, "Twilight of the Gridiron," *Washington Post Magazine* May 5, 1974; Harold Brayman, *The President Speaks Off-the-Record: Historic Evenings with America's Leaders, the Press, and Other Men of Power at Washington's Exclusive Gridiron Club* (Princeton: Dow Jones Books, 1976), 766; James Aronson, *Deadline for the Media: Today's Challenges to Press, TV, and Radio* (Indianapolis: Bobbs-Merrill, 1972), 179–80.

58.   Aronson, *Deadline for the Media*, 181–82; Chalmers M. Roberts, *The Washington Post: The First 100 Years* (Boston: Houghton Mifflin, 1977), 429; Marzof, *Up from the Footnote*, 100–2; Maurine Beasley and Sheila Gibbons, *Women in Media: A Documentary Source Book* (Washington: Women's Institute for Freedom of the Press, 1977), 138–41.

59.   *Washington Daily News*, February 22, 1971; Journalists for Professional Equality to Carl Albert, February 19, 1971, Gridiron Club papers, Library of Congress.

60.   J. V. Reistrup to Jack Bell, February 19, 1971; Jerald F. terHorst to Charles A. Perlick Jr. March 3, 1971, Bob Dole to John W. Jarrell, March 16, 1971, Gridiron Club papers; *Washington Star*, February 25, 1971; *Washington Post*, February 26, 1971; *New York Times*, April 3, 1972.

61.   Minutes, April 6, May 12, November 12, December 4, 1971, letter from eleven members to Jack Bell, September 24, November 1, 1971, Gridiron Club papers; *Washington Post*, December 9, 1971; *Washington Star*, December 5, 1971.

62.   Katharine Graham, *Personal History* (New York: Knopf, 1997), 417–19; *Washington Star*, November 7, 1971, February 11, April 9, 16, 1972; Shirley Chisholm, "Guess Who's Not Coming to the Gridiron Club Dinner?" in Robert O. Blanchard, ed., *Congress and the News Media* (New York: Hastings House, 1974), 149–53; Journalists for Professional Equality press release, February 10, 1972, Edmund S. Muskie to Edgar A. Poe, February 25, 1972, Arthur

Krock to Poe, April 14, 1972, Humphrey speech, April 1972, Barry Goldwater to Edgar Allen Poe, April 11, 1972, Minutes, April 8, 1972, Gridiron Club papers; *New York Daily News*, March 4, April 29, 1972; *Washington Post*, April 9, 10, 1972; *New York Times*, April 3, 1972; Ann Wood, "Journalists Protest: Gridiron Drag Show Is a Drag," *Chicago Journalism Review* (May, 1972); Brayman, *The President Speaks Off-the-Record*, 802–4.

63.   Krock to Marshall McNeil, April 12, 1971, and to Edgar Poe, January 18, 1972, Krock memorandum, April 19, 1972, Krock papers; *New York Times*, April 3, 1972; Minutes, February 1, November 10, 1972, January 5, October 9, December 8, 1973, Gerald Ford remarks to Gridiron, December 8, 1973, Gridiron Club papers; *Washington Star*, November 11, 1972, March 10, 1973, February 8, 1974.

64.   Brayman, *The President Speaks Off-the-Record*, 782–83, 795–97; Walter T. Ridder, "Gridiron Club Records for 1974," Minutes, November 9, 1974, Gridiron Club papers; *Washington Star-News*, March 24, 1974; *Washington Post*, April 6, 8, 1974; *New York Times*, April 8, 14, 1974; Arthur Krock to Charles L. Bartlett, October 17, 1961, Krock papers; *New York Daily News*, April 13, 1974; "It's a Hit!!" News Release, March 16, 1974, Journalists for Professional Equity, Ann Wood papers.

65.   *Washington Post*, November 10, 1974, February 8, 1975; *Washington Star*, February 8, 1975, January 15, 1976; *New York Daily News*, March 26, 1977; Lucian Warren, to Jim Free, July 22, 1980, Gridiron Club papers; Brayman, *The President Speaks Off-the-Record*, 834; "Party," *People* (March 31, 1975); Reporters Committee for Freedom of the Press to Ann Wood and Friends, May 21, 1975, Ann Wood papers.

66.   McClendon oral history, 67; McClendon, *Mr. President! Mr. President!* 264.

67.   Amanda Spake, "Thirty Years at the White House," *Washington Post Magazine* (October 21, 1990), 19; Helen Thomas, *Dateline: White House*, xviii; Stephen Hess, *The Washington Reporters* (Washington: Brookings Institution, 1981), 67–69; Stephen Hess, *Live from Capitol Hill! Studies of Congress and the Media* (Washington: Brookings Institution, 1991), 116–17.

68.   Martha Griffiths oral history, 88–90, Former Members of Congress oral history project, Library of Congress; Beth J. Harpaz, *The Girls in the Van: Covering Hillary* (New York: St. Martin's Press, 2001), 3, 219–20, 239.

Chapter Nine

1.   William Small, *To Kill a Messenger: Television News and the Real World* (New York: Hastings House, 1970), 13; Philip J. Hilts, "CBS: The Fiefdom and the Power in Washington," *Washington Post Potomac Magazine* (April 21, 1974), 27; Bill Leonard, *In the Storm of the Eye: A Lifetime at CBS* (New York: Putnam, 1987), 187; Ernest Leiser to all correspondents, March 5, May 8, 1964, Walter Cronkite papers, Institute for News Media History, University of Texas.

2.   Author interview with Fred Graham; Fred Graham, *Happy Talk: Confessions of a TV Newsman* (New York: W. W. Norton, 1990), 41; Bob Schieffer, *This Just In: What I Couldn't Tell You on TV* (New York: Putnam, 2003), 126–28.

3.   Turner Catledge to Arthur Krock, March 18, 1952, Clayton Knowles to Catledge, March 19, 1952, Catledge to Krock, June 17, 1952, Gene Giancarlo to Jack Gould, July 14, 1952, Emmit Holleman to Catledge, August 1, 1952, Turner Catledge papers, Mississippi State University.

4.   Advertisement, *Broadcasting*, 87 (July 29, 1974), 59; Av Westin, *Newswatch: How TV Decides the News* (New York: Simon and Schuster, 1982), 11.

5.   Sig Mickelson, *Booknotes* interview, January 7, 1990, C-SPAN; Sig Mickelson, "Television News Has Come of Age," *The Quill*, 47 (November 1959), 83–84.

6.   Glenn C. Altschuler and David I. Grossvogel, *Changing Channels: America in TV Guide* (Urbana: University of Illinois Press, 1992), 158–60; Steven Zousmer, *TV News Off-Camera: An Insider's Guide to Newswriting and Newspeople* (Ann Arbor: University of Michigan Press, 1987), 22–23, 92; *Washington Post*, January 5, 2000.

7.   Patricia Henry Yeomans, ed., *Behind the Headlines with Bill Henry* (Los Angeles: Ward Ritchie, 1972) 159–60; Barbara Matusow, *The Evening Stars: The Making of the Network*

News Anchor (Boston: Houghton Mifflin, 1983), 64, 53, 96–97; Theodore F. Koop oral history, 7–8, Broadcast Archives, University of Maryland.

8.   Marion Elizabeth Rodgers, ed., *The Impossible H. L. Mencken: A Selection of His Best Newspaper Stories* (New York: Doubleday, 1991), iii, 382, 385; Reuven Frank, *Out of Thin Air: The Brief Wonderful Life of Network News* (New York: Simon & Schuster, 1991), 12–15; Edward Bliss, *Now the News: The Story of Broadcast Journalism* (New York: Columbia University Press, 1991), 208–10; Marlene Sanders and Marcia Rock, *Waiting for Prime Time: The Women of Television News* (New York: Harper & Row, 1988), 8–10; Marion Marzolf, *Up from the Footnote: A History of Women Journalists* (New York: Hastings House, 1977), 157–62.

9.   Mickelson, "Broadcast News Has Come of Age," 15; Don Hewitt, *Tell Me a Story: Fifty Years and Sixty Minutes in Television* (New York: Public Affairs Press, 2001), 44, 94; Hewitt, "Lets Not Compete with the Sitcoms: What's Become of Broadcast Journalism," *Vital Speeches of the Day*, 64 (November 1, 1997), 50; Thomas Frensch, ed., *Television New Anchors: An Anthology of Profiles of the Major Figures and Issues in United States Network Reporting* (Jefferson, N.C.: McFarland, 1993), 54.

10.   Frank, *Out of Thin Air*, 413; Elmer W. Lower, "Broadcasting—The Young Giant," *Dateline: 1976, Journalism in the United States, The First 200 Years*, 22–23, from the papers of the Overseas Press Club of America, American Heritage Center, University of Wyoming, Laramie; Stanley Cloud and Lynne Olson, *The Murrow Boys: Pioneers on the Front Lines of Broadcast Journalism* (Boston: Houghton Mifflin, 1996), 286–89; Eric Sevareid to Chester Morrison, May 24, 1955, Eric Sevareid papers, Library of Congress.

11.   Mickelson, "Broadcast News Has Come of Age," 83; *Washington Post*, June 22, 1979; Leonard, *In the Storm of the Eye*, 38, 66; Frank, *Out of Thin Air*, 32–33; Reuven Frank, *Booknotes* interview, September 15, 1991, C-SPAN; Louis M. Lyons, ed., *Reporting the News: Selections from Nieman Reports* (New York: Atheneum 1968), 192–96; Sig Mickelson, *The Decade That Shaped Television News: CBS in the 1950s* (Westport, Conn.: Praeger, 1998), 5; Cabell Phillips, et al., *Dateline: Washington: The Story of National Affairs Journalism in the Life and Times of then National Press Club* (Garden City, N.Y.: Doubleday, 1949), 91–92.

12.   *The Postwar Congress and the Media*, Freedom Forum video documentary, 1996, episode 5; Frensch, ed., *Television New Anchors*, 55; Martha Roundtree to Blair Moody, February 28, 1946, Blair Moody papers, Michigan Historical Collection, University of Michigan; Eric Sevareid to Harriet Van Horn, December 8, 1949, Sevareid papers; Sig Mickelson, *Booknotes* interview, January 7, 1990, C-SPAN; "The Battling Panelists," *Newsweek*, 47 (January 16, 1956), 78; *Broadcast Pioneers Library Reports*, 8–11 (Winter/Spring 1988, Summer/Fall 1989), 48.

13.   Eric Sevareid to John Day, October 2, 1956, Sevareid papers; Turner Catledge to Arthur Krock, April 23, 1953, Arthur Krock papers, Princeton University; author interview with Richard Harwood; *The Postwar Congress and the Media*, episode 5; Eric Alterman, *Sound and Fury: The Washington Punditry and the Collapse of American Politics* (New York: HarperCollins, 1992), 93, 97, 157; *Washington Post*, December 4, 1988, November 7, 1993.

14.   Douglass Cater, *The Fourth Branch of Government* (Boston: Houghton Mifflin, 1959), 104–5; *Evening Star*, January 3, 1947; *Time*, 62 (November 2, 1953), 49; Bryson Rash oral history, 75, 77, Broadcast Archive, University of Maryland; Charles L. Fontenay, *Estes Kefauver: A Biography* (Knoxville: University of Tennessee Press, 1980), 164–68.

15.   William Henry Moore, *The Kefauver Committee and the Politics of Crime, 1950–1952* (Columbia: University of Missouri Press, 1974), 168–71, 183–89; Gregory C. Lisby, "Early Television on Public Watch: Kefauver and His Crime Investigation," *Journalism Quarterly*, 62 (Summer 1985), 236–38; Ivan Doig, "Kefauver versus Crime: Television Boosts a Senator," *Journalism Quarterly*, 39 (Autumn 1962), 483–90; Jeanine Derr, "'The Biggest Show on Earth': The Kefauver Crime Committee Hearings," *Maryland Historian*, 17 (Fall/Winter 1986); *New York Times*, March 14, 18, 20, 1951; *Evening Star*, March 25, 1951.

16.   Lisby, "Early Television on Public Watch," 238–41; "And May the Best Man Win!" *Time* convention guide, 1952, 4; *New York Times*, March 25, 1951; *Washington Daily News*, May 28,

1951; Doig, "Kefauver versus Crime," 490; Ronald Garay, *Congressional Television: A Legislative History* (Westport Conn.: Greenwood, 1984), 37–46.

17.   Mike Michaelson interview, Lisby, "Early Television on Public Watch," 241; *New York Times*, June 25, 1951; Garay, *Congressional Television*, 50–54; Martin Agronsky to Robert B. Chiperfield, May 20, 1953, Executive Committee meetings, January 14, 1952, May 5, 1955, Minutes of the Radio and Television Correspondents Association; Thomas G. Abernathy oral history, 48–50, Former Members of Congress, Library of Congress.

18.   *Congressional Record*, 95th Cong., 1st sess., E5353; *Washington Star*, January 1, 1953; Edwin R. Bayley, *Joe McCarthy and the Press* (Madison: University of Wisconsin Press, 1981), 56–57, 166–67, 176–83, 203–9; *New York Times*, November 14, 1954; *Washington Star*, June 3, 5, 1954; Elmer W. Lower to Sig Mickelson, May 5, 1954, Sevareid papers; Leonard H. Goldenson with Marvin J. Wolf, *Beating the Odds: The Untold Story behind the Rise of ABC: The Stars, Struggles, and Egos That Transformed Network Television by the Man Who Made It Happen* (New York: Charles Scribner's Sons, 1991), 117, 274; Sally Bedell Smith, *In All His Glory: The Life of William S. Paley, the Legendary Tycoon and His Brilliant Circle* (New York: Simon and Schuster, 1990), 361–68; Brian Thornton, "Published Reaction When Murrow Battled McCarthy," *Journalism History*, 29 (Fall 2003), 143; Robert J. Donovan and Ray Scherer, *Unselect Revolution: Television News and American Public Life, 1948–1991* (New York: Cambridge University Press, 1992), 23–34; commentary by Daniel Schorr and George Herman, American Film Institute, April 22, 2004.

19.   Executive Committee meetings, June 3, November 2, 1953, minutes of the Radio and Television Correspondents Association; Bryson Rash oral history, 36–38; Norris Cotton, *In the Senate: Amidst the Conflict and the Turmoil* (New York: Dodd, Mead, 1978), 56; Joint Committee on the Organization of Congress, *Hearings on the Organization of Congress* (Washington: Government Printing Office, 1965), 439.

20.   George Dixon, *Leaning on a Column* (Philadelphia: Lippincott, 1961), 109–11; Douglass Cater, "Every Congressman a Television Star," *The Reporter*, 12 (June 16, 1955), 26–28.

21.   Cater, *Fourth Branch of the Government*, 104–5; Haynes Johnson, address to the Society for History and the Federal Government, March 23, 1990; Drew Pearson, "Can TV Be Saved?" *Esquire*, 60 (December 1963), 210, 292–94; Ray Elton Hebert, ed., *The Press in Washington* (New York: Dodd, Mead, 1966), 98; Roy McGhee oral history, 120, Senate Historical Office; *New York Times*, July 25, 1952; David Brinkley, *11 Presidents, 4 Wars, 22 Political Conventions, 1 Moon Landing, 3 Assassinations, 2,000 Weeks of News and Other Stuff on Television and 18 Years of Growing Up in North Carolina* (New York: Knopf, 1996), 65.

22.   Koop oral history, Sig Mickelson oral history, 9, Broadcast Archives, University of Maryland; Walter Cronkite, *A Reporter's Life* (New York: Knopf, 1996), 4, 57–60, 154, 157–65, 176, 184; Walter Cronkite to Sig Mickelson, March 31, 1980, Sig Mickelson papers, Institute for News Media History, University of Texas; Mickelson, *The Decade That Shaped Television News*, 29; "Water Cronkite Seminars," *MBNews: The Museum of Broadcasting Newsletter*, 11 (Winter 1987), 28; Desmond Smith, "TV News Did Not Just Happen. It Had to Invent Itself," *Smithsonian*, 20 (June 1989), 74–78.

23.   Eric Sevareid, ed., *Candidates 1960: Behind the Headlines in the Presidential Race* (New York: Basic, 1959), 186; Frank, *Out of Thin Air*, 90–101; Reuven Frank, *Booknotes* interview; September 15, 1991, C-SPAN; Frensch, ed., *Television News Anchors*, 51; David Brinkley, *Brinkley's Beat: People, Places, and Events That Shaped My Time* (New York: Knopf, 2003), 165–67; Brinkley, *11 Presidents*, 100; Lyric Wallwork Winik, "A Voice of His Own," *Washingtonian*, 33 (July 1995), 55–56.

24.   *New York Times*, August 17, 1956; *Washington Star-News*, October 26, 1973; Brinkley, *Brinkley's Beat*, xi; Brinkley, *11 Presidents*, 45–46, 54, 85–87, 103, 107–10; Frank, *Out of Thin Air*, 110–12; Winik, "A Voice of His Own," 55, 128–29; Mickelson, *The Decade That Shaped Television News*, 210–12; Edward Jay Epstein, *News from Nowhere: Television and the News* (New York: Random House, 1973) 194–95; Matusow, *The Evening Stars*, 100–3; Scherer, "Television

News in Washington," 106–7; Frensch, ed., *Television News Anchors*, 45, 48; *Washington Post*, June 13, 2003.

25. Fred W. Friendly, *Due to Circumstances beyond Our Control . . .* (New York: Vintage, 1967), 157, 166; Goldenson, *Beating the Odds*, 140, 150; Frank, *Out of Thin Air*, 133–34; Reuven Frank, *Booknotes* interview, September 15, 1999, C-SPAN; Robert E. Kintner, "Broadcasting and the News," *Harper's*, 230 (April, 1965), 52–54; Milton Viorst, *Hustlers and Heroes: An American Political Panorama* (New York: Simon and Schuster, 1971), 100–15.

26. Susan and Bill Buzenberg, eds., *Salant, CBS, and the Battle for the Soul of Broadcast Journalism* (Boulder, Col.: Westview, 1999), 47; Eric Sevareid to Richard Salant, April 22, 1963, Sevareid papers; Mickelson oral history, 94; Harry Reasoner, *Before the Colors Fade* (New York: Knopf, 1981), 19–20, 26, 167.

27. Hebert, ed., *The Press in Washington*, 97–100; Sig Mickelson, *The Electric Mirror: Politics in the Age of Television* (New York: Dodd, Mead, 1972), 43, 172–73; Craig Allen, *Eisenhower and the Mass Media: Peace, Prosperity, and Prime-Time TV* (Chapel Hill: University of North Carolina Press, 1993), 47–63; Brinkley, *11 Presidents*, 125–26; Brinkley interview on *Television and the Presidency*, Freedom Forum video documentary, 1994.

28. Russell Baker, *The Good Years* (New York: William Morrow, 1989), 326; Eric Sevareid, "Who Will Win in 1960?" *Esquire*, 52 (December 1959), 123; Ben Bradlee, *A Good Life: Newspapering and Other Adventures* (New York: Simon & Schuster, 1995), 211; Newton Minow, et al., *Presidential Television*,(New York: Basic, 1973), 38; John F. Kennedy, "Television: A Force in Politics," *TV Guide* (November 14, 1959), 6–7; Ruth Young Watt oral history, 303, Senate Historical Office; Press Panel oral history, 19–20, John F. Kennedy Library; George Aiken oral history, 2, John F. Kennedy Library; Robert E. Kintner, "Television and the World of Politics," *Harper's*, 230 (May 1965), 121–23; *New York Times*, March 22, 1998.

29. Winik, "A Voice of His Own," 128; Willard A. Edwards oral history, Truman Library, 54–56; Walter Trohan, *Political Animals: Memoirs of a Sentimental Cynic* (Garden City, N.Y.: Doubleday, 1975), 190, 261; Hiebert, ed., *The Press in Washington*, 100; Small, *To Kill a Messenger*, 226; Frank, *Out of Thin Air*, 167–68; Pierre Salinger, *With Kennedy* (Garden City, N.Y.: Doubleday, 1966), 58, 112; Robert Pierpoint, *At the White House: Assignment to Six Presidents* (New York: Putnam, 1981), 69–70; Merriman Smith, *The Good New Days* (New York: Bobbs-Merrill, 1962), 215–16.

30. Author interview with Neil MacNeil; Eric Sevareid to Richard Salant, April 22, 1963, Salant to Sevareid, April 25, 1963, Sevareid papers; Leonard, *In the Storm of the Eye*, 90; Reasoner, *Before the Colors Fade*, 41–42, 123; Frank, *Out of Thin Air*, 180–84.

31. "CBS Evening News with Walter Cronkite, Half-Hour Nightly Series Starting September 2, 1963," news release, Cronkite papers; "CBS and NBC: Walter vs. Chet and Dave," *Newsweek*, 62 (September 23, 1963), 62–65; Mickelson, *The Decade That Shaped Television News*, 217.

32. Author interview with Roger Mudd; David Schoenbrun, *On and Off the Air: An Informal History of CBS News* (New York: Dutton, 1989), 160; Mike Mosettig interview on "Covering the Kennedy Assassination," PBS *NewsHour*, November 22, 2003; Tom Brokaw, *Booknotes* interview, March 7, 1999, C-SPAN.

33. Philip J. Hilts, "CBS: The Fiefdom and the Power in Washington," *Washington Post Potomac Magazine* (April 21, 1974), 11–12.

34. Eric Sevareid to Alexander Kendrick, April 9, 1959, Sevareid papers; Cloud, *The Murrow Boys*, 334–36; Howard K. Smith, *Events Leading Up to My Death: The Life of a Twentieth-Century Reporter* (New York: St. Martin's, 1996), 223, 241, 256, 259, 265–67, 279.

35. Eric Sevareid to Charles Collingwood, April 14, 1959, Collingwood to Sevareid, April 16, 1959, Sevareid papers; "Ready, Washington?" *Newsweek*, 59 (February 12, 1962), 81; Schoenbrun, *On and Off the Air*, 140–46, 151–53; Gary Paul Gates, *Airtime: The Inside Story of CBS News* (New York: Harper & Row, 1978), 357.

36. Schoenbrun, *On and Off the Air*, 146–48; Buzenberg, eds., *Salant, CBS, and the Battle for the Soul of Broadcast Journalism*, 216–18; Hewitt, *Tell Me a Story*, 71–72.

37. Eric Sevareid to Bill Small, July 12, 1963, Sevareid papers; Graham, *Happy Talk,* 30; Roger Mudd, *Booknotes* interview, June 6, 1999, C-SPAN; Hilts, "CBS," 14, 26–28.

38. Schorr, *Staying Tuned,* 185–86; Bob Schieffer and Gary Paul Gates, *Booknotes* interview, August 13, 1989, C-SPAN; Schieffer, *This Just In,* 119–21, 126, 130.

39. Bob Schieffer comments at the Third National Heritage Lecture, Russell Senate Office Building, March 3, 1994; Lee Graham, "Women Don't Like to Look at Women," *New York Times Magazine* (May 24, 1964), 55; Sanders and Rock, *Waiting for Prime Time,* 8–10, 51; Marzolf, *Up from the Footnote,* 157–62; *New York Times,* October 19, 1997; Nancy Dickerson oral history, 1–3, Lyndon B. Johnson Library; Nancy Dickerson, *Among Those Present: A Reporter's View of Twenty-five Years in Washington* (New York: Random House, 1976), 4, 9, 14–15, 19–23, 31; Darrell St. Claire oral history, 230, Senate Historical Office; *Washington Post,* October 19, 1997.

40. Dickerson oral history, Johnson Library, 21–23; Dickerson oral history, 3, Broadcast Archives, University of Maryland; Dickerson, *Among Those Present,* 33–35.

41. Dickerson oral history, 6–8, Johnson Library; Dickerson, *Among Those Present,* 40, 60–61, 134; Sarah McClendon, *My Eight Presidents* (New York: Wyden, 1978), 52, 207; Winzola McLendon and Scottie Smith, *Don't Quote Me! Washington Newswomen and the Power Society* (New York: Dutton, 1970), 144–46; Smith, *Good New Days,* 216.

42. Altschuler and Grossvogel, *Changing Channels,* 140; Dickerson, *Among Those Present,* 85–86, 88, 124–25; McClendon, *My Eight Presidents,* 207; McLendon and Smith, *Don't Quote Me!* 151–52; John F. Dickerson, "On Her Trail," *Time,* 156 (November 13, 2001), 47–48; Barry Gottehrer, "Television's Princess of the Press Corps," *Saturday Evening Post,* 237 (October 31, 1964), 36–37; Johnson telephone call with Mike Mansfield, September 28, 1964, Johnson Library.

43. "Bulldozer," *Newsweek,* 63 (March 16, 1963), 56; Walter Cronkite to Frank Swider, September 22, 1964, Fred Friendly to CND Organization, February 12, 1965, Cronkite papers; Eric Sevareid, "Observations on the CBS 'News Analysis' Policy," 1957, Sig Mickelson to Sevareid, July 26, 1957, Sevareid to Richard Salant and Blair Clark, September 10, 1963, Sevareid memo, May 4, 1965, Sevareid papers.

44. Roger Mudd, *Booknotes* interview, June 6, 1999, C-SPAN; Gates, *Airtime,* 245–47; Small, *To Kill a Messenger,* 147; Special Joint Committee on the Organization of Congress, *The Organization of Congress,* 79th Cong., 1st sess., (1945), 188–93; "Mudd, Roger (Harrison)," *Current Biography Yearbook, 1981* (New York: H. W. Wilson, 1982), 311–14; Charles and Barbara Whalen, *The Longest Debate: A Legislative History of the 1964 Civil Rights Act* (Washington: Seven Locks, 1985), 158; author interview with Roger Mudd; Roger Mudd, Marya McLaughlin Lecture, Marymount University, February 16, 2000.

45. Minutes of the Radio and Television Correspondents Association, December 12, 1962, Joseph F. McCaffrey to Mike Mansfield, April 28, 1970, Radio and Television Correspondents Association; Small, *To Kill a Messenger,* 256–58; "Mudd into Gold," *Newsweek,* 63 (June 22, 1964), 74; Roger Mudd interviewed on *The Postwar Congress and the Media,* episode 3; author interviews with Roger Mudd and Bob Barr.

46. Author interview with Roger Mudd; Small, *To Kill a Messenger,* 258; Whalen, *The Longest Debate,* 199; "Mudd into Gold," 74; *Washington Post,* May 4, 1964; Warren Weaver, *Both Your Houses: The Truth about Congress* (New York: Praeger, 1973), 15; Mudd interviewed in *The Postwar Congress and the Media,* episode 3; Westin, *Newswatch,* 149–50; Gates, *Airtime,* 111–17, 249, 264–65.

47. Author interview with Roger Mudd; Matusow, *The Evening Stars,* 16–17; Dan Rather with Mickey Herskowitz, *The Camera Never Blinks, Adventures of a TV Journalist* (New York: William Morrow, 1977), 159–65, 195; Schieffer, *This Just In,* 262–64; "Mudd, Roger (Harrison)," 314.

48. Sam Donaldson, "The State of Television News: In the Business to Make Money," *Vital Speeches of the Day,* 64 (January 1, 1998), 169; Small, *To Kill a Messenger,* 252–53; author interview with Fred Graham; Roger Mudd, Marya McLaughlin Lecture, Marymount Uni-

versity, February 16, 2000; Garrick Utley, *You Should Have Been Here Yesterday* (New York: Public Affairs, 2000), 80.

49. Daniel J. Boorstin, *The Image: A Guide to Pseudo-Events in America* (New York: Atheneum, 1987 [1961]), 7–44; Sophy Burnham, "Telling It Like It Isn't," *New York*, 1 (September 16, 1968), 22–27; Small, *To Kill a Messenger*, 286.

50. William M. Hammond, *Public Affairs: The Military and the Media, 1962–1968* (Washington: Center of Military History, 1988), 184–95; Daniel C. Hallin, *The "Uncensored War": The Media and Vietnam* (New York: Oxford University Press, 1986), 184–91; Friendly, *Due to Circumstances beyond Our Control . . .*, 213–65; Reasoner, *Before the Colors Fade*, 132–35; see also Todd Gitlin, *The Whole World Is Watching: Mass Media in the Making & Unmaking of the New Left* (Berkeley: University of California Press, 1980).

51. Sander Vanocur, "How the Media Massaged Me," *Esquire*, 77 (January 1972), 84–85; Vanocur, Freedom Forum session, National Archives, September 20, 2000; George Christian, *The President Steps Down: A Personal Memoir of the Transition of Power* (New York: Macmillan, 1970), 195; Small, *To Kill a Messenger*, 19, 263; "Report from Vietnam by Walter Cronkite," February 27, 1968, transcript, Cronkite papers; Hallin, *The "Uncensored War,"* 167–74.

52. "Two Decades of Crisis between Nixon and the Media," *Broadcasting*, 87 (August 19, 1974), 22–23; Irwin F. Gellman, *The Contender: Richard Nixon: The Congress Years, 1946–1952* (New York: Free Press, 1999), 95; Douglass Cater, "Who Is Nixon? What Is He?" *The Reporter*, 15 (November 27, 1958), 9–13; Stewart Alsop, notes on interview with Richard Nixon, April 23, 1958, Joseph and Stewart Alsop papers, Library of Congress.

53. David Halberstam, *The Powers That Be* (New York: Knopf, 1979), 600–1; *Washington Post*, June 11, 2003; Jeb Stuart Magruder, *An American Life: One Man's Road to Watergate* (New York: Atheneum, 1974), 4–5, 53–55; John D. Ehrlichman, *Witness to Power: The Nixon Years* (New York: Simon and Schuster, 1982), 274–75; John Clark Pratt, ed., *Vietnam Voices: Perspectives on the War Years, 1941–1982* (New York: Viking Penguin, 1984), 403–4; Walter Lippmann, "The Problem of Vietnam," *Newsweek*, 74 (December 1, 1969), 27; Hammond, *Public Affairs: The Military and the Media, 1968–1973*, 159–65.

54. Richard Nixon, *RN: The Memoirs of Richard Nixon* (New York: Grosset & Dunlap, 1978), 409–12; H. R. Haldeman, *The Haldeman Diaries: Inside the Nixon White House* (New York: Putnam, 1994), 87, 97–99, 104–6, 109; Brinkley, *11 Presidents*, 123; *New York Times*, December 18, 1972.

55. Patrick J. Buchanan, *Right from the Beginning* (Boston: Little, Brown, 1988), 292–93; Robert W. Peterson, *Agnew: The Coining of a Household Word* (New York: Facts on File, 1972), 55–80; Jules Witcover, *White Knight: The Rise of Spiro Agnew* (New York: Random House, 1972), 296–97, 449; Ehrlichman, *Witness to Power*, 146; John C. Spear, *Presidents and the Press: The Nixon Legacy* (Cambridge, Mass.: MIT Press, 1984), 113–17; John R. Coyne Jr., *The Impudent Snobs: Agnew vs. the Intellectual Establishment* (New York: Arlington House, 1972), 265–70; Herbert G. Klein, *Making It Perfectly Clear* (Garden City, N.Y.: Doubleday, 1980), 168–72; Alan Crawford, *Thunder on the Right: The "New Right" and the Politics of Resentment* (New York: Pantheon, 1980), 165–70, 206–7; Marvin Barett, ed., *Survey of Broadcast Journalism, 1969–1970* (New York, Grosset and Dunlap, 1970), 32, 37.

56. Herbert J. Gans, *Deciding What's News: A Study of* CBS Evening News, NBC Nightly News, Newsweek, *and* Time (New York: Random House, 1979), 358; Westin, *Newswatch*, 145–46; Brinkley, *11 Presidents*, 124; Frank, *Out of Thin Air*, 293–96, 325–26; Walter Cronkite on Eric Sevareid, National Public Radio, February 12, 2004; "Agnew's Complaint: The Trouble with TV," *Newsweek*, 74 (November 24, 1969), 88–92; Dennis T. Lowry, "Agnew and the Network TV News: A Before/After Content Analysis," *Journalism Quarterly*, 48 (Summer 1971), 205–10.

57. Edith Efron, *The News Twisters* (Los Angeles: Nash, 1971), 1–47; John Chamberlain, *A Life with the Printed Word* (Chicago: Regnery Gateway, 1982), 97; William A. Rusher, *The Rise of the Right* (New York: National Review, 1993), 171; John Corry, *TV News and the Dominant Culture* (Washington: The Media Institute, 1986), 5–15, 54.

58.   Eric Sevareid, "Journalism: The Relationship between the Print and Electric Media," *Vital Speeches of the Day*, 42 (July 1, 1976), 564; Reasoner, *Before the Colors Fade*, 167–69, 203; William A. Rivers, *The Adversaries: Politics and the Press* (Boston: Beacon, 1970), 167; Richard H. Rovere, "Letter from Washington," *New Yorker*, 45 (November 29, 1969), 165–68; Don Fry, ed., *Believing the News* (St. Petersburg, Fla.: Poynter Institute, 1985), 167; Gates, *Airtime*, 266–68, 412; Wells Church to Stephen McCormick, March 17, 1965, Radio and Television Correspondents Association; Fred Graham, *Booknotes* interview, March 16, 1990, C-SPAN; see also Lewis S. Feuer, "Why Not a Commentary on Sevareid?" *National Review*, 27 (August 15, 1975), 874–76.

59.   Buzenberg, eds., *Salant, CBS, and the Battle for the Soul of Broadcast Journalism*, 86–99; "The Selling of the Pentagon," in Barrett, ed., *Survey of Broadcast Journalism, 1970–1971*, 32–49, 151–71; John E. O'Connor, ed., *American History/American Television: Interpreting the Video Past* (New York: Ungar, 1983), 256–78; *Washington Post*, December 1, 1997; Mudd interview in *The Postwar Congress and the Media*, episode 3.

60.   Rather, *The Camera Never Blinks*, 213–33; "Salant Says Media Shouldn't Wallow in Watergate," *Broadcasting*, 87 (September 30, 1974), 35–36; Powers, *The Newscasters*, 196; Gates, *Airtime*, 301–16; Schieffer, *This Just In*, 201; Lesley Stahl, *Reporting Live* (New York: Simon & Schuster, 1999), 16–18; Daniel Schorr, *Clearing the Air* (Boston: Houghton Mifflin, 1977), 15, 18; Hilts, "CBS," 28.

61.   Author interview with Roger Mudd; Schorr, *Clearing the Air*, 30–34; Schorr, *Staying Tuned*, 241–43, 246–47; "Delayed Reaction: No More Commentaries Immediately after Presidential Speeches on CBS," *Newsweek*, 81 (June 18, 1973), 74; Buzenberg, eds., *Salant, CBS, and the Battle for the Soul of Broadcast Journalism*, 79–81, 108–9; Hilts, "CBS," 36; James A. Capo, "Network Watergate Coverage Patterns in Late 1972 and Early 1973," *Journalism Quarterly*, 60 (Winter 1983), 595–602; Dom Bonafede, "The Washington Press—Competing for Power with the Federal Government," *National Journal*, 14 (April 17, 1982), 669.

62.   Rather, *The Camera Never Blinks*, 233; interview with Fred Graham; Graham, *Happy Talk*, 142–57.

63.   Haldeman, *White House Diary*, 118, 127–28, 147, 161–62, 169, 179–80, 356–57; Ehrlichman, *Witness to Power*, 103; Rather and Gates, *The Palace Guard*, 300–2; Nixon, *RN*, 674–75; "Historical Coverage for Historic Events," *Broadcasting*, 87 (July 29, 1974), 29–30; "Nixon's Days in Court Are TV's, Too; Impeachment Coverage Makes History," *Broadcasting*, 87 (August 5, 1974), 18–22.

64.   Schieffer, *This Just In*, 123–25; author interview with Fred Graham; Schorr, *Clearing the Air*, 113–20; Schorr, *Staying Tuned*, 256–57; Donaldson, "The State of Television News," 169; Peter J. Boyer, *Who Killed CBS? The Undoing of America's Number One News Network* (New York: Random House, 1988), 235; Frank, *Out of Thin Air*, 361; Hilts, "CBS," 34.

65.   Bonafede, "The Washington Press—Competing for Power with the Federal Government," 664; Leonard, *In the Storm of the Eye*, 13, 18–34; Peter McCabe, *Bad News at Black Rock: The Sell-Out of CBS News* (New York: Arbor House, 1987), 14–15.

66.   Brinkley, *11 Presidents*, 232–33; "The Unmuddling of Mudd," *Time*, 116 (July 14, 1980), 75; "Anchor away at NBC," *Newsweek*, 102 (August 8, 1983), 76; Roger Mudd, *Booknotes* interview, June 6, 1999, C-SPAN.

67.   Stahl, *Reporting Live*, 93, 135; Utley, *You Should Have Been Here Yesterday*, 134–35; Gans, *Deciding What's News*, 19–21, 264, 285; Westin, *Newswatch*, 12.

68.   James David Barber, "Not the *New York Times*: What Network News Should Be," *Washington Monthly*, 11 (September 1979), 14–21; "News Doctors: Taking Over TV Journalism?" *Broadcasting*, 87 (September 9, 1974), 21–28; Gabriel Pressman, "Local Newscasts—A Continuing Identity Crisis," *Television Quarterly*, 11 (Summer 1974), 25–26; Boyer, *Who Killed CBS?* 14–15, 51, 89–90, 87; Julius K. Hunter and Lynne S. Gross, *Broadcast News: The Inside Out* (St. Louis: C.V. Mosby, 1980), 50–51, 262.

69.   *Washington Post*, December 6, 2002; *New York Times*, December 6, 2002; Julian Rubinstein, "The Emperor of the Air," *New York Times Magazine* (December 29, 2002), 38–39; Reuven

Frank, *Booknotes* interview, September 15, 1991, C-SPAN; Zousmer, *TV News Off-Camera*, 45; Matusow, *The Evening Stars*, 222–46; Ted Koppel and Kyle Gibson, *Nightline: History in the Making and the Making of Television* (New York: Random House, 1996), 4–7; Marc Gunther, *The House That Roone Built: The Inside Story of ABC News* (Boston: Little, Brown, 1994), 5–9; Judith Hennessee, "The Press's Very Own Barbara Walters Show," *Columbia Journalism Review*, 14 (July/August 1976), 23; Marvin Barrett and Zachary Sklar, *The Eye of the Storm* (New York: Lippincott & Crowell, 1980), 53–57.

70.   Ron Powers, *The Newscasters* (New York: St. Martin's, 1977), 3–5, 30–35; Sevareid, "Journalism: The Relationship between the Print and Electric Media," 566; Ron Rosenbaum, "The Man Who Married Dan Rather," *Esquire*, 98 (November 1982), 53–64; Sig Mickelson, *From Whistle Stop to Sound Bite: Four Decades of Politics and Television* (New York: Praeger, 1989), 162; Westin, *Newswatch*, 204–28; Boyer, *Who Killed CBS?* 135–45; Edwin Newman, "Some Thoughts about the News Business," *Television Quarterly*, 20 (Summer 1983), 36; Ed Joyce, *Prime Times, Bad Times* (New York: Doubleday, 1988), 86–88, 94–95; interview with Fred Graham.

71.   Schieffer, *This Just In*, 296–97; Graham, *Happy Talk*, 31, 208–10 214–16, 222–23, 233, 247; Fred Graham, *Booknotes* interview, March 16, 1990, C-SPAN; Ron Chew, "Collected Stories," *Museum News* (November/December 2002), 32; author interview with Roger Mudd.

72.   *New York Times*, April 17, 1988; Boyer, *Who Killed CBS?* 14–15, 51, 89–90, 87; Hunter and Gross, *Broadcast News*, 50–51, 262.

73.   "Why TV News Has Been Losing Its Audience," *Business Week*, 54 (April 16, 1984), 137, 141; "The Past as Prologue," in Marvin Barrett, ed., *Broadcast Journalism, 1979–1981* (New York: Everest House, 1982), 145–46; Joyce, *Prime Times, Bad Times*, 320; Ken Auletta, *Booknotes* interview, October 16, 1991, C-SPAN; Peter Benjaminson, "Bernard Shaw," in *Contemporary Authors*, vol. 119 (Detroit: Gale Research, 1987), 329–33; Bernard Shaw interview on *Larry King Live*, CNN, March 8, 2001.

74.   Max Frankel, "Full-Text TV," *New York Times Magazine* (February 5, 1995), 32; Gunther, *The House That Roone Built*, 122; William Powers, "This Year's Model," *National Journal*, 34 (May 19, 2001), 1,512; *The Postwar Congress and the Media*, episode 5.

75.   Author interview with Brian Lamb; Julius Duscha, "Whitehead? Who's Whitehead?" *The Progressive*, 37 (April 1973), 39–43; William Small, "Mischief in Washington," *Television Quarterly*, 10, (Spring 1973), 46–49; "After Whitehead," *Broadcasting*, 87 (August 19, 1974), 20–21; "A Sadder Whitehead Leave OTP," *Broadcasting*, 87 (August 26, 1974), 17–18; *New York Times*, December 19, 20, 1972; *Washington Post*, March 19, 1998.

76.   James Lardner, "The Anti-Network," *New Yorker*, 70 (March 14, 1994), 51–53; Stephen Frantzich and John Sullivan, *The C-SPAN Revolution* (Norman: University of Oklahoma Press, 1996), 5–6, 17–18, 27–28, 126–27; Howard Kurtz, *Hot Air: All Talk, All the Time* (New York: Random House, 1996), 151–70; Brian Lamb, "Debunking the Myths," Address to the National Press Club, January 6, 1997, C-SPAN; author interview with Mike Michaelson; Hewitt, "Lets Not Compete with the Sitcoms," 50.

77.   "How Is Broadcast News Changing?" *Larry King Live*, CNN, June 13, 2000; J. Fred MacDonald, *One Nation under Television: The Rise and Decline of Network TV* (New York: Pantheon, 1990), 269–71; Tad Friend, "It's You Know, About Opinions and Stuff," *New York Times Magazine* (June 16, 1997), 34–39; Abigail Pogrebin, "Lack Attack," *Brill's Content*, 2 (February 1999), 94–98; *New York Times*, March 18, 2002; Neil Hickey, "Cable Wars," *Columbia Journalism Review*, 41 (January/February 2003), 12–15.

78.   Goldenson, *Beating the Odds*, 3; Philip S. Cook, Douglas Gomery, and Lawrence W. Lichty, *The Future of News: Television-Newspapers-Wire Services-News Magazines* (Baltimore: Johns Hopkins University Press, 1992), xxvi–xxvii; *Washington Post*, October 30, 1999; Hewitt, "Lets Not Compete with the Sitcoms," 49.

79.   William Sheehan remarks at Eisenhower Seminar, Gettysburg College, October 28, 2000; Gunther, *The House That Roone Built*, 137–42, 208, 342, 347; Frank, *Out of Thin Air*, 409–13;

Reuven Frank, *Booknotes* interview, September 15, 1991, C-SPAN; Jerry W. Knudson, *In the News: American Journalists View Their Craft* (Wilmington, Del.: Scholarly Resources, 2000), 193.

80. Stahl, *Reporting Live*, 146–47, 184, 197; Fred Graham, *Booknotes* interview, March 16, 1990, C-SPAN; Graham, *Happy Talk*, 217–18, 264; Jonathan Alter, "CBS As Lightening Rod," *Newsweek*, 105 (April 29, 1985), 56; Charles Babington, "Helms & Co.: Plotting to Unseat Dan Rather," *Columbia Journalism Review*, 23 (July/August 1985), 47–51; Ken Auletta, *Booknotes* interview, October 16, 1991, C-SPAN; *New York Times*, March 10, 1987, March 22, 1998; *Washington Post*, November 11, 1999.

81. Fred Graham, *Booknotes* interview, March 16, 1990, C-SPAN; McCabe, *Bad News at Black Rock*, 207–8, 282, 294–95; Sanders and Rock, *Waiting for Prime Time*, 1–2; Timothy E. Cook, "Senators and Reporters Revisited," *Civility and Deliberation in the United States Senate* (Lawrence, Kan.: Robert J. Dole Institute, 1999), 31; *Washington Post*, March 10, 1987; *New York Times*, September 20, 1985, July 17, 1986, March 10, 1987; Schieffer, *This Just In*, 359.

82. Dan Rather interview on *Larry King Live*, July 4, 2002, CNN; Donaldson, "The State of Television News," 168–71; *Washington Post*, September 24, 2000; *News in the Next Century: Profile of the American News Consumer* (New York: Radio and Television News Directors Foundation, 1996), 4–13, 17–24; Hewitt, "Lets Not Compete with the Sitcoms," 48; Andie Tucher, "You News," *Columbia Journalism Review*, 35 (May/June 1997), 26–30; Robert MacNeil, "Doing Things Differently: The *MacNeil/Lehrer Report*," *Television Quarterly*, 19 (Summer 1982), 17–19; Robert MacNeil, *The Right Place at the Right Time* (New York: Penguin, 1990), 297–325.

83. Utley, *You Should Have Been Here Yesterday*, 257–58; *Washington Post*, January 22, 1991; Perry M. Smith, *How CNN Fought the War* (New York: Carol, 1991), 23–42; Douglas Kellner, *The Persian Gulf TV War* (Boulder, Col.: Westview, 1992), 90, 133, 143; Thomas B. Allen, et al., *War in the Gulf* (Atlanta: Turner Publications, 1991), 13, 119–20, 232–36; Stephen Engleberg, "Open Your Mind," *American Journalism Review*, 21 (March 1999), 37–39.

84. Ed Henry, "The Old Man and the Web," *Capital Style*, 3 (March 2000), 30; Dan Rather, *Booknotes* interview, July 25, 1999, C-SPAN; *New York Times*, June 8, October 12, 1998, January 17, August 5, 2001; *Washington Post*, December 2, 1999, August 12, 2003; *Wall Street Journal*, January 15, 2001; Eric Alterman, "The Not Obviously Insane Network," *The Nation*, 273 (October 1, 2001), 10; Neil Hickey, "Is Fox News Fair?" *Columbia Journalism Review*, 36 (March/April 1998), 30–34; John Fund, "Out-Foxing the Experts," *WSJ.com Opinion Journal*, February 9, 2001; John Fund, "Remembering Rowly Evans," *WSJ.com Opinion Journal*, May 26, 2001; Jack White, "Washington Journal," C-SPAN, November 15, 2002; *The Hill*, November 20, 2002, September 24, 2003.

85. Steve M. Barkin, *American Television News: The Media Marketplace and the Public Interest* (Armonk, N.Y.: M.E. Sharpe, 2003), 165–67; Dan Rather, *Booknotes* interview, July 25, 1999, Tom Brokaw, *Booknotes* interview, March 7, 1999, C-SPAN; "How Is Broadcast News Changing?" *Larry King Live*, CNN, June 13, 2000; Richard Zoglin, "Newscast in Overdrive," *Time*, 149 (February 17, 1997), 76–78; *New York Times*, March 22, 1998; Neil Braun, "Broadcasting in the Age of Infinite Choice," *Vital Speeches of the Day*, 63 (October 1, 1997), 754; *New York Times*, May 4, 1998; *Washington Post*, February 17, 1997, October 1, 1999; Tucher, "You News," 26–30; *Milwaukee Journal Sentinel*, February 26, 1998; James McCarthey, "News Lite," *American Journalism Review*, 19 (June 1997), 20.

86. *CBS Evening News*, September 15, 2003; Frank Rich, "The Weight of an Anchor," *New York Times Magazine* (May 19, 2002), 36; *New York Times*, November 14, 2001; Roger Mudd, *Booknotes* interview, June 6, 1999, C-SPAN; Walter Cronkite on Eric Sevareid, National Public Radio, February 12, 2004; *USA Today*, January 14–16, 2000.

Chapter Ten

1. John Corry, *My Times: Adventures in the News Trade* (New York: Grosset/Putnam, 1993), 131; Fred Graham, *Happy Talk: Confessions of a TV Newsman* (New York: W. W. Norton, 1990), 65–66.

2. Barry Sussman, *The Great Coverup: Nixon and the Scandal of Watergate* (New York: New American Library, 1974), 21; Charles Peters, "Why the White House Press Didn't Get the Watergate Story," *Washington Monthly*, 5 (July/August 1973), 7–15; Jack W. Germond, *Fat Man in a Middle Seat: Forty Years of Covering Politics* (New York: Random House, 1999), 98; David S. Broder, *Behind the Front Page: A Candid Look at How the News Is Made* (New York: Simon & Schuster, 1987), 167.

3. Roy L. McGhee oral history, 100, Senate Historical Office; Lesley Stahl, *Reporting Live* (New York: Simon & Schuster, 1999), 16–20; *Washington Post*, June 14, 1992; Katharine Graham, *Personal History* (New York: Knopf, 1997), 468–69.

4. Ray Eldon Hiebert, ed., *The Press in Washington* (New York: Dodd, Mead, 1966), 13–14; Jules Whitcover, "Washington: The News Explosion," *Columbia Journalism Review*, 8 (Spring 1969), 23; Alan Ehrenhalt, "Political Science and Journalism: Bridging the Gap," *Perspectives on Politics*, 1 (March 2003), 127; William Greider, "Reporters and Their Sources: Mutual Assured Seduction," *Washington Monthly*, 14 (October 1982), 10–19.

5. William Safire, "Off the Record: Obey the Lindley Rule of Sourcemanship," *New York Times Magazine* (May 23, 2004), 16; Edward J. Epstein, "Journalism and Truth," *Commentary*, 57 (April 1974), 36–40; *Washington Post*, March 7, April 6, 2004.

6. Roger Mudd, Marya McLaughlin Lecture, Marymount University, February 16, 2000.

7. Jim Bellows, *The Last Editor: How I Saved the* New York Times, *the* Washington Post, *and the* Los Angeles Times *from Dullness and Complacency* (Kansas City: Andrews McMeel, 2002), 95–96; Benjamin C. Bradlee, *The Theodore H. White Lecture* (Cambridge, Mass.: John F. Kennedy School of Government, 1991), 13; Thomas M. Franck and Edward Weisband, eds., *Secrecy and Foreign Policy* (New York: Oxford University Press, 1974), 170–72; James McCartney, "Must the Media Be 'Used'?" *Columbia Journalism Review*, 8 (Winter 1969–1970), 36; Anthony Marro, "When the Government Tells Lies," *Columbia Journalism Review*, 23 (March/April 1985), 30–34; Leon V. Sigal, *Reporters and Officials: The Organization and Politics of Newsmaking* (Lexington, Mass.: D.C. Heath, 1973), 56–58; *Washington Post*, January 2, 1972; Peters, "Why the White House Press Didn't Get the Watergate Story," 7.

8. Andrew Patner, *I. F. Stone, A Portrait* (New York: Pantheon, 1988), 55–56, 99–105; James Deakin, *Straight Stuff: The Reporters, the White House and the Truth* (New York: William Morrow, 1984), 102–3; Michael Gartner interview with Benjamin C. Bradlee, "The First Rough Draft of History," *Smithsonian*, 33 (October/November 1982), 37; Jack Anderson with Daryl Gibson, *Peace, War, and Politics: An Eyewitness Account* (New York: Forge, 1998), 66; Carol Williams and Irwin Touser, *The* Washington Post: *Views from the Inside* (Englewood Cliffs, N.J.: Prentice-Hall, 1976), 54; Leonard Downie Jr., *The New Muckrakers* (Washington: The New Republic, 1976), 7–10; John H. Bunzel, ed., *Political Passages: Journeys of Change through Two Decades, 1968–1988* (New York: Free Press, 1988), 35.

9. *Washington Post*, April 22, 1978; Walter Lippmann, *Drift and Mastery: An Attempt to Diagnose the Current Unrest* (New York: Mitchell Kennerley, 1914), 4–6, 25; Anderson, *Peace, War, and Politics: An Eyewitness Account*, 415; Donald A. Ritchie, *Press Gallery: Congress and the Washington Correspondents* (Cambridge, Mass.: Harvard University Press, 1991), 179–94.

10. Fred Freed, "Paul Y. Anderson," *Esquire*, 29 (March 1948), 102; U.S. Congress, House of Representatives, *Report of the Special Committee Authorized by Congress to Investigate the East St. Louis Riots*, 65th Cong., 2nd sess., H. Doc. 1231, 24.

11. Paul Y. Anderson, "The Press and the Federal Government," in the *Congressional Record*, 72nd Cong., 1st sess., 15624; Anderson, "The Scandal in Oil," *The New Republic*, 37 (February 6, 1924), 277–79. Thomas L. Stokes, *Chip off My Shoulder* (Princeton, N.J.: University of Princeton Press, 1940), 143.

12. School of Public and International Affairs, Princeton University, *Conference on the Press, April 23–25, 1931* (Washington: Printing Corporation of America, 1931), 73; Edmund B. Lambeth, "The Lost Career of Paul Y. Anderson," *Journalism Quarterly*, 60 (Autumn 1983),

401–6; Freda Kirchwey, et al., *Where Is There Another? A Memorial to Paul Y. Anderson* (Norman, Okla.: Cooperative Books, 1939), 17–20; Freed, "Paul Y. Anderson," 101–4; Irving Dillard, "Anderson, Paul Y.," *Dictionary of American Biography*, supplement 2 (New York: Charles Scribner's Sons, 1958), 13–15; Walter Trohan, *Political Animals: Memoirs of a Sentimental Cynic* (Garden City, N.Y.: Doubleday, 1975), 116; Marquis Childs, *Witness to Power* (New York: McGraw-Hill, 1975), 39; *New York Times*, November 1, December 7, 1938; *Washington Star*, December 6, 1938; *Washington Post*, December 7, 1938; *St. Louis Post-Dispatch*, December 7, 1938; Alexander F. Jones to William Randolph Hearst, March 10, 1953, Eugene Meyer papers, Library of Congress.

13.   Freed, "Paul Y. Anderson," 101; Kenneth G. Crawford, *The Pressure Boys: The Inside Story of Lobbying in America* (New York: Julian Messner, 1939), vii.

14.   Merriman Smith, *The Good New Days* (Indianapolis: Bobbs-Merrill, 1962), 210; author interview with Don Larrabee; Richard Langham Riedel, *Halls of the Mighty: My 47 Years at the Senate* (Washington: Robert B. Luce, 1969), 120–21; Jack Anderson with James Boyd, *Confessions of a Muckraker: The Inside Story of Life in Washington during the Truman, Eisenhower, Kennedy, and Johnson Years* (New York: Random House, 1979) 298; John Hohenberg, *The New Front Page* (New York: Columbia University Press, 1966), 79; Clark R. Mollenhoff, *Investigative Reporting: From Courthouse to White House* (New York: Macmillan, 1981), 14–20; *Washington Post*, March 3, 1991.

15.   James H. Dygert, *The Investigative Journalist: Folk Heroes of a New Era* (Englewood Cliffs, N.J.: Prentice-Hall, 1976), 50–51; Mollenhoff, *Investigative Reporting*, 148–50, 194–203, 217; Robert F. Kennedy, *The Enemy Within* (New York: Harper & Brothers, 1960), 7, 55, 237–38; Arthur M. Schlesinger Jr., *Robert F. Kennedy and His Times* (Boston: Houghton Mifflin, 1978), 143–48, 157; Ruth Young Watt oral history, 176–77, 190, Senate Historical Office; John L. McClellan, *Crime without Punishment* (New York: Durell, Sloan and Peace, 1962), 32–33; see also Clark R. Mollenhoff, *Tentacles of Power, The Story of Jimmy Hoffa* (Cleveland: World, 1965).

16.   Clark R. Mollenhoff, *Washington Cover-Up* (Garden City, N.Y.: Doubleday, 1962), 10, 17, 54, 106–8, 177; Mary S. McAuliffe, "Dwight D. Eisenhower and Wolf Ladejinsky: The Politics of the Declining Red Scare, 1954–55," *Prologue*, 14 (Fall 1982), 109–27; Robert H. Ferrell, ed., *The Diary of James C. Hagerty: Eisenhower in Mid-Course, 1954–1955* (Bloomington: Indiana University Press, 1983), 154; *New York Times*, June 1, 1970.

17.   Hiebert, ed., *The Press in Washington*, 197–216; George Smathers oral history, 145, Rein Van der Zee oral history, 22, Senate Historical Office; *Chicago Tribune*, March 3, 1991; William L. Rivers, *The Opinionmakers* (Boston: Beacon, 1967), 155; Clark Mollenhoff, *Despoilers of Democracy: The Real Story of What Washington Propagandists, Arrogant Bureaucrats, Mismanagers, Influence Peddlers, and Outright Corrupters Are Doing to Our Federal Government* (Garden City, N.Y.: Doubleday, 1965), 282–90; Mollenhoff, *Investigative Reporting*, 204–16, 280–304; Dygert, *The Investigative Journalist*, 48; Charles Roberts oral history, 69, Johnson Library.

18.   Timothy Crouse, *The Boys on the Bus* (New York: Random House, 1973), 237; William Safire, *Before the Fall: An Inside View of the Pre-Watergate White House* (Garden City, N.Y.: Doubleday, 1975), 91; Mollenhoff to Hanson Baldwin, February 9, 1965, Arthur Krock papers, Princeton University; Herbert G. Klein, *Making It Perfectly Clear* (Garden City, N.Y.: Doubleday, 1980), 422; Clark R. Mollenhoff, *Game Plan for Disaster: An Ombudsman's Report on the Nixon Years* (New York: W. W. Norton, 1976), 23, 26–29.

19.   H. R. Haldeman, *The Haldeman Diaries: Inside the Nixon White House* (New York: Putnam, 1994), 74.

20.   Mollenhoff, *Game Plan for Disaster*, 32–36, 39–44, 47–50, 62–64, 126, 134–35; Klein, *Making It Perfectly Clear*, 173; John W. Dean III, *Blind Ambition: The White House Years* (New York: Simon & Schuster, 1976), 317; Crouse, *The Boys on the Bus*, 237–38; *New York Times*, May 31, June 1, 1970.

21. Mollenhoff, *Game Plan for Disaster*, 142–43, 183, 203–7, 227; Mollenhoff, *Investigative Reporting*, 318–38; Stanley I. Kutler, ed., *Abuse of Power: The New Nixon Tapes* (New York: Free Press, 1997), 128.

22. Mollenhoff, *Game Plan for Disaster*, 237–41; Crouse, *The Boys on the Bus*, 235–241; Dygert, *The Investigative Journalist*, 52–53; *Chicago Tribune*, March 3, 1991; *New York Times*, March 4, 1991; Barney Collier, *Hope and Fear in Washington (The Early Seventies): The Story of the Washington Press Corps* (New York: Dial, 1975), 215–20.

23. Mollenhoff, *Investigative Reporting*, 353; Dygert, *The Investigative Journalist*, vii, 7–8, 59; Jack Anderson, *Washington Exposé* (Washington: Public Affairs Press, 1967), 111; Brit Hume, "Inside Story: How Jack Anderson Gets All Those Hot Columns," *Washingtonian*, 9 (August 1974), 99–120. William L. Rivers, *The Other Government: Power & the Washington Media* (New York: Universe, 1982), 117–29; Lenora Williamson, "2 Pulitzer Prizes Applaud Piercing of Gov't Secrecy," *Editor & Publisher*, 105 (May 6, 1972), 9–11; "Reston Complains of 'Tricky' Nixon News Machinery," *Editor & Publisher*, 105 (April 29, 1972), 56.

24. Kutler, *Abuse of Power*, 8–9; William M. Hammond, *Public Affairs: The Military and the Media, 1962–1968* (Washington: Center of Military History, 1988), 217; *Washington Post*, March 16, 1983, January 18, 1993; Robert Garcia, "Leak City," *American Politics*, 2 (August 1987), 23–24.

25. Joseph L. Rauh oral history, Harry S. Truman Library; Edward J. Epstein, "Journalism and Truth," *Commentary*, 57 (April 1974), 36–40; William Lambert and Thomas Powers, letters to the editor, *Commentary*, 58 (August 1974), 5–7, 10; *Washington Post*, July 20, 1982; see also John F. Stacks, "The Art of the Leak," *Time*, 151 (February 16, 1998), 54

26. Richard Rayner, "Existential Cowboy," *New Yorker*, 74 (May 18, 1998), 69; Alicia C. Shepard, "Off the Record," *Washingtonian*, 38 (September 2003), 62, 102; Mollenhoff, *Investigative Reporting*, 5–6, 12, 201.

27. *The White House Transcripts* (New York: Bantam, 1974), 83; Carl Bernstein and Bob Woodward, *All the President's Men* (New York: Simon & Schuster, 1974), 71–72, 112, 243; Sussman, *The Great Coverup*, 111; David Halberstam, *The Powers That Be* (New York: Knopf, 1979), 615; James Mann, "Deep Throat: An Institutional Analysis," *Atlantic Monthly*, 269 (May 1992), 106–12.

28. Jim Hougan, *Secret Agenda: Watergate, Deep Throat, and the CIA* (New York: Random House, 1984), 284–85; Halberstam, *The Powers That Be*, 637–41; Katharine Graham interview, Newseum.

29. Cartha "Deke" DeLoach, *Hoover's FBI: The Inside Story by Hoover's Trusted Lieutenant* (Washington: Regnery, 1995), 5, 11, 408; Athan G. Theoharis and John Stuart Cox, *The Boss: J. Edgar Hoover and the Great American Inquisition* (Philadelphia: Temple University Press, 1988), 408, 413–16; Richard Nixon, *RN: The Memoirs of Richard Nixon* (New York; Grosset & Dunlap, 1978), 474–75, 513; Jonathan Aitken, *Nixon: A Life* (Washington: Regmery, 1993), 412–14; William C. Sullivan with Bill Brown, *The Bureau: My Thirty Years in Hoover's FBI* (New York: W. W. Norton, 1979), 193, 211–17, 251–57; Ovid Demaris, *J. Edgar Hoover: As They Knew Him* (New York: Carroll & Graff, 1994 [1975]), 251.

30. W. Mark Felt, *The FBI Pyramid: From the Inside* (New York: Putnam, 1979), 182–88, 208, 211–13, 277 510–23; Sanford J. Ungar, *FBI* (Boston: Atlantic Monthly Press, 1975), 278, 508–9, 522–24; Mollenhoff, *Investigative Reporting*, 321; U.S. House of Representatives, 94th Cong., 1st sess., Subcommittee of the Committee on Government Operations, *Inquiry into the Destruction of Former FBI Director J. Edgar Hoover's Files and FBI Recordkeeping* (Washington: Government Printing Office, 1975); see also Greg Bradsher, "Thank you very, very much . . . J. Edgar Hoover," *The Record: News from the National Archives and Records Administration*, 4 (September 1997), 16–17.

31. *Washington Post*, May 16–18, 25, June 3, 1972, June 17, 1997; Haldeman, *The Haldeman Diaries*, 460; Sussman, *The Great Coverup*, 110; Adrian Havill, *Deep Truth: The Lives of Bob Woodward and Carl Bernstein* (Seacaucus, N.J.: Carol, 1993), 71; Downie, *The New Muckrakers*, 21–29; Shepard, "Off the Record," 60–62; Colin L. Powell with Joseph E. Persico, *My*

American Journey (New York: Random House, 1995), 420; Bob Woodward commentary, Brody Public Policy Forum, University of Maryland, October 16, 2002.

32. The FBI's final report on Watergate cited Carl Bernstein's attempted contacts with FBI agents, but none of Woodward's. O. T. Jacobson to the Director, "Watergate Investigations, OPE Analysis," July 5, 1975, 48, 76, file # 139-4089, Federal Bureau of Investigation; *Washington Post*, 19 June 1972; Bernstein and Woodward, *All the President's Men*, 23–25; *Washington Post*, June 20, 21, 1972; Felt, *The FBI Pyramid*, 248; U.S. Senate, Committee on the Judiciary, *Nomination of Louis Patrick Gray III* (Washington: Government Printing Office, 1973), 64, 115, 123–24, 632.

33. Keith W. Olson, *Watergate: The Presidential Scandal That Shook America* (Lawrence: University Press of Kansas, 2003), 51–52; *Nomination of L. Patrick Gray III*, 117; Bruce Oudes, ed., *From the President: Richard Nixon's Secret Files* (New York: Harper & Row, 1989), 502–9; Haldeman, *The Haldeman Diaries*, 474–75; Select Senate Committee on Presidential Campaign Activities, *Presidential Campaign Activities of 1972* (Washington: Government Printing Office, 1977–1974), 3,815–20, 3,843–47; Richard Helms with William Hood, *A Look over My Shoulder: A Life in the Central Intelligence Agency* (New York: Random House, 2003), 3–11.

34. Dean, *Blind Ambition*, 93, 117; Jacobson to the Director, "Watergate Investigations, OPE Analysis," July 5, 1975, 47–48, FBI; Felt, *The FBI Pyramid*, 248–52, 291–92; Unger, *FBI*, 532; *Presidential Campaign Activities*, 3,477, 3,504–5, 3,530, 3,533, 3,540 3,546–47, 3,832; Felt, *The FBI Pyramid*, 255–57; Ronald Kessler, *The FBI* (New York: Pocket, 1993), 268–69; *The White House Transcripts* (New York: Bantam, 1974), 77–78; Helms, *A Look over My Shoulder*, 12–13.

35. Felt, *The FBI Pyramid*, 258; *Nomination of L. Patrick Gray III*, 3,478, 3,515; James McCord, "What the FBI Almost Found," *Armed Forces Journal International*, 110 (August 1973), 57 [reprinted in *Presidential Campaign Activities of 1972*, 3,848]; Dean, *Blind Ambition*, 123.

36. Ellis Cose, *The Press* (New York: William Morrow, 1989), 61–62; Sussman, *The Great Coverup*, 103; Stanley I. Kutler, *The Wars of Watergate: The Last Crisis of Richard Nixon* (New York: Random House, 1990), 226; Bernstein and Woodward, *All the President's Men*, 59, 72–73, 86–87; *Nomination of Louis Patrick Gray III*, 53, 64, 3,512–13; Felt, *The FBI Pyramid* 225, 248–49.

37. *The White House Transcripts*, 63; Felt, *The FBI Pyramid*, 224, 259; Bernstein and Woodward, *All the President's Men*, 76; Mann, "Deep Throat," 110; *Washington Post*, September 18, 28, 1972.

38. Bernstein and Woodward, *All the President's Men*, 130–35; Sussman, *The Great Coverup*, 113; *Washington Post*, October 10, 1972; Dean, *Blind Ambition*, 141.

39. Kutler, *Abuse of Power*, 159, 170–71; Felt, *The FBI Pyramid* 225, 248–49; *Washington Post*, October 25, 1972; Halbestam, *The Powers That Be*, 648–49; Bernstein and Woodward, *All the President's Men*, 173, 189, 195–96.

40. Don Fry, ed., *Believing the News* (St Petersburg, Fl.: Poynter Institute, 1985), 124; *Congressional Record*, 92nd Cong., 2nd sess., 36800; John W. Dean III, *Lost Honor* (Los Angeles: Stratford, 1982), 69, 272, 281–82, 317; Sussman, *The Great Coverup*, 146; see also Charles Peters, *How Washington Really Works* (New York: Addison-Wesley, 1992), 10.

41. Stahl, *Reporting Live*, 19; John Dean, *Lost Honor*, 271; Graham, *Personal History*, 468–69; *Presidential Campaign Activities of 1972*, 3,889.

42. Kutler, *The Wars of Watergate*, 246–47, 268–70; Kutler, *Abuse of Power*, 246; *The White House Transcripts*, 78; Nixon, *RN*, 778; Felt, *The FBI Pyramid*, 278, 287–88; *Nomination of Louis Patrick Gray III*, 661–62, 666–71, 3,490; Joseph C. Spear, *Presidents and the Press: The Nixon Legacy* (Cambridge, Mass.: MIT Press, 1984), 191–92; Bernstein and Woodward, *All the President's Men*, 268–71, 306–7.

43. Edward Jay Epstein, "Did the Press Uncover Watergate?" *Commentary*, 58 (July 1974), 21–24; Edward J. Epstein, "Journalism and Truth," *Commentary*, 57 (April 1974), 36–40; William Lambert, letter to the editor, and Epstein's replies to letters to the editor, *Commentary*, 58 (August 1974), 5–7, 10, 12; Julia Cameron, "A Portrait of the Investigative Re-

porter as a Young, Rich, Sexy, Glamorous Star," *Washingtonian*, 9 (May 1974), 91; Kessler, *The FBI*, 269–70.

44. Peters, "Why the White House Press Didn't Get the Watergate Story," 12; Robert Sam Anson, "The Best of Times, the Worst of Times," *Esquire*, 119 (March 1993), 109; Kutler, *Abuse of Power*, 99; Max Frankel, *The Times of My Life and My Life with the* Times (New York: Random House, 1999), 340, 344–46; David Margolick, "Clash of the *Times* Men," *Vanity Fair* (December 1999), 196.

45. Bob Thompson, "The Hersh Alternative," *Washington Post Magazine* (January 28, 2001), 9–15, 20–27; Rael Jean Isaac, "The Cult of Seymour Hersh," *Weekly Standard*, 37 (July/August 2004), 17–21; Alfred Balk and James Boylan, eds., *Our Troubled Press; Ten Years of the* Columbia Journalism Review (Boston: Little, Brown, 1971), 119–24; Seymour Hersh, "Role Models," *Columbia Journalism Review*, 41 (May/June 2001), 51; Gup David Rubien, "Brilliant Careers: Seymour Hersh," *Salon* (January 18, 2000); Dean, *Lost Honor*, 272; Kutler, *Abuse of Power*, 453.

46. *Washington Post*, June 14, 1992; Thomas Powers's letter to the editor of *Commentary*, 58 (August 1974), 7, 10; Peters, "Why the White House Press Didn't Get the Watergate Story," 7–15.

47. James L. Aucoin, "The Re-emergence of American Investigative Journalism, 1960–1975," *Journalism History*, 21 (Spring 1995), 3–15; Michael Schudson, *Discovering the News: A Social History of American Newspapers* (New York: Basic, 1978), 187–92; Ron Chepesiuk, Haney Howell, and Edward Lee, *Raising Hell: Straight Talk with Investigative Journalists* (Jefferson, N.C.: McFarland, 1997), 45; Deakin, *Straight Stuff*, 102–3; Scott Sherman, "The Avenger: Sy Hersh, Then and Now," *Columbia Journalism Review*, 43 (July/August 2003), 36; Sigal, *Reporters and Officials*, 119–30; Norman L. Rosenberg, *Protecting the Best Men: An Interpretive History of the Law of Libel* (Chapel Hill: University of North Carolina Press, 1986), 235, 243–57.

48. Robert Pack, "Inside the *Post*," *Washingtonian*, 18 (December 1982), 144–47, 198–208; Cose, *The Press*, 91–97; Bradlee, *A Good Life*, 461–64; Tom Kelly, *The Imperial* Post: *The Myers, the Grahams, and the Paper That Rules Washington* (New York: William Morrow, 1983), 275–81; Todd Gitlin, "The Clinton-Lewinsky Obsession," *Washington Monthly*, 30 (December 1998), 18; *Washington Post*, July 20, 1982, March 26, 2002.

49. Chepesiuk, Howell, and Lee, *Raising Hell*, 14; Cose, *The Press*, 109–12; Bradlee, *A Good Life*, 435–52; Graham, *Personal History*, 598–99; Kelly, *The Imperial* Post, 255–69; Monica Langley and Lee Levine, "Broken Promises," *Columbia Journalism Review*, 27 (July/August 1988), 22; Steve Weinberg, "The Secret Sharer," *Mother Jones*, 17 (May/June 1992), 54, 59; *Washington Post*, April 11, 1984, May 26, 2002; Bob Woodward, *Booknotes* interview, June 23, 1991, C-SPAN.

50. Stephen Engelberg, "Open Your Mind," *American Journalism Review*, 21 (March 1999), 37–39.

51. Author interview with Don Oberdorfer; *Washington Post*, April 18, 1993; Paul Starobin, "A Generation of Vipers," *Columbia Journalism Review*, 34 (March/April 1995), 26–32; Meg Greenfield, *Washington* (New York: Public Affairs, 2001); Jules Witcover, "'Gotcha' Journalism Not Necessarily Better," *The Hill*, July 26, 1995; *New York Times*, December 28, 1998.

52. *Washington Times*, January 22, February 27, July 23, 1992.

53. James B. Stewart, *Blood Sport: The President and His Adversaries* (New York: Simon & Schuster, 1996), 184–86, 207–8; Haynes Johnson, *Divided We Fall: Gambling with History in the Nineties* (New York: W.W. Norton, 1994), 357; Ted Gup, "Eye of the Storm," *Columbia Journalism Review*, 40 (May/June 2001), 32–38; *Washington Post*, March 7, August 11, November 30, 1993, April 3, 1994; Terry Eastland, "Beltway Journalism," *National Review*, 45 (June 21, 1993), 39–40; Joe Klein, *The Natural: The Misunderstood Presidency of Bill Clinton* (New York: Doubleday, 2002), 99–100.

54. *The Hill*, December 6, 2000; Gitlin, "The Clinton-Lewinsky Obsession," 15; David Blum, "Working the Bimbo Beat," *George*, 5 (May 1999), 63; *Washington Post*, February 19, 1978;

Alicia C. Shepard, "The Isikoff Factor," *American Journalism Review,* 20 (December 1998), 22–31.

55. Larry J. Sabato and S. Robert Lichter, *When Should the Watchdogs Bark? Media Coverage of the Clinton Scandals* (Washington: Center for Media and Public Affairs, 1994), 29, 31; Ann Coulter, "Spikey & Me," *George*, 5 (May 1999), 48; Alicia C. Sheppard, "A Scandal Unfolds," *American Journalism Review*, 20 (March 1998), 22; Anthony Marro, "Active Reporter or Passive Conspirator?" *Columbia Journalism Review*, 38 (May/June 1999), 61.

56. Michael Isikoff, *Uncovering Clinton: A Reporter's Story* (New York: Crown, 1999); Blum, "Working the Bimbo Beat," 63.

57. Hillary Rodham Clinton, *Living History* (New York: Simon & Schuster, 2003), 406–7, 452–53; Marvin Kalb, *One Scandalous Story: Clinton, Lewinsky, and Thirteen Days That Tarnished American Journalism* (New York: Free Press, 2001), 267–68; Steven Brill, "Pressgate," *Brill's Content*, 1 (August 1998), 132; *Washington Post*, February 13, 16, March 1, 5, 6, 9, 15 1998, June 14, 16, 1998, May 22, 2000; Brill, "Pressgate," 132, 149.

58. *New York Times*, October 31, 1998, January 21, September 14, 1999; *Washington Post*, November 9, 1998, March 12, 1999, July 11, 13, 18, 20, October 7, 2000; Gilbert Cranberg, "Starr's Office Claims Source Confidentiality Privilege," *Editor & Publisher*, 131 (December 26, 1998), 38; Byron York, "The Ordeal of Charles Bakaly," *American Spectator*, 33 (September 2000), 28–33, 76.

Chapter Eleven

1. *Washington Post*, March 22, 1981.

2. Ibid., January 12, 15 2002; Nancy Reagan interview on *Larry King Live*, CNN, July 17, 2001; Roger Wilkins, *A Man's Life: An Autobiography* (Woodbridge, Conn.: Ox Bow, 1982), 329; Meg Greenfield, *Washington* (New York: Public Affairs, 2001), xxiii, 127–28, 164–65.

3. Marlin Fitzwater, *Booknotes* interview, November 5, 1995, C-SPAN; *Washington Post*, March 25, 1981; Sidney Blumenthal, *Our Long National Daydream: A Political Pageant of the Reagan Era* (New York: Harper & Row, 1988), 87.

4. Oswald Garrison Villard, *Some Newspapers and Newspaper-Men* (New York: Knopf, 1923), 170–92; *Washington Post*, 3 March 1921.

5. Will Irvin, *Propaganda and the News, or What Makes You Think So?* (New York: Whittlesey House, 1936), 101; Silas Bent, *Ballyhoo: The Voice of the Press* (New York: Boni and Liveright, 1927), 234–35; Oliver Knight, ed., *I Protest: Selected Disquisitions of E. W. Scripps* (Madison: University of Wisconsin Press, 1966), 209–10; Simon Michael Bessie, *Jazz Journalism: The Story of the Tabloid Newspaper* (New York: Dutton, 1938), 177–79; Villard, *Some Newspapers and Newspaper-Men*, 176, 189; Oswald Garrison Villard, *The Disappearing Daily: Chapters in American Newspaper Evolution* (New York: Knopf, 1944), 193–94; Walter Trohan, *Political Animals: Memoirs of a Sentimental Cynic* (Garden City, N.Y.: Doubleday, 1975), 50.

6. Villard, *Some Newspapers and Newspaper-Men*, 172; Lawrence Sullivan, *All about Washington* (New York: John Day, 1932), 185–86; Constance McLaughlin Green, *Washington: Capital City, 1879–1950*, vol. 2 (Princeton, N.J.: Princeton University Press, 1962), 213–14, 260–72; Chalmers M. Roberts, *The* Washington Post: *The First 100 Years* (Boston: Houghton Mifflin, 1977), 134–58.

7. Eugene Meyer oral history, 697–707, Columbia University; Roberts, *The* Washington Post, 189–95; John E. Drewry, ed., *More* Post *Biographies* (Athens: University of Georgia Press, 1947), 194; *Washington Evening Star*, June 1, 1933.

8. *Washington Post*, July 18, 1959; Drewry, ed., *More* Post *Biographies*, 194–95; Tom Kelly, *The Imperial* Post: *The Meyers, the Grahams and the Paper That Rules Washington* (New York: William Morrow, 1983), 59; Milton Friedman and Anna Jacobson Schwartz, *The Great Contraction, 1929–1933* (Princeton, N.Y.: Princeton University Press, 1965), 81–93, 120–21; Leo C. Rosten, *The Washington Correspondents* (New York: Harcourt, Brace, 1937), 232–33; Marguerite Young, "Ignoble Journalism in the Nation's Capital," *American Mercury*, 34 (February 1935), 240.

9.   Meyer oral history, 709, 720; Raymond Clapper, *Watching the World* (New York: Whittlesey House, 1944), 21–22; Roberts, *The* Washington Post, 203; *Washington Post*, March 26–28, 1934, January 26, 1936; Kelly, *The Imperial* Post, 57–66; Drewry, ed., *More* Post *Biographies*, 203.

10. Franklyn Waltman to Eugene Meyer, March 24, 1936, Eugene Meyer papers, Library of Congress; *Washington Post*, July 18, 1959; Felix Morley, *For the Record* (South Bend, Ind.: Regnery/Gateway, 1979), 261–71, 277.

11. Drewry, ed., *More* Post *Biographies*, 199–202; Morley, *For the Record*, 285; *Washington Post*, July 18, 1959, July 9, 1982.

12. Eugene Meyer to Oscar Lawler, February 4, 1938, Alexander F. Jones to Meyer, May 2, 1950, Meyer papers; Charles Fisher, *The Columnists* (New York: Howell, Soskin, 1944), 290–95; Morley, *For the Record*, 277, 284–86, 321, 346–47; Drewry, ed., *More* Post *Biographies*, 197–98, 201–3; Katharine Graham, *Personal History* (New York: Knopf, 1997), 85, 94–99, 103–4.

13. Hedley Donovan, *Right Place, Right Times; Forty Years in Journalism Not Counting My Paper Route* (New York: Henry Holt, 1989), 72–86; Hedley Donovan, *Booknotes* interview, February 27, 1990, C-SPAN; Carol Williams and Irwin Touster, *The* Washington Post: *Views from the Inside* (Englewood Cliffs, N.J.: Prentice-Hall, 1976), 37–38; Chalmers Roberts, *First Rough Draft: A Journalist's Journal of Our Times* (New York: Praeger, 1973), 18–20, 93.

14. Villard, *The Disappearing Daily*, 187–92; W. M. Kiplinger, *Washington Is Like That* (New York: Harper & Brothers, 1942), 129; *Washington Post*, July 18, 1959.

15. Meyer oral history, 785–86; David Halberstam, *The Powers That Be* (New York: Knopf, 1979), 218–19; Susan E. Tifft and Alex S. Jones, *The Trust: The Private and Powerful Family behind the New York Times* (Boston: Little, Brown, 1999), 207–8.

16. George Smathers oral history, Senate Historical Office, 5–9.

17. *Washington Post*, September 23, 1979, April 5, 1998; Herbert Block, *Herblock: A Cartoonist's Life* (New York: Macmillan, 1993), 114; "History of WTOP and WTOP-TV," and Granville Klink Jr. oral history, 23–24, Broadcasting Archives, University of Maryland.

18. Alexander F. Jones to Eugene Meyer, May 2, 1950, announcement to advertisers, 1954, Raoul Blumberg to Meyer, July 16, 1954, Meyer papers; author interviews with Kristie Miller and James Sayler; Paul F. Healy, *Cissy: The Biography of Eleanor M. "Cissy" Patterson* (Garden City, N.J.: Doubleday, 1966), 371–415; Ronald Kessler, *The Sins of the Father: Joseph P. Kennedy and the Dynasty He Founded* (New York: Warner, 1996), 310; Richard Norton Smith, *The Colonel: The Life and Legend of Robert R. McCormick, 1880–1955* (Boston: Houghton Mifflin, 1997), 491–518; J. Russell Wiggins letter to *Washington Post Book World* (March 21, 1993), 14; *Washington Star*, August 7, 1981; *Washington Post*, April 5, 1998; Halberstam, *The Powers That Be*, 224.

19. Block, *Herblock*, 97–107, 114–16, 153–55; Herbert Block, *Booknotes* interview, November 14, 1993, C-SPAN; *Washington Post*, December 31, 1995, October 8, 2001.

20. Edwin R. Bayley, *Joe McCarthy and the Press* (New York: Pantheon, 1981), 148–51; Graham, *Personal History*, 199–200; Nicholas von Hoffman, *Citizen Cohn* (New York: Doubleday, 1988), 217; *Washington Post*, February 13, 1977, September 13, 1985, October 16, 2001.

21. David M. Oshinsky, *A Conspiracy So Immense: The World of Joe McCarthy* (New York: Free Press, 1983), 114; Roberts, *The* Washington Post, 322; John Earl Haynes, "The 'Spy' on Joe McCarthy's Staff: The Forgotten Case of Paul H. Hughes," *Continuity: A Journal of History*, 14 (Spring/Fall 1990), 21–61.

22. Turner Catledge to Philip L. Graham, February 26, 1953, Turner Catledge papers, Mississippi State University; Halberstam, *The Powers That Be*, 223–25; James Reston, *Deadline: A Memoir* (New York: Random House, 1991), 209, 349–52; "The Troubled Press," *Fortune*, 24 (February 1952), 164; Block, *Herblock*, 116; A. Kent MacDougall, ed., *The Press: A Critical Look from the Inside* (Princeton, N.J.: Dow Jones Books, 1972), 13–23; Ben Bradlee, *Booknotes* interview, October 29, 1995, C-SPAN; Edward T. Folliard to Eugene Meyer, June 23, 1955, Meyer papers.

23. "Guest at Breakfast," *Time*, 67 (April 16, 1956), 64–72; 48; Block, *Herblock*, 175; *Washington Post*, July 18, 2001; Katharine Graham oral history, Lyndon B. Johnson Library, 13; Graham, *Personal History*, 257–58, 284; Montague Kern, Patricia W. Levering, Ralph B. Levering, *The Kennedy Crises: The Press, the Presidency and Foreign Policy* (Chapel Hill: University of North Carolina Press, 1983), 18; Kelly, *The Imperial* Post, 123–24; Theodore H. White, *The Making of the President 1965* (New York: Atheneum, 1965), 407–14; Roberts, *First Rough Draft*, 191; Bernard C. Cohen, *The Press and Foreign Policy* (Princeton, N.J.: Princeton University Press, 1963), 137–38.

24. Osborn Elliott, *The World of Oz* (New York: Viking, 1980), 1–6, 38; Osborn Elliott, letter to the editor, *Newsweek*, 138 (August 20, 2001), 12; Ben Bradlee, *A Good Life: Newspapering and Other Adventures* (New York: Simon & Schuster, 1995), 223–53.

25. Roberts, *The* Washington Post, 361–63; Graham, *Personal History*, 301–38; Elliot, *The World of Oz*, 25–29; Donovan, *Right Place, Right Times*, 330; "Guest at Breakfast," 64, 71–72; Carol Felsenthal, *Power, Privilege, and the* Post: *The Katharine Graham Story* (New York: Putnam, 1993), 445; J. Russell Wiggins letter to *Washington Post Book World* (March 21, 1993), 14.

26. Graham, *Personal History*, 379–80; MacDougall, ed., *The Press*, 17–18; Henry Brandon, *Special Relationships: A Foreign Correspondent's Memoirs from Roosevelt to Reagan* (New York: Atheneum, 1988), 181; Laurence Leamer, *Playing for Keeps in Washington* (New York: Dial, 1977), 15–22; Michael Gartner interview with Benjamin C. Bradlee, "The First Rough Draft of History," *American Heritage*, 33 (October/November 1982), 48; Bradlee, *A Good Life*, 277.

27. Norman Sherman, "'Who the Hell Was That?' 'He's the Editor of the *Post*.' 'Jesus, I Thought He Was Your Bookie,'" *Washingtonian*, 9 (July 1974), 66; Gartner, "The First Rough Draft of History," 33; author interview with Don Oberdorfer; Leonard Downie Jr., *The New Muckrakers* (Washington: New Republic Books, 1976), 29–30; Martin Walker, *Powers of the Press; Twelve of the World's Influential Newspapers* (New York: Adama, 1984), 255; Ellis Cose, *The Press* (New York: William Morrow, 1989), 40–43; MacDougall, ed., *The Press*, 18–19; Nicholas von Hoffman, "Post Toastie: Bradlee," *The Nation*, 261 (October 23, 1995), 470; Turner Catledge to Tom Wicker, July 14, 1966, Catledge papers; Roberts, *The* Washington Post, 394, 406–7; Ben H. Bagdikian, *Double Vision: Reflections on My Heritage, Life, and Profession* (Boston: Beacon, 1995), 229.

28. Gartner, "The First Rough Draft of History," 44–45; Laura Longley Babb, ed., *Of the Press, by the Press, for the Press (and Others, Too)* (Washington: Washington Post Company, 1974), 175; Nicholas von Hoffman, *Left at the* Post (Chicago: Quadrangle, 1970), 7–9, 13–18; von Hoffman, "Post Toastie," 470–1.

29. *Washington Post*, April 4, 1993; David Remnick, "Last of the Red Hots," *New Yorker*, 71 (September 18, 1995), 80–81; Leon V. Sigal, *Reporters and Officials: The Organization and Politics of Newsmaking* (Lexington, Mass.: D.C. Heath, 1973), 40–41; George Wilson, *Booknotes* interview, July 16, 1989, C-SPAN; Robert B. Sims, *The Pentagon Reporters* (Washington: National Defense University Press, 1983), 49–55.

30. James Reston to Turner Catledge, November 25, 1962, Catledge to Reston, March 19, 1963, Catledge to Robert Phelps, December 19, 1966, Catledge papers.

31. Harrison Salisbury to Clifton Daniel, March 15, 1966, Catledge papers; Harrison Salisbury, *A Time of Change: A Reporter's Tale of Our Time* (New York: Harper & Row, 1988), 317; Tifft and Jones, *The Trust*, 463–64; Dom Bonafede, "The *New York Times* Washington Desk," *Washington Journalism Review*, 1 (September/October 1979), 20–25.

32. Richard Pollak, ed., *Stop the Presses, I Want to Get Off!* (New York: Random House, 1974), 164–72; Max Frankel, *The Times of My Life and My Life with the* Times (New York: Random House, 1999), 328–38; Bradlee, *A Good Life*, 310–12; Stanford Unger, *The Paper & the Papers: An Account of the Legal and Political Battles over the Pentagon Papers* (New York: Dutton, 1972), 15–16.

33. Roberts, *First Rough Draft*, 319–24; Daniel Ellsberg, *Secrets: A Memoir of Vietnam and the Pentagon Papers* (New York: Viking, 2002), 391–93, 425; Bagdikian, *Double Vision*, 1–14.

34. Author interview with Don Oberdorfer; Bagdikian, *Double Vision*, 15–33; Graham, *Personal History*, 445; Bradlee, *A Good Life*, 315–23.

35. Brandon, *Special Relationships*, 286; author interview with Richard Harwood; Babb, ed., *Of the Press*, 79–81; "The *Washington Post* Went up the Hill with 550,000 Men," *Washingtonian*, 5 (February 1970), 46–47; Howard Bray, *The Pillars of the Post: The Making of a News Empire in Washington* (New York: W. W. Norton, 1980), 44–57; *Congressional Record*, 90th Cong., 2nd sess., 28,800–1; *New York Times*, July 18, 2001; *Washington Post*, January 11, 2004; James S. Doyle, "Has Money Corrupted Washington Journalism?" *Nieman Reports*, 53/54 (Winter 1999/Spring 2000), 49–51.

36. David Margolick, "Clash of the *Times* Men," *Vanity Fair*, 62 (December 1999), 208; Ungar, *The Papers & the Papers*, 149–50; David Rudenstine, *The Day the Presses Stopped: A History of the Pentagon Papers Case* (Berkeley: University of California Press, 1996); Bagdikian, *Double Vision*, 24–28; Frankel, *The Times of My Life and My Life with the* Times, 340–41; Floyd Abrams, "The Pentagon Papers a Decade Later," *New York Times Magazine* (June 7, 1981), 76, 95.

37. Frankel, *The Times of My Life and My Life with the* Times, 335–45; Sherman, "'Who the Hell Was That?'" 110; Remnick, "Last of the Red Hots," 78; *Washington Post*, January 21, 2001.

38. Gartner, "The First Rough Draft of History," 34–38; author interview with Don Oberdorfer.

39. William Greider, *Who Will Tell the People: The Betrayal of American Democracy* (New York: Simon & Schuster, 1992), 296; James Fallows, "Big Ben," *Esquire*, 85 (April 1976), 144, 146; Sigal, *Reporters and Officials*, 22–23; *Washington Post*, April 19, 1981; Joseph Nocera, "Making It at the *Washington Post*," *Washington Monthly*, 10 (January 1979), 14–16; Bagdikian, *Double Vision*, 230–38; Leamer, *Playing for Keeps in Washington*, 36–38; MacDougall, ed., *The Press*, 19–21; Mary McGrory oral history, Washington Press Club Foundation, 48; Sherman, "'Who the Hell Was That?'" 66.

40. Lou Cannon, *Reporting: An Inside View* (Sacramento: California Journal Press, 1977), 3–7; Carl Bernstein and Bob Woodward, *All the President's Men* (New York: Simon & Schuster, 1974), 220; Stephen Bates, ed., *If No News, Send Rumors: Anecdotes of American Journalism* (New York: Henry Holt, 1989), 224; Leamer, *Playing for Keeps in Washington*, 43–44; *Washington Post*, March 20, 2001.

41. *Washington Post*, June 14, 1992, July 23, 2001; Bradlee, *A Good Life*, 337, 350; Martin L. Fleming, *Inside the* Washington Post (New York: Vantage, 1996), 159–60; Bob Woodward and Carl Bernstein commentary, Brody Public Policy Forum, University of Maryland, October 16, 2002.

42. Fallows, "Big Ben," 142; *Washington Post*, June 14, 1992, October 27, 2002.

43. Walker, *Powers of the Press*, 258; William Greider, "Aftergate," *Esquire*, 84 (September 1975), 99–100; *Washington Post*, February 11, 1998; Leamer, *Playing for Keeps in Washington*, 44–45; Bradlee, *Booknotes* interview, October 29, 1995, C-SPAN.

44. Babb, ed., *Of the* Press, 184–92; Fleming, *Inside the* Washington Post, 23–28, 42, 49–65, 77–79, 114–15, 127–35; *Washington Star*, January 5, 1976; Graham, *Personal History*, 515–40; *Washington Post*, March 6, 2004.

45. Author interview with Don Oberdorfer; *Washington Post*, July 18, 2001, March 6, 2004; *New York Times*, July 18, 2001; *Baltimore Sun* editorial, July 18, 2001.

46. J. Russell Wiggins to Eugene Meyer, July 2, 1954, Meyer papers; Bradlee, *A Good Life*, 343; "No Room in the Pool," *Newsweek*, 81 (January 1, 1973), 14, 17.

47. Jim Bellows, *The Last Editor: How I Saved the* New York Times, *the* Washington Post, *and the* Los Angeles Times *from Dullness and Complacency* (Kansas City: Andrews McMeel, 2002), 15–33, 224; Kelly, *The Imperial* Post, 271–73; interview with James Sayler; Fleming, *Inside the* Washington Post, 60–72; Greg Easterbrook, "Who Will Catch the Falling *Star*?" *Washington Monthly*, 12 (May 1981), 14–15; *Washington Post*, February 4, 1978; *Washington Star*, August 7, 1981.

48. McGrory oral history, 48, 57; Peter Benjaminson, *Death in the Afternoon: America's News-paper Giants Struggle for Survival* (Kansas City: Andrews, McMeel & Parker, 1984), 85–108; Bellows, *The Last Editor*, 169–92.

49. McGrory oral history, 70–71; Donovan, *Right Place, Right Times*, 437; Easterbrook, "Who Will Catch the Falling *Star*?" 13–26; William Boot, "Time Inc.'s 'Unbiased' Satellite," *Columbia Journalism Review*, 20 (May/June 1981), 43–48; *Washington Star*, July 23, August 7, 1981.

50. Graham, *Personal History*, 596–97; Gay Jervey, "In Search of Maureen Dowd," *Brill's Content*, 2 (June 1999), 90; Howard Kurtz, *Media Circus: The Trouble with America's Newspapers* (New York: Random House, 1993), 348–53; McGrory oral history, 73.

51. *Washington Star*, July 24, August 7, 1981; Michael Kilian and Arnold Sawislak, *Who Runs Washington?* (New York: St. Martin's, 1982), 163; Gartner, "The First Rough Draft of History," 43.

52. *Washington Post*, May 22–23, 2002; Bryan Abas, "Inside the Paper That God Wanted: A Nonbeliever's Account of Life at the Reverend Moon's *Washington Times*," *Columbia Journalism Review*, 23 (May/June 1984), 47–49; Leonard Downie Jr. *Booknotes* interview, April 7, 2002, C-SPAN; James M. Jeffords, *My Declaration of Independence* (New York: Simon & Schuster, 2001), 93; Nurith C. Aizenman, "Stop Dissing the *Washington Times*!" *Washington Monthly*, 29 (May 1997), 26–29; Craig Crawford, "The Readings of Sun Myung Moon," *National Journal*, 29 (May 21, 1997), 1,294; Dante Chinni, "The Other Paper," *Columbia Journalism Review*, 41 (September/October 2002), 47.

53. Aizenman, "Stop Dissing the *Washington Times*!", 26–36; Nelson Mandela, *Long Walk to Freedom: The Autobiography of Nelson Mandela* (Boston: Little, Brown, 1994), 453; *The Hill*, September 6, 1995; *Washington Times*, January 22, February 27, March 20, July 23, 1992.

54. Stephen Goode, "Right to Laugh," *Insight*, 17 (August 13, 2001), 10–12, 32; *Washington Times*, December 11, 1997; *Washington Post*, May 22–23, 2002.

55. Leonard Downie Jr. interview, *Booknotes*, April 7, 2002, C-SPAN; Allen Neuharth, *Confessions of an S.O.B.* (New York: Doubleday, 1989), 255–62; Kurtz, *Media Circus*, 36–63; *Washington Post*, July 1, 1984, April 23, 2004; see also Peter Prichard, *The Making of McPaper* (New York: Andrews, McMeel & Parker, 1987).

56. E. J. Dionne Jr., *Why Americans Hate Politics* (New York: Simon & Schuster, 1991), 203–4; Greider, *Who Will Tell the People*, 294–95, 298–99.

57. *Washington Star*, January 5, 1976; Nocera, "Making It at the *Washington Post*," 20; Cannon, *Reporting: An Inside View*, 10–11, 35, 91; Babb, ed., *Of the Press*, 21–23; *Washington Post*, December 18, 1977, January 28, 1995; January 30, June 23, 1996, March 20, 2001; Laura Longley Babb, ed., *The* Washington Post *Guide to Washington* (New York: McGraw-Hill, 1976), xii, 85; Don Fry, ed., *Believing the News* (St Petersburg, Fla.: Poynter Institute, 1985), 54.

58. *Washington Post* May 8, 1962; Bray, *Pillars of the Post*, 163, 173–76; Richard W. Lee, ed., *Politics & the Press* (Washington: Acropolis, 1970), 119–20; Cose, *The Press*, 104; Judith Martin, *The Name on the White House Floor, and Other Anxieties of Our Times* (New York: Coward, McCann & Geoghean, 1972), 13.

59. Lee, ed., *Politics & the Press*, 121–23; Jules Witcover, "Washington's White Press Corps," *Columbia Journalism Review*, 8 (Winter 1969–1970), 46; Kay Mills, *A Place in the News: From the Women's Pages to the Front Pages* (New York: Dodd, Mead, 1988), 181; Bradlee, *A Good Life*, 279–84; Ben W. Gilbert, *Ten Blocks from the White House: Anatomy of the Washington Riots of 1968* (New York: Frederick A. Praeger, 1968), ix–xiv.

60. Dorothy Gilliam oral history, Washington Press Foundation, 68, 79–81, 115–20; Maria Braden, *She Said What? Interviews with Women Newspaper Columnists* (Lexington: University Press of Kentucky, 1993), 113; Mills, *A Place in the News*, 179–82.

61. Gilliam oral history, 68–109, 121–23; Braden, *She Said What?* 114–15; Alicia Mundy, "Getting Personal," *Washingtonian*, 28 (June 1993), 52, 125–26.

62. Gilliam oral history, 126–27; Jill Nelson, *Volunteer Slavery: My Authentic Negro Experience* (Chicago: The Noble Press, 1993), 86–88; 384; Nathan McCall, *Makes Me Wanna Holler: A Young Black Man in America* (New York: Random House, 1994), 381–84.

63. *Washington Post*, September 28, 1980, April 19, 1981; *After "Jimmy's World": Tightening Up in Editing, a Report by the National News Council* (New York: National News Council, 1981); Bradlee, *A Good Life*, 435–52; Patrice Gaines, *Laughing in the Dark: From Colored Girl to Woman of Color—A Journey from Prison to Power* (New York: Doubleday, 1994), 241–43; Nathan McCall, *Booknotes* interview, March 6, 1994, C-SPAN; David S. Broder, *Behind the Front Page: A Candid Look at How the News Is Made* (New York: Simon & Schuster, 1987), 309–13; Fleming, *Inside the* Washington Post, 162–63; Remnick, "Last of the Red Hots," 76.

64. Alicia C. Shepard, "High Anxiety," *American Journalism Review*, 15 (November 1993), 19–24; Nelson, *Volunteer Slavery*, 137; *Washington Post*, December 11, 1987.

65. *Washington Post*, January 20, 1990, April 14, 1991 September 21, 1995, January 11, 1999; David K. Shipler, "Blacks in the Newsroom: Progress? Yes, but. . ." *Columbia Journalism Review*, 37 (May/June 1998), 26–32; Ruth Shalit, "Race in the Newsroom," *New Republic*, 213 (October 2, 1995), 20–37; "Shalit Makes Posties Quake," *Washingtonian*, 31 (November 1995), 12; Alicia C. Shepard, "Too Much Too Soon?" *American Journalism Review*, 17 (December 1995), 34–39; *Montgomery (Maryland) Journal*, October 2, 1995; *New York Times*, January 12, 1998.

66. Leonard Downie Jr., *Booknotes* interview, April 7, 2002, C-SPAN; Jeffrey Toobin, "The Regular Guy," *New Yorker*, 76 (March 20, 2000), 99; Amy Waldman, "Class, Not Race," *Washington Monthly*, 27 (November 1995), 27; Fallows, "Big Ben," 45; *New York Times*, January 12, 1998; *Washington Post*, June 5, 2002.

67. *Washington Post*, October 18, 1992, February 11, 1998, June 5, September 29, 2002; Leonard Downie Jr. and Robert G. Kaiser, *The News about the News: American Journalism in Peril* (New York: Knopf, 2002), 63–110; Leamer, *Playing for Keeps in Washington*, 56; Nocera, "Making It at the *Washington Post*," 13; Warren Berger, "Leonard Downie," *USAir Magazine*, 3 (January 1996), 59–60; Leonard Downie Jr., *Justice Denied: The Case for Reform of the Courts* (New York: Praeger, 1971), 8–9, 23.

68. Toobin, "The Regular Guy," 94–101; Walker, *Powers of the Press*, 260; Scott Sherman, "Stability: Donald Graham's *Washington Post*," *Columbia Journalism Review*, 41 (September/October 2002), 40–49; Harry Jaffe, "Katharine the Great," *Salon* (July 18, 2001); Michael Scherer, "The Post Company's New Profile," *Columbia Journalism Review*, 41 (September/October 2002), 44; Don Campbell, *Inside the Beltway: A Guide to Washington Reporting* (Ames: Iowa State University Press, 1991), 9.

Chapter Twelve

1. *Washington Post*, January 21, 2001.

2. Anthony Smith, *Goodbye Gutenberg: The Newspaper Revolution of the 1980s* (New York: Oxford University Press, 1980), 73–134; David H. Weaver and G. Cleveland Wilhoit, *The American Journalist in the 1990s: U.S. News People at the End of an Era* (Mahwah, N.J.: Lawrence Erlbaum Associates, 1996), 49–50, 60–72; J. D. Lasica, "Net Gain," *American Journalism Review*, 18 (November 1996), 20–33.

3. Sig Mickelson interview with Stan Swinton, February 18, 1974, Sig Mickelson papers, Institute for News Media History, University of Texas; author interview with Bob Petersen; Chip Rowe, "A Journalist's Guide to the Internet," *American Journalism Review*, 17 (January/February 1995), 30–34; Carl Sessions Stepp, "The X Factor," *American Journalism Review*, 18 (November 1996), 34–37; Howell Raines, "My Times," *The Atlantic*, 293 (May 2004), 50; *Washington Post*, June 9, 1996; *The Hill*, October 30, 2002.

4. Lasica, "Net Gain," 27; Carol Pogash, "Cyberspace Journalism," *American Journalism Review*, 18 (June 1996), 30; Michael Kinsley, "Slate Goes Free," *Slate* (February 13, 1999).

5. On the alternative press see Laurence Leamer, *The Paper Revolutionaries: The Rise of the Underground Press* (New York: Simon & Schuster, 1972), Lauren Kessler, *The Dissident Press:*

Alternative Journalism in American History (Beverly Hills, Calif.: Sage, 1984), and Abe Peck, *Uncovering the Sixties: The Life and Times of the Underground Press* (New York: Citadel, 1991). Carl Sessions Stepp, "The New Journalist," *American Journalism Review*, 18 (April 1996), 19–23; Pogash, "Cyberspace Journalism," 26–31; *The Hill*, November 16, 1994, September 3, 1997; Matt Welch, Mallory Jensen, and Jacqueline Reeves, "Blogworld and Its Gravity," *Columbia Journalism Review*, 42 (September/October 2003), 2; Ann Coulter interview, August 11, 2002, *Booknotes*, C-SPAN.

6. Bill Kovach and Tom Rosenstiel, *Warp Speed: America in the Age of Mixed Media* (New York: The Century Foundation Press, 1999), 1–9, 43–50; Philip Seib, *Going Live: Getting the News Right in a Real-Time, Online World* (New York: Rowman & Littlefield, 2001), 37–46.

7. *The Drudge Report*, August 11, 1997; *Sidney Blumenthal and Jacqueline Jordan Blumenthal v. Matt Drudge and America Online, Inc.*; Sidney Blumenthal, "The Clinton Presidency and America's Future," Speech, April 23, 1998, John F. Kennedy School of Government, Harvard University, televised on C-SPAN.

8. Sidney Blumenthal, *The Clinton Wars* (New York: Farrar, Straus, and Giroux, 2003), 191–207; *The Observer*, August 17, 2003; *Washington Post*, June 16, 1997; Michael Shnayerson, "Sid Pro Quo," *Vanity Fair*, 61 (May 1998), 94; David Armstrong, *A Trumpet to Arms: Alternative Media in America* (Los Angeles: J. P. Tarcher, 1981), 22.

9. Sidney Blumenthal, *The Permanent Campaign* (New York: Simon & Schuster, 1982, [1980]), 2–7, 12–13, 40, 47–49, 78–79, 260–61, 283–334; *Washington Post*, July 30, 1986; K. L. Billingsley, "Free Matt Drudge," *Heterodoxy* (October 1997); Blumenthal, speech "The Clinton Presidency and America's Future"; Dana Milbank, "Sid's Id," *New Republic*, 219 (October 12, 1998), 11.

10. Blumenthal, *The Clinton Wars*, 212–13; *Washington Post*, June 16, 1997; Shnayerson, "Sid Pro Quo," 94.

11. Martin Schram, *The Great American Video Game: Presidential Politics in the Television Age* (New York: William Morrow, 1987), 133–36; Sidney Blumenthal, *Our Long National Daydream: A Political Pageant of the Reagan Era* (New York: Harper & Row, 1988), 3–4, 8–9, 87.

12. Blumenthal, *The Clinton Wars*, 213–14; R. Emmett Tyrrell Jr. *The Conservative Crack-Up* (New York: Simon & Schuster, 1992), 288; David Frum, *Dead Right* (New York: Basic, 1994), 75–76; Sidney Blumenthal, *The Rise of the Counter-Establishment: From Conservative Ideology to Political Power* (New York: Times Books, 1986), xiii, 3–10, 123, 159, 180–81; Blumenthal, *Our Long National Daydream*, xiv, xvii, 250–55; David Horowitz, *Sex, Lies & Vast Conspiracies* (Los Angeles: Second Thought Books, 1998), 24–26; Horowitz, "Don't Look Back," *Salon*, October 25, 1999; David Horowitz interview, April 13, 1997, *Booknotes*, C-SPAN; Horowitz, "Sid 'Vicious' Blumenthal," *Townhall.com*, June 2, 2003; Horowitz, *Radical Son: A Journey through Our Times* (New York: Free Press, 1997), 376–79.

13. Paul Starobin, "A Generation of Vipers: Journalists and the New Cynicism," *Columbia Journalism Review*, 33 (March/April 1995), 27–32; Christopher Hitchens, "Thinking Like an Apparatchik," *Atlantic Monthly*, 292 (July/August 2003), 131; Joanne Weintraub, "Tina Brown's *New Yorker*," *American Journalism Review*, 17 (April 1995), 21–24; Stefan Kanfer, "Tina Brown and the Coming Decline of Celebrity Journalism," *Columbia Journalism Review*, 37 (September/October 1998), 42–44; William Powers, "Tina and the Tinseling of Washington," *National Journal*, 30 (July 25, 1998), 1,756–58.

14. *Washington Post*, July 29, 1994, January 28, 1995, June 16, 1997, March 3, 1999, April 5, May 9, 2003, April 3, 2004; *New York Times*, April 6, 2003; *The Hill*, June 18, 1997; Eric Alterman, "Anonymous No Longer," *The Nation*, 265 (December 8, 1997), 6; Michael Kelly, "Our Hero," *The New Republic*, 215 (December 2. 1996), 6; Michael Kelly, "The Road to Paranoia," *The New Yorker*, 71 (June 29, 1995), 67; David Carr, "Paper Trail," *Washington City Paper*, February 27–March 6, 1998; Blumenthal speech, "The Clinton Presidency and America's Future."

15. Sidney Blumenthal, "The Ruins of Georgetown," *New Yorker*, 72 (October 21 & 28, 1996), 235–36; *Washington Post*, June 16, 22, 1997, February 7, 1999; *Communication from the Office of the Independent Counsel, Kenneth W. Starr, Transmitting Supplemental Materials to*

the Referral to the United States House of Representatives, September 9, 1998 (Washington: Government Printing Office, 1998), part 1, pp. 1606–1, 168, 177, 179–80, 191; Milbank, "Sid's Id," 11; Shnayerson, "Sid Pro Quo," 47; *Congressional Record*, 106th Cong., 1st sess., S1246.

16.   *Salon,* April 5, 2001; Matt Drudge, "Anyone with a Modem Can Report on the World," address before the National Press Club, June 2, 1998; *Drudge Report*, January 17, 1999; Matt Drudge with Julia Phillips, *Drudge Manifesto* (New York: New American Library, 2000), 24, 27; Robert Scheer, "Dinner with Drudge," *Online Journalism Review* (July 16, 1998); David McClintick, "Town Crier for the New Age," *Brill's Content,* 1 (November 1998), 115; *New York Times*, March 12, 1998.

17.   Drudge, "Anyone with a Modem Can Report on the World"; Annette N. Markham, *Life Online: Researching Real Experience in Virtual Space* (Walnut Creek, Calif.: AltaMira, 1998), 52; Drudge, *Drudge Manifesto*, 27–29; McClintick, "Town Crier for the New Age," 115; Denise Hamilton, "Right Knight," *Miami NewTimes.Com,* 1997; Nicholas Negroponte, "Reintermediated," *Wired,* 5 (September 1997), 208.

18.   The change in attitude was a worldwide phenomenon. In 1990, at his first press conference after twenty-seven years of imprisonment, Nelson Mandela noticed that reporters were as eager to learn about his personal feelings and relationships as his political thoughts. "This was new to me," he wrote; "when I went to prison [in 1962], a journalist would never had thought of asking questions about one's wife and family, one's emotions, one's most intimate moments." Nelson Mandela, *Long Walk to Freedom: The Autobiography of Nelson Mandela* (Boston: Little, Brown, 1994), 496; Lewis Lapham, "The King's Pleasure," *Harper's,* 252 (March 1976), 13–181; see also Gail Collins, *Scorpion Tongues: Gossip, Celebrity, and American Politics* (New York: William Morrow, 1998).

19.   Scott Shuger, "Deep Dish a la Modem: To Get the Latest Industry Gossip, Contact Matt Drudge," *Los Angeles Magazine,* 41 (September 1996), 32; Shuger, "Drudge Report: 'A Network of Whispers,'" *Salon* (April 18, 1996); Michele Botwin, "The Early Bird Media Critic: Scott Shuger of 'Today's Paper,'" *Online Journalism Review* (February 26, 1999); *Drudge Report*, January 17, 1999; McClintick, "Town Crier for the New Age," 114.

20.   NBC news broadcaster John Chancellor reviewed the changing use of the media by the candidates in the 1992 election in Arthur M. Schlesinger Jr., ed., *Running for President: The Candidates and Their Images*, vol. 2 (New York: Simon & Schuster, 1994), 439–45; Benjamin R. Barber, *The Truth of Power: Intellectual Affairs in the Clinton White House* (New York: W. W. Norton, 2001), 82, 120–21; Sidney Blumenthal, "The Syndicated Presidency," *New Yorker* (April 5, 1993), 42–47; Dee Dee Myers interview for "The Clinton Years," *Nightline*, ABC-News, 2001.

21.   McClintick, "Town Crier for the New Age," 113–16; *Washington Post*, June 4, 2001; Jonathan Broder, "A Smear Too Far," *Salon* (August 15, 1997); Jonathan Broder, "Libel Suit Tests the Limits of Freewheeling Net Speech," *Salon* (August 29, 1997); *Blumenthal v. Drudge*; Drudge, *Drudge Manifesto*, 29; Michael Isikoff, *Uncovering Clinton: A Reporter's Story* (New York: Crown, 1999), 167.

22.   Jonathan Broder, "A Smear Too Far," *Salon*, August 15, 1997; *Washington Post*, August 12, 28, 1997; Drudge, "Anyone with a Modem"; Sean Paige, "What Makes Sidney Vicious?" *Insight,* 15 (March 1, 1999), 43; Barb Palser, "Charting New Terrain," *American Journalism Review,* 21 (November 1999), 25–31; Will Rodger, "Net Case Liable to Impact Libel," *Inter@ctive Week* (March 30, 1998); Lasica, "Net Gain," 29.

23.   Broder, "Libel Suit Tests the Limits of Freewheeling Net Speech,"; "Net News: Journalism in Search of a Niche," *The Freedom Forum and Newseum News,* 5 (January/ February 1998), 6; *Washington Post,* August 30, 1997; *New York Times*, March 12, 1998; *CNN Interactive*, April 23, 1998; Susan Estrich, "White House Pops Susan Estrich for *USA Today* Op-Ed on Drudge," *Drudge Report,* December 1, 1997.

24.   Scott Rosenberg, "Drudge Falls for Yahoo Hackers' Nonsense," *Salon* (December 11, 1997); Michael Kinsley, "In Defense of Matt Drudge," *Time*, 151 (February 2, 1998), 41; McClintick, "Town Crier for the New Age," 114; Horowitz, *Sex, Lies, & Vast Conspiracies*, 15–28; Horowitz,

Radical Son, 376–79; Horowitz, *Booknotes* interview, C-SPAN April 13, 1997; Horowitz, "Sid 'Vicious' Blumenthal,"; Ledeen letter, *Washington Post*, March 6, 1987; Barbara Ledeen and Michael Ledeen depositions, July 30, 1998, *Blumenthal v. Drudge*; Hamilton, "Right Knight."

25.   *Drudge Report*, January 18, 1998; Haynes Johnson, *The Best of Times: America in the Clinton Years* (New York: Harcourt, 2001), 292–93; Alicia C. Shepard, "A Scandal Unfolds," *American Journalism Review*, 20 (March 1998), 21–28; McClintick, "Town Crier for the New Age," 118–19; Drudge address to the National Association of Radio Talk Show Hosts, May 1, 1999; Drudge, "The Media Should Apologize," address before the Wednesday Morning Club, September 10, 1998; Mike McCurry interview, "The Clinton Years," *Nightline*, ABC-News, 2001.

26.   Joseph Lelyveld, "In Clinton's Court," *New York Review of Books*, 50 (May 29, 2003), 12; *Drudge Report*, January 17, 1999; Jeffrey Toobin, *A Vast Conspiracy: The Real Story of the Sex Scandal That Nearly Brought Down a President* (New York: Random House, 1999), 233; Mike Godwin, "Drudging Admiration," *Salon* (Febrary 2, 1998); Joan Didion, "Clinton Agonistes," *New York Review of Books*, 45 (October 22, 1998), 18–22; David Corn, "Cyber Speed on Journalism," *Online Journalism Review* (March 1, 1998).

27.   *Drudge Report*, October 6, November 13, 1998.

28.   Blumenthal, *The Clinton Wars*, 401, 408; *Starr Report*, part 1, 184, 199; Milbank, "Sid's Id," 10; Barber, *The Truth of Power*, 282; *Drudge Report*, February 2, 1998; David Horowitz, "Paging Joe McCarthy," *Salon* (February 23, 1998); *New York Post*, September 18, 1998; Carl M. Cannon, "Hillary's Brain," *Weekly Standard*, 3 (February 23, 1998), 21–25.

29.   Drudge address to the National Association of Radio Talk Show Hosts; *Washington Post*, August 3, 1998; *Drudge Report*, February 25, 1998; *Starr Report*, part 1, 191, 206; *Washington Post*, March 1, 1998; Jonathan Broder, "Blumenthal Blasts Starr as He Exits Grand Jury Room," *Salon* (February 27, 1998); Milbank, "Sid's Id," 9; David Carr, "Paper Trail," *Washington City Paper* (February 27–March 6, 1998); Isikoff, *Uncovering Clinton*, 389–90.

30.   Bob Schieffer, *This Just In: What I Couldn't Tell You on TV* (New York: Putnam, 2003), 362; Nicol C. Rae and Colton C. Campbell, *Impeaching Clinton: Partisan Strife on Capitol Hill* (Lawrence: University of Kansas Press, 2004), 60–64.

31.   *New York Times*, March 12, 1998; *Washington Post*, September 16, 1998.

32.   *Roll Call*, October 12, 1998; "Hubris, Thy Name Is Blumenthal, or Will *Blumenthal v. Drudge* Bring Down Bill Clinton," *No Holds Barred: A Journal of Republican Thought, Political News, and Other Ramblings*, 1998; Christopher J. Barr, "The Rivera File," *No Holds Barred*, August 24, 1998; Daniel J. Harris and Teresa Hampton, "White House Knew about Hyde Affair before Attempts to Leak it to Media Started," *Capitol Hill Blue*, October 13, 1998; "Sidney Blumenthal's Perjury Trap," *The Weekly Standard*, 3 (September 28, 1998), 2.

33.   Drudge, "Anyone with a Modem"; "Titans of 'tude," *Newsweek*, 133 (January 18, 1999), 32; McClintick, "Town Crier for the New Age," 124; Robert Scheer, "Murdoch Presents: The Sludge Report," *Online Journalism Review* (January 12, 1999); *Washington Post*, November 15, 17, 18, 1999, November 13, 2000; *Drudge Report*, November 18, 30, 1999.

34.   *Congressional Record*, 106th Cong., 1st sess, S135–36, S240–41, S1246–54; *Washington Post*, January 28, February 7–12, 1999; *Washington Times*, February 8, 1999; *New York Times*, February 4, 10, 15, 1999; Joe Conason, "Taking It Out on Sid," *Salon* (February 9, 1999); Jonathan Broder, "Critics Lie in Wait for Blumenthal," *MSNBC News* (February 2, 1999); Sidney Blumental, "Presidents & Democracy," speech at Princeton University, November 9, 1999, broadcast on C-SPAN; David P. Shippers with Alan P. Henry, *Sellout: The Inside Story of President Clinton's Impeachment* (Washington: Regnery, 2000), 264–66, 280; Christopher Hitchens, "I'll Never Eat Lunch in this Town Again," *Vanity Fair*, 62 (May 1999), 72–80; Blumenthal, *The Clinton Wars*, 600–19; Joshua Micah Marshall, "Stalking Sidney Blumenthal," *Salon* (February 9, 1999); Craig Winneker, "The Defiant One," *Capital Style*, 2 (June 1999), 28–35.

35.   *Washington Post*, November 16, 2000; Blumenthal, *The Clinton Wars*, 784.

36. Roger Parloff, "If This Ain't Libel . . ." *Brill's Content*, 4 (Fall 2001), 95–113; *Drudge Report*, May 1, 2001; *Washington Post*, May 2, 2001; "Drudge Wins," *WSJ.com*, May 2, 2001.

37. William Powers, "Clown Time Is Over," *National Journal*, 33 (May 12, 2001), 1,432; Powers, "You Can't Hide Your Spying Eyes," *National Journal*, 31 (March 13, 1999), 703–4; Camille Paglia, "Drudge Match," *Radar Magazine* (June 2003); *Washington Post*, March 15, 2004.

38. *Washington Post*, May 13, June 12, November 2, 1998; *New York Times*, July 16, 2001; Charles Lane, "To Tell the Truth," *The New Republic*, 218 (May 25, 1998); Stephen Glass, "Hack Heaven," *The New Republic*, 218 (May 18, 1998), 11–12; Adam L. Penenberg, "Faked Out," *Forbes Digital Tool*, June 1, 1998; Robert Scheer, "When the News Proves to Be Fiction." *Online Journalism Review* (June 23, 1998); Buzz Bissinger, "Shattered Glass," *Vanity Fair*, 61 (September 1998), 180–90; "To Our Readers," *The New Republic*, 218 (June 1, 1998), 8–9, (June 29, 1998), 8, 10; "To Our Online Readers," *The New Republic* (July 20, 1998).

39. Pete Danko, "Print Media in Glass Houses," *Wired News* (May 13, 1998); Adam L. Penenberg, "Lies, Damn Lies, and Fiction," *Forbes Digital Tool* (May 11, 1998).

40. Mark Hall, "One-to-One Politics in Cyberspace," *Media Studies Quarterly*, 11 (Winter 1997), 97–103; Chip Brown, "Fear.Com," *American Journalism Review*, 21 (June 1999), 55, 68; Pogash, "Cyberspace Journalism," 31; *New York Times*, July 27, 1998; Michael Oreskes, "Navigating a Minefield," *American Journalism Review*, 21 (November 1999), 20–25.

41. *New York Times*, August 3, 1998; *Washington Post*, May 12, 1999, May 17, 2000; Paul Farhi, "The Dotcom Brain Drain," *American Journalism Review*, 22 (March 2000), 30–33; Joel Simon with Carol Napoitano, "We're All Nerds Now: The Digital Reporting Revolution Is Research Warp Speed. Here's Why," *Columbia Journalism Review*, 37 (March/April 1999), 20.

42. Larry Pryor, "Old Media Firms Dig a Grave with Shoveware," *Online Journalism Review* (April 9, 1999); Jeffrey A. Perlman, "Print Sites Still Wary of Chatting It Up," *Online Journalism Review* (May 6, 1999); Brown, "Fear.Com," 67.

43. *Washington Post*, July 13, 2003; "Newspapers and the Internet," *The Economist*, 352 (July 17, 1999), 17–19; "How Is Broadcast News Changing?" *Larry King Live*, CNN, June 13, 2000; Leonard Downie Jr. and Robert G. Kaiser, *The News about the News: American Journalism in Peril* (New York: Knopf, 2002), 203–6, 214–15; Leonard Downie Jr., *Booknotes* interview, April 7, 2002, C-SPAN.

44. Matt Welch, "Is Reliance on the AP Draining the Life from Online News?" *Online Journalism Review*, (May 20, 1999); "Missouri J-Dean Deplores Dependence on Wire News," *Editor & Publisher*, 105 (May 20, 1972), 11; *New York Times*, January 31, 2000.

45. *Washington Post*, January 11, 2000; *New York Times*, March 20, 2000; Brendan I. Koerner, "Click Here for Britney!" *Washington Monthly*, 33 (July/August 2001), 25–30; Alicia C. Shepard, "Get Big or Get Out," *American Journalism Review*, 22 (March 2000), 22–29; Jim Monk, "Broadband Is for 'Losers': Matt Drudges the Dot-coms," *Online Journalism Review* (August 23, 2000); The Project for Excellence in Journalism, *The State of the News Media 2004: An Annual Report on American Journalism*, Journalism.org.

46. "Business: The Failure of New Media," *The Economist*, 356 (August 19, 2000), 53–55; Paul Farhi, "Surviving in Cyberspace," *American Journalism Review*, 22 (September 2000), 23–27; William Powers, "This Year's Model," *National Journal*, 33 (May 19, 2001), 1,512; *Wall Street Journal*, January 15, 2001; *New York Times*, January 7, 2001; *Washington Post*, February 21, April 9, 2001; Mallory Jensen, "A Brief History of Weblogs," *Columbia Journalism Review*, 42 (September/October 2003), 22.

47. Author interview with Vigdor Schreibman; *The Hill*, February 7, April 3, 1996; *New York Times*, February 26, 1996; Schreibman, "An Idea Whose Time Has Come: FINS Lays Plans for Internet Press Galleries at US Capitol," FINS, February 27, 1996.

48. *Roll Call*, April 1, 17, June 3, 1996, June 8, 29, 2000; *The Hill*, April 3, 1996, April 18, 2002; Sinéad O'Brien, "Press Passes for Online Journalists," *American Journalism Review*, 22 (June 2000), 12.

49. Michael Bloomberg and Matthew Winkler, *Bloomberg by Bloomberg* (New York: John Wiley, 1997), 91–99; Paul Sperry, "Is Bloomberg New 'Bully' on Block?" *WorldNetDaily*, September

9, 2002; William Roberts to Paul Sperry, February 8, 2002, Standing Committee of Correspondents.

50. Joseph Farah, "Why I'm Not a Conservative," June 13, 2002, Farah, "Stalinists in the Press Gallery," August 20, 2002, Farah, "Breakthrough for New Media," February 11, 2003, Tom Ambrose, "The Pending Demise of WorldNetDaily?" February 5, 2003, Paul Sperry, "Rogues' Gallery of Press-Pass Holders," September 4, 2002, Paul Sperry, "Press Cops Surrender, Grant WND Credentials, September 12, 2002, "Senate Weighs Reforms after WND Press Battle," February 11, 2003, *WorldNetDaily;* transcript, *In the Matter of the Appeal of WorldNetDaily,* April 15, 2002, Standing Committee of Correspondents; *Roll Call,* April 18, 2002, January 20, 2003.

Epilogue

1. *Today Show* transcript, NBC, September 11, 2001.

2. "The Age of Indifference," 1990, Kimberly Parker and Claudia Deane, "Ten Years of the Pew News Interest Index," 1997, "Terror Coverage Boosts News Media's Image," 2001, online reports of *The Pew Research Center for the People & the Press;* Stephen Hess and Marvin Kalb, eds., *The Media and the War on Terrorism* (Washington: Brookings Institution Press, 2003), 283.

3. Kenneth T. Walsh, *Feeding the Beast: The White House Versus the Press* (New York: Random House, 1996), 76–78; John Anthony Maltese, *Spin Control: The White House Office of Communications and the Management of Presidential News* (Chapel Hill: University of North Carolina Press, 1992), 215–20; Arthur E. Rowse, *Drive-By Journalism: The Assault on Your Need to Know* (Monroe, Maine: Common Courage, 2000), 31–48; Leonard Downie Jr. and Robert G. Kaiser, *The News about the News: American Journalism in Peril* (New York: Knopf, 2002), 234–43; *Bangor Daily News,* August 4, 1997; *Milwaukee Journal Sentinel,* February 26, 1998; *Washington Post,* November 19, 2001.

4. Lucinda Fleeson, "Where Are the Watchdogs?" *American Journalism Review,* 23 (July/August 2001), 36–46.

5. Robert D. Putnam, *Bowling Alone: The Collapse and Revival of American Community* (New York: Simon and Schuster, 2000), 35–42, 218–21.

6. Doyle McManus, *Columbia Journalism Review,* 41 (September/October 2002), 52; *Washington Post,* April 8, 2004.

7. Frank Rich, "All the President's Stink," *New York Times Magazine* (August 15, 1999), 42; *Washington Post,* January 6, 18, 1999; Marvin Kalb, *One Scandalous Story: Clinton, Lewinsky, and Thirteen Days That Tarnished American Journalism* (New York: Free Press, 2001), 7–9, 263.

8. *Washington Post,* November 29, 2000; Kelly Patricia O'Meara, "Media Culpas," *Insight,* 16 (December 11, 2000), 10–11.

9. *New York Times,* December 17, 2000; *USA Today,* December 26, 2000.

10. *Washington Post,* September 14, 2001; Susan Paterno, "Ignoring the Warning," *American Journalism Review,* 23 (November 2001), 25–27; Kathleen Hall Jamieson and Paul Waldman, *The Press Effect: Politicians, Journalists, and the Stories That Shape the Political World* (New York: Oxford University Press, 2003), 163–64.

11. Peter Jennings quoted in *A Front-Row Seat to History,* documentary film for the exhibit *September 11: Bearing Witness to History,* Smithsonian National Museum of American History; Allison Gilbert, Phil Hirschkorn, Melinda Murphy, Robyn Walensky, and Mitchell Stephens, eds., *Covering Catastrophe: How Broadcast Journalists Reported September 11, 2001* (Chicago: Bonus Books, 2002), 9–29.

12. Barton Gellman, "The Cloud Rolled toward Us, and We Had to Run," *American Journalism Review,* 23 (October 2001), 23–25; *Washington Post,* September 13, 2001; *Wall Street Journal,* April 12, 2002.

13. "First Reporter on Scene at Pentagon on 9/11 Looks Back," *CNN Saturday Morning News,* September 7, 2002.

14. Hess and Kalb, eds., *The Media and the War on Terrorism*, 278–79; Gilbert, et al., eds., *Covering Catastrophe*, 61–69, 91–92.

15. Bob Schieffer, *This Just In: What I Couldn't Tell You on TV* (New York: Putnam, 2003), 394–95; Gilbert, et al., eds, *Covering Catastrophe*, 73–74.

16. *New York Times*, September 12, 2001; *Wall Street Journal*, September 12, 2001; author interviews with Elaine Povitch and Helen Dewar.

17. *Washington Post*, September 12, 2001; Schieffer, *This Just In*, 395–97.

18. Suzanne Huffman, *Women Journalists at Ground Zero: Covering Crisis* (Lanham, Md.: Rowman & Littlefield, 2002), 135–39; *New York Times*, September 12, 2001; David McCullough, "Recalling 9-11," *Humanities: The Magazine of the National Endowment for the Humanities*, 24 (May/June 2003), 43.

19. *Washington Post*, September 12–14, 2001; Tish Durkin, "Dial 9/11 for Absurdity and Nobility; Hold the Profundity," *National Journal*, 33 (September 15, 2001), 2,801; *New York Times*, September 12, 2001.

20. "A Scarred Capital," *The Economist*, 360 (September 15, 2001), 17.

21. Peter Jennings in *A Front-Row Seat to History*; *New York Times*, September 12, 2001; *Washington Post*, September 12, 2001; William Powers, "Features Our Front," *National Journal*, 33 (September 29, 2001), 3,017.

22. Lori Robertson, "We Have a Breaking Story . . . " *American Journalism Review*, 23 (October 2001); William Powers, "Being There," *National Journal*, 33 (September 15, 2001), 2,844–45; Sylvester and Huffman, *Women Journalists at Ground Zero*, 51–57.

23. *Wall Street Journal*, September 12, 2001; Marc Fisher, "Meeting the Challenge," *American Journalism Review*, 23 (October 2001), 18–21; Barbie Zelizer and Stuart Allan, eds., *Journalism after September 11* (New York: Routledge, 2002), 73; *Washington Post*, September 12, 2001.

24. Zelizer and Allan, eds., *Journalism after September 11*, 124–25; Downie and Kaiser, *The News about the News*, 215; Pamela Parker and Christopher Saunders, "Tragedy Results in Web News Gridlock," Internetnews.com (September 11, 2001); Wayne Robins, "The Web Fails Its First Big Test," *Editor and Publisher*, 134 (September 17, 2001), 4–5; *Wall Street Journal*, September 12, 2001; Barb Palser, "Not So Bad," *American Journalism Review*, 23 (November 2001), 49–53.

25. *The Hill*, October 3, 2001; *Washington Post*, September 12, 2001; *New York Times*, September 12, 2001; Zelizer and Allan, eds., *Journalism after September 11*, 127–30; Welch, "Blogworld and Its Gravity," 24.

26. Stephen Seplow, "Tactical Shift," *American Journalism Review*, 23 (December 2001), 38–43; Christopher Hanson, "Over Here: We're All War Correspondents Now," *Columbia Journalism Review*, 40 (November/December 2001), 25; Nina Easton, "Unsung Heroes," *American Journalism Review*, 24 (May 2002), 48–53.

27. Ted Gup, "Working in a Wartime Capital: An Uneasy Quiet and a Sense of Mission," *Columbia Journalism Review*, 41 (September/October 2002), 21–27; Sherry Ricchiairdi, "The Anthrax Enigma," *American Journalism Review*, 23 (December 2001), 18–23.

28. Walter Shapiro and Gwen Ifill quoted in *Columbia Journalism Review*, 41 (September/October 2002), 22, 27.

29. Warren Strobel, Nina Totenberg, and Sally Quinn quoted in *Columbia Journalism Review*, 41 (September/October 2002), 26, 30, 42; Jamieson and Waldman, *The Press Effect*, 130–64; *Washington Post*, January 7, 2002.

30. Fred Barnes, "The Press in Time of War," *The Weekly Standard*, 7 (December 3, 2001), 31–33; *New York Times*, November 7, 2001; *Washington Post*, November 9, 2001, June 24, 2002; Nina J. Easton, "Left in the Lurch," *American Journalism Review*, 24 (January/February 2002), 38–43.

31. Downie and Kaiser, *The News about the News*, 28, 63–64; Lucia Moses, "Reading a Trend," 16, Joe Strupp, "That'll Be the Day: Local Stories Take a Back Seat," *Editor and Publisher*, 134 (October 22, 2001), 17.

32.   Todd Shields, "Washington Pressed for Access," *Editor and Publisher*, 134 (October 22, 2001), 6. Sherman, "The Avenger: Sy Hersh, Then and Now," 41; Gup, "Working in a Wartime Capital," 21; *The Hill*, February 26, 2003; Zelizer and Allan, eds., *Journalism after September 11*, 12–13.

33.   Eric Alterman, "What Liberal Media?" *The Nation*, 276 (February 24, 2003), 14; Steve Piacente, "Cutting Furthest from the Heart," *Columbia Journalism Review*, 41 (September/October 2002), 36; "9/11/03," *Columbia Journalism Review*, 42 (September/October 2003), 7.

Index